BOLD WORDS

BOLD WORDS

A Century of Asian American Writing

**Edited by RAJINI SRIKANTH and
ESTHER Y. IWANAGA**

Rutgers University Press
New Brunswick, New Jersey, and London

Library of Congress Cataloging-in-Publication Data

Bold words : a century of Asian American writing / edited by Rajini Srikanth and
Esther Yae Iwanaga.
    p. cm.
    Includes bibliographical references and indexes.
    ISBN 0-8135-2965-4 (alk. paper)—ISBN 0-8135-2966-2 (pbk. : alk. paper)
    1. American literature—Asian American authors. 2. Asian Americans—
Literary collections. 3. American literature—20th century. 4. Asian
Americans—Biography. I. Srikanth, Rajini. II. Iwanaga, Esther Yae.

PS508.A8 B65 2001
810.8'0895'0904—dc21

00-068346

British Cataloging-in-Publication data for this book is available from the British
Library

This collection copyright © 2001 by Rutgers, The State University
For copyrights to individual pieces please see Copyrights and Permissions,
pp. 437–440.

Manufactured in the United States of America

—For my mother, Hema Srinivasan,
who continually surprises me with her boldness.

—To the memory of my father, Morio Iwanaga,
and to my son, Matthew Morio Altieri

Contents

PART 2

POETRY

Contents

viii

PART 3

FICTION

Contents

xi

ĐRAMA

Acknowledgments

We thank Peter Nien-chu Kiang for his vision and support at the University of Massachusetts, Boston; Meena Alexander, Gary Pak, Eileen Tabios, and Roberta Uno for their enthusiastic commitment to the anthology and for the energy they brought to their essays; Walter Lew for drawing our attention to the poetry of Frances Chung; the Asian American Writers Workshop for help in locating the whereabouts of numerous writers in the collection; Monique T. D. Truong for helping us track down many of the anthology's Vietnamese American writers and Luis H. Francia for contact information on Filipino/a American writers; Geraldine Kudaka and Steven Leigh Morris for help in reaching one of our writers; WoongSoon Lee and Sophia Kim for their help with the biographical notes; Vrunda Stampwala for her transcription of Meena Alexander's interview; Leanne Hirata for generously sending us a dictionary of Hawaiian words; Yuan Hsi Fan for the line art for the map of Korea. Wellesley College and the University of Massachusetts, Boston, for help in paying for permissions.

Esther Iwanaga thanks Vivian Zamel for her encouragement and active support.

Rajini Srikanth thanks her students for their appreciation of the complex relationship between aesthetics and politics.

Introduction

RAJINI SRIKANTH

A century of Asian American writing has generated a forceful cascade of bold words; Esther and I felt a turn-of-the-century impulse to plunge into this waterfall and try to re-create the amazement and invigoration of that experience for others. In taking on this task, we were keenly aware of the difficulties embedded within the project. Given the extraordinary heterogeneity of Asian America and the sudden explosion in the number of publications of poetry, fiction, and memoir by Asian Americans, there is a certain presumptive quality to imagining that one could put together an anthology of Asian American literature and pull off the feat with reasonable success.

Admittedly, there already exist available anthologies of Asian American literature: a brief and *very incomplete* list of collections published from 1989 includes *The Forbidden Stitch: An Asian American Women's Anthology* (1989), *Unbroken Thread: An Anthology of Plays by Asian American Women* (1993), *Charlie Chan Is Dead: An Anthology of Contemporary Asian American Fiction* (1993), *Growing Up Asian American* (1993), *Premonitions: The Kaya Anthology of New Asian North American Poetry* (1995), *Under Western Eyes: Personal Essays from Asian America* (1995), *On a Bed of Rice: An Asian American Erotic Feast* (1995), *Flippin': Filipinos on America* (1996).[1] But these are either genre specific or ethnicity specific, and some restrict themselves to one thematic perspective or one gender. These anthologies have been of immeasurable value in drawing attention to the robust creative writing energies among Asian Americans and in amplifying steadily the voices of Asian America so that they are now impossible to ignore or treat cursorily. They have provided us with the springboard, the launching pad, to our collection because they testify to the quantity and quality of the available material, an impressive body of work that calls for organization and a navigational chart.

The few anthologies that do cross ethnic, genre, and gender boundaries to encompass diverse writings—*Aiiieeeee! An Anthology of Asian American Writers* (1974) and *Asian American Literature: A Brief Introduction and Anthology* (1996),[2] for example—reproduce traditional paradigms of Asian American literature, a model that privileges writing by East Asian Americans, that illuminates California-centric experiences, that focuses on the United States as the primary site of emotional allegiance. It seems almost a truism to say that Asian America today is undergoing rapid demographic changes, and yet it needs saying so that we remind ourselves constantly of the problematic nature of that construction and reflect upon the implications of these demographic changes on the composition of our classrooms and the pedagogical approaches we employ. The last twenty years have seen extraordinary increases in the numbers of South and Southeast Asian immigrants (sometimes as high as 150 percent in certain regions), leading to classrooms in which fifth-generation Japanese Americans sit alongside immigrant Vietnamese Americans.[3] With the rapid growth of Asian American populations in the Midwest, South, and Northeast, intercultural contact can no longer be described solely from a California-centric perspective. Shirley Lim's recent volume, *Asian-American Literature: An Anthology* (2000),[4] like *Bold Words,* attempts to expand the representational boundaries of previous collections. But *Bold Words* differs from Lim's collection in its organization and in its emphases.

Bold Words tries to re-create the sense of a vast and incompletely knowable Asian America that is implicit in Stephen Sumida's presidential address at the 1999 conference of the Association for Asian American Studies (AAAS):

> We need one another as sources for what we ourselves do not know, even while our own institutions demand that each of us be an expert in the entire universe of things Asian American and no doubt Asian too, culturally and biologically, because usually they are too narrow to hire enough of us to complement one another on our own campuses. So I am not saying that we should each, or in cliques, be secure in our specialties and let others do the work we think marginal but needed outside our zones of comfort. There are already immense gaps among us in our respective knowledge and practices in Asian American studies, our epistemologies, our pedagogies, and our politics. Think now of how exhilarating it is for us to be humbled and learning about things we never knew, even while we ourselves are presuming to teach our students about what they never knew.[5]

We have tried in the compilation of *Bold Words* to convey the impression of a complicated set of realities, the wide range of experiences of Asians in the United States.

In the first 2000 issue of the *Journal of Asian American Studies,* editors John Liu and Gary Okihiro assess the trajectory of the field's development since its inception. Acknowledging a level of institutionalization of Asian American studies on college campuses, Liu and Okihiro offer a succinct position statement of the current state of the field:

> To serve the community was a founding principle in the establishment of Asian American studies programs. Over the past three decades, the complexity of this community has increased with the continuous migration of ethnically diverse Asian populations into an ever-changing U.S. political economy. Some of the political and intellectual currents generated by this development are renewed debates among scholars and activists as to who comprises the community served by Asian American studies. What criteria are to be used and who determines these criteria in assessing the quality and worth of the scholarship now being produced? . . . Transitory answers to the questions emerging from the new multiplicities of Asian American communities include the . . . articulation of new theoretical orientations to encompass issues such as sexuality and diasporic/transnational cultural identities. (2–3)[6]

Guest editors Shirley Hune and Phil Nash of this millennial issue of JAAS remind us that "[t]ensions about power and influence have also emerged with debates over the regional domination of AAS [Asian American Studies], namely, California-centrism, and more recently around the development of canons and a center in the field" (10).[7] They reiterate that discussions around issues of "community, pedagogy, and paradigms . . . require the field to consider new frameworks for the future if AAS is to be more inclusive, comprehensive, and dynamic" (11). The challenges posed by Sumida, Liu, Okihiro, Hune, and Nash are particularly urgent in light of the numerous programs and departments of Asian American studies that have recently been established or which are to be set up in the near future. A *New York Times* article states, "There are at least 43 undergraduate programs—twice as many as a decade ago" at campuses in different regions of the country.[8] Moreover, programs are emerging in such "unexpected locales as Arizona, Illinois, and Texas."[9] *Bold Words* sees the current turbulence in the field as an opportunity to stimulate new ways of seeing, knowing, and teaching Asian America and the multiplicity of Asian American experiences.

Reconciling Literature with Ethnography: An Uneasy Alliance

We organized *Bold Words* by genre to underscore the literary value of the writings. We wanted to work against the prevailing tendency to read works by ethnic writers as documents to be mined for the "authentic" ethnic experience. Thus, we also stayed away from organization by ethnic group. Similarly, we eschewed a thematic organization, so as to avoid having to frame and suggest limits to the experiences of Asian Americans around identifiable or defined themes. We wish the reader to take from a poem, story, or personal essay any theme or themes that present themselves as possibilities. If readers feel that they have entered unfamiliar territory, so be it. We want them to delineate their own landmarks, create their own paths. Within each genre, the materials are chronologically organized so as to give to readers a historical picture of the deployment of the genre among Asian American writers. We hope that readers will notice both the changes in and persistence of issues within each genre.

There are images and narratives that make visible early Asian American experiences ("In the Land of the Free," "Seventeen Syllables," "The Founding of Yuba City"); protest narratives boldly and aggressively criticize the dominant culture and claim a space on American soil ("Railroad Standard Time," excerpt from *No-No Boy*, "The Grandfather of the Sierra Nevada Mountains," "Cincinnati"); characters yearn for belonging in the United States ("Fredo Avila," "Recipe") and come to the bitter realization that a sense of belonging is elusive ("They Don't Think Much about Us in America," excerpt from *Assimilation*); sharp memories of other homelands seize one's imagination ("Show and Tell," "Pa," "Ceylon"). Commingled with these themes are those that declare the power of art ("News of the World," excerpt from *A Cab Called Reliable*), the pull of sexual desire (excerpt from *Where the Body Meets Memory*, "The Chocolatier"), and revel in the use of pidgin ("The Valley of the Dead Air"). We hope that readers notice parallels and differences in style, characterization, tone, and setting.

Keeping Up with Controversy

Even as we insist that readers throw themselves into the literary experience of Asian America, we recognize that a knowledge of the current debates within the field of Asian American literary studies provides a useful framework to enhance engagement with the material. In the Asian American poetry, fiction, memoirs, and plays that are being published at an astonishing rate today, there is no longer an exclusive concern with claiming voice, space, and power within the United States, although these imperatives are by no means absent; increasingly, writings by Asian Americans are invoking countries in Asia, Latin America, and Africa, regions of the far-flung Asian diaspora. Along with decentering the United States so that it is no longer necessarily featured as the primary stage of the text's action, the literature is also spotlighting Latin America, the Caribbean, and Canada as sites of rich and complex histories of Asians.

In recent years, there appear to be two not-unconnected trajectories developing within Asian American studies: one thrust of scholarship, activism, and creative work centered primarily in the United States, and the other arcing to include ancestral homelands and diasporic locations outside the United States. The development of internet technology, easily reproducible and distributable multimedia such as video and audiotapes, and relatively easy travel have facilitated the creation and maintenance of transnational links. It is now possible to speak of global communities of, for example, diasporic Vietnamese whose contact networks span France, Australia, Canada, and the United States, or diasporic South Asians widely dispersed in the United Kingdom, Canada, the United States, the Caribbean, Singapore, and South Africa. I would argue that the local (or domestic) and diasporic (or transnational) are not oppositional states of being within Asian American communities. Individuals make highly intricate maneuvers on the one hand to be active locally in their neighborhoods and towns in the United States and, on the other, to be connected transnationally to ancestral countries and to people who are part of the diaspora of these original homelands. What one needs, then, at this immensely complex juncture in Asian American literary studies, is a perspective that brings to the surface the interplay in Asian American literature between the global and local, between the pull of other nations and the pull of the United States, between the resurrection of other histories and the erasure of these same histories, between the United States as an external colonizing power and the United States as an internal "colonizer" (of certain groups—Native Americans, inner-city residents, for example), between the ideal of democracy espoused at home and the support of dictators abroad, between the promise of the United States and its realities.

The transnational and global sentiment among many Asian Americans is, perhaps, a phenomenon both to be celebrated and to be viewed with some alarm. Sau-ling Wong was among the first Asian American scholars to caution against an undue fascination among researchers and educators with non-U.S.

trajectories of the experiences of Asian Americans. The 1968 student strikers of San Francisco State fought hard to claim full membership for Asian Americans in the U.S. sociopolitical landscape, she argues; to embrace uncritically the phenomenon of transnationalism is to risk undermining the gains for which the students labored.[10] Arif Dirlik echoes Wong's sentiment, urging the commitment to local issues as a priority over transnational concerns.[11]

For Asian Americans, the tension between the local and the transnational, between a U.S.-centered existence and transnational involvement, is particularly urgent. Because they are seen as perpetual foreigners regardless of the length and generational depth of their stay in the United States, one wonders whether Asian Americans' emotional and economic links with ancestral homelands function as a kind of insurance policy against the risk of being held in suspicion at the slightest provocation.[12]

In this time of relatively easy transnational travel and communication, the opportunity to trace one's own and one's ancestors' multiple historic locations has compelling force. Some of the stories and poems in *Bold Words* explore the pull of other geographies—for example, Frances Chung's untitled poem, Ginu Kamani's "The Goddess of Sleep," Indran Amirthanayagam's "Ceylon," Andrew Lam's "Show and Tell." The literary creations of Filipino/a, Vietnamese, and South Asian Americans carry the imperatives of peoples from once-colonized nations who retain a fierce connection to these ancestral homelands as they watch them emerge into self-sustaining countries. The condition of being postcolonial and of being diasporic does not necessarily imply an abrogation of one's civic responsibilities in the nation of one's residence. Perhaps we need to move beyond a bipolar perspective and accept that Asian America is comprised of the sensibilities of *both* fifth-generation Chinese Americans *and* first-generation immigrant Vietnamese. It may be that our understanding of the complexity of forces affecting such urgent issues as political participation, interethnic relations (both among minority groups and between the majority and minority groups), activism, and economic and educational justice among all Asian Americans can be enhanced if we construct a vision of belonging in the United States that combines the local and the global.[13]

Cutting Edge Asian America

One remarkable location in which a new and cutting-edge vision of Asian American literature is being enacted daily is the Asian American Writers' Workshop (AAWW) in New York City. Established in 1990 as "a non-profit literary arts organization dedicated to the creation, development, publication and dissemination of literature by Asians living in America," the AAWW's many facets of operation are noteworthy for the range of Asian American ethnicities featured, the diversity of issues addressed, and the vast database of authors maintained.[14] In fact, the AAWW enabled us to contact many of the authors included in this anthology when we were not able to reach them through other avenues. The workshop runs a very successful bookstore with over two thousand titles which include Asian American poetry, fiction, drama, essays, and literary and cultural criticism. It offers creative writing workshops conducted by writers from many Asian American ethnicities—for example, Amitava Kumar (South Asian), Ralph Peña (Filipino), Susan Choi (Korean), and Christian Langworthy (Vietnamese) have been among those who have run workshops in their particular genre. I point to the ethnicities of the writers because AAWW's active outreach to communities that have often felt marginalized in Asian America cannot go unacknowledged. Within the workshop, there is a vibrant exchange of ideas among diverse Asian Americans (between first-generationers and those who have been embedded for multiple generations in the United States; between queer and straight, multiracial and monoracial Asian Americans; between diasporics and U.S.-centered individuals; and among people from the various ethnicities that are comprised in Asian America). Perhaps New York City, with its complex mix of Asian American ethnicities, facilitates this nontraditional approach to Asian American literature. In addition to publishing three ethnicity-specific anthologies (*Contours of the Heart: South Asians Map North America, Flippin': Filipinos on America,* and *Watermark: Vietnamese American Poetry and Prose*) and two poetry anthologies (*Quiet Fire: A Historical Anthology of Asian American Poetry* and *Black Lightning: Poetry in Progress*),[15] the workshop has illuminated the New York City Asian American experience in two recently released anthologies (*The Nuyorasian Anthology: Asian American Writings about New York City* and *Tokens? The NYC Asian American Experience on Stage*).[16] The latter two publications go a long way toward balancing the West-coast dominated settings and images of Asian American literature.

Aesthetics and Politics: Debates and Divides

In 1998, the Asian American Writers Workshop conferred the Asian American Literary Award on Japanese Hawaiian author Lois-Ann Yamanaka's controversial novel *Blu's Hanging* (1997).[17] In doing so, the workshop signaled the centrality of literary craft to its mission, thereby eschewing the complicated tangle of politics and aesthetics that marked the reception of the novel at the 1998 conference of the Association for Asian American Studies. In June of 1998, the AAAS membership voted to rescind the literary award it had made to Yamanaka for *Blu's Hanging*. A resolution introduced by the association's Filipino American caucus called for a revocation of the award on the grounds that the novel gratuitously stereotyped Filipino Hawaiians as sexual predators (and so reinforced negative images of Filipino men prevalent in Hawai'i). The ultimate passage of the resolution was not without its wrenching dilemmas for many members of the association. I raise the issue not to rehash a painful event that many would prefer to move beyond, but rather to draw attention to the complex intersection between aesthetics and politics that marks a critical moment in Asian American studies today.

Writers who sent in statements to the association decried what they saw as literary policing and emphatically declared an author's right to creative freedom. The members introducing the resolution asserted that they weren't calling for censorship—because they weren't demanding that the book be removed from bookstores or classrooms; in fact, they welcomed active discussion of the book, they said—but were asking that the association not endorse what they saw as the internal racism of the book by giving it an award. The association, they argued, had been established to create a pan-ethnic coalition of diverse Asian American scholars, educators, and others involved in the study of Asian America; therefore, given the genesis of the association, the divisiveness generated by the award was counterproductive to the association's objectives.

The discipline of Asian American studies has metamorphosed to the point at which such ideological debates are likely to emerge on multiple fronts (the diasporic versus U.S.–centered focus of the field described above is one such front, for example). Rather than lament the development of such debates, I would argue that they attest to the growing vitality and complexity of the field. In March 2000, at the sixth annual conference of the Asian Pacific American Law Students Association at Harvard University, one of the panels focused on the "changing paradigms in Asian American literature." Panel organizers asked the speakers to consider the extent to which Asian American writers' works ought to have ethnic "resonance" and to engage with the "social and political implications of Asian American literature":

> Writers have tremendous power to capture individual and collective representations of our community. Literature is a central slice of the ongoing enterprise of defining our "conglomerate ethnic image," and in turn informs our macro understandings of race and identity that are reflected in jurisprudence and other social structures. . . .
>
> How is the new generation of writers addressing the tension between their artistic and political roles? Do they see their works as sending important political messages, or do they reject any sort of political typecasting in favor of "art for art's sake"? Does the question of connecting art and politics require us to think beyond these dichotomies? Do these artists presenting new visions believe they have an obligation to debunk stereotypes in their portrayal of Asian American characters? What obligations are there to "represent" the community and attendant issues of family, immigration, and discrimination?[18]

Thinking of aesthetics (art) and politics as mutually exclusive facets of a literary work is not a constructive approach to Asian American writing. One cannot legislate themes, nor can one demand that writers and poets render certain situations in preference to others. Creativity cannot perform under duress. Poet Christian Langworthy and novelist Samantha Chang, two of the panel's four speakers, explained that for them the relationship between aesthetics and politics is continually in flux, continually subject to new formations, and never predictable. In correspondence with me, Langworthy remarked, "If themes inherent to being an Asian American exist, then they exist very implicitly in my writing, so that I see them only after reading my work. I would like to place *War Child* [his forthcoming novel] under what is called 'global literature.' It is neither about Asian America, Asian, nor is it about Americans, but its themes are not uncommon to the rest of the world."

The Anthology

We put together *Bold Words* to reflect the impact of new social, cultural, political, and economic forces on present-day Asian America. We cover all genres, and in our selections encompass regional, ethnic, and thematic diversity. Of the selections, those by Chinese American writers number 11, Filipino/a 12, Japanese 14, Korean 8, South Asian 11, Southeast Asian 9, bi/multiracial 5. Our gender split is almost equal: 38 women and 32 men. Undoubtedly there are still gaps: for instance, we acknowledge the relative paucity of gay/lesbian writing and writing by bi/multiracial people in our collection.

Each genre section is introduced by a recognized practitioner in the genre. These section introductions provide varied frameworks within which to consider the genres. An interview that Esther and I did with Meena Alexander introduces the memoir section. Alexander, whose memoir, *Fault Lines* (1993), and personal essay collection, *The Shock of Arrival: Reflections on Postcolonial Experience* (1996) have received high acclaim,[19] describes memoir as the "intersection between what one is driven to say but cannot say in the shadow of where words fall." There's an unfinished quality to memoir, says Alexander, a rawness that is not an attribute of poetry or fiction (Alexander is a widely published poet as well). "We don't want too much perfection [in a memoir], because you think, 'What the hell is this? Is it for real?'"

Eileen Tabios, editor of *Black Lightning: Poetry in Progress* and herself an accomplished poet, urges us to savor the poems as *poems,* to "[r]ead the poems for what they say to [us], rather than through the clouds of context in which the poetry of their authors has been featured, whether as works by writers-of-color, creations from a multicultural canon, songs from a diaspora, or hymns from Asian America." But she also cautions us against completely adopting the aesthetic posture or a posture divorced from social and political concerns, because factors such as "racism and objectification have afflicted Asian America."

Gary Pak, fiction writer from Hawai'i, voices amazement and not a little unease at the flood of new writers: "Yes, I must admit, the throes of being a has-been brushed me wildly while reading those stories of the many, many unknown names of this new generation of Asian American fiction writers. (And I thought I was in this 'new' generation!) And the real reason—I've had to be honest to myself—is that these writers are good. *Damn,* these writers are *good,* most of them transcending your typical 'Asian American' topics." His undisguised sense of surprise reminds us of the remarkable demographic changes that have taken place within Asian America in the last twenty years and the rapidly expanding realms of Asian American experience.

Roberta Uno, Artistic Director of New WORLD Theater in Amherst, Massachusetts, introduces the drama section. She offers a rich overview of innovative Asian American playwrights and performing artists while reminding us of the urgent need to document and preserve their work so that it does not "evaporat[e] with its final performance." Uno draws attention to the challenges that Asian American theater must address in the new millennium: going "outside the box" of ethnic-specific issues, situating work in community-based settings, collaborating with other racial and ethnic groups, incorporating transnational cultural and artistic influences, engaging with "alternative social and political contexts (feminist, multiracial, and/or queer, for example)" and breaking "the confines of a bicoastal geography." Her closing paragraphs read like an invocation, as she lists numerous performing artists and theater companies that are transforming the landscape of Asian American theater.

Bold Words gives readers a nuanced snapshot of Asian American literature at this critical moment of self-examination and paradigmatic redefinitions. The available literature is immense in scope and rich in its multiplicity of voices. Asian Americans are bold writers—whether they're writing about Asian Americans or about others, whether they're placing their narratives in the United States or elsewhere. Their creations are so numerous and so compelling as to have an undeniable impact on the shape of the American literary landscape.

Notes

1. Shirley Geok-lin Lim and Mayumi Tsutakawa, eds., *The Forbidden Stitch: An Asian American Women's Anthology* (Corvallis, Oreg.: Calyx Books, 1989); Roberta Uno, ed., *Unbroken Thread: An Anthology of Plays by Asian American Women* (Amherst: University of Massachusetts Press, 1993); Jessica Hagedorn, ed., *Charlie Chan Is Dead: An Anthology of Contemporary Asian American Fiction* (New York: Penguin, 1993); Maria Hong, ed., *Growing Up Asian American* (New York: Avon Books, 1993), Walter K. Lew, ed., *Premonitions: The Kaya Anthology of New Asian North American Poetry* (New York: Kaya Production, 1995); Garrett Hongo, ed., *Under Western Eyes: Personal Essays from Asian America* (New York: Anchor Books, 1995); Geraldine Kudaka, ed., *On a Bed of Rice: An Asian American Erotic Feast* (New York: Anchor Books, 1995); Luis H. Francia and Eric Gamalinda, eds., *Flippin': Filipinos on America* (New York: Asian American Writers Workshop, 1996)

2. Frank Chin, Jeffrey Paul Chan, Lawson Fusao Inada, and Shawn Wong, eds., *Aiiieeeee! An Anthology of Asian American Writers* (Washington, D.C.: Howard University Press, 1974); Shawn Wong, ed., *Asian American Literature: A Brief Introduction and Anthology* (New York: HarperCollins, 1996).

3. See Linda Trinh Vo, "The Vietnamese American Experience: From Dispersion to the Development of Post-Refugee Communities," *Asian American Studies: A Reader,* eds., Jean Yu-wen Shen Wu and Min Song (New Brunswick, N.J.: Rutgers University Press, 2000), 290–305. For the most up-to-date population trends in Asian America, see also United States census data at internet address <http://www.census.gov/population/www/pop-profile/apipop.html>. For annual immigration data by country of origin, see United States Immigration and Naturalization Service data at internet address <http://www.ins.usdoj/text/aboutins/statistics/annual>.

4. Shirley Geok-lin Lim, ed., *Asian-American Literature: An Anthology* (Lincolnwood, Ill.: NTC/Contemporary Publishing Group, 2000).

5. Stephen H. Sumida, "Presidential Address Presented at the Association for Asian American Studies Annual Meeting, Philadelphia, Pennsylvania, April 2, 1999," *AAAS Newsletter* 16.2 (May 1999): 9.

6. John M. Liu and Gary Y. Okihiro, "Introduction," *Journal of Asian American Studies* 3.1 (February 2000): 1–5.

7. Shirley Hune and Phil Tajitsu Nash, "Reconceptualizing Community,

Pedagogy, and Paradigms: Asian American Studies and Higher Education," *Journal of Asian American Studies* 3.1 (February 2000): 7–15.

8. Somini Sengupta, "Asian-American Programs Are Flourishing at Colleges," *New York Times* June 9, 1999: A24.

9. Peter Monaghan, "A New Momentum in Asian-American Studies," *The Chronicle of Higher Education* 45.30 (April 2, 1999): A16.

10. Cynthia Sau-ling Wong, "Denationalization Reconsidered: Asian American Cultural Criticism at a Theoretical Crossroads," *Amerasia Journal* 21.1, 2 (1995): 1–27.

11. Arif Dirlik, "Asians on the Rim: Transnational Capital and Local Community in the Making of Contemporary Asian America," in *Across the Pacific: Asian Americans and Globalization.* ed. Evelyn Hu-Dehart, Asia Society, New York (Philadelphia: Temple University Press, 1999), 29–60.

12. The recent case against Wen Ho Lee is a good example of the suspicion attaching to Asian Americans' loyalty to the United States. For another example, see L. Ling-chi Wang, "Race, Class, Citizenship, and Extraterritoriality: Asian Americans and the 1996 Campaign Finance Scandal," *Amerasia Journal* 24.1 (1998): 1–21. The internment of 110,000 Japanese Americans during World War II is, of course, one of the first injustices resulting from the assumed disloyalty of Asian Americans.

13. For a fascinating collection of essays discussing, in a general sense, the relationship between local commitments and global responsibilities, see Joshua Cohen, ed., *For Love of Country: Debating the Limits of Patriotism* (Boston: Beacon Press, 1996).

14. Asian American Writers' Workshop, *Annual Report 1999* (New York: Author, 1999).

15. Sunaina Maira and Rajini Srikanth, eds., *Contours of the Heart: South Asians Map North America* (1996); Barbara Tran, Monique T. D. Truong, and Luu Truong Khoi, eds., *Watermark: Vietnamese American Poetry and Prose* (1998); Juliana Chang, ed., *Quiet Fire: A Historical Anthology of Asian American Poetry, 1892–1970* (1996); Eileen Tabios, ed., *Black Lightning: Poetry in Progress* (1998); (all titles, New York: Asian American Writers Workshop).

16. Bino A. Realuyo, ed., *The Nuyorasian Anthology: Asian American Writings about New York City* ; Alvin Eng, ed., *Tokens? The NYC Asian American Experience on Stage* (both titles, New York: Asian American Writers Workshop, 1999).

17. Lois-Ann Yamanaka, *Blu's Hanging* (New York: Farrar, Straus and Giroux, 1997).

18. Harvard Asian Pacific American Law Students Association, "Breaking the Writer's Block: Changing Paradigms in Asian American Literature," in *Visions and Voices: New Horizons for the Next Millennium* (The Sixth Annual National Asian American Conference on Law and Public Policy), (Cambridge, Mass.: docupress, 2000), 13.

19. Meena Alexander, *Fault Lines* (New York: The Feminist Press, 1993) and *The Shock of Arrival: Reflections on Postcolonial Experience* (Boston: South End Press, 1996).

PART 1

MEMOIR

Introduction

The Voice That Passes through Me: An Interview with Meena Alexander

ESTHER IWANAGA AND RAJINI SRIKANTH

In your essay on your reaction to reading The Waves, *you quote Virginia Woolf as saying that the body "goes before me like a lantern down a dark lane, bringing one thing after another out of darkness into a ring of light." Could you speak about your sense of the relationship between memoir writing as an activity of the mind and memoir writing as a memory of the muscles—the kind of bodily recovery of what's hidden deep within one's bones and muscles that Woolf speaks of.*

I write, as you know, across genres. I hopscotch, in one or two different squares or placing both feet in the same square and then I think of the different kinds of writing, the different voices that come from the same body. But all of them draw on an instinct for what cannot in the end be spoken. Which might be a weird thing for a writer to say, but that's really what drives me as a writer: the intersection between what one is driven to say and yet cannot say in the shadow of where words fall. And I mean words written in multiple languages, because I grew up in India on the borders of languages and I traveled a great deal as a child.

Memory is very central for me in what I'm doing at the moment. I'm going for what I cannot remember but has left a vacancy in my head. It is a visceral thing. I'm writing poems, but I'm also writing a prose book, a very simple book. It's going to have a different kind of voice than *Fault Lines* or *Manhattan Music,* which are both jagged in their own ways. I just ended a section in this book with the grandfather figure clutching a window, and thirty years later I had the child going into the room and finding and holding onto the window. That is going to be the transition between two chapters, but there's thirty years in between because I'm playing with different times.

Thank God we have long lives. There was a time when I was pretty young, writing at thirteen—and I would think, "Oh, seventeen is finished. If you haven't done it by seventeen, it's over." Now I understand why we've been given a gift of long lives. We are able to recuperate and retrieve, so I feel as though I'm self-inventing at this point in my own history. Between '88 and '96, I wrote a lot and I wrote very fast. It was a "coming to America" kind of writing. I felt that I had to write in order to be, and now I'm doing something else. In other words, writing can be writing in order to understand that those different pieces of time and those different spaces that I've lived in are just parts of a life. Now it's as if I'm writing to uncover the very small details that make up a child's life because it is a child's story. The fact that these details are spread over different places, different territories, different cultures doesn't matter except and insofar as it impacts on the child. So the map is different.

I'm trying to go back so that what is for me now is all of a piece with what was before. Not that the shadows don't fall or the barbed wire or the gaps, but it is of the same piece of voice. It's almost about entering into a dream state, blending these multiple zones together so that the work of memory and the work of cultural transformation become part and parcel of setting up a new imaginary. I think that's the task of all of us who are sitting at this table. There's a sense that one is laying something down because it has to be done—there's nothing else in place. I remember David Mura saying to me a few years ago, "It's so weird, Meena. We're not that old, but there's a whole other generation for whom we are older." Then we both agreed: "In ten years, it's going to be totally different." There's an extraordinary sense of an explosion of writing. I think it comes precisely because of the energy that comes out of necessity.

You said that writing, especially memoir writing, is a way in fact to translate what is very visceral and bring it into the zone of language. Part of me is comparing that with fiction writing, which I see as qualitatively different. In memoir writing you are writing to fill a gap of things that cannot be linguistically articulated. In fiction, I almost feel that it's a construction of something that you're, how do I put this—

Fiction is like creating an architecture, because you already have the materials—you polish and plane down; they are handed to you. With the work I'm doing now, I was thinking to write a memoir and then I thought, "No, I couldn't do it that way." I wanted a structure that I could enter into.

It seems as if there is more muscle and bone in memoir.

With memoir, there's always a sense that you're doing it for the first time and you're doing it because you have to do it; nobody else's life is like yours. I think that is the impulse behind memoir, the places where stuff can't be articulated. That pushes us back to Woolf's idea of a memory of the body.

I think it's important to be able to do different kinds of writing. Some writing, like an open poem, is very vulnerable. But whatever kind of writing you engage in, it is part of this task of creating an imaginary which then might take the place of where histories cannot render up the visible. For instance, there's work done in India now by people like Ritu Menon and Urvashi Butalia about women during Partition who were abducted, raped, forcibly taken away from their families, and then after Partition they were taken back to the old home. But of course everything had changed. Among the very interesting things that have come up in these oral histories is that there are things that people can't talk about. Not just don't want to talk about, but can't talk about. And then it will be the silences, the places in the way the body moves or doesn't move that will have to tell that story. I think that is the task of this zone of the imaginary. For writers, our job is to go where talk doesn't attach.

Adrienne Rich, whom I admire greatly, said once, "If you're a writer, you have to go where the fear is," and that's what it's all about. That's one of the things that memoir—good memoir—does. It goes there. I think good poetry goes there. I think good fiction goes there. For a poet, there's a kind of crystallization of the image which memoir doesn't quite permit. Certain things are possible because you crystallize them, you hold them up to the light. Whereas when you deal with memoirs, there's always a sense that there's a living person. It's part of the stamp of veracity which is very different from fiction or poetry. It's a genre that most closely attaches us to reality, whatever that is.

So it's always incomplete in some way.

It has to be because there's always the hand that wrote it.

So you can't offer up in a memoir the kind of perfection that a poetic image gives you.

No, you can't. And yet, there are some extraordinary memoirs that seem to in bits, and yet we are also suspicious if they do too much of it. We don't want too much perfection, because you think, "What the hell is this? Is it for real?" Then of course you have to ask yourself, "Why are there so many memoirs now?" I think it's because people really want to talk about their lives.

Traditionally, memoir was used to look back at a life well lived, to articulate an organized narrative of all one's deeds and to trace a recognizable trajectory of development from childhood to an advanced period of one's life. Lately, there has been an explosion of memoir writing among Asian Americans—yourself, Shirley Lim, David Mura, Lydia Minatoya, Abraham Verghese, Garrett Hongo, to name a few. Clearly, these writers are not at the end of their careers. What role do you think memoir writing of this kind—in the thick of one's life and work—plays for the artist?

I started *Fault Lines* and I went to India to interview my mother. She said, "This is ridiculous. You can't write a memoir. You either have to be very famous or very old, and you're neither. Look at me, I'm not even seventy myself." She was actually quite offended that I would write a memoir. She felt it was a totally inappropriate project, and how would I feel if Svati [her daughter] came to me and said, "I want to write a memoir." I would feel very nervous.

But there's a sense that some piece of your life is not in place, so something has to be constructed in order for the future to begin. That's a very grandiose way of putting it. It makes it sound like I'm involved in a town planning project. I really don't mean that. When I was writing *Fault Lines* the kids were little and I was waking up at four to write. It was an enormous necessity. I was terrified because I thought when I finished it, I would just die. There's a sense of wanting to achieve one's life which in some way feels very unfinished and raw. I get the feeling that memory has to be constructed—not that it should come into being but that it should be constructed. This is the project of revisionism that we're all engaged in in some fashion or other.

For Asian Americans, even for those who are born and raised in this country, there is a way in which memory can be disjunctive. It makes us exiles from ourselves. If you are an immigrant or born of migrant parents and you are a minority in a country, you live in a racialized reality. There is a way in which what you remember from your parents becomes a way of authenticating what cannot be rendered visible in a majority culture. It's a very powerful tug of memoir. It says, "Yes, this really happened. This is the way my parents, my grandparents lived and I know you don't believe it." It's as if as soon as you said that, then it's extraordinary because there are so many other people who are like you, which you can't know till you get to that point of saying.

Memoirs can have a capacity to cut across into the realm of myth, which brings us to the question of cultural translation. There are historical materials which are part of our cultural memory, part of the public space in which we grow up that also inevitably suppresses and cuts away and mutilates in silence. It's the task of the zone of the imaginary to render some of the silences into speech. You remember, but beyond just remembering you are offered the construction of a future. There is always that future project built into the task of memory.

It's almost as though you construct a certain self to carry you forward.

Which is a construction, you have to acknowledge. It's made up, but the made-up has many important uses. What is made up for you is truth for the one who comes after you. It seems to me that in the deepest type of memoir is the tug for what cannot be spoken. I think that's what drives people: What cannot be spoken cannot enter into history—and so you write a memoir. I am always plagued by a sense of incompletion, which is why one keeps writing. Otherwise I would have felt that I'm done. I would just paint my nails or something.

Memoir takes you to places where language hasn't been before. In writing you need to extract language from somewhere. Does that extraction give you the power then to shape poetry? I know it's not cause and effect, but it's a totally different relationship to language.

Writing memoir prose is like getting into the rough material. But it isn't just digging something out, it's also laying it down. That's the crucial piece for memoir we must not forget. It isn't just that when you extract the material you are closer to the crudeness and rawness of your life. It's that when you make the structure, you're putting it back in place and saying, "This is my life." That's very important. Whereas in a poem, unfortunately—I mean I love poetry, it's what's closest to my heart—when you finish a poem you don't really have a bridge back. A poem just kind of leaves you there; it closes you out. I suffer when I finish a poem. Even if there's a momentary clarity, a release.

Also when you write a memoir, there is always the boundary of the historical present within which the text is being composed and to which it will return. This is not the case for poetry, for better and for worse. In other words, poetry creates quite precisely the illusion that it is raised up above the material. When you pick up a powerful poem or a very good novel, you feel that you've entered a life and a world, but you don't quite have the sense that you're going through someone's experience in the same way, which is what the access to memoir writing requires.

The other critical question you haven't really raised but implied is the whole question of the author, the figure of the author. If you write a memoir, people think they know you, because what is in the book is thought to be attachable quite seamlessly to the body of the writer. That's one of the dangers but also one of the enormous attractions of the memoir. So many people have called and said, "I know all about you, but you don't know me." Is that part of the price you pay for this constant clarification? But of course the I keeps changing. I don't really know myself.

What makes David Mura reveal himself?

I think for him it's part of the coding of history—the task of making up a history so that sexuality for him and the play of the erotic are also part of the same world: lynched black men and the colors of the desire we go between. Where do you belong? I think the erotic is terribly important because it is our most primitive affiliation.

In many of your writings, you speak of a splintered and splintering of self, but you write of such a self with a kind of fascination for its power. Is there a power in this splintering? If so, how do you tap into it as an artist rather than succumb in despair to its force?

The graduate students at CUNY [City University of New York] had a conference and asked me to moderate a panel on thinking back through our mothers and fathers. One of the things that suddenly struck me was the question of affiliation. My poem "Illiterate Heart" begins with Wordsworth and the Indian Mahakavi both coming up to me and saying, basically, "How can you write poetry?" One because I'm not English, and the other because I'm not male. So for me the question of affiliation is very painful and difficult. It has to involve a splintering and a reattachment.

At the conference, as I was listening to these papers on literary revisionism and the choice of affiliation, it suddenly came to me that there's a real power in going backwards into history and choosing the ground from which you write. Very often the ground from which you write will be another voice, another writer. What you have is a process of de-creation. You used the word splintering and I actually like the word de-creation; Simone Weill uses it in her writings. It involves an emptying out and a waiting upon so that the question of process is clarified, if only very briefly. There is a way in which one has to lose in order to compose, and it has to do with the way in which we make sense—in other words, an ability to lose what is taken for granted and considered solid and central, already there and readily given into the hold of words. So when you choose a literary forebear there is something revealing and integral, because you are also placing yourself in a one-to-one relationship with that person's process. I think my job is both to have the power of someone standing behind me but also to say that where the shadow falls is not where I stand, because I cannot ever have that seamless canonical affiliation.

For me, the global piece is really an accident of biography. When I was young, I was shuttling between India and North Africa. My father was in the Indian government and posted abroad. I wanted to be a writer and I thought, "How can I ever be a real writer because to be a real writer you have to grow up in one place. What kind of creature am I?" I was forced to stand apart, and coming to America was very exciting. I felt that in America, I could allow colliding memories to emerge inside me. Here there is this diasporic space, for better and worse, and I feel that it's made me the writer that I am. In order to write, not only did I have to deal with what was outside the door, but I also had to hearken back to these very early memories of moving between India and North Africa. As a child you remember these things so vividly—the steamer, people living in the hold. What does a child think? We're all going someplace, and why are we going? It was very early in me, a deep unrest about the question of location.

Theresa Cha is very important to me. If she were alive, we would be almost the same age. One of the things that comes out of her work is the partition of Korea and the war. In this book I'm writing, I'm thinking a great deal about the partition of India and the figure of Gandhi. As Asian American writers living here, bringing within us these histories of which we have memories and experiences, we're able to use this edge of dislocation in North America to render up an image of what cannot be spoken of just in terms of partitions of nations. There's some shifting, sliding—What is the opposite of discrepancy? Consonance—between these two worlds, involving the question of memory and of making up a future, a future where things are torn and split and cannot be stitched back together and there's a great deal that's been buried in silence. The question of a whole new identity is up for grabs. A minor literature—what is that? A literature that is born in the conditions of marginalization.

To be in the margin is also a very powerful position.

It can be, if you use it creatively. But it can also be deadening and destructive. If you are able to transform it, it can be powerful precisely because you've put into a play of opposition what is normally taken for granted.

Another reason lots of people are working on memory now is this burden of ethnic violence. It's no accident that the upsurge of ethnic violence in the construction of new nationhood stands side by side with a problem of amnesia which may be termed the end of memory. There's a whole other conversation underlying this which involves the questions of degradation, brutality, and cruelty that exist in may parts of the world.

I have been thinking a lot about the Diallo case recently, and actually there are lines sitting there on the kitchen counter, some lines I want to use for a poem.[1] What happened to him is part of our world and that's a very hard thing about New York City. For a long time I didn't want to think about the Diallo case, but then my son got involved in Providence, in a protest against police brutality, and once I'm drawn in, I'm drawn in. So you go where you have to go. But the fact that Amadou Diallo was standing in the doorway haunts me.

It's not like he was standing in the street; he was in his doorway. These are lives that are lived out at the threshold site. And there's a terrible unease about that. A terrible power. Do you go in, do you go out? If you stand in the door, what can you remember, what must you forget? What is it that passes through you? For me, it is the voice that passes through me—not that it's me, but it's what passes through me—that is very possible. I would never say it's me, because it's not. I don't know how else to express it.

March 18, 2000

Meena Alexander

9

Note

1. Amadou Diallo, an immigrant from West Africa, was killed by New York city police on February 4, 1999.

How My Stories Were Written

CARLOS BULOSAN

A few years ago, I wrote for the *Writer* a brief article revealing the compelling force that propelled me from an obscure occupation to the rewarding writing of short stories. That *force* was anger born of a rebellious dissatisfaction with everything around me.

When I sold my first story, I was still a laborer at a fish cannery in San Pedro, California. But immediately afterward letters came asking me how I became a writer, pointedly emphasizing the fact that I have a very limited formal education, and why was I writing proficiently in a language which is not my own?

The making of a writer is not by accident. It takes years of painstaking preparation, whether one knows or not that he is on the path of a writing career; of extensive reading of significant contemporary writings and the classics of literature, and of intensive experimental writing, before one is ready to synthesize reading, writing and experience into a solid premise from which one should begin a difficult career as a writer.

But the type of writing which flows from such a premise depends completely on the sensibility of the individual and his ability to crystallize his thoughts; whether he would interpret reality and maintain that art is not alien to life but a transmutation of it in artistic terms, or indifferently deny life and completely escape from it, as though the immediacy of man's problems of existence were not the concern of the writer.

I did not know what kind of a writer I would become. Not having known any writer personally, I had to grope my way in the dark. And what a heartbreaking journey that was! I thought I could write commercial stories for the high-paying slick magazines—and thus I wrote dozens of stories that came back as fast as I sent them out. Then the foolish notion came to me that the literary magazines were my natural field, since the literary story seemed to me the easiest thing to write; so dozens of stories again came back as fast as I sent them out.

Remember that these stories dealt with a life that was unknown to me. I wrote about imagined experiences of body and mind, put words in the mouths of characters that were ridiculously alien to them, it seems to me now. I even carefully plotted: the compulsive beginning, the staggering anti-climax or denouement, and the heartwarming or heartbreaking climax.

You see, I denied myself: my own experiences seemed irrelevant, my own thoughts seemed innocuous, my own perceptions seemed chaotic and ambiguous. These are some of the dilemmas of the beginner.

It was only when I began to write about the life and people I have known that a certain measure of confidence began to form as my periscope for future writing. And as this confidence grew and took a definite shape, I discovered that the actual process of writing was easy—almost as easy as breathing.

I wrote about my family and the village where I had been born. I wrote about my friends and myself in America, placing my characters in localities familiar to me, and always wrapping them up in contemporary events. Except, of course, my stories based on Philippine folk tales and legends. But even these were given a background known to me. And more, I humanized my legendary and folktale characters, so that reading them, it would be impossible to determine which is fact and which is the flight of imagination.

I have written many stories of this type. I will now tell you about the vast storehouse of rich material with which my childhood world endowed me so generously that I can go on indefinitely writing folkwise stories based on the hard core of reality. It is about an old man in my childhood.

It is true there are mountains which are green all the year round bordering the northside of the province of Pangasinan, my own native province, in the island of Luzon. It is true there is a fertile valley under the shadows of these mountains from which the peasants have been scratching a living since the dawn of Philippine history. And these simple peasants, backward still in their ways and understanding of the world, have not yet discarded the primitive tools that their forefathers had used centuries before them, in the beginning of a settlement that was to become the most densely packed population section of the island. The passing of time and the intensification of settlers in this valley helped preserve a common folklore that was related from mouth to mouth and from generation to generation, until it was no longer possible to distinguish which tale was indigenous to the people living there and which one was borrowed from the other tribes and molded into their own. But the telling of these tales was so enchanting, so uncommonly charming, that no man now questions the truth of their origin and the validity of their existence in times past.

It is also true that there is a village called Mangusmana, where I had been born, in this valley where a wayward river runs uncharted and waters the plains on its journey to the open seas. Here the farmers plant rice when the rains come from the mountains to the north, and corn when the sun shines, and sugarcane when soothing winds blow from the other horizon in the south and sometimes in the west, so that the fields are verdant with vegetation every day of the year.

But it is also true that when the moon was bright in the sky an old man whose age no one could remember because he was born long, long ago, in the era of the great distress of the land, who came down from his mysterious dwelling in the mountains and walked in our village and the children stoned him when he did not tell his tales of long ago: now it is true that he sometimes sat under a mango tree at the edge of the village to relate a story over a cup of red wine or when he was given a handful of boiled rice, and the children would scatter attentively on the grass around him, and the men and women would stand silently further away to catch every word, because there was no telling when he had a new tale about the people who had wandered and lived and died in that valley ages ago.

It happens that it is also true, that I heard this old man tell his tales many a time when I was a little boy. At first he did not notice my presence among the crowd of children that listened to him, but as time went by he began to notice me until at last he concentrated his telling to me.

"I have noticed your attentiveness," he said to me one day. "Do you believe these tales?"

"I believe them, Apo Lacay," I told him.

"But why?" he demanded. "These are merely the tales of an old and forgotten man who has lived beyond his time. There are others who can tell you more fascinating stories of what is happening today."

"There is wisdom in your words, Apo Lacay," I said respectfully. "Besides, I will go away some day and I would like to remember what kind of people lived here a long time past."

"You will go to a land far away," he asked. There was a sudden gleam in his eyes but just as suddenly it vanished, and a deep melancholy spread across his wrinkled face. "But you will never return, never come back to this valley."

I could not answer him then, or the day after, or long afterward—not even when I came to this land far away, remembering him.

"Everybody dies, but no man comes home again," he said sadly. "No man comes to bathe in the cool water of the river, to watch the golden grain in the fields, to know the grandeur of the meadow lark on the wing. No man comes back to feel the green loam of the land with his bare feet, to touch the rich soil with his loving hands, to see the earth move under him as he walks under his silent skies."

"I will come back, Apo Lacay," I said.

He looked at me silently and long, then there were tiny tears in his eyes.

"Son," he said at last, touching my head with his faded hands, "I will go home now."

He reached for his cane and walked away. He did not come again. Many years passed, and everybody thought he was dead. And then that year of my grand awakening, I decided to look for the old man. I went to the mountains and looked for him, sleeping in several forests and crossing many ravines and hills, shouting in the wind and climbing the tallest trees to see some signs of human habitation on the caves that dotted the mountainside. And at last I found him sitting by a small stream.

"Good morning, Apo Lacay," I greeted him.

He stirred but his face was lifted toward the sun.

"I came to say goodbye," I told him.

"So it is you," he said. "I thought you left long ago."

"Now is the time, Apo Lacay," I said. "But tell me this: is it not dangerous to live all by yourself in the mountains?"

"What is there to fear in the night? The beasts, the birds, the trees, the storms and tempests—would you be afraid of them? There is nothing to fear in the night, in the heart of night. But in the daylight among men, there is the greatest fear."

"But why, Apo Lacay?"

"In the savage heart of man there dwells the greatest fear among the living."

" But man has a mind."

"That is the seed of all the fear. The mind of man. The beast in the jungle with his ferocious fangs is less dangerous than man with his cultivated mind. It is the heart that counts. The heart is everything, son.

"Is that why you tell the kind of stories you have told us? To make us laugh?"

"Laughter is the beginning of wisdom."

"There is perhaps a great truth in what you have just said. That is why I came to see you. I will leave our country soon and I would like to remember all your stories."

"But why? In that land where you are going, will the people give you something to eat when you retell them? Will you not be afraid the children will stone you?"

"I don't know, Apo Lacay. But this I know: if the retelling of your stories will give me a little wisdom of the heart, then I shall have come home again."

"You mean it will be your book as well as mine? Your words as well as my words, there in that faraway land, my tales going around to the people? My tales will not be forgotten at last?"

"Yes, Apo Lacay. It will be exactly like that, your books as well as mine.

He was silent for a long time. He made a fire by the stream, sat by it and contemplated deeply. Then it seemed to me, watching him lost in thought, he had become a little boy again living all the tales he had told us about a vanished race, listening to the gorgeous laughter of men in the midst of abject poverty and tyranny. For that was the time of his childhood, in the age of great distress and calamity in the land, when the fury of an invading race impaled their hearts in the tragic cross of slavery and ignorance. And that was why they had all become that way, sick in soul and mind, devoid of humanity, living like beasts in the jungle of their captivity. But this man who had survived them all, surviving a full century of change and now living in the first murmurs of a twilight and the dawn of reason and progress, was the sole surviving witness of the cruelty and dehumanization of man by another man, but whose tales were taken for laughter and the foolish words of a lonely old man who had lived far beyond his time.

When I looked at him again he was already dead. His passing was so quiet and natural that I did not feel any sadness. I dug a grave by the stream and buried him with the soft murmur of the trees all around me. Then I walked down the mountains and into the valley of home, but which was no longer a home. Sometime afterward I boarded a big boat that took me to this land far away.

And now in America, writing many years later, I do not exactly know which were the words of the old man of the mountains and which are mine. But they are his tales as well as mine, so I hope we have written stories that really belong to everyone in that valley beautiful beyond any telling of it.

The Grandfather of the Sierra Nevada Mountains (From *China Men*)

MAXINE HONG KINGSTON

The strike began on Tuesday morning, June 25, 1867. The men who were working at that hour walked out of the tunnels and away from the tracks. The ones who were sleeping slept on and rose as late as they pleased. They bathed in streams and shaved their moustaches and wild beards. Some went fishing and hunting. The violinists tuned and played their instruments. The drummers beat theirs at the punchlines of jokes. The gamblers shuffled and played their cards and tiles. The smokers passed their pipes, and the drinkers bet for drinks by making figures with their hands. The cooks made party food. The opera singers' falsettos almost perforated the mountains. The men sang new songs about the railroad. They made up verses and shouted Ho at the good ones, and laughed at the rhymes. Oh, they were madly singing in the mountains. The storytellers told about the rise of new kings. The opium smokers when they roused themselves told their florid images. Ah Goong sifted for gold. All the while the English-speaking China Men, who were being advised by the shrewdest bargainers, were at the demons' headquarters repeating the demand: "Eight hours a day good for white man, all the same good for China Man." They had probably negotiated the demons down to nine-hour shifts by now.

The sounds of hammering continued along the tracks and occasionally there were blasts from the tunnels. The scabby white demons had refused to join the strike. "Eight hours a day good for white man, all the same good for China Man," the China Men explained to them. "Cheap John Chinaman," said the demons, many of whom had red hair. The China Men scowled out of the corners of their eyes.

On the second day, artist demons climbed the mountains to draw the China Men for the newspapers. The men posed bare-chested, their fists clenched, showing off their arms and backs. The artists sketched them as perfect young gods reclining against rocks, wise expressions on their handsome noble-nosed faces, long torsos with lean stomachs, a strong arm extended over a bent knee, long fingers holding a pipe, a rope of hair over a wide shoulder. Other artists drew faeries with antennae for eyebrows and brownies with elvish pigtails; they danced in white socks and black slippers among mushroom rings by moonlight.

Ah Goong acquired another idea that added to his reputation for craziness: The pale, thin Chinese scholars and the rich men fat like Buddhas were less beautiful, less manly than these brown muscular railroad men, of whom he was one. One of ten thousand heroes.

On the third day, in a woods—he would be looking at a deer or a rabbit or an Injun watching him before he knew what he was seeing—a demon dressed in a white suit and tall hat beckoned him. They talked privately in the wilderness. The demon said, "I Citizenship Judge invite you to be U.S. citizen. Only one bag gold." Ah Goong was thrilled. What an honor. He would accept this invitation. Also what advantages, he calculated shrewdly; if he were going to be jailed for this strike, an American would have a trial. The Citizenship Judge unfurled a parchment sealed with gold and ribbon. Ah Goong bought it with one bag of gold. "You vote," said the Citizenship Judge. "You talk in court, buy land, no more chinaman tax." Ah Goong hid the paper on his person so that it would protect him from arrest and lynching. He was already a part of this new country, but now he had it in writing.

The fourth day, the strikers heard that the U.S. Cavalry was riding single file up the tracks to shoot them. They argued whether to engage the Army with dynamite. But the troops did not come. Instead the cowardly demons blockaded the food wagons. No food. Ah Goong listened to the optimistic China Men, who said, "Don't panic. We'll hold out forever. We can hunt. We can last fifty days on water." The complainers said, "Aiya. Only saints can do that. Only magic men and monks who've practiced." The China Men refused to declare a last day for the strike.

The foresighted China Men had cured jerky, fermented wine, dried and strung orange and grapefruit peels, pickled and preserved leftovers. Ah Goong, one of the best hoarders, had set aside extra helpings from each meal. This same quandary, whether to give away food or to appear selfish, had occurred during each of the six famines he had lived through. The foodless men identified themselves. Sure enough, they were the shiftless, piggy, arrogant type who didn't worry enough. The donors scolded them and shamed them the whole while they were handing them food: "So you lived like a grasshopper at our expense." "Fleaman." "You'll be the cause of our not holding out long enough." "Rich man's kid. Too good to hoard." Ah Goong contributed some rice crusts from the bottoms of pans. He kept how much more food he owned a secret, as he kept the secret of his gold. In apology for not contributing richer food, he repeated a Mohist saying that had guided him in China: "'The superior man does not push humaneness to the point of stupidity.'" He could hear his wife scolding him for feeding strangers. The opium men offered shit and said that it calmed the appetite.

On the fifth and sixth days, Ah Goong organized his possessions and patched his clothes and tent. He forebore repairing carts, picks, ropes, baskets. His work-habituated hands arranged rocks and twigs in designs. He asked a reader to read again his family's letters. His wife sounded like herself except for the polite phrases added professionally at the beginnings and the ends. "Idiot," she said, "why are you taking so long? Are you wasting the money? Are you spending it on girls and gambling and whiskey? Here's my advice to you: Be a little more frugal. Remember how it felt to go hungry. Work hard." He had been an idle man for almost a week. "I need a new dress to wear to weddings. I refuse to go to another banquet in the same old dress. If you weren't such a spendthrift, we could be building the new courtyard where we'll drink wine among the flowers and sit about in silk gowns all day. We'll hire peasants to till the fields. Or lease them to tenants, and buy all our food at market. We'll have clean fingernails and toenails." Other relatives said, "I need a gold watch. Send me the money. Your wife gambles it away and throws parties and doesn't disburse it fairly among us. You might as well come home." It was after one of these letters that he had made a bonus checking on some dud dynamite.

Ah Goong did not spend his money on women. The strikers passed the word that a woman was traveling up the railroad and would be at his camp on the seventh and eighth day of the strike. Some said she was a demoness and some that she was a Chinese and her master a China Man. He pictured a nurse coming to bandage wounds and touch foreheads or a princess surveying her subjects; or perhaps she was a merciful Jesus demoness. But she was a pitiful woman, led on a leash around her waist, not entirely alive. Her owner sold lottery tickets for the use of her. Ah Goong did not buy one. He took out his penis under his blanket or bared it in the woods and thought about nurses and princesses. He also just looked at it, wondering what it was that it was for, what a man was for, what he had to have a penis for.

There was rumor also of an Injun woman called Woman Chief, who led a nomadic fighting tribe from the eastern plains as far as these mountains. She was so powerful that she had four wives and many horses. He never saw her though.

The strike ended on the ninth day. The Central Pacific announced that in its benevolence it was giving the workers a four-dollar raise, not the fourteen dollars they had asked for. And that the shifts in the tunnels would remain eight hours long. "We were planning to give you the four-dollar raise all along," the demons said to diminish the victory. So they got thirty-five dollars a month and the eight-hour shift. They would have won forty-five dollars if the thousand demon workers had joined the strike. Demons would have listened to demons. The China Men went back to work quietly. No use singing and shouting over a compromise and losing nine days' work.

There were two days that Ah Goong did cheer and throw his hat in the air, jumping up and down and screaming Yippee like a cowboy. One: the day his team broke through the tunnel at last. Toward the end they did not dynamite but again used picks and sledgehammers. Through the granite, they heard answering poundings, and answers to their shouts. It was not a mountain before them any more but only a wall with people breaking through from the other side. They worked faster. Forward. Into day. They stuck their arms through the holes and shook hands with men on the other side. Ah Goong saw dirty faces as wondrous as if he were seeing Nu Wo, the creator goddess who repairs cracks in the sky with stone slabs; sometimes she peeks through and human beings see her face. The wall broke. Each team gave the other a gift of half a tunnel, dug. They stepped back and forth where the wall had been. Ah Goong ran and ran, his boots thudding to the very end of the tunnel, looked at the other side of the mountain, and ran back, clear through the entire tunnel. All the way through.

He spent the rest of his time on the railroad laying and bending and hammering the ties and rails. The second day the China Men cheered was when the engine from the West and the one from the East rolled toward one another and touched. The transcontinental railroad was finished. They Yippee'd like madmen. The white demon officials gave speeches. "The Greatest Feat of the Nineteenth Century," they said. "The Greatest Feat in the History of Mankind," they said. "Only Americans could have done it," they said, which is true. Even if Ah Goong had not spent half his gold on Citizenship Papers, he was an American for having built the railroad. A white demon in top hat tap-tapped on the gold spike, and pulled it back out. Then one China Man held the real spike, the steel one, and another hammered it in.

While the demons posed for photographs, the China Men dispersed. It was dangerous to stay. The Driving Out had begun. Ah Goong does not appear in railroad photographs. Scattering, some China Men followed the north star in the constellation Tortoise the Black Warrior to Canada, or they kept the constellation Phoenix ahead of them to South America or the White Tiger west or the Wolf east. Seventy lucky men rode the Union Pacific to Massachusetts for jobs at a shoe factory. Fifteen hundred went to Fou Loy Company in New Orleans and San Francisco, several hundred to plantations in Mississippi, Georgia, and Arkansas, and sugarcane plantations in Louisiana and Cuba. (From the South, they sent word that it was a custom to step off the sidewalk along with the black demons when a white demon walked by.) Seventy went to New Orleans to grade a route for a railroad, then to Pennsylvania to work in a knife factory. The Colorado State Legislature passed a resolution welcoming the railroad China Men to come build the new state. They built railroads in every part of the country—the Alabama and Chattanooga Railroad, the Houston and Texas Railroad, the Southern Pacific, the railroads in Louisiana and Boston, the Pacific Northwest, and Alaska. After the Civil War, China Men banded the nation North and South, East and West, with crisscrossing steel. They were the binding and building ancestors of this place.

Ah Goong would have liked a leisurely walk along the tracks to review his finished handiwork, or to walk east to see the rest of his new country. But instead, Driven Out, he slid down mountains, leapt across valleys and streams, crossed plains, hid sometimes with companions and often alone, and eluded bandits who would hold him up for his railroad pay and shoot him for practice as they shot Injuns and jackrabbits. Detouring and backtracking, his path wound back and forth to his railroad, a familiar silver road in the wilderness. When a train came, he hid against the shaking ground in case a demon with a shotgun was hunting from it. He picked over camps where he had once lived. He was careful to find hidden places to sleep. In China bandits did not normally kill people, the booty the main thing, but here the demons killed for fun and hate. They tied pigtails to horses and dragged chinamen. He decided that he had better head for San Francisco, where be would catch a ship to China.

Perched on hillsides, he watched many sunsets, the place it was setting, the direction he was going. There were fields of grass that he tunneled through, hid in, rolled in, dived and swam in, suddenly jumped up laughing, suddenly stopped. He needed to find a town and human company. The spooky tumbleweeds caught in barbed wire were peering at him, waiting for him; he had to find a town. Towns grew along the tracks as they did along rivers. He sat looking at a town all day, then ducked into it by night.

At the familiar sight of a garden laid out in a Chinese scheme—vegetables in beds, white cabbages, red plants, chives, and coriander for immortality, herbs boxed with boards—he knocked on the back door. The China Man who answered gave him food, the appropriate food for the nearest holiday, talked story, exclaimed at how close their ancestral villages were to each other. They exchanged information on how many others lived how near, which towns had Chinatowns, what size, two or three stores or a block, which towns to avoid. "Do you have a wife?" they asked one another. "Yes. She lives in China. I have been sending money for twenty years now." They exchanged vegetable seeds, slips, and cuttings, and Ah Goong carried letters to another town or China.

Some demons who had never seen the likes of him gave him things and touched him. He also came across lone China Men who were alarmed to have him appear, and, unwelcome, he left quickly; they must have wanted to be the only China Man of that area, the special China Man.

He met miraculous China Men who had produced families out of nowhere—a wife and children, both boys and girls. "Uncle," the children called him, and he wanted to stay to be the uncle of the family. The wife washed his clothes, and he went on his way when they were dry.

On a farm road, he came across an imp child playing in the dirt. It looked at him, and he looked at it. He held out a piece of sugar; he cupped a grass-blade between his thumbs and whistled. He sat on the ground with his legs crossed, and the child climbed into the hollow of his arms and legs. "I wish you were my baby," he told it. "My baby." He was very satisfied sitting there under the humming sun with the baby, who was satisfied too, no squirming. "My daughter," he said. "My son." He couldn't tell whether it was a boy or a girl. He touched the baby's fat arm and cheeks, its gold hair, and looked into its blue eyes. He made a wish that it not have to carry a sledgehammer and crawl into the dark. But he would not feel sorry for it; other people must not suffer any more than he did, and he could endure anything. Its mother came walking out into the road. She had her hands above her like a salute. She walked tentatively toward them, held out her hand, smiled, spoke. He did not understand what she said except "Bye-bye." The child waved and said, "Bye-bye," crawled over his legs, and toddled to her. Ah Goong continued on his way in a direction she could not point out to a posse looking for a kidnapper chinaman.

Explosions followed him. He heard screams and went on, saw flames outlining black windows and doors, and went on. He ran in the opposite direction from gunshots and the yell—*eekha awha*—the cowboys made when they herded cattle and sang their savage songs.

Good at hiding, disappearing—decades unaccounted for—he was not working in a mine when forty thousand chinamen were Driven Out of mining. He was not killed or kidnapped in the Los Angeles Massacre, though he gave money toward ransoming those whose toes and fingers, a digit per week, and ears grotesquely rotting or pickled, and scalped queues, were displayed in Chinatowns. Demons believed that the poorer a chinaman looked, the more gold he had buried somewhere, that chinamen stuck together and would always ransom one another. If he got kidnapped, Ah Goong planned, he would whip out his Citizenship Paper and show that he was an American. He was lucky not to be in Colorado when the Denver demons burned all chinamen homes and businesses, nor in Rock Springs, Wyoming, when the miner demons killed twenty-eight or fifty chinamen. The Rock Springs Massacre be-

gan in a large coal mine owned by the Union Pacific; the outnumbered chinamen were shot in the back as they ran to Chinatown, which the demons
burned. They forced chinamen out into the open and shot them; demon
women and children threw the wounded back in the flames. (There was a rumor of a good white lady in Green Springs who hid China Men in the Pacific
Hotel and shamed the demons away.) The hunt went on for a month before
federal troops came. The count of the dead was inexact because bodies were
mutilated and pieces scattered all over the Wyoming Territory. No white min-
ers were indicted, but the government paid $150,000 in reparations to victims'
families. There were many family men, then. There were settlers—abiding
China Men. And China Women. Ah Goong was running elsewhere during the
Drivings Out of Tacoma, Seattle, Oregon City, Albania, and Marysville. The
demons of Tacoma packed all its chinamen into boxcars and sent them to
Portland, where they were run out of town. China Men returned to Seattle,
though, and refused to sell their land and stores but fought until the army
came; the demon rioters were tried and acquitted. And when the Boston police
imprisoned and beat 234 chinamen, it was 1902, and Ah Goong had already
reached San Francisco or China, and perhaps San Francisco again.

In Second City (Sacramento), he spent some of his railroad money at the
theater. The main actor's face was painted red with thick black eyebrows and
long black beard, and when he strode onto the stage, Ah Goong recognized the
hero, Guan Goong; his puppet horse had red nostrils and rolling eyes. Ah
Goong's heart leapt to recognize hero and horse in the wilds of America. Guan
Goong murdered his enemy—crash! bang! of cymbals and drum—and left his
home village—sad, sad flute music. But to the glad clamor of cymbals entered
his friends—Liu Pei (pronounced the same as Running Nose) and Chang Fei.
In a joyful burst of pink flowers, the three men swore the Peach Garden Oath.
Each friend sang an aria to friendship; together they would fight side by side
and live and die one for all and all for one. Ah Goong felt as warm as if he
were with friends at a party. Then Guan Goong's archenemy, the sly Ts'ao
Ts'ao, captured him and two of Liu Pei's wives, the Lady Kan and the Lady
Mi. Though Ah Goong knew they were boy actors, he basked in the presence
of Chinese ladies. The prisoners traveled to the capital, the soldiers waving
horsehair whisks, signifying horses, the ladies walking between horizontal
banners, signifying palanquins. All the prisoners were put in one bedroom, but
Guan Goong stood all night outside the door with a lighted candle in his hand,
singing an aria about faithfulness. When the capital was attacked by a common enemy, Guan Goong fought the biggest man in one-to-one combat, a
twirling, jumping sword dance that strengthened the China Men who watched
it. From afar Guan Goong's two partners heard about the feats of the man
with the red face and intelligent horse. The three friends were reunited and
fought until they secured their rightful kingdom.

Ah Goong felt refreshed and inspired. He called out Bravo like the demons
in the audience, who had not seen theater before. Guan Goong, the God of
War, also God of War and Literature, had come to America—Guan Goong,
Grandfather Guan, our own ancestor of writers and fighters, of actors and
gamblers, and avenging executioners who mete out justice. Our own kin. Not
a distant ancestor but Grandfather.

In the Big City (San Francisco), a goldsmith convinced Ah Goong to have his gold made into jewelry, which would organize it into one piece and also delight his wife. So he handed over a second bag of gold. He got it back as a small ring in a design he thought up himself, two hands clasping in a handshake. "So small?" he said, but the goldsmith said that only some of the ore had been true gold.

He got a ship out of San Francisco without being captured near the docks, where there was a stockade full of jailed chinamen; the demonesses came down from Nob Hill and took them home to be servants, cooks, and baby-sitters.

Grandmother liked the gold ring very much. The gold was so pure, it squished to fit her finger. She never washed dishes, so the gold did not wear away. She quickly spent the railroad money, and Ah Goong said he would go to America again. He had a Certificate of Return and his Citizenship Paper.

But this time, there was no railroad to sell his strength to. He lived in a basement that was rumored to connect with tunnels beneath Chinatown. In an underground arsenal, he held a pistol and said, "I feel the death in it." "The holes for the bullets were like chambers in a beehive or wasp nest," he said. He was inside the earth when the San Francisco Earthquake and Fire began. Thunder rumbled from the ground. Some say he died falling into the cracking earth. It was a miraculous earthquake and fire. The Hall of Records burned completely. Citizenship Papers burned, Certificates of Return, Birth Certificates, Residency Certificates, passenger lists, Marriage Certificates—every paper a China Man wanted for citizenship and legality burned in that fire. An authentic citizen, then, had no more papers than an alien. Any paper a China Man could not produce had been "burned up in the Fire of 1906." Every China Man was reborn out of that fire a citizen.

Some say the family went into debt and sent for Ah Goong, who was not making money; he was a homeless wanderer, a shiftless, dirty, jobless man with matted hair, ragged clothes, and fleas all over his body. He ate out of garbage cans. He was a louse eaten by lice. A fleaman. It cost two thousand dollars to bring him back to China, his oldest sons signing promissory notes for one thousand, his youngest to repay four hundred to one neighbor and six hundred to another. Maybe he hadn't died in San Francisco, it was just his papers that burned; it was just that his existence was outlawed by Chinese Exclusion Acts. The family called him Fleaman. They did not understand his accomplishments as an American ancestor, a holding, homing ancestor of this place. He'd gotten the legal or illegal papers burned in the San Francisco Earthquake and Fire; he appeared in America in time to be a citizen and to father citizens. He had also been seen carrying a child out of the fire, a child of his own in spite of the laws against marrying. He had built a railroad out of sweat, why not have an American child out of longing?

The Faintest Echo of Our Language

CHANG-RAE LEE

My mother died on a bare January morning in our family room, the room all of us favored. She died upon the floor-bed I had made up for her, on the old twin mattress from the basement that I slept on during my childhood. She died with her husband kneeling like a penitent boy at her ear, her daughter tightly grasping the soles of her feet, and her son vacantly kissing the narrow, brittle fingers of her hand. She died with her best friend weeping quietly above her, and with her doctor unmoving and silent. She died with no accompaniment of music or poetry or prayer. She died with her eyes and mouth open. She died blind and speechless. She died, as I knew she would, hearing the faintest echo of our language at the last moment of her mind.

That, I think, must be the most ardent of moments.

I keep considering it, her almost-ending time, ruminating the nameless, impossible mood of its ground, toiling over it like some desperate topographer whose final charge is to survey only the very earth beneath his own shifting feet. It is an improbable task. But I am continually traveling through that terrible province, into its dark region where I see again and again the strangely vast scene of her demise.

I see.

Here before me (as I now enter my narrative moment), the dying-room, our family room. It has changed all of a sudden—it is as if there has been a shift in its proportion, the scale horribly off. The room seems to open up too fast, as though the walls were shrinking back and giving way to the wood flooring that seems to unfurl before us like runaway carpet. And there, perched on this crest somehow high above us, her body so flat and quiet in the bed, so resident, so immovable, caught beneath the somber light of these unwinking lamps, deep among the rolls of thick blankets, her furniture pushed to the walls without scheme, crowded in by the medicines, syringes, clear tubing, machines, shot through with the full false hopes of the living and the fearsome calls of the dead, my mother resides at an unfathomable center where the time of my family will commence once again.

No one is speaking. Except for the babble of her machines the will of silence reigns in this house. There is no sound, no word or noise, that we might offer up to fill this place. She sleeps for a period, then reveals her live eyes. For twelve or eighteen hours we have watched her like this, our legs and feet deadened from our squatting, going numb with tired blood. We sometimes move fitfully about, sighing and breathing low, but no one strays too far. The living room seems too far, the upstairs impossible. There is nothing, nothing at all outside of the house. I think perhaps it is snowing but it is already night and there is nothing left but this room and its light and its life.

People are here earlier (when?), a group from the church, the minister and some others. I leave her only then, going through the hallway to the kitchen. They say prayers and sing hymns. I do not know the high Korean words (I do not know many at all), and the music of their songs does not comfort me. Their one broad voice seems to be calling, beckoning something, bared in some kind of sad invitation. It is an acknowledgment. These people, some of them complete strangers, have come in from the outside to sing and pray over my mother, their overcoats still bearing the chill of the world.

I am glad when they are finished. They seem to sing too loud; I think they are hurting her ears—at least, disturbing her fragile state. I keep thinking, as if in her mind: *I'm finally going to get my sleep, my sleep after all this raw and painful waking, but I'm not meant to have it. But sing, sing.*

When the singers finally leave the room and quickly put on their coats I see that the minister's wife has tears in her eyes: so it is that clear. She looks at me; she wants to say something to me but I can see from her stunted expression that the words will not come. Though I wanted them earlier to cease I know already how quiet and empty it will feel when they are gone. But we are all close together now in the foyer, touching hands and hugging each other, our faces flushed, not talking but assenting to what we know, moving our lips in a silent, communal speech. For what we know, at least individually, is still unutterable, dwelling peacefully in the next room as the unnameable, lying there and waiting beside her, and yet the feeling among us is somehow so formidable and full of hope, and I think if I could hear our thoughts going round the room they would speak like the distant report of ten thousand monks droning the song of the long life of the earth.

Long, long life. Sure life. It had always seemed that way with us, with our square family of four, our destiny clear to me and my sister when we would sometimes speak of ourselves, not unlucky like those friends of ours whose families were wracked with ruinous divorce or drinking or disease—we were untouched, maybe untouchable, we'd been safe so far in our isolation in this country, in the country of our own house smelling so thickly of crushed garlic and seaweed and red chili pepper, as if that piquant wreath of scent from our mother's kitchen protected us and our house, kept at bay the persistent ghosts of the land who seemed to visit everyone else.

Of course, we weren't perfectly happy or healthy. Eunei and I were sometimes trouble to my parents, we were a little lazy and spoiled (myself more than my sister), we didn't study hard enough in school (though we always received the highest marks), we chose questionable friends, some from broken families, and my father, who worked fourteen hours a day as a young psychiatrist, already suffered from mild hypertension and high cholesterol.

If something happened to him, my mother would warn me, if he were to die, we'd lose everything and have to move back to Korea, where the living was hard and crowded and where all young men spent long years in the military. Besides, our family in Korea—the whole rest of it still there (for we were the lone émigrés)—so longed for us, missed us terribly, and the one day each year when we phoned, they would plead for our return. What we could do, my mother said, to aid our father and his struggle in this country, was to relieve his worry over us, release him from that awful burden through our own hard work which would give him ease of mind and help him not to die.

My mother's given name was Inja, although I never once called her that, nor ever heard my sister or even my father address her so. I knew from a young age that her name was Japanese in style and origin, from the time of Japan's military occupation of Korea, and I've wondered since why she chose never to change it to an authentic Korean name, why her mother or father didn't change the names of all their daughters after the liberation. My mother often showed open enmity for the Japanese, her face seeming to ash over when she spoke of her memories, that picture of the platoon of lean-faced soldiers burning books and scrolls in the center of her village still aglow in my head (but from her or where else I don't know), and how they tried to erase what was Korean by criminalizing the home language and history by shipping slave labor, draftees, and young Korean women back to Japan and its other Pacific colonies. How they taught her to speak in Japanese. And as she would speak of her childhood, of the pretty, stern-lipped girl (that I only now see in tattered rust-edged photos) who could only whisper to her sisters in the midnight safety of their house the Korean words folding inside her all day like mortal secrets, I felt the same burning, troubling lode of utter pride and utter shame still jabbing at the sweet belly of her life, that awful gem, about who she was and where her mother tongue and her land had gone.

She worried all the time that I was losing my Korean. When I was in my teens, she'd get attacks of despair and urgency and say she was going to send me back to Korea for the next few summers to learn the language again. What she didn't know was that it had been whole years since I had lost the language, had left it somewhere for good, perhaps from the time I won a prize in the first grade for reading the most books in my class. I must have read fifty books. She had helped me then, pushed me to read and then read more to exhaustion until I fell asleep, because she warned me that if I didn't learn English I wouldn't be anybody and couldn't really live here like a true American. *Look at me,* she'd say, offering herself as a sad example, *look how hard it is for me to shop for food or speak to your teachers, look how shameful I am, how embarrassing.*

Her words frightened me. But I was so proud of myself and my prolific reading, particularly since the whole year before in kindergarten I could barely speak a word of English. I simply listened. We played mostly anyway, or drew pictures. When the class sang songs I'd hum along with the melody and silently mouth the strange and difficult words. My best friend was another boy in the class who also knew no English, a boy named Tommy. He was Japanese. Of course, we couldn't speak to each other but it didn't matter; somehow we found a way to communicate through gestures and funny faces and laughter, and we became friends. I think we both sensed we were the smartest kids in the class. We'd sit off by ourselves with this one American girl who liked us best and play house around a wooden toy oven. I've forgotten her name. She'd hug us when we "came home from work," her two mute husbands, and she would sit us down at the little table and work a pan at the stove and bring it over and feed us. We pretended to eat her food until we were full and then she'd pull the two of us sheepish and cackling over to the shaggy remnants of carpet that she'd laid down, and we'd all go to sleep, the girl nestled snuggly between

Tommy and me, hotly whispering in our ears the tones of a night music she must have heard echoing through her own house.

Later that year, after a parents' visiting day at school, my mother told me that Tommy and his family were moving away. I didn't know how she'd found that out, but we went to his house one day, and Tommy and his mother greeted us at the door. They had already begun packing, and there were neatly stacked boxes and piles of newspapers pushed to a corner of their living room. Tommy immediately led me outside to his swing set and we horsed about for an hour before coming back in, and I looked at my mother and Tommy's mother sitting upright and formally in the living room, a tea set and plate of rice cookies between them on the coffee table. The two of them weren't really talking, more smiling and waiting for us. And then from Tommy's room full of toys, I began to hear a conversation, half of it in profoundly broken English, the other half in what must have been Japanese, at once breathy and staccato, my mother's version of it in such shreds and remnants that the odd sounds she made seemed to hurt her throat as they were called up. After we said goodbye and drove away in the car, I thought she seemed quiet and sad for me, and so I felt sadder still, though now I think that it was she who was moved and saddened by the visit, perhaps by her own act. For the momentary sake of her only son and his departing friend, she was willing to endure those two tongues of her shame, one present, one past. Language, sacrifice, the story never ends.

Inside our house (wherever it was, for we moved several times when I was young) she was strong and decisive and proud; even my father deferred to her in most matters, and when he didn't it seemed that she'd arranged it that way. Her commandments were stiff, direct. When I didn't listen to her, I understood that the disagreement was my burden, my problem. But outside, in the land of always-talking strangers and other Americans, my mother would lower her steadfast eyes, she'd grow mute, even her supremely solemn and sometimes severe face would dwindle with uncertainty; I would have to speak to a mechanic for her, I had to call the school myself when I was sick, I would write out notes to neighbors, the postman, the paper carrier. Do the work of voice. Negotiate *us,* with this here, now. I remember often fuming because of it, this one of the recurring pangs of my adolescence, feeling frustrated with her inabilities, her misplacement, and when she asked me one morning to call up the bank for her I told her I wouldn't do it and suggested that she needed "to practice" the language anyway.

Gracious God. I wished right then for her to slap me. She didn't. Couldn't. She wanted to scream something, I could tell, but bit down on her lip as she did and hurried upstairs to her bedroom, where I knew she found none of this trouble with her words. There she could not fail, nor could I. In that land, her words sang for her, they did good work, they pleaded for my life, shouted entreaties, ecstasies, they could draw blood if they wanted, and they could offer grace, and they could kiss.

But now—and I think, *right now* (I am discovering several present tenses)— she is barely conscious, silent.

Her eyes are very small and black. They are only half opened. I cannot call up their former kind shade of brown. Not because I am forgetting, but because it is impossible to remember. I think I cannot remember the first thing about her. I am not amnesiac, because despite all this *I know everything about her.* But the memories are like words I cannot call up, the hidden vocabularies of our life together. I cannot remember, as I will in a later narrative time, her bright red woolen dress with the looming black buttons that rub knobbly and rough against my infant face; I cannot remember, as I will soon dream it, the way her dark clean hair falls on me like a cloak when she lifts me from the ground; I cannot remember—if I could ever truly forget—the look of those soft Korean words as they play on her face when she speaks to me of honor and respect and devotion.

This is a maddening state, maybe even horrifying, mostly because I think I must do anything but reside in this very place and time and moment, that to be able to remember her now—something of her, anything—would be to forget the present collection of memories, this inexorable gathering of future remembrances. I want to disband this accumulation, break it apart before its bonds become forever certain.

She wears only a striped pajama top. Her catheter tube snakes out from between the top buttons. We know she is slipping away, going fast now, so someone, not me, disconnects the line to her food and water. The tube is in her way. These last moments will not depend on it. Her line to the morphine, though, is kept open and clear and running.

This comforts me. I have always feared her pain and I will to the end. Before she received the automatic pump that gives her a regular dosage of the drug, I would shoot her with a needle at least five times a day.

For some reason I wish I could do it now:

I will have turned her over gently. She will moan. Every movement except the one mimicking death is painful. I fit the narrow white syringe with a small needle, twisting it on tight. I then pull off the needle's protective plastic sheath. (Once, I will accidentally jab myself deep in the ring finger and while I hold gauze to the bloody wound she begins to cry. I am more careful after that.) Now I fill the syringe to the prescribed line, and then I go several lines past it; I always give her a little more than what the doctors tell us, and she knows of this transgression, my little gift to her, to myself. I say I am ready and then she lifts her hips so I can pull down her underwear to reveal her buttocks.

I know her body. The cancer in her stomach is draining her, hungrily sucking the life out of her, but the liquid food she gets through the tube has so many calories that it bloats her, giving her figure the appearance of a young girl who likes sweets too well. Her rump is full, fleshy, almost healthy-looking except for the hundreds of needle marks. There is almost no space left. I do not think it strange anymore that I see her naked like this. Even the sight of her pubic hair, darkly coursing out from under her, is now, if anything, of a certain more universal reminiscence, a kind of metonymic reminder that not long before she was truly in the world, one of its own, a woman, fully alive, historical, a mother, a bearer of life.

I feel around for unseeable bruises until I find a spot we can both agree on.

"Are you ready?" I say. "I'm going to poke."

"*Gu-rhaeh,*" she answers, which, in this context, means some cross between "That's right" and "Go ahead, damn it."

I jab and she sucks in air between her teeth, wincing.

"*Ay, ah-po.*" *It hurts.*

"A lot?" I ask, pulling the needle out as straight as I can, to avoid bruising her. We have the same exchange each time; but each time there arises a renewed urgency, and then I know I know nothing of her pains.

I never dreamed of them. Imagined them. I remember writing short stories in high school with narrators or chief characters of unidentified race and ethnicity. Of course this meant they were white, everything in my stories was some kind of white, though I always avoided physical descriptions of them or passages on their lineage and they always had cryptic first names like Garlo or Kram.

Mostly, though, they were figures who (I thought) could appear in an *authentic* short story, *belong* to one, that no reader would notice anything amiss in them, as if they'd inhabited forever those visionary landscapes of tales and telling, where a snow still falls faintly and faintly falls over all of Joyce's Ireland, that great muting descent, all over Hemingway's Spain, and Cheever's Suburbia, and Bellow's City of Big Shoulders.

I was to breach that various land, become its finest citizen and furiously speak its dialects. And it was only with one story that I wrote back then, in which the character is still unidentified but his *mother* is Asian (maybe even Korean), that a cleaving happened. That the land broke open at my feet. At the end of the story, the protagonist returns to his parents' home after a long journey; he is ill, feverish, and his mother tends to him, offers him cool drink, compresses, and she doesn't care where he's been in the strange wide country. They do not speak; she simply knows that he is home.

Now I dab the pinpoint of blood. I'm trying to be careful.

"*Gaen-cha-na,*" she says. *It is fine.*

"Do you need anything?"

"*Ggah,*" she says, flitting her hand, "*kul suh.*" *Go, go and write.*

"What do you want? Anything, anything."

"*In-jeh na jal-leh.*" *Now I want to sleep.*

"Okay, sleep. Rest. What?"

"*Boep-bo.*" *Kiss.*

"Kiss."

Kiss.

This will be our language always. To me she speaks in a child's Korean, and for her I speak that same child's English. We use only the simplest words. I think it strange that throughout this dire period we necessarily speak like this. Neither of us has ever grown up or out of this language; by virtue of speech I am forever her perfect little boy, she my eternal righteous guide. We are locked in a time. I love her, and I cannot grow up. And if all mothers and sons converse this way I think the communication must remain for the most part unconscious; for us, however, this speaking is everything we possess. And although I wonder if our union is handicapped by it I see also the minute discoveries in the mining of the words. I will say to her as naturally as I can—as I could speak only years before as a child—*I love you, Mother,* and then this thing will happen, the diction will take us back, bridge this moment with the others, remake this time so full and real. And in our life together, our strange language is the bridge and all that surrounds it; language is the brook streaming through it; it is the mossy stones, the bank, the blooming canopy above, the ceaseless sound, the sky. It is the last earthly thing we have.

My mother, no longer connected to her machine, lies on the bed on the floor. Over the last few hours she suffers brief fits and spasms as if she is chilled. She stirs when we try to cover her with the blanket. She kicks her legs to get it off. Something in her desires to be liberated. Finally we take it away. Let her be, we think. And now, too, you can begin to hear the indelicate sound of her breathing; it is audible, strangely demonstrative. Her breath resonates in this house, begins its final cadence. She sounds as though she were inhaling and exhaling for the very first time. Her body shudders with that breath. My sister tries to comfort her by stroking her arms. My mother groans something unintelligible, though strangely I say to myself for her, *Leave me alone, all of you. I am dying. At last I am dying.* But then I stroke her, too. She keeps shuddering, but it is right.

What am I thinking? Yes. It is that clear. The closer she slips away, down into the core of her being, what I think of as an origin, a once-starting point, the more her body begins to protest the happening, to try to hold down, as I am, the burgeoning, blooming truth of the moment.

For we think we know how this moment will be. Each of us in this room has been elaborating upon it from the very moment we gained knowledge of her illness. This is the way it comes to me, but I think we have written, each of us, the somber epic novel of her death. It has taken two and one-half years and we are all nearly done. I do not exactly know of the others' endings. Eunei, my sister (if I may take this liberty), perhaps envisioning her mother gently falling asleep, never really leaving us, simply dreams of us and her life for the rest of ever. I like that one.

My father, a physician, may write that he finally saves her, that he spreads his hands on her belly where the cancer is mighty and lifts it out from her with one ultimate, sovereign effort. Sometimes (and this ought not be attributed to him) I think that his entire life has come down to this struggle against the palpable fear growing inside of his wife. And after she dies, he will cry out in a register I have never heard from his throat as he pounds his hand on the hardwood above her colorless head, *"Eeh-guh-moy-yah? Eeh-guh-moy-yah?"* *What is this? What is this?* It—the cancer, the fear—spites him, mocks him, this doctor who is afraid of blood. It—this cancer, this happening, this time— is the shape of our tragedy, the cruel sculpture of our life and family.

In the ending to my own story, my mother and I are alone. We are always alone. And one thing is certain; she needs to say something only to me. That is why I am there. Then she speaks to me, secretly. What she says exactly is unclear; it is enough, somehow, that she and I are together, alone, apart from everything else, while we share this as yet unborn and momentary speech. The words are neither in Korean nor in English, languages which in the end we cannot understand. I hear her anyway. But now we can smile and weep and laugh. We can say goodbye to each other. We can kiss, unflinching, on our mouths.

Then she asks if I might carry her to the window that she might see the new blossoms of our cherry tree. I lift her. She is amazingly light, barely there, barely physical, and while I hold her up she reaches around my neck and leans her head against my shoulder. I walk with her to the window and then turn so that she faces the tree. I gaze longingly at it myself, marveling at the gaudy flowers, and then I turn back upon her face, where the light is shining, and I can see that her eyes have now shut, and she is gone.

But here in this room we are not alone. I think she is probably glad for this, as am I. Her breathing, the doctor says, is becoming labored. He kneels and listens to her heart. "I think we should be ready," he says. "Your mother is close." He steps back. He is a good doctor, a good friend. I think he can see the whole picture of the time. And I think about what he is saying: *Your mother is close.* Yes. Close to us, close to life, close to death. She is close to everything, I think; she is attaining an irrevocable nearness of being, a proximity to everything that has been spoken or written or thought, in every land and language on earth. How did we get to this place? Why are we here in this room, assembled as we are, as if arrayed in some ancient haunted painting whose grave semblance must be known in every mind and heart of man?

I count a full five between her breaths. The color is leaving her face. The mask is forming. Her hand in mine is cold, already dead. I think it is now that I must speak to her. I understand that I am not here to listen; that must be for another narrative. I am not here to bear her in my arms toward bright windows. I am not here to be strong. I am not here to exchange goodbyes. I am not here to recount old stories. I am not here to acknowledge the dead.

I am here to speak. Say the words. Her nearness has delivered me to this moment, an ever-lengthening moment between her breaths, that I might finally speak the words turning inward, for the first time, in my own beginning and lonely language: Do not be afraid. It is all right, so do not be afraid. You are not really alone. You may die, but you will have been heard. Keep speaking— it is real. You have a voice.

From *Among the White Moon Faces:*
An Asian-American Memoir of Homelands

SHIRLEY GEOK-LIN LIM

I became an American politically with the birth of my child. I may have been a blackbird, flying into Boston as a disheveled traveler uncertain whether I was choosing expatriation, exile, or immigration. But I had no such doubts about my unborn child. He would be an American child of Jewish and Asian descent.

Native-born children carry the cultural imprint of Americanism in a way that their immigrant parents cannot. If they become encumbered by nostalgia and regret, like their parents, this consciousness of another country cannot undermine the infant primacy of an American homeland. I wanted my child to possess the privileges of a territorial self, even as I had as a young Malaysian. "Out of the cradle endlessly rocking," the folding into and unfolding out of a social space and a people. While all citizens are guaranteed juridically their claim to a place in the United States, not every claim is unquestioned, nor is that place certain. Poverty, skin color, sex, disease, disability, any difference can arouse suspicion and exclusion. I did not expect my child to be safe from these discriminations, but I wished, at least for his infancy, the primal experience of bonding with an American homeland. In this desire, I marked myself as a U.S. citizen, and I finally began the process for citizenship.

Without relatives and with only my college colleagues for a community, pregnancy was a lonely, isolating experience. One morning I had to be in New York City for an interview with the Immigration and Naturalization Office. The train rattled through the underground tunnels into Grand Central Station, shaking its entire length. On any other morning I would have been absorbing its energy, bouncing with it, waiting eagerly to emerge into the day outside and to merge into the anonymity of coats and boots and shining shop windows.

Now, overcome with nausea, I munched furiously on Saltine crackers. My seatmate pretended not to see the crumbs that fell like dandruff over my black winter coat. My stomach heaved and rumbled. It was aching to throw up, but there was nothing inside, only dry lumps of baked flour like wet cement chuting down to settle my hunger pangs.

The doors opened and everyone pushed out. I was a black fish gathered up in the net of bodies. The bodies carried me out of the train and up the stairs through other tunnels. I could not slow my stride; my legs trundled like part of a centipede's hundred pairs. I had no will in this morning rush hour's masses. Slowly my head was turning dark, and I felt myself lose consciousness. The centipede was rushing down a flight of steps toward the downtown Lexington. Just ahead the subway cars were spilling with other bodies, and a mechanical voice was announcing, "Keep clear of the closing doors. Keep clear of the closing doors." The feet rushed faster, faster down the steps.

But I could not keep up. I sat down on the steps, despite the press of bodies behind me. The river backed up, split open, then swirled around the boulder that was myself. I put my head down between my knees. The concrete steps were black and brown with grime. The dirt had piled up along the backs of the steps, bits of fresh candy wrappers still colored blue and gold, brown filter tips and butts with shredded tobacco falling out. I could see only a little piece of concrete. The rest was filled with moving legs, tan and khaki pants, blue dungarees, suede heels, frayed hems and silk-bound hems, unwashed sneakers split at the sides, white leather sneakers squeaking new, dirt-crusted workboots with soles like floors. No one stopped to ask why I was sitting on the steps of Grand Central Station. I was grateful for the city's impersonality: I could have been sitting by the abyss of the Grand Canyon listening to the rush of the wind among the bent piñon and ponderosa pines. The huge ingrained ugliness of New York's subways appeared as much a force of nature as the Grand Canyon's wind-scrubbed beauty; I was as invisible in the midst of thousands of hurrying feet as a hiker lost on the canyon's red-scarp edge.

On Saint Valentine's Day 1980, four months pregnant, I stood in a hall in White Plains and swore allegiance to the flag and to the republic for which it stands. There must have been about two hundred others there that morning, more white than brown, and there was a festive mood in the hall as the black-robed justice congratulated us. This is the crucible of America, the moment when the machinery of the state opens its gate and admits irrevocably those aliens who have passed the scrutiny of its bureaucrats—language tests, history tests, economic tests, social tests. Tests that impress with the enormous and amazingly indifferent power of representative Americans to deny you identity, tests that force you to compliance, tests for inclusion that threaten exclusion. So my patriotism on my first day as an American citizen was not unbounded. Scooping a piece of buttermilk pancake from its puddle of maple syrup at the International House of Pancakes where I had gone to celebrate my passage into American identity, I felt alien in a different way, as if my ambivalence toward the United States must now extend inward to an ambivalence toward myself. No longer a traveler, I was included in my accusations of America.

My morning sickness disappeared after three months. I swelled and swelled, fifty pounds above my normal weight, half as much as I was, a red plum tomato in my cotton summer frock. We had moved to Westchester County, fifty miles out of Manhattan, two years earlier, and while Charles commuted to teach in Manhattan, I fell in love with the Westchester suburbs for the first time. The May days were busy with Queen Anne's lace, day lilies, Dutchmen's-breeches, and flourishing sumac. I fretted over a strand of bright orange butterfly weed that had sprung up by Route 100, waving above the still gray water of the Croton Reservoir, just below our white-and-green colonial home. It was too exotic, an endangered wildflower, in plain view, with the red-winged blackbirds flashing among the sumac bushes. Sure enough in a few days the butterfly weed blossoms, winged like palpitating floaters that its milky sap invites, were gone. Some passing human had picked them, robbing the seeds that would have borne more orange wings for the years after.

We practiced huffing and puffing. The gynecologist's receptionist had me down as a *mater primigravida*. The term conjured the images of the Virgin Mary from those faraway convent days: the gravely tragic countenance, the graceful folds of cloak and robes concealing a thickened waistline. A pregnant woman oppressed by secrets, social isolation, poverty, married to a man not the father of her baby, that central story never told directly, the story of woman's delight in childbearing. The narrowing of the story to simply mother and infant, the man far away in the clouds or discreetly in the background, together with the oxen and donkeys. A celibate woman's fantasy, a revenge story for women harrowed by men's demands and commands.

I was lucky. Charles was tender and attentive, but all that deep breathing and panting came to nothing. At almost nine pounds, the baby had to be sprung out of my bony pelvic cage by a scalpel. As the nurses rushed me into the operating room, my temperature rising precipitously each minute and the fetal temperature mounting to life-threatening degrees, I focused on the life in my body. It, he, she was ready to emerge from the container which was myself. The event of childbirth is violent and bloody. As if experiencing her death, the mother cannot change course. She endures and, if she is able and wise, assists in the moment of expulsion. When the anesthesiologist crammed the plastic apparatus into my throat like a giant obscene penis, I willed my body to relax, to float like the lotus yielding its seeds to the light. At that moment I felt the cold swab of the anesthetic-soaked cotton like the curve of a scimitar across my abdomen and lost consciousness.

The nine months of pregnancy had been a slowly swelling swoon into domesticity, marked by giddy strolls through aisles of baby perambulators, crib mobiles, bath toys, terry-cloth books, hooded towels, fuzzy blue, brown, and white rabbits, dogs, lions, unicorns, Smurfs, bears and more bears, an instant cornucopia of infant goods for infant-obsessed Americans. But once my son was born, strenuously hungry and alert, it became clear I could not simply buy him a life.

I had entered U.S. society through the workplace, taking my seat in department meetings and at conference sessions as a colleague. My husband's parents were dead, he was estranged from his only brother, and all my brothers were in Malaysia. It mattered that we spent Easter, Passover, Memorial Day, Labor Day, Hanukkah, Christmas, and New Year's Eve alone, but it didn't matter that much. Occasionally a colleague invited us to a department picnic or a department brunch. But babies do not socialize through English departments. I was tormented by the fear that my son would grow up isolated, as I was, in the United States. I did not wish my son to be lonely the way we were. He was an American, whatever that was, and I wanted him to have the full plenitude of his world, not the shadowy existence of a green-card holder.

The myth of assimilation became a pressing reality as soon as I brought my son home from Northern Westchester Hospital. A child's society is his parents': cut off from the umbilical cord, he is nonetheless tied to the company his mother keeps. Or does not keep, in my case. It may have been important for my imagination to maintain the distance of the resident alien, but I wanted something different for my son. Despite the absence of an extended community, I wanted for him to have a pride of belonging, the sense of identity with a homeland, that which I had possessed as a Chinese Malaysian for a brief time in my youth. I wanted Gershom to be able to run for the presidency of the United States if that was what he wished.

The passage of assimilation began at the earliest age. Anxiously I accepted every birthday invitation that came his way from the Montessori mothers. Together, Gershom and I shopped for Mattel educational toys, boxes with differently shaped mouths and blocks, cobblers' benches, multicolored xylophones, huge plastic contraptions that invited baby fists to punch and ring and pull and pat. I chose the opulent set, the more expensive version of a brand-name product, while Gershom sat in his thrift-store stroller, pointing at each large package within reach. We drove down numerous Yorktown and Somers circular dead-ends, clutching party invitations and directions in one hand. His bottom still padded with diapers, he waddled among pink-cheeked, blond, and blue-eyed toddlers. I sat with the mommies, an alien among a dozen or so white women, an awkward mismatch among the grandmothers furiously snapping Nikons at the cake and chubby faces and the fathers with rolling video cameras. A college teacher years older than the young homemakers with junior executive husbands, I held my breath and sat very gingerly on the new sofas in these strangers' split-level ranches, where lavish bathrooms were cleaner than the shelters of billions of other humans. I could not afford contemptuous segregation or condescending kinship if I wished Gershom to have a full human connection with America.

Malls and department-store aisles do not discriminate. Everything is for sale to everyone. But women do. Mothers, keeping a wary eye on their scrambling pebble-picking children in playgrounds, do. Fathers, arriving to pick up their toddlers after work, loosening their ties by the Montessori entrance, do. If I could hope to have Gershom pass into Middle America in wall-to-wall carpeted living rooms, we never succeeded in the public playgrounds among anonymous whites.

Weekends and summers Gershom and I set forth to Reis Park, Leonard Park, Muscoot Farm, and assorted town fairs and parades. Cautiously I let him loose in the sandbox, retreated to one side where other mothers stood under the shade of birches and oaks and cast their eyes sidewise on the little spaders and grubbers. There were no homesteaders here, only transient visitors who might or might not return another afternoon. Was it the chip on my shoulder that sounded the alarm? I watched enviously as strangers veered toward each other and began exchanging intimacies of toilet training and bedwetting. I imagined their eyes were already measuring their toddlers' compatibility, one pink hand patting another pink hand's castle.

My olive-skinned child had dark handsome eyes and thick dark hair. He was oblivious to social slight as he scrambled up the teeter-totter. There was no one to teeter with him. The other children had wandered away with their parents who strolled off deep in conversation. I called out to him, placed my weight on two legs so that my body did not pull the balance down, and planted the illusion that between us we could move the teeter-totter up and down, up and down.

I had approached being alone in the United States as inevitable. It was a lonely society, even lonelier for an Asian immigrant whose train seat next to her usually remained untaken till the car was full. But what I accepted as my position in the United States I felt keenly as unacceptable for my son. A grievance gnawed in me, perhaps the displaced desires for assimilation, a growing anger that, despite his birth here in the United States, his childhood was still marked by the perception of my foreignness.

I began to ask my colleagues, "When did your family come to the United States?"

"Oh, I don't know. My grandfather was a Prussian officer, so I must be third generation."

"My mother came after World War I; got out just before Hitler. What does that make me? A second generation?"

"I came over from Manchester to do my master's at New York University. Never went home."

"Well, I'm not an American citizen. I still have my Canadian passport."

"Of course, my husband's parents are from Sicily. They are horribly traditional."

All these recent origins. All these immigrants. But the stiffness and tentativeness, the distinct charge of distance that marked one as alien and outsider, was directed chiefly to those who did not look white European.

There are many ways in which America tells you don't belong. The eyes that slide around to find another face behind you. The smiles that appear only after you have almost passed them, intended for someone else. The stiffness in the body as you stand beside them watching your child and theirs slide down the pole, and the relaxed smile when another white mother comes up to talk. The polite distance as you say something about the children at the swings and the chattiness when a white parent makes a comment. A polite people, it is the facial muscles, the shoulder tension, and the silence that give away white Americans' uneasiness with people not like them. The United States, a nation of immigrants, makes strangers only of those who are visibly different, including the indigenous people of the continent. Some lessons begin in infancy, with silent performances, yet with eloquent instructions.

Struggling through the maniacal traffic on the Taconic State Parkway after teaching at the college, I picked my son up from the baby-sitter each evening with a rush of relief, relief that he was still there in the world despite my disappearance for almost nine hours, relief at the end of another separation. I nuzzled his smooth round cheek, no texture as sensuous as my baby's skin, and held his body to mine, his warm breath and growing bulk filling me with the most intense emotions of safety and completion and of fear also.

But the weekends with a cranky baby and a busy husband sometimes stretched long and tense. I could not understand the volatility of my feelings at unexpected moments.

The first week of my son's life I cried easily. My body hurt constantly from this bond, these surges of emotion that physically pulled the milk out of my body. My nipples wept milk each time I thought of this other being, not so tiny at almost nine pounds, already insistent on his own drives, staring unblinking at me, mouth tugging at my breasts, his fists puckered and gradually uncurling ready to push and punch.

We hung a rope of bells above the crib, a mirror, so he could see himself, so he could learn to beat the bells and make a noise upon the world. Gratefully I surrendered myself to his unscheduled feeding, his fretful demands, his nightly wails, the unending rounds of diaper changes, baths, laundries, doctor visits. Satiated with mother love, I had no time for unhappiness.

He was barely two feet tall, and usually I saw him as a vulnerable, weak infant. I was afraid to leave him alone in a room, out of my sight. His slightest cry or fuss would rouse me. Accustomed to nursing on demand through the night, he would stir and wake up crying if I were not sleeping beside him. We dismantled his crib and bought a futon as it was easier for me to lie down beside him to pacify him. His intense dependency was addictive, drugged me so I had to drink jolts of coffee to keep me awake through the day. I was confused by reports that mothers should allow their babies to cry through the night to teach them to sleep alone and by my inability to do so. On the few occasions we lay rigid in bed listening to him screaming, he threw up so violently that we feared he would choke and had to rush in to change his clothes and bedding. Finally, despite the medical advice and the fear that we were contributing to a future pathology, we gave up on our attempt to wean him. In many non-Western societies, babies slept with their mothers till they were older, we told each other.

Why not in our home?

Violence, like racism, imprinted from childhood, can never be totally eradicated. My rage at my baby was all the more terrifying to me in contrast to my usual intimate protectiveness. He was so small and weak, but he struggled to have his way. The shame I suffered when my father beat me was the same shame I felt when I hit my son, only fourteen months old.

Barely walking, Gershom had already learned to say no. "No" was like his fist which waved before the mirror and which rang the bells. He beat us with it. "No, no!" he shrieked, even when he meant yes. It was the lever that pulled his mother back and forth, back and forth. He was terrified when this lever did not work, as if he could no longer see himself in the mirror. With this word he commanded us to turn back from the front door, like a fast rewind of a videotape, and to reenact the earlier scene, erasing the action that had so offended him. He believed time was plastic and recoverable, that he could control events, even to replaying them exactly the way he wanted them to be. When the television cartoon displeased him, he yelled, "No!" then cried because the television set would not replay for him the cartoon he had in mind. He regressed from godlike power to mere human frustration; his rages went on for months.

Like him I too was suddenly enraged. One night, after I had tried unsuccessfully to get him to sleep by himself, I shook him hard, and roared, "Go to sleep, damn you, go to sleep!" He gave me a startled look, then threw up, the white-spotted vomit splattering my face, his sheets, the carpet. Once, hurrying someplace, burdened with his bags, his obstinate weight, I heard him whine. He wriggled, protesting at our errand, and the bags fell. My slap left a red palm print on his cheek, and he wailed. I did not admit my guilt. He was bad, bad, bad. But I remembered my father's anger, and I was afraid of myself.

Then I slapped Gershom in front of Jane and Milton. It was true that Jane and Milton, who came up to northern Westchester every weekend, escaping the West Side, were comfortable people to be around, pleasant because safe. Some weekends they would invite us to drop by their country home, a convenient mile away. Their son, Ferdie, two years older than Gershom, was fascinated by a creature even smaller than himself. I looked forward to visiting their home, a cozy jumble of small dark rooms, set among several acres of brambly blackberries, pines, and overgrown rhododendrons, a wilderness which Jane's grandparents had bought just before the Depression as an inexpensive summer cottage to escape the city's dangerous polio-ridden streets.

That afternoon, the October Sunday streamed blue and gold outdoors. We sat in the one sunlit room, an expanded kitchen, around the scrubbed kitchen table. Gershom was babbling in the highchair while we waited for the kettle to boil. He was familiar with Jane and Milton, and at fourteen months, his confidence was overweening.

The cup of herbal tea steamed up my face, raising a different kind of gold in the kitchen. A placid boredom filled the cluttered kitchen, where every counter space was taken up with brown shopping bags from Waldbaums, packed tight with coffee, sodas, carrots, cabbages, toilet paper, cereals, packages of matzos and bagels, honey jars, and assorted cookies, comestibles that Jane and Milton carried off every Sunday to their Manhattan apartment to see them through the week. Gershom, smiling in the highchair, beat my arm with his fist as I leaned, elbows forward, to inhale the dusky steam.

"Chinese children do not hit their parents," I said. By the kitchen Jane was pouring the water for her tea bag, and Ferdie, his nose dripping from a cold, was tugging at her skirt for an ice-cream cone they had just refused him.

Bang! Again the pudgy fist hit out. It didn't hurt, but I felt myself flush. "Don't do that!" I warned. "Children should never hit their mothers!"

I suddenly imagined him an adult. There was a panic that if I could not stop him then, make him obey, everything would be lost. "Chinese children must respect their parents," the tape played in my head. A few minutes later, as I listened to Milton, elbows on the table, and blew on my mint tea, Gershom slapped my arm a third time, and chuckled as my elbow gave way. I did not think; my arm flew across the table, and the slap left red finger bruises on his face.

Milton stopped talking and raised his eyebrows. I heard Jane saying, "All right, Ferdie, if you'll come outside I'll give you your ice cream," and the sound of the kitchen door opening and shutting.

Strangely, Gershom didn't cry. Perhaps it was Milton's presence at the table, the adult's sudden wary silence and look of surprise, that stopped him. He lowered his head, bit his lip, then pretended to eat his cookie. I saw shame in Milton's averted glance. In that moment, I saw through Milton's eyes the scene of my own childhood; it was excruciating. The shame prevented me from picking the baby up; it spoke in a stifled insistent voice, "Chinese children do not hit their parents!" It forced me to stay in my chair sipping the flat mint tea, while Jane and Milton politely talked about Ferdie's ear infections, and led me home, where I cuddled my baby tearfully, because I hadn't meant to slap him.

The shame did not prevent me from hitting him again. Sometimes it was a smack on a diaper-cushioned bottom; or a slap on the hand, sharp enough to cause a pucker and a wail. Each time I felt shame and defiance, mixed with panic: panic that he was not me, he was hatefully not me; defiance against the shame that insisted that what I was doing was wrong.

The last time I slapped him, it was in front of my husband. Not yet two, Gershom was fussing about putting on his shoes. "Hold still while I put on your other shoe!" I said. Sitting on the stairs, he continued to wriggle. His foot slipped out of my hands and the tiny sneaker fell down. As unreflecting and as quick as a branch in a wind storm my hand went up. Whap! Startled I watched the vivid shape of my palm print on his cheek turn crimson.

Charles stood at the top of the stairs, a calm presence. "I'll put your sneakers on for you," he said, and reached down for the baby. A few minutes later we were out of the door, nothing discussed.

The red finger marks on the cheek faded after an hour, but in that silent hour I rehearsed the scene through Charles's eyes, seeing with no excuses my adult size, the actual littleness of my baby, and finally that I was repeating those very scenes of brutality that my father had wreaked on me.

There were no more slaps after that morning, although I continued to struggle with stubborn outbursts of rage, an adamantine insecurity that would turn my child into my enemy were my reason less supported by my love for him. Once started, the cycle of family violence may never end. Only the consciousness of one's own precarious position in the cycle can contain the violence. To change the blow to a caress, the sharp and ugly words to careful explanation, the helpless choking rage to empathy, that is my struggle as a mother: to form a different love.

The consciousness of family as love and violence all in one, and the power to stop the violence, whether practiced by men or women, is, for me, a feminist consciousness. I could only unravel the repetitions of fear and rage by understanding myself as a woman: a girl-child seizing autonomy rather than suffering damage, but damaged still by that premature forced growth, a young woman fearing independence but fearing dependency more.

For women breaking out of closed societies, the break itself is traumatic. Liberation hurts. Feminism must prepare women for struggle not comfort. Women who look for comfort reject feminism's lessons, but without those struggles, we can never move out of our parents' houses.

I did not understand my place as a feminist until very late. In 1982, while my husband remained in New York, I returned to teach for a semester at the National University of Singapore. My son was just two years old, and my mother had been asking to meet him. I intended for the six months to be a private retreat, when my son could be with his grandmother, and I might work out my still unsettled ambivalences with her. However, much of my time there when not teaching became taken up with defining a public sense of a female self.

Unbeknown to me, my first book of poems had brought me public attention in Malaysia and Singapore. Published as part of the Writing in Asia series, it had won one of the most significant international awards ever given to a "local" writer. Still, when the Singapore newspaper, *The Straits Times,* interviewed me, the reporter asked about my husband's response to my success, and the article featured a photograph of me playing with my handsome toddler. Times Books International had also published a collection of my stories that year, a number of which had appeared among the top ten of the *Asiaweek* short-story competition. *Asiaweek* had published both the prize-winning story and an extensive interview. But when some junior college students came to interview me for their newspaper, they wanted to know why my stories centered on women characters. After La Leche Club invited me to speak to its members, the papers carried a short news item about my talk on breast-feeding. It was an uneasy period for me. For all my early struggles and professional visibility, once back in Singapore I was inevitably, inextricably woman. Wife, mother, and breast—I was continuously addressed as such.

From *My Own Country: A Doctor's Story of a Town and Its People in the Age of AIDS*

ABRAHAM VERGHESE

In the fall, the mountains of Tennessee glowed like molten lava in every direction. Pine needles crackled underfoot and stuck to the carpet in our house, bringing their scent within. Every day a cluster of leaves collected in the niche between the windshield and the bonnet of my car. The leaves were so brittle that they snapped and popped in my fingers when I tried to lift them out intact.

At Mountain Home, the lawns were covered with a fiery carpet of leaves. They were plastered against the wire fence, caught like fish in a net, until the VA groundskeepers came and picked the fence clean.

The giant oak tree near the old skating pond stood unshakable. Every year it grew more familiar. When I went jogging, I began at this oak tree, stretching my calf muscles while leaning against it. Where once low branches had extended out, there were now big hollows. If no one was around, I wrapped my arms around its trunk and hugged it like an old friend, breathed in its fragrance, felt the reassuring scrape of bark against my skin. With the flesh of my arms joined to the tree, my feet between its knobby roots, I felt connected to Mountain Home, to my adopted country, to the earth. I wanted to stop time.

But despite its placid veneer, the VA was abuzz with change. Rumor had it that we were slated not only for the construction of "bed towers" but also for the construction of a new nursing home and domiciliary. Change had also come about in the form of new faculty recruits. Two of my former fellow residents had returned to Mountain Home as junior faculty after completing fellowships in hematology and oncology. We who had stalked these hallways at all hours, dressed in scrub suits, now watched others ruling the hospital during the night's quiet hours. In the corridors we exchanged secret smiles, thought about how once we had plotted revolution, had considered blowing up the radiology department to inject some life into that sluggish section.

Every subspecialty division was adding new members. Steve and I were recruiting for an additional infectious diseases faculty member. We found Felix Sarubbi, an academician who had been on the faculty at the University of North Carolina at Chapel Hill before joining the Asheville VA. He was well published—a true scholar—and was well known in academic infectious diseases circles.

Fil plunged right into the business of infectious disease consultation at the VA and Miracle Center. For a while, my workload was divided in half: Fil rounded at the Miracle Center and saw consults there for a week while I covered the VA. The next week we reversed roles. Fil scheduled a half-day clinic of his own at the University Practice Group and began not only to see new HIV-infected persons, but also to get to know some of my old patients in follow-up.

I could not imagine such luxury. There was one week where I played tennis every day, clocking out of the VA at 4 P.M. like everyone else.

But the workload was decreased for only a short while. Soon we were seeing twice the number of consults from the Miracle Center; there was a perception that since there were two of us we could handle more. There were more calls from Northside Hospital. And HIV patients were now coming from far and wide; we each saw at least one or two new patients a week. Now that we were using AZT, with its propensity to cause anemia, we had to follow blood counts closely. As a result, we saw our patients at more frequent intervals than before AZT.

On a Thursday morning, October 1987, my beeper went off at 6 A.M. The answering service informed me that Dr. J, a dentist, wanted me to call him at home. I had never heard of Dr. J. He was from a nearby town.

He apologized profusely for disturbing me so early and he sounded distraught. His voice was high-pitched and faint, and I could hear the country in his accent lurking under a thin layer of gentrification.

He told me he had performed a difficult extraction the previous afternoon. That night, he had discovered that the patient was HIV positive. The patient, Ethan Nidiffer, was under my care.

The tooth had been a deeply embedded molar. He had to cut the gum to expose the tooth. Then he had chipped at bone. The tooth had not wanted to come out. He finally had to split it into four pieces and lever it out. "There was blood everywhere, blood on my hands . . ."

"Were you wearing gloves?"

"Gloves, yes. But nothing else. I mean I never thought—"

"Were you wearing goggles, a mask?"

"I had my glasses on. No mask. . . . There was blood everywhere. Blood on my glasses. It must have fallen on my skin . . ." Here his voice broke. "Dr. Verghese, I'm so scared. I feel like my life is over. Do you think I will get AIDS?"

"No, no, no. You should be fine—"

"—Are you sure? I haven't slept all night." He was crying now. "My wife and I . . . we have small children. . . . I'm thinking of giving up dentistry altogether. . . . I'd just as soon raise cattle or move away. . . . If the Lord spares me, I swear I'll be a farmer or something else, but not dentistry. . . ."

His diction had slipped way back toward east Tennessee. I spent a long time reassuring him: he hadn't cut himself, he had no open wounds, he was wearing glasses—he had little to fear. I was a little embarrassed and taken aback by his emotional outburst. I gently asked him if he did not use gloves and goggles on *all* patients? Was he not aware of the need for barrier precautions?

"Well, who would have thought in Tennessee. I mean I know when you spoke to us . . ."

I had given a talk at the Sheraton, three weeks before, to the county dental society. Dr. J had evidently been there. The topic was AIDS and the talk was extremely well attended. The question-and-answer session went on for half an hour. I had spelled it out then, emphasized the "AIDS iceberg": there were many more HIV-infected persons than most of them realized; they needed to treat *everyone* they saw as if he were infected. From some of their questions I could tell that they were not using barrier precautions on every patient. (Will Johnson told me he had stopped going to his regular dentist, an old family friend, because despite telling the dentist he had hepatitis B, he could not seem to get him to use gloves.)

The dentists in town either did not believe there was as much HIV as I was telling them, or were relying on their ability to sniff "them" out from among their other patients; prune "them" from their patient rosters.

I asked Dr. J how he found out the patient had HIV. Obviously the patient had not volunteered this information before the procedure.

"Dr. Verghese, you promise you won't be mad if I tell you? The person who told me was only trying to help. I don't want him to get into trouble . . ."

I insisted he tell me. My tone was commanding. If he wanted me to commiserate with him, have me reassure him and cite statistics for him, he better tell me.

"It was the pharmacist from Z_____ Drugs. Ethan Nidiffer went there to fill a prescription for penicillin. The pharmacist called me at home and asked me if I knew I had just operated on an AIDS person. I know you're going to be upset with the pharmacist, but if he hadn't told me, I wouldn't have known. Ethan Nidiffer is one of your patients, isn't he?"

"If he was, I could not possibly tell you. I would be violating his confidentiality. I would be doing what the pharmacist did. I do think it was highly inappropriate, *highly* inappropriate and unprofessional of the pharmacist to call you and tell you."

"But shouldn't the patient have told me? What about *my* risk?"

"The patient certainly should have—I'm not for a moment supporting what the patient did. Had I known, I would have insisted he tell you. And if this is a patient of mine, you can be sure I will speak to him. And I feel for you, I hate that this had to happen to you. I'm glad that from your description of events it doesn't sound to me like you are at risk. But it's important that you use precautions as if every single person you bring an instrument to is potentially infected with the virus."

"If I ever operate again."

I concentrated now on calming Dr. J down. We went over carefully the transmission of the virus. I pointed out to him that there were reports of at least five hundred health care workers with needlesticks from AIDS patients and only one or two had contracted the virus in this way. Dr. J's exposure, at worst, constituted a "splash" and was of extremely low risk. We went over universal precautions, and it was clear Dr. J had only been giving universal precautions lip service. "I just couldn't imagine in this town . . ." he kept repeating.

We were on the phone for another twenty minutes. I was angry with the pharmacist, annoyed with the mewling tone of the dentist, and irritated with Ethan Nidiffer.

I arranged for Dr. J to get the HIV test done and to repeat it again in six weeks and six months. When I hung up, he seemed calmer than when we had first talked.

Ethan Nidiffer, the dentist's patient, was, in his own words, an "over-the-hill Tennessee queen." He was in his late sixties, and if you saw him on the street you would have thought of him as someone's uncle or grandfather. He had silvery hair combed straight back, walked with a stoop, and had severe emphysema, which made him pause in midsentence to get a breath. Polyester pants with front slit pockets and western shirts with a polyester blazer were his regular dress. He looked very much like a veteran, which he was, though since he had private insurance he never went to the VA for care. The skin on the back of his hands and on his face was shiny and very thin; it was also as fragile as tissue paper from years of taking cortisone for his emphysema. An inhaler rattled in his pocket alongside his car keys. He had stopped smoking and quit the heavy drinking in the past few years, but despite that was in a delicate state. To have found out he was HIV positive was a cruel blow so late in his life. When I first saw him, I was much more concerned about his emphysema than about his HIV infection.

Ethan was bitter about the HIV. He had not been very promiscuous, at least by his own account. He had held a steady job in town for thirty-odd years and had taken an early retirement because of his lung problems. He was in the closet and, though unmarried, had never given anyone cause to do more than speculate that he was gay.

His sexual activity of choice had consisted of performing oral sex on others. Now he rarely left his house. He claimed that for years there were at least four married men who stopped by his house every week for him to perform this service. I had once asked him, "What do *you* get out of it? Do you come yourself?" He shook his head and smiled: "No, but you wouldn't understand, Doc." He said he could count on the fingers of one hand the number of times he had engaged in rectal intercourse. But his luck had been bad because one of those "fingers" gave him HIV infection.

I had sent him to Duke to see if he would be eligible for the AZT trials on early HIV infection. Duke entered him into a randomized, placebo-controlled trial. I was to do some of his follow-up blood work in my office and send it on to them. When I saw him a month after the enrollment, it was clear to me that he was getting placebo. AZT induces a very characteristic change in the size of the red blood cell that is apparent in one of the indices measured on a routine blood count.

A part of me was sorely tempted to tell him he was on placebo and for him not to bother going to Duke. The five-hour drives across the mountain were torture for him; in summer, it was hell to breathe in Durham whether you had lung disease or not, so oppressive and humid was the air. Ethan struggled for days after each visit. Yet he went religiously every couple of weeks until he himself was sure he was getting placebo, at which point he dropped out.

Ethan had managed to keep the fact of his HIV infection hidden. I doubt that my office staff for one moment thought of him as an HIV-infected patient, but for the fact that he was seeing me. There was a bluff, good-ole-boy, old-fashioned heartiness in his manner, in the way he greeted the nurses, flirted with them. There was no trace of effeminacy, only a hint of punctiliousness in his mien that was quite allowable in a confirmed bachelor. When we were in the exam room alone, he was looser, his conversation more risqué, and his manner intimate and confiding. Above all, Ethan Nidiffer abhorred the loud "flaming queens." That adjective popped up often in his conversation. He himself was an "old queen," or a "Tennessee queen," but never a *flaming* queen. He was the only patient I had met who was critical of ACT-UP and felt the cause was already lost since the public had come to associate homosexuality with the loud angry images of ACT-UP protesters or members of Queer Nation.

"How can they possibly respect us if we don't conduct ourselves in a manner that they can identify with?"

Since Ethan was still in the closet, what other choice did the "public" have but to go by those who were willing to speak out?

As we got to know each other better, it became clear that Ethan understood that his two secrets would eventually come out; that, in fact, his neighbors and his sisters had a pretty good idea about why he was unmarried so long, and why the majority of his visitors were younger males.

I decided to call Ethan. It took several rings before Ethan came to the phone. His voice was muffled and I could hear him panting from the effort.

I had no plan of what I was to say to Ethan. What was I calling for? To chastise him? I told him what had transpired.

"I know. The dentist already called me. He was mad at me."

"I think you should have told him."

"Well I asked him when he called. I said, 'If I had told you, would you have done the operation?' He didn't say nothing. He kept quiet."

"I *am* sorry the pharmacist betrayed your confidence, acted in such an unprofessional manner, I—"

"Well, don't worry, Doc. He's just a snake, is all there is to it. And, Doc, *I'm* not going to worry about any of that. I dialed eight dentists in three counties. I called till my fingers were just tired of dialing. I gave them a false name, I said I was HIV and needed a tooth pulled—the tooth was killing me, honest to God—and not a one of them would do it, and they wouldn't give me a name of someone who would."

"Didn't you have a regular dentist? All these years—"

"Well, let me tell you about my regular dentist! A few months ago I got a letter from his office saying he would not be able to see me any longer and asking if I wanted my records forwarded to a particular dentist."

"Why?"

"Tell *me*, Doc! You figure it out. I guess he's known me for years, had his suspicions and figured the way he would protect himself is get all the nellies out of his practice!"

"So how did you pick Dr. J____?"

"Well, I just got tired of calling and calling and telling the truth. I just picked one—any one. To tell you the truth I don't know how come I picked him. Why, every one of them has a big-old ad in the Yellow Pages like a goddamn used-car dealer: WE WELCOME NEW PATIENTS or SPECIALIZE IN NERVOUS PATIENTS, or LATEST TECHNOLOGY or stuff like that. I figured that was me. I was nervous, new, and in need of the latest technology!"

What could I say? I could certainly see his point of view.

I tried to decide whether I should call the pharmacist and tell him off for what was a clear violation of ethics. Z Drugs was a new store, struggling to survive at a time when all around them the large drugstore chains were cutting prices and offering more sophisticated services such as home intravenous therapy and home health care. The one time I had gone to fill a prescription for myself at that pharmacy, the proprietor had been very solicitous, almost fawning. He was six-foot-six and towered over me. As opposed to the genuine warmth a Tennessean can project by being himself, the pharmacist's sugar-coating, his dated used-car-dealer sweetness rang hollow. On the other hand, he had at least been a face and a name I could deal with on a personal level, unlike the large chains. He asked me to never hesitate to call him, he showed me how every patient's record was on computer, how his was in fact a modern operation. He gave me a huge discount on my prescription. I called in prescriptions to his store whenever the patient expressed no preference and lived in that general area.

When AZT came along, I called him and several other pharmacists and asked if they would stock the drug. They jumped at the opportunity: the average patient would spend $8,000 to $10,000 on AZT every year.

I heard complaints from several AIDS patients who said they were made to feel uneasy in the store. After they dropped their prescriptions off and sat down to wait, there would be pin-drop silence behind the counter. There was not a doubt in the patient's mind that the pharmacist had conveyed the nature of the prescription to the other employees behind the counter. Eventually the patient's name would be called and he would step up to the counter, where every eye would watch him as he paid for the drug and then marched bravely down the aisle and out of the store. Otis had overheard a remark from one of the women in the store about "God's revenge." He vowed never to return.

I kept sending patients to that pharmacy primarily because the arrangement was already in place and, so far, the pharmacist himself had been professional, even if his staff may not have been. But this incident with the dentist and Ethan was the last straw. I would not send any more patients to him. But I decided I would not call him and chastise him. The damage was done.

As I mulled over these thoughts, the phone rang. It was my friendly pharmacist. His tone was not that friendly anymore.

"I heard from Dr. J_____ that you weren't happy with what I did. I thought I would call you and see if you wanted to speak to me."

"I wasn't planning to call you. But now that you have called me, yes, I thought it was quite unprofessional of you to call the dentist on my patient. It does not inspire confidence—"

He interrupted me. His tone was defiant: He said he felt an obligation to warn the dentist, to "take care of my doctors," as he put it. He saw it as his civic responsibility. He didn't see anything wrong with what he had done.

I let him go on. It was clear to me that he knew he had overstepped his boundary, been unprofessional, but he was not about to admit it. Instead he was going to hide behind the shield of civic responsibility, of duty to God and country.

I waited till he was done. I asked him, "Didn't you think of the possibility of calling *me* first? After all, it was my patient. If you were going to get involved, why not call me and let me deal with it, instead of taking it on yourself to break the patient's confidentiality?"

There was a silence. "Well, I guess I could have done that."

"Am I to assume now that you will take it on yourself to call any other doctor who happens to be seeing the thirty-odd patients who fill AZT at your store? So that you can tell the doctor the patient has AIDS?"

He had no reply.

"You see, I'm afraid I can't in good faith send you my patients because I don't think I can be sure of your not betraying their confidence."

Now he dropped all pretense. The obsequious, fawning tone that he usually used with me was completely gone and in its place was this snapping, testy tone that revealed him for what he was: a weasel in sheep's clothing. His voice was dripping with hate: "Well, I don't want your business either. It doesn't matter to me one bit. And I don't want any of your patients. I'll just take care of *my* doctors. Suits me fine."

He hung up on me.

The words "foreign doctor" rang in my ears, even though he had not said them. My intuition was so strong that I could not write my discomfort off to paranoia. I caught the undertone, and all day the memory kept me uneasy.

Sometimes it was possible to have the illusion that I was so much a part of the town, so well integrated, that I even looked like the townsfolk. But at times like this, I walked around gingerly, seeking my footing with great caution.

Sometimes I felt that I was accepted only as long as they needed me, as long as I could be of service to them. I had fought the clannishness of the Indian community, felt embarrassed by their refusal to integrate. But now I wondered, did they understand something I did not?

But even within the Indian community, the issue of belonging was not so simple. The north Indians were starting to have their own gatherings; the same was true of the south Indians. The Sikhs, in keeping with tumultuous events in India, no longer felt themselves in the mainstream Indian community; their poorly concealed delight in Indira Gandhi's death did not sit well with the rest of the Indians. The Pakistanis, who till then had fit under the general rubric of "Indian," now increasingly met by themselves. And to all these groups, I was an outsider of sorts: an Indian born in Africa. Was there ever going to be a place in this world for me to call my own?

That evening, I told Rajani the story of the dentist and my subsequent words with the pharmacist. She could see I was agitated.

"He didn't actually *say* 'foreigner,' right? You just felt like he said it."

"No, he didn't *say* it. But, yes, I feel as if he said it."

Rajani could not see the point of my uneasiness. Her sympathies were with the dentist. And she was tired of losing my time and attention. She had once said to me, after seeing me come home yet again at an odd hour after answering a summons from the Miracle Center, "You have a choice, you know. You don't *have* to do the AIDS stuff; if you were full-time at the VA you would have more regular hours, you would have no involvement with the Miracle Center. You could just opt to be full-time VA."

"But it's not like cardiology or hematology," I had said. "There is no one out there doing infectious diseases. If I didn't do it, if Fil didn't do it, then there would be no one for these patients."

"It would work out. The point is you have a choice. You're choosing to do what you are doing, so you can't complain about the hours."

My conversation with the pharmacist and the reporting of it to Rajani seemed to exaggerate my feeling of alienation. And my alienation had so much to do with the fact that I was taking care of persons with AIDS. I wondered if subconsciously Rajani viewed me the same way the pharmacist viewed me: tainted by the people I took care of?

That evening, my motorcycle mechanic friend, Darryl, dropped by. Over the years, Darryl and I had worked out a barter system: he took care of my motorcycle and I helped with his kids' medical needs. Now, as a sacrifice for being a father, I had sold the motorcycle. Rajani had argued that it was dangerous and hardly fitting for a father of two kids and I had very reluctantly agreed. Still, Darryl came by from time to time, and I often went by his shop to admire a Norton or an old Indian that he was restoring.

Darryl and I started in the living room with a beer, and when he wanted to smoke, we moved out to the porch—Rajani could not abide the smell of cigarettes in the house. On the porch we had another beer. Steven stayed with us until Rajani summoned him up to bed. I debated telling Darryl the story of the pharmacist, but decided against it. I could not gauge how Darryl would respond: I could not handle a crack about "homos" or a response other than the one I had. Instead, we talked motorcycles and then marriage—specifically Darryl's marriage, which was not going well. While he talked, Darryl pulled out a reefer. Its acrid smell was nostalgic, but the memories it brought back were all of more alienation: Ethiopia in the throes of a war, India on the eve of my departure for America.

When Darryl finally left, I stumbled upstairs, red-eyed, my mind racing, my discomfort having only increased. Rajani handed me the kids who were too excited to sleep. She said, "*You* put them to bed then." I didn't think she took kindly to Darryl and perhaps she had smelled the reefer.

I studied the map on Steven's wall as I carried the baby. Idaho. Montana. Iowa. South Dakota. Texas. Was there some place in this country where I could walk around anonymously, where I could blend in completely with a community, be undistinguished by appearance, accent or speech?

Still carrying the baby and telling Steven to wait, I went down to the basement and pulled out my guitar, which I had not touched in over a year. I came back to the kids' room and Jacob allowed me to put him in his crib. I began to sing to the two of them. I sang song after song, with barely a pause.

It seemed like hours later that I looked up to see Steven and the baby both fast asleep. And staring at me from the doorway across the room was my beautiful wife, a puzzled look on her face. I didn't know how long she had been there watching me.

Rajani loved me, wanted to help me, wanted to make my life easier, wanted our marriage to work. But looking at me as I sat there bleary-eyed, thumping out tunes, singing like a college kid, the floor that separated us was like an abyss that could not be bridged. As she walked away, I found myself crying, but without the heart to call out to her because I didn't know what to say. I didn't think words could fix us. Our lives had changed. I was going to have to find some compromise.

From *Where the Body Meets Memory*

DAVID MURA

My friend Alexs, who's black, thinks that I'm reckless in my willingness to share secrets. "You write about sleeping with all sorts of women and pornography, about the ways race has affected your personal life. Me, I reveal as little as possible." He laughs. "Every moment I am not being pursued by some governmental authority is a blessed moment. . . . The less you know about me, the better. The longer I live.

"The thing I worry about is this: Do you give people too much ammunition to condemn you? You give very little counterbalancing information. I'm talking about the contrast between your craziness early in your life and your balance and security now and how openly you talk about the changes you've gone through. You run the risk of demonizing yourself."

I tell him that I'm trying to explore what my life says about the issues of sexuality and race. The ways I hurt Susie and others in my early life are part of that exploration. I know people will criticize me not only for what I've done but also for writing about it. It goes with the territory. But what's the alternative? Pretending it didn't happen, that such issues don't exist?

Alexs and I met a few years ago when we were both giving a reading at a local college. It was his invitation that led me to do my first performance piece in a series he was curating. Eventually, we ended up doing a show together about our friendship and Asian American–African American relations. He's taught me a lot about race, how much I don't know about the lives of African Americans. We talk constantly about how our attitudes toward writing are shaped by our racial backgrounds. For instance, there's our relationship with our fathers.

"To talk about my father and how hard he worked and how strong my family was and how that has led to my success—all that balances what is automatically the demonology that's associated with African American men," Alexs said recently.

His words made me feel I needed to think more about my father in relationship to the issues of race, that perhaps I've not been as generous with my father as I could be.

Alexs said this may be so, but he thought our jobs were different. "What I want to do is to say, 'No, there is a gentle spirit in African America.' Humanizing the African American male. For you, your work is about exposing the madness that is in the civilized caricature of Asian America."

• • •

In his great *Black Skin, White Masks,* Frantz Fanon examines a black neurotic, Jean Veneuse, who uses his blackness as the sole explanation of his psychic condition. For Veneuse, there is no inner solution to his lack of concrete contact with others. The causes are all external. Such a person, says Fanon, isn't interested in health or psychological equilibrium. If the social difference between blacks and whites did not exist, Veneuse "would have manufactured it out of nothing" in order to remain entrenched in his own self-hatred.

Trapped in feelings of inferiority, Veneuse clings to the sense that his skin color is a flaw; a loner, he accepts the separation imposed on him by the color line. At the same time, he wants "to elevate himself to the white man's level," and his "quest for white flesh"—he constantly seeks out white women—is part of that attempt. Veneuse's acceptance of the color line dooms him, says Fanon. It keeps Veneuse from seeing that the world must be restructured and, with it, his own psyche.

I first read Fanon around 1985. It was a couple of years after Susie and I had finally gotten married and just before I was to leave for Japan. I was in New York, studying Japanese at Columbia, and finding it more difficult than I could have imagined. At times I retreated into other reading. I had some vague sense that Fanon had written a book about revolutions called *The Wretched of the Earth*. But for some reason I started with *Black Skin, White Masks*.

I was riding the subway home from class, still new enough to New York to be captivated by the advertisements in Spanish and the mixture of languages on the train, two old women conversing in Russian, a Hasid reading a Hebraic text, two Chinese girls with their schoolbooks, not to mention the various dialects coming from the black and brown mouths around me. I had a long train ride to Brooklyn Heights, and I settled into my book. I came to the passages on the black man who constantly sleeps with white women, how he has the illusion that his sense of inferiority will be erased by doing so. Somehow crossing the color line sexually will prove himself as good as a white man.

In an instant I understood what I'd been doing all those years.

What had long been unconscious had suddenly become conscious. Fanon had laid it all out before me. I'd elevated whiteness, I'd inculcated its standards of beauty, I'd believed on some deep level in the myth of white superiority. That was part of my sickness, part of the colonizing of my sexuality. I felt that every white woman who rejected me somehow reaffirmed both my sense of a color line and my sense of debasement.

Here, I realized, was a truth that neither therapy nor my work on family systems nor addiction had ever addressed. None of that psychological thinking had ever considered very deeply the context of race.

As the years have passed, I've come to feel both liberated and entrapped, penetrated and critiqued by Fanon. For in his dissection of Veneuse, I see a counterpart to my lifelong perception of myself as a "loser," an outsider unable to make "concrete contact with his fellow man." Veneuse's wish to blame each flaw and defeat on skin color seems to echo my explanations of my sexual insecurity: I was a Japanese in a white world. It was as if I sometimes could see no other cause for my neuroses, the flaws in my psyche.

In recent years, as I've grown further and further away from the madness of my twenties, as I've come to see how lucky I've been in my life, I've finally stopped looking at myself as someone who's always going to get the short end, as someone whose identity must be based on being a victim. I'm happily married, with a wonderful family. The young man who went out haunting the bars, searching for sexual trysts, for some confirmation from women, particularly white women—that's simply not me anymore.

Still, I don't think the original imprinting, this colonizing, ever completely leaves. You just learn to choose other ways, you learn another response.

When I traveled to Japan in 1985, I realized that my reading of Fanon helped deepen my experience there, my questioning of identity. It wasn't just that I was encountering various aspects of Japanese culture or that my experience there enabled me to imagine more deeply the lives of my grandparents and therefore the lives of my parents. The presence of Japanese faces and media images made me much more aware of how culture shapes how we see our bodies and the bodies of those around us. A telling instance occurred one afternoon in the Seibu Theater in the Ginza, when I was watching *Out of Africa*. Buoyed by months of living in a culture where everyone looked like me, where my racial and cultural background was not neglected, I suddenly found myself looking at Meryl Streep, Klaus Maria Brandauer, and Robert Redford and the characters they play—Karen Blixen (a.k.a. the writer Isak Dinesen), her husband, and her lover—in an entirely different light. The moment occurred when Blixen is taken by her husband for the first time to their farm in Kenya and all the African servants come out to greet them. It's night, and the movie tries to impart a sense of the heroine traveling into an unknown space. Always the focus is on what the Meryl Streep character is going through; her face and form were blown up at the center of the frame.

Despite this, I realized I felt bored with her character. I'd seen the great white bwana story and the romance of Europeans in Africa a hundred times before. What I wanted to know about, what I knew little about, were the minds of the Africans around Blixen, the Kenyans who, two decades later, would organize the Mau Maus and the revolt which gained independence for Kenya. What was the interior life behind those black faces? I found I couldn't keep both the Meryl Streep character and the black faces at the center of my attention at the same time. I had to choose. Indeed, I had been choosing all my life. Only now I was withdrawing attention, affection, curiosity, from the white face at the center of the picture and giving it to the black faces. I was striking a new balance. And the world looked differently. I saw that this was a form of cultural and political power, the almost unconscious and instantaneous granting of priority to faces of one skin color over another.

After I came back from Japan, on a visit to Boston, I happened to attend an African American literary conference. It was the first time I had ever been surrounded by a group of black writers. I was pleasantly surprised at how everyone embraced the aesthetic "Art is political." At the time, I had been arguing with white Minnesota writers about this issue, and I was relieved to be in a place where this was not a question. But more importantly, it also forced me to ask questions about why there seemed such a discrepancy between the white Minnesota writers I knew and the black writers at this conference.

Slowly, I began writing work that was more and more explicit about my sexuality, trying to articulate connections between sexuality and race. One of these poems, "The Colors of Desire," opened with a section entitled "Photography of a Lynching, circa 19_." The poem began with a photograph of a lynching, which it then connected with my viewing of the pornographic film *Behind the Green Door,* where a black man makes love to a white woman, and the way that image focused on the taboo of miscegenation. The poem was one of my first attempts to move beyond Japanese American issues and history into a broader racial context. The initial section ended with me leaving the porno movie theater in a hash-laced haze:

> *I left that theater, bolted from a dream into a dream.*
> *I stared at the cars whizzing by, watched the light change,*
> *red, yellow, green, and the haze in my head from the hash,*
> *and the haze in my head from the image, melded together,*
>   *reverberating.*
> *I don't know what I did afterwards. Only, night after night,*
> *I will see those bodies, black and white (and where am I,*
>   *the missing third?), like a talisman, a rageful, unrelenting release.*

I showed a version of this poem to an all-white workshop I was attending in Vermont. Some of the members of the workshop were confused as to what I meant by the phrase "the missing third." I conceded that perhaps there were some technical problems and that the poem could be clearer, but I also argued that their response brought up certain racial issues. The poet teaching the workshop disagreed.

After class, I pressed my point again. I wasn't bothered by the fact that I'd received criticism about my poem; I'd been in enough workshops to be used to that. I was bothered by the unexamined racial assumptions the teacher had made.

"After all," I said, "if you tell a white person that there's a man sitting in an X-rated movie theater, they'll probably think it's a white man. If you tell a black person, they'll probably think it might be either a white man or a black man. But if you tell that to an Asian person, they'll at least entertain the possibility that the man might be Asian, and therefore the figure which might be missing from the binary opposition of black and white would be an Asian."

He finally admitted I might have a point.

Still, I could tell he wasn't happy. He'd decided that I was difficult, someone bent on making my own power play. A pain in the ass.

A few weeks after the Vermont workshop, I read the same version of "The Colors of Desire" to an Asian American studies conference. None of the Asian Americans I asked seemed confused about the phrase "the missing third."

A couple of years after this, in 1989, when I first began traveling around the country, I noticed the reception to my poems differed depending on the racial mixtures of the audience. A poem which sometimes seemed difficult or extreme to white audiences did not seem so to audiences of color. I was forced to confront the fact that I could not write for both audiences at once. And I had to ask what were the differences in the lives of people of color that could explain their responses. I realized the deeper I went into my own life and into the lives of my community, the farther away I traveled from the preconceptions of a white audience. I would not exclude the lives of whites from my writings; but I also would not write for their approval or in fear of their responses.

In a later version of "The Colors of Desire," I added an image of my father stepping onto a segregated bus in Jerome, Arkansas, confronting the line between the white and black passengers. "How did he know," the poem asks, "where to sit?"

These lines were written in response to Bill Hosokawa's *Nisei: The Quiet Americans* and a passage where he describes the Japanese Americans getting onto segregated buses in the South during World War II. Over and over I thought about this passage, which describes a telling point in American history:

The evacuees who were sent to Arkansas had been astonished to find they were regarded as white by the whites and colored by the blacks. The whites insisted the Japanese Americans sit in the front of the bus, drink from the white man's fountain and use the white man's rest rooms even though suspecting their loyalty to the nation. And the blacks embarrassed many a Nisei when they urged: "Us colored folks has got to stick together."

If there was no middle ground in the South's polarized society of black and white, in the rest of the country after the war, a Nisei could live as a yellow-skinned American without upsetting too many people, and he also discovered it was not particularly difficult to be accepted into the white man's world.

Most Japanese Americans of my father's generation decided to sit in the front of the bus. And many are guilty of the same racist attitudes toward blacks as white Americans. But whatever their attitudes toward blacks, Japanese Americans made an understandable choice when confronted with the segregated buses: Sit where the power is. Don't associate yourself with those who are more oppressed than you; don't become partners with the powerless if you can avoid it.

Of course, blacks and other people of color in this country know when Japanese Americans and other Asian Americans are assenting to an honorary white status. When we play that card. And as long as we do that, there's little reason for other people of color to trust us.

But there is a paradox in this choice, a paradox many Japanese Americans wish to avoid. In making their choice, the Japanese Americans are no less connected to blacks than to whites. The racial identity of Japanese Americans was formed not just by the internment camps or by their dealings with whites, but also against the backdrop of race relations involving blacks and other people of color. There was an unspoken message all about them in the camps, especially in the South: Things are bad now, but they could be worse. We aren't lynching your kind. Yet.

Do I overdramatize? A threat doesn't have to be carried out to be effective.

What were the charges that prompted the lynchings in the South where my father was interned? They were that a black man had raped, or had sex with, a white woman or even that he had simply "recklessly eyeballed" her. Behind this grotesque violence was the fear of the black man's sexuality. But there was also the fear of the white woman's sexuality, the need to rein in her desires. There was also the couplings, many of them rapes, between white men and black women, which occurred in the past and left most American blacks with some white blood. This was part of a history everyone knew about, but no one talked about publicly. What was talked about was the hatred of black men, of what they represented as sexual beings.

The body tells us we are human, one species. We can copulate and procreate across color lines. This is a horrible unspeakable truth in a society where the sexual segregation of the races is still the norm. It brings up the suspicion that we all may be, after all, only human. That some are not destined by God or nature to be inferior, to have less of society's power and bounty.

Amidst this immense desire by whites to suppress blacks, the Japanese American did not call up the same vehement fears. Of course, during the war fears about Japanese Americans were certainly exacerbated. But these fears didn't carry the same sexual charge that the fear of blacks did; there was the fear of the "sneakiness" of the "Japs," the seeming insanity of their "banzai" methods of fighting. This is not to say, though, that white America was prepared then to entertain the thought of interracial coupling with Japanese Americans.

Did my father think of such issues when he looked across the floor at a Nisei dance in 1949 and saw my mother and said to his friend, "That's the girl I'm going to marry"? I don't think so. It would have seemed natural as rain to my father that he would marry another Nisei.

From *Ono Ono Girl's Hula*

CAROLYN LEI-LANILAU

ONO ONO GIRL'S *Hula* (aka Introduction)

This is about the sacred and sweet: nobody "in their right mind" will talk about this but I'll try. This is about intimacy: About animals in the trees—like Daphne or big and older folks who still like to play in mud. This is something beyond English which cannot Truly be understood in English. If owls and sharks could tell this story in words, then these are the words they would translate their lives into. This is the real: no right, no wrong. Only feelings, good feelings. Here male and female mate. Other varieties come after. First there is Papa and Wākea, *wahine* and *kane*. First, there is the pretty and strong complex aroma. Who is this? *li hing mui, kahili* ginger, *lau lau* singing, "Time to eat."

My mouth licks owl's genitals while owl shrieks longing for me who cannot be human.

Crying, I beg shark to chew me hard. Dig . . . dig me deep.

Help yourself to my bloodline. Pull and knot the cords freely.

Tattoo your thrust in the small of my spine.

Protect my sacred ears which lengthen from my heart to brain.

Stay until you can: linger no longer in this ordinary tradition, in which calmly, we are alive briefly.

Ono Girl's Song poorly, poorly translates into English. With the exception of Hawaiian, her natural body, other languages are not sufficient. To know *Ono* Girl, to really know *Ono* Girl, one must struggle with her shy and often frightening dance. Among her family—her *hānai 'ohana,* the family who adopted her, she is named *Ono Ono* Girl because of her lovely body which creates comfort in everyone to be so delighted and relaxed: happy to "share in her great enthusiasm for living." *Ono* Girl invites you to eat life. Eat love, eat more, fall asleep in love waking up to live, fall down, fall down again, deep.

Cry hard and pick up, dance and dance singing, laugh and laugh dancing. Go ahead, have a good cry. Isn't the song, life is such beauty? *Nani*, so so nani

Five Thirty Hawaiian Time; Eight Thirty Somewhere Else

This is weird. Today is the second day at home and, as usual, I can't figure out who I am and how old I am? Yesterday, I was among the eighty-year-old Long's Drugstore Vetrans followed by the Fook Yuen Sunday Brunch crowd. As usual, every day that I'm here, I'll be eating like it is always my first meal and my first good meal in a long time. When I mentioned this to Aunty

Mabel—you remember her?—she kindly reminded me of the Maryknoll days when "you looked like a basketball." Nonetheless, having left the soupy grayness of cold; collectively shared personal angst; the art biz scene; the Giants in combat; my kid about to bunt for college; my in and out husband; the Hawaiians and our evolutionary jokes, I find myself *here,* the other zone, the notquite, the fiftieth state but not really, international but American: it's a vacation to most people but it's home—that is HOME, hOme, hoME—for the rest of us, the plantation and cannery workers; the *maka'āinana,* siblings and descendants of the slop man, *lei* ladies, missionaries now not so well respected but still feared; still the best to all who left for better or worst.

Today, ma and I did our regular Long's Drugs ritual, which we do within the first forty-eight hours of my arrival. This done, in tandem with my eating of *Gau Chee Mien* at the Golden Eagle Restaurant, I am free to then proceed to visiting aunties, cousins, and maybe a bit of self-discovery! Whee, freedom.

What did I do today? I found myself impulsively walking two blocks from my mother's house to the Varsity Theater, which I have been dying to do for years. The heat sent me today. Man, this is hot weather. How do people *work* in this weather? And how do they study? Don't kid yourself: if you make it through the University of Hawai'i, you should really pat yourself on the back—except of course—if you get your degree in tourism, which is a free ride and all the coupons you can get. Gotta tell you something—am I kidding myself to imagine that I could return home to think and *work* in this weather? I could faint in this weather. I could sleep in this weather. I am already attuned to shopping for brief periods of time at *Ala Moana* in this weather. Boy, folks like to eat and shop and shop and eat here—even at Summer Session I heard a guy treat the subject of "refried beans on special at Safeway, nonfat," but he was behind a cubicle so I couldn't see him. He did mention chips too, and almond rocca. Man, people are always talking and dreaming food and shopping. Eh, I can get into fights very easily in this weather: the trick is in the breathing. Just breathe and walk to the bathroom, look out at the enticing *ti/ki* leaves, the palms shaking their *'ōkole,* the bluest sky in the world, and return like a god.

I can eat this weather. The *pakalana,* white ginger, *pīkake,* and stephanotis at my mother's house hypnotize any rational senses. I hate the idea of air conditioning—breathing recycled dust particles day in and out—but work in this natural weather, I don't know. How about all the people who jog, play tennis, drive in stop-and-go butt to butt, walk-with-the-umbrella, or wait-for-the-bus in the sun in this weather? Maybe if I was located at another spot with breeze and surf lying in and out mixing with just the right amount of sand, maybe if there was Hawaiian music and a black-and-white silent movie featured before my eyes, then maybe the story would be different, but meanwhile while the heat influences my body and psyche, I gotta adjust to it.
Da end. Whoa da moss.

On the way to Varsity Theater, I passed my childhood. The Marciels who played music all the time and smooched under the green orange tree and hugged and called each other "dahling." He played the bass and she, the piano, to the beast of a sa-lid, I mean solid one-two, one two three beat, and they sang like love birds nectar in their eyes and throats—their romantic house followed by Mrs. Aguiar, who worked for Liberty House, and always showed us the gorgeous red dress that she intended to be buried in. When I was a kid and used to walk past her house with those red kind of bushes, I used to always hope that she would get her wish. Now that those bushes have been replaced with a chain-link fence, you realize that dreams and symbols change, but you can't get too deep into this kind of thing in Hawai'i, not in this heat, not when the overt manifestations *appear* like tradition—especially the First Day.

Maybe it's those *haole* magazines that give me theese kind ideas; maybe anybody can see this if you take a heat break.

The Zanes now live in the Marciel house. Mr. Zane is always polishing his car and willing to practice my Mandarin with me. Lately, my mother has been scolding me about not being able to understand my Hakka because of a strong *guo yu* accent.

One day Mrs. Zane was visiting and my mother was yakking to somebody on the telephone. That was the perfect opportunity for me and Mrs. Zane to speak both Hakka and *guo yu*. As I switched, she followed. Mrs. Zane can speak several dialects of Hakka as well as many dialects of Mandarin. As we were talking stories, I asked Mrs. Zane if she could understand me when I spoke Hakka to her.

"I understand you Perfectly," she exclaimed sm(hi)iiling,
which could only make me wonder what my mother is really saying to me.

Later, over cigarettes and beer on a warm and rainy 4th of July, their lovely daughter Dottie and I laughed about our families as I started the coals for the barbeque that me and ma would always remember. It was so great sitting under the carport, our backs to the street as we wondered if the bananas were ripe enough to be picked.

Then the very Best happened: ma and I ate the potato salad and seaweed and short ribs while we watched white people on television celebrating the holiday in DC. Why were We watching white people watch somebody entertain them? It definitely was an audience of white folks with no Marion Barry around. Eventually though, I remembered that I had purchased these sparklers which I had hoped would return a feeling from my childhood. NOPE. They were duds, but as I was outside in the warm dark, the memory of the fig tree behind me, *pakalana* strongly chanting near plumeria flashing its hot scent into the stillness, I saw a rainbow in the night and ran inside to grab ma by the elbow. Poor ma. So much excitement! and romantic in the backyard among the *ti* leaves and avocado tree.

man oh Man, I wanted to cry I was so happy! I held that bone and skin next to me loving Loving my mother in a way that I was unprepared for. We leaned against each other to watch the silent worlds of Blake and Confucius, Walt Disney, and our ancestors spring and flood our eyes with neon zeal. Of course, we joked: it was so intense. So mother-daughter. The measurement of time beneath the arches of our feet tasting so so *ono*.

Here I must cross the street for a sentence or two. Mrs. Eaton would be surprised if I don't mention her especially since we are now cousins through the Crowinburgs. Especially since her eighty-seven-year-old cousin Joe is the current flame of me and Annette—bless his heart—but beware of how my family uses the terms "sweetheart," "lover," "boyfriend": we don't care. It's just to kiss up to that insecure male ego—EXcept for Mr. Kumalae (so cute in his bermuda shorts), whose daddy made *ukulele*. Hakka girls say whatever we please leaving smoke or dust or heaven while our big gorgeous feet speed away.

Beyond Mrs. Aguiar house live Mr. and Mrs. Kumalae, who are the real *ali'i* of the neighborhood. Mrs. Kumalae, a Hakka girl from School Street, is ninety and she looks young! And she is bright and super together. What is her secret? maybe her Hawaiian husband, her daily walk, and picking ma's white ginger. She picks ginger everyday "to make the flowers come out more." And now, she's picking *pakalana*—those so small hard to pick easy to bruise so so good to smell *pakalana*. And you wanna know what for? for me! She picks enough *pakalana* until she has enough to make me a three-strand *lei*. Can you believe it! Nobody does this kind of stuff on the mainland. Nobody's gonna take the time to be so nice. This could only happen in Hawai'i.

My mother's boyfriend Mr. Pang lives across from the Kumulae's. Ma actually hates Mr. Pang but she started a habit a long time ago by calling the Egg Man, the Laundry Man, the Gas Station Man—any guy who was sweet with her was her "boyfriend." Mr. Pang only lacks a number in the long line of Mildred's boyfriends. Now but, ma got young REcycle boy-Man. He, tall. He, cute. He say, "Aunty, I hang clothes for you."

The other night we were sitting in the livingroom which everyone in the world can look through because we have louvers and it is so hot that they have to be open because we are natural air purists. You get used to it after years of humiliation and self-consciousness. Anyway, we were sitting there oppressed by the heat and *ayecudiyou!* I jump up in the power-ranger stance and with my two arms and hands extended as machine guns point out my mother's latest and most god-like boyfriend, the *mo'o*. Who is *mo'o*? a gecko or common lizard to most of the world. But to *HERE*, any uncontrollable anything is deemed vicious and worthy of death. My mother's heart leaped for the spray. I said, "Forget it. You won't see it soon enough." Oh, Mildred was agitated, she wanted that *mo'o* dead. It just reminded her of when daddy was alive and she used to get after him to kill the *mo'o*, but when he couldn't, she proudly "wouldn't speak to him for days." My mother, Miss Perfect, wouldn't speak to my father because he couldn't—maybe *wouldn't*—kill a lizard!

After the Mesicks' house, I don't know too many houses except for Elmo Wong's—the tall cigar man who had those beautiful rainbow plumerias in his yard. Now, there are new houses with new plants. There is actually some lively and lovely style with the house that has squash and beans languishing in its front yard next to its relative cement structure with fertile *boo look* and green grass. Talk about green grass, the only green grass on the street is owned by these folks and the Japanese Chamber of Commerce, that has the most imposing structure on the street nearer to the University side. It was already Big, but it had to resurrect to become bigger. So, my little street goes commercialand I don't know just how much I hate that new structure because I read that there's a gallery there now . . . maybe if it continues to be so upscale, I could walk down the street, drink a *skoosh* bit of *sake* and *bonzai, pal mal merci.*

This is what I was inhaling on the way to the Varsity, which during the Sixties I had heard had become a lecture hall! My baby memory of a theater where I walked to on the weekends with a dime in my hands. Sometimes, I ran barefeet with only that dime between my fingers. I can't remember how many black-and-white matinees were like vitamins to me. Me and the usually empty theater like it was today for this uneventful foreign film called
"White." Sometimes I got jujubes stuck in my teeth. Once, at the water fountain,
I even saw my older sister at the same movie that I was at!
That movie theater means something to me.
If I try real hard, maybe I can remember going to the movies with my mother at night, a real excitement because then we would always race home against the thought of burglars or rapists or who-know-whats.
Now we walk to the bank, which is next door to the theater, or the other bank, which is across the street—the banks that you can not wear dark glasses or a hat into because of all the robberies. For real, **can not.**

Thank god, the Varsity is still there at five dollars and ninety cents heavier. The soda fountain across the street *hele* on to somewhere else and so did this *keiki. Pau hana*

An Den

By ten o'clock in the morning, it is too hot. Seven o'clock at night or morning, too hot already. Whoh man. On the way from my mother's house (it used to be my parents' house until my daddy went to be with the *'ohana'aumākua*), some of the sounds remind me of China. The constant pounding, rat-tat-tatting; the whizz of some fanning-like drill from the dentist's office; but more monsterish is the old guy who yesterday was repainting the blue utility pipe who today is sitting on a wooden stool and shaving the grass by hand. By hand! cut-ting the damn grass by hand! what? the Japanese Chamber of Commerce can not give the guy one hand lawn mowa? Gotta have so much art. I can't decide if I'm jealous, in love or am diss-gusted with the Japanese: art in the food; art with tea; art when you give a gift; always so neat—the old man was very artful—by hand!

It is so darn hot
soo Hot so so hohTT
(becuss we are so sSensitiff, ov coss)
—summertime, middle of the afternoon by Bay area standards and the colors
in the shower blossoms, the ordinary red hibiscus, the clutches and bunches of
aloe plants which everyone has incase of an emergency which never happens
while the aloe continues to regenerate—the swampiness of birthing is blinding.

The shower trees which the elder cousins and aunties hate because of the *dead*
shower blossoms that they have to rake to keep the yard looking so green and
soft and nice. Man, those shower blossoms possessed me to imagine that I was
a young pretty bride season after season. Even as an old fut I still feel so excited to see those cumulus happenings of yellow and buff and rouge and
passionfruit orange, rainbow pink, and lemonade. Blonde and shave ice strawberry, pineapple, *mai tai,* tutti-frutti, papaya, french, and lipstick deep kisses
parasols tree after tree, street after street near the canals in Chinatown; along
King Street infront of all those concrete buildings with air conditioners sticking out looking so ugly; where Honolulu Stadium use to be which is now a
lovely park for babies to learn to walk and old folks take their daily at 5:30
am. Those showers are here to stay, tourists or not. Sovereignty or not. Who
takes care of the shower trees? Aye, can learn something from the shower tree,
eh!

Oh oh oh, the strong smell from the fried fast goodies and plumeria and water
floating in the heat—Auʻē, I feel sex in around and overboard: the *maʻi lele* is
not only *kaona* but biting; and tickling my psyche and body and *imua*—English not enough!

I am so glad that I lived in China because I can see some overlapping of China
in Oakland and now I can see some overlapping of China here, but I doubt if
any other culture can ever overlap in China because it's pretty hard to influence 1.2 billion knuckleheads. They're not good at jokes unless it is at your expense—poor tings: that's what they're used to.

Wait a second—wait second, I heard that now, Christianity is a big thing in
China, though the Christians are getting killed. And actually, most of the Chinese who made it to Hawaiʻi didnot go back to Zhong Guo. Granpa married
tūtū and they were happy: he never wanted no mo China. He learned to speak
Hawaiian, *ʻōlelo o Hawaiʻi* and he never spoke Loong Doo again. My other
granpa made it to Kohala and sent for my pretty pretty granma with the
smooth sweet big feet and they fought for the rest of their lives but they never
wanted to go back to China either.
When daddy was alive, we couldn't be Hawaiian but now that it is safe to be
Hawaiian, ma teaching all these Hawaiian words which I did not know she
knew. She said *tūtū* never spoke English, always always gently spoke beautiful
Hawaiian. Was so so kind to ma. But Then, Chinese was a step up from
Hawaiian and even though daddy was half Uygur which is like Turk and
Loong Doo, he sucked in, "he was Chinese except with *tūtū*. So now, my

Chinese mother is teaching me Hawaiian. Maybe someday even the Chinese can let loose when it's safe.

Which brings me to the secrets. A long time ago, my mother said, "Nobody gives out the recipe." but me,

I *waha nui* **big mouth,** I goin essay everyting.

For the past two days I have been reading John Charlot's work on *Kamapua'a* and something about the politics of literature or something. Good ting that *haole* grew up here—I went to school wit his brudder, Peter—anyway he went write dat he got the material from here and dere and put um togeter and went come up with dis pretty good *haole*/local resource material 'cause maybe I going use John as a reference for my unique syntax.

Anyways, yesterday, while I *liao* with my Hakka *'ohana*, I learned something: *Pikai!*

the rain come down!

Laughing and laughing so loud my aunties accused me of being Portuguese.

Teasing, we slice each other's breath with kung fu daggers, flips, trips, and poetry.

Those old ladies are viciously funny and got nothing on their minds except a good time and having the last sound.

They not so smart sometime. They not so right but they love imagining they being right.

And they love drama.

They would never own up to it but they love staring in a down-to-earth and up-to-Las Vegas opera. No wonder I am so goddamn dramatic. Those Hakka women know how to put on a show, and the secret of club membership is speaking their esoteric but very user-friendly public language. Once you can joke in Hakka, you're in. While I don't know how to play the conventional gambling games, I know those girls love to gamble and they love fast thinking, an' good laugh and Action.

When you spend the afternoon at Nelia's having lunch, it is *de rigueur* to pass the time gracefully, so you need to keep the action moving by being able to comment quickly in Hakka and English. Your English must be taut and somewhere in the realm of the obnoxious but your Hakka can be Rude, ssssSexual, sec-ular, conTemptuous, Vain, VULgar, hiStoric, INdulgent. It can be incorrect and everyone will raid the wrongdoer with fierce justice met. I mentioned some phrases that the younger of the sisters, Aunty Alma, was unaware of, and she was promptly educated by the two elder dowagers. Even I knew the proverbs—though I knew them only in English. And guess what? when I began dropping some phonemes in Hawaiian, the aunties didn't react. They were either feeling sorry for their sister my mother or Maybe, I am coming home often enough so that they are getting used to what a headache I was as a child and maybe in their senior years they cannot tell the difference or bother to care. Though they pretend not to know a lot of Hawaiian they know a lot! My Hakka grandpa loved Hawaiian, spoke and danced Hawaiian whenever his *mane'o* kicked the *kino*.

"Of couse!" they always exclaim!

"ov cuss!"

Pa
From *First They Killed My Father:*
A Daughter of Cambodia Remembers

LOUNG UNG

December 1976

Time passes by slowly. We are in the middle of our summer because the air is hotter and drier now. It seems to be about four months since Keav died. Though the family does not talk about her, my heart still weeps when I remember that she is no longer with us.

The government continues to reduce our food rations. I am always hungry and all I think about is how to feed myself. Each night, my stomach growls and aches as I try to sleep. Our family remains dependent on Khouy and Meng to bring us food whenever they can steal away from their camp to visit us. However, the Angkar keeps them so busy that they are unable to visit us as often as before.

We live under the constant fear of being discovered as supporters of the former government. Every time I see soldiers walking in our village, my heart leaps and I fear they are coming for Pa. They don't know that Pa is not a poor farmer, but how long will it be before they realize we are all living a lie? Everywhere I go I am obsessed with the thought that people are staring at me, watching me with suspicious eyes, waiting for me to mess up, and give away our family secret. Can they tell by the way I talk, or walk, or look?

"They know," I overhear Pa whisper to Ma late one night. Lying on my back next to Chou and Kim, I pretend to be asleep. "The soldiers have taken away many of our neighbors. Nobody ever talks of the disappearances. We have to make preparations for the worst. We have to send the kids away, to live somewhere else, and make them change their names. We must make them leave and go to live in orphanage camps. They must lie and tell everyone that they are orphans and don't know who their parents are. This way, maybe, we can keep them safe from the soldiers and from exposing one another."

"No, they are too young," Ma pleads with him. Unable to stop my eyes from twitching, I roll over to my side. Ma and Pa become quiet, waiting for me to go back to sleep. Staring at Kim's back, I force myself to breathe regularly.

"I want them to be safe, to live, but I cannot send them away. They are too young and cannot defend themselves. Not now but soon." His voice trails off.

Beside Chou, Geak kicks and moans in her sleep, almost as if she senses impending doom. Ma picks her up and puts her down between Pa and herself. I roll over once more, this time facing Chou's back. I spy Ma and Pa asleep facing each other on their sides with Geak in the middle, their hands touching above Geak's head.

The next evening, while sitting with Kim outside on the steps of our hut, I think how the world is still somehow beautiful even when I feel no joy at being alive within it. It is still dark and the shimmering sunset of red, gold, and purple over the horizon makes the sky look magical. Maybe there are gods living up there after all. When are they going to come down and bring peace to our land? When I focus my eyes back on the earth, I see two men in black walking toward us with their rifles casually hanging on their backs.

"Is your father here?" one of them asks us.

"Yes," Kim answers. Pa hears them and comes out of the hut, his body rigid as our family gathers around him.

"What can I do for you?" Pa says.

"We need your help. Our ox wagon is stuck in the mud a few kilometers away. We need you to help us drag it out."

"Could you please wait for a moment so that I can talk to my family?" The soldiers nod to Pa. Pa and Ma go inside the hut. Moments later, Pa comes out alone. Inside, I hear Ma sobbing quietly. Opposite the soldiers, Pa straightens his shoulders, and for the first time since the Khmer Rouge takeover, he stands tall. Thrusting out his chin and holding his head high, he tells the soldiers he is ready to go. Looking up at him, I see his chest inflates and exhales deeply, and his jaw is square as he clenches his teeth. I reach up my hand and lightly tug at his pant leg. I want to make him feel better about leaving us. Pa puts his hand on my head and tousles my hair. Suddenly he surprises me and picks me up off the ground. His arms tight around me, Pa holds me and kisses my hair. It has been a long time since he has held me this way. My feet dangling in the air, I squeeze my eyes shut and wrap my arms around his neck, not wanting to let go.

"My beautiful girl," he says to me as his lips quiver into a small smile. "I have to go away with these two men for a while."

"When will you be back, Pa?" I ask him.

"He will be back tomorrow morning," one of the soldiers replies for Pa. "Don't worry, he'll be back before you know it."

"Can I go with you, Pa? It's not too far. I can help you." I beg him to let me go with him.

"No, you cannot go with me. I have to go. You kids be good and take care of yourselves," and he puts me down. He walks slowly to Chou and takes Geak from her arms. Looking into her face, he cradles her and gently rocks her back and forth before bending and gathering Chou into his arms also. His head high and his chest puffed out like a small man, Kim walks over to Pa and stands quietly next to him. Letting go of Chou and Geak, Pa stoops down and lays both hands on Kim's shoulders. As Kim's face crumbles, Pa's face is rigid and calm. "Look after your Ma, your sisters, and yourself," he says.

Pa walks away with a soldier on either side of him. I stand there and wave to him. I watch Pa's figure get smaller and smaller, and still I wave to him, hoping he will turn around and wave back. He never does. I watch until his figure disappears into the horizon of red and gold. When I can no longer see Pa, I turn around and go inside our house, where Ma sits in the corner of the room crying. I have seen Pa leave the house many times in Phnom Penh, but I have never seen her this upset. In my heart I know the truth, but my mind cannot accept the reality of what this all means.

"Ma, don't cry, the soldiers said Pa will be back tomorrow morning." I lay my hand on hers. Her body shakes at my touch. I walk outside to where my siblings are sitting on the step and sit next to Chou, who holds Geak in her arms. Together we wait for Pa, sitting on the stairs, staring at the path that took him away. We pray it will bring Pa back to us tomorrow.

As the sky turns black, the clouds rush in to hide all the stars. On the steps, Chou, Kim, Geak, and I sit waiting for Pa until Ma orders us in to sleep. Inside the hut, I lie on my back, my arms folded across my chest. Chou and Kim breathe deeply, quietly, but I do not know if they are asleep. Ma is on her side, facing Chou. She has one arm around Geak, and the other rests above Geak's head. Outside the wind blows in the branches, and the leaves rustle and sing to each other. The clouds part, and the moon and stars shine and give life to the night. In the morning, the sun will come up and the day creatures will wake. But for us, time stands still that night.

I wake up the next morning to see Ma sitting on the steps. Her face is swollen and she looks like she has not slept all night. She is crying softly to herself and is miles away. "Ma, is Pa back yet?" Not answering me, she squints her eyes and continues to look at the path that took Pa away. "The soldiers said Pa would come back in the morning. I guess he's late. He's late, that's all. I know he will return to us." As I speak, my lungs constrict and I gasp for air. Fighting for breath, my thoughts race and I wonder what this all really means. It is morning and Pa is not back! Where is he? I sit with my siblings, facing the road, looking for Pa. I think up reasons why Pa is late returning to us. The wagon is broken in the mud, the oxen would not move, the soldiers needed Pa to help them fix the wagon. I try to believe my excuses and make them reasonable, but my heart is filled with fear.

Telling the chief we are ill, we receive permission to stay home. All morning and afternoon, we wait for Pa to walk back to us. When night comes, the gods again taunt us with a radiant sunset. "Nothing should be this beautiful," I quietly say to Chou. "The gods are playing tricks on us. How could they be so cruel and still make the sky so lovely?" My words tug at my heart. It is unfair of the gods to show us beauty when I am in so much pain and anguish. "I want to destroy all the beautiful things."

"Don't say such things or the spirits will hear," Chou warns me. I don't care what she says. This is what the war has done to me. Now I want to destroy because of it. There is such hate and rage inside me now. The Angkar has taught me to hate so deeply that I now know I have the power to destroy and kill.

Soon darkness covers the land and still Pa has not returned. We sit on the steps waiting for him together in silence. No words are exchanged as our eyes search the fields waiting for him to come home. We all know that Pa will not return, but no one dares to say it out loud for it will shatter our illusion of hope. With darkness, the flies disappear and the mosquitoes appear to feast on our flesh. Ma holds Geak in her arms. Every once in a while, Ma's arms fan Geak's body to chase away the mosquitoes. As if picking up on Ma's pain, Geak kisses her cheek softly and caresses her hair.

"Ma, where's Pa?" Geak asks, but Ma only responds with silence.

"Go inside, all you kids, go inside," Ma tells us in a tired voice.

"You should come in with us. We can all wait inside," Chou says to her.

"No, I'd rather wait out here and greet him when he returns." Chou takes Geak from Ma and goes into the hut. Kim and I follow her, leaving Ma sitting on the steps by herself, waiting for Pa to return.

Listening to Geak and Chou breathing softly, my eyes stay wide open. After he hid from the soldiers for twenty months, they finally found him. Pa always knew he couldn't hide forever. I never believed he couldn't. I cannot sleep. I worry about Pa, and about us. What will become of us? We have taken our survival for granted. How will we survive without Pa? My mind races and fills my head with images of death and executions. I have heard many stories about how the soldiers kill prisoners and then dump their bodies into large graves. How they torture their captives, behead them, or crack their skulls with axes so as not to waste their precious ammunition. I cannot stop thinking of Pa and whether or not he died with dignity. I hope they did not torture him. Some prisoners are not dead when they are buried. I cannot think of Pa being hurt this way, but images of him clawing at his throat, fighting for air as the soldiers pile dirt on him flood my mind. I cannot make the pictures go away! I need to believe Pa was killed quickly. I need to believe they did not make him suffer. Oh Pa, please don't be afraid. The images play over and over again in my head. My breath quickens as I think about Pa's last moment on earth. "Stop thinking, stop or you'll die," I hiss to myself. But I cannot stop.

Pa told me once that the really old monks could leave their bodies and travel the world as spirits. In my mind, my spirit leaves my body and flies around the country, looking for Pa.

I see a big group of people kneeling around a big hole. There are already many dead people in the hole, their bodies sprawled on top of each other. Their black pajama clothes are soaked with blood, urine, feces, and small white matter. The soldiers stand behind the new group of prisoners, casually smoking a cigarette with one hand, while the other holds onto a big hammer with clumps of hair sticking to its head.

A soldier leads another man to the edge of the hole—my heart howls with agony. "It's Pa! No!" The soldier pushes on Pa's shoulders, making him kneel like the others. Tears stream out of my eyes as I whisper thanks to the gods that the soldier has blindfolded Pa. He is spared from having to see the executions of many others. "Don't cry, Pa. I know you are afraid," I want to tell him. I feel his body tense up, hear his heart race, see tears flowing out from under the blindfold. Pa fights the urge to scream as he hears the sound of a hammer crack the skull next to him, smashing into it. The body falls on top of the others with a thump. The other fathers around Pa cry and beg for mercy but to no avail. One by one, each man is silenced by the hammer. Pa prays silently for the gods to take care of us. He focuses his mind on us, bringing up our faces one by one. He wants our faces to be the last things he sees as he leaves the earth.

"Oh Pa, I love you. I will always miss you." My spirit cries and hovers down over him. My spirit wraps invisible arms around him, making him cry even more. "Pa, I will always love you. I will never let you go." The soldier walks up to Pa, but I will not let him go. The soldier cannot hear or see me. He cannot see my eyes burn into his soul. "Leave my Pa alone!" My eyes dare not

blink as the soldier raises the hammer above his head. "Pa," I whisper, "I have to let you go now. I cannot be here and live." Tears wash across my body as I fly away, leaving Pa there by himself.

Back in the hut, I slide next [to] Chou. She opens her arms and takes me in. Our bodies cradling each other, we cry. The cool air chills the beads of sweat on my skin, making my teeth chatter. Beside us, Kim holds on tight to Geak.

"Pa, I cannot bear to think that you struggled for breath lying on top of the others in that hole. I must believe the soldier took pity and used one of his bullets on you. I cannot breathe, Pa. I am sorry I had to let you go." My mind swirls with pain and anger. The pain grows larger in my stomach. The pain spasm convulses as if it is eating away my linings. Turning on my side, I dig my hands into my stomach and squeeze it violently to make the physical pain stop. Then the sadness surrounds me. Dark and black it looms over me, pulling me deeper and deeper into it. And then it happens again. It is almost as if I am somewhere else for the moment and I simply black out the part of me that feels emotion. It is as if I am alive but not alive. I can still hear the faint noise of Ma's muffled cries outside, but I do not feel her pain. I do not feel anything at all.

Ma is up before anyone else the next morning. Her face is all puffy, her eyes are red and swollen shut. Chou gives Ma some of the very little food we have left, but she will not eat. I join them on the steps, daydreaming about our lives back in Phnom Penh when I was happy. I cannot allow myself to cry because once I do I will be lost forever. I have to be strong.

By the third day, we all know that what we feared most has happened. Keav, and now Pa, one by one, the Khmer Rouge is killing my family. My stomach hurts so much I want to cut it open and take the poison out. My body shivers as if evil has entered it, making me want to scream, beat my hands against my chest, and pull out my hair. I want to close my eyes and blank out again, but I don't know how to do it at will. I want my Pa here in the morning when I wake up! That night I pray to the gods, "Dear gods, Pa is a very devout Buddhist. Please help my Pa return home. He is not mean and does not like to hurt other people. Help him return and I will do anything you say. I will devote my entire life to you. I will believe you always. If you cannot bring Pa home to us, please make sure they don't hurt him, or please make sure Pa dies a quick death."

"Chou," I whisper to my sister, "I am going to kill Pol Pot. I hate him and I want to make sure he dies a slow and painful death."

"Don't say such things or you will get hurt."

"I am going to kill him." I do not know what he looks like, but if Pol Pot is the leader of the Angkar then he is the one responsible for all the miseries in our lives. I hate him for destroying my family. My hate is so strong it feels alive. It slithers and moves around in the pit of my stomach, growing bigger and bigger. I hate the gods for not bringing Pa back to us. I am a kid, not even seven years old, but somehow I will kill Pol Pot. I don't know him, yet I am certain he is the fattest, slimiest snake on earth. I am convinced that there is a monster living inside his body. He will die a painful, agonizing death, and I pray that I will play a part in it. I despise Pol Pot for making me hate so deeply. My hate empowers and scares me, for with hate in my heart I have no room for sadness. Sadness makes me want to die inside. Sadness makes me want to kill myself to escape the hopelessness of my life. Rage makes me want to survive and live so that I may kill. I feed my rage with bloody images of Pol Pot's slain body being dragged in the dirt.

"As long as we don't know for certain that your pa is dead, I will always have hope that he is alive somewhere," Ma declares to us the next morning. My heart hardens at her words, knowing I cannot allow myself the luxury of hope. To hope is to let pieces of myself die. To hope is to grieve his absence and acknowledge the emptiness in my soul without him.

Now that I have accepted the truth, I worry about what will happen to Ma. She was very dependent on Pa. He had always been there to make things easier for her. Pa was raised in the country and was accustomed to hardship. In Phnom Penh, we had live-in housekeepers to do just about everything for us. Pa was our strength and we all needed him to survive, especially Ma. He was good at surviving and knew best what to do for us.

I hope Pa comes to me again tonight. I hope he visits me in my sleep and meets me in my dreams. I saw him last night. He wore his tan military uniform from the Lon Nol government. His face was once again round like the moon and his body was soft. He was so real standing next to me, big and strong like he was before the war.

"Pa!" I run to him and he picks me up. "Pa, how are you? Did they hurt you?"

"Don't worry." He tries to soothe me.

"Pa, why did you leave us? I miss you so much it hurts my stomach. Why didn't you come and find me? Pa, when will you come and find us? If I go to the orphanage camp will you be able to find me?" I rest my head on his shoulder.

"Yes, I will."

He's my Pa, and if he says that he will find me, I know he will.

"Pa, why does it hurt so much to be with you? I don't want to hurt, I don't want to feel."

"I am sorry you are hurt. I have to go." Hearing this, I grip his arms tighter, refusing to let go. "Pa, I miss you so much. I miss sitting on your lap like I did in Phnom Penh."

"I have to go, but I will look after you always," Pa says softly, putting me down on the ground. I hold on to his finger and beg him not to leave me.

"No! No! Stay. Pa, stay with us. Please, don't leave. I miss you and I am scared. What will happen to us? Where will you go? Take me with you!"

Pa looks at me, his eyes brown and warm. I reach out my hands to him, but the farther I reach, the farther away he moves until he fades away completely.

My body fights to sleep when the sun shines through our door to tell us it is morning. I want to stay asleep forever just so I can be with him. In the real world, I don't know when I will ever see Pa again. Slowly, I open my eyes with Pa's face still lingering in my vision. It is not the face of the gaunt old man the soldiers took away but the face of the man I once thought was a god.

It was during our trip to Angkor Wat that I first thought Pa was a god. I was only three or four years old then. With my hand in Pa's, we entered the area of Angkor Thom, one of the many temple sites there. The gray towers loomed large before us like stone mountains. On each of the towers, giant faces with magnificent headdresses looked out in different directions over our land. Staring at the faces I exclaimed, "Pa, they look like you! The gods look like you!" Pa laughed and walked me into the temple. My eyes could not leave those huge round faces, with their almond-shaped eyes, flat noses, and full lips—all of Pa's features!

Waking up I try to hold on to these images of Pa even as we resume our lives without him. Ma returns to the field, working twelve to fourteen hours a day and leaves Geak behind with Chou. With Geak toddling after us, Chou and I and the other children work in the gardens and do menial labor in the village. It has been over a month since Pa was taken away. Ma seems to have recovered and is trying to get on with her life, but I know I will never see her truly smile again. Sometimes late at night, I am awakened by the sound of Ma sobbing on the steps, still waiting for Pa. Her body slumped like an old woman, she leans against the door frame, her arms wrapped around herself. She looks out into the field at the path Pa once walked, crying and longing for him.

We miss him terribly and Geak, being so young, is the only one able to vocalize our loneliness, by continuing to ask for Pa. I am afraid for Geak. She is four years old and has stopped growing because of malnutrition. I want to kill myself knowing that it was I who stole the food from her mouth that one night. "Your Pa will bring us lots of food when he returns," Ma tells Geak when she asks for Pa.

The soldiers come to our village more and more often now. Each time they leave, they take fathers from the other families. They always come in pairs—though never the same pair twice—with their rifles and casual excuses. When they come, some villagers try to hide their fathers by sending them off to the woods or having them be conveniently gone. But the soldiers wait, standing around the chief's house, slowly smoking their cigarettes as if they have all the time in the world. After they finish the pack, they walk to the victim's hut and loud cries and screams from inside follow. Then there's only silence. We all know they feed us lies about the fathers coming back the next morning. Still there is nothing we can do to stop them. No one questions these disappearances, not the chief, not the villagers, not Ma. I hate the soldiers now as much as I hate the Angkar and their leader, Pol Pot. I etch their faces into my memory and plan for the day when I can come back and kill them.

There have been rumors in the village that Pa was not killed in a Khmer Rouge mass execution. Rumors spread that the soldiers made Pa a prisoner on a faraway mountain and tortured him every day. But he survived and escaped to the top of the mountains. The soldiers, hunting for him, have not been able to catch him. People passing by our village say they have seen someone fitting Pa's description. They tell tales of Pa forming his own army, trying to recruit more soldiers to fight the Khmer Rouge. Upon hearing these rumors, Ma's face lights up and her eyes shine once again with hope. For a few days, she walks off to work with a little more life in her step and even twelve hours later the glimmer of a smile is still on her face. At night, she continuously fusses over our appearance, wiping the dirt off our faces, combing the knots out of our hair. She believes the stories wholeheartedly. "If he has escaped, it will not be long now before he comes searching for us. Until we know for sure of his fate, we must never give up hope." Once again, she devotes herself to sitting on the steps waiting for Pa's return.

Weeks pass after we hear the rumors about Pa and still he has not returned. I know Ma misses him and believes he is alive somewhere. Eventually, she stops waiting for him and tries once more to resume her life. Time passes slowly without Pa in our lives. Even with our own ration of food, our survival depends on our older brothers bringing more food to us each week. When Khouy gets sick, coughing up blood, we are forced to fend for ourselves. Khouy is a strong young man, but he pushes himself too hard at work. His work consists of constantly loading and unloading one hundred kilograms of rice onto trucks to be sent to China. Meng also cannot come because the soldiers are keeping him busy with work. We are all very worried for them both.

Life is hard without Pa. People in the village look down on Ma because she is not good at field work. It is too dangerous to have friends so she does not talk to anyone. The villagers also look down on her white skin and often make rude comments about "lazy white people." To my surprise, Ma becomes a hard worker and is surviving without Pa. On the days when Ma is assigned to work with fifteen other village women fishing for shrimp in nearby ponds, I go with her, leaving Chou behind with Geak. My job in the group includes fetching water for the shrimp catchers, helping untangle their nets, and separating the shrimp from weeds. Though hungry, we are not allowed to eat the shrimp we catch because it belongs to the village and must be shared with all. If anyone is caught stealing, the chief can publicly humiliate her, take away her possessions, and beat her. The punishments for such acts are grave, but our hunger does not allow this to stop us from sometimes stealing.

"Loung," Ma calls me. "I need some water, come here." She stands up and wipes her brows with her sleeve, leaving a trail of mud on her face. Scooping a coconut shell of water out of the bucket, I run over and hand it to her. "Here," she whispers, "give me your hand fast while no one is looking." Ma turns around and takes another careful look at the others to make certain we are not being watched. She quickly gives me a handful of baby shrimp as she takes the water cup from me. "Quick, eat them while no one is looking." Without hesitation, I shove the raw crawling baby shrimp into my mouth, shells and all. They taste of mud and rotten weeds. "Chew quickly and swallow," Ma tells me. "Now, you look out for me while I eat some. If anyone is looking, call me." I see Ma in a very different light now and have more pride in her strength. Somehow, one way or another, we find ways to stay alive.

PART 2

POETRY

Introduction
Absorbing and Being Absorbed by Poetry

EILEEN TABIOS

> The dragons on the back of a circular bronze mirror
> swirl without end. I sit and am an absorbing form.
>
> **—ARTHUR SZE**

I sit before a manuscript I received as a gift: the poems in *Bold Words*. I have
read them all and am returning to an excerpt from "The Redshifting Web" by
Arthur Sze. To paraphrase this poet whose clear-eyed openness to the world
has taught me as much as his words about the grace that is poetry, I absorb the
moments of molten gold wrought by this book's twenty-nine poets.

I turn to a goblet on my desk and raise the thin crystal to the white light
embracing St. Helena, California, where I recently moved from New York
City. Within its hold lies a swirling liquid poured from a bottle of Philip Togni
Cabernet. The wine is colored dark red—and I recall Mother's gift of a ruby
bracelet. I notice glycerine leaving visible tracks against the wine glass—and I
recall a long afternoon looking at London behind rain streaming across a hotel window in a manner similar to the liquid coating my glass. I raise the wine
and revel in its bouquet, inhaling aromas of vanilla, leather, oak, and herbs—
and I recall the scent of my grandparents' tobacco fields in the Philippines
where I once frolicked as a little girl. Finally, I take my first sip; the wine does
not disappoint with its rich and concentrated tannic taste bearing elements of
plums and blackberries, leather and smoked meats—and I recall a set of memories involving goats: a backyard barbecue in Vallejo which, in turn, evoked an
alley in Kathmandu where I had stared at the long-whiskered animals peering
at me from second-story windows.

Once more, I return to Arthur Sze's poem: "as moments coalesce, [I] see to
travel far is to return." Yes, it is time to return to the poems themselves. Are
these "Asian American" poems? After the seminal anthology *Premonitions*
(1995)[1] edited by Walter Lew required over five hundred pages to even come
close to displaying the range and diversity of Asian American poets, I am considering the challenge posed to any scholar, editor, or critic asked to put together a collection representing "Asian American" poetry.

Such a task occurred for the editors of *Bold Words* amidst a growing
recognition at the turn of the century that there may be no such thing as
"Asian America." Perhaps the label was once—for some, is still—convenient
for addressing the invisibility of certain writers within the so-called literary
canon of the United States, as addressed by the first anthology I read described
as Asian American poetry: the groundbreaking *The Open Boat* edited by Garrett Hongo.[2] But, unless all such anthologies can bear at least five hundred

pages of poems, does not the label also work to reduce the presentation of diversity within its community?

As I consider what to say about the poems in *Bold Words,* which is described as an Asian American anthology encompassing a century of writing, *I sit and am an absorbing form.* And it occurs to me that much wisdom might be available in simplicity: what I wish to suggest to you, Dear Reader, is to read and interact directly with the poems themselves. Read the poems for what the poems say to you, rather than through the clouds of context in which the poetry of their authors has been featured, whether as works by writers of color, creations from a multicultural canon, songs from a diaspora, or hymns from Asian America. These poems are not tokens—let alone tokens of something that artificially exists, or may not exist, called "Asian America." These poems are poems.

These poems are poems—what does that mean? I suggest that poems have their own lives separate from what is said about them, and that they exist so that you, Dear Reader, may respond *directly* to them and not to what I or anyone else would say *about* them. A poem, or any work of art, can engender a space for interaction with the audience—there is no need to predefine the nature of that engagement. Indeed, I suggest that poems ask you to respond to them in the way I responded earlier in this essay to the experience of tasting Philip Togni's Cabernet. Like poetry, wine can be about nostalgia—linking a smell, sight, taste, and feel to a prior experience by the wine drinker. Thus, one can hear oenophiles relating wine to such things as "grilled lamb," "tobacco," "blackberries," "the smell of wet hay," "dust," or "gravel." Notwithstanding phrases that may seem overreaching, the wine lovers are trying to relate the experience to their memories—is this not how one may also read a poem? That is, a poem transcends its author's autobiography when it manages to articulate a space where different readers will feel a variety of emotional responses to the same words—a variety of reactions because each reader bears a different set of memories.

Consequently, I don't wish to present the poems in this book within only one context, for example "Asian America." I don't ever wish to tell readers how to respond to Art. How can I? Dear Reader, you and I are different people. For instance, how can you mirror my response to Janice Mirikitani's poem "Recipe" unless you were (with) me as a teenager attending Gardena High School with someone we shall call "Julia." Gardena, California, contains one of the largest Japanese American communities in the mainland United States. Julia was an unprepossessing-looking girl who easily got lost in the crowd. The first time I *noticed* her was when she arrived at school one day bearing the feature of "round eyes" for which Mirikatani wrote her recipe-poem. Julia apparently had attained the desired result, complete with double eyelids, through bodily surgery rather than through the use of Scotch tape and black eyeliner as suggested in Mirikatani's poem. As I envisioned the scalpel slitting the smooth seamless slopes of Julia's eyelids, I winced.

It is the same wince I felt upon first reading Mirikitani's poem. But you, Dear Reader, who's never met Julia or someone like her, might respond differently. You might look at the poem and think it a comment on society's views on what defines Beauty; that the poem uses the recipe format to reference the importance of food in Asian social interactions; that the directive "Cleanse face" rather than "wash face" implies something dirty about the Asian face; and that the overall focus on "face" relates to the masks attributed to and, indeed, worn by some Asian Americans.

Both responses are equally valid—my response of a deeply-felt shudder or the latter reaction I imagined from a reader sensitized to read the poem in an Asian American context. I share both interpretations because I believe that most if not all of the poets in *Bold Words*—to the extent they even consider their poems' audiences—would not wish to privilege one type of response over another. Do you need to have the phrase "Asian America" running through your mind to appreciate Li-Young Lee's love poem, "This Room and Everything in It"? Lee sings: "This desire, perfection. / Your closed eyes my extinction / . . . The sun is / God, your body is milk // . . . it had something / to do with love." Faced with these words, I wish only to move out of the poem's way.

In another example, one of my friends read Vince Gotera's poem "Beetle on a String," a poem set in the Philippines. My friend loved the poem because it reminded her of similar childhood play in New Orleans. "The poem," my friend added, "made me realize how intimate this vast world can be." As my friend did, Dear Reader, go directly to the poems themselves. Read and trust your responses—or lack thereof—to the poems. *Sit and be an absorbing form.* The direct relationship between reader and poem unencumbered by critics, academics and theorists (or writers of poetry introductions) is the most honest, most passionate, and most true interaction.

I confess that I am also reluctant to contextualize poems because I believe it is impossible to fully capture the poem in talking about it; one can experience the poem without verbalizing the experience. The impossibility of defining the golden moments called "poems" relates, I believe, to the experience of the poem being formed significantly by what the reader gives to it. *Empathy*— with its related intangibles that have been called "heart," "spirit," "grace," and "compassion"—is crucial if one is to engage with the poem, whether in writing or reading it. Thus, in discussing the poetry in *Bold Words,* I am left inarticulate—and wish to remain inarticulate—in addressing the humanity of the poet and reader that would determine their experience with a poem. But I can address poetic form.

Many of the poems in *Bold Words* use a narrative which allows the poets to share stories: Alfred Yuson's cooptation of the Pop artist-icon in "Andy Warhol Speaks to His Two Filipino Maids"; Garrett Hongo's moving description of how Los Angeles in October "seethes like a billboard under twilight" in "Yellow Light"; Chitra Divakaruni's heart-rending evocation of the sacrifices of Punjabi immigrant farmers in "The Founding of Yuba City"; Lawson Inada's urgent love cries in "Filling the Gap"; Cathy Song's deft riff on miserliness in "A Conservative View"; the sensuality of chocolate in Tina Koyama's "The Chocolatier"; and the way memories refuse to die in Linh Dinh's "The Dead." These poems explain why Meena Alexander was moved to write, "We must always return / to poems for news of the world."

I wish to address poetic form because the presence of Marilyn Chin in *Bold Words* reminded me of the controversial book *The Best of The Best American Poetry* edited by Harold Bloom.[3] This anthology was culled from the 1988–1997 *Best American Poetry* annuals. The 1996 volume, guest-edited by Adrienne Rich and featuring many ethnic American writers such as Chin and Kimiko Hahn, was the only volume not represented in Bloom's compendium. Indeed, Bloom attacked this volume as one where he "failed to discover more than an authentic poem or two." Bloom explains, "That 1996 anthology . . . seems to me a monumental representation for the enemies of the aesthetic who are in the act of overwhelming us." *Us?* Bloom continues, "It is of a badness not to be believed, because it follows the criteria now operative: what matters most are race, gender, sexual orientation, ethnic origin, and political purpose of the would-be poet" (15–16).

After reading Bloom's essay, I immediately recalled Chin's counsel in my book which interviews fifteen Asian American poets, *Black Lightning: Poetry In Progress.*[4] Chin notes, "My advice to young poets is to cultivate a strong stomach for rejection. The dominant society will tell you that you may not enter the canon, because what you have to say does not matter to them."

This is not the place to rebut Bloom and those who feel the way he does. But I wish to note this issue—and for young Asian American poets reading this book, to offer encouragement—because it is not likely to go away. How can it? Poems are not mere words; they are living creatures. Bloom is entitled to his opinions—but should not his criticism directly address the "badness" of the poems rather than the overall approach of the poems in addressing "race, gender, sexual orientation, ethnic origin and political purpose"? Poets write poems based on their concerns. For example, Mitsuye Yamada's poem "Thirty Years Under" evokes a disgraceful period in U.S. history when Japanese Americans were interned in camps: "there is nothing more / humiliating / more than beatings / more than curses / than being spat on // like a dog." Such a poem needs to exist. The alternative is, as Yamada writes, to "travel blind." Let me repeat the excerpt from Alexander's poem "News of the World" and continue it one line further: "We must always return / to poems for news of the world / or perish for the lack."

How can Asian American poets ignore their culture, ethnicity, and community in writing poems? The question evokes what I consider to be a dead-on assessment by poet and critic John Yau which he shares in *Black Lightning*, "The identity issue is a major issue not being addressed by modernist and post-modernist poets. It's not been addressed by later modernist poets because many often want to assimilate and be part of the mainstream and, thus, do not question the mainstream's use of identity, how it fixes them with a narrow possibility. It's not being addressed by post-modernists because they say the author is dead. But why is the author dead at a point when demographics have changed such that all these people who were once marginalized and silenced can now talk—but during a period when the author is supposedly dead" (390)?

Identity, of course, is a critical issue for the Asian American community where the silencing of poets may mean the silencing of history or translate to invisibility within "mainstream" culture. Indeed, one of *Bold Words*'s strengths lies in how—as an Asian American collection—it includes the work of ethnicities less published than East Asians: Vietnamese, Filipino and South Asian American poets. Indran Amirthanayagam recalls how a civil war devastated a country now lost to him in "Ceylon":"(Pity the poor lion, / pity the poor tiger, / the cobra, the elephant, / the fish and fowl / the birds and beasts / who see their jungle cut down / to build huts / for knife throwers guns / bombs rapists / thieves of every color // who come to drink the milk / and eat the bread / of young boys and girls / who've always been told, // when the beggar comes / give something, give something you like / like your life.)"

Whatever poetry's unique demands may be, they are not necessarily divorced from a poet's social concerns. Some Asian American poets who do not "talk story" in their poems do so in opposition to a sociological reading of their works which often prevails among critics and academics. The latter response, however, still reflects a poet's social consciousness. Thus, when it comes to poetic form the Asian American poet's concerns—to the extent one understands that such factors as racism and objectification have afflicted Asian America—might also lead to the rupturing of traditional poetic forms which predominate in the literary mainstream. I, for one, am interested in disrupting narrative in my poems as a result of exploring issues of colonialism and postcolonialism. In this book, one may interpret form as opposition through Jessica Hagedorn's bow to Black vernacular in her poem "Smokey's Getting Old," written during a period in which she was searching for a language that also evoked the hybrid "Taglish," a combination of Tagalog and English; Walter Lew's gorgeous use of the page as a field in "Ch'onmun Hak"; Lois-Ann Yamanaka's use of Hawaiian "local" language in "Kala Gave Me Anykine Advice Especially about Filipinos When I Moved to Pahala"; and, naturally, Janice Mirikitani's recipelike structure in "Recipe."

A significant number of Asian American poets have addressed and continue to push the boundaries of poetic form: Mei-mei Berssenbrugge (whose groundbreaking poems informed by a feminist perspective turn politics into astoundingly beautiful art), Yau, Myung Mi Kim, as well as more emerging poets such as Catalina Cariaga, Tan Lin, Brian Kim Stefans, Sianne Ngai, Nick Carbo, and Oliver de la Paz. (I specify these poets partly because they have published at least one poetry collection.) When one understands that the twenty-first century is unlikely to leave behind the race-based atrocities or diaspora-induced anguish that have afflicted Asian America, it makes sense to me that many Asian American poets also would write *in opposition*.

Nonetheless, it is the slippery nature of art that as soon as one attempts to categorize it, the art slips away. As a poet—thus, practitioner—I realize that before poets come to write something that is later labeled "oppositional" they may have intended something else, including simply trying to develop their craft. Sometimes, a poem is just a poem—or, as Eric Chock writes in "Strawberries" and which I choose to read as a metaphor for this point: "I'm just an ordinary man / who loves strawberries. / I love to grab the green fuzziness / in my gathered fingertips / and dip the seedy point in sour cream / and brown sugar / and into my waiting lips. / Mmmm, that's a sweet kiss worth / repeating all night, / just an ordinary man / loving his strawberries. / And I don't want to have to think / who picked them with / what brown illegal alien fingers, / back bent under the California sun."

In other words, a poem by an Asian American poet can be read, too, for pleasure alone rather than within a particular context. This possibility again highlights the importance of the reader investing attention in reading a poem, for it is that investment which will cause the poem to mature. Indeed, I mentioned earlier that *Bold Words* is admirable for including members of ethnicities not as well represented by older Asian American anthologies. However, the more that one widens the net cast to round up poets for a collection, the more one may see commonalities of experience: the pensiveness of reminiscence in Agha Shahid Ali's "In Search of Evanescence"; the meditation/mediation on dying in Bao-Long Chu's "The Bitterness of Bodies We Bear"; the questioning of laws in Luis H. Francia's "Walls"; the anticipation of returning to a childhood home in Reetika Vazirani's "Reading the Poem about the Yew Tree"; and an immigrant's invisibility in Alfrredo Navarro Salanga's "They Don't Think Much about Us in America."

This "universality" makes sense, and only emphasizes again the critical role of the reader in making poems live. Critics have written about how humanity relates to common experiences in the remote past when many of our propensities were acquired as adaptations to environment. In a recent conversation, the Filipino poet Bino A. Realuyo said, "I look at a page the way I have always looked at a canvas because I used to paint. Our eyes have an intense desire for symmetry. Even those who try to go against nature by drawing asymmetrical lines eventually create beauty through abstraction—one reason why the avant-garde never quite remains avant-garde for long is because they eventually fulfill our human desire for beauty."

In other words, poems live through the exercise of the shared humanity among and between poets and readers. You, the Reader, play a critical role in the life of a poem. The poem is a hand reaching out and it lives only if you yourself reach out and clasp that hand. I return to Arthur Sze's poem which—like many of this poet's works—is marked by his ability to find connections among varied elements within the universe. The open-minded and open-hearted empathy in Sze's words may teach much about how one may write and read a poem: "I absorb the weight of a pause when it tilts / the conversation in a room. I absorb the moments / he sleeps holding her right breast in his left hand / and know it resembles glassy waves in a harbor / in descending spring light. Is the mind a mirror? / . . . I absorb the stench of burning cuttlefish bone, / and as moments coalesce see to travel far is to return." Dear Reader, *sit and be an absorbing form.*

The editors of this volume asked me to predict some trends in Asian American poetry. I believe there will be a continued diversity in poetic styles without departing from the stories in poets' communities— they are not mutually exclusive. This point seems rather basic, until one understands that a major tension in contemporary American poetry has been the debate between the idea of language as material and the idea that the poem is rooted in the ego. This paradigm cannot adequately address Asian American poetry. For Asian American poets, the poem is not separable from culture even when the form would seem to suggest less focus than overt narrative indicates on issues related to identity.

It is apt for poetry to combine two seemingly opposing positions—the reader's subjectivity and the importance of the poet's biography. As Meena Alexander noted in *Black Lightning,* "The poem on the page is only the tip of the iceberg. Most of what endures, turning into the soil of the poem, is carried within, unseen, even worldless" (195). Autobiography matters, *and* the Poem also transcends autobiography.

In fact, it seems to me that being an Asian American poet lends itself to transcending not just canonical views on "form" but poetry itself, to work in other categories such as fiction and essays. As one who edits in addition to writing, I consider all of my activities integral to being a poet, particularly as an Asian American poet. Garrett Hongo, David Mura, and others who also write both prose and poetry have spoken about the importance of providing criticism concurrent with creating their poems. In particular, I recall Mura once saying that he writes memoirs partly to lay out a context for his poems—that otherwise no one else might do so, or do so in a manner that Mura would appreciate.

As Arthur Sze notes in his introduction to *Black Lightning,* "critical discussion of Asian American poetry lag[ged] behind artistic accomplishment. The discourse tend[ed] to center on race and identity, and . . . [is] just beginning to address theory and practice and the polysemous nature of the work" (1). However, by offering a poetry-in-progress format, *Black Lightning* allowed poets to comment on their own writing processes rather than the more common practice of having others critique their works. One reviewer said the book damned the notion that there is no "I" behind poems (this has become my favorite review of the book).

The best poems resonate, leave behind a simmering feeling in response to their words. The same occurs with wine: long after the wine has been swallowed, its aftermath lingers along the edges of your tongue. What we might call "resonance" in a poem is what oenophiles call "finish" for wines. For me, I often say about a moving poem, "It has a long finish" rather than "It resonates." The poetry in *Bold Words* reverberates in a manner I need not define for you. Dear Reader, simply *sit and be an absorbing form.*

Let me share some of what resonates for me from the poems in *Bold Words*: questions, not answers. Christian Langworthy's question, "Why does autumn undress the way you do?" Meena Alexander's question, "What ink can inscribe them now / the young of Tiananmen?" Marilyn Chin's question, "What shall we cook tonight? / Perhaps these six tiny squid / lined up so perfectly on the block?" Vince Gotera's question, "It makes me shiver now / to wonder what thoughtless boy holds my string?" Cathy Song's question, "How else are you going to get those damn pa-kes to share?" Jessica Hagedorn's question, "did you / come with yr daddy in 1959 / on a second-class boat crying all the while / cuz you didn't want to leave the barrio"? Alfrredo Navarro Salanga's question, "Who cares?"

I introduce the poetry in *Bold Words* by asking you, Dear Reader, "Which poem(s) shall transport you with a long finish?"

Notes

1. Walter K. Lew, ed., *Premonitions: The Kaya Anthology of New Asian North American Poetry* (New York: Kaya Production, 1995).

2. Garrett Hongo, ed., *The Open Boat: Poems from Asian America* (New York: Anchor Books, 1993).

3. Harold Bloom, ed., *The Best of the Best American Poetry* (New York: Scribners, 1998).

4. Eileen Tabios, ed., *Black Lightning: Poetry in Progress* (New York: Asian American Writers Workshop, 1998).

(Untitled)

FRANCES CHUNG

The young man dressed in white is a barber at
the airport. He teases you in Spanish. When
you answer him in Spanish he follows you down
the corridors of waiting rooms. His father
was Chinese and came from Hong Kong. His last
name is Jung. His mother is Mexican. When
his parents died seven years ago, he came to
this country to be a barber. He wants to learn
Chinese. He has a book in his shop for this
purpose, but the language is difficult to learn.
When he questions you, you lie to him and say
you have a husband. He looks disappointed,
smiles and walks away in the direction of the
men's room. You are on the way to Lima.

Filling the Gap

LAWSON FUSAO INADA

When Bird died, I didn't mind:
I had things to do—

polish some shoes, practice
a high school cha-cha-cha.

I didn't even know
Clifford was dead:

I must have been
lobbing an oblong ball
beside the gymnasium.

I saw the Lady
right before she died—

dried, brittle
as last year's gardenia.

I let her scratch an autograph.

But not Pres.

Too bugged to boo, I left
as Basie's brass
booted him off the stand
in a sick reunion—

tottering, saxophone
dragging him like a stage-hook.

When I read Dr. Williams'
poem, "Stormy,"
I wrote a letter of love and praise

and didn't mail it.

After he died, it burned my desk
like a delinquent prescription . . .

I don't like to mourn the dead:
what didn't, never will.

And I sometimes feel foolish
staying up late,
trying to squeeze some life
out of books and records,
filling the gaps
between words and notes.

That is why
I rush into our room to find you
mumbling and moaning
in your incoherent performance.

That is why
I rub and squeeze you
and love to hear your
live, alterable cry against my breast.

Lawson Fusao
Inada

79

Thirty Years Under

MITSUYE YAMADA

I had packed up
my wounds in a cast
iron box
sealed it
labeled it
do not open . . .
ever . . .

and traveled blind
for thirty years

until one day I heard
a black man with huge bulbous eyes
say
there is nothing more
humiliating
more than beatings
more than curses
than being spat on

like a dog.

Cincinnati

MITSUYE YAMADA

Freedom at last
in this town aimless
I walked against the rush
hour traffic
My first day
in a real city
where

no one knew me.

No one except one
hissing voice that said
dirty jap
warm spittle on my right cheek.
I turned and faced
the shop window
and my spittled face
spilled onto a hill
of books.
Words on display.

In Government Square
people criss-crossed
the street
like the spokes of
a giant wheel.

I lifted my right hand
but it would not obey me.
My other hand fumbled
for a hankie.

My tears would not
wash it. They stopped
and parted.
My hankie brushed
the forked
tears and spittle
together.

I edged toward the curb
loosened my fisthold
and the bleached laced
mother-ironed hankie blossomed in
the gutter atop teeth marked
gum wads and heeled candy wrappers.

Everyone knew me.

Smokey's Getting Old
(for Smokey Robinson)

JESSICA HAGEDORN

hey Nellie,
how long you been here? did you
come with yr daddy in 1959
on a second-class boat   crying all the while
cuz you   didn't want to leave the barrio
the girls back there
who wore their hair loose
lots of orange lipstick & movies on Sundays
Quiapo market in the mornings
yr grandma chewing red tobacco
roast pig
(yeah . . . and it tastes good)

hey Nellie,
did you have to live in Stockton
with yr daddy
and talk to old farmers
who immigrated in 1941;   did yr daddy
promise you
to a fifty-eight year old bachelor
who stank of cigars
and did you run away
to San Francisco
go to Poly High
rat yr hair
hang around Woolworth's
Chinatown at three in the morning
go to the Cow Palace & catch
Smokey Robinson
cry at his gold jacket
dance
every Friday night at the Mission
go steady with Ruben
(yr daddy can't stand it
cuz he's a spik)

and the sailors
you dreamed of in Manila

with yellow hair
did they take you to the beach
to ride the ferris wheel?
Life's Never Been So Fine!

you & Carmen harmonize
"Be My Baby" by the Ronettes
and 1965 you get laid at a party
(Carmen's house)   and Ruben marries you
and you give up harmonizin'

Nellie,
you sleep without dreams
and remember the barrios
and how it's all the same

Manila,
the Mission,
Chinatown,
East L.A., Harlem, Fillmore Street,
and you're getting kinda fat
and Smokey Robinson's getting old

but yr son
has learned to jive
to the Jackson Five

"i don't want to /
but i need you / seems like /
i'm always / thinkin' of you /
though / you do me wrong now /
my love is strong / now /
you really
got a hold on me . . ."

Recipe

JANICE MIRIKITANI

Round Eyes

Ingredients: scissors, Scotch magic transparent tape,
eyeliner—water based, black.
Optional: false eyelashes.

Cleanse face thoroughly.

For best results, powder entire face, including eyelids.
    (lighter shades suited to total effect desired)

With scissors, cut magic tape $1/16$" wide, $3/4$"–$1/2$" long—
depending on length of eyelid.

Stick firmly onto mid-upper eyelid area
    (looking down into handmirror facilitates finding
    adequate surface)

If using false eyelashes, affix first on lid, folding any
Excess lid over the base of eyelash with glue.

Paint black eyeliner on tape and entire lid.

Do not cry.

Why Is Preparing Fish a Political Act?

JANICE MIRIKITANI

Preparing fish
each Oshogatsu
I buy a gleaming rock cod,
pink, immaculately gutted.
Each year, a respectable fish
that does not satisfy
(hard as I try)
to capture flavors
once tasted.

Grandmother's hands
washing, scaling, cleaning
her fish,
saved each part,
guts, eggs, head.
Her knife, rusted
at the handle screws
ancient as her curled fingers.
Her pot, dented,
darkened, mottled with age
boiled her brew
of shoyu
sweetened with ginger and
herbs she grew
steamed with blood, water.
Nothing wasted.

Someone once tried to sell her
a set of aluminum
pots, smiling too much, called her
mamasan.
Her silence thicker than
steaming shoyu,
whiter than sliced bamboo root
boiled with fish heads.

Preparing fish
is a political act.

Yellow Light

GARRETT HONGO

One arm hooked around the frayed strap
of a tar-black patent-leather purse,
the other cradling something for dinner:
fresh bunches of spinach from a J-Town *yaoya,*
sides of split Spanish mackerel from Alviso's,
maybe a loaf of Langendorf; she steps
off the hissing bus at Olympic and Fig,
begins the three-block climb up the hill,
passing gangs of schoolboys playing war,
Japs against Japs, Chicanas chalking sidewalks
with the holy double-yoked crosses of hopscotch,
and the Korean grocer's wife out for a stroll
around this neighborhood of Hawaiian apartments
just starting to steam with cooking
and the anger of young couples coming home
from work, yelling at kids, flicking on
TV sets for the Wednesday Night Fights.

If it were May, hydrangeas and jacaranda
flowers in the streetside trees would be
blooming through the smog of late spring.
Wisteria in Masuda's front yard would be
shaking out the long tresses of its purple hair.
Maybe mosquitoes, moths, a few orange butterflies
settling on the lattice of monkey flowers
tangled in chain-link fences by the trash.

But this is October, and Los Angeles
seethes like a billboard under twilight.
From used-car lots and the movie houses uptown,
long silver sticks of light probe the sky.
From the Miracle Mile, whole freeways away,
a brilliant fluorescence breaks out
and makes war with the dim squares
of yellow kitchen light winking on
in all the side streets of the Barrio.

She climbs up the two flights of flagstone
stairs to 201-B, the spikes of her high heels

clicking like kitchen knives on a cutting board,
props the groceries against the door,
fishes through memo pads, a compact,
empty packs of chewing gum, and finds her keys.

The moon then, cruising from behind
a screen of eucalyptus across the street,
covers everything, everything in sight,
in a heavy light like yellow onions.

The Gift

LI-YOUNG LEE

To pull the metal splinter from my palm
my father recited a story in a low voice.
I watched his lovely face and not the blade.
Before the story ended, he'd removed
the iron sliver I thought I'd die from.

I can't remember the tale,
but hear his voice still, a well
of dark water, a prayer.
And I recall his hands,
two measures of tenderness
he laid against my face,
the flames of discipline
he raised above my head.

Had you entered that afternoon
you would have thought you saw a man
planting something in a boy's palm,
a silver tear, a tiny flame.
Had you followed that boy
you would have arrived here,
where I bend over my wife's right hand.

Look how I shave her thumbnail down
so carefully she feels no pain.
Watch as I lift the splinter out.
I was seven when my father
took my hand like this,
and I did not hold that shard
between my fingers and think,
Metal that will bury me,
christen it Little Assassin,
Ore Going Deep for My Heart.
And I did not lift up my wound and cry,
Death visited here!
I did what a child does
when he's given something to keep.
I kissed my father.

Urban Love Songs
after Tzu Yeh

WING TEK LUM

You stop to watch the Mandarin ducks.
The rest of us continue on to the flamingo lagoon.
I would like to ask what attracts you to them.
But my feet keep walking, I don't look back.

• • •

From a piece of cloth I cut out a heart.
In the laundromat it is washed and dried.
I can spend whole hours watching it toss and tumble.
I wonder if you feel the same way as I.

• • •

I wave as you enter; you take your seat smiling.
This same coffee shop now feels crowded.
We whisper to each other:
all eyes have noticed something's changed.

• • •

I've bought a new phone and an answering machine
because I know you will be calling.
Here's the number, which only you will have.
I plan to change the tape every hour on the hour.

• • •

Our friends are laughing.
They say we sit so close in your old Buick
it has become second nature for me
to exit on the same side as you.

• • •

Pinocchio's back!
Let's relive that night at the drive-in
when I whispered that his nose was giving me ideas
and you got into my pants for the first time.

• • •

You drop the laundry off going to work.
I bring the bag back when I come home.

Neatly folded, your underthings are left on the bed
—I wish to respect certain cabinets as yours.

. . .

You shut the window rushing to your covers
complaining of the cold night.
I need fresh air, but am willing to compromise.
Let's just pull up the sash halfway, okay?

. . .

We hunt for photos in my parents' storeroom.
Look how young I was and full of dreams.
On the way out you brush against a cobweb.
Your flailing arms make me afraid.

. . .

A firetruck screams through my heart.
Douse the flames! Douse the flames!
I awake to find my pillow soaked with sweat.
For a moment I thought it was my tears.

. . .

You've stacked your boxes neatly by the door.
I find atop one Chinese poems I had bought for us.
Quietly I take the book out.
I resolve to tell you this after you have moved.

. . .

For my clogged sink I called a plumber.
When my cat got ill I took her to the vet.
My heart is broken
—I will not ask you to come to mend me.

. . .

Last night you made me so mad.
I've resolved never ever to speak to you again.
I regret having to put my foot down so.
I'm sending you a telegram to let you know.

. . .

One friend I know cut her hair short.
Another shaved his beard without regrets.
I would walk this city naked and bald
if ever I thought I could be free of you.

. . .

After you, I took up jogging.
I wore through my running shoes in no time.

One night I chucked them down into the trash chute.
See how trim I am these days!

      • • •

Once I bought a single chrysanthemum on a stem.
We watched it blossom, red and full.
Those times now bring a smile to me
finding its brown petals as I sweep the floor.

The Chocolatier

TINA KOYAMA

Find a special spot on your body
and use it, he tells us, like *this,* and he touches
chocolate to his lip again and again,
closing his eyes. Spurning all
thermometers, he waits for the perfect moment
to slide truffle centers deep
into a bowl of cooling chocolate.
It's all a matter of patience, he says,
for while the science of chocolate
is the altered crystalline structure
of sugar, the art
is treating it with love.
I nod along with the class and pretend
to take notes, all the while

melting in his arms, falling
for his every tempered word: my hair
is a riverful of dark couverture,
my eyes the color of ephemere truffles.
I could learn to love
a man like this, his hands at first cool
then warming the way a square
of chocolate takes after the tongue.

I could learn to wait
for a man like this, but he no longer
waits for me: the chocolatier dips truffles now, one
by one, by hand, holding each
not as he might the breast of a woman
he loves but perhaps of a woman he once loved, then slowly
let go. Chocolate, treated right, will love you
back, he says. Look at that shine,
as if the light belonged there
in the dark.

Strawberries

ERIC CHOCK

Leave me alone.
I'm just an ordinary man
who loves strawberries.
I love to grab the green fuzziness
in my gathered fingertips
and dip the seedy point in sour cream
and brown sugar
and into my waiting lips.
Mmmm, that's a sweet kiss worth
repeating all night,
just an ordinary man
loving his strawberries.
And I don't want to have to think
who picked them with
what brown illegal alien fingers,
back bent under the California sun
that used to belong to his forefathers anyway.
I don't wanna know that the price of cream
is American decadence that the rest of the world
would never dream of spending,
or that sugar is giving me an insulin rush
or that the strawberries were sprayed with EDB
causing me cancer.
I don't wanna know these things
so don't bother me!
I'm just an ordinary man
who loves strawberries that come to me
past striking cashiers at Safeway,
that come to me in green plastic baskets
that will not decompose, but fill the air
with toxic fumes as they're incinerated
in the city dump polluting Hawaii's air and ocean,
plastic containers, a petroleum by-product
that the Arabs are processing
to enable the rich to buy the homes
of movie stars in Beverly Hills,
to buy whole hotels in Miami
or L.A. or New York,
while the rest of their people in poverty pray,

bowing their heads to the ancient ground
while all the oil flows out of the deserts
to America to grease the great machine
that grows the strawberries that I love,
sent by diesel trucks to the coast,
and by jet to Hawaii
where I can sit on my bed
and enjoy the pleasures of an ordinary man,
kissing that sweet kiss all night long,
without a care in the world.

Eric Chock

95

This Room and Everything in It

LI-YOUNG LEE

Lie still now
while I prepare for my future,
certain hard days ahead,
when I'll need what I know so clearly this moment.

I am making use
of the one thing I learned
of all the things my father tried to teach me:
the art of memory.

I am letting this room
and everything in it
stand for my ideas about love
and its difficulties.

I'll let your love-cries,
those spacious notes
of a moment ago,
stand for distance.

Your scent,
that scent
of spice and a wound,
I'll let stand for mystery.

Your sunken belly
is the daily cup
of milk I drank
as a boy before morning prayer.

The sun on the face
of the wall
is God, the face
I can't see, my soul,
and so on, each thing
standing for a separate idea,
and those ideas forming the constellation
of my greater idea.
And one day, when I need

to tell myself something intelligent
about love,

I'll close my eyes
and recall this room and everything in it:
My body is estrangement.
This desire, perfection.
Your closed eyes my extinction.
Now I've forgotten my
idea. The book
on the windowsill, riffled by wind . . .
the even-numbered pages are
the past, the odd-
numbered pages, the future.
The sun is
God, your body is milk . . .

useless, useless . . .
your cries are song, my body's not me . . .
no good . . . my idea
has evaporated . . . your hair is time, your thighs are song . . .
it had something to do
with death . . . it had something
to do with love.

From "In Search of Evanescence"

AGHA SHAHID ALI

3

When on Route 80 in Ohio
I came across an exit
to Calcutta

the temptation to write a poem
led me past the exit
so I could say

India always exists
off the turnpikes
of America

so I could say
I did take the exit
and crossed Howrah

and even mention the Ganges
as it continued its sobbing
under the bridge

so when I paid my toll
I saw trains rush by
one after one

on their roofs old passengers
each ready to surrender
his bones for tickets

so that I heard
the sun's percussion
on tamarind leaves

heard the empty cans of children
filling only with the shadows
of leaves

that behind the unloading trucks
were the voices of vendors
bargaining over women

so when the trees
let down their tresses
the monsoon oiled and braided them

and when the wind again parted them
this was the temptation
to end the poem this way:

The warm rains have left
many dead on the pavements

The signs to Route 80
all have disappeared

And now the road is a river
polished silver by cars

The cars are urns
carrying ashes to the sea

Agha Shahid Ali

99

Andy Warhol Speaks to His Two Filipino Maids

ALFRED A. YUSON

Art, my dears, is not cleaning up
after the act. Neither is it washing off
grime with the soap of fact. In fact
and in truth, my dears, art is dead

center, between meals, amid spices
and spoilage. Fills up the whitebread
sweep of life's obedient slices.

Art is the letters you send home
about the man you serve. Or the salad
you bring in to my parlor of elites.
While Manhattan stares down at the soup

of our affinities. And we hear talk of coup
in your islands. There they copy love
the way I do, as how I arrive over and over

again at art. Perhaps too it is the time
marked by the sand in your shoes, spilling
softly like rumor. After your hearts I lust.
In our God you trust. And it's your day off.

Not Much Art

INDRAN AMIRTHANAYAGAM

I hear there isn't much art
in the bombing of Jaffna.

Planes fly overhead
and crews pick up
bombs and fling
them down on houses.

On houses, mind you,
no attempt to dig out
guerrillas hiding in bush empires.

No soldier to soldier combat
in the old man on a bicycle
fleeing his burning compound.

I hear from friends
who watch CNN
that a Norwegian crew

made it in and sent
a report for broadcast
in the post-midnight hour,

the scrambly witchy time
when Americans learn
the darknesses of dark lands,

at that hour, even America
is dark watching the Dark Star
attack its sister or father.

How shall the night end,
drummed?   Our eyes punched
                        we sleep.

Versed?   Blindfolded

                        we sleep.

Brush stroked?

            Eyes wide open,

                        we sleep.

There isn't much art
in pill-taking
or the whiskey toothbrush

or 500 laps on one foot
to tire it out   before working
the other foot to tire that out,

when each minute the heart
aches, and lungs draw
cigarettes,   not peace pipes,

when each minute
sons and daughters
raped and murdered

visit the beachhead
of your dreams
bloated and wild-eyed,

and you run
that foot faster
and faster

punch your eyes out
blindfold them
and tear the cloth off,

and in the white dark
fling the balls out
to meet the arriving dreams,

to receive them whole
blood pumped and pumped,
balls soaring
sockets in attendance.

Ceylon

INDRAN AMIRTHANAYAGAM

The head is cold, the cigarette
cold, the bomb
             cold,
the wind
the Sun
the white wedding flower
             cold,

The man who reads the papers,
wrapped in a sheet,
door barred with books
a typewriter, broom
a few cans of fish
a kerosene stove

reads of horses
in flying colors   at Epsom,
of the Queen in her palace
who cries about her common wealth,

so many jewels
so many black bus conductors
so many bits of bus and flesh
near the Fort, the Pettah

where the Tamil shopkeepers
used to make their daily bread,
and build houses in Wellawatte,
now all gone.

In Toronto,
rice and curry
a fist fight,

in Madras
rice and curry
a camp for boys,

grenades and jungle skins
accurate marks man ship
off boats down the barrels
of the Army's gunships.

And the bus on the jungle road
the military checkpoint
the men in uniform, sandals
on their feet, who came to kill

(The sandals was how we could tell
these were terrorists)

No big black boots
marching to the temple
to grab a few young girls
and caress their breasts
and break them down,
"dirty bloody hymens."

No minister with portfolio
at night with soldiers
to hatch the plan   to burn
the Jaffna Public Library

its ola leaf eggs,
its precious historical chicks,
its grand medicinal tapestry
of Ceylon Tamil life served
to wolves, *lion*-hearted men—
    (Pity the poor lion,
    pity the poor tiger,
    the cobra, the elephant,
    the fish and fowl
    the birds and beasts
    who see their jungle cut down
    to build huts
    for knife throwers   guns
    bombs rapists
    thieves of every color
    who come to drink the milk
    and eat the bread
    of young boys and girls
    who've always been told,

        when the beggar comes
        give something, give something you like
                like your life.)

The Floral Apron

MARILYN CHIN

The woman wore a floral apron around her neck,
that woman from my mother's village
with a sharp cleaver in her hand.
She said, "What shall we cook tonight?
Perhaps these six tiny squid
lined up so perfectly on the block?"

She wiped her hand on the apron,
pierced the blade into the first.
There was no resistance,
no blood, only cartilage
soft as a child's nose. A last
iota of ink made us wince.

Suddenly, the aroma of ginger and scallion fogged our senses,
and we absolved her for that moment's barbarism.
Then, she, an elder of the tribe,
without formal headdress, without elegance,
deigned to teach the younger
about the Asian plight.

And although we have traveled far
we would never forget that primal lesson
—on patience, courage, forbearance,
on how to love squid despite squid,
how to honor the village, the tribe,
that floral apron.

Kala Gave Me Anykine Advice Especially about Filipinos When I Moved to Pahala

LOIS-ANN YAMANAKA

No whistle in the dark
or you call the Filipino man
from the old folks home across your house
who peek at you already from behind
the marungay tree, the long beans
in front of his face;

he going cut across your backyard
from the papaya tree side
when you whistle the Filipino love call,
then take you when you leave your house
for buy jar mayonnaise for your madda
from the superette.

Then he going drag you to his house,
tie you to the vinyl chair,
the one he sit on outside all day,
and smile at you with his yellow teeth
and cut off your bi-lot with the cane knife.
He going fry um in Crisco for dinner.
That's what Kala told me.

No sleep with your feet to the door.
No sleep with your hair wet,
Kala said, or you going be like Darlene Ebanez
who run around her house na-ked
and nobody can stop her when she like that.
She take her two fingers
and put um up her bi-lot.
That's what you not supposed to do, Kala said,
the Bible said so that's why.

No clip your toenails at night.
And no wear tight jeans or
Felix going follow you home with his blue Valiant
when you go plantation camp side past
the big banyan tree, past the sugar mill,
past the pile of bagasse, down your dirt road.

Kala said he rape our classmate Abby already
and our classmate Nancy even if he get one
girlfriend senior in high school
and his father one cop.

Kala told me no use somebody's deodorant
or I going catch their b.o.
No make ugly faces or my nose going be pig
and my eyes Japanee.
And no tell nobody the words she tell me.
Nobody. Especially the word she told me today.
Okay.   Okay.   The word is *cremation*.

The graveyard man he sew all the holes
on your body shut with dental floss, Kala said;
your eyes, your nose, your mouth,
your belly button, your okole hole
and yeah, even your bi-lot so the gas
cannot escape when he shove you in the brick oven.

Watch out for the Filipino man, Kala said,
he eyeing my black dog, Melba,
he eyeing my baby goat
that my uncle caught for me up Mauna Kea,
the small green papayas on my tree.

A Conservative View

CATHY SONG

Money, my mother
never had much.
Perhaps that explains her life's
philosophy, the conservation of money,
the idea of money as a natural resource,
the sleepless nights worrying
whether there is enough of it.
According to her current calculations,
there isn't.

I used to think it was because she is Chinese,
proud of the fact that her practical
nature is due to her Chinese blood.
"We do not spoil our children"
she is fond of saying as an explanation
for never having given in to our demands.
"Take care of the needs but not the wants" is another.

Place a well-behaved child
in front of her and my mother will say,
"Chinese, eh?"
She believes Japanese and Korean
parents spoil their children.
"Doormats to their kids."
And the bok gwai?—well,
they ship their offspring to camp or boarding school, right?
For the Chinese, discipline begins at home.
And it begins with teaching the value of money.

There are two things in life
my mother vows never to pay for:
gift wrapping and parking.
It hurts her to cough up change for the meter.
Lucky is any day she can pull
into an empty space with time still running.
I was convinced my friends knew
that the birthday gifts I presented at parties
were wrapped in leftover sheets of our bathroom wallpaper.
—"Eh, how come dis paypa so tick?"

My mother's thrift frowns on the frivolous—
like singing in the shower
(it's a waste of water).
Her clear and practical sentences
are sprinkled with expressions
semantically rooted to the conservation of money.
They pepper her observations like expletives—
"Poho" if we bought something we couldn't use.
"Humbug" if we have to go out and buy
something we don't need.
"No need"—her favorite expression of all.

On shopping trips to the mall
she'll finger something soft and expensive,
letting her fingers linger on the exquisite
cut and fabric of a garment
when suddenly she'll exclaim,
like a kung fu battle cry,
"Pee-sa!"
(the one word she borrows liberally
from her Korean in-laws),
shuddering and releasing the price tag
as if she'd been bitten by a snake.

My sister and I agree
she takes the price of things too personally.
Every morning there is her wake-up call—
"Diapers on sale at Longs."
"Price of lettuce up at Star."—
as though she were reporting the Dow Jones Industrial Average.
If I answer in the negative
to her interrogative
"Did you use coupons to buy that?"
—*that* being chicken thighs or toilet paper,
I feel guilty,

My father doesn't help matters.
He has heard enough from Mother
about Koreans being big spenders, show-offs—
"champagne taste on a beer budget"—
to have his revenge.
He thinks Mao Tse-tung is the best
thing that ever happened to China.
"How else are you going to get those damn pa-kes to share?"

The Founding of Yuba City

CHITRA DIVAKARUNI

Let us suppose it a California day
bright as the blinding sea that brought them
across a month of nights
branded with strange stars
and endless coal shoveled
into a ship's red jaws.
The sudden edge of an eucalyptus grove,
the land fallow and gold to the eye, a wind
carrying the forgotten green smell
of the Punjab plains.

They dropped back, five or maybe six,
let the line straggle on. The crew's song
wavered, a mirage, and sank
in the opaque air. The railroad owed them
a month's pay, but the red soil
glinted light.
Callused from pounding metal into earth,
their farmer's hands
ached to plunge into its moisture.
Each man let it run pulsing
through his fingers,
remembered.

The sun fell away. Against its orange,
three ravens, as in the old tales. Was it good luck
or bad? They weren't sure.
Through the cedars, far light
from a window on a white man's farm.
They untied their waistbands,
counted coins, a few crumpled notes.
They did not fear
work. Tomorrow they would find jobs,
save, buy the land soon. Innocent
of Alien Laws, they planned their crops.
Under the sickled moon the fields
shone with their planting:
wheat, spinach, the dark oval wait

of potatoes beneath the ground, cauliflowers
pushing up white fists toward the light.

The men closed their eyes, turned their faces
to the earth's damp harvest-odor.
In their dreams their wives' red skirts flamed
in the Punjab noon. Slender necked women
who carried on their heads
rotis and *alu,*
jars of buttermilk for the farmers' lunch.
When they bent to whisper love
(or was it farewell)
their hibiscus-scented hair fell like tears
on the faces of the husbands
they would not see again.

A horned owl gliding on great wings
masked the moon. The men stroked the soil,
its soft warm hollows. Not knowing
how the wheels of history
grind over the human heart, they
smiled in their sleep.

Note: Yuba City, settled by Punjab farmers
around 1910, is now a thriving Indian
community in Northern California. Until the
1940s, the Alien Land Laws precluded nonwhite
immigrants from owning land, and immigration
restrictions prevented their families from joining
them. A number of the original settlers were
never reunited with their families.

Prints

CHRISTIAN LANGWORTHY

The day was brisk and windy, the thunderheads
rolled wet leaves over the city, leaves
pressed onto the blackened streets like Japanese prints.
The fresh scent of a new rain hangs in the air.
I am thinking of you. Must be thinking of you.
Thoughts of you come only like this.
Why does autumn undress the way you do?

Yesterday, I thought of black umbrellas.
I had read Max Jacob's
"Black Umbrellas" a few weeks back,
so perhaps that was why, the bodies like mushroom stems—
rigid, damp, and cold, coping with the heavy rain
as best they could, each tethered
to the cold wet streets.

Today, the wet streets are smudged with the colors
of passing cars and buses
and shining headlights. I am thinking of you.
The way you are in my head is like a painting
speaking to a stranger years later.
The city hums with life, a city of elevated
trains, wires, and fire escapes waiting
for someone's misfortune.
Brown, wet leaves lay flattened
against the black, slick streets. I think of the Japanese
prints we saw together at the Institute
and of a haiku by Basho.

Reading the Poem about the Yew Tree

REETIKA VAZIRANI

Reading the poem about the yew tree,
I realize I do not recall the trees of my youth,
the particular leafy shapes and blooming seasons and their
    moist odors in the heat.
I could look them up in a tree guide
and mend the holes in my memory—
but then it would not be my memory,
it would be the guide's.

All I remember today is the rapid chatter
of tea-colored women,
their plump arms, fingers reaching out
to pinch us when we were small;
lips passing hushed remarks
about others in the town, like branches shifting in the wind.
The grown-ups talked as if they hadn't heard
any local news but had to inquire after rumors.
You mean to say she is tolerating that scoundrel Gopal?
(though they'd all been to the wedding).
And their voices always verged on anticipation,
as if waiting for a great event to unfold—
a heavy rain to cool the grass
or the breeze with some news.
But they were indoors perpetually expecting another guest
    to arrive,
so that when the somebody appeared
they would congratulate the guest in unison:
See that, we were just speaking of you,
you will live long.
Now, planning a trip to my homeplace,
I'm told our friends are gone, have moved or passed away.
But I imagine the same kinds of trees are growing now as then,
and they will be expecting me when I arrive.

News of the World

MEENA ALEXANDER

We must always return
to poems for news of the world
or perish for the lack

Strip it
block it with blood
the page is not enough
unless the sun rises in it

Old doctor Willi writes
crouched on a stoop
in Paterson, New Jersey.

I am torn by light

She cries into her own head.
The playing fields of death
are far from me. In Cambodia I carried
my mother's head in a sack
and ran three days and nights
through a rice field

Now I pick up vegetables
from old sacking and straighten
them on crates: tomatoes
burning plums, cabbages hard
as bone. I work in Manhattan.

The subway corrupts me
with scents the robed Muslims sell
with white magazines
with spittle and gum

I get lost underground

By Yankee Stadium
I stumble out
hands loaded down
fists clenched into balls

A man approaches
muck on his shirt
his head, a battering ram
he knows who I am

I stall:
the tracks flash
with a thousand suns.

Meena Alexander

The Young of Tiananmen

MEENA ALEXANDER

If I had crimson I would write with it
for the battle of Tiananmen
raise garlands of orchids, roses
blood-sucking Venus Trap flowers

For the young with black silken hair
unstrapping fear from their thighs
raising it aloft like a banner, singing
"China, newborn China, be our shield."

If I had indigo I would write with it
for the battle of Tiananmen
raise garlands of hooks, eyes,
burst bone, torn cartilage
mucus that shines with death

For the young with black silken hair
unstrapping fear from their thighs
raising it aloft like a banner singing
"China, newborn China, be our shield."

But old men with glue in their
bones, wax in their hip sockets
flesh in their teeth cracked
sticks, whips, ropes with rusty nails

Tanks rolled, guns coughed
tear gas choked them in pitiful
sobs: the young of Tiananmen.
From a far country I sing

As blood swallowed them whole
they became our blood
as the sun swallowed them whole
they became children of the sun

What ink can inscribe them now
the young of Tiananmen?

They Don't Think Much about Us in America

ALFRREDO NAVARRO SALANGA

ALFRREDO NAVARRO SALANGA

Q. Do you feel you are free to express your ideas adequately?
A. Of course, yes. I live in America.
—From an interview with an exile

The only problem is
they don't think much
      about us
in America.
      That's where Manila's
just as small as Guam is:
      dots
on a map, points east,
      China
looming up ahead. Vietnam
more popular
      (because of that war).
They don't think much
      about
expats, either:

Until they stink up
      their apartments
with dried fish.
      Or worry those
next in line at the fish shops
—that's where they insist
      on getting
fish heads
Along with the fillet: "They're good
for soup, you know."
      But distance helps—
all the same.

That's what it is—it's all the same:
so we hit the New York Times
      and get
a curdled editorial.

Who cares?
The Washington Post can say as much
and the Potomac still
        won't be changing course.

It's here, back home,
        where the curdling
begins; where minds can melt
        like so much cheese.

Walls

LUIS H. FRANCIA

I know about laws
how well they set up walls

Do's in a small room
Don'ts in a labyrinth of huge halls

I know about
official trust
how they apportion it
Like chunks of bad
meat for the hungry

I know all about the smooth
wall in the law
difficult to see

but I keep bumping
against it

how it hides what's true
By telling me I'm a
swell fella
Filipino brother
(no you're no bother at all)
but   it's the other   way
around

I know its surfaces
very well
How when you try to
climb it   you
find you've
fallen farther

than before

Beetle on a String

VINCE GOTERA

When I was a kid, I walked bugs on a leash.
This was in the Philippines, where my parents
and I moved when I was a toddler, trading
foggy San Francisco for Manila's typhoons.

Actually, it was an idyllic place for a child—
warm evenings drenched in the sweet scent
of sampaguita flowers, but most of all,
a huge universe of enthralling insects

filling the night with buzzing and clicks, strobe
flashes of their glow-in-the-dark wingflicks.
It was my father who showed me how to catch
a scarab beetle in the cup of your hand, wait

for the wings to subside and close, then loop a thread
between thorax and carapace, tying it off—
not too tight— to allow the insect to fly
on a two-foot-long lasso. I remember

how I would smile and laugh, maybe five
or six years old, as a beetle would circle my head
like a whirring kite, iridescent green in the sun,
the thread stretched almost to the breaking point.

At night, I would tie my beetles to the round knobs
on my dresser drawers and be soothed to sleep
by a lullaby of buzzing. By morning, the beetles
were always dead, weights hung on string.

Those long nights must have been horrible.
Straining your body to shift an immovable weight,
unable to evade the swooping flight
of predators, banging again and again hard

against the dead wood, brought up short
by that unforgiving tether, cutting off
your pulsing blood every time, the long tube
of your heart quivering. It makes me shiver now

to wonder what thoughtless boy holds my string?

天文学

WALTER K. LEW

Early on we learned
That when we couldn't see the face
It was still there
Later, we covered that
Wound up with speech. But words also
Disappeared, could not
Repeat forever
And more and more
Things would not return to us
When we said them. Here, they said
Learn this.
        A song, a story
And though things are no longer near

You will see how they have changed.

      •

À la fin tu es las des rêves nouvelles

Though we can't know in the end if it is *all* a spell

Who would to be asked?

The beginning of questions we can hardly face

Perhaps it's a dream I had when five

And remembered as real when fifteen, permanent
Blur and diffraction   [Diffraction in my depths
In my depths.

It doesn't matter: there are
Equations, they tell us
Facts about the light its
Aberration and flawing

               We make our laws up out of

                  fear and tenacity

                                        and find in them

                                        faits about the light, its

                                        aberration and flawing

                                        Whenever a planet

                    Wheels all hell-like
Grinding in the wrong

                                        [Azimuth or angle of
                                        Right-ascension: coordinates

                    Deep in the lake of the heart

Zenith

BARBARA TRAN

On the other end of the line,
my mother drones on.

It does not matter what she says,
these are sounds I cannot repeat.

Though I could translate her words for you,
it is in the tone that her message lies.

And this is why, after trying all day,
I am only able to write this at night.

This is the tone I have been seeking:
this hour, the eleventh,

the anticipated end of a cycle,
like the eleventh month

and the anticipated closing
of an old year—

the way we knew our grandmother
would close her eyes.

We should have known then
that she had already left us,

knowing how often
we forgot her

by the number of times
her clock was allowed to unwind.

She relied on the sun
and the trees

and the degree of intimacy
between them,

the way my mother
and I

rely on distance,
only speaking on the phone

and then
in different languages.

The Bitterness of Bodies We Bear

BAO-LONG CHU

Tonight, my father combs my mother's hair down her back,
his hand gliding like a falcon over dark water. The years
since the war have bound them skin to skin, bone to bone.
She leans against him, or he against her, but beyond their bodies
embracing, merging, beyond this night, I see the certain, unbearable
grief of my mother's dying: a flaming coal in my father's mouth.

This vision, this impossible flower on fire I hold in my mouth
is nameless even as it names my life, names the hours and years
I see myself shadowed in a house, the shadow of my back
looming like a blackbird on the wall. Who can swallow this bone,
this shard of the future? This is the sorrow of bodies we must bear:
skin, tears, hair we shed. We eat the bitterness of bodies. Bodies

we love we embrace in brief repose, only to send off each body's
death with sighs, with prayers, with words, with our mouths
open, sweet with words. Even across sorghum fields and years,
even oceans and years, my father and mother will come back,
witnesses to this pain, relentless as the blood-flow between bones.
What I see is not my father standing behind my mother, her bare

back lovely, long against the length of his torso, but the unbearable
backside of Buddha turning away. What I see is my father's mouth,
a burning rose falling from it as he weeps over my sister's body
on Tu Do Street; what I see is the floating water, yellow backs
of monks heading up the hill where they will burn. I recall years
of waiting, waiting for a brother to come home. Finally his bones

came to us in a jar from across oceans. My mother took his bones,
white ashes between her hands, and breathed in the love of a body
she had endured. Believe me: this has everything to do with how I bear
my love for you—no, not my love of flesh to flesh, mouth to mouth
(though your mouth on my thigh and the curve of your back
are my nightly defeats). *These long mornings and years*

to come promise nothing, you say. But, love, the passing years
cannot undo; they deepen, shore the love, harden the lust we bear.
Come, let me take you in as my mother took in the love of a body

like a lover's grief for a body, her mouth taking in the powdered bones
of my brother, let me take you in as my father will soon, with his mouth,
take in my mother's death, his tongue holding onto, not pushing back,

the iron taste of death. Tonight, while you thrust your back
to me and against the coming years, I'll testify with my mouth
the truth of the body I bear: in you, I'll last beyond heart, blood, bone.

The Dead

LINH DINH

The nine-year-old hockey puck
Bounced from the fender of an olive truck
Now bounces a leather ball on his forehead.
The old lady who scrounged potted meat
From foreign men lying in a mortar pit
Now sells gold jewelry in Santa Barbara.
The dead are not dead but wave at pretty strangers
From their pick-up trucks on Bolsa Avenue.
They sit at Formica tables smoking discount cigarettes.
Some have dyed their hair, changed their name to Bill.
But the living, some of them, like to dig up the dead,
Dress them in native costumes, shoot them again,
Watch their bodies rise in slow motion.

Sister Play

LAN DUONG

Sometimes we slept together
because there were not enough beds.
Our legs were like father's pliers
when he tried to play the handyman;
They would lock
together at night, tight and unrelenting.
Our legs, hard and muscular, because we took
after our stout mother,
the shapely calves reminding us
where we came from, that we inherited more than just
pimply backs and an ironic fear of men,
but that we could endure and endure
for a long time after that too.
We used each other as levers to breathe,
and we held on because we had to. Like
the time we played on the slide
and the brown bark on the ground was "FIRE!"
We tried to keep from sliding down, hanging on
to one another, with fingers not yet
painted with the brush of puberty.
Sister 3 on top (because she was older and taller)
and "HOLD ON!" then laughter.
Our bits of legs struggling against
the smooth evil of aluminum.
And sweet-smelling, child-sweat making it slicker
and "FIRE!" was all around.
We played until the slide was no longer hot,
but cool and indifferent.
We left the playground with the brown of bark
on our elbows and we slept that night,
our fingers laced, our strong legs
hurting a little from our play, muscled the other
and we lay entwined,
stronger than an umbilical cord.

From The Redshifting Web

ARTHUR SZE

The dragons on the back of a circular bronze mirror
swirl without end. I sit and am an absorbing form:
I absorb the outline of a snowy owl on a branch,
the rigor mortis in a hand. I absorb the crunching sounds
when you walk across a glacial lake with aquamarine
ice heaved up here and there twenty feet high.
I absorb the moment a jeweler pours molten gold
into a cuttlefish mold and it begins to smoke.
I absorb the weight of a pause when it tilts
the conversation in a room. I absorb the moments
he sleeps holding her right breast in his left hand
and know it resembles glassy waves in a harbor
in descending spring light. Is the mind a mirror?
I see pig carcasses piled up from the floor
on a boat docked at Wanxian and the cook
who smokes inadvertently drops ashes into soup.
I absorb the stench of burning cuttlefish bone,
and as moments coalesce see to travel far is to return.

Projections
(*from Edison's proposal for the kinetoscope*)

CHRISTIAN LANGWORTHY

We see May & hear it perfectly as if
Whole illusions presented actual
Performances. A complete opera
Years before a place may have taken it.

I'm working on this new eye.
Just as my ears record your voice
From the phonographic motion—
How you move, my love, moves me.

I'm experiencing difficulties interpreting
And must find a name for this device.
Content's origins remain unclear—
Non-existent frame by frame as proposed.

I had a man sing the other day.
Photographed the singing as he was him.
Then I gave a long concert with stills
To arrest all his motions and gesticulations.

He sang himself through all his ranges,
But instead I heard your voice fading away.
Unfocused, the eye laments for the circle
To capture the movement, yet not to exceed it.

PART 3

FICTION

Introduction
In That Valley Beautiful Beyond

GARY PAK

The struggle of man against power is the struggle of memory against forgetting.
—**MILAN KUNDERA**, *THE BOOK OF LAUGHTER AND FORGETTING*

And now in America, writing many years later, I do not exactly know which
were the words of the old man of the mountains and which are mine. But they
are his tales as well as mine, so I hope we have written stories that really belong
to everyone in that valley beautiful beyond any telling of it.
—**CARLOS BULOSAN**, "HOW MY STORIES WERE WRITTEN"

I

This is one of the hardest essays for me to write.

I've been asked to write an essay that discusses the developmental history
of Asian American fiction within the context of Asian American literature, to
position myself within this history, and to offer a prognosis about the future of
the genre in terms of thematic observations and issues. If this assignment had
been given to me twenty years ago—perhaps even ten—ʻaʻole pilikia, no problem. There was not a whole lot of history, or, maybe better stated, there was
not a whole lot that *I* was aware of in terms of a broad-based Asian American
literature. Twenty years ago I could have rattled out names like John Okada,
Louis Chu, Hisaye Yamamoto, Carlos Bulosan, Toshio Mori, and the like,
those bold writers who dared to venture into an uncharted territory. Of
course, there were others, such as Sui Sin Far, Yong Sil Kang, and Kim Ronyoung, whose work I'd read years later. And there were, of course, other writers whom I was introduced to, such as Wing Tek Lum, Janice Mirikitani,
Maxine Hong Kingston, Shawn Wong, et cetera, et cetera, et cetera, and—
and—and—of course—I can't forget—Uncle Frank Chin. Those were the writers who filled their sails with the tumultuous winds of the '60s and '70s and
showed that they were genuine descendants of the aforementioned first generation of Asian American writers. If you had asked me ten—perhaps even
five—years ago who the contemporary Asian American writers were, I could
have rattled off perhaps 60 to 70 percent of the entire list in a handful of
blinks. What a distinction, huh?

If knowing some of these writers on a first name basis gave me a sense of security entering the '90s, forget about it for the twenty-first century. For now
comes this anthology, edited by Esther Iwanaga and Rajini Srikanth, entitled
Bold Words: A Century of Asian American Writing, an anthology that, in my
initial impression—to say the very least—has been successful at intimidating me.

A few months ago I accepted the offer of Esther Iwanaga to write the introduction to the fiction section of this anthology. I thought I had a good grip on "what was happening." I thought I knew somewhat of "the know" about "who is who." To be frank, as a practitioner of the craft, I thought I was a small part of the cutting edge of the discipline. But after scanning the list of fiction writers to be included in the collection and reading the selected work of mostly every one of these writers, I was aghast at what little I knew of the recent developments in Asian American writing. Who are these people? Where have they come from? How did so many books by these writers get published by the big-name presses? And—and—and—where—where do I stand?

Yes, I felt intimidated, perhaps even a bit xenophobic—to tell you the truth—a kind of defensive feeling that fired up my street instincts: *Something's being taken from me, and I'm not going to just sit back and observe this robbery like a goddamn wuss. Who are these damn writers, Patricia Chao, Gina Apostol, Eric Gamalinda, Nurul Kabir, Ginu Kamani, Patti Kim, et al, et al, et al?*

Phew! I noted to myself. Okay. Some of these names are familiar, some of these names I have personal touches with and/or have admired for a number of years. There's even my name there on the list. Okay. Okay. Take hold of yourself, local boy from Hawai'i with a short fuse. Come on, release this insecurity. Release this . . . jealousy.

But still, I was not without—could not dispel—this "being swept-away feeling," not unlike how a piece of cogitating driftwood on a muddy shore would feel, wishing desperately that one day someone will pick it up—rescuing it from the tedium of tide in, tide out—and position it on some significant place in a dry, warm, secure living room or kitchen or den; or despairing at the more realistic possibility that its fate will take it drifting toward the empty infinity of horizon or sinking to the bottomless forgetting ocean, disintegrating with the bottom muck of ages.

Yes, I must admit, the throes of being a has-been brushed me wildly while reading those stories of the many, many, unknown names of this new generation of Asian American fiction writers. (And I thought I was in this "new" generation!) And the real reason—I've had to be honest to myself—is that these writers are good. *Damn,* these writers are *good,* most of them transcending your typical "Asian American" topics. A lot of experimenting, the taking of narrative chances. Yeah—okay—so there are your typical Asian American mother/daughter sweet stories, your cross-generational stuff, your intercultural relationship jive. (Can we ever get away from at least nuances of these topics? Maybe after the revolution.)

But where the hell do I fit in? Am I still a part of this field or what?

(It is with some kind of—positive—purgative effect that I am writing this piece.)

Okay—okay. So let's get down to business. What are these so-called writers talking about, writing about? About their relationship with their mothers, their grandmothers? About having to deal with inferior-racial complex cuz of their Asian ancestry in a white-bread-and-mayonnaise land? About having to eat kim chee and kal bi when they would rather be grinding burgers and fries and shakes? About the big choice between marrying an Asian looker to placate the family or marrying a haole to go with that evanescent romantic ride à la *Titanic* and *Sleepless in Seattle* and the rest of sitcom Haolewood's b.s. fantasy trap, et cetera. (Eh Fred Ho—Where is the Asian love? Where are the Asian/ethnic American romantic leads?) Let me be bored. Let me plod through this latest last gasp of ethnic pain and torment and feel another chapter of insecurity and letdown and the haole taking the Third World woman from the clutches of the evil Yellow, puddle-colored men (boys?)—and—and the additional ferment of advanced wuss-hood. But let me check out these writers a bit more.

II

Back in 1974, when I was fresh out of college and spending my new sense of "freedom" roaming the streets in Europe, I came across on a remnant table outside of an obscure bookstore near a train station in Bradford, England, a hard-cover copy of Richard Kim's novel *Lost Names,* a work that I believe to be now out of print. My college buddy Roy and I were on our way south to Birmingham to visit a couple of his distant relatives, then to Stratford-upon-Avon to catch some Shakespeare, then to London to check on the hard rock scene. When I came upon the name Richard Kim in black letters against an off-white background, while browsing over the colorful spines of hundreds of books, I stopped, digested thoughtfully the moment, then greedily scooped up the book. Christ! As I read the jacket notes, I could not help but marvel—really, shaken with ethnic pride—that a Korean American writer was published by a *foreign* press and that the book was placed on a bookstore table in—of all places—England! I had known the name before, Richard Kim, being familiar with his first book, *The Martyred.* I studied the author's photo on the inside back flap. Yeah, he looked Korean, that handsome ruggedness that advertised, "Don't tread on me." I searched my pocket for change and bought the book for 20p, a bargain. This pride that I felt, of course, I had experienced infrequently ("infrequently" is being optimistic). One of the activities that I had enjoyed in my free time in Boston, where I did my undergraduate studies, was to roam between the remnant tables in the many bookstores, but I had never found anything that came close to fueling/feeding my deepening, troubling ethnic consciousness. (The closest I had ever come to touching that evolving level of understanding was the time I discovered, in a Kenmore Square bookstore, the first volume of Mao's *Selected Works*; to this day, he's still my favorite political philosopher.) Finding Richard Kim, Korean American writer, in 1974 was one of those freak arrangements in nature, a startling event similar to meeting a neighborhood friend in some faraway, blown-off-the-map place like the Orkney Islands (no, that didn't happen to me; and yes, I did visit the Orkney Islands). In Richard Kim, I felt a connection to a developing tradition—for lack of a better description—that I could say, without having to rationalize so deeply, was my own, just as my friend Roy could claim Shakespeare without batting an eye.

Yes, I did feel connected to the artist, to the book, in a strange ambiguous way that at the time I could not articulate well (though I could feel it in my gut: right on, we got an ethnic minority on the scene, stirring up something;

but hey, could you write about something else besides living in the "old country"?) Perhaps what attracted me to this book and its author was the haan inside of me, that eternal suffering and agony that supposedly all Koreans feel (more so among Korean females, for obvious reasons), no matter if they are twice or thrice or however many times removed from that supposed appendage of China. Perhaps it was the haan of being a Korean American in a white-bread-and-mayonnaise land. Perhaps it was the haan deepened by being Asian/ethnic American in a white-bread-and-mayonnaise land.

But I can remember, at the same time I was smiling with discovery in that grayish Bradford afternoon, the always present cynicism. Browsing through the book while on the train toward Birmingham, I wondered, "Is this another book about growing up in the old country, that so rigidly signified 'Motherland'?" Although I did feel connected to this experience, via stories told to me by my grandparents, still my heart yearned for something more contemporary, more meaningful and relevant to my own circumstances, my own—yeah, I guess you can call it "American"—existence. I read the first few chapters, but the story didn't "hit" me, didn't shake me with enthusiastic relevance. It was okay, a good story, but I had an expanding appetite for experiment and invention, and the conventional narrative style didn't jazz me. Where else can I turn for my Joyce, Kerouac, and Faulkner?

III

If I had done any research then, in 1974 or those whenabouts, I would have surprisingly uncovered a significant number of other Asian American voices, such as Yong Sil Kang, Sui Sin Far, John Okada, and Louis Chu; and, of course, from my local heritage, John Shirota, John Dominis Holt, and Milton Murayama. All of these writers did write about an Asian American experience. But I didn't do any of that homework; perhaps more to the point, I wasn't given any of that homework when I needed it. All that my professors knew— all of them continental haoles, mostly male—was the literature of their world, of their desires, of their perspectives; and their *their* of course meant universal, as in the canon. Too, I did not have the research tools available to me anyway, having matriculated to a private East Coast university in the early 1970s where "Asian American" probably meant to the continental haoles more Asian—as in "foreigner"—than American. (Who's the foreigner anyway?)

How in the hell could I find out about Louis Chu's New York Chinatown life when back then during my undergraduate years the stronger pull was Walden Pond—that geographic/romantic icon of the hegemonic consciousness called American Renaissance—which was just a few miles down Route 2? Didn't we all have (according to our memory, which sometimes is called liar) a copy of Thoreau's microcosmic universe radiating in the back pocket of our pants?[1]

IV

In Carlos Bulosan's "How My Stories Were Written,"[2] a young Bulosan becomes enthralled by the powerful storytelling of an old, outcast villager. When the old man questions why Bulosan believes in his tales and not stories by younger, more accepted storytellers, Bulosan answers, "There is wisdom in your words, Apo Lacay. . . . Besides, I will go away some day and I would like to remember what kind of people lived here a long time past." There is a gleam of promise in the old man's eyes, but that quickly fades. "But you will never return," the old man flatly says, "never come back to this valley." With "tiny tears in his eyes," the old man walks away from young Carlos and begins his trek back to the mountains.

Years later, when Bulosan has a "grand awakening" and decides to return to the valley, he looks for the old storyteller, and after "several forests" and "many ravines and hills," he discovers the man "sitting by a small stream." In a dialectical exchange between teacher-student and student-teacher, in voices that are both didactic and rhapsodic, Bulosan and the old man come to a transcendence:

> "I will leave our country soon and I would like to remember all your stories."
>
> "But why? In that land where you are going, will the people give you something to eat when you retell them? Will you not be afraid the children will stone you?"
>
> "I don't know, Apo Lacay. But this I know: if the retelling of your stories will give me a little wisdom of the heart, then I shall have come home again."
>
> "You mean it will be your book as well as mine? Your words as well as my words, there in that faraway land, my tales going around to the people? My tales will not be forgotten at last?"
>
> "Yes, Apo Lacay. It will be exactly like that, your books as well as mine."

A short while after, the old man dies, "[h]is passing . . . so quiet and natural that [Bulosan does] not feel any sadness." Years later, as Bulosan looks over the body of work that he has accomplished since leaving his village and coming to America, he remarks with the hope that "we have written stories that really belong to everyone in that valley beautiful beyond any telling of it."

V

Stories that really belong to everyone in that valley beautiful beyond any telling of it. In that valley beautiful beyond. In that valley beautiful . . . beyond.

VI

Like Bulosan, we've come far from this valley and have—as writers of fiction, as writers of Asian descent—written our stories to mark our memories of these valleys, and not without the urgency that Bulosan suggests when he says to the old storyteller, "If the retelling of your stories will give me a little wisdom of the heart, then I shall have come home again." And as my first epigraph suggests, we are struggling also against the power that wants us to forget, wants us to dis-member ourselves from our past, from our present and from—of course—our future.

But let's take Bulosan's words further: We have also gone beyond this valley, have discovered other valleys here in America, and are telling/writing our stories about living in these new valleys. We have created—are creating—our stories of our ancestors' valleys beautiful and of these valleys beautiful now, now beyond. It is unquestionable that we should never forget these visions that empower our consciousness, our being, our community.[3] And it is overwhelming—for me—to see our tradition develop and extend to prosaic dimensions infinite. (Thank you, Richard Kim, for being part of this start-up.) Our stories have taken off beyond "the-anxieties-of-influence" literary. Rather, our literature is a synthesis of visions of our ancestors, and our present and future living in the belly of the beast. We've come a long way, baby, and we've done this in such an explosively short time. Just look at the diversity of recent linguistic landmarks, such as Theresa Hak Kyung Cha's cerebral trip in that uncanny verbal/mnemonic/historic wormhole,[4] *DICTEE;* or, even more recent, expatriate local writer Carolyn Lei-lanilau's verbal masturbatory *Ono Ono Girl's Hula,* an extraordinarily orgasmic journey into the be-coming consciousness of a Chinese/Hawaiian/Local/Woman.[5]

What follows are stories by writers who defined Asian American literature in the '60s and '70s and '80s. But *Bold Words* also includes *impressive* new writers who are expanding the definition of the literature of Asian America. And how are they writing their stories? Well, in my humble opinion, they are setting up a new standard. Check out, for example, the polychromatic points of view in Monique T. D. Truong's "Seeds" and in the nightmarish selection from Patricia Chao's novel, *Monkey King.* And consider the subdued yet striking characterizations in the excerpt from Susan Choi's *The Foreign Student* and in "Mrs. Sen's," a short story by Jhumpa Lahiri, who won the 2000 Pulitzer Prize for fiction. Or the brave linguistic experiment in ambiguity by Zack Linmark. And take note of the investigations in cultural re/dis/placement in Andrew Lam's "Show and Tell" and in the excerpt from Patti Kim's novel, *A Cab Called Reliable* (note especially the protagonist's cadenced description of her mother that resounds with a Jamaica Kincaidesque quality).

So . . . what are we writers doing? Let me say this simply: We writers are not only redefining Asian American fiction. Rather, we are redefining *American* literature; we are telling the stories of America that already *is*. What is here. What is beyond.

VII

Gentle reader, angry reader, sophisticated reader: Take this collection gently and separate the pages with soft touches and gentle proddings. Smell these pages. Smell the ink. Smell that fresh book smell that promises a reading pleasure. Then read these selections—in a small nook of a public library, on your favorite chair, during your lunch break, before going to sleep, before you have sex. Enjoy the moments, the linguistic ride to the crest, roller coasting up and down the face of the growing blue wave that trembles and feathers and spurts you with bubbly water. Ride the face and lick the airy drops that form on the wave's hairy lips. Work your way through the unfolding sections that are tumbling over you with power and brashness, splashing and slathering its juices over your face. And crouch hard to the end where you will fall, on your face into a shallow bed of water with sand swirling all over you as the wave crashes and dissipates into relaxing foam. Sit in the foam, watch with half-folded eyelids the coming sets peeling over and rushing toward you with flourishing whispers. Then, when—and only when—you are brave enough to realize that time is pacing on, when your groin speaks the wordless desire for more, rise from this foamy bliss, plod through the push/pull of current and begin your quest out—again—for another ride in.

Gary Pak

139

Notes

1. Later, back in Hawai'i, while romanticizing about my attachment to the '60s and '70s, I'd swear that, while hitchhiking down the Mass Turnpike to visit my cousin and her husband—my only family for three thousand miles—at UMass at Amherst, a dog-eared paperback copy of *Walden* was warming my butt with its regional relevance; that I actually hitchhiked with this copy I can't truly say right now.

2. See this essay in the memoir section of this anthology.

3. When asked the question by critic Brenda Kwon, "How did you decide to become a writer?" as a part of an interview that was included in *Words Matter: Conversations with Asian American Writers,* ed. King-Kok Cheung (Honolulu: University of Hawai'i Press, 2000), I answered, "There were many stories to be told in Hawai'i, in my family, in the community, and they were important stories. Looking at my son who was just born, I felt that maybe we should write these stories down, commit them to paper, so that my son and others would be able to read them and have that as part of their cultural experience" (304).

4. Here I freely use this term of physics. In its scientific usage, a wormhole is an "umbilical cord" that theoretically may connect two different universes or time-space continuums. It is a term used when discussing the possibilities of time travel.

5. An excerpt from *Ono Ono Girl's Hula* appears in the memoir section.

In the Land of the Free

SUI SIN FAR

I

"See, Little One—the hills in the morning sun. There is thy home for years to come. It is very beautiful and thou wilt be very happy there."

The Little One looked up into his mother's face in perfect faith. He was engaged in the pleasant occupation of sucking a sweetmeat; but that did not prevent him from gurgling responsively.

"Yes, my olive bud; there is where thy father is making a fortune for thee. Thy father! Oh, wilt thou not be glad to behold his dear face. 'Twas for thee I left him."

The Little One ducked his chin sympathetically against his mother's knee. She lifted him on to her lap. He was two years old, a round, dimple-cheeked boy with bright brown eyes and a sturdy little frame.

"Ah! Ah! Ah! Ooh! Ooh! Ooh!" puffed he, mocking a tugboat steaming by.

San Francisco's waterfront was lined with ships and steamers, while other craft, large and small, including a couple of white transports from the Philippines, lay at anchor here and there off shore. It was some time before the *Eastern Queen* could get docked, and even after that was accomplished, a lone Chinaman who had been waiting on the wharf for an hour was detained that much longer by men with the initials U.S.C. on their caps, before he could board the steamer and welcome his wife and child.

"This is thy son," announced the happy Lae Choo.

Hom Hing lifted the child, felt of his little body and limbs, gazed into his face with proud and joyous eyes; then turned inquiringly to a customs officer at his elbow.

"That's a fine boy you have there," said the man. "Where was he born?"

"In China," answered Hom Hing, swinging the Little One on his right shoulder, preparatory to leading his wife off the steamer.

"Ever been to America before?"

"No, not he," answered the father with a happy laugh.

The customs officer beckoned to another.

"This little fellow," said he, "is visiting America for the first time."

The other customs officer stroked his chin reflectively.

"Good day," said Hom Hing.

"Wait!" commanded one of the officers. "You cannot go just yet."

"What more now?" asked Hom Hing.

"I'm afraid," said the first customs officer, "that we cannot allow the boy to go ashore. There is nothing in the papers that you have shown us—your wife's papers and your own—having any bearing upon the child."

"There was no child when the papers were made out," returned Hom Hing. He spoke calmly; but there was apprehension in his eyes and in his tightening grip on his son.

"What is it? What is it?" quavered Lae Choo, who understood a little English.

The second customs officer regarded her pityingly.

"I don't like this part of the business," he muttered.

The first officer turned to Hom Hing and in an official tone of voice, said:

"Seeing that the boy has no certificate entitling him to admission to this country you will have to leave him with us."

"Leave my boy!" exclaimed Hom Hing.

"Yes; he will be well taken care of, and just as soon as we can hear from Washington he will be handed over to you."

"But," protested Hom Hing, "he is my son."

"We have no proof," answered the man with a shrug of his shoulders; "and even if so we cannot let him pass without orders from the Government."

"He is my son," reiterated Hom Hing, slowly and solemnly. "I am a Chinese merchant and have been in business in San Francisco for many years. When my wife told to me one morning that she dreamed of a green tree with spreading branches and one beautiful red flower growing thereon, I answered her that I wished my son to be born in our country, and for her to prepare to go to China. My wife complied with my wish. After my son was born my mother fell sick and my wife nursed and cared for her; then my father, too, fell sick, and my wife also nursed and cared for him. For twenty moons my wife care for and nurse the old people, and when they die they bless her and my son, and I send for her to return to me. I had no fear of trouble. I was a Chinese merchant and my son was my son."

"Very good, Hom Hing," replied the first officer. "Nevertheless, we take your son."

"No, you not take him; he my son too."

It was Lae Choo. Snatching the child from his father's arms she held and covered him with her own.

The officers conferred together for a few moments; then one drew Hom Hing aside and spoke in his ear.

Resignedly Hom Hing bowed his head, then approached his wife. "'Tis the law," said he, speaking in Chinese, "and 'twill be but for a little while—until tomorrow's sun arises."

"You, too," reproached Lae Choo in a voice eloquent with pain. But accustomed to obedience she yielded the boy to her husband, who in turn delivered him to the first officer. The Little One protested lustily against the transfer; but his mother covered her face with her sleeve and his father silently led her away. Thus was the law of the land complied with.

II

Day was breaking. Lae Choo, who had been awake all night, dressed herself, then awoke her husband.

"'Tis the morn," she cried. "Go, bring our son."

The man rubbed his eyes and arose upon his elbow so that he could see out of the window. A pale star was visible in the sky. The petals of a lily in a bowl on the windowsill were unfurled.

"'Tis not yet time," said he, laying his head down again.

"Not yet time. Ah, all the time that I lived before yesterday is not so much as the time that has been since my little one was taken from me."

The mother threw herself down beside the bed and covered her face.

Hom Hing turned on the light, and touching his wife's bowed head with a sympathetic hand inquired if she had slept.

"Slept!" she echoed, weepingly. "Ah, how could I close my eyes with my arms empty of the little body that has filled them every night for more than twenty moons! You do not know—man—what it is to miss the feel of the little fingers and the little toes and the soft round limbs of your little one. Even in the darkness his darling eyes used to shine up to mine, and often have I fallen into slumber with his pretty babble at my ear. And now, I see him not; I touch him not; I hear him not. My baby, my little fat one!"

"Now! Now! Now!" consoled Hom Hing, patting his wife's shoulder reassuringly; "there is no need to grieve so; he will soon gladden you again. There cannot be any law that would keep a child from its mother!"

Lae Choo dried her tears.

"You are right, my husband," she meekly murmured. She arose and stepped about the apartment, setting things to rights. The box of presents she had brought for her California friends had been opened the evening before; and silks, embroideries, carved ivories, ornamental lacquer-ware, brasses, camphorwood boxes, fans, and chinaware were scattered around in confused heaps. In the midst of unpacking the thought of her child in the hands of strangers had overpowered her, and she had left everything to crawl into bed and weep.

Having arranged her gifts in order she stepped out on to the deep balcony.

The star had faded from view and there were bright streaks in the western sky. Lae Choo looked down the street and around. Beneath the flat occupied by her and her husband were quarters for a number of bachelor Chinamen, and she could hear them from where she stood, taking their early morning breakfast. Below their dining-room was her husband's grocery store. Across the way was a large restaurant. Last night it had been resplendent with gay colored lanterns and the sound of music. The rejoicings over "the completion of the moon," by Quong Sum's firstborn, had been long and loud, and had caused her to tie a handkerchief over her ears. She, a bereaved mother, had it not in her heart to rejoice with other parents. This morning the place was more in accord with her mood. It was still and quiet. The revellers had dispersed or were asleep.

A roly-poly woman in black sateen, with long pendant earrings in her ears, looked up from the street below and waved her a smiling greeting. It was her old neighbor, Kuie Hoe, the wife of the gold embosser, Mark Sing. With her was a little boy in yellow jacket and lavender pantaloons. Lae Choo remembered him as a baby. She used to like to play with him in those days when she had no child of her own. What a long time ago that seemed! She caught her breath in a sigh, and laughed instead.

"Why are you so merry?" called her husband from within.

"Because my Little One is coming home," answered Lae Choo. "I am a happy mother—a happy mother."

She pattered into the room with a smile on her face.

• • •

The noon hour had arrived. The rice was steaming in the bowls and a fragrant dish of chicken and bamboo shoots was awaiting Hom Hing. Not for one moment had Lae Choo paused to rest during the morning hours; her activity had been ceaseless. Every now and again, however, she had raised her eyes to the gilded clock on the curiously carved mantelpiece. Once, she had exclaimed:

"Why so long, oh! why so long?" Then apostrophizing herself: "Lae Choo, be happy. The Little One is coming! The Little One is coming!" Several times she burst into tears and several times she laughed aloud.

Hom Hing entered the room; his arms hung down by his side.

"The Little One!" shrieked Lae Choo.

"They bid me call tomorrow."

With a moan the mother sank to the floor.

The noon hour passed. The dinner remained on the table.

III

The winter rains were over: the spring had come to California, flushing the hills with green and causing an ever-changing pageant of flowers to pass over them. But there was no spring in Lae Choo's heart, for the Little One remained away from her arms. He was being kept in a mission. White women were caring for him, and though for one full moon he had pined for his mother and refused to be comforted he was now apparently happy and contented. Five moons or five months had gone by since the day he had passed with Lae Choo through the Golden Gate; but the great Government at Washington still delayed sending the answer which would return him to his parents.

• • •

Hom Hing was disconsolately rolling up and down the balls in his abacus box when a keen-faced young man stepped into his store.

"What news?" asked the Chinese merchant.

"This!" The young man brought forth a typewritten letter. Hom Hing read the words:

> Re Chinese child, alleged to be the son of Hom Hing, Chinese merchant, doing business at 425 Clay Street, San Francisco.
>
> Same will have attention as soon as possible.

Hom Hing returned the letter, and without a word continued his manipulation of the counting machine.

"Have you anything to say?" asked the young man.

"Nothing. They have sent the same letter fifteen times before. Have you not yourself showed it to me?"

"True!" The young man eyed the Chinese merchant furtively. He had a proposition to make and he was pondering whether or not the time was opportune.

"How is your wife?" he inquired solicitously—and diplomatically.

Hom Hing shook his head mournfully.

"She seems less every day," he replied. "Her food she takes only when I bid her and her tears fall continually. She finds no pleasure in dress or flowers and cares not to see her friends. Her eyes stare all night. I think before another moon she will pass into the land of spirits."

"No!" exclaimed the young man, genuinely startled.

"If the boy not come home I lose my wife sure," continued Hom Hing with bitter sadness.

"It's not right," cried the young man indignantly. Then he made his proposition.

The Chinese father's eyes brightened exceedingly.

"Will I like you to go to Washington and make them give you the paper to restore my son?" cried he. "How can you ask when you know my heart's desire?"

"Then," said the young fellow, "I will start next week. I am anxious to see this thing through if only for the sake of your wife's peace of mind."

"I will call her. To hear what you think to do will make her glad," said Hom Hing.

He called a message to Lae Choo upstairs through a tube in the wall.

In a few moments she appeared, listless, wan, and hollow-eyed; but when her husband told her the young lawyer's suggestion she became as one electrified; her form straightened, her eyes glistened; the color flushed to her cheeks.

"Oh," she cried, turning to James Clancy, "You are a hundred man good!"

The young man felt somewhat embarrassed; his eyes shifted a little under the intense gaze of the Chinese mother.

"Well, we must get your boy for you," he responded. "Of course"—turning to Hom Hing—"it will cost a little money. You can't get fellows to hurry the Government for you without gold in your pocket."

Hom Hing stared blankly for a moment. Then: "How much do you want, Mr. Clancy?" he asked quietly.

"Well, I will need at least five hundred to start with."

Hom Hing cleared his throat.

"I think I told to you the time I last paid you for writing letters for me and seeing the Custom boss here that nearly all I had was gone!"

"Oh, well then we won't talk about it, old fellow. It won't harm the boy to stay where he is, and your wife may get over it all right."

"What that you say?" quavered Lae Choo.

James Clancy looked out of the window.

"He says," explained Hom Hing in English, "that to get our boy we have to have much money."

"Money! Oh, yes."

Lae Choo nodded her head.

"I have not got the money to give him."

For a moment Lae Choo gazed wonderingly from one face to the other; then, comprehension dawning upon her, with swift anger, pointing to the lawyer, she cried: "You not one hundred man good; you just common white man."

"Yes, ma'am," returned James Clancy, bowing and smiling ironically.

Hom Hing pushed his wife behind him and addressed the lawyer again: "I might try," said he, "to raise something; but five hundred—it is not possible."

"What about four?"

"I tell you I have next to nothing left and my friends are not rich."

"Very well!"

The lawyer moved leisurely toward the door, pausing on its threshold to light a cigarette.

"Stop, white man; white man, stop!"

Lae Choo, panting and terrified, had started forward and now stood beside him, clutching his sleeve excitedly.

"You say you can go to get paper to bring my Little One to me if Hom Hing give you five hundred dollars?"

The lawyer nodded carelessly; his eyes were intent upon the cigarette which would not take the fire from the match.

"Then you go get paper. If Hom Hing not can give you five hundred dollars—I give you perhaps what more that much."

She slipped a heavy gold bracelet from her wrist and held it out to the man. Mechanically he took it.

"I go get more!"

She scurried away, disappearing behind the door through which she had come.

"Oh, look here, I can't accept this," said James Clancy, walking back to Hom Hing and laying down the bracelet before him.

"It's all right," said Hom Hing, seriously, "pure China gold. My wife's parent give it to her when we married."

"But I can't take it anyway," protested the young man.

"It is all same as money. And you want money to go to Washington," replied Hom Hing in a matter of fact manner.

"See, my jade earrings—my gold buttons—my hairpins—my comb of pearl and my rings—one, two, three, four, five rings; very good—very good—all same much money. I give them all to you. You take and bring me paper for my Little One."

Lae Choo piled up her jewels before the lawyer.

Hom Hing laid a restraining hand upon her shoulder. "Not all, my wife," he said in Chinese. He selected a ring—his gift to Lae Choo when she dreamed of the tree with the red flower. The rest of the jewels he pushed toward the white man.

"Take them and sell them," said he. "They will pay your fare to Washington and bring you back with the paper."

For one moment James Clancy hesitated. He was not a sentimental man; but something within him arose against accepting such payment for his services.

"They are good, good," pleadingly asserted Lae Choo, seeing his hesitation.

Whereupon he seized the jewels, thrust them into his coat pocket, and walked rapidly away from the store.

IV

Lae Choo followed after the missionary woman through the mission nursery school. Her heart was beating so high with happiness that she could scarcely breathe. The paper had come at last—the precious paper which gave Hom Hing and his wife the right to the possession of their own child. It was ten months now since he had been taken from them—ten months since the sun had ceased to shine for Lae Choo.

The room was filled with children—most of them wee tots, but none so wee as her own. The mission woman talked as she walked. She told Lae Choo that little Kim, as he had been named by the school, was the pet of the place, and that his little tricks and ways amused and delighted every one. He had been rather difficult to manage at first and had cried much for his mother; "but children so soon forget, and after a month he seemed quite at home and played around as bright and happy as a bird."

"Yes," responded Lae Choo. "Oh, yes, yes!"

But she did not hear what was said to her. She was walking in a maze of anticipatory joy.

"Wait here, please," said the mission woman, placing Lae Choo in a chair. "The very youngest ones are having their breakfast."

She withdrew for a moment—it seemed like an hour to the mother—then she reappeared leading by the hand a little boy dressed in blue cotton overalls and white-soled shoes. The little boy's face was round and dimpled and his eyes were very bright.

"Little One, ah, my Little One!" cried Lae Choo.

She fell on her knees and stretched her hungry arms toward her son.

But the Little One shrunk from her and tried to hide himself in the folds of the white woman's skirt.

"Go'way, go'way!" he bade his mother.

The Story of a Letter

CARLOS BULOSAN

When my brother Berto was thirteen he ran away from home and went to Manila. We did not hear from him until eight years later, and he was by that time working in a little town in California. He wrote a letter in English, but we could not read it. Father carried it in his pocket all summer, hoping the priest in our village would read it for him.

The summer ended gloriously and our work on the farm was done. We gathered firewood and cut grass on the hillsides for our animals. The heavy rains came when we were patching up the walls of our house. Father and I wore palm overcoats and worked in the mud, rubbing vinegar on our foreheads and throwing it around us to keep the lightning away. The rains ceased suddenly, but the muddy water came down from the mountains and flooded the river.

We made a bamboo raft and floated slowly along the water. Father sat in the center of the raft and took the letter from his pocket. He looked at it for a long time, as though he were committing it to memory. When we reached the village church it was midnight, but there were many people in the yard. We tied our raft to the riverbank and dried our clothes on the grass.

A woman came and told us that the priest had died of overeating at a wedding. Father took our clothes off the grass and we put them on. We untied our raft and rowed against the slow currents back to our house. Father was compelled to carry the letter for another year, waiting for the time when my brother Nicasio would come home from school. He was the only one in our family who could read and write.

When the students returned from the cities, Father and I went to town with a sack of peanuts. We stood under the arbor tree in the station and watched every bus that stopped. He heated a pile of dry sand with burning stones and roasted peanuts. At night we sat in the coffee shop and talked with the loafers and gamblers. Then the last students arrived, but my brother Nicasio was not with them. We gave up waiting and went back to the village.

When summer came again we plowed the land and planted corn. Then we were informed that my brother Nicasio had gone to America. Father was greatly disappointed. He took the letter of my brother Berto from his pocket and locked it in a small box. We put our minds on our work and after two years the letter was forgotten.

Toward the end of my ninth year, a tubercular young man appeared in our village. He wanted to start a school for the children and the men were enthusiastic. The drummer went around the village and announced the good news. The farmers gathered in a vacant lot not far from the cemetery and started building a schoolhouse. They shouted at one another with joy and laughed aloud. The wind carried their laughter through the village.

I saw them at night lifting the grass roof on their shoulders. I ran across the fields and stood by the well, watching them place the rafters on the long bamboo posts. The men were stripped to the waist and their cotton trousers were rolled up to their thighs. The women came with their earthen jars and hauled drinking water, pausing in the clear moonlight to watch the men with secret joy.

Then the schoolhouse was finished. I heard the bell ring joyfully in the village. I ran to the window and saw boys and girls going to school. I saw Father on our carabao, riding off toward our house. I took my straw hat off the wall and rushed to the gate.

Father bent down and reached for my hands. I sat behind him on the bare back of the animal. The children shouted and slapped their bellies. When we reached the school yard the carabao stopped without warning. Father fell to the ground and rolled into the well, screaming aloud when he touched the water. I grabbed the animal's tail and hung on to it till it rolled on its back in the dust.

I rushed to the well and lowered the wooden bucket. I tied the rope to the post and shouted for help. Father climbed slowly up the rope to the mouth of the well. The bigger boys came down and helped me pull Father out. He stood in the sun and shook the water off his body. He told me to go into the schoolhouse with the other children.

We waited for the teacher to come. Father followed me inside and sat on a bench behind me. When the teacher arrived we stood as one person and waited for him to be seated. Father came to my bench and sat quietly for a long time. The teacher started talking in our dialect, but he talked so fast we could hardly understand him.

When he distributed some little Spanish books, Father got up and asked what language we would learn. The teacher told us that it was Spanish. Father asked him if he knew English. He said he knew only Spanish and our dialect. Father took my hand and we went out of the schoolhouse. We rode the carabao back to our house.

Father was disappointed. He had been carrying my brother's letter for almost three years now. It was still unread. The suspense was hurting him and me, too. It was the only letter he had received in all the years that I had known him, except some letters that came from the government once a year asking him to pay his taxes.

When the rains ceased, a strong typhoon came from the north and swept away the schoolhouse. The teacher gave up teaching and married a village girl. Then he took up farming and after two years his wife gave birth to twins. The men in the village never built a schoolhouse again.

I grew up suddenly and the desire to see other places grew. It moved me like a flood. It was impossible to walk a kilometer away from our house without wanting to run away to the city. I tried to run away a few times, but whenever I reached the town, the farm always called me back. I could not leave Father because he was getting old.

Then our farm was taken away from us. I decided to go to town for a while and live with Mother and my two little sisters. Father remained in the village. He came to town once with a sack of wild tomatoes and bananas. But the village called him back again.

I left our town and traveled to other places. I went to Baguio in the northern part of the Philippines and worked in the marketplace posing naked for American tourists who seemed to enjoy the shameless nudity of the natives. An American woman, who claimed that she had come from Texas, took me to Manila.

She was a romantic painter. When we arrived in the capital she rented a nice large house where the sun was always shining. There were no children of my age. There were men and women who never smiled. They spoke through their noses. The painter from Texas asked me to undress every morning; she worked industriously. I had never dreamed of making a living by exposing my body to a stranger. That experience made me roar with laughter for many years.

One time, while I was still in the woman's house, I remembered the wide ditch near our house in the village where the young girls used to take a bath in the nude. A cousin of mine stole the girls' clothes and then screamed behind some bushes. The girls ran about with their hands between their legs. I thought of this incident when I felt shy, hiding my body with my hands from the woman painter. When I had saved a little money I took a boat for America.

I forgot my village for a while. When I went to a hospital and lay in bed for two years, I started to read books with hunger. My reading was started by a nurse who thought I had come from China. I lied to her without thinking of it, but I told a good lie. I had no opportunity to learn when I was outside in the world but the security and warmth of the hospital gave it to me. I languished in bed for two years with great pleasure. I was no longer afraid to live in a strange world and among strange peoples.

Then at the end of the first year, I remembered the letter of my brother Berto. I crept out of bed and went to the bathroom. I wrote a letter to Father asking him to send the letter to me for translation. I wanted to translate it, so that it would be easy for him to find a man in our village to read it to him.

The letter arrived six months later. I translated it into our dialect and sent it back with the original. I was now better. The doctors told me that I could go out of the hospital. I used to stand by the window for hours asking myself why I had forgotten to laugh in America. I was afraid to go out into the world. I had been confined too long, I had forgotten what it was like on the outside.

I had been brought to the convalescent ward when the Civil War in Spain started some three years before. Now, after the peasants' and workers' government was crushed, I was physically ready to go out into the world and start a new life. There was some indignation against fascism in all civilized lands. To most of us, however, it was the end of a great cause.

I stood at the gate of the hospital, hesitating. Finally, I closed my eyes and walked into the city. I wandered all over Los Angeles for some time, looking for my brothers. They had been separated from me since childhood. We had had, separately and together, a bitter fight for existence. I had heard that my brother Nicasio was in Santa Barbara, where he was attending college. Berto, who never stayed in one place for more than three months at a time, was rumored to be in Bakersfield waiting for the grape season.

I packed my suitcase and took a bus to Santa Barbara. I did not find my brother there. I went to Bakersfield and wandered in the streets asking for my brother. I went to Chinatown and stood in line for the free chop-suey that was served in the gambling houses to the loafers and gamblers. I could not find my brother in either town. I went to the vineyards looking for him. I was convinced that he was not in that valley. I took a bus for Seattle.

The hiring halls were full of men waiting to be shipped to the canneries in Alaska. I went to the dance halls and poolrooms. But I could not find my brothers. I took the last boat to Alaska and worked there for three months. I wanted to save money so that I could have something to spend when I returned to the mainland.

When I came back to the West Coast, I took a bus to Portland. Beyond Tacoma, near the district where Indians used to force the hop pickers into marriage, I looked out the window and saw my brother Berto in a beer tavern. I knew it was my brother although I had not seen him for many years. There was something in the way he had turned his head toward the bus that made me think I was right. I stopped at the next town and took another bus back to Tacoma. But he was already gone.

I took another bus and went to California. I stopped in Delano. The grape season was in full swing. There were many workers in town. I stood in the poolrooms and watched the players. I went to a beer place and sat in a booth. I ordered several bottles and thought long and hard of my life in America.

Toward midnight a man in a big overcoat came in and sat beside me. I asked him to drink beer with me without looking at his face. We started drinking together and then, suddenly, I saw a familiar face in the dirty mirror on the wall. I almost screamed. He was my brother Nicasio—but he had grown old and emaciated. We went outside and walked to my hotel.

The landlord met me with a letter from the Philippines. In my room I found that my letter to Father, when I was in the hospital, and the translation of my brother Berto's letter to him, had been returned to me. It was the strangest thing that had ever happened. I had never lived in Delano before. I had never given my forwarding address to anybody. The letter was addressed to me at a hotel I have never seen before.

It was now ten years since my brother Berto had written the letter to Father. It was eighteen years since he had run away from home. I stood in the center of my room and opened it. The note attached to it said that Father had died some years before. It was signed by the postmaster of my town.

I bent down and read the letter—the letter that had driven me away from my village and had sent me half-way around the world—read it the very day a letter came from the government telling that my brother Berto was already serving in the Navy—and the same day that my brother Nicasio was waiting to be inducted into the Army. I held the letter in my hand, and suddenly, I started to laugh—choking with tears at the mystery and wonder of it all.

"Dear Father [my brother wrote]:
    America is a great country. Tall buildings. Wide good land. The people walking. But I feel sad. I am writing you this hour of my sentimental.
                                                                Your son—Berto."

He Who Has the Laughing Face

TOSHIO MORI

The simplest thing to say of him is that he is sad and alone but is laughing all the time. It would definitely put him in a hole and everybody would understand and say what a sad story, what an unhappy man he is, what bravery there is in the world. But that is not the story. He is a very common man. His kind is almost everywhere, his lot is the ordinary, the most common, and that is why he is so lost and hidden away from the spotlight.

He, the Japanese, was sitting on the park bench on Seventh and Harrison, looking and gazing at the people without much thought but looking just the same and this being Sunday he was taking his time about it, taking all the time in the world, to belong to this great world or to discover why he is so unhappy, sad and alone. But he did not think for long, he did not sit down and probe like great philosophers do. Instead he simply sat and pretty soon from his sadness, and aloneness, he began to smile, not from happiness, not from sadness, and this is where I saw his face, not a handsome one but common and of everyday life.

His name does not matter, it makes no difference, although it is Tsumura. I found him sitting on the park bench on Seventh and Harrison when I looked up from a book I was reading under a tree. And before one begins to guess and attempt to judge a person right who is a stranger, there is an adventure. I sat, pretending to read the book, and all the time watching this individual who was like all or any of the park bench sitters on Sundays. By the time I began to guess who he was and what he did, he was someone of immense proportions, someone living close to me or someone I know and talk to. And then suddenly, unexpectedly, he would laugh. Not a crazy laugh. He would laugh the kind no one pays attention to. Or if someone pays attention and hears him that someone will believe the man had seen something funny in the park or in the street or had listened to something amusing, and let it go. But that is not all. He did not look queer, he looked the part of others—out for rest.

When I began to guess who he was and what he did there was no stopping of human curiosity and there was no end of mental adventure that is inward and centralized on intuition. What was he laughing at? I wanted to know. Who was he, what does he do for a living? I sat and guessed many times.

He looked like a writer or an artist or a composer with his sad face detached from laughter. But he was laughing almost all the time and smiling as if the world was a part of him. He looked like an idiot, laughing when there was no outward evidence of laughing matter and sense. But idiot he could not be— he was too polished, too well groomed to lead a causeless life. Could he be a priest, a clergy? Could he be the one to lead others and could he by chance come among the people to mix without identity, without the strings attached to him? But on Sunday! Sunday is the clergyman's busy day and also, Sunday is the day anyone may possibly be in the park. At one time I believed he was a grocer or a manager of a dry goods store or the proprietor of a flower shop. So it went but it did not end.

One Monday morning I saw him out early in the park, sitting and looking the same as he did the day before and on other Sundays, watching the race of people and of machinery and of time passing through the earth with the same lazy, easy eyes of Sunday and looking unhurried and unflustered and still living, in spite of the fact that this was the restless weekday, the day of sweat and toil and misery and no church bells ringing. He sat without words, like other days, simply sitting and laughing at intervals unconsciously, unaware of human ears and human eyes listening and noticing and probing him. He sat without austerity, without a wit of sadness, sitting, basking, drinking, not singing dramatically in the opera or in the arena, not writing to bring tears or happiness, not using, not playing, not living heroically in one word perhaps, but alive, basking today, a living presence, a phenomenon of life that is here awhile and gone without an answer.

And then on Tuesday I saw him again, and again on Wednesday, Thursday, Friday till I began to believe I have been following a man of leisure or a man out of work or on pension. This assumption, however, was short lived. He did not make an appearance for a week, leaving myself sitting under a tree, waiting with anticipation and with nervousness that the man will not appear again. When I sat and watched for a week and he did not come, I was certain I had lost him, the individual who had become someone big, the man who instantly had charged the park on Seventh and Harrison with life and interest. I sat and read my book regretting the opportunity I had lost to identify him, to put him down as he was, to seek him out through words and gestures the man he really was in the material atmosphere.

But the Japanese returned to the park bench one Sunday, returning with laughter intact and with the sadness creased in his face, looking unchanged as the time I had first noticed him, looking and laughing at intervals, unexpectedly and inconspicuously, occupying a place on the park bench, occupying simply and quietly and lost in the mass of Sunday faces.

This time I did not hesitate to go up to the park bench and address him. I said hello and he looked at me not surprised and smiled. I told him I had been sitting under the tree reading books for weeks and that I had seen him come and sit down on the park bench for weeks and that for a week I had missed him and feared that something must have happened or more dreadful, that he was not to appear at the park bench again.

"Sit down," he said.

He made room for me. We sat and talked a good hour or more. He said his name was Tsumura, and he was from Shinano prefecture in Japan. I said my parents were from Hiroshima prefecture and he said he knew a number of people from Hiroshima.

"I was afraid I had lost you, that I would not see you again," I said.

The man laughed. "You need not be afraid," he said. "I am always here. I am not rich and I do not travel."

"What do you do?" I said.

He said he worked for Hinode Laundry Co. He said he was a truck driver calling at the houses and offices all over the East Bay. He said he had been working for fourteen years at the same place and sometimes he worked only part time which was why I saw him on weekdays for a long stretch.

A moment later he said he had to go. He said the supper at the laundry house was at six and he must go now to be on time. We said good-bye and promised that we would meet again. Not a word did he say about the sadness of his face and his life. And I did not ask why he is sad and why he is laughing all the time. We did not speak a word of it, we did not like to be foolish and ask and answer the problem of the earth, and we did not have to. Every little observation, every little banal talk or laughing matter springs from the sadness of the earth that is reality; every meeting between individuals, every meeting of society, every meeting of a gathering, of gaiety or sorrow, springs from sadness that is the bed of earth and truth.

And so when he said he was a laundry truck driver and had come to the park for breath of air which is no different from the wind that hits him while driving, all that matters is that he is a laundry truck driver, a man living in the city, coming to the park for a pause, not for great thoughts or to escape the living of life, but to pause and laugh, unbitterly and unsentimentally, not wishing for dreams, not expecting a miracle, not even accepting the turn of the next hour or the next second.

And this is the greatest thing happening today: that of a laundry truck driver or an equivalent to such who is living and coming in and out of parks, the homes, the alleys, the dives, the offices, the rendezvous, the vices, the churches, the operas, the movies; all seeking unconsciously, unawaredly, the hold of this sadness, the loneliness, the barrenness, which is not elusive but hovering and pervading and seeping into the flesh and vegetation alike, churning out potentially the greatness, the weakness, and the heroism, the cowardice; and therefore, leaving unfinished all the causes of sadness, unhappiness, and sorrows of the earth behind in the laughter and the mute silence of time.

Seventeen Syllables

HISAYE YAMAMOTO

The first Rosie knew that her mother had taken to writing poems was one evening when she finished one and read it aloud for her daughter's approval. It was about cats, and Rosie pretended to understand it thoroughly and appreciate it no end, partly because she hesitated to disillusion her mother about the quantity and quality of Japanese she had learned in all the years now that she had been going to Japanese school every Saturday (and Wednesday, too, in the summer). Even so, her mother must have been skeptical about the depth of Rosie's understanding, because she explained afterwards about the kind of poem she was trying to write.

See, Rosie, she said, it was a *haiku*, a poem in which she must pack all her meaning into seventeen syllables only, which were divided into three lines of five, seven, and five syllables. In the one she had just read, she had tried to capture the charm of a kitten, as well as comment on the superstition that owning a cat of three colors meant good luck.

"Yes, yes, I understand. How utterly lovely," Rosie said, and her mother, either satisfied or seeing through the deception and resigned, went back to composing.

The truth was that Rosie was lazy; English lay ready on the tongue but Japanese had to be searched for and examined, and even then put forth tentatively (probably to meet with laughter). It was so much easier to say yes, yes, even when one meant no, no. Besides, this was what was in her mind to say: I was looking through one of your magazines from Japan last night, Mother, and towards the back I found some *haiku* in English that delighted me. There was one that made me giggle off and on until I fell asleep —

It is morning, and lo!
I lie awake, comme il faut,
sighing for some dough.

Now, how to reach her mother, how to communicate the melancholy song? Rosie knew formal Japanese by fits and starts, her mother had even less English, no French. It was much more possible to say yes, yes.

It developed that her mother was writing the *haiku* for a daily newspaper, the *Mainichi Shimbun,* that was published in San Francisco. Los Angeles, to be sure, was closer to the farming community in which the Hayashi family lived and several Japanese vernaculars were printed there, but Rosie's parents said they preferred the tone of the northern paper. Once a week, the *Mainichi* would have a section devoted to *haiku,* and her mother became an extravagant contributor, taking for herself the blossoming pen name, Ume Hanazono.

So Rosie and her father lived for awhile with two women, her mother and Ume Hanazono. Her mother (Tome Hayashi by name) kept house, cooked, washed, and, along with her husband and the Carrascos, the Mexican family hired for the harvest, did her ample share of picking tomatoes out in the sweltering fields and boxing them in tidy strata in the cool packing shed. Ume Hanazono, who came to life after the dinner dishes were done, was an earnest, muttering stranger who often neglected speaking when spoken to and stayed busy at the parlor table as late as midnight scribbling with pencil on scratch paper or carefully copying characters on good paper with her fat, pale green Parker.

The new interest had some repercussions on the household routine. Before, Rosie had been accustomed to her parents and herself taking their hot baths early and going to bed almost immediately afterwards, unless her parents challenged each other to a game of flower cards or unless company dropped in. Now if her father wanted to play cards, he had to resort to solitaire (at which he always cheated fearlessly), and if a group of friends came over, it was bound to contain someone who was also writing *haiku*, and the small assemblage would be split in two, her father entertaining the non-literary members and her mother comparing ecstatic notes with the visiting poet.

If they went out, it was more of the same thing. But Ume Hanazono's life span, even for a poet's, was very brief—perhaps three months at most.

One night they went over to see the Hayano family in the neighboring town to the west, an adventure both painful and attractive to Rosie. It was attractive because there were four Hayano girls, all lovely and each one named after a season of the year (Haru, Natsu, Aki, Fuyu), painful because something had been wrong with Mrs. Hayano ever since the birth of her first child. Rosie would sometimes watch Mrs. Hayano, reputed to have been the belle of her native village, making her way about a room, stooped, slowly shuffling, violently trembling (*always* trembling), and she would be reminded that this woman, in this same condition, had carried and given issue to three babies. She would look wonderingly at Mr. Hayano, handsome, tall, and strong, and she would look at her four pretty friends. But it was not a matter she could come to any decision about.

On this visit, however, Mrs. Hayano sat all evening in the rocker, as motionless and unobtrusive as it was possible for her to be, and Rosie found the greater part of the evening practically anaesthetic. Too, Rosie spent most of it in the girls' room, because Haru, the garrulous one, said almost as soon as the bows and other greetings were over, "Oh, you must see my new coat!"

It was a pale plaid of grey, sand, and blue, with an enormous collar, and Rosie, seeing nothing special in it, said, "Gee, how nice."

"Nice?" said Haru, indignantly. "Is that all you can say about it? It's gorgeous! And so cheap, too. Only seventeen-ninety-eight, because it was a sale. The saleslady said it was twenty-five dollars regular."

"Gee," said Rosie. Natsu, who never said much and when she said anything said it shyly, fingered the coat covetously and Haru pulled it away.

"Mine," she said, putting it on. She minced in the aisle between the two large beds and smiled happily. "Let's see how your mother likes it."

She broke into the front room and the adult conversation and went to stand in front of Rosie's mother, while the rest watched from the door. Rosie's mother was properly envious. "May I inherit it when you're through with it?"

Haru, pleased, giggled and said yes, she could, but Natsu reminded gravely from the door, "You promised me, Haru."

Everyone laughed but Natsu, who shamefacedly retreated into the bedroom. Haru came in laughing, taking off the coat. "We were only kidding, Natsu," she said. "Here, you try it on now."

After Natsu buttoned herself into the coat, inspected herself solemnly in the bureau mirror, and reluctantly shed it, Rosie, Aki, and Fuyu got their turns, and Fuyu, who was eight, drowned in it while her sisters and Rosie doubled up in amusement. They all went into the front room later, because Haru's mother quaveringly called to her to fix the tea and rice cakes and open a can of sliced peaches for everybody. Rosie noticed that her mother and Mr. Hayano were talking together at the little table—they were discussing a *haiku* that Mr. Hayano was planning to send to the *Mainichi*, while her father was sitting at one end of the sofa looking through a copy of *Life*, the new picture magazine. Occasionally, her father would comment on a photograph, holding it toward Mrs. Hayano and speaking to her as he always did—loudly, as though he thought someone such as she must surely be at least a trifle deaf also.

The five girls had their refreshments at the kitchen table, and it was while Rosie was showing the sisters her trick of swallowing peach slices without chewing (she chased each slippery crescent down with a swig of tea) that her father brought his empty teacup and untouched saucer to the sink and said, "Come on, Rosie, we're going home now."

"Already?" asked Rosie.

"Work tomorrow," he said.

He sounded irritated, and Rosie, puzzled, gulped one last yellow slice and stood up to go, while the sisters began protesting, as was their wont.

"We have to get up at five-thirty," he told them, going into the front room quickly, so that they did not have their usual chance to hang onto his hands and plead for an extension of time.

Rosie, following, saw that her mother and Mr. Hayano were sipping tea and still talking together, while Mrs. Hayano concentrated, quivering, on raising the handleless Japanese cup to her lips with both her hands and lowering it back to her lap. Her father, saying nothing, went out the door, onto the bright porch, and down the steps. Her mother looked up and asked, "Where is he going?"

"Where is he going?" Rosie said. "He said we were going home now."

"Going home?" Her mother looked with embarrassment at Mr. Hayano and his absorbed wife and then forced a smile. "He must be tired," she said.

Haru was not giving up yet. "May Rosie stay overnight?" she asked, and Natsu, Aki, and Fuyu came to reinforce their sister's plea by helping her make a circle around Rosie's mother. Rosie, for once having no desire to stay, was relieved when her mother, apologizing to the perturbed Mr. and Mrs. Hayano for her father's abruptness at the same time, managed to shake her head no at the quartet, kindly but adamant, so that they broke their circle and let her go.

Rosie's father looked ahead into the windshield as the two joined him. "I'm sorry," her mother said. "You must be tired." Her father, stepping on the starter, said nothing. "You know how I get when it's *haiku*," she continued, "I forget what time it is." He only grunted.

As they rode homeward silently, Rosie, sitting between, felt a rush of hate for both—for her mother for begging, for her father for denying her mother. I wish this old Ford would crash, right now, she thought, then immediately, no, no, I wish my father would laugh, but it was too late: already the vision had passed through her mind of the green pick-up crumpled in the dark against one of the mighty eucalyptus trees they were just riding past, of the three contorted, bleeding bodies, one of them hers.

Rosie ran between two patches of tomatoes, her heart working more rambunctiously than she had ever known it to. How lucky it was that Aunt Taka and Uncle Gimpachi had come tonight, though, how very lucky. Otherwise she might not have really kept her half-promise to meet Jesus Carrasco. Jesus was going to be a senior in September at the same school she went to, and his parents were the ones helping with the tomatoes this year. She and Jesus, who hardly remembered seeing each other at Cleveland High where there were so many other people and two whole grades between them, had become great friends this summer—he always had a joke for her when he periodically drove the loaded pick-up up from the fields to the shed where she was usually sorting while her mother and father did the packing, and they laughed a great deal together over infinitesimal repartee during the afternoon break for chilled watermelon or ice cream in the shade of the shed.

What she enjoyed most was racing him to see which could finish picking a double row first. He, who could work faster, would tease her by slowing down until she thought she would surely pass him this time, then speeding up furiously to leave her several sprawling vines behind. Once he had made her screech hideously by crossing over, while her back was turned, to place atop the tomatoes in her green-stained bucket a truly monstrous, pale green worm (it had looked more like an infant snake). And it was when they had finished a contest this morning, after she had pantingly pointed a green finger at the immature tomatoes evident in the lugs at the end of his row and he had returned the accusation (with justice), that he had startlingly brought up the matter of their possibly meeting outside the range of both their parents' dubious eyes.

"What for?" she had asked.

"I've got a secret I want to tell you," he said.

"Tell me now," she demanded.

"It won't be ready till tonight," he said.

She laughed. "Tell me tomorrow then."

"It'll be gone tomorrow," he threatened.

"Well, for seven hakes, what is it?" she had asked, more than twice, and when he had suggested that the packing shed would be an appropriate place to find out, she had cautiously answered maybe. She had not been certain she was going to keep the appointment until the arrival of mother's sister and her husband. Their coming seemed a sort of signal of permission, of grace, and she had definitely made up her mind to lie and leave as she was bowing them welcome.

So as soon as everyone appeared settled back for the evening, she announced loudly that she was going to the privy outside, "I'm going to the *benjo*!" and slipped out the door. And now that she was actually on her way, her heart pumped in such an undisciplined way that she could hear it with her ears. It's because I'm running, she told herself, slowing to a walk. The shed was up ahead, one more patch away, in the middle of the fields. Its bulk, looming in the dimness, took on a sinisterness that was funny when Rosie reminded herself that it was only a wooden frame with a canvas roof and three canvas walls that made a slapping noise on breezy days.

Jesus was sitting on the narrow plank that was the sorting platform and she went around to the other side and jumped backwards to seat herself on the rim of a packing stand. "Well, tell me," she said without greeting, thinking her voice sounded reassuringly familiar.

"I saw you coming out the door," Jesus said. "I heard you running part of the way, too."

"Uh-huh," Rosie said. "Now tell me the secret."

"I was afraid you wouldn't come," he said.

Rosie delved around on the chicken-wire bottom of the stall for number two tomatoes, ripe, which she was sitting beside, and came up with a left-over that felt edible. She bit into it and began sucking out the pulp and seeds. "I'm here," she pointed out.

"Rosie, are you sorry you came?"

"Sorry? What for?" she said. "You said you were going to tell me something."

"I will, I will," Jesus said, but his voice contained disappointment, and Rosie fleetingly felt the older of the two, realizing a brand-new power which vanished without category under her recognition.

"I have to go back in a minute," she said. "My aunt and uncle are here from Wintersburg. I told them I was going to the privy."

Jesus laughed. "You funny thing," he said. "You slay me!"

"Just because you have a bathroom *inside*," Rosie said. "Come on, tell me."

Chuckling, Jesus came around to lean on the stand facing her. They still could not see each other very clearly, but Rosie noticed that Jesus became very sober again as he took the hollow tomato from her hand and dropped it back into the stall. When he took hold of her empty hand, she could find no words to protest; her vocabulary had become distressingly constricted and she thought desperately that all that remained intact now was yes and no and oh, and even these few sounds would not easily out. Thus, kissed by Jesus, Rosie fell for the first time entirely victim to a helplessness delectable beyond speech. But the terrible, beautiful sensation lasted no more than a second, and the re-

Fiction

158

ality of Jesus' lips and tongue and teeth and hands made her pull away with such strength that she nearly tumbled.

Rosie stopped running as she approached the lights from the windows of home. How long since she had left? She could not guess, but gasping yet, she went to the privy in back and locked herself in. Her own breathing deafened her in the dark, close space, and she sat and waited until she could hear at last the nightly calling of the frogs and crickets. Even then, all she could think to say was oh, my, and the pressure of Jesus' face against her face would not leave.

No one had missed her in the parlor, however, and Rosie walked in and through quickly, announcing that she was next going to take a bath. "Your father's in the bathhouse," her mother said, and Rosie, in her room, recalled that she had not seen him when she entered. There had been only Aunt Taka and Uncle Gimpachi with her mother at the table, drinking tea. She got her robe and straw sandals and crossed the parlor again to go outside. Her mother was telling them about the *haiku* competition in the *Mainichi* and the poem she had entered.

Rosie met her father coming out of the bathhouse. "Are you through, Father?" she asked. "I was going to ask you to scrub my back."

"Scrub your own back," he said shortly, going toward the main house.

"What have I done now?" she yelled after him. She suddenly felt like doing a lot of yelling. But he did not answer, and she went into the bathhouse. Turning on the dangling light, she removed her denims and T-shirt and threw them in the big carton for dirty clothes standing next to the washing machine. Her other things she took with her into the bath compartment to wash after her bath. After she had scooped a basin of hot water from the square wooden tub, she sat on the grey cement of the floor and soaped herself at exaggerated leisure, singing "Red Sails in the Sunset" at the top of her voice and using da-da-da where she suspected her words. Then, standing up, still singing, for she was possessed by the notion that any attempt now to analyze would result in spoilage and she believed that the larger her volume the less she would be able to hear herself think, she obtained more hot water and poured it on until she was free of lather. Only then did she allow herself to step into the steaming vat, one leg first, then the remainder of her body inch by inch until the water no longer stung and she could move around at will.

She took a long time soaking, afterwards remembering to go around outside to stoke the embers of the tin-lined fireplace beneath the tub and to throw on a few more sticks so that the water might keep its heat for her mother, and when she finally returned to the parlor, she found her mother still talking *haiku* with her aunt and uncle, the three of them on another round of tea. Her father was nowhere in sight.

At Japanese school the next day (Wednesday, it was), Rosie was grave and giddy by turns. Preoccupied at her desk in the row for students on Book Eight, she made up for it at recess by performing wild mimicry for the benefit of her friend Chizuko. She held her nose and whined a witticism or two in what she considered was the manner of Fred Allen; she assumed intoxication and a British accent to go over the climax of the Rudy Vallee recording of the pub conversation about William Ewart Gladstone; she was the child Shirley Temple piping, "On the Good Ship Lollipop"; she was the gentleman soprano of the Four Inkspots trilling, "If I Didn't Care." And she felt reasonably satisfied when Chizuko wept and gasped, "Oh, Rosie, you ought to be in the movies!"

Her father came after her at noon, bringing her sandwiches of minced ham and two nectarines to eat while she rode, so that she could pitch right into the sorting when they got home. The lugs were piling up, he said, and the ripe tomatoes in them would probably have to be taken to the cannery tomorrow if they were not ready for the produce haulers tonight. "This heat's not doing them any good. And we've got no time for a break today."

It *was* hot, probably the hottest day of the year, and Rosie's blouse stuck damply to her back even under the protection of the canvas. But she worked as efficiently as a flawless machine and kept the stalls heaped, with one part of her mind listening in to the parental murmuring about the heat and the tomatoes and with another part planning the exact words she would say to Jesus when he drove up with the first load of the afternoon. But when at last she saw that the pick-up was coming, her hands went berserk and the tomatoes started falling in the wrong stalls, and her father said, "Hey, hey! Rosie, watch what you're doing!"

"Well, I have to go to the *benjo*," she said, hiding panic.

"Go in the weeds over there," he said, only half-joking.

"Oh, Father!" she protested.

"Oh, go on home," her mother said. "We'll make out for awhile."

In the privy Rosie peered through a knothole toward the fields, watching as much as she could of Jesus. Happily she thought she saw him look in the direction of the house from time to time before he finished unloading and went back toward the patch where his mother and father worked. As she was heading for the shed, a very presentable black car purred up the dirt driveway to the house and its driver motioned to her. Was this the Hayashi home, he wanted to know. She nodded. Was she a Hayashi? Yes, she said, thinking that he was a good-looking man. He got out of the car with a huge, flat package and she saw that he warmly wore a business suit. "I have something here for your mother then," he said, in a more elegant Japanese than she was used to.

She told him where her mother was and he came along with her, patting his face with an immaculate white handkerchief and saying something about the coolness of San Francisco. To her surprised mother and father, he bowed and introduced himself as, among other things, the *haiku* editor of the *Mainichi Shimbun*, saying that since he had been coming as far as Los Angeles anyway, he had decided to bring her the first prize she had won in the recent contest.

"First prize?" her mother echoed, believing and not believing, pleased and overwhelmed. Handed the package with a bow, she bobbed her head up and down numerous times to express her utter gratitude.

"It is nothing much," he added, "but I hope it will serve as a token of our great appreciation for your contributions and our great admiration of your considerable talent."

"I am not worthy," she said, falling easily into his style. "It is I who should make some sign of my humble thanks for being permitted to contribute."

"No, no, to the contrary," he said, bowing again.

But Rosie's mother insisted, and then saying that she knew she was being unorthodox, she asked if she might open the package because her curiosity was so great. Certainly she might. In fact, he would like her reaction to it, for personally, it was one of his favorite *Hiroshiges*.

Rosie thought it was a pleasant picture, which looked to have been sketched with delicate quickness. There were pink clouds, containing some graceful calligraphy, and a sea that was a pale blue except at the edges, containing four sampans with indications of people in them. Pines edged the water and on the far-off beach there was a cluster of thatched huts towered over by pine-dotted mountains of grey and blue. The frame was scalloped and gilt.

After Rosie's mother pronounced it without peer and somewhat prodded her father into nodding agreement, she said Mr. Kuroda must at least have a cup of tea after coming all this way, and although Mr. Kuroda did not want to impose, he soon agreed that a cup of tea would be refreshing and went along with her to the house, carrying the picture for her.

"Ha, your mother's crazy!" Rosie's father said, and Rosie laughed uneasily as she resumed judgment on the tomatoes. She had emptied six lugs when he broke into an imaginary conversation with Jesus to tell her to go and remind her mother of the tomatoes, and she went slowly.

Mr. Kuroda was in his shirtsleeves expounding some *haiku* theory as he munched a rice cake, and her mother was rapt. Abashed in the great man's presence, Rosie stood next to her mother's chair until her mother looked up inquiringly, and then she started to whisper the message, but her mother pushed her gently away and reproached, "You are not being very polite to our guest."

"Father says the tomatoes . . ." Rosie said aloud, smiling foolishly.

"Tell him I shall only be a minute," her mother said, speaking the language of Mr. Kuroda.

When Rosie carried the reply to her father, he did not seem to hear and she said again, "Mother says she'll be back in a minute."

"All right, all right," he nodded, and they worked again in silence. But suddenly, her father uttered an incredible noise, exactly like the cork of a bottle popping, and the next Rosie knew, he was stalking angrily toward the house, almost running in fact, and she chased after him crying, "Father! Father! What are you going to do?"

He stopped long enough to order her back to the shed. "Never mind!" he shouted. "Get on with the sorting!"

And from the place in the fields where she stood, frightened and vacillating, Rosie saw her father enter the house. Soon Mr. Kuroda came out alone, putting on his coat. Mr. Kuroda got into his car and backed out down the driveway onto the highway. Next her father emerged, also alone, something in his arms (it was the picture, she realized), and, going over to the bathhouse woodpile, he threw the picture on the ground and picked up the axe. Smashing the picture, glass and all (she heard the explosion faintly), he reached over for the kerosene that was used to encourage the bath fire and poured it over the wreckage. I am dreaming, Rosie said to herself, I am dreaming, but her father, having made sure that his act of cremation was irrevocable, was even then returning to the fields.

Rosie ran past him and toward the house. What had become of her mother? She burst into the parlor and found her mother at the back window watching the dying fire. They watched together until there remained only a feeble smoke under the blazing sun. Her mother was very calm.

"Do you know why I married your father?" she said without turning.

"No," said Rosie. It was the most frightening question she had ever been called upon to answer. Don't tell me now, she wanted to say, tell me tomorrow, tell me next week, don't tell me today. But she knew she would be told now, that the telling would combine with the other violence of the hot afternoon to level her life, her world to the very ground.

It was like a story out of the magazines illustrated in sepia, which she had consumed so greedily for a period until the information had somehow reached her that those wretchedly unhappy autobiographies, offered to her as the testimonials of living men and women, were largely inventions: Her mother, at nineteen, had come to America and married her father as an alternative to suicide.

At eighteen she had been in love with the first son of one of the well-to-do families in her village. The two had met whenever and wherever they could, secretly, because it would not have done for his family to see him favor her—her father had no money; he was a drunkard and a gambler besides. She had learned she was with child; an excellent match had already been arranged for her lover. Despised by her family, she had given premature birth to a stillborn son, who would be seventeen now. Her family did not turn her out, but she could no longer project herself in any direction without refreshing in them the memory of her indiscretion. She wrote to Aunt Taka, her favorite sister in America, threatening to kill herself if Aunt Taka would not send for her. Aunt Taka hastily arranged a marriage with a young man of whom she knew, but lately arrived from Japan, a young man of simple mind, it was said, but of kindly heart. The young man was never told why his unseen betrothed was so eager to hasten the day of meeting.

The story was told perfectly, with neither groping for words nor untoward passion. It was as though her mother had memorized it by heart, reciting it to herself so many times over that its nagging vileness had long since gone.

"I had a brother then?" Rosie asked, for this was what seemed to matter now; she would think about the other later, she assured herself, pushing back the illumination which threatened all that darkness that had hitherto been merely mysterious or even glamorous. "A half-brother?"

"Yes."

"I would have liked a brother," she said.

Suddenly, her mother knelt on the floor and took her by the wrists. "Rosie," she said urgently, "Promise me you will never marry!" Shocked more by the request than the revelation, Rosie stared at her mother's face. Jesus, Jesus, she called silently, not certain whether she was invoking the help of the son of the Carrascos or of God, until there returned sweetly the memory of Jesus' hand, how it had touched her and where. Still her mother waited for an answer, holding her wrists so tightly that her hands were going numb. She tried to pull free. Promise, her mother whispered fiercely, promise. Yes, yes, I promise, Rosie said. But for an instant she turned away, and her mother, hearing the familiar glib agreement, released her. Oh, you, you, you, her eyes and twisted mouth said, you fool. Rosie, covering her face, began at last to cry, and the embrace and consoling hand came much later than she expected.

Hisaye Yamamoto

163

From *No-No Boy*

JOHN OKADA

The Kumasakas had run a dry-cleaning shop before the war. Business was good and people spoke of their having money, but they lived in cramped quarters above the shop because, like most of the other Japanese, they planned some day to return to Japan and still felt like transients even after thirty or forty years in America and the quarters above the shop seemed adequate and sensible since the arrangement was merely temporary. That, he thought to himself, was the reason why the Japanese were still Japanese. They rushed to America with the single purpose of making a fortune which would enable them to return to their own country and live adequately. It did not matter when they discovered that fortunes were not for the mere seeking or that their sojourns were spanning decades instead of years and it did not matter that growing families and growing bills and misfortunes and illness and low wages and just plain hard luck were constant obstacles to the realization of their dreams. They continued to maintain their dreams by refusing to learn how to speak or write the language of America and by living only among their own kind and by zealously avoiding long-term commitments such as the purchase of a house. But now, the Kumasakas, it seemed, had bought this house, and he was impressed. It could only mean that the Kumasakas had exchanged hope for reality and, late as it was, were finally sinking roots into the land from which they had previously sought not nourishment but only gold.

Mrs. Kumasaka came to the door, a short, heavy woman who stood solidly on feet planted wide apart, like a man. She greeted them warmly but with a sadness that she would carry to the grave. When Ichiro had last seen her, her hair had been pitch black. Now it was completely white.

In the living room Mr. Kumasaka, a small man with a pleasant smile, was sunk deep in an upholstered chair, reading a Japanese newspaper. It was a comfortable room with rugs and soft furniture and lamps and end tables and pictures on recently papered walls.

"Ah, Ichiro, it is nice to see you looking well." Mr. Kumasaka struggled out of the chair and extended a friendly hand. "Please, sit down."

"You've got a nice place," he said, meaning it.

"Thank you," the little man said. "Mama and I, we finally decided that America is not so bad. We like it here."

Ichiro sat down on the sofa next to his mother and felt strange in this home which he envied because it was like millions of other homes in America and could never be his own.

Mrs. Kumasaka sat next to her husband on a large, round hassock and looked at Ichiro with lonely eyes, which made him uncomfortable.

"Ichiro came home this morning." It was his mother, and the sound of her voice, deliberately loud and almost arrogant, puzzled him. "He has suffered, but I make no apologies for him or for myself. If he had given his life for Japan, I could not be prouder."

"Ma," he said, wanting to object but not knowing why except that her comments seemed out of place.

Ignoring him, she continued, not looking at the man but at his wife, who now sat with head bowed, her eyes emptily regarding the floral pattern of the carpet. "A mother's lot is not an easy one. To sleep with a man and bear a son is nothing. To raise the child into a man one can be proud of is not play. Some of us succeed. Some, of course, must fail. It is too bad, but that is the way of life."

"Yes, yes, Yamada-san," said the man impatiently. Then, smiling, he turned to Ichiro: "I suppose you'll be going back to the university?"

" I'll have to think about it," he replied, wishing that his father was like this man who made him want to pour out the turbulence in his soul.

"He will go when the new term begins. I have impressed upon him the importance of a good education. With a college education, one can go far in Japan." His mother smiled knowingly.

"Ah," said the man as if he had not heard her speak, "Bobbie wanted to go to the university and study medicine. He would have made a fine doctor. Always studying and reading, is that not so, Ichiro?"

He nodded, remembering the quiet son of the Kumasakas, who never played football with the rest of the kids on the street or appeared at dances, but could talk for hours on end about chemistry and zoology and physics and other courses which he hungered after in high school.

"Sure, Bob always was pretty studious." He knew, somehow, that it was not the right thing to say, but he added: "Where is Bob?"

His mother did not move. Mrs. Kumasaka uttered a despairing cry and bit her trembling lips.

The little man, his face a drawn mask of pity and sorrow, stammered: "Ichiro, you—no one has told you?"

"No. What? No one's told me anything."

"Your mother did not write you?"

"No. Write about what?" He knew what the answer was. It was in the whiteness of the hair of the sad woman who was the mother of the boy named Bob and it was in the engaging pleasantness of the father which was not really pleasantness but a deep understanding which had emerged from resignation to a loss which only a parent knows and suffers. And then he saw the picture on the mantel, a snapshot, enlarged many times over, of a grinning youth in uniform who had not thought to remember his parents with a formal portrait because he was not going to die and there would be worlds of time for pictures and books and other obligations of the living later on.

Mr. Kumasaka startled him by shouting toward the rear of the house: "Jun! Please come."

There was the sound of a door opening and presently there appeared a youth in khaki shirt and wool trousers, who was a stranger to Ichiro.

"I hope I haven't disturbed anything, Jun," said Mr. Kumasaka.

"No, it's all right. Just writing a letter."

"This is Mrs. Yamada and her son Ichiro. They are old family friends."

Jun nodded to his mother and reached over to shake Ichiro's hand.

The little man waited until Jun had seated himself on the end of the sofa. "Jun is from Los Angeles. He's on his way home from the army and was good enough to stop by and visit us for a few days. He and Bobbie were together. Buddies—is that what you say?"

"That's right," said Jun.

"Now, Jun."

"Yes?"

The little man looked at Ichiro and then at his mother, who stared stonily at no one in particular.

"Jun, as a favor to me, although I know it is not easy for you to speak of it, I want you to tell us about Bobbie."

Jun stood up quickly. "Gosh, I don't know." He looked with tender concern at Mrs. Kumasaka.

"It is all right, Jun. Please, just this once more."

"Well, okay." He sat down again, rubbing his hands thoughtfully over his knees. "The way it happened, Bobbie and I, we had just gotten back to the rest area. Everybody was feeling good because there was a lot of talk about the Germans' surrendering. All the fellows were cleaning their equipment. We'd been up in the lines for a long time and everything was pretty well messed up. When you're up there getting shot at, you don't worry much about how crummy your things get, but the minute you pull back, they got to have inspection. So, we were cleaning things up. Most of us were cleaning our rifles because that's something you learn to want to do no matter how anything else looks. Bobbie was sitting beside me and he was talking about how he was going to medical school and become a doctor—"

A sob wrenched itself free from the breast of the mother whose son was once again dying, and the snow-white head bobbed wretchedly.

"Go on, Jun," said the father.

Jun looked away from the mother and at the picture on the mantel. "Bobbie was like that. Me and the other guys, all we talked about was drinking and girls and stuff like that because it's important to talk about those things when you make it back from the front on your own power, but Bobbie, all he thought about was going to school. I was nodding my head and saying yeah, yeah, and then there was this noise, kind of a pinging noise right close by. It scared me for a minute and I started to cuss and said, 'Gee, that was damn close,' and looked around at Bobbie. He was slumped over with his head between his knees. I reached out to hit him, thinking he was fooling around. Then, when I tapped him on the arm, he fell over and I saw the dark spot on the side of his head where the bullet had gone through. That was all. Ping, and he's dead. It doesn't figure, but it happened just the way I've said."

The mother was crying now, without shame and alone in her grief that knew no end. And in her bottomless grief that made no distinction as to what was wrong and what was right and who was Japanese and who was not, there was no awareness of the other mother with a living son who had come to say to her you are with shame and grief because you were not Japanese and thereby killed your son but mine is big and strong and full of life because I did not weaken and would not let my son destroy himself uselessly and treacherously.

Ichiro's mother rose and, without a word, for no words would ever pass between them again, went out of the house which was a part of America.

Mr. Kumasaka placed a hand on the rounded back of his wife, who was forever beyond consoling, and spoke gently to Ichiro: "You don't have to say anything. You are truly sorry and I am sorry for you."

"I didn't know," he said pleadingly.

"I want you to feel free to come and visit us whenever you wish. We can talk even if your mother's convictions are different."

"She's crazy. Mean and crazy. Goddamned Jap!" He felt the tears hot and stinging.

"Try to understand her."

Impulsively, he took the little man's hand in his own and held it briefly. Then he hurried out of the house which could never be his own.

His mother was not waiting for him. He saw her tiny figure strutting into the shadows away from the illumination of the street lights and did not attempt to catch her.

As he walked up one hill and down another, not caring where and only knowing that he did not want to go home, he was thinking about the Kumasakas and his mother and kids like Bob who died brave deaths fighting for something which was bigger than Japan or America or the selfish bond that strapped a son to his mother. Bob, and a lot of others with no more to lose or gain than he, had not found it necessary to think about whether or not to go in the army. When the time came, they knew what was right for them and they went.

What had happened to him and the others who faced the judge and said: You can't make me go in the army because I'm not an American or you wouldn't have plucked me and mine from a life that was good and real and meaningful and fenced me in the desert like they do the Jews in Germany and it is a puzzle why you haven't started to liquidate us though you might as well since everything else has been destroyed.

And some said: You, Mr. Judge, who supposedly represent justice, was it a just thing to ruin a hundred thousand lives and homes and farms and businesses and dreams and hopes because the hundred thousand were a hundred thousand Japanese and you couldn't have loyal Japanese when Japan is the country you're fighting and, if so, how about the Germans and Italians that must be just as questionable as the Japanese or we wouldn't be fighting Germany and Italy? Round them up. Take away their homes and cars and beer and spaghetti and throw them in a camp and what do you think they'll say when you try to draft them into your army of the country that is for life, liberty, and the pursuit of happiness? If you think we're the same kind of rotten Japanese that dropped the bombs on Pearl Harbor, and it's plain that you do or I wouldn't be here having to explain to you why it is that I won't go and protect sons-of-bitches like you, I say you're right and *banzai* three times and we'll sit the war out in a nice cell, thank you.

And then another one got up and faced the judge and said meekly: I can't go because my brother is in the Japanese army and if I go in your army and have to shoot at them because they're shooting at me, how do I know that maybe I won't kill my own brother? I'm a good American and I like it here but you can see that it wouldn't do for me to be shooting at my own brother; even if he went back to Japan when I was two years old and couldn't know him if I saw him, it's the feeling that counts, and what can a fellow do? Besides, my mom and dad said I shouldn't and they ought to know.

And after the fellow with the brother in the army of the wrong country sat down, a tall, skinny one sneered at the judge and said: I'm not going in the army because wool clothes give me one helluva bad time and them O.D. things you make the guys wear will drive me nuts and I'd end up shooting bastards like you which would be too good but then you'd only have to shoot me and I like living even if it's in striped trousers as long as they aren't wool. The judge, who looked Italian and had a German name, repeated the question as if the tall, skinny one hadn't said anything yet, and the tall, skinny one tried again only, this time, he was serious. He said: I got it all figured out. Economics, that's what. I hear this guy with the stars, the general of your army that cleaned the Japs off the coast, got a million bucks for the job. All this bull about us being security risks and saboteurs and Shinto freaks, that's for the birds and the dumbheads. The only way it figures is the money angle. How much did they give you, judge, or aren't your fingers long enough? Cut me in. Give me a cut and I'll go fight your war single-handed.

Please, judge, said the next one. I want to go in your army because this is my country and I've always lived here and I was all-city guard and one time I wrote an essay for composition about what it means to me to be an American and the teacher sent it into a contest and they gave me twenty-five dollars, which proves that I'm a good American. Maybe I look Japanese and my father and mother and brothers and sisters look Japanese, but we're better Americans than the regular ones because that's the way it has to be when one looks Japanese but is really a good American. We're not like the other Japanese who aren't good Americans like us. We're more like you and the other, regular Americans. All you have to do is give us back our home and grocery store and let my kid brother be all-city like me. Nobody has to know. We can be Chinese. We'll call ourselves Chin or Yang or something like that and it'll be the best thing you've ever done, sir. That's all, a little thing. Will you do that for one good, loyal American family? We'll forget the two years in camp because anybody can see it was all a mistake and you didn't really mean to do it and I'm all yours.

There were others with reasons just as flimsy and unreal and they had all gone to prison, where the months and years softened the unthinking bitterness and let them see the truth when it was too late. For the one who could not go because Japan was the country of his parents' birth, there were a thousand Bobs who had gone into the army with a singleness of purpose. In answer to the tall, skinny one who spouted economics, another thousand with even greater losses had answered the greetings. For each and every refusal based on sundry reasons, another thousand chose to fight for the right to continue to be Americans because homes and cars and money could be regained but only if they first regained their rights as citizens, and that was everything.

And then Ichiro thought to himself: My reason was all the reasons put together. I did not go because I was weak and could not do what I should have done. It was not my mother, whom I have never really known. It was me, myself. It is done and there can be no excuse. I remember Kenzo, whose mother was in the hospital and did not want him to go. The doctor told him that the shock might kill her. He went anyway, the very next day, because though he loved his mother he knew that she was wrong, and she did die. And I remember Harry, whose father had a million-dollar produce business, and the old man just boarded everything up because he said he'd rather let the trucks and buildings and warehouses rot than sell them for a quarter of what they were worth. Harry didn't have to stop and think when his number came up. Then there was Mr. Yamaguchi, who was almost forty and had five girls. They would never have taken him, but he had to go and talk himself into a uniform. I remember a lot of people and a lot of things now as I walk confidently through the night over a small span of concrete which is part of the sidewalks which are part of the city which is part of the state and the country and the nation that is America. It is for this that I meant to fight, only the meaning got lost when I needed it most badly.

Then he was on Jackson Street and walking down the hill. Through the windows of the drugstore, the pool hall, the cafés and taverns, he saw groups of young Japanese wasting away the night as nights were meant to be wasted by young Americans with change in their pockets and a thirst for cokes and beer and pinball machines or fast cars and de luxe hamburgers and cards and dice and trim legs. He recognized a face, a smile, a gesture, or a sneer, but they were not for him, for he walked on the outside and familiar faces no longer meant friends. He walked quickly, guiltily avoiding a chance recognition of himself by someone who remembered him.

From *Clay Walls*

KIM RONYOUNG

I did not mind losing Bertha as a friend. I was confident the judge could keep Lucerne Luke from John, but Bertha would try to fill me with doubts. As long as Luke was in custody I considered John safe and found me a new friend.

I met Jane on my way to school. We started right in talking to one another. When she saw me at recess, she said, "Let's meet after school and walk home together." When we discovered that we were going to be in the same gym class, we jumped and squealed with delight.

"Which team are you going to sign up for?" I asked.

"Let's sign up for volleyball," she suggested.

We stood in line together. At my insistence, she stood in front of me. She was shorter and more petite than I. Just like Momma would want me to be, I thought.

"Is your hair naturally curly?" I asked. "It's so pretty."

"Sort of. I don't need a perm, but I have to set it if I want it this curly." She pulled a shiny black curl straight then let it spring back.

"Mine's like wire. A perm makes it all kinky. I hate it," I said.

She ran her hand over my straight bobbed hair. "It's black and silky like my mother's," she said.

We had moved up to the sign-up table. Jane gave the teacher her full name and my heart sank into my shoes. Her last name was Nagano, a Japanese name. Every March First and just about every day in between, Koreans reminded each other to hate the Japanese. She signed up for volleyball and waited for me.

"Next!" the teacher snapped.

I gulped. "Faye Chun."

"Speak up. I can't hear you," the teacher bellowed.

I cleared my throat. "C-h-u-n," I spelled it for her. "Faye with an 'e'."

"F-e-y?" she asked.

I wanted to die. "No. F-a-y-e." I said.

"Which team?" she asked impatiently.

I had been struggling with that same question as soon as learned Jane's full name, wondering if I should end the friendship now.

"Volleyball," Jane told the teacher. "We want to be on the same team."

"Volleyball's filled up." The teacher looked over the sign-up sheets. "There's space in baseball and basketball."

It was being decided for me, I thought with relief. "Basketball," I said.

Jane tugged at my arm. "How about baseball? I'm too short for basketball." She turned to the teacher. "Can the two of us sign up for baseball?"

The teacher sighed as she erased Jane's name from the volleyball column and wrote our names on the sheet marked 'baseball'.

Jane linked her arm in mine. "Let's share lockers," she said.

"Okay," I said, convinced there could be no harm in sharing lockers.

After school, we parted at the corner of Normandie Avenue and 37th Street, promising each other to meet in the morning. I skipped all the way home. I ran into the house and told Momma, "I have a new friend. Her name is Jane."

"That's nice. Bring her home sometime," Momma said.

"She lives kind of far from here, way on the other side of Normandie."

"Some Saturday, then," Momma suggested.

"It would be too hard for her to find us," I said and went to my room to change my clothes.

Whenever I came home late from school, Momma knew it was because I had stayed at the corner of Normandie and 37th to play with Jane. To keep her from worrying, I told Momma, "Jane's a straight A student. She's very popular, the president of the Scholarship Society."

"I'm glad she's a nice girl. Why don't you invite her over?"

"She spends most of her time studying," I said.

Jane had invited me to her house several times, but I had made excuses without ever telling her about March First. She knew that on Thursdays I had to meet Momma at the bus stop with the baby carriage, but she was not convinced by my excuses on other days.

"My mother wants you to come for dinner. When can you come?" Jane asked.

"My mother wants you to come to our house too, but she's busy with her work so I have to cook. That's why I can't come to your house on any night," I said. For good measure I added, "My mother would give me permission if I asked her, but I won't because it's too hard for her to do her work and cook too." I made myself sound noble while lying to her.

It was harder for me to lie to Momma. I told her everything Jane and I did without ever telling her Jane's last name. Then one Thursday morning, Momma told me something that changed everything.

The early morning light was shining on Momma's hands. "Mr. Seligman likes my work. He thinks I am good enough to teach other women," Momma said.

"That's good," I said, gathering my books to leave for school.

"Better bring John's wagon to the bus stop. The carriage is too broken down. I'm going to bring work for some of the ladies in the neighborhood."

"You'll have to carry more handkerchiefs on the bus. Why don't they go to Seligman's themselves?" I said, making my way to the door.

"The ladies asked me to do it. They don't speak English very well. They need the work and it will mean a commission for me."

"What ladies?" I looked at the clock on the mantel. I would have to hurry if I did not want to miss Jane.

"Oh you know. Mrs. Kano, Mrs. Watanabe, and Mrs. Hiroshi. You're going to be late if you don't leave now," she said.

I stopped in my tracks. Those were Japanese names. I took my hands off the doorknob and walked to the table. "You're bringing work for *them*?"

"It's strictly business. Run along or your friend will leave without you," she said, waving me out.

I opened my mouth to speak, but decided it could wait and ran out the door.

I had missed Jane in the morning, but we met after school as usual. She was never late on Thursdays, knowing that I had to meet Momma at the bus stop. "Race you," she said, challenging me. "Skipping," she added.

We laughed harder than we skipped and collapsed at the corner. Panting, our hair clinging to our damp faces, our cheeks red with heat, we stayed sprawled on the cement sidewalk. "My sisters are putting a skit together. Ask your mother if you can come for dinner tomorrow night," Jane said. "It will be fun."

I sat up and looked straight at her. "You know what? I think I'll just do that."

Her eyes grew wide. "Swell!" she said.

At home, I brushed off John's wagon and pulled it to meet Momma. I could hardly wait for her to get off the bus. We packed the bundles into the wagon and started for home.

"You've brought a lot of work for the Japanese ladies. When are they coming to the house?" I asked.

"This evening."

"Momma, Jane Nagano asked me over for dinner tomorrow. It's Friday so I don't have to do my homework. Can I go?" I spewed it out when all along I had planned to work up to it gradually.

"Nagano? So that's why you've never brought her home," she said.

I felt the perspiration form under my arms. "I guess I forgot to tell you . . ."

"Don't lie to me, Faye." Momma stepped out of the way as the wagon swerved.

"I didn't mean to lie. I was afraid you wouldn't let me keep Jane as a friend." I started to walk faster.

She quickened her pace to keep up with me. "You know what the Japanese have done to our people."

"Not Jane. She's the nicest girl I've ever met."

"You know the rule. No Japanese friends."

I walked even faster, raising my voice to cover the distance between us. "What about Mrs. Kano, Mrs. Watanabe, and Mrs. Hiroshi?"

"I've told you. It's strictly business. That's not the same as you and Jane." She stopped to shout at me. "Faye! You wait for me!"

Tears began to fill my eyes and blurred my vision. "Jane's my friend."

"What? I can't hear you! Stop where you are," she ordered.

When she caught up with me, I blurted out, "I haven't got anyone. You're always at that stupid table." I couldn't stop myself. "The boys are always out together. Papa's gone and I don't have anyone." I threw down the handle of the wagon and ran into the house.

I was under the cover of my bed when I heard Momma drop the bundles of unsewn handkerchiefs on the table. I hid my head under the pillow when she came into my room.

"I'm sorry you're so miserable," she said. "Everything would be different if your Papa were here taking care of us." She sat on the edge of the bed. "We'd be rich if we were in Korea. None of us would have to work. But we came back to America because the Japanese were so cruel and there was no freedom."

"Jane could never be cruel," I said. "You're the one who's being cruel, keeping me from being her friend."

"You should be spanked for saying that," she said, bringing down her hand on my seat. "I guess you'll just have to find out for yourself. I'm going to give you permission to go to Jane's house to play. But you cannot have dinner with them. Is that clear?" She stood up and left the room.

I couldn't help myself. I laughed into my pillow.

I tried to sleep, shutting my eyes tightly to invite sleep to come, unable to keep from popping them open to see if the night was over. Jane and I had giggled at every word when I told her I could come to her house. I smiled in the dark remembering. When tired of waiting for sleep, I began to worry. Momma was usually right. I thought of torture chambers and Koreans shouting "Mansei!" My head began to ache. I ran the conversation with Jane through my mind again and tried to forget that she was Japanese. Sleep finally came when I decided what dress I would wear to Jane's house.

"Do you like *arare*?" Jane asked.

"I love it." I often craved the sugar and soy sauce coating on the Japanese rice cracker.

"We always have some with our tea," she said.

"I love it," I said again and smiled.

The outside of her house looked like mine: three steps led to a cement porch and an asphalt shingled roof pitched over the one-story wood-framed house. But her porch was bigger. Hers was large enough to hold a swing and a half-dozen potted ferns. Jane held the screendoor open and I stepped into what, until that moment, had been forbidden territory. The sharp smell of camphorwood pushed at my nostrils. The rooms were arranged like those in my house and the furniture were similar to ours, but nothing seemed like home. Not a scratch on the tables or a speck of dust anywhere. Hanging perfectly straight on the wall were two pictures: one of Mount Fujiyama and the other of the Crown Prince of Japan. Snapshots of Jane's family were turned just-so on the mantelpiece.

"Your house is nice," I whispered.

Jane smiled and led me to a man dressed in a gray suit. He was sitting in a large green easy chair reading a newspaper. Jane bowed. "Father, this is Faye Chun." The newspaper came down and he nodded. Momma would have said he was dignified-looking. I could not imagine him prying anyone's fingernails with bamboo sticks, but I was relieved when he returned to reading his paper.

"Excuse us, father. I'll take Faye into the kitchen to meet mother." She bowed to the newspaper then led me out of the room.

"Is your father going out?" I asked in a whisper.

"No. Why?"

"He's wearing a suit."

"He always wears a suit," Jane said as she pushed on the kitchen door. "Why are you whispering?"

I shrugged my shoulders. "I don't know."

Mrs. Nagano was a few inches shorter than Momma and looked as soft as a pillow. She smiled warmly and raised her hand to approximate my height. "Tall girl," she said. I was shorter than she but a half a head taller than Jane. "American food," Mrs. Nagano declared, nodding her head in agreement with herself. "I made Japanese dinner. Too bad you can't stay. You have tea with Jane. I bring to the dining room."

Jane's sisters were also in the kitchen: older sisters I had heard about. Margaret, the eldest, had pushed aside the salt and pepper shakers and the bottle of soy sauce to make room for her books at the kitchen table. She was the studious one, the sister Jane wanted to be like. Dale, the middle sister, was helping Mrs. Nagano prepare the meal. They stopped what they were doing to say "hi".

I knew that Jane had an older brother. "He's in Japan attending school," she said. She put her lips to my ear. "He's really there to meet a girl. My parents want him to marry a girl from Japan. They think the girls in L.A. are too Americanized." Jane looked at me in surprise when I told her that no one could make my brothers live in Korea just to find a girl. "Doesn't your mother care about family tradition?" she asked.

"Oh sure. We're *yangbans*," I said.

"What's that?"

I paused, wondering where to begin. "Never mind, it's too hard to explain."

Jane took me by the arm. "Come on. I'll show you our family shrine."

At the back of the house, in a glassed-in porch overlooking the garden, potted plants had been carefully arranged around a high narrow table. Two lacquered urns stood on the table. "My grandparents' ashes," Jane said softly.

"I'll stay here," I said, backing into the hallway.

Jane bowed to the urns before joining me. "You're not afraid, are you?"

"No," I lied. The thought of having anyone's ashes in the house sent a shiver through me.

"Tea, tea, tea," Mrs. Nagano sang as she pushed through the swinging door. As the aroma of toasted *arare* mixed with the fragrance of camphorwood, I recognized the scent I had associated with Jane. Out on the streets in the sunshine, when we played and perspired, Jane emitted a mystifying and elusive trace of a smell that I was not able to identify. In her house, the odor was strong and pervasive. I suddenly felt like an intruder, barging in, making discoveries that were none of my business.

Mrs. Nagano waited while Mr. Nagano folded his newspaper. He took the cup from her hands. "Aah, the tea smells good," he said as he ran his nose over the cup. "There's nothing like green tea from Japan. Don't you agree, Faye?"

"Uh, well, uh," I stammered. "My mother usually makes coffee."

"Jane tells me your parents are from Korea," he said, as if they should know about Japanese green tea.

"I think the tea we drink is Chinese," I said.

As he nodded, he brought his cup to his lips and blew gently. "Do you speak Korean?" he asked before taking a sip.

"Yes. We speak it at home. My mother's English isn't very good." To keep him from thinking Momma was stupid, I quickly added, "But she speaks Japanese and can read Chinese."

He raised his eyebrows. "Is that so?" He put down his cup. "Where did she learn?"

"In Korea. She had to."

He was quiet for a moment then said, "I see. Did she teach you Japanese?"

I shook my head. That was the last thing in the world she would do. Momma always sounded angry when she spoke Japanese, as if she were punishing each word as it came out of her mouth.

My mouth was dry but I hesitated to bring the teacup to my lips, afraid I would hit my teeth and spill the tea. I helped myself to more *arare*.

Jane took my arm and shook it gently. "I wish you could stay for dinner. My sisters prepared a skit for tonight. We take turns on Friday nights entertaining each other. It's their turn and they said it's going to be funny. Please stay."

"Jane," Mr. Nagano interrupted. "Do not insist. Faye's mother has her reasons and we must respect them. Perhaps your sisters can give their skit now. Call them in and ask your mother to join us."

It was settled. All Papa had to do was say something and it was settled too. Only he would have said all that in half the number of words. On second thought, Papa would not have said any of it. We never entertained one another at home.

The ladies came from the kitchen and took their places. Mrs. Nagano turned a dining chair toward the parlor, brushed off imaginary crumbs, then sat on the edge of the seat. Jane took my hand and we sat on the floor in front of the performers. I began to feel warm with excitement. My skin tingled as I waited in anticipation.

Margaret moved in close behind Dale until no one could see her. As Dale put her hands behind her back, Margaret brought her hands around and tucked them into the pockets of Dale's apron.

How clever, I thought. Margaret's hands were to appear as if they belonged to Dale.

"Ladies and gentlemen. My first number will be 'Home Sweet Home'," Dale announced with Margaret's hands clasped in front of her. Margaret raised her hand to Dale's lips while Dale cleared her throat. As Dale burst into song, Margaret's arms floated in the air like Jeanette McDonald's in *Naughty Marietta*.

I thought it was wonderful and wanted to roll on the floor with delight. "Bad manners," Momma would have said, so I noticed the way Jane laughed and followed her example with a delicate lilting laugh. When Dale ended with ". . . there's no-o place like home," my sides ached from having restrained my laughter. I applauded loudly.

For their second act, the performers exchanged places. Margaret began her monologue. "A child said, 'What is grass?' fetching it to me with full hands . . ." Dale's graceful hand movements accompanied the poem. I became entranced. Momma would recite poetry to me, but always in Korean. ". . . Or I guess it is the handkerchief of the Lord," Margaret was saying. The words gave significance to Momma's work, I thought. She ended with, "And now it seems to me the beautiful uncut hair of graves".

"Oh, Margaret. That was nice," I said. "Did you write it?"

She laughed. "I wish I had. It's from *The Grass,* by Walt Whitman."

Mrs. Nagano said something to Mr. Nagano. I recognized the word *"Chosen-jin"* and knew it was about me. I felt ill at ease. Was it about my ignorance of Walt Whitman? I wondered, or about the way I laughed, or the way I don't drink Japanese green tea? Was it about my being Korean? We had our opinions about the Japanese; perhaps they had formed some about us. Did Jane have to beg her parents for permission to invite me to her house?

Mr. Nagano smiled at Dale and Margaret with approval. "You have improved a great deal. You have developed duplicity into a fine art. It is difficult to tell if you are two acting as one or one acting as two."

The word 'duplicity' opened a crack in my memory. I had tried desperately to forget a secret, tried so hard that I could never forget. I remembered Captain Yamamoto of the Taiyo Maru.

I stood up. "I have to go now," I said.

Everyone looked surprised.

"I have to help my mother," I explained.

Mrs. Nagano nodded. "Wait. I'll wrap some *arare* for you." She started for the kitchen.

"No. No, please. No, thank you," I said.

"No?" She turned back. "Next time, you stay for dinner," she said.

"I'll walk you to the corner," Jane offered.

"Never mind. You stay here. I'll see you on Monday," I said, making my way toward the door.

Not until I was out on the street headed for home did a sense of relief come over me.

The sun was down. I walked rapidly. Someone could be hiding behind the thick stumps of the palm trees, someone like Lucerne Luke. What did Mrs. Nagano say? It was driving me crazy not to know.

In the open space of a vacant lot, I stopped to break off a few clusters of baby-pink roses. The Cecile Brunner bloomed over a neglected heap of dead branches. As I turned away, the hem of my dress hooked itself on a thorn. Several threads broke as I pulled free. Nuts, I muttered to myself. I looked to see if there was anyone around. "Damn!" I said aloud.

I hurried homeward as the twilight breeze stirred the scent of narcissus and wild roses. " 'a scented gift . . .' something . . . something 'dropped.'" I wished I could remember the poem. My birthday was coming soon. I could teach John the skit. Papa would sit in the wing chair. Momma would turn her chair toward the parlor, and Harold could sit where he wanted. Momma could make coffee and Papa would not have to wear a suit. It would be a birthday party and everyone would be polite to one another.

I turned the corner to our street and broke into a trot. *The Grass,* by Walt Whitman. I'll look it up at the library.

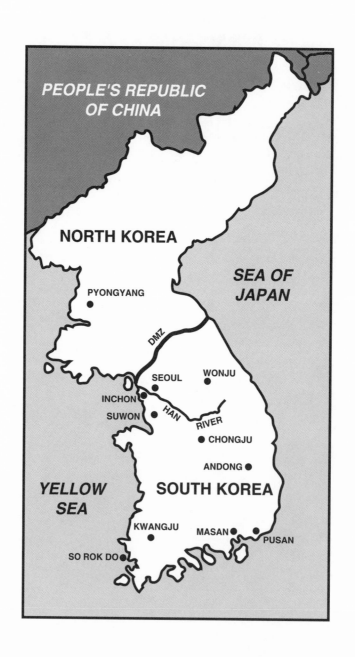

Melpomene Tragedy
From *DICTEE*

THERESA HAK KYUNG CHA

She could be seen sitting in the first few rows. She would be sitting in the first few rows. Closer the better. The more. Better to eliminate presences of others surrounding better view away from that which is left behind far away back behind more for closer view more and more face to face until nothing else sees only this view singular. All dim, gently, slowly until in the dark, the absolute darkness the shadows fade.

She is stretched out as far as the seat allows until her neck rests on the back of the seat. She pulls her coat just below her chin enveloped in one mass before the moving shades, flickering light through the empty window, length of the gardens the trees in perfect a symmetry.

The correct time beyond the windows the correct season the correct forecast. Beyond the empty the correct setting, immobile. Placid. Extreme stillness. Misplaces nothing. Nothing equivalent. Irreplaceable. Not before. Not after.

The submission is complete. Relinquishes even the vision to immobility. Abandons all protests to that which will appear to the sight. About to appear. Forecast. Break. Break, by all means. The illusion that the act of viewing is to make alteration of the visible. The expulsion is immediate. Not one second is lost to the replication of the totality. Total severance of the seen. Incision.

April 19
Seoul, Korea

Dear Mother,

    4. 19. Four Nineteen, April 19th, eighteen years later. Nothing has changed, we are at a standstill. I speak in another tongue now, a second tongue a foreign tongue. All this time we have been away. But nothing has changed. A stand still.

    It is not 6. 25. Six twenty five. June 25th 1950. Not today. Not this day. There are no bombs as you had described them. They do not fall, their shiny brown metallic backs like insects one by one after another.

The population standing before North standing before South for every bird that migrates North for Spring and South for Winter becomes a metaphor for the longing of return. Destination. Homeland.

No woman with child lifting sand bags barriers, all during the night for the battles to come.

There is no destination other than towards yet another refuge from yet another war. Many generations pass and many deceptions in the sequence in the chronology towards the destination.

You knew it would not be in vain. The thirty six years of exile. Thirty-six years multiplied by three hundred and sixty-five days. That one day your country would be your own. This day did finally come. The Japanese were defeated in the world war and were making their descent back to their country. As soon as you heard, you followed South. You carried not a single piece, not a photograph, nothing to evoke your memory, abandoned all to see your nation freed.

From another epic another history. From the missing narrative. From the multitude of narratives. Missing. From the chronicles. For another telling for other recitations.

Our destination is fixed on the perpetual motion of search. Fixed in its perpetual exile. Here at my return in eighteen years, the war is not ended. We fight the same war. We are inside the same struggle seeking the same destination. We are severed in Two by an abstract enemy an invisible enemy under the title of liberators who have conveniently named the severance, Civil War. Cold War. Stalemate.

I am in the same crowd, the same coup, the same revolt, nothing has changed. I am inside the demonstration I am locked inside the crowd and carried in its movement. The voices ring shout one voice then many voices they are waves they echo I am moving in the direction the only one direction with the voices the only direction. The other movement towards us it increases steadily their direction their only direction our mutual destination towards the other against the other. Move.

I feel the tightening of the crowd body to body now the voices rising thicker I hear the break the single motion tearing the break left of me right of me the silence of the other direction advance before . . . They are breaking now, their sounds, not new, you have heard them, so familiar to you now could you ever forget them not in your dreams, the consequences of the sound the breaking. The air is made visible with smoke it grows spreads without control we are hidden inside the whiteness the greyness reduced to parts, reduced to separation. Inside an arm lifts above the head in deliberate gesture and disappears into the thick white from which slowly the legs of another bent at the knee hit the ground the entire body on its left side. The stinging, it slices the air it enters thus I lose direction the sky is a haze running the streets emptied I fell no one saw me I walk. Anywhere. In tears the air stagnant continues to sting I am crying the sky remnant the gas smoke absorbed the sky I am crying. The streets covered with chipped bricks and debris. Because. I see the frequent pairs of shoes thrown sometimes a single pair among the rocks they had carried. Because. I cry wail torn shirt lying I step among them. No trace of them. Except for the blood. Because. Step among them the blood that will not erase with the rain on the pavement that was walked upon like the stones where they fell had fallen. Because. Remain dark the stains not wash away. Because.

I follow the crying crowd their voices among them their singing their voices unceasing the empty street.

There is no surrendering you are chosen to fail to be martyred to shed blood to be set an example one who has defied one who has chosen to defy and was to be set an example to be martyred an animal useless betrayer to the cause to the welfare to peace to harmony to progress.

It is 1962 eighteen years ago same month same day all over again. I am eleven years old. Running to the front door, Mother, you are holding my older brother pleading with him not to go out to the demonstration. You are threatening him, you are begging to him. He has on his school uniform, as all the other students representing their schools in the demonstration. You are pulling at him you stand before the door. He argues with you he pushes you away. You use all your force, all that you have. He is prepared to join the student demonstration outside. You can hear the gun shots. They are directed at anyone.

Coming home from school there are cries in all the streets. The mounting of shouts from every direction from the crowds arm in arm. The students. I saw them, older than us, men and women held to each other. They walk into the *others* who wait in *their* uniforms. Their shouts reach a crescendo as they approach nearer to the *other side.* Cries resisting cries to move forward. Orders, permission to use force against the students, have been dispatched. To be caught and beaten with sticks, and for others, shot, remassed, and carted off. They fall they bleed they die. They are thrown into gas into the crowd to be squelched. The police the soldiers anonymous they duplicate themselves, multiply in number invincible they execute their role. Further than their home further than their mother father their brother sister further than their children is the execution of their role their given identity further than their own line of blood.

You do not want to lose him, my brother, to be killed as the many others by now, already, you say you understand, you plead all the same they are killing any every one. You withstand his strength you call me to run to Uncle's house and call the tutor. Run. Run hard. Out the gate. Turn the corner. All down hill to reach Uncle's house. I know the two German shepherd dogs would be guarding one at each side, chained to their house they drag behind them barking. I must brave them, close my eyes and run between them. I call the tutor from the yard, above the sounds of the dogs barking. Several students look out of the windows. They are in hiding from the street, from their homes where they are being searched for. We run back to the house the tutor is ahead of me, when I enter the house the tutor is standing in front of him. You cannot go out he says you cannot join the D-e-m-o. *De. Mo.* A word, two sounds. Are you insane the tutor tells him they are killing any student in uniform. Anybody. What will you defend yourself with he asks. You, my brother, you protest your cause, you say you are willing to die. Dying is part of it. If it must be. He hits you. The tutor slaps you and your face turns red you stand silently against the door your head falls. My brother. You are all the rest all the others are you. You fell you died you gave your life. That day. It rained. It rained for several days. It rained more and more times. After it was all over. You were heard. Your victory mixed with rain falling from the sky for many days afterwards. I heard that the rain does not erase the blood fallen on the ground. I heard from the adults, the blood stains still. Year after year it rained. The stone pavement stained where you fell still remains dark.

Eighteen years pass. I am here for the first time in eighteen years, Mother. We left here in this memory still fresh, still new. I speak another tongue, a second tongue. This is how distant I am. From then. From that time. They take me back they have taken me back so precisely now exact to the hour to the day to the season in the smoke mist in the drizzle I turn the corner and there is no one. No one facing me. The street is rubble. I put my palm on my eyes to rub them, then I let them cry freely. Two school children with their book bags appear from nowhere with their arms around each other. Their white kerchief, their white shirt uniform, into a white residue of gas, crying.

I pass a second curve on the road. You soldiers appear in green. Always the green uniforms the patches of camouflage. Trees camouflage your green trucks you blend with nature the trees hide you you cannot be seen behind the guns no one sees you they have hidden you. You sit you recline on the earth next to the buses you wait hours days making visible your presence. Waiting for the false move that will conduct you to mobility to action. There is but one move, the only one and it will be false. It will be absolute. Their mistake. Your boredom waiting would not have been in vain. They will move they will have to move and you will move on them. Among them. You stand on your tanks your legs spread apart how many degrees exactly your hand on your rifle. Rifle to ground the same angle as your right leg. You wear a beret in the 90 degree sun there is no shade at the main gate you are fixed you cannot move you dare not move. You are your post you are your vow in nomine patris you work your post you are your nation defending your country from subversive infiltration from your own countrymen. Your skin scorched as dark as your uniform as you stand you don't hear. You hear nothing. You hear no one. You are hidden you see only the prey they do not see you they cannot. You who are hidden you who move in the crowds as you would in the trees you who move inside them you close your eyes to the piercing the breaking the flooding pools bath their shadow memory as they fade from you your own blood your own flesh as tides ebb, through you through and through.

> You are this
> close to this much
> close to it.
> Extend arms apart just so, that much. Open
> the thumb and the index finger just so.
> the thumb and the index finger just so.
> That much
> you want to kill the time that is oppression itself.
> Time that delivers not. Not you, not from its
> expanse, without dimension, defined not by its

limits. Airless, thin, not a thought rising even
that there are things to be forgotten. Effortless. It
should be effortless. Effort less ly
the closer it is the closer to it. Away and against
time ing. A step forward from back. Backing
out. Backing off. Off periphery extended. From
imaginary to bordering on division. At least
somewhere in numerals in relation to the
equator, at least all the maps have them at least
walls are built between them at least the militia
uniforms and guns are in abeyance of them.
Imaginary borders. Un imaginable boundaries.

Suffice more than that. SHE opposes Her.
SHE against her.
More than that. Refuses to become discard
decomposed oblivion.
From its memory dust escapes the particles still
material still respiration move. Dead air stagnant
water still exhales mist. Pure hazard igniting flaming
itself with the slightest of friction like firefly. The loss
that should burn. Not burn, illuminate. Illuminate by
losing. Lighten by loss.
Yet it loses not.
    Her name. First the whole name. Then syllable by
syllable counting each inside the mouth. Make them
rise they rise repeatedly without ever making visible
lips never open to utter them.
Mere names only names without the image not *hers*
hers alone not the whole of *her* and even the image
would not be the entire
her fraction *her* invalid that inhabits that rise
voluntarily like flint
pure hazard dead substance to fire.
    Others anonymous *her* detachments take her place. Anonymous against
her. Suffice that should be nation against nation suffice that should have been
divided into two which once was whole. Suffice that should diminish human
breaths only too quickly. Suffice Melpomene. Nation against nation multiplied
nations against nations against themselves. Own. Repels her rejects her expels
her from *her* own. Her own is, in, of, through, all others, *hers*. Her own who
is offspring and mother, Demeter and Sibyl.
    Violation of *her* by giving name to the betrayal, all possible names, inter-
changeable names, to remedy, to justify the violation. Of *her*. Own. Unbegot-
ten. Name. Name only. Name without substance. The everlasting, Forever.
Without end.
    Deceptions all the while. No devils here. Nor gods. Labyrinth of decep-
tions. No enduring time. Self-devouring. Devouring itself. Perishing all the
while. Insect that eats its own mate.

Suffice Melpomene, arrest the screen en-trance flickering hue from behind cast shadow silhouette from back not visible. Like ice. Metal. Glass. Mirror. Receives none admits none.

Arrest the machine that purports to employ democracy but rather causes the successive refraction of *her* none other than her own. Suffice Melpomene, to exorcize from this mouth the name the words the memory of severance through this act by this very act to utter one, *Her* once, Her to utter at once, *She* without the separate act of uttering.

Railroad Standard Time

FRANK CHIN

"This was your grandfather's," Ma said. I was twelve, maybe fourteen years old when Grandma died. Ma put it on the table. The big railroad watch, Elgin. Nineteen-jewel movement. American made. Lever set. Stem wound. Glass face-cover. Railroad standard all the way. It ticked on the table between stacks of dirty dishes and cold food. She brought me in here to the kitchen, always to the kitchen to loose her thrills and secrets, as if the sound of running water and breathing the warm soggy ghosts of stale food, floating grease, old spices, ever comforted her, as if the kitchen was a paradise for conspiracy, sanctuary for us *juk sing* Chinamen from the royalty of pure-talking China-born Chinese, old, mourning, and belching in the other rooms of my dead grandmother's last house. Here, private, to say in Chinese, "This was your grandfather's," as if now that her mother had died and she'd been up all night long, not weeping, tough and lank, making coffee and tea and little foods for the brokenhearted family in her mother's kitchen, Chinese would be easier for me to understand. As if my mother would say all the important things of the soul and blood to her son, me, only in Chinese from now on. Very few people spoke the language at me the way she did. She chanted a spell up over me that conjured the meaning of what she was saying in the shape of old memories come to call. Words I'd never heard before set me at play in familiar scenes new to me, and ancient.

She lay the watch on the table, eased it slowly off her fingertips down to the tabletop without a sound. She didn't touch me, but put it down and held her hands in front of her like a bridesmaid holding an invisible bouquet and stared at the watch. As if it were talking to her, she looked hard at it, made faces at it, and did not move or answer the voices of the old, calling her from other rooms, until I picked it up.

A two-driver, high stepping locomotive ahead of a coal tender and baggage car, on double track between two semaphores showing a stop signal was engraved on the back.

"Your grandfather collected railroad watches," Ma said. "This one is the best." I held it in one hand and then the other, hefted it, felt out the meaning of "the best," words that rang of meat and vegetables, oils, things we touched, smelled, squeezed, washed, and ate, and I turned the big cased thing over several times. "Grandma gives it to you now," she said. It was big in my hand. Gold. A little greasy. Warm.

I asked her what her father's name had been, and the manic heat of her all-night burnout seemed to go cold and congeal. "Oh," she finally said, "it's one of those Chinese names I . . ." in English, faintly from another world, woozy and her throat and nostrils full of bubbly sniffles, the solemnity of the moment gone, the watch in my hand turned to cheap with the mumbling of a few awful

English words. She giggled herself down to nothing but breath and moving lips. She shuffled backward, one step at a time, fox trotting dreamily backward, one hand dragging on the edge of the table, wobbling the table, rattling the dishes, spilling cold soup. Back down one side of the table, she dropped her butt a little with each step then muscled it back up. There were no chairs in the kitchen tonight. She knew, but still she looked. So this dance and groggy mumbling about the watch being no good, in strange English, like an Indian medicine man in a movie.

I wouldn't give it back or trade it for another out of the collection. This one was mine. No other. It had belonged to my grandfather. I wore it braking on the Southern Pacific, though it was two jewels short of new railroad standard and an outlaw watch that could get me fired. I kept it on me, arrived at my day-off courthouse wedding to its time, wore it as a railroad relic/family heirloom/grin-bringing affectation when I was writing background news in Seattle, reporting from the shadows of race riots, grabbing snaps for the 11:00 P.M., timing today's happenings with a nineteenth-century escapement. (Ride with me, Grandmother.) I was wearing it on my twenty-seventh birthday, the Saturday I came home to see my son asleep in the back of a strange station wagon, and Sarah inside, waving, shouting through an open window, "Goodbye, Daddy," over and over.

I stood it. Still and expressionless as some good Chink, I watched Barbara drive off, leave me, like some blonde white goddess going home from the jungle with her leather patches and briar pipe sweetheart writer and my kids. I'll learn to be a sore loser. I'll learn to hit people in the face. I'll learn to cry when I'm hurt and go for the throat instead of being polite and worrying about being obnoxious to people walking out of my house with my things, taking my kids away. I'll be more than quiet, embarrassed. I won't be likable anymore.

I hate my novel about a Chinatown mother like mine dying, now that Ma's dead. But I'll keep it. I hated after reading *Father and Glorious Descendant, Fifth Chinese Daughter, The House That Tai Ming Built.* Books scribbled up by a sad legion of snobby autobiographical Chinatown saps all on their own. Christians who never heard of each other, hardworking people who sweat out the exact same Chinatown book, the same cunning "Confucius says" joke, just like me. I kept it then and I'll still keep it. Part cookbook, memories of Mother in the kitchen slicing meat paper-thin with a cleaver. Mumbo jumbo about spices and steaming. The secret of Chinatown rice. The hands come down toward the food. The food crawls with culture. The thousand-year-old living Chinese meat makes dinner a safari into the unknown, a blood ritual. Food pornography. Black magic. Between the lines, I read a madman's detailed description of the preparation of shrunken heads. I never wrote to mean anything more than word fun with the food Grandma cooked at home. Chinese food. I read a list of what I remembered eating at my grandmother's table and knew I'd always be known by what I ate, that we come from a hungry tradition. Slop eaters following the wars on all fours. Weed cuisine and mud gravy in the shadow of corpses. We plundered the dust for fungus. Buried things. Seeds plucked out of the wind to feed a race of lace-boned skinnys, in high-school English, become transcendental Oriental art to make the dyke-ish spinster teacher cry. We always come to fake art and write the Chinatown book like bugs come to fly in the light. I hate my book now that Ma's dead, but I'll keep it. I know she's not the woman I wrote up like my mother, and dead, in a book that was like everybody else's Chinatown book. Part word map of Chinatown San Francisco, shop to shop down Grant Avenue. Food again. The wind sucks the shops out and you breathe warm roast ducks dripping fat, hooks into the neck, through the head, out an eye. Stacks of iced fish, blue and fluorescent pink in the neon. The air is thin soup, sharp up the nostrils.

All mention escape from Chinatown into the movies. But we all forgot to mention how stepping off the streets into a faceful of Charlie Chaplin or a Western on a ripped and stained screen that became caught in the grip of winos breathing in unison in their sleep and billowed in and out, that shuddered when cars went by . . . we all of us Chinamans watched our own MOVIE ABOUT ME! I learned how to box watching movies shot by James Wong Howe. Cartoons were our nursery rhymes. Summers inside those neon-and-stucco downtown hole-in-the-wall Market Street Frisco movie houses blowing three solid hours of full-color seven-minute cartoons was school, was rows and rows of Chinamans learning English in a hurry from Daffy Duck.

When we ate in the dark and recited the dialogue of cartoon mice and cats out loud in various tones of voice with our mouths full, we looked like people singing hymns in church. We learned to talk like everybody in America. Learned to need to be afraid to stay alive, keeping moving. We learned to run, to be cheerful losers, to take a sudden pie in the face, talk American with a lot of giggles. To us a cartoon is a desperate situation. Of the movies, cartoons were the high art of our claustrophobia. They understood us living too close to each other. How, when you're living too close to too many people, you can't wait for one thing more without losing your mind. Cartoons were a fine way out of waiting in Chinatown around the rooms. Those of our Chinamans who every now and then break a reverie with, "Thank you, Mighty Mouse," mean it. Other folks thank Porky Pig, Snuffy Smith, Woody Woodpecker.

The day my mother told me I was to stay home from Chinese school one day a week starting today, to read to my father and teach him English while he was captured in total paralysis from a vertebra in the neck on down, I stayed away from cartoons. I went to a matinee in a white neighborhood looking for the MOVIE ABOUT ME and was the only Chinaman in the house. I liked the way Peter Lorre ran along non-stop routine hysterical. I came back home with Peter Lorre. I turned out the lights in Pa's room. I put a candle on the dresser and wheeled Pa around in his chair to see me in front of the dresser mirror, reading Edgar Allan Poe out loud to him in the voice of Peter Lorre by candlelight.

The old men in the Chinatown books are all fixtures for Chinese ceremonies. All the same. Loyal filial children kowtow to the old and whiff food laid out for the dead. The dead eat the same as the living but without the sauces. White food. Steamed chicken. Rice we all remember as children scrambling down to the ground, to all fours and bonking our heads on the floor, kowtowing to a dead chicken.

My mother and aunts said nothing about the men of the family except they were weak. I like to think my grandfather was a good man. Even the kiss-ass steward service, I like to think he was tough, had a few laughs and ran off with his pockets full of engraved watches. Because I never knew him, not his name, nor anything about him, except a photograph of him as a young man with something of my mother's face in his face, and a watch chain across his vest. I kept his watch in good repair and told everyone it would pass to my son someday, until the day the boy was gone. Then I kept it like something of his he'd loved and had left behind, saving it for him maybe, to give to him when he was a man. But I haven't felt that in a long time.

The watch ticked against my heart and pounded my chest as I went too fast over bumps in the night and the radio on, on an all-night run downcoast, down country, down old Highway 99, Interstate 5. I ran my grandfather's time down past road signs that caught a gleam in my headlights and came at me out of the night with the names of forgotten high school girlfriends, BELLEVUE KIRK-LAND, ROBERTA GERBER, AURORA CANBY, and sang with the radio to Jonah and Sarah in Berkeley, my Chinatown in Oakland and Frisco, to raise the dead. Ride with me, Grandfather, this is your grandson the ragmouth, called Tam-pax, the burned scarred boy, called Barbecue, going to San Francisco to bury my mother, your daughter, and spend Chinese New Year's at home. When we were sitting down and into our dinner after Grandma's funeral, and ate in front of the table set with white food for the dead, Ma said she wanted no white food and money burning after her funeral. Her sisters were there. Her sisters took charge of her funeral and the dinner afterwards. The dinner would most likely be in a Chinese restaurant in Frisco. Nobody had these dinners at home anymore. I wouldn't mind people having dinner at my place after my fu-neral, but no white food.

The whiz goes out of the tires as their roll bites into the steel grating of the Carquinez Bridge. The noise of the engine groans and echoes like a bomber in flight through the steel roadway. Light from the water far below shines through the grate, and I'm driving high, above a glow. The voice of the tires hums a shrill rubber screechy mosquito hum that vibrates through the chassis and frame of the car into my meatless butt, into my tender asshole, my pelvic bones, the roots of my teeth. Over the Carquinez Bridge to CROCKETT MAR-TINEZ closer to home, roll the tires of Ma's Chevy, my car now, carrying me up over the water southwest toward rolls of fog. The fat man's coming home on a sneaky breeze. Dusk comes a drooly mess of sunlight, a slobber of cheap pawnshop gold, a slow building heat across the water, all through the milky air through the glass of the window into the closed atmosphere of a driven car, into one side of my bomber's face. A bomber, flying my mother's car into the unknown charted by the stars and the radio, feels the coming of some old night song climbing hand over hand, bass notes plunking as steady and shady as reminiscence to get on my nerves one stupid beat after the other crossing the high rhythm six-step of the engine. I drive through the shadows of the bridge's steel structure all over the road. Fine day. I've been on the road for sixteen hours straight down the music of Seattle, Spokane, Salt Lake, Sacramento, Los Angeles, and Wolfman Jack lurking in odd hours of darkness, at peculiar alti-tudes of darkness, favoring the depths of certain Oregon valleys and heat and moonlight of my miles. And I'm still alive. Country'n'western music for the night road. It's pure white music. Like "The Star-Spangled Banner," it was the first official American music out of school into my jingling earbones sung by sighing white big tits in front of the climbing promise of FACE and Every Good Boy Does Fine chalked on the blackboard.

She stood up singing, one hand cupped in the other as if to catch drool slipping off her lower lip. Our eyes scouted through her blouse to elastic straps, lacy stuff, circular stitching, buckles, and in the distance, finally some skin. The color of her skin spread through the stuff of her blouse like melted butter through bread nicely to our tongues and was warm there. She sat flopping them on the keyboard as she breathed, singing "Home on the Range" over her shoulder, and pounded the tune out with her palms. The lonesome prairie was nothing but her voice, some hearsay country she stood up to sing *a capella* out of her. Simple music you can count. You can hear the words clear. The music's run through Clorox and Simonized, beating so insistently right and regular that you feel to sing it will deodorize you, make you clean. The hardhat hit parade. I listen to it a lot on the road. It's that get-outta-town beat and tune that makes me go.

Mrs. Morales was her name. Aurora Morales. The music teacher us boys liked to con into singing for us. Come-on opera, we wanted from her, not them Shirley Temple tunes the girls wanted to learn, but big notes, high long ones up from the navel that drilled through plaster and steel and skin and meat for bone marrow and electric wires on one long titpopping breath.

This is how I come home, riding a mass of spasms and death throes, warm and screechy inside, itchy, full of ghostpiss, as I drive right past what's left of Oakland's dark wooden Chinatown and dark streets full of dead lettuce and trampled carrot tops, parallel all the time in line with the tracks of the Western Pacific and Southern Pacific railroads.

Batista and Tania Aparecida Djapan
From *Through the Arc of the Rain Forest*

KAREN TEI YAMASHITA

Change came to Kazumasa Ishimaru as suddenly as I had come into his life. Kazumasa realized that as long as he had me for a companion, he would never be alone in life. He would always share the adventure of life with his ball, and with that strong sense of support, Kazumasa stepped away from all his years with the Japanese railroads and took the first flight out of Haneda for what he believed might be a distant but familiar place, São Paulo, Brazil.

Kazumasa had seen an NHK documentary about the Japanese in Brazil. Most of the Japanese who had immigrated there seemed to live in a quaint clump in an urban setting much like Tokyo. Then there were those who lived in the countryside growing Chinese cabbage, daikon and tea. But it was not just the idea of gravitating toward other Japanese outside of Japan nor even that he had seen just about everything there was to see in Japan. Something drew Kazumasa and me irresistibly to Brazil.

Kazumasa had a cousin who had been traveling in South America after passing his college examinations and before entering college. This cousin had stopped in Rio de Janeiro with his backpack and sat out on the beach at Ipanema. He sat there all morning and afternoon and evening, the balmy breeze caressing his thick hair and the sand and salt air peppering his face and arms. The bronzed women and men sauntered by, wet, warm and carefree, and Kazumasa's cousin began to weep. He sent his regrets to the University of Keio and never returned to Japan.

Kazumasa's mother kept in touch with her nephew in Brazil because Brazil seemed to be the sort of place that might absorb someone who was different. Not that her son Kazumasa had not done extremely well for himself in Japan. Kazumasa was, after all, the man who had saved hundreds, perhaps thousands, of lives by his painstaking and accurate calculations of track deterioration. But Kazumasa's mother worried about her son's happiness, about arranging a happy marriage, about the future and the nature of true happiness. While others in the family sneered at her nephew's decision to abandon his studies at Keio for an uncertain future in Brazil, Kazumasa's mother privately praised his courage. It was she who noticed me hanging sadly over Kazumasa's nose and realized that her son's possibilities for happiness in Japan had exhausted the limits of those tiny islands. "Your cousin Hiroshi, remember?" She pulled the address out of a small notebook. "He lives in São Paulo now. Go see him."

Soon after arriving in São Paulo, Kazumasa and I got a job with the São Paulo Municipal Subway System. Hiroshi had arranged the interview and had pulled some strings with somebody who knew somebody else, but considering our background and experience in the field, the São Paulo Municipal Subway System was more than fortunate to retain our services. We also began to get freelance jobs in other states to check out their railways. Once again, Kazumasa and I had the opportunity to go out on the road. Unlike Japan, Brazil was massive, inefficient, encumbered by bureaucracy, graft and poverty. Kazumasa took me, his precision ball, into this tropical and elusive mess like a beachcomber with a metal detector on Coney Island on the Fourth of July. I did not, of course, complain. I was as oblivious to the heat, the humidity, the insects and the stink of sweating humanity as I was to graft and poverty. And Kazumasa met this sudden change in our lives with optimism and resilience; anything was better than that circular Tokyo train.

Kazumasa took his cue from his cousin Hiroshi who seemed nonchalant about the mess and calmly walked Kazumasa through the bureaucratic arrangements of renting a comfortable apartment with a maid on the fourteenth floor of a high-rise, not too far from the subway offices.

Kazumasa was drawn to the sunlight flooding his apartment through the large windows. We stood there together in the window looking out, a prism of light spinning off my shiny surface. Kazumasa looked down at the scenes on the street and in the tenements below. The activity down there was a clutter of street people, children and dogs, women hanging wash from their windows, lovers snatching caresses in the shadows, workers restoring brick walls and tile roofs, men and women playing cards and drinking, dancing and swearing, loving and fighting. As the days passed, Kazumasa found himself observing one scene in particular—the back porch at one end of a tenement house. He found that by focusing beyond me onto the continuing saga of what he soon came to think of as "his" back porch, he began to feel a special intimacy with this new country, to share his cousin's gentle but continuing passion.

• • •

Kazumasa's back porch happened to belong to Batista Djapan, who had rented the room and the porch it opened onto for the past five years. Batista worked in a document processing service as a clerk-runner, which the Brazilians call *despachantes*. Batista caught buses and subways and scurried all over the city with a vinyl briefcase filled with documents needing signatures on as many as ten pages of their forms. He always had a little extra money and a joke to bribe a slow bureaucrat into signing something at the bottom of the bureaucratic stack. Batista handled business for lawyers, small companies and individuals. He knew all the side doors, how far the laws could be bent before they would break, and what anyone from a clerk to a *delegado* might consider enough to buy a beer. Batista considered his business a craft by which he survived, paid his rent, gave Tania Aparecida and her mother some spending money, and had a few coins for a *cafézinho* in the morning and a beer after work.

Batista was a man with a joke on the tip of his tongue, a penchant for gossip, cynical about politics, passionate about soccer, and painfully jealous of Tania Aparecida. He could turn a phrase, sing a song, play the guitar. He was Catholic, cursed the priests and practiced Candomblé. He was an observer of the philosophy of life in the tropics summed up by the statement "There is no sin below the equator." Despite the scarcity of food in the cement metropolis, he continued to live as if mangoes and papayas could be had from the trees, fish from the rivers and manioc from the red earth, all in the abundance of a continuing Eden on earth. Batista was a mellow and handsome mixture of African, Indian and Portuguese, born on a farm near Brasilia in Goiás and raised in the urban outskirts of São Paulo. He was childish and heroic, genuine and simple. He was the sort of man every Brazilian knew and sensed in their hearts.

Batista's wife, Tania Aparecida, came and went as she pleased. When she did not live with Batista, she lived with her mother a few tenements down the street. Her coming and going, however, did not please Batista, who could be seen dragging his wife home at some odd hour of the night or prodding her toward her kitchen with the end of a baguette at dinnertime. "When a man comes home at night, he should have a supper waiting! I'm nearly dead from hunger."

"I took Mama to the movies, poor thing. It was a scary movie. She didn't want to be alone at night, Batista," Tania Aparecida protested.

"It's your fault for taking her to the movies in the first place!"

"Oh, Batista," Tania Aparecida cooed. "You would have liked this movie."

Batista relented, "What was the movie about?"

She grabbed the baguette and jammed it in Batista's stomach. "So you're hungry are you?" she taunted and scurried up the stairs.

"Crazy woman!" Batista yelled after her.

Batista and Tania Aparecida were passionately in love, but they were also always fighting. They had no children, and Batista continually accused Tania Aparecida of never being home long enough to have children in the first place.

Every day, Kazumasa and I peered down from our window on the fourteenth floor to observe Batista's life. We saw Tania Aparecida in the afternoons, washing bundles of clothing and hanging them to dry on the lines on the sunny veranda. We saw Batista struggle out on Sunday mornings, heavy with a hangover and cursing his team and that idiot player Pedro-Paulo who overshot the goal on an easy penalty kick. We saw Batista and Tania Aparecida dance on the veranda at night and scream at each other in the morning. We saw Tania's corpulent mother hit Batista on the head with the side of her bag. We saw everything—the friends, the good times and the bad—but one day Kazumasa and I saw Batista arrive, balancing his vinyl briefcase on his head and carefully carrying in the palms of his hands a single pigeon.

Batista had found the wounded pigeon on the sidewalk as he stepped off the bus on his way home. The pigeon trembled helplessly as people scurried in both directions without noticing the grey thing on the pavement. Batista instinctively scooped the pigeon up from the ground just before a bicycle would have pressed its delicate head into the concrete.

At home, Batista examined the pigeon carefully, taped its ailing foot and tucked it to bed in a box in a warm place above his refrigerator. In the morning he remembered to buy a bag of birdseed and to invest in a small cage. As the days passed, the pigeon grew stronger, hopped around Batista's veranda and took short running flights to the window sill. Soon it was strong enough to fly again, but it did not leave Batista's veranda.

After awhile, Tania Aparecida would come to take down her wash only to find that the pigeon had managed to seat itself on the clothesline and oblige her labor by soiling her clean sheets. "If you don't put that pigeon away, I'm going to cook it for dinner!" she would yell at Batista, but Tania Aparecida did not mean it. She had noticed a change in Batista since the pigeon had come to live with them. Batista no longer tarried so long in the bar after work, but hurried back to their veranda to look after the pigeon. He was always occupied now with the pigeon, giving it a bath, grooming it, mixing some new concoction of vitamins and meal for its supper.

"Isn't this the most beautiful pigeon you have ever seen?" he boasted to Tania Aparecida as if it were his own child. That was it. Tania Aparecida brushed aside a tear. The pigeon was the child they could never seem to have. What a difference a simple bird made to their lives now.

As the days passed, Batista became more and more involved in caring for his pigeon. He wandered into bookstores looking for books about pigeons. He spent evenings in the city library reading everything he could find about pigeons. He searched out and spoke with other people who cared for pigeons, observed their methods and listened to their ideas. He became so immersed in the study of pigeons that Tania Aparecida, who had welcomed the change in him, began to have feelings of envy. Occasionally Batista remembered his old habit of dragging Tania Aparecida home from her mother's, but now he seemed to do it as an afterthought, without the old conviction. Batista, once an avid conversationalist about soccer and women and politics, could now only think, live and talk about pigeons.

One day, it became more than Tania Aparecida could take. Batista had forgotten her birthday and spent the day with a fellow pigeon enthusiast. Tania Aparecida stomped down the steps of the veranda with Batista's pigeon in a cage. She took the pigeon on a bus to the end of the line in Santo Amaro and tossed the pigeon out of the cage. That was the end of her competition, she thought crossly. She was ready to have the old Batista back.

Tania Aparecida took the long bus trip home with a muddled sense of relief and fear. By the time she got off the bus and walked up the stairs to the veranda, she was remorseful. It was only a poor pigeon after all. She met Batista at the bottom of the steps and cried out her apologies. She had really meant no harm. She had been jealous.

Batista looked quizzically at Tania Aparecida and led her up the stairs to the sunny veranda, where the pigeon was flapping around in a pan of bath water after a long flight from Santo Amaro. The sputtering water around the pigeon seemed to bathe it in a soft mist of colored light. It looked at Tania Aparecida forgivingly, nodding its head from side to side. She wrapped her arms around Batista and wept with shame.

"It's all right, Tania." Batista was not angry. "I haven't been able to summon the courage to do what you did. I mean,"—he kissed her lightly on the forehead—"to try the pigeon out in flight. I didn't have enough faith that it would return. Now we know. It is a good carrier pigeon!" Batista was joyful.

From that time on, Batista and Tania Aparecida and the pigeon went everywhere together on the weekends. He would put the pigeon in its cage and she would would pack a lunch. They would board buses and head to the seaside or travel to the hills and fish in the streams. Sometimes they would visit Tania's cousins in the rural interior and spend the day picking fruit and chewing sugar cane. And from every place they went, they sent the pigeon flying home to the tenement veranda in the city.

Batista then got the idea to time the pigeon's flights, making note of the time he let the pigeon free, while Tania's mother and the neighborhood children waited excitedly with a watch on the veranda at home. Batista always sent a message—a riddle or joke—home with the pigeon which the children clamored around to read with laughter and wonder. As the flights became a regular event, Kazumasa could see on any Saturday or Sunday the children gather from every end of the tenement to read the notes brought by the pigeon. For some reason, no matter how simple nor how silly, the messages brought by the pigeon were more wonderful and exciting than a voice on a telephone.

• • •

So it was that Kazumasa and I had come to live in Brazil. Kazumasa had no idea at the time how this simple pastime of staring out his window on the tenement scene below might affect his own future. These things I knew with simple clairvoyance. I also knew that strange events far to our north and deep in the Amazon Basin, events as insignificant as those in a tiny northeastern coastal town wedged tightly between multicolored dunes, and events as prestigious as those of the great economic capital of the world, New York, would each cast forth an invisible line, shall I say, leading us to a place they would all call the Matacão.

The Valley of the Dead Air

GARY PAK

The day after Jacob Hookano died, that old hermit who had lived at the very end of Waiola Valley, a bad air from the ocean came in and lingered over the land. The residents of the valley thought that a Kona wind had brought in that rotten smell from the mangroves and mud flats of the coastal area, and they waited impatiently for another wind to take the smell away.

As Leimomi Vargas said succinctly, "Jus' like old Jacob wen fut and dah fut jus' stayin' around."

And stay around it did, for weeks. There seemed no end. The residents prayed for that new wind to blow the obstinate smell away, but no wind came and the air became stagnant and more foul as if the valley were next to an ancient cesspool that had suddenly ruptured after centuries of accumulations. The malodor permeated the wood of the houses, it tainted the fresh clothes hung to dry, and it entered the pores of everyone, making young and old smell bad even after a good scrubbing. The love lives of the residents became nonexistent.

"We gotta do somet'ing 'bout dis hauna," Joseph Correa complained. The retired sewers worker from the City and County sat on a chair under the eaves of an old abandoned store that fronted the main road.

"Yeah, but what?" said Bobby Ignacio. He turned his gaunt, expressionless face towards Correa, then returned to his meditation of birds eating the ripened fruits of a lichee tree across the road.

"You know, Bobby," Correa said in a voice shaded ominously, "I betchu dah gov'ment is behind all dis. Look how long dis hauna stay heah. Long time already. If was jus' one nat'ral t'ing, dah wind already blow 'em away."

Ignacio, a truck farmer up the road in the valley, spat disconsolately into the wild grass growing on the side of the store.

"But I tell you dis, Bobby. I betchu one day dah gov'ment goin' come down heah and dey goin' brag how dey can take dis hauna away. And den they *goin'* take 'em away. But I betchu little while aftah dat, dey goin' come back and try ask us for do dem one favor. You watch." Correa nodded his head. "No miss."

The farmer shrugged his narrow shoulders. "But you know what everybody saying?"

"Who everybody?"

"Everybody."

"So what everybody saying?"

"Dey saying old Jacob dah one doing all dis."

The old retiree nervously stretched out his tired legs, his head twitched a few times, then he looked out languidly towards the mango trees across the road.

"I nevah had no problems with old Jacob," Correa said weakly. "I was always good to him. I nevah talk stink 'bout him or anything li' dat."

The smell persisted, and somehow it infected the rich, famous soil of the valley. The earth began to emit a terrible odor of rotten fish. While plowing one corner of his sweet potato field, Tats Sugimura uncovered a hole full of fish scales and fish bones. He didn't think anything of it until his wife complained to him later how fishy everything smelled. The bad smell of the valley had numbed his nose so Tats couldn't smell anything worth shit now. His wife, on the other hand, had a super-sensitive nose and she often would sniff the air in her kitchen and know exactly what the Rodriguez family was cooking a quarter of a mile down the road.

"Tats, you wen dump some rotten fish around here or what?" she said. Sugimura shook his head. He wasn't the talking type, even with his wife. "Den whas dat stink smell?"

He thought of telling her about the fish scales and bones, then he thought that perhaps a bunch of stray cats had had a feast in that corner of his field. The fish were probably tilapia or catfish the cats had caught in the nearby stream. But he was tired from working all day under the hot sun and in the stifling humid air and he didn't have the energy to describe to his wife what he had seen. The fish scales and fish bones were unimportant, and he shrugged his thin, wiry shoulders and said nothing.

But something bad was in the soil. When Tats and the other sweet potato farmers began harvesting their produce a few days later, they found abnormally small sweet potatoes, some having the peculiar shape of a penis.

"How dah hell we goin' sell dis kine produce?" complained Earl Fritzhugh, a part-Hawaiian sweet potato farmer. "Dey goin' laugh at us. So small. And look at dis one. Look like one prick!"

"Somet'ing strange goin' on in dis valley," said Darryl Mineda, another farmer. "Get dah story goin' around dat old Jacob doin' all dis to get back."

"Get back at who?" Fritzhugh asked irately.

"At us."

Fritzhugh looked at Mineda incredulously. "At us? Why dat old Hawaiian like get back at us fo'? He wen live by himself. Nobody wen bother him."

Mineda shook his head. "Somebody tol' me all dah land in dis valley used to be his family's land, long time ago. Den dah Cox family wen come in and take dah land away from his family. Somet'ing 'bout Jacob's family not paying dah land tax or water tax or somet'ing li' dat, and dah haole wen pay instead."

"But what got to do with us? I not responsible. Dah haole wen do it. Not me."

Mineda shrugged his shoulders.

"Eh, I was good to dah old man," Fritzhugh said. "I nevah bother him. When he used to go up and down dis road, he nevah said not'ing to me, so I never say not'ing to him." He paused. "But I wonder who goin' get his land now he ma-ke. He no mo' children, eh?"

Mineda shrugged his shoulders again. "Maybe das why," Mineda said.

"Maybe das why what?"

"Maybe das why he got all salty. Nobody pay attention to him. Nobody talk story with him. Nobody go bother him."

"So what you goin' do? Dah buggah dead already."

"What . . . you no believe in dah spirits?"

"Eh, no fut around."

"No. I asking you one simple question. You believe in dah kine Hawaiian spirits or what?"

"Yeah, I believe in dat kine," Fritzhugh said, looking warily across his sweet potato field, then back to Mineda's furrowed face. "But so what? Why . . . you think he wen curse dah valley or what?"

Mineda looked at this feet. He was silent for a while. "Crazy," he said finally. "All of dis. And how we going sell our produce to dah markets?"

A white car with the state emblem on the doors came by the store one day. Correa sat up and stared into the car curiously. Then he nodded his head. "You see, Bobby, you see," he said. "What I tol' you. Dah gov'ment goin' come down heah and try get somet'ing from us. I tol' you all along, dis hauna was from dah gov'ment. What I tol' you?"

Ignacio leaned forward, squinting his eyes to read the emblem. "Department of Agriculture," he muttered. He slouched back into his seat.

"What I tol' you, eh, Bobby? Look, dah Japanee going come out and he goin' try smooth talk us. You watch."

"Fritzhugh wen call dem fo' come down and try figure out whas wrong with dah dirt."

"Look dah buggah, nice clean cah, air conditionah and everyt'ing," Correa said sardonically, pretending he had not heard what his friend had said.

The man got out of the car and went up to the two men.

"Yes, sir," Correa said officiously. "What can I do fo' you today?"

The man crimped his nose at the fetid air. "You know where I can find Earl Fritzhugh?"

"Yeah-yeah. He live up dah valley. Whas dis fo'?" Correa asked.

"He called me about some problems you farmers having over here. Something about the soil."

"Not dah soil," Correa said. "Dah air. You cannot smell how hauna dah air is?"

The man nodded his head. "Yes . . . yes, the air kind of stink. Smell like rotten fish."

"Smell like somebody wen unload one big pile shit in dah middle of dah valley."

The man from the state grinned.

"So why you come," Correa asked pointedly, "and not one guy from dah Department of Air?"

The man from the state looked at Correa with dying interest. "You can tell me where Earl Fritzhugh lives?" he asked Ignacio.

"Yeah, brah," Ignacio said, pointing up the valley road. "You go up this road, maybe one mile into the valley. You goin' pass one big grove bamboo on the right side. The farm right after that going be the Fritzhugh farm. No can miss 'em."

The man thanked him, then got back into the car and left.

"You better call up Fritzhugh and tell him dah Japanee comin' up question him," Correa said.

Ignacio waved the flies away from his face, then spat into the grass.

There was nothing wrong with the soil, the state worker told them a few days after he had come up and taken samples to the downtown laboratory. Nothing was wrong. The farmers left that meeting with remorse. Then what was wrong with the crops?

A day later heavy rains came, and for three days the whole valley was inundated with torrents and flash floods. The residents welcomed the storm, for they believed that the rains would wash the soil of the inscrutable poison and cleanse the air of the bad smell. But came the fourth day and a bright sun and when the residents smelled the air again, the odor was still there, now more pronounced than ever and denser. It was as if the storm had nurtured the smell like water nourishes plants.

"You did anyt'ing to old Jacob?" people were now asking each other. And the answer was always, "No . . . but did you?" And when the informal polling was completed, it was determined that everybody in the valley had left old Jacob alone. But they all cast accusing looks at one another, as if everyone else but themselves were responsible for the curse that old Jacob seemed to have thrown over the once peaceful and productive valley.

One morning a haole salesman came to the doorsteps of one of the houses.

"Heard you folks here were having problems with fires," he said in a jovial voice, a Mid-Western accent.

"No," Tats Sugimura's wife said sourly. "Not fires. The smell. You cannot smell dah stink smell?"

The haole laughed. "Well, you know what they say," he said.

"No, what dey say?" Harriet said.

"They say that if you can't see it, then you can surely smell it." He laughed again. Harriet was about to ask who had said that when the salesman segued quickly into a sales pitch about a new fire prevention system his company was now offering in the area. And, for a limited time, he concluded, they would install the entire system without charge.

"We not interested," Harriet Sugimura said. "Go away. Go talk to somebody else."

"But you don't understand," the salesman said. "Along with this fire prevention system comes our new, revolutionary, home-odors maintenance system. And for a limited time, we will give it to you free if you purchase our fire prevention system. Here . . . smell this."

The salesman took out a small aerosol can and sprayed it inside the Sugimuras' house from the front door. Instantly, the spray cleared the air of the ugly smell that Harriet had almost gotten used to and the whole living room smelled fresh like roses.

"Your system can do this?" she gasped with delight.

"Yes, and more. Why, because our system is computer-controlled, you don't have to lift a finger. Everything will be done automatically."

Harriet's face beamed with promise. It had been so long since she smelled the scent of flowers. "So how much is it?"

"Retail, it sells for eight-hundred and fifty dollars. But for this limited offer, we will sell it to you for two-hundred and fifty dollars."

"Two-hundred-fifty!"

"Well, if you know of a friend or neighbor or family who would want this system too, I can give it to you for two-twenty-five."

"Hmm. Wait, let me call my neighbor."

Soon, the entire valley was buzzing on the telephone lines talking about that new machine that would wipe out the bad smell in the homes. If the valley was going to stay bad smelling, that didn't mean the homes had to have that smell, too. So almost every other household bought one of those systems, and the salesman, being a nice guy, even reduced the price by another twenty-five dollars, prepayment, stating emphatically that the company was now making only a twenty-dollar profit from each unit sold. The residents waited impatiently for that big brown truck that the haole promised would bring the fire-prevention-home-odor-maintenance system, and they waited past the promised three days delivery period, but the truck never came.

The smell worsened to the point that every other person in the valley was getting a constant headache.

"Somet'ing has to be done about the smell," Ignacio said. "If we cannot do anyt'ing about it, den we gotta take dis to the state."

"Nah, how you can do dat?" Correa said. "Dah state already wen say dey cannot do not'ing about it."

"But something gotta be done," Ignacio said.

"Something gotta be done," Harriet Sugimura said to her husband, sheepishly, a few days after her husband, for the first time in seven years, had lost his temper when she told him how she had spent their tax refunds.

"If this smell continue on, I'm getting the hell out of this valley," Pat Fritzhugh said to her husband.

"Me, too," Fritzhugh replied.

"You know what the problem is?" Leimomi Vargas said to her neighbor, Elizabeth Kauhale. "The problem is nobody honest wit' everybody else. I betchu somebody wen get the old man real angry. Really angry. And das why he wen curse the valley wit' dis stink fut smell before he ma-ke."

"I think you right, Lei," Elizabeth said sadly. "We gotta be honest wit' each other. Das dah only way."

"Then maybe the old man going take back the curse," Lei said.

"Maybe we should go get one kahuna bless dah friggin', stinkin' place," Elizabeth said.

"You nevah know the old man was one kahuna?"

"I know, but he dead."

"Still yet."

"But I t'ink you right. We gotta get to the bottom of this. Find all the persons responsible for him cursing the valley. Then make them offer somet'ing to the old man's spirit. Or somet'ing like that. Whachu t'ink?"

So from that conversation, the two women went door to door, struggling with the others to be honest. For starts, Lei told about the time when she was a small girl and she went up to the old man's place and stole an egg from one of his hens. And Elizabeth said one time she saw her brother throw a rock at the old man as he was climbing the road to his hermitage, and because her brother was now living on the Big Island, she would take responsibility for his wrong action. Then, slowly, the others began to unfold their stories of wrong-doings against the old man, even Joseph Correa, who admitted that he wronged old Jacob when they were young men growing up in the valley and wooing the same girl and he had told her parents that Jacob didn't have a prick and that he was a mahu. About the only person who hadn't sinned against Jacob was Tats Sugimura, who lived the next lot down from Jacob's. In fact, he had been kind to Jacob, giving him sweet potatoes and letting him use his water at the far end of the field (where Tats had found the fish scales and bones, though Tats couldn't figure out that that was where Jacob used to clean his fish).

So they organized representatives from each household of the valley to go up the road and pay their homage to Jacob's vindictive soul. They went to his place one late Saturday afternoon when the sun was beginning to set behind the mountains, parking their cars and trucks at the end of the dirt road where the road turned into a trail that led into Jacob's forbidden plot of land. They brought taro, sweet potatoes, corn, watermelons, yams, several 'awa roots, a dozen cans of meat, a basket of freshly laid eggs, a tub of fish and another tub of crawling crabs, loads of ti leaves, bunches of green bananas, and a fifth of good bourbon so that Jacob could wash all of the offerings down. They silently climbed the narrow path that the valley road turned into, winding up through dense brush and trees towards old Jacob's place. Lei was the only one in the contingent who had been up to Jacob's place before, but that was years and years ago and all she had seen were the dilapidated chicken coops, and everyone's senses were suspended in fear, not knowing what they might expect or see at the end of the trail.

Finally, they reached a flat clearing where they saw a sweeping view of the precipitous mountain range. They searched anxiously for his house until finally Elizabeth Kauhale found it hanging a few feet above the ground, with vines attaching it to a giant kukui tree. It was made out of scrap wood and looked like a big crate with a small opening on the side where a tattered rope ladder hung down. The box house began to swing and there was heard hollow laughter coming from within. The entourage retreated a few steps, their faces blanched with the expectation that Jacob's ghost might leap out after them. The laughing stopped, and they quickly dropped their offerings in an untidy heap under Jacob's pendular house, not daring to glance up the rope ladder. Then, hurriedly, they filed down the trail.

When they reached the bottom, they stopped, looked back, and made sure everyone who had gone up was back down. After they finished counting heads, they ambled off to their cars, murmuring among themselves how they hoped things would come out all right and the smell would leave the valley. Then, suddenly, there came loud, crackling laughter from deep in the valley that made the plants and trees shake. Everyone crammed into whosesoever's car was nearest. They raced down the road and did not stop until, breathless and terrified and worried for their very lives, they were down at the old abandoned store, and here they sat speechless until Leimomi Vargas shouted at the top of her lungs, "I think dis is all silly—us guys getting our pants scared off our 'okoles!"

Embarrassed smiles came upon everyone's face and there was heard some nervous laughter. Someone suggested that they celebrate in the memory of old Jacob, and, without further ado, they voted unanimously to go back to their homes and get what they had to eat and bring it all back down to the abandoned store where they would party for the rest of the night. So the people who were in the wrong cars got out and into the cars they had originally gone up the road with, and they all went back home and took boxes of chicken or beef or squid or whatever they had out of the freezers and thawed them under warm running water; the Ignacios brought down a pig Bobby had slaughtered that morning; the Fritzhughs brought a big barrel of fish their oldest son had caught that day; and Tats Sugimura trucked down a load of his miniature, mutant sweet potatoes; and the others went into backyards and lopped off hands of bananas and picked ears of corn and mangoes and carried off watermelons from the fields; and they brought all that food and all the beer and whiskey they had in their homes down to the store. Earl Fritzhugh and his two sons chopped up a large kiawe tree and made a roaring fire in the empty lot next to the store, and everyone pitched in and cooked the copious amounts of food in that sweet-smelling, charcoal inferno. Bobby Ignacio and friends—Earl Fritzhugh, Fritzhugh's youngest son, Sonny Pico's two boys and his daughter, Tats Sugimura's brother and Joseph Correa—brought down their ukes and guitars and a washtub bass and provided the entertainment that lasted exactly three nights and two days. And when the festivities finally ended—the smoke from the kiawe fire was still smoldering strongly—everyone at the old store began hugging each other and then meandered off to their homes.

But before they fell into deep sleep, Earl Fritzhugh and his wife made love for the first time since the smell began putrefying the air of the valley. And so did Tats and Harriet Sugimura. And there were at least a dozen or so illegitimate liaisons committed that festive time—for one, Elizabeth Kauhale saw her teenage son go in the bush with Bobby Ignacio's willowy daughter—which was probably the reason why weeks ahead there would be more festivities when three of those liaisons would be legitimized, and why months later, on the same day, there would be added three new members to the community.

And before he slept, old Joseph Correa dragged his feet to the old cemetery next to the clapboard Catholic Church, and there he laid a bunch of wild orchids on the grave of his beloved wife, Martha, and he sat down on the soft, wet ground, though it was a struggle for his brittle old legs to do so, and he sang that song that was a favorite of his wife—"Pua Lilia"—because his wife's middle name was Lilia, and he had often sung that song to her when she was alive and he had sung that song to her when she was dying. And after that song, he gazed up the valley and apologized once again to his former friend,

Jacob Hookano, for saying those damaging things about him in the past. "But she was worth fighting for," he said with a choke in his voice. "And you can see, my friend," he added with a touch of jealousy, "that you with her right now."

When the people of the valley finally woke up the next morning, or the next afternoon—or whenever—the first thing they noticed was the smell. The fresh clean smell of the ocean. It was the smell of salt, and the warm winds that carried it over the valley swept up to the highest ridges of the mountains, and there the warm air married with the cold dampness and thick clouds formed, and soon, with the shift in the trades, rain began to fall over the silent, peaceful valley.

Rated-L
From *Rolling the R's*

R. ZAMORA LINMARK

The movie is titled *Making Love* so it's rated-R. It stars ex-Angel Kate Jackson as Claire, a TV executive producer; ex-Rookie Michael Ontkean as Zack, a doctor; and *Clash of the Titans* Perseus, Harry Hamlin, as Bart, the novelist.

Vicente lies. Tells his mother he's going over to Florante's to work on a school project. Extra credit if handed in early. He asks for money in case they decide to order pizza from Magoo's. Six blocks and ten minutes later, he's riding in the back seat of Chantelle's black Rabbit, next to Exotica blushing her cheekbones cotton-candy pink.

Florante lies. Tells Lolo Tasio he's going over to Edgar's because Edgar has commissioned him to start writing his biography. He asks for money in case they decide to order pizza from Magoo's. Ten minutes later, he's sitting between Vicente and Exotica, who's thickening her lashes with Cover Girl's 24–hour mascara.

Edgar doesn't lie. Tells his parents he's going to see *Making Love* because it received three-and-a-half stars. Because it's about a closeted married man who breaks his silence. His father throws a fit; his mother sneaks a five-dollar bill into his pocket. Ten minutes later, he's sitting on the front seat, occasionally turning around to watch Exotica paint her lips watermelon-red.

The show has already started when they enter the dark, crowded room. Exotica whispers to meet in front of the lobby when the movie is over. Before they find their separate seats, Zack and Claire have already moved into a newly bought home with a fireplace in the master bedroom. Vicente finds a vacant seat next to a man leaning close to the woman beside him.

Zack lies. Tells Claire there is nothing the matter with him. His job is stressful. It's made him tired and moody; that's all. He turns from her, does not tell her how Bart and he faced each other, bare-chested.

Bart lies. Tells Zack he doesn't believe in love or relationships. His writing comes first. It takes all his time, consumes all his energy. He likes Zack, but not enough. It's too much to handle, too complicated—and his writing comes first.

Claire doesn't lie. Tells her boss she needs time off. To save her eight years of marriage. A baby will do it. She confronts Zack, tells him he's shut her off from his life. She wants back in. For emphasis, she breaks the china but not his silence. It's driving her mad.

For a week, Claire leaves; out of town on business—a job promotion. For a week, Zack and Bart wrap their arms around each other. Making love in front of the fireplace.

The theater is dead quiet except for Zack's and Bart's breathing made crisp by the kindling. The man next to Vicente shifts in his seat. Vicente feels the hairs of the man's arm brush his skin. He imagines himself and the man in front of a fireplace with Zack and Bart. The four of them wrapped in each other's arms, watching the ritual of flames.

Zack doesn't lie. He breaks his silence, tells Claire he's been unfaithful. There have been midnight kisses; his name is Bart. But Bart is gone. Claire tells Zack there's still hope—perhaps a psychiatrist. She doesn't need sex. Zack says it wouldn't be fair to either of them.

The man rubs his arm softly against Vicente's. Vicente feels the hairs dance like reeds on a stormy night.

Claire doesn't lie. Tells Zack she's happy for him. Very happy. Because she's happy with Larry and their one-year-old son Rupert. She kisses Zack on the cheek. He tells her he's happy, very happy for her. Tells her he's happy with his new life and lover in New York City. Claire and Zack kiss and hug. Goodbye, Claire. Bye, Zack.

As the credits begin to roll, the first bars of the title track, sung by Roberta Flack, swim across the silent room.

Here, close to our feelings
We touch again
We love again

The man glances at the woman beside him, her eyes fixed on Zack's car coasting down the winding road. He slowly moves his arm away from Vicente's.

And now neither one of us
Is breaking

Vicente turns his head, drops his chin against his shoulder, and furtively watches the man watch the roundness of the woman's lips, how they tighten to form a smile.

Our Lady of Kalihi
From *Rolling the R's*

R. ZAMORA LINMARK

Virgin Mary lives at the top of Monte Street right below King Kamehameha School, but you don't have to be from Kalihi Valley to know that. You can be riding the skyslide in front of Gibson's department store, lining up to visit the USS *Arizona* at Pearl Harbor, going on a buta hunt at Camp Erdman, or climbing the thirteen deadly steps near Morgan's corner, but the millisecond you turn towards Kalihi Valley, or even think to, you see her: A woman walking out of a mountain carrying a baby in her left hand and a crystal ball in her right, her melancholy eyes always open, always gazing down.

She isn't like the other Virgins. She bears no fancy names like Regina Cleri or Medjugorje, or Maria del Monte, but simply, Our Lady of the Mount.

She doesn't talk to children like Queen of Fatima, who is also called Mama Mary, because her mouth is veiled with asbestos. She can't dance when you blast the car stereo and shine your headlights on her, like Mary in Diamond Head Cemetery, because her feet are bound by a fat green snake with a pitchfork tongue. She isn't Asian-looking like La Naval, whose almond-shaped face, high cheekbones, slanty eyes, and flawless gown earned her a free trip around the world. And she won't heal the sick like Our Lady of Lourdes or perform miraculous feats like Our Lady of Mediatrix of All Grace, who showered the earth with roses, because a year after she was proclaimed Our Lady of the Mount, a hurricane stormed into the island and turned it into a garbage dump.

The buffeting winds jolted everyone and everything, including Our Lady of the Mount, whose tin-foil tiara and head were flung out into the Pacific Ocean. For months she stood decapitated at the top of the hill, waiting for Father Pacheco to collect enough donations to buy her a new head. When she was finally given the chance to think and see again, the parish of Our Lady of the Mount Church was a penny away from filing bankruptcy, for her disaster-proof head cost more than an arm and a leg. It was so expensive it came with a free crown and a makeover fit for a Halston runway show: Sophisticated with the jaguar eyes of Bianca Jagger, pout of Sophia Loren, cheekbones of Lauren Hutton, arched brows of Brooke Shields, and the attitude of a Studio 54 Disco Mama.

As you grapple your way up Monte Street with a bouquet of roses in your hand, you wonder if this mascaraed diva ramping out of the mountain is the same one that spoke like a dream the first time you collapsed before her. In front of the green snake that grins at you from around her feet, you offer her the roses wilting in your hand and look up at her newly acquired face. She does not look at you sweetly or serenely as before, but points her catty eyes toward the ships anchored at Pearl Harbor, prowling to see which sailor will crown her Notre Dama de Noche.

A New Beginning

JOHN YAU

I had a job interview the next afternoon and needed to buy some new clothes. My girlfriend was at work and I was on my own. I went to the bank shortly before it closed and took out one hundred and forty dollars. That left twenty-eight in the account and a few hours to kill before I headed for the stores.

A hundred and forty dollars, seven crisp twenties. It was the most money I had had in my pocket since I had a job washing dishes the first summer after high school. I still remember my first pay check: Forty-nine dollars, forty-seven cents for forty-eight hours a week. It was the first steady job I had and it was nearly the last.

I'm thinking: What kind of clothes? A sports jacket, white shirt, and tie. Maybe some shoes. Pants, definitely pants. A suit, could I buy a suit? No, I couldn't buy a suit. I had never bought a suit. My mother bought me a suit once, a shiny black thing, when I was about to graduate from the eighth grade and enter high school. I hated it, wore it for the class photograph, and then stuck it in the closet, where it is still collecting dust next to my boy scout uniform. Hated that too. Wouldn't wear it either, and got myself thrown out.

A sports jacket, how do you buy a sports jacket?

I didn't know these things then. I thought buying clothes was a sign of failure, an admission that you wanted to join the hamster division of the human race and spend your days running inside a wheel.

A friend of mine, who had also spent his nights and days in bars, staggering into walls, sleeping on the floor, because the bed was too far from the front door, once told me: "The worst thing about being a drunk is you never buy shoes that fit. I didn't know that until I was sober, I thought my feet were supposed to hurt. I thought the pain was some kind of necessary proof, that it connected me to the earth."

Sneakers, dungarees, denim shirt, black leather jacket—not the clothes you wear to a job interview, not if you want to get the job. My girlfriend and I lived in a big unheated loft in Chinatown then, and I was walking around Lower Manhattan, telling myself: It's easy, you just walk in the store and pick out what you want. But I didn't know what I wanted, I didn't have the tiniest iota of a clue. A sports jacket. I might as well have been taking an exam in physics, it was that abstract to me.

Did I go into more than one bar or was it just that one? The Doll Pit, a seedy topless bar for delivery boys, truck drivers, security guards, post office employees, and, sometimes, the Wall Street, baby-faced, junior execs that ventured that far north during lunch hour or wanted to kill an hour or two after work, swell their chests up and flex their muscles before going home to their studios or one bedroom apartments filled with examples of all the right things in it.

The Doll Pit lived up to its name. It was an all-black room with a horseshoe bar, a small, mirrored runway for the dancers and a loud, blinking jukebox full of disco. Music for undulators, shakers, twisters, teasers, and, as I called them back then, the bunny robots. It was a theater with a ramshackle stage and an audience peppered with guys that would have been shooed away from the Roman Forum.

The layers of encrusted black paint soaked up all the daylight that managed to crawl under the thick black front door, made it hard to see how dirty it actually was in there. There was a frayed red carpet around the bar, though it looked like someone had poured a mixture of cabbage and old confetti on the floor. A gold-framed mirror stretched across the black wall behind the bar so the audience got simulvision, front and back views of the dancers. There was beer on tap and the hard liquor was under the bar.

If you were smart, you didn't ask for anything by brand name. Knowing the name of a liquor meant you were smart enough to have graduated from college and gotten a good job, but stupid enough to pay extra on top of the extra the bartender already charged you.

It's dumb to walk into a topless bar if you have a hundred and forty dollars in your pocket, twenty-eight in the bank, and no steady job. It's even dumber if you go there in the middle of the afternoon. The drinks cost more than in a regular bar. Even the beer costs more. You start drinking in the cool cave of a topless bar in the afternoon and suddenly, like Dracula, you know you have lots of time staring down at you.

I knew all the topless bars in Lower Manhattan and how late they stayed open. I also knew about the bars that didn't have names and opened their doors at midnight or later. The ones that stayed open until 9:00 A.M. I drank in bars where beautiful transvestites lip-synched to Page, Minelli, and Streisand, and I drank in darker ones where firemen danced with waiters and cab drivers. I didn't discriminate. If they served alcohol, I'd go there. But midnight was a long way off and I had to buy a sports jacket, a tie, shirt, and shoes. It was a Herculean labor. I figured a couple of beers and a few naked dancers would smooth the way.

I didn't notice the sun go down. There was no window and you don't think about those kinds of things when you're sitting in a topless bar, swilling down beer or bourbon or both, watching bored women bouncing around, shaking their breasts as if they were frogs attached to batteries.

If you do any thinking in a topless bar, which is hard to imagine given what the place is called, it's in the third person. He, you think to yourself. He can and he will when he wants to. He, it is clear to me now, didn't know how and couldn't admit it.

I was proud of the fact that I was drinking slow and steady, like a submarine sneaking up on its target, and still had most of my money in my pocket. The only plan I had when I went to the bank that afternoon was to hold onto enough money until it was dark. I knew I wanted to buy my clothes after the sun went down, but I wasn't sure why.

One of my favorite ways of communing with nature back then was to drink as much as I possibly could as fast as I could. It made me understand the laws of gravity on a cellular level. I could feel cosmic particles drifting through the vast, empty regions of my brain. I was sure I could hear the little explosions of surplus activity in my veins. Lying in a park, more than once I fell asleep on a bench or under it, I swear I could feel the earth tilting toward or away from the sun.

When you're drunk, you slip, if you're lucky, into a different form of motion, and dance on the ribbon between the laws of gravity and the parapets of imagination.

I was a Sufi pressed between the smoky pages of alcohol, a genie waiting to jump back into the bottle. I wanted to find the amber snake whose fangs were full of sweet, sweet poison. Well, this Sufi must have been dancing somewhere behind his eyes when she came up and asked me if I could give her change for a dollar, because she needed to use the phone. I handed her some change, watched her hand slide the dollar onto the bar, watched her walk off to the phone.

Dark brown pony tail, white cotton blouse, red Dacron skirt, nylons, and low, black patent leather heels. A familiar type; the office worker. Miss Pony Tail was probably a secretary in one of the buildings a few blocks further south, down toward the World Trade Center. Most likely, she lived in Queens or Brooklyn. Maybe Staten Island. She was short but not overweight. She had a figure, I could see that. What's she doing in a place like this? Oh well, I didn't even see what she looked like. Back to the business at hand. Another beer, another dancer, and then off to the store.

Back then I didn't know that lots of stores stayed open really late. Not that it wouldn't have mattered anyway. I didn't know that I could have staggered into some place at around eleven and found what I needed to wear, that is if I had any money left and knew what I wanted. I probably never intended to buy clothes that day, though certainly on my way out of the bank, through its revolving door, happy that I got to smile at my favorite teller, a Jamaican woman who had both ears pierced twice, but often only wore earrings in one ear, two large red tears that morning, I thought that I was on my way to buying clothes and getting a job.

The job offer: Teaching college freshmen how to write sentences and, if they got that far, compositions. The bottom of the educational barrel is crammed with fish you don't want to shoot or bruise because each of them represents money for a college's coffers.

The real job: Putting more money in a school's bank account so they will thank you and throw you a few scraps. I suppose the difference between a hunting dog and me was that the four-legged worker knew how to carry his prey back to the master, while I was supposed to convince the students that one day, because of this class, they would all be able to leap gracefully from their crummy little barrels to big fancy models, ones that looked like new cars and freshly painted apartments on nice streets somewhere. I was supposed to convince a classroom full of faces, the eager, the sullen, and the blank, that I was a locksmith who could help them open any door.

The assignment: Describe what it was like to make love on your parents' plastic covered couch. If you were allowed to kill someone, who would it be? If you ever used the word spic, kike, chink, faggot, nigger, wop, bitch, please explain in a three-paragraph essay what this word means to you.

Yes, Professor Schooner, I understand this job has a lot of responsibility. Yes, I understand what the word, responsibility, means. Yes, I realize that I am their only gateway to the future, that I am what stands between them and success, and that I must help them reach their goals.

The future: a shot of bourbon straight up and a cold beer in a frosted glass. Thanks, how much do I owe you? I must have been trying to see China through the bottom of my dirty glass because I didn't realize Miss Pony Tail had slid onto the stool beside me.

"What are you drinking?"

"Bourbon and beer."

"My name's Lisa."

"Glad to meet you."

"You have a name."

"Yeah, I think so. I'm not sure. Call me Doc, all my friends call me Bill."

Lisa laughs. "You know what I was doing, I was making a call because I wanted to get high. You know what I mean?"

"Yeah, I know what you mean. I do it every chance I get."

What Lisa meant was heroin. I thought she meant something else: marijuana, hash, maybe opium. For some reason, I was thinking of the medicinal opium I once had. Maybe because it was the same color as the cabbage and confetti carpet. A friend of mine mailed me some. It looked like a red clay cigar. I was wishing I had some more. Or I just didn't care. She said "high" and I said "yeah." That was enough. Who needs to know how to write a sentence?

"But I need some money and I gotta take a cab. Do you like me? You're sweet. We could both get high. It'll only cost thirty dollars, plus the cab. Fine stuff, really fine stuff."

"Thirty dollars, plus cab. Suppose I give you fifteen, pay for the cab. I'll just go with you," I say, as if I were escorting someone to the hospital so they can visit a friend.

"You don't want some." Lisa is incredulous. "You sure you don't want some?"

"Well, maybe. Who knows?" I answer, shrugging my shoulders.

By now I realize that I haven't quite translated what Lisa is talking about.

It sounds like, it looks like. Surprise, you wake up in a stainless steel chamber and realize that you've just reached the last chapter of your future. Gee, sir, but that was kind of quick. Can I go back and try again? No, not this time. Good luck, here, spin the big wheel. Oh dear, in ten years you get to come back as a three-legged kangaroo or maybe, if you're really lucky, an albino newt. Meanwhile, we'll just spend a little time together in here and get to know each other real well.

"Where did you say we were going?" I ask, knowing it didn't matter, knowing the only answer that would have surprised me was if Lisa had said, a clothing store. Given that we were just in a topless bar, I doubt she was inspired to buy a new wardrobe.

Lisa and I are in the cab, snuggling. It's dark out. Shit, I think to myself, I bet the stores are closed. How did it get so late so quick? Shit, my girlfriend's probably wondering where I am. I ought to call her. You can't call from a cab, stupid. Besides, what are you going to say? Oh, hi honey. I'm in a cab with this young woman who has just put my hand inside her blouse and licked her lips. Funny, she's not wearing lipstick. I didn't notice that before. Oh honey, don't worry, I'm too drunk to do anything but grope her.

Somehow we get there and, as promised, I pay the cabby. Lisa leads the way. We're walking down a dark street with no streetlights, they're all busted, on the Lower East Side, somewhere around Avenue C. Lisa is a homing pigeon and heads straight for a building with no lights and no windows, all boarded up except for this one hole punched in through the cement blocks that have been used to fill the doorway and first floor windows. These are serious, industrious little fuckers, I realize, and I'm about to meet them.

"Hey Ramon."

Lisa is halfway through the hole. I'm looking at the pleated red skirt riding up her legs, looking at her legs, short but shapely, well muscled, topped by a black garter belt. I didn't expect to see that there and I'm thinking: Gee, she's going to get her skirt dirty or tear her nylons if she climbs all the way in, which she does when she hears a whistle and an all-clear from a voice perched high above her, in the shadows.

I'm standing there, looking at the hole when Lisa puts her arm back through it and waggles her fingers.

"It's okay. Ramon's already here. C'mon."

We climb three eerily lit flights of stairs. There are cheap metal lamps suspended by thickly insulated orange wires hanging down from one of the bannisters on the upper floors. I realize there's water trickling down the walls. Had it been raining when I was in the bar? It's as if we were in a cave somewhere out in Nevada, above the high desert plain, two prospectors digging for gold.

We get to the third floor and, like moths, head for the light at the end of the hall. I begin slowing down, letting Lisa take the lead.

Ramon and another man, who never said his name, are waiting in the room, like priests ready to guide us to the electric chair. There's one lamp facing the wall and four devotional candles, the kind you can get in any supermarket or bodega, on a table, along with a metal spoon and two hypodermics. Two gouged wooden chairs. An old lumpy mattress is pressed up against the far wall, by a boarded-up window. Gray sheet and khaki green army blanket. No pillow.

On the walls our shadows are rising and falling, like Balinese puppets rowing away from some hideous sea creature. I listen hard, but I can't quite hear what the storyteller is saying.

I give Ramon fifteen dollars. That's the deal Lisa and I made in the cab. It was after I said I'd give her the money that she began unbuttoning her blouse. I saw a mole above her pale right breast with white lace, almost like a doily, decorating the top of her pink satin bra.

Lisa was a secretary who wore frilly underwear, as well as a junkie with a habit. This was something I was just beginning to learn. There's no such thing as mutually exclusive personalities. Everybody was more than one.

"What about you?" Ramon asks nonchalantly. "Aren't you going to join the party?"

I try to act equally nonchalant.

"No, not tonight," I answer, shrugging my shoulders, as if it were my loss rather than Ramon's.

"Oh, you're a weekend shooter."

Whew. Yes, that's what I am, a weekend shooter. I'll know what to say the next time I'm standing on the third floor of an abandoned building on the Lower East Side, talking to a dealer with eyes that are like black, bottomless holes.

"Yeah, you know how it is," which was my way of saying, I think that's what I was doing, I had a job during the week. I didn't of course, but I wasn't going to tell Ramon that I had lots of time on my hands, that after tonight I wasn't even sure where I would be living, and that I still had more than fifty dollars in my pocket. No way.

I sensed that it was okay, that they weren't going to make me roll up my sleeves and prove to them that I was a weekend junkie. Ramon and his silent companion didn't suspect that I was an undercover cop. Besides, in the mid '70's in New York, the idea of a long-haired Chinese undercover cop busting dealers and junkies was just too preposterous to even begin considering. There are fairytales and there are fairytales.

Yes, along with a sports jacket, tie, shirt, and shoes, I had thought about going to a barber shop that afternoon, something I hadn't done since I was fourteen. It was going to be a big day. I was going to join the human race. But standing there in a dimly lit room, watching a woman, who was in her mid twenties, tying a belt around her arm, I knew that I had decided to postpone this decision a little while longer. It was too big a jump, too rash an impulse to have followed all the way through. I wanted to stay where I was a little longer.

Ramon looked at Lisa shooting up and then at me, who was standing beside her, and, I swear, he winked.

Did we stand on one of the dark landings afterwards and kiss? Did she try to unzip my pants? Did I push her against the wall and begin pulling up her skirt? No. I was glad to be walking down the stairs, glad to be climbing out of the cave, and standing on a empty dark street, breathing the dirty night air.

Somehow that night we found a cab that took us out of there, back to The Doll Pit. After my girlfriend and I broke up, I used to go there all the time, usually around midnight. I would sit at the bar with the waiters who had just gotten off their jobs in Chinatown, most of them still in uniform: white shirts, black pants, white socks, black shoes. A checkerboard. The cooks and dishwashers didn't bother to change. A black room full of men in stained white uniforms, kind of like a hospital or abattoir.

I used to think that I might get to see the waiters and cooks slumped down in their chairs, jerking off into their white hats. But that only happened after midnight in the Pagoda Palace, a movie theater right across from where my girlfriend and I lived. They showed porno flicks from Hong Kong, with subtitles in English and French should you want to follow the plot.

We, my girlfriend and I, went there couple of times. We learned it was better not to sit too close to anyone else. People who go to porno flicks after midnight have an invisible wall around them and it's best not to get too close to the wall, much less its inhabitant. I know, because I've been on both sides of that wall.

Yes, Lisa and I went back to the bar where we first met, and I had another drink or two. She leaned on my arm, drowsily batted her eyelashes and asked me what time I was getting up. She told me she had to get up in the morning and go to work.

"Do you have an alarm clock? I need an alarm clock. My boss will kill me if I go to work late one more morning."

"No, I don't have an alarm clock. Sorry."

I was lying, of course. Everyone has an alarm clock.

Well, my girlfriend had an alarm clock, that's true. It was one [of] the things she unpacked when we moved in together. But I wasn't about to go back there and ask her if I could borrow it for my friend, Lisa. Besides, my interview wasn't until three, and I didn't want to get up in the morning.

You see, I did know a few things back then. I knew Lisa was a junkie who needed an alarm clock, that I was guy who didn't know how to buy a sports jacket, and that we weren't a match made in heaven.

Kim

JANA MONJI

Can you keep from hating a roommate who gets all the looks? You know, the one that makes a man's pulse jump just walking across the floor. Of course, sometimes it helped that the skirt was so short bare cheeks flashed brazenly from the black thong worn underneath. And Kim took time. Each painful step of the patent leather stiletto radiated forbidden pleasures and broadcasted the smothering scent of Opium, Kim's trademark perfume for these nights.

"Those silly white bitches think you need breasts. You just need attitude. Look like yes, but say no. Men like what they can't have," Kim would say.

I learned a lot about life from Kim. It was like Aesop's city mouse and country cousin fable. When I first came to L.A., I was prepared for hitting the books—living in a library. But I didn't belong in L.A. and certainly not in Hollywood.

I found Kim through an ad in the *L.A. Weekly.* The rents in Hollywood were cheaper than Westwood. It wasn't the best way to find future roommates, but I didn't know that then. There was so much I didn't know.

Kim was willing to teach me. After a month, Kim squinted, looking at me like a piece of blank canvas, and said, "You know, you could be real good looker. Hot stuff. You just need little change." Kim smiled, tossing the long waves of auburn hair, permed out of its natural straightness.

I don't know what I like about Kim. Our bond was perhaps dependent on bridges built on false assumptions of sameness—the Asian factor. But I had never known war nor sold spring to quiet my stomach. Kim had.

Kim warned me about white men. "They only want one thing, girl," Kim would say, winking. "Madonna even knows that. You make good life here, you learn that fast."

"What about Asian men?" I asked one day when Kim had finally convinced me to forgo the usual sweat pants and ponytail and was deciding how to achieve an attractive but tasteful hairstyle for me.

"Asian boys, they nothing but paper dragons. They too afraid to spit fire, but they make good bonfire," Kim said with a throaty laugh steeped in bitterness.

Our bedrooms were separated by rattan screens and curtains. But these were walls, just the same. "Privacy is only a state of mind," my mother once said. I saw that in Kim, too. With curtains pulled, Kim was alone and I was too. Otherwise, Kim's futon folded up into a chair for company and with the throw pillows, my bed was a couch.

Kim had been a student, but was not caught up in the Hollywood movie rush. "My life, like this shit," Kim once said, turning on the garbage disposal to whirl away the remains of our stir-fry dinner. When Kim was working, doing makeup or hair on a shoot, I had no roommate. Otherwise, Kim would sleep late and watch grainy videos borrowed from Vietnamese friends.

When Kim's money thinned down to pennies in a jar, Kim worked at a local Vietnamese-Chinese restaurant owned by a nice woman Kim called "Mother-lady." Kim's real mother belonged to another world that Kim had left behind. This Mother-lady had a big heart. Her real children were bits of dust—ashes in a man's war. At least, she thought they were dead.

We were her city orphans, sent to give her good karma and comfort. She liked feeding us. Kim and I were both so thin—like baby birds who have to be brought food and too stupid to get it by yourself, she would say.

But we ate a lot. Kim took me to the best cheap eats. "Don't worry. Floor dirty, but kitchen clean. I never get sick here, not like American hamburger shit," Kim would sniff with disgust.

Other times, Kim fretted about my safety. "If you out too late, call. No funny look, call. Call. Don't wait for MTA," Kim would say, then, picking me up in a very dented white Datsun B210, "Good brakes, so-so tires. No one want steal. That best car for Hollywood."

Despite little changes, some of which I admit I liked, I never let Kim take over my appearance. Still, Kim never gave up. "You could be hot stuff, real hot number girl." I just nodded and went back to my books.

Listening to Madonna on a shiny yellow Walkman, Kim would sometimes dance half-naked to empty air as I studied. Our building had paper-thin walls, and our neighbor, a sickly thin old woman who rarely left her apartment, would complain loudly if Kim's antiquated stereo broke her serenity. Then *bang, bang, bang,* went the old woman's cane against the wall.

On hot days, Kim would leave the door open, dancing madly, and sometimes catch our neighbor watching. The old lady didn't approve of the life Kim led, but she still worried. We returned the favor, shopping for her.

Kim would yell from the kitchen, "I go market. You need something?" The old lady would poke her head out ten minutes later. Holding a worn purse in hand, she counted out the dollars and pennies.

After knocking three times on her door, Kim would leave the old lady's small items on the hallway floor. Then, with our door open, Kim would dance passionately while putting everything away in our kitchen. Unless I was studying, Kim would try to get me dancing. "You need to relax, baby-girl," Kim would say. But as with all of Kim's wildness, I resisted until the summer sun melted my reserve.

With the quarter over, I was locked in a mind-numbing dead-end summer job.

"Let's celebrate summer, baby-girl," Kim said. "I give you my fuck-me look special." I gave in. "Trust me, baby-girl. You look nice yuppie tomorrow. I make sure," Kim said, and fiendishly began the transformation. Opening up a great hot-pink plastic tool box, Kim washed my hair, cut and sprayed. "My mother taught me how. You know, best bucks go to best-looking girl," Kim laughed. "Now, we go shopping."

For me, Kim favored black miniskirts and stiletto heels. "Show some flesh, not too much. Don't want to be mistaken for Miss Saigon," Kim said sarcastically. Kim wore tastefully tight black pants with rather understated silk shirts.

We went to small clubs at first, but as Kim saw my confidence grow, we tried better places. Sometimes, the bouncers were only letting in certain girls and very few couples. One night, we couldn't get in at all. Kim didn't mind if white guys with Rolexes got in while we waited. Kim winked and said, "Kiss ass. I get even. You see, next time we have good laugh."

The next weekend, Kim came out dressed in high black platforms, a skin-tight leather miniskirt studded with silver and a low-cut black blouse. "You not shocked, baby-girl," Kim said with wide-eyed coyness. "Beauty, it's just dust and imagination," Kim said, blowing face powder off a brush. It held the lamplight briefly, sparkling as we began our enchanted evening.

Jana Monji

This time, the bouncer took one look at Kim's long smooth legs and smiled as if his brain had evaporated. Kim stooped over sideways to give him a good view, pretending to pull up the stockings—not quickly, but slowly. "Give man his money's worth, baby-girl. Gotta sell merchandise," Kim hissed with a false smile.

After that, we always got in. The club managers, those white men with slick ponytails and overly bright smiles, liked having Kim there. Asian girls were exotic, but humble enough to not cause trouble. We never went to Asian hangouts dressed like this. Kim advised, "We live two worlds. One, real. Two, white boy fantasy."

It was a game. Meat on the market for slobbering dogs that couldn't afford the entry fee. Kim's standard lose-them line was, "You nice fella, but my family don't like no white boys. But white boys so nice looking and fun to dance with. I can't bring you home. No, I can't go your place. I get killed if I don't make breakfast for old man. My cousin, here, she same. We neighbors."

Kim would smile and feign shyness.

Kim got to know all the bouncers by name so if some Romeo got too hot, we would call for help from our bouncer friends. "You know, we good girls. We don't want no trouble," Kim would say coyly.

Summer nights became our realm of magic. After selecting our costumes and taping for cleavage ("I learn this from pageant," Kim confided), we would meet in the bathroom. Our mirror ritual would begin with careful plucking of facial hair. "I no like Brooke Shields. Look like man or horse," Kim would say.

We would sponge on foundation and then lightly brush our faces, necks and shoulders with Kim's "fairy dust" mixture of translucent powder, rice polishings and pearlescent eye shadow for an otherworldly glow.

Then we would brush two different tones of brow to form expressive eyebrows. "Think young Liz Taylor," Kim would chant softly. Then, Kim would whisper, "Delicately—no Connie Chung eye," while applying eyeliner for both of us. We would then curl, mascara, powder and re-mascara our eyelashes.

Eye shadow swept up from our eyes to our eyebrows, blending from wine purple to a soft pink at the crest of our brows. After a slight whisper of rouge, we applied lipstick—first outlining our lips with pencil. Kim favored China red or blood reds while I used rose colors. Kim would mousse and lightly spray our hair.

We applied perfume. Opium for Kim ("It like history, you know. China and white man," Kim once explained.) and Shalimar for me. Kim had bought me a bottle as a surprise one day. "I think it you," Kim explained noncha-lantly. Pulling on our black stockings and slipping into high heels we walked incognito, nighttime creatures feeding off the fantasies of strangers.

But it couldn't last like that, could it? I had seen those two watching us. Sometimes they would just stare at us, panting like dogs hoping for a phantom meal. I mentioned them to Kim, but Kim laughed them off. "They frightened we too hot for them. We are."

But one full moon, we slipped into an abyss, falling before we even knew we were in danger.

We were sitting down, drinking Perrier, when the two watchers sat down on the stools next to us. The shorter man was muscular, sweaty and tanned with stubble glistening on his chin. He sat next to Kim. He leaned over and said something to Kim. Kim shot me a look of disgust, but still got up to dance. Kim was a good dancer. I liked watching Kim dance.

The taller man also favored that Don Johnson *Miami Vice* sleaze look. He came and sat next to me, touching my leg and taking hold of my thigh. "Don't," I said as I tried to squirm out of his reach. He relaxed his hold and asked me if I wanted a drink. I could feel his fingers stroking my inner thigh as he ordered two margaritas. His fingers stole under my skirt; I tried to push him away, but he tightened his grip until it hurt. Then he kissed me like a slobbering bulldog, tasting of stale alcohol, stinking of Old Spice.

Kim saw, then began looking for a bouncer. Turning Kim's face, the short man pulled Kim toward him. I couldn't catch the eye of the nearest bouncer boy; he was socializing a new girl at the club—a bleached blonde.

The margaritas came. I gave mine to the man's pants and jumped up. Kim joined me as I stormed out the door. Kim shot a kiss at the same bouncer who had just scored the blonde's phone number. Kim shouted, pointing with a black sequined bag toward the two men, "We too hot for those boys. You cool them off?"

We escaped into the night, our heels beating an erratic retreat cadence. When we reached the car, Kim, unlocking the passenger door, offered me com-fort by kissing my forehead, nose and lips. Kim looked solemnly into my eyes for a moment before I got in. I felt unclean, but now curiously excited by the feel of soft hairless skin slipping tenderly against my own.

Kim couldn't erase my fear; I was shaking in the car. Kim cursed and chanted, coaxing the Datsun into action. Finally, we jumped into traffic. Kim held my hand, turning every now and then to smile and say a comforting word until we got home.

Kim kissed me, like a lover, while opening the building's front door, and then hurried me inside. "I sorry, baby-girl; I never want you get hurt. You don't know men. You be okay. I make you some tea." Kim stroked my hair and murmured gently.

That night we slept together. Kim stroked me like I was a lost kitten. "You baby-girl, not ready for city. You gotta be tough, baby-girl. Okay, I be tough enough for both."

That next morning, Saturday, Kim went out early to work at the restaurant. "Tonight we have quiet dinner, okay, baby-girl? We have good talk. You rest. I be back, maybe eight?"

At seven-thirty, the doorbell rang. I thought Kim was laden down with goodies from Mother-lady and couldn't open the door, so I opened it. There they stood—those two men.

"You damn cock-teasing dykes," the taller one began. I screamed and tried to shut the door. "Where's your friend?" the shorter one asked. They checked our rooms, ripping open the curtains and pushing aside the rattan screens, destroying the barriers like cobwebs of Asian dreams. "Get out," I cried, trying to grab the phone. But the tall one ripped it off the wall. I tried to escape.

"I'll show you what a real man feels like," the tall one said, grabbing me. Slobbering like a rabid dog, he gave me a deep-tongued kiss before throwing me onto the sofa. The throw pillows that gave my bed a different daytime reality scattered. Tightly pinned down, I couldn't breathe. He tried to get me out of my pants. With his massive bulldog mouth, he swallowed my face. I bit his lip, and he slapped me hard. The shock made me momentarily stop kicking. I kept thinking "Breathe" and "No."

"You dykes are afraid of real men, but you'll like it," he grunted in my ear. "You just need a good one." He grated me with sandpaper stubble, stinking of Old Spice. My pants were off and now he forced my hand down to touch his slimy dull weapon. I turned my face away, to breathe. I prayed for life and death, unable to choose.

"Hey, white boy. You no real man. You don't know real man when you see one." Greasy from the heat of Mother-lady's kitchen, Kim stood defiant at the doorway, holding plastic grocery bags.

"Who the hell are you?" said the tall man. His grip relaxed enough for me to squirm from under him. The short man couldn't speak.

"You don't know me, white boy? I tell you, you don't know nothing," Kim laughed sarcastically. Kim put down the bags and sauntered up to the short man, walking his Saigon slut strut and running his fingers up the man's chest. "You remember me, white boy? Last night, you say you win toss-up. I yours. You say you give me good time."

Stepping back, Kim leaned against the kitchen counter and slowly unwound the bun. Letting out a tide of wavy auburn hair, Kim smiled slyly. The scent of Opium and rancid sesame seed oil engulfed us.

The tall man looked back at me. "You—you—" he stuttered.

The short man only shuddered. Kim said nothing, but coyly stood straight, presenting himself with a great flourish of his hands. He began to laugh wildly, recklessly. And then he just posed, smiling with his hand on his hip.

I laughed hysterically. "I'm the only woman here, you stupid assholes."

"No," the short man shook nervously. Looking at me, he muttered, "She said you were always jealous."

"White boys like me best. That why. Who want me first?" Kim smiled coyly. "White boys like rice queens with tight asses." The short man shook his head. "Maybe you hit wrong club, white boy. Go look for white love. Maybe you get three-way boy love."

"No," the short man said. "I like women."

"White boy don't even know woman when he see," Kim laughed.

"I know women," the taller man stuttered, staring uneasily at Kim.

"But you've never seen him naked. I have," I screamed.

Our neighbor popped her head in. "I called the police. You better go. We don't want no trouble here."

They left puzzled and angry. Afraid to touch Kim or look at me. Before they reached the front door, Kim called out and exposed himself. With a defiant laugh, Kim slammed our door.

Kim embraced me in his sinewy arms and fed me from cartons of food, scolding me like a mother bird feeding her chick. "Baby-girl, I told you about white men. You believe now? Don't worry, baby-girl. I no paper dragon. I keep you safe."

Seeds

MONIQUE T. D. TRUONG

Two American ladies wish to retain a cook—27 rue de Fleurus. See caretaker's office, first floor.

"Yes, yes, they are still looking for a cook. You'll have to come back in an hour or two when they have returned from their drive. Just knock on those large doors to your left. They lead to the studio. What did you say your name was?"

"Binh. Binh Nguyen."

"Beene? Beene, yes, that's easy enough on the tongue. You seem like a nice boy. Let me give you, let's say, a bit of advice—don't blink an eye."

"What?"

"Don't blink an eye. Do you understand?"

"No."

"Well, let's say, the two Americans are a bit unusual. Well, you'll see that for yourself as soon as the doors to the studio are opened."

"Did you say 'studio?' Painters?"

"No, no, a writer and, ummm, a companion. But that's not the point! They are très gentilles, très gentilles."

"And?"

"Well, no point, really. Except. Except, you should call her by her full name, Madame GertrudeStein. Always, Madame GertrudeStein. Just think of it as one word."

"Is that it? What about the other one?"

"Oh, yes, certainly, her name is Alice Toklas. She prefers Madame Alice."

"And?"

"Well, that's it. That's it."

"I'll be back in an hour then. Good-bye, Monsieur."

• • •

Two American ladies wish—

Sounds more like a proclamation than a help-wanted ad.

Well, of course, two American ladies in Paris these days would only "wish" because to wish is to receive; to want, well, to want is just not American. I congratulated myself on this rather apt and piquant piece of social commentary. Now if only I knew how to say "apt" and "piquant" in French, I could stop congratulating myself and strike up a conversation with the "petit garçon" sitting three park benches over. Ah, the irony of acquiring a foreign tongue is that you amass just enough cheap, serviceable words to fuel your desires and never, never enough lavish, imprudent ones to feed them.

It is true that there are some French words I have picked up quickly, in fact, words I can't remember never knowing. Like I had been born with them in my mouth, like they were the seeds and pits of a sour fruit that someone else ate and stuffed ungraciously into my own.

"Ungraciously? Ungraciously? *Troi oi*, I'll tell you who is ungracious. It's you, you ungracious, disrespectful, disappearing lout of a son. I taught you how to say 's'il vous plaît,' 'merci,' 'Monsieur,' 'Madame,' so that you could work in the Governor-General's house. Your oldest brother, he started out like you. At the age of ten, he was just the boy who picked up after Madame's 'petit chouchou' after it did its business in every corner of the house, warping the wood floors with its shit and urine. Now, he's thirty and a sous-chef! Wears a crisp white apron and knows more French words than the local school teacher. He says that soon he's going to be promoted to. . . ."

I have discovered only one true and constant thing in my life. It is that my father's anger has no respect for geography. Mountains, rivers, oceans, and seas, these things that would have otherwise kept an average man locked onto the hectare of land which he was raised from birth to call home; these things have never kept my father from honing in on me, pinpointing my location, and making me pay my respects. While his body lies deep in the ground of Saigon, his anger sojourns with his no-good son on a Parisian park bench.

Even here, he's found me.

"Unemployed and alone," he surmises, distilling my life into two sad, stinging words.

I try to protect myself with a knowing smirk. "Oh, you again? I thought I was dead to you, old man? 'No son of mine leaves a good job at the Governor-General's to be a cook! A cook on some leaky boat for sailors who don't even know how to say "please" or "thank you" in their own language not to mention in French. Old whores become *cooks* on boats, not any son of mine,' you said."

Sometimes, I cannot give enough thanks to your Catholic god, that you, my dear and violent father, are now merely cobbled together from my unwavering sense of guilt and my telescopic memories of brutalities lived long ago. Because a retort like that, a challenge like that, would have extracted from you nothing less than a slap in the face and a punch in the stomach. But now, my dear and violent father, who art up in heaven, you *will* dissipate in the face of my calm, cool smirk.

"Unemployed and Alone," however, obstinately refuse to retreat and demand that I address their needs before September disappears into October.

• • •

Two American ladies wish to retain a cook—

Hmmm . . . Americans. Hope their French is not as wretched as mine. What a fine household we would make, hand movements and crude drawings to supplement our mutual use of a secondhand language.

Though, contrary to what my father would tell you, the vocabulary of servitude is not built upon your knowledge of foreign words but rather on your ability to swallow them. Not your own, of course, but your Monsieur and Madame's.

The first thing I learned at the Governor-General's house was that when Monsieur and Madame were consumed by their lunatic displeasure at how the floors had been waxed, how the silver had been polished, or how the "poulet" had been stewed, they would berate the household staff, all fifteen of us, in French. But not the patois of dumbed-down French coupled with atonal attempts at Vietnamese that they'd normally used with us. No, this was a pure variety reserved for dignitaries and obtuse Indochinois servants. It's as if Monsieur and Madame were wholly incapable of expressing their finely wrought rage in any other language but their own.

Of course, we would all bow our heads and act repentant, just like the Catholic priest had taught us. Of course, we would all stand there blissful in our ignorance of the nuances, wordplays and double entendres of that language which was seeking desperately to assault us. Oh, naturally, some words would slip through, but for the most part we were all rather skilled in the refusal and rejection of all but the most necessary.

Minh-The-Sous-Chef, as my father had renamed him, was always telling us how the French never tired of debating why the Indochinois of a certain class are never able to master the difficulties, the subtleties, the winged eloquence of the French language. I now suspect that this is a topic of discussion for the ruling class everywhere. So enamored with their differences, language and otherwise, that they have lost the instinctual ability to detect the defiance of those who serve them.

Minh-The-Sous-Chef used to be just Anh Minh, my oldest brother and the only brother who today can make me think of home. No one would have enjoyed this park bench and the shade of these forlorn chestnut trees more than he would have. Anh Minh believed absolutely and passionately that the French language would save us, would welcome us into the fold, would reward us with kisses on both checks. His was not an abstract belief. No, it was grounded in the kitchen of the Governor-General's house. He insisted that after Monsieur and Madame tasted his Omelette à la Bourbonnaise, his Coupe Ambassadrice, his Crème Marquise they would have no need to send for a French chef de cuisine to replace old Claude Chaboux. My father, like a soothsayer, declared that soon there would be the first Vietnamese chef de cuisine in the Governor-General's house.

So while the rest of us stood there dumbly experiencing the balletic surges of Monsieur and Madame's tirade, Anh Minh, alone, stood in agony. Lashed and betrayed by all those words he had adopted and kept close to his heart. Wounded.

Minh-The-Wounded, I began calling him in my prayers.

Old Chaboux died and a young Jean Blériot arrived from France to don the coveted title. Now, only an act of god, a bout of malaria, or a lustful look at Madame would hasten the departure of Chef Blériot, as he insisted on being called.

May 11, 1922, began the reign of Chef Blériot. Anh Minh stayed on in the kitchen of the Governor-General's to serve under yet another French chef, to cover for him once he begins to reek of rum, to clean after him once he can no longer see where the rim of the pot begins, sending handfuls of shallot and dashes of oil to season the tile floor. And me, what was I supposed to do? Twenty years old and still just a "garde-manger" sculpting potatoes into perfect little spheres, carving chunks of turnips into swans with the arc of their necks as delicate as Blériot's fingers, fingers that I instinctively wanted to taste. Equipped with skills and desires that no man would admit to having, what was I supposed to do?

• • •

Two American ladies wish to retain a cook— 27 rue de Fleurus.

Prosperous enough area of town and two American ladies must have enough to pay a nice wage.

One of my skills, really it's more like a sleight of hand, that I've secured since coming to this city is an acumen for its streets. I know where they reside, where they dissolve discreetly into one another, where they inexplicably choose to rear their unmarked heads. A skill born from the lack of other skills, really. When each day is mapped for you by a wanton display of street names, congesting the pages of the help-wanted's; when you are accompanied by the stench of unemployability, well, you too will be forced into an avid, adoring courtship with the streets of this city.

Oh, I must admit that in truly desperate times, my intimate knowledge of the city has saved me. A mistress with a heart.

"Name any street. Go ahead, any street. I'll tell you where it is, Left Bank or Right Bank, exact locale even. Rue de Fleurus? It's that little street off the boulevard Raspail, near the Luxembourg Gardens."

I've earned at least several dozen glasses of marc that way. Frenchmen, Drunkmen love a challenge. The listeners, if any, often will ask me to repeat myself. Seems that my accented French is even hard on the ears of laborers. Once it's clear that I am there for their amusement, well, the rest is a transcendent performance. Fortunately, for me, I have no idea how to say "transcendent performance" in French because otherwise I would be compelled to brag and ruin the surprise. And they are always surprised. And they always try again. They'll name the street where their great-aunt Sylvie lived, where their butcher is located, where they last got lost; and then, when truly desperate, they'll name a street on one of the islands that cleave this city. By then, I am gone because too often their surprise deviates into anger.

"How can this little Indochinois, who can't even speak proper French, who can't even say more than a simple sentence, who can't even understand enough to get angry over the jokes that we are making at his expense; how can this Indochinois know this city better than me?"

It's like I promised them a bag of rotten apples and then they opened it and found, well, *me*. "Come see the little Indochinois who knows this city better than any Parisian!" All I need is a little monkey dressed in a suit better than my own, and I could join the ranks of the circus freaks, half-man-half-woman sword swallowers, and now "Binh-The-Human-Map-of-Desperation!"

But, these are hardly skills to impress any potential Monsieur and Madame with.

I have been in this city now for over three years. I have interviewed with and even worked for an embarrassing number of households. In my experience, they break down into two categories. No, in fact, there are three. The first are those who after a cat-like glimpse at my face will issue an immediate rejection, usually non-verbal. A door slam is an uncommonly effective form of communication. No discussion, no references required, no "Will you want Sundays off?" Those, while immediately unpleasant, I prefer.

Type-twos are those who may or may not end up hiring you but who will nonetheless insist on stripping you with questions, like an indelicate physical examination. Type-twos often behave as if they've been deputized by the French government to ferret out and to document exactly how it is that I have come to inhabit these hallow shores.

"In Paris. Three years."

"Where were you before?"

"Marseilles."

"Where were you before that?"

"Boat to Marseilles."

"Boat? Yes, well, obviously. Where did that boat sail from?"

"Alexandria."

"Alexandria?"

"Yes, Egypt."

And so like a courtesan, forced to perform the dance of the seven veils, I grudgingly reveal the names, one by one, of the cities that have imperceptibly carved their names into me, leaving behind the scar tissue that form the bulk of who I am.

"Hmmm . . . you say you've been in Paris for three years? Now, let's see, if you left Indochine when you were twenty, that would make you. . . ."

"Twenty-seven, Madame."

"Four years unaccounted for!" You could almost hear them thinking.

Most Parisians can ignore and even forgive you for not having the refinement to be born amidst the ringing bells of their cathedrals, especially if you were born instead amidst the ringing bells of the replicas of their cathedrals, erected in far off colonies to remind them of the majesty, the piety of home. This is all to say that as long as Monsieur and Madame can account for your whereabouts in their city or in one of their colonies, well, then they can trust that the Republique and the Catholic Church have had their watchful eyes on you.

But now that I have exposed myself as a subject who has strayed, lived a life unchecked, ungoverned, undocumented, and unrepentant, I am again suspect. Before, I was no more of a threat than a cloistered nun. Now, Madame glares at me to see if she can detect the deviant sexual practices that I have surely picked up and am now, without a doubt, proliferating under the very noses of the city's Notre Dames. Madame now worries whether she can trust me with her little girls.

"Ah, Madame. You have nothing to worry about. I have no interest in your little girls. Your boys . . . well, that is their choice." She should hear me thinking.

The odds are stacked against me with this second type. I know. But I find myself again and again shamefully submitting. All those questions, I deceive myself each time; all those questions must mean that I have a chance. And so, I stay on, eventually serving myself forth like a scrawny roast pig only to be told "thank you, but no thank you."

"Thank you? Thank you? You should applaud! A standing ovation would not be inappropriate," I think each time. "I've just given you a story filled with exotic locales, travel on the open seas, family secrets, un-Christian vices. Thank you, will not suffice."

My self-righteous rage burns until I am forced to concede that I, in fact, have told them nothing. This language that I dip into like a dry inkwell has failed me. It made me take flight with weak wings and watched me plummet into silence. I am unable to tell them anything but a list of cities; some they've been to and others a mere dot on a globe, places they'll only touch with the tips of their fingers and never the soles of their feet. I am forced to admit that I am, to them, nothing but a series of destinations with no meaningful expanses in between.

"Thank you. But no thank you."

The third type, I call the "collectors." They are always good for several weeks and sometimes even several months worth of work. The interviews they conduct are professional, even mechanical. Before I can offer the usual inarticulate boast about my "good omelettes," I am hired. Breakfast, lunch and dinner to be prepared six days a week. Sundays off. Some immediately delegate the marketing to me. Others insist on accompanying me for the first week to make sure that I know the difference between a "poularde" and a "poulette."

I rarely fail them. Oh, of course, I have never been able to memorize nor keep an accurate tally of the obsessive assortment of words that the French have devised for this animal that is the center, the stewed, fricasseed, sautéed, stuffed heart, of every Frenchman's home. Fat chickens, young chickens, newly-hatched chickens, old wiry chickens . . . all are awarded with their very own name, a noble title of sorts, in this language, which can afford to be so drunk and extravagant towards what lies on the dinner table.

"A chicken" and "Not this chicken." These are the only words I need to navigate the poultry markets of this city. Communicating in the negative is not the quickest and certainly not the most esteemed form of expression, but for those with few words to spare it is the magic spell, the incantation which opens up an otherwise inaccessible treasure trove. Wielding my words like a rusty kitchen knife, I can ask for, reject, and ultimately locate that precise specimen which will grace tonight's pot.

And yes, for every coarse, misshapen phrase, for every blundered, dislocated word, I pay a fee. A man with a borrowed, ill-fitting tongue, I cannot compete for this city's attention. I cannot participate in the lively lover's quarrel between it and its inhabitants. I am a man whose voice is a harsh whisper in a city which loves a melody. No longer able to trust the sound of my own voice, I carry a small speckled mirror which shows me my face, my hands, and assures me that I am still here.

Becoming more animal-like with each displaced day, I scramble to seek shelter in the kitchens of those who will take me. Every kitchen is a homecoming, a respite, where I am the village elder, sage and revered. Every kitchen is a familiar story that I can relate and embellish with saffron, cardamom, bay laurel, and lavender. In their heat and in their steam, I allow myself to believe that it is the sheer speed of your hands, the flawless measurement of your eyes, the science of your tongue, that is rewarded. During these restorative intervals, I am no longer the mute who begs at this city's steps. Three times a day, I orchestrate and they sit with slacken jaws. Silenced. Mouths preoccupied with the taste of foods so familiar, and yet with every bite even the most parochial of palates detect redolent notes of something which they have no words to describe. They are, by the end, overwhelmed by an emotion which they do not know, a nostalgia for places they've never been.

I never willingly depart these havens. I am content to grow old in them, calling the stove my lover, calling the copper pans my children. But "collectors" are never satiated by my cooking. They are ravenous and compulsive. The honey that they covet lies inside my scars.

They are subtle in their tactics. A question slipped in with the money for the weekly food budget. A follow-up twisted inside a compliment for last night's dessert. Three others disguised as curiosity about the recipe for yesterday's soup. In the end, they are indistinguishable from the type-twos except for the defining core of their obsession. They have no interest in where I have been or what I have seen. They crave the fruits of exile, the bitter juices and the heavy hearts. They yearn for a taste of the pure, sea salt sadness of the outcast whom they've brought into their homes. And I am but one within a long line of others. The Algerian who was orphaned by a famine, the Turkish girl violated by her uncle, the Pakistani driven out of his village because his shriveled left hand was a sign of his mother's misdeeds. These are the wounded trophies who have preceded me.

It is not that I am unwilling. I've sold myself in exchange for less. Under their gentle guidance, their velvet questions, even I can disgorge enough pathos and cheap souvenir tragedies to sustain them. They are never gluttonous in their desires, rather the opposite. Methodical. A measured, controlled dosage is part of the thrill.

No, I am driven out by my own willful hands. Yes, it is only a matter of time. After so many weeks of having that steady, soft light shined at me, I begin to forget the demarcations, the barbed-wire rules of such engagements. I forget that there will be days when it is I who will have the craving, the red raw need to expose all my neglected, unkempt days. And I forget that I will wait, like a supplicant at the temple's gate, until all the rooms of the house are somber and silent.

When I am abandoned by their sweet-voiced catechism, I forget how long to braise the ribs of beef, whether chicken is best steamed over wine or broth, where to buy the sweetest trout . . . I neglect the pinch of cumin, the sprinkling of lovage, the scent of lime. And, in these ways, I compulsively write, page by page, the letters of my resignation.

Fredo Avila

GINA APOSTOL

Fredo Avila's dream was to travel to Beverly Hills, California, in the U.S.A., to be a contestant in "The Price is Right."

"Have you ever seen a group of happier people?" he said to me. "Everyone is so happy: look at how they all cheer wildly when the camera falls on them—and they're just the audience, not even contestants. It's just like heaven."

He acknowledged that winning a prize was mere luck, yes; it required only a talent at guessing. He'd once seen a Chinese man on the show who could hardly speak English—"dollar" and "car" were all he could sputter—but he knew his numbers, and he could point. He won a grand piano and a bath tub.

What would he, Fredo Avila, do if he won a bathtub? He'd plant it in his backyard, he would, near the bougainvilleas on the street. No more pumping on the *bomba,* slaving on the jetmatic pump for him, Fredo Avila. He'd hire someone to fetch water in pails and line them by his bath tub, while he, Fredo Avila, "The Price is Right" champion, would sit in splendor for all his neighborhood to see. He'd be in his jockeys, of course, new nylon swimming trunks, as he lay in his free, glistening bathtub in the open, Filipino air.

All of us in Barugo knew what Fredo's dream was. We all knew Fredo: in real life, he was our town's boxer. Stocky and squat, with a mean right jab and always steady on his feet, Fredo Avila won fights in towns as far south as Ormoc. He whipped to shreds and pathos lesser men right next door in Calingcaguing, all on the strength of his feet's stubborn steadiness and his "good conditioning," the hours he spent sparring in the space below my uncle's sala, on the dirt floor where the pigs were also kept for slaughtering on fiesta days.

He fought during fiesta bouts, when the gambling mood was contagious, and my uncle, the mayor, had a decent excuse for getting drunk and singing *Please Release Me* and *Besame Mucho*. There was always a smell of jubilation, hectic mindless happiness, and the plaster odor of Salonpas around Fredo when I saw him. But that's because I always remember him amid intensities, in the middle of fiesta fever when all men are friends until the next round of beer.

Fredo didn't drink, and whenever he fought a fiesta match, scheduled always before the Angelus so that the concerns of the body never interfered with the silence of the soul, he would return promptly to my uncle's house, win or lose, jawbone bloodied or intact, to watch "The Price is Right" at six o'clock.

"Heretic and blasphemer!" my aunt would say, crossing herself as the Angelus bells tolled. She was sick of having Fredo at the house at the Angelus hour, turning on the TV as if he owned it. But my uncle, the mayor, allowed him free reign of the house. And then, after a raced rendition of her prayers, my aunt would settle next to Fredo, to watch with sainted exclamations, "Sus-mariosep!" the genius of generosity in Bob Barker's parade. With loud awe, she'd comment on washers, dryers, steel machines of all shapes, gadgets imagined beyond delirium: lawn mowers for her stretch of crabgrass, answering machines for the municipal office, which had the sole telephone in the entire town, and electronic flea collars for her doomed pigs.

Shows were beamed via satellite from Manila, way up north, a twenty-four-hour bus ride away (including the three-hour dawn wait for a ferry from Allen, Samar). In Manila, we imagined, the show was beamed in miraculous simulcast from Beverly Hills. We got the show a month after, as was our due—when sophisticates in Manila were tired of hoarding it from losers in the province. I remember Fredo once punched a pomaded visitor from Manila, when the man told him who would win the trip to Venice, Italy, in the jackpot portion of the show. That's what he got for showing off.

We all had our dreams. Mine was merely to study in Manila, maybe take commerce or philosophy in Letran or San Beda, like my uncle, the mayor, who had flunked both schools. Spinoza "Chong" Botictic, my good high school friend, wanted to meet Jaworski, the basketball player. But he wished for a specific type of meeting: after a game in overtime, when Jaworski broke a tie in the last four seconds, hitting a three-point shot from the exact, requisite distance. Jaworski always did that in Chong's dreams, and he'd hit Fernandez, the enemy's center, right on the jaw, too, secretly, in that suave way of his. Chong wanted Jaworski to blind Fernandez forever. But that last was only extra. In his dream, Chong would then jump onto the court while the Ginebra team raised their sweaty arms in victory, embracing everyone, including Chong. At that opportune moment, he would meet Jaworski, shaking his hand with all due respect and coming up with something like: "Sic transit gloria mundi" or "Ad maiorem del gloriam," something witty like that. That's so Jaworski would know he had smart fans, even the ones from the provinces.

"Hope you take a bath after you meet him," we heckled Chong when he told us his dream. "Those guys smell like pigshit after they play."

"Shit," Tio Sequiel, my uncle's cousin, said, slapping my shoulder. "You won't find me crapping in my pants to dream of Jaworski's smelly armpits, let me tell you.

Chong was ready to leave the room. He was fifteen, and he hardly had any hair on his face, although he was still fertilizing a mustache he had started months ago: he cried easily, in sniffles.

"Get off his back, Exequiel," someone said from the back of the room. Then we heard a snort and a hand banging on the table.

It was Fredo. He'd been playing solitaire while a variety show from Manila was on.

"He's entitled to his ambition," Fredo said more quietly, laying still more cards on the table without skipping a hand. "That's what he has. And besides, you smell like a cow in sweat everyday: you're just a champion of the chamberpots."

Everyone knew about Tio Sequiel's historic diuretic trouble, handed down to males in his branch of the family for three verifiable generations. We all

agreed it was this that made Tio Sequiel chronically red-faced and excitable—
and simple-minded in the bargain.

"Oh yeah," he said, flustered and blushing. "So what kind of champion are
you? Champion of elbow boxing?"

We couldn't believe Tio Sequiel's guts. We stood up, scraping chairs and
shaking heads. I held on to Tio Sequiel's steamy arm, and some of us rose as if
casually but really to block Fredo's view of Tio Sequiel, crazy red man. We
didn't dare touch Fredo.

The truth was, I don't remember anyone referring even once to the baffling
time a few months before when Fredo in his last known fight knocked a man
out by elbowing him in the face, gashing cheek and jaw. He won in points but
lost by this foul. He returned from Ormoc to Barugo with no comment, our
compassionate curiosity unrewarded.

Since then, Fredo had refused to fight, fiesta or not.

Fredo merely looked in contempt at our timid shuffling about the room
and then swept cards cleanly off the table.

"Another dead end," he muttered to the cards then left the house. He'd lost
his game of solitaire.

I thought of this scene some months later when I heard the news about Fredo.
Eusebia the midwife and tolerated quack doctor told me all about it: Fredo
was going to America.

Secretly, Fredo had been sending letters to America, addressed to California, for three years. He sent his letters through the next town's post, so that
not even Claudia, postwoman and bigbreasted notary public, would know
about it. One day inexplicably he got a letter back. "Congratulations!" it said
in red, block letters visible from outside the envelope. Claudia expertly peered
through it and memorized the return address: "The Price is Right," Beverly
Hills, California, U.S.A.

Fredo received the letter without immediately opening it. But news spread
that afternoon that Fredo had called upon the intsik Go Long Tiu and had
borrowed a sum rumors judged to be three thousand to maybe half a hundred
mil—the wealth of a sugarman or the prized futurity of a pedigreed cock; big
bucks he'd pay off with his winnings from "The Price is Right."

It was all over Barugo: Fredo had won the solitaire stakes, hit the jackpot,
caught the secret of the royal flush. He was going to America.

"Dreams are wounds," said Eusebia, snapping wisdom from the air as was
her duty as a quack. "But with Fredo, who knows? God smiles slantwise on
simple men."

Fredo soon left for Manila to arrange his booking for abroad: this at least
he imparted to us, but before we could arrange the farewell drinking feast and
happy-tearful backslapping and stabbing. And still the town glowed with the
pure miracle of his departure. Flagrant hopes and undeclared dreams took
shape and vigor in its wake. Chong talked with simple certainty about his
meeting with Jaworski. Men filled cockpits with avid knowledge of how their
luck would change. Tio Sequiel dreamed on his chamberpot of blonde women,
chrome cars, white Christmas and other metallurgical treasures of Beverly
Hills, saying "Sonamagun" and "Damn" as if he were Fredo Avila in Califor-

nia. And my aunt prayed the Angelus with more fervor and speed than usual and, without any surprise, played bingo as if with a mad streak of clairvoyance, winning the salad casseroles and paired candlesticks with all the ease of the indecently charmed.

As for me, I did go to Manila that June, studying philosophy, accounting and many other wisdoms, in those first months, many of the books I read seemed to refer directly or casually to Fredo Avila's imminent appearance on "The Price is Right": for his destiny was now a constant puzzle to me: how do dreams come true?

There was the stodgy plodding over ledgers, balancing credits and debits with optic and cumulative anxiety: in accounting, there was no triumph but stability, no virtue apart from diligence and care. In my classes in religion, we were shown images of Saint Anthony in the desert, Saint Jerome before his skull and pen, men of abstinence and learning whose holiness was directly proportional to what flesh they had on their chins. And in the stories of philosophers, most clearly I would see Fredo Avila: Thales with the vision that led him to the hole in the well, Pythagoras of the singular solitude and madness over beans. In my twisted, one-track state of mind, I saw how Fredo Avila was one with mystics, philosophers and accountants: he stuck to one cause with the purity of a historical ascetic, stubborn and faithful to his dream, against odds, against distance, time, fate, and against reason.

In December of that year, Fredo was to appear on "The Price is Right." Claudia the postwoman knew about it before Amanda, Fredo's wife, did: she had a talent with penknives on sealed envelopes. Amanda and her two children were invited as guests of honor at my uncle's house when the day arrived. It must be explained that my uncle, the mayor, had one of two television sets in the town of Barugo. Go Long Tiu owned the other, but no one but flies and a cat had ever entered the Chinese man's house; he lived alone with his cat, sacks of flour and rice his millers sent him, and tins of money and creditor's bills that he stashed under his mattress like a good man of Guangdong.

My aunt made pudding with pig's intestines, leche flan, rice cakes in pastel colors, pancit and pork jumba. Amanda entered bearing vegetables; it was said that Fredo had taken her savings from her earnings as a vegetable vendor, along with the money from Go Long Tiu, and left her only with the garden plot and two pudgy-cheeked kids who looked eerily like the Santo Nino. We pinched the kids when they came in, their cheeks lumpy like the unpigmented, flour-faced Christ's; as the Angelus bells tolled, we did our quick stumbled prayers; then we turned the TV on.

It was a gathering of the town's worthies: drunks, gossips, the compassionate and the wise. Chong's father, Enoch Botictic de Enage, held center position, being the town's most learned man: he was a constantly crocked former teacher of philosophy and defrocked Jesuit whose last nod to his youthful learning was the naming of his children, Archimedes, Heraclitus, Baruch and Spinoza—more commonly known to us, respectively, as Boy, Bigboy, Bulldog and Chong. Chong's brother Heraclitus, aka Bigboy, despised "The Price is Right" because he favored "Jeopardy"—"You have to think to play it," he said, "unlike that stupid game, where even if all you did was fart, you'd win." But even he was present that night.

"Heraclitus, give me the odds on Fredo's name being called," his father said to him.

"What's infinitesimal?" Bigboy said. He spoke often in stupid riddles we forgave him for because his father was, after all, made crazy by intelligence.

None of us had any doubts that Fredo would be chosen from the audience right from the start. When the names were called and three exultant white ladies and a longhaired man came forward, we were puzzled.

"There's Fredo!" someone yelled as the camera panned on a group of wildly clapping people. But no one could tell for sure.

The first prizes were two sets of billiard balls.

"What's the use of billiard balls without a pool table. What a stupid game," said Chong's father, already red from tuba, incendiary coconut wine I was still not allowed to drink, except in secret.

Then the pool table was shown, a richly green board: you could tell from its harsh color how new it was.

"See, see," Tio Sequiel sneered at Mr. Botictic, elbowing him.

The professor merely shrugged, drinking.

"Ssh!" my aunt said.

A blonde woman won the round. She looked like a version of Claudia, chest pendulous and torso abridged, except that she was from Texas.

"Where the best chickens are raised," Tio Sequiel said; with chickens, he was a man of learning.

She was to bid on—suspense and gasp, in Beverly and Barugo—a trip to Honolulu!

"Pearl Harbor!" Chong said.

"Waikiki, aloha oe," we answered.

The woman squealed as the fake view of Hawaii was displayed.

She played a game called Circus Gong. She pounded on a board that then rose up a vertical range of prices. When the board stopped under what she believed to be the cost of the trip, she hit the board with an oversized hammer.

"Twenty thousand dollars?" my uncle guessed.

"No, in American money, maybe five hundred dollars," Tio Sequiel said. "Big difference between dollars and pesos, you know."

The woman pressed the button at five thousand. The trip cost four.

"Poor woman," my aunt said. "But she still gets prizes after the show. No one loses in America. Unlike in that game with Jeanne Young, where you can win corniks."

Her scorn for all Filipino goods increased phenomenally when she watched "The Price is Right"; you could measure her disgust.

"There's Fredo," someone yelled again.

But the camera was too quick, although the blackhaired man at the end of the row looked blurredly like Fredo in California, pensive and robust in light-tremored sunglasses.

A woman won a xylophone complete with sticks and pedal. Another narrowly guessed the price of Funai 5–Setting Whirlpool Bath.

I liked best the models, Diane and Janis, who lay on the beds or played the musical prizes with delicate, otherworldly gestures.

The four original contestants had either won or been disqualified except for the young man with long hair. I can tell you the sequence of play in "The Price is Right" even in my sleep. The announcer calls four players; the winner of the first round of price-guessing gets to play a game. After the games, one player is added to the three remaining slots, to make a constant four, and each player tries to win a spot in the game-playing segments. You could remain in contention until the end of the show, until you get lucky. This was the case now with the longhaired guy. A crowd of people cheered crazily whenever he made his wrong bid. And it was becoming clear to me that Fredo Avila's dream was going to end in obscurity, without even the witless consolation of bidding too high or too low on a barbecue from Amata.

The second to the last number was called, and the spotlights raised hope again among the crowd of Californians, Omahans, Nashvilleans, Mormons, Yosemiteans, Cherokees and Presbyterians, all the great gamut of Americans on the set of "The Price is Right."

Looking at them, I'd wonder why people never looked like that on "Charlie's Angels," with their necks seemingly attached directly to their earlobes, or with bare, splotched, broad faces that made one think momentarily of the dangers of frontal nudity. I'd feel bad for them; it was like they were America's secret people, these people forever barred from primetime.

"There's Fredo!" someone yelled again.

And sure enough, a name was called out.

The camera panned above a cheering mop of heads. Someone stood up: a t-shirted man in shining boat-heeled boots, boxer-shouldered and sunglasses-less—Fredo Avila in California took the long steps down, "Come on down!" to his place in the spotlight as a self-made man.

We were stunned in Barugo.

Long afterwards, we would replay the moment when Fredo took his place before the stage, and Bob Barker asked him, a propos of everything, "Where are you from?"

"Barugo, Leyte, in the Philippines, Sir!"

But that didn't happen until Fredo won the round's bid, edging out the longhaired man by a hair of a dollar or two, winning for himself a high-tech, mirrored, 4-speed bubblegum machine.

History was made on "The Price is Right" when Fredo ascended and stood next to Bob Barker, he of Miss Universe fame.

"What diction!" my aunt would say of Bob when she heard him say "a neeeeew car!" I'd keep correcting her, saying diction meant choice of words, not enunciation; and anyway, Rod the announcer said those things, not Bob. But I myself coveted Bob Barker's smoothness and charm and practiced in a mirror the way he smiled and waved his hands, his charm stuck permanently to him like a gun in a gangster's hand.

The man with the best diction in America and Fredo, the best-conditioned man in Barugo, stood side by side. Fredo's head didn't reach quite as high as the knot in Bob Barker's tie, and he looked strangely like a stunted cowboy in his tall, gleaming boots.

"And what do you do, Fredo?"

"Boxer," Fredo said promptly. And he added: "Bej-etable vendor, too."

We hooted in Barugo and gave high fives.

And I remember every single second of Fredo Avila's appearance on "The Price is Right." He had the best prize of all, a Chevy Nova waiting in the wings as he picked out numbers from a jumble of oversized cards in Bob Barker's hands. I remember the luminous quality of each minute in which he guessed: wrong, wrong, wrong. I see the erect posture of Fredo Avila in the shining moment when the actual price of the Chevy Nova was revealed and Bob Barker shook Fredo's hand, waving good-bye, Fredo Avila waving to the crowd, almost saluting—good-bye, losing the Chevy Nova and the chance at the showcase that the longhaired man won, of course. The boy, for he was a student, we learned, from Clyde, Ohio ("Nowhere place," Heraclitus sneered, forgetting where he was in the excitement of the moment), won his bid finally in the next round and garnered, in all, a trampoline, a trailer and a trip to Tokyo, Japan: $18,000 in prizes! The crowd went wild because, it turned out, the longhaired boy's entire fraternity was with him on the show, perfect recipients of the trampoline's elastic high.

Then Rod, the man in the hat, announced the prizes every contestant would take home, win or lose, and they were shown on the screen in still photographs without the happy complicity of the models' hands: Geritol Extend Vitamin Capsules, Seminole Flea Collars that glow in the dark, and Vita Bikini Underwear for men and women at home or on the beach—"Sexy as you wanna be!"

No one expected Fredo home after his appearance on "The Price is Right." We knew, for instance, that when a group of Leyte Girls Scouts left for the U.S. on a goodwill tour, they'd return with someone missing: in their case, the assistant scoutmistress who stopped over and vanished in Milwaukee. We hear that now she has a successful thousand-dollar business buying groceries for rich, old people who've "lost their qualities of mind," she wrote. Then there's Claudia's fabled, filthy-rich cousin who paid thirty thousand pesos to buy a nurse's certificate, and there she is in Passaic, New Jersey, sending pictures home of her pink Mitsubishi Eclipse and herself in Washington, D.C., shaking the large-as-life hands of Ronald Reagan: my aunt swears it was him—as if you couldn't tell him apart from cardboard.

I imagined Fredo staying behind in California, outstaying his visa to become, perhaps, a flyweight contender in fights in Fayetteville, Nevada, or a strong-armed burger flapper in McDonald, New York. He had achieved his dream: he was a self-made man in America.

I returned to Barugo in the summer. Instead of a boxing match, my uncle had arranged a marathon for the fiesta of Saint Jude; streamers lined the paved parts of the town's streets, and coconut wine and lemonade stands stood ready at the corners as the bus drove into town. I had arrived on the day of the fiesta, wishing almost that I hadn't returned. I didn't know what my sickness was all about—the nausea I felt as I saw the familiar turns and tin roofs of my hometown, the usual layabouts gathered about the corner near my uncle's house drinking tuba and wasting their lives as if they were immortal. Bums, of all the people I know, seemed most fixedly to have some hold on the notion of eternity.

I hung around on the street with my bags stickered "Letran" and a guilt in my lack of affection as people surged around my uncle's house, where it seemed the marathon was to begin.

"Danilo!" my aunt cried from the window. "That's my nephew, the future accountant!" she said excitedly to her cronies in the house.

"Manila boy," the Botictic brothers passed by—Boy, Bigboy, Bulldog, and Chong.

"Letran, ha." Heraclitus swiped at the sticker on my bag. "Big deal."

I thought of why I must be more sophisticated even than Heraclitus, because I had spent a year in Manila, a city boy studying philosophy. But I couldn't remember, in this dust, what I had become, what I had done in the city, the books that had wrought what changes, what made me superior, a man with significant dreams. It seemed that the suddenly stable ground of arrival had left me sick, reeling.

"Watching the race?" I asked. I pulled a lone, crushed cigarette from my pocket, the one I had had since the beginning of my trip. "Who's the main contender?"

"Fredo, of course."

"New guy? From Barugo or no?"

"You joking? Fredo Avila, I mean."

"The boxer? He's home?"

"Yeah. No one knows what happened," Chong volunteered seriously. He had always been my favorite among the brothers. His mustache now vied with his Adam's apple in temerity, in serious growth. He was still as skinny as a lizard. "Immigration got him maybe. Bad luck."

"Stupidity," Heraclitus corrected.

Chong was quiet. Heraclitus continued:

"Yeah, formerly of Beverly Hills, back to Barugo. He didn't even have talent for hiding."

"Works for Go Long Tiu now. Him and his kids. Hauls flour and stuff. You should see him," Chong said.

"But still," said Bulldog knowledgeably, "he's the best-conditioned man in Leyte. He'll win this race. No one can touch Fredo."

I smoked my limp, pocket-shredded Camel as I digested the news.

"But he's not really Fredo anymore," Chong said suddenly.

"What?" I asked.

"So he's a disguise now? He's really Gary Cooper?" Heraclitus laughed.

"I don't know," said Chong. "He doesn't box. He doesn't even talk."

A makeshift stage fronted my uncle's house. The vice-mayor made his speech, then my uncle, the mayor, made a longer one. Finally, the runners were called to their places, and I looked for Fredo Avila. He was in the middle, a runner with a number like the rest of them. I looked for a momentous change in the way he looked, in his stance before the crowd. He looked as sturdy as before: but he was so small as the TV screen had made him out to be. But I was taller now, a veteran of the city, Manila boy and future accountant: disoriented by arrival and queasy in the stomach. I coughed from the cigarette smoke and waved at Fredo.

"Hey, Fredo."

A visitor from Manila, a Barugo boy who became a judge in the big city, rose to the makeshift stage to speak. I walked over to Fredo.

"Hey, Fredo. What's up."

He nodded at me without really looking.

"When did you get back? How was America, ha, Fredo? The blonde chicks and all?"

Fredo still stood like a brick man with big shoulders. I did notice the bulk in his stomach, a bulge unthinkable in the boxing champion of old.

I poked him in the stomach.

"So what was America like, ha? Eating all those steaks and ham?"

Fredo wiped his brow. It's quite true: the summer sun blazed almost painfully.

"What did you find in America, Fredo?" He looked at me, and I thought— I had gone too far: one didn't mess with Fredo.

"Danielboy," he said finally. He held my arm: his touch was firm, and I remember his expression of seriousness, like a teacher. It was the Fredo of old, the Fredo who lounged on the dirt floor of my uncle's house, stacking up cards. "Danny, did you know there is dust in America?"

The race started early with a boy from Calingcaguing in the lead, Fredo following close behind. "Go, Fredo, go!" Tio Sequiel and other drunkards waved him on. Barugo's dust flew in Barugo's sun. Young kids in slippers, bearing ice candy, brought up the rear, laughing and shouting. I rode in my uncle's jeep to get to the finishing line, leisurely following the runners' route. Dust was dense, adding to my discomfort; the paved road was pocked with pork-barrel providence; my uncle waved benignly as we passed the crowds. We were about to turn into a dirt road, a shortcut to the end of the line, when the fiesta crowd turned into a commotion, and someone ran after my uncle's jeep.

"Mayor, mayor, stop!"

I turned around, kneeling on my seat to look.

It seemed that the race had halted.

"He collapsed, right in the middle of the road, mayor."

"Who is it?"

"The boxer."

"Fredo Avila."

We rushed him to the nearest hospital, which was three towns away. In his delirium he kept saying, with spirit and old feistiness: "Come on down!"

The opinion in the town was—Fredo's body was well-conditioned, but his heart was foolish: should boxers run marathons? But still, they shook their heads, saying: "The best-conditioned man—how could that be?"

He died on the day of his heart attack, an end that astounded even rumor.

"From Beverly Hills to Barugo—only to die," Tio Sequiel shook his head and spat. "Foolish!" How could that be?

He left his wife the high-tech, 4-speed, mirrored bubblegum machine. To his mother, a bottle of Geritol Extend. He lost the Seminole Flea collar on the trip home, pilfered from his bag by someone possibly deranged. On his deathbed, in the last throes of glory as he raved in delirium: "Boxer, sir! From the Philippines, sir!" he wore the sum of his dream's progress, Vita bikini briefs, coral pink, for men and women at home or on the beach. Sexy as You Wanna Be.

How could it be? I vomited on the jeep on the way to the hospital, vomited days after at home and at the funeral; my aunt forced me to bed before the lines formed to walk to Fredo Avila's grave. I had the most serious case of intestinal flu Eusebia the quack had ever seen.

"You vomiting your life out, man? Coughing up even your dreams?" she said, pasting leaves and hot wild forest roots against my chest.

I rested my head against her arm, my cheeks hot.

"It's the spirit of absence," she said to my aunt. "He needs to rest, to see his world again as if he had never left."

A Difference of Background

NURUL KABIR

Is life ever free of problems? If your worries are waved away with a magic wand, just wait, your mind will create new problems out of thin air for you. Thus I never thought being a taxi cab driver was as pitiful a fate as many of my compatriots thought. Like anything in life, one must make the best of it. There were ill-mannered passengers, robbers in the heart of the night, and perhaps, yes, not so much money at the end of the week to compensate for the loneliness in which I drove through endless circles. But that was okay. If you knew the impossible situation I was in in another land far away and the chance that brought me to this country, like the kindly ocean current washing a weary swimmer to a desolate shore, you would understand right away. Without a soul to welcome me in this vast teeming metropolis, with the heels of my shoes worn out by my search all over the great city for work—any kind of work— life as a taxi cab driver was simple and blessed, a precious love found after a lifetime of wandering. I meant to be forever grateful to the fellow countryman through whose intercession this came to be, Saladin.

Saladin, dear friend! How fragile is gratitude! It shatters one day into pieces and becomes dust. Vengeance lives longer. I look at Saladin across the table as he wolfs down another dish of murag biriyani. He asks why is it that I cook so well for him, so much, and he asks this in a light way because he actually believes that this is his due. He does not go very deep into any matter these days, he never suspects the trap he has fallen in. Revenge, I tell you, is indeed sweet. And let me tell you, it takes many forms. There is revenge you take after much planning and waiting, like medicine in one gulp, and there is revenge that requires no effort on your part, that Fate hands you on a platter. If the latter be yours, take care of the gift well, for it is as pleasurable as the quenching of daily thirst, as long-lasting as your life.

When my eyes first set on him I saw a handsome young man, possessed of qualities which would never be mine. He was studying at a great university, and at the party in his house he was surrounded by others as glamorous as himself. I had never been to any such event before. Mine were the modest get-togethers the people of my background have, simple people who never erase from their hearts the memories of other lives in the homeland far away. Men sit around in a room warmed by their camaraderie and exchange their tales and the women gather in another room with their housewives' talk. Many were the cold nights when I returned home late from such gatherings to my single bare room, the awareness of fellowship in my heart like a candlelight in the darkness.

Saladin's party was different, I could tell straight away. The women and men were in the same hall, talking, drinking wine, laughing, as if it was completely natural for everybody to be together. They were mostly foreigners, and by that I don't mean white Americans, because of course everybody knows some Americans. They are easier to befriend than many compatriots even though the friendships with them are far less likely to last as long. Well, in Saladin's house there were men and women from all four corners of the globe. Foreign students, professors, artists, filmmakers. In the midst of these people was Saladin himself, the center of attention in the distinguished crowd. Elegantly dressed in a black silk shirt and black slacks, a brown leather belt around his waist, he was of medium height and slim, had sharp features and a mass of curly hair. A dark complexion on such a handsome figure accentuated his serious mien, his grave and deliberate manner of conversing. Of such a person mothers back at home would say to their daughters, "He comes from a fine family."

I hesitated between entering the crowd of people and leaving quietly when I caught Saladin's eyes. He paused in his talk to a beautiful foreign woman to throw me a look. It was not quite a greeting, but the hint of a nod that acknowledged my existence. Soon he came to meet me. He came over and measured me with a look that went from feet to head. We made our introductions.

"Have you had dinner? Would you like a sandwich?" he asked in a voice made soft with grace.

The sandwiches on the big trays were delicate, perfect, like items of show in glass cases. But how was I to have one here in front of these people? "I ate," I replied.

Saladin gave me a glance of unease. He helped himself to a sandwich and resumed questioning me. Did he not already know all about me? Soon he came to the point.

"You have looked for work?" he asked, as he threw me another sideways look and his lips played out a faint smile. Or was it a sneer?

"From the day I landed."

"Do you have a degree?"

"A student in the polytechnic."

"No papers?"

"I hear you can get by," I offered. Indeed I knew *deshis* who got by very well without documents, working around the clock with no more than six hours of sleep. I could do that, yes.

"Difficult," Saladin replied, looking away at the crowd in the middle of the hall.

"You can do nothing?" I asked in anxiety, nagged by fresh worries. The hope with which I had come to him was very high; I had been told that Saladin could get me work even without the "papers."

He bent his head without replying. A young man with very short, very blond hair came near us and Saladin greeted him warmly, as if they had not met in a long time. I was forgotten.

Well, Saladin got me my taxi job soon after that meeting. How happy I was then! Just this foothold is what I needed to succeed in this country. My boss, the owner of several cars, didn't speak much with me even though he was a *deshi,* but I could see he thought well of me because of my connection with Saladin. He could have given the job to anybody else. He gave it to me because he had a respect for learned people like Saladin. He noticed, I think with a bit of fear, that I too read books. I am not the average high-class Bangladeshi who goes from the university to a cushy job, but I like to pick up a book here and there and try to learn something from it. Driving a taxi cab is thus quite a good occupation because you can read in the cab when waiting for customers. Often I would pull off to some side road to be away from passengers and just read.

On one such night none other than Saladin came up to my cab and surprised me while I was reading a book. I think he thought a bit better of me from that point on. Previously he may have thought that I was completely outside of his cultured society. We chatted a little on that drive. He took my phone number. Soon thereafter I got calls from him inviting me to come to his parties. I went a couple of times even though it was hard to get time off from my taxi cab shifts, even for critical matters. Each time I went I marveled at how Saladin, a fellow countryman, mixed so easily with women and foreigners. This was not something I could do, nor could my other *deshi* friends. An inexplicable hesitation stood in my way even when I knew what to say. It was different with the brown people from Mexico, Puerto Rico, and other Spanish-speaking countries who also lived in this city in great numbers, ordinary people like me, taxi cab drivers, construction workers, building cleaners. Through a halting foreign language I sensed a familiarity and an equality that loosened my tongue and made easy the affectionate slap on the back. They conveyed a warmth that I never expected from the upper-class *deshi* or Indian. Pakistanis I never liked anyway. They come to me as if we are brothers but they already forget what their army did in Bangladesh in 1971 in the name of religion.

So with the taxi cab work and my getting to know people like Saladin, I began to feel settled in the USA. I was bringing home a steady income and no longer lived off my card. Soon I would be able to send some money back home. Soon there would be other things . . . Things looked so good that one day I gave Saladin a phone call inviting him to dinner at my house. He accepted my invitation and I was truly happy. I had moved up in life by my friendship with so great a character. I was okay, like any one of those young well-heeled people I saw chatting away at the cafés, like Saladin himself. I had never gone in to any café but with my new found confidence I felt I could go in one day and sit at a table in an elegant café, just like that.

We had indeed become closer. At Saladin's insistence I used his first name only, dropping the respectful "Bhai" after the name. A rose is a not rose by any other name, otherwise why do people who come here change names? Without the appellation Saladin indeed appeared as someone like me, born under the same sun. He was someone with a better start, but still no more than another human being looking at the world through windows that were perhaps no clearer or wider than my own.

"Why are you here?" he asked me shortly after we began our meal.

"Why is anybody here? To survive."

"Money?"

"Yes," I hesitated, feeling trapped and yet convinced of my innocence.

"Why are you here?" I asked back.

"Me?" he replied taken aback. "The university I go to has the best film department in this country."

"You want fame?"

"You don't understand. I plan to make movies. Good ones."

He was different because he was a student. He was not here just to get a job. He was going to make movies. Movies with great messages that would change people's way of thinking, give them new dreams, offer solace in life through epic stories. He would be an "America-returned" movie maker in Bangladesh, living and conversing with other gifted people like himself. Sometime in the future.

I looked at him and could think of nothing good to say. Doubt grows insidiously and I was no longer secure about my little happiness. "A job is to survive, no matter what you do . . . ," I offered in a weak defense.

"You should not be so content. People do not respect a cab driver," he replied in a silky voice.

"You can not see their worth?" Anxiety was clouding my mind like a cold fog. Someone had applied a cold wet towel to my temple.

"Me? With me it is different. Why, in Bangladesh my family always accepted the servant as our own family member," Saladin replied quickly, with a note of irritation.

"The servant is a family member?" Can this be true? "Does he eat from the same table as everybody else?" I asked.

Saladin's face contorted in an ugly expression of anger. He stared at me under clenched brows. "Just what do you mean by that?" he whispered with a quiet vehemence.

Did I exceed my limits? But how could I back down?

I realized soon that we were not talking about the situations we each happened to find ourselves in at the moment, but about faceless fears that lurked deep inside our souls and the clashing philosophies of life they gave seed to. From the heights of his future glory, Saladin saw me without ambition, content with the little I had achieved and irritatingly incapable of comprehending the greatness of his dreams and of himself. I had missed his point, probed too deep on chance remarks, challenged assumptions he was not prepared to question and, somewhere, a raw nerve was touched. He was now speaking to another untiring and loyal, invisible listener, defending before an unknown judge his image that I had put on the dock. He had me in mind but he was no longer talking to me. He talked with a quiet violence about people who fall unawares into American banality, ignorant people who apply American norms to our culture without understanding "the parameters," who waste away their life amounting to nothing more than fodder for American materialism. I chewed small mouthfuls of my food slowly while he went on talking. "What irks me most, after the unthinking slide into degeneracy," he continued, "is that it is for no great cause, for no goals worth speaking of, that *deshis* shamelessly exploit the goodwill of others, as if help from other expatriates is a God-given right that can never be denied but must come unconditionally, no matter what, as if by virtue of a common nationality all personal deficiencies must be forgiven and forgotten." I had long finished eating and given up trying to reply honestly to anything he said; neither was I interested in agreeing and saying nice things just to placate Saladin. Instead I filled and refilled my glass with water and sipped it while Saladin talked away in a monotone, his mind stalking the woods and forests of a world none but he was familiar with. I sipped the water and looked askance at him trying hard to conceal my growing impatience. I only wanted him to leave.

That evening with Saladin may have faded from my mind long ago if it was not for a curious thing that happened afterwards. I lost my job in a week's time.

Now, I can not prove this but I am convinced that it was because of Saladin. I don't know just what he told my boss but it could easily have been any number of well-known secrets about me. I have no doubt everything he said was true. My boss didn't have to explain. The coldness in his voice, the paucity of his words, the averted look all told me that nothing I could do or say to him would change the decision. He no longer "needed me." He had made up his mind well before he talked with me. The only person who could help would have been Saladin, but Saladin never returned my calls. Now, if you think Saladin was not behind my getting fired, do you think he didn't even know about what had happened to me? He knew! My boss would respond to just a vibe from him! He knew very well!

I kept phoning Saladin and always his answering machine took my anxious messages. That he never got back to me was proof enough that he was the man responsible. Suspicion became bitterness, became a dull hatred that profiled Saladin and all he stood for. To drop me like that! I wanted to tell him what I thought of his speeches, his fancy parties, his high culture. For days I walked alone in the streets looking for work and thinking of nothing else but Saladin. He didn't care. I will make him care. He will not see me. I will pin him down. I will make him admit a thousand times over and more, he is false, false, false.

Arrogant, know-it-all who knows nothing!

I never got him. Life began to overtake me again, and yes, I had to give up trying to see him. But the desire for hitting him, attacking him in some way, that did not go away. Do you like being the lowly bug that somebody can just walk over without even a thought? What does it matter that I had no higher education, that I did not throw big parties, that I was only a cab driver? Is my worth less as a human being? From a hot gas that enveloped my brain the desire for revenge sublimated and condensed and became part of my beating heart. It was responsible for the new, stronger person I became, it was a source of strength in hard times. It was indeed a gift from Saladin that I cherished and did not want to see eroded by time, a talisman against despair. I worked harder, I saved every penny, I made new friends. And yet a certain lightness of spirit ebbed away and disappeared. Secretly, in rare moments by myself in the cab, in my bare room late at night, looking at the far sky through the small window, I would remind myself that life was not given for enjoyment but for becoming strong and to grow so nobody could demean me. The stars up there in the darkness would be my guide, their constancy my inspiration. Like them, I would live by my own truth. I had no need of praise or appreciation from the world. If others looked at me and saw nothing more than a taxi driver, I would still know all the good hidden by that label. Without university degrees I could still learn; shut in a taxi cab or in this little room I would travel infinite vistas. I would know myself, find my truth, make peace with my life, and I would let the disdain of others fall at my feet like flightless spears.

Time is an anomaly. The minutes slide grudgingly but the years fly by. They fly by and their gifts are removed, away from sight, till a long way along life's path they are unveiled in the very bosom of the present. More than a decade had gone by when one pleasant summer evening I found myself walking along a peaceful street lined with low offices placed between shops and residences. The blue of the sky had deepened to a purple and a beautiful full moon rested low on the horizon just above the houses. The yellow street lights had come on above my head. One of the windows was of a small real estate office, with color photographs of properties to be sold on the glass pane. I do not know what mysterious hand of fate made me pause to look at these photos, but I did. My glance went past them and fell on a brown face inside. There in that room was Saladin, working late, all by himself in this street corner real estate office! My heart beat fast and my throat became dry. I went in.

Ah! The unease of his eyes when they meet mine! "Saladin. How are you!" I said in a joy only half-affected.

"Quite well. What can I do for you?" He gave me a hard stare. He remembered me, but he did not want to.

I persisted. "You are working late, and all by yourself!"

"As you can see."

"Don't you make movies?"

"No. I work here, no time for movies."

How I admired his practical sense!

"Are you married and with children?"

"None of those things for me."

He had expected to hear worse things. I saw before me the very same arrogance and I remembered perfectly well my resolutions, but I was a small boy tiptoeing to catch the most desired butterfly in an open field. Fear of losing him calmed my feverish mind. I gave up any thought of talking about the past. A strange idea that I had never anticipated took hold of me. I had to go back to the scene of the crime, to the past, and I had to take him back there with me! The terrible accusations and the insults I had phrased and rephrased in my mind for precisely this encounter were pitiful drops of water that would never slake my thirst for revenge. That demanded life—warm, living blood. It required friendship.

Yes, I found out about how Saladin came to where he was today. With care and affection and patience, between visits he accepted reluctantly at first and then with resignation and habit, in light comments and masked excuses, he traced out the path from the great movie-maker he was to have been, the mover and shaker of society, the beacon of enlightenment, to the real estate agent he is today. I didn't need him to tell me the ending, for it was written all over him: his face, harassed by the real estate deals narrowly missed; his eyes, glazed by the late hours over boring descriptions of houses he wanted rich people to buy through him; his body, soft and bloated beyond recognition by virtue of the sedentary life he led; his mind, swimming in schemes to snatch away closures from his colleagues and incapable now of passions other than the square footage and location of houses, their prices, mortgage payments. This real estate agent was very far from the man whom I had one day met with trepidation and awe. This man was quite middle-class, harmless.

We come from different backgrounds and we meet today in another land, more equal than twins. This friendship is perfidy, you say? Yes, it is. I have no remorse. But know that it is a faithful friendship. No brotherhood is stronger than mine for Saladin. Friendship takes many forms and flows from many fountains, and who is to say that ours was not destined to be this? The human heart is mysterious. Like the photo developed from a negative, its source can be the inverse of what the eyes see. Revenge can be the seed of love, from which grows a fruit of exquisite taste, no less true than friendship from any other tree, all the more true because vengeance requires precisely that.

Fiction

Elvis of Manila

ERIC GAMALINDA

He looked at himself in the bathroom mirror and felt a twinge of remorse. The lightbulb over his head hissed like a heckler, casting a pale, jaundiced sheen over his unshaven face.

"I'm not going out on that stage tonight," he called out to someone in the bedroom.

"Of course you are," a woman answered him. "Everyone will be disappointed if you don't show up. You're the star of the show." Her last—encouraging—statement was immediately drowned out by the whir of a hair dryer.

"Let Mario Lanza be the star this time," he said, rubbing his chin. "He deserves a break."

"Honey, Mario Lanza died two years ago. Don't you remember? Choked on a piece of steak. Champagne brunch at the Odyssey. We were *there.*"

He stared at his face, remembering. Then, without taking his eyes off the mirror, he stripped his shirt off and pinched his love handles. "The Everly Brothers then," he said. "They're still around, aren't they?"

"Honey, the Everly Brothers were never as big as you."

"Or that new girl, Barbra Streisand."

The hum of the dryer stopped. "She *is* good," the woman in the bedroom said. "Sounds so much like Barbra. I swear, I can't tell sometimes if she's actually singing or just lip-synching, you know?"

"There you go," he said, and began to shave. "Let her steal the show."

In the mirror he saw the woman walking into the bathroom. Her hair had been teased to a kind of pouf. Her face was pale and pasty; she was holding a matte pressed powder case in her hand. She walked behind him and ran the other hand against his bare back. "Honey," she said. "*Nobody* steals the show from Elvis."

For close to a decade he was the Elvis Presley of Manila. Not just an Elvis—for there were hundreds of Elvises all over the archipelago, including a novelty act from Baguio who once sang *Blue Suede Shoes* dressed in feathered headgear and loincloth. He was *the* Elvis. Patsy and Pugo, the hosts of the talent search program *Tawag ng Tanghalan,* proclaimed him no less after he beat a succession of pretenders for eight consecutive weeks. Immediately after winning the grand prize, Sampaguita Pictures signed him up, and he swivelled his hips and snarled seductively for a good number of box office hits.

He was going to be immortal. He knew it, watching the *colegialas* squeal and faint in the studios of Channel 9. He could feel it in his bones when they went on tour, out in barrios light years away from Manila where farm maidens swooned as he gyrated on *entablados* festooned with buntings and balloons.

He went stumping on the campaign trail with a succession of politicians, and no shift in political power ever faded his star. He told Manila to vote for Lacson, and they did. Then he told them to vote for Villegas, and Lacson was out. He sang for Marcos, and Marcos returned the favor by giving him top billing at his inaugural ball, where Imelda, despite a butterfly-sleeved *terno* that seemed to make all movement impossible, danced the twist with him for a couple of minutes. And when Marcos declared martial law in 1972, he was still on centerstage, urging people to support the New Society.

Soon after that, however, for reasons he could never fathom, Elvis—the *real* Elvis—went out of style. No, worse: he became *baduy*. Disco edged him out of the clubs, the restaurants, the cocktail bars along Roxas Boulevard, the dancefloors of swanky hotels. His records disappeared from the shops, only to resurface in bargain bins along Calle Raon, where they sold two for the price of one. Kids cringed and giggled whenever *Love Me Tender* crooned over the radio. They thought it was too sentimental; they thought Elvis was too *smooth*. And the real Elvis had turned ugly and bloated like a stuffed turkey in Memphis, where nothing was happening.

He, however, remained Elvis of Manila. He could never shake that image, just as Elvis could never stop being Elvis. Once he got invited to perform at the noontime television extravaganza, *Student Canteen*. To his horror he was presented in a series of novelty acts, all of them clones. There was James Taylor of the Philippines, all nasal twang and hair. And then a sorry copy of the Village People who sang the Village People's songs—in Tagalog. And then two sets of the Eagles, both of them rendering *Hotel California* as faultlessly as the original.

Sometime after that, he met his future wife, a lab technician from Malabon, and he decided to give up being Elvis. It all happened naturally, not unlike molting, and with very little ceremony—he woke up one morning and decided, with little forethought, to shave off his sideburns. When he saw Lally later that afternoon, she merely remarked, "You shaved."

"Yes," he said.

"It looks good," she said.

Not that she wasn't interested in his career, or his history. She was young then, and she wanted a life, which meant a life beyond his being Elvis. She kept an album of his interviews and press shots and sometimes they looked at it and he told her stories about the crowds, the politicians, the midnight trips to nowhere. She liked it when hairdressers at Minda's Beauty Shoppe gasped, "You're married to Elvis of Manila?" But she felt relieved when that phase was over. She kept the album on a shelf, like a relic.

And Elvis of Manila felt he was transforming, but the transformation was gradual and painful. He welcomed it nonetheless, because when the crowds lost interest in him, he lost interest in the business. It was like that, he kept telling himself. You can't love with a one-way mirror. He wanted to get a job, but people kept telling him Elvis shouldn't be working as a sales clerk or an insurance agent. Finally, his wife got a post in a food lab in Encino, California, and they packed their bags and left the country one rainy day in August. He accompanied her on a tourist visa, but it was easy to stay on in those days, and lawyers were more than willing to take his case. He found a job as a filing clerk in a travel agent's office right next to Lally's lab. People in the Filipino grocery stores in Los Angeles still recognized him, but as the months wore on they got tired of yelling, "Hoy, Elvis!" and let him shop in peace. Soon he became not Elvis, but his real self, and he no longer felt uneasy writing his own name: Eddie Valdez. One evening he sat alone in their apartment in Encino and wrote his name over and over, saying it under his breath like a mantra, or a mike test.

He was happy being Eddie Valdez until the Filipino community, or the ragtag, nebulous diaspora that represented it, decided to stage Nostalgia Night at the Civic Center in Pasadena and called for a meeting three months before the concert. The show was for the benefit of the victims of the eruption of Mount Pinatubo. Nobody knew where Mount Pinatubo was except that it was making summer ten degrees hotter in Southern California, but they all pitched in: the Tribung Iloko, the Bisaya Confederation, the Veterans' Association and the Filipino Christian Renewal Association, among others.

The benefit was being coordinated by Sweetheart Pantig, who had immigrated to California around the time that Eddie Valdez and his wife did. They had known her from way back when they played marathon mah-jong sessions in her duplex in the Valley. Sweetheart was a mean mah-jong player and had wiped out many a Manila celebrity's savings.

"Where are you getting the money to put up the show this time, ha?" someone was asking Sweetheart when Eddie Valdez and his wife walked into the conference room of the Civic Center.

"Oy, I sued the nursing home that was taking care of my mother, they were treating her like garbage, *puta*," Sweetheart replied. "Oy, here comes Elvis."

"You look as gorgeous as ever," Eddie Valdez said, bussing her on both cheeks. "You don't look a day older." Sweetheart must have gained fifty pounds since her recent hysterectomy.

"Oy, Lally," Sweetheart said. "You watch your husband. He hasn't lost his touch. All the matronas will be running after him."

"Let them find their own Elvis," Lally said, walking towards a service tray burdened with rice cakes. There was little she could do to hide her annoyance every time Sweetheart, or anybody, teased them like that. "Is this *puto* real?" she asked, to change the subject.

"*Loka*, nobody makes real *puto* in America," Sweetheart said. "They're flour cakes. Very good, though. Shirley made them." The woman she referred to, a tiny, elderly lady sitting in an armchair, waved a tiny, ring-encrusted hand at Lally.

"Shirley *Temple*?" Lally gasped.

The elderly lady smiled and nodded her head. She primped her hair more out of reflex than vanity—her once much-envied peroxide ringlets which she flaunted in the heyday of Sampaguita Pictures were now clipped short. Beside her, sitting in another armchair and vigorously waving a fan across her face, was Carmen Miranda, once the rage of Philippine television, but now, thanks to plastic surgery performed during a visit to Manila, a raspy matron with her face pulled back to a look of perpetual surprise. Next to her were the Everly Brothers, Juanito and Alberto, who still had enough hair to sculpt into teddy boy waves with megahold gel, but who had both gained considerably around the girth. (Rumor had it, Sweetheart later confided to Lally, that they could only perform with their guitars tilted upwards, against their beer bellies, like a koto.) Then there was John Travolta, who had won the title in *Student Canteen* and even danced for Denny Terio during the semifinals of *Dance Fever* in Manila. And there was a younger performer whose name was Anna Marie Lepanto. She could sing any song, even Tagalog *kundiman,* like Barbra Streisand, and for the show she wouldn't mind being called Barbra of the Philippines, even if she had lived in California since she was seven.

They discussed the line-up of performers—including Filipino versions of Matt Monroe, Simon and Garfunkel, the Four Tops and Bob Dylan ("Ay," Sweetheart exclaimed, "he's better than Bob Dylan—he can *sing!*"). But when they began discussing the sequence of performances, they reached an impasse, because Carmen Miranda wanted to be the finale.

"No," Shirley Temple insisted, "Elvis should be the finale. Rock 'n' roll is a hard act to follow."

"We're not talking about acts," Carmen Miranda protested. "We're talking about who the people want to see most. I've been in more than two dozen films, many of them with Leopoldo Salcedo. I am not *just* Carmen Miranda."

"I've been in movies myself," Shirley Temple said.

"When you were a little *girl,* Shirley," Carmen Miranda said. "That's how they *remember* you."

"But if I hadn't come to the States—"

"Coming here had nothing to do with it," Carmen Miranda said. "You either last or you don't—"

"I was just trying to be helpful," Shirley Temple said. Tears were beginning to well in her eyes, not unlike the way they did when she made audiences cry in movie theaters.

"All right," Sweetheart cut in. "We'll draw lots."

"You're kidding," protested Carmen Miranda.

"It's the only way," said Sweetheart. "I don't want any hard feelings here. We're doing this for a *cause.*"

They threw their names in a Tupperware bowl, including those of the absent performers, and finally drew a list. The Everly Brothers were to open the show, followed by Shirley Temple, then Simon and Garfunkel, Matt Monroe, the Four Tops, Barbra Streisand, Bob Dylan, and John Travolta. Carmen Miranda would follow, and the show would close with Elvis. The line-up seemed satisfactory for most, though predictably Carmen Miranda stormed out of the meeting and threatened to convince her fellow Ilocanos to boycott the show.

As they filed out of the room, Anna Marie Lepanto walked beside Eddie Valdez and said, "I'm so glad you get to close the show. I mean, Carmen Miranda's probably OK, but she seems a bit, like, *dated.*"

Lally slipped her arm around Eddie's and said, "Honey, you chose the perfect word."

"Have you ever been to Graceland?" Anna Marie wanted to know. "I mean, for research or whatever. You being Elvis and all."

"No," Eddie Valdez said. "I wanted to, but it just seemed so—well, distant—"

"We wanted to go there for our second honeymoon," Lally interrupted him. "But we went to Las Vegas instead. We won six hundred dollars on the slot machine."

"Oh, how wonderful," Anna Marie said.

"Beginner's luck," Lally said.

Later that evening, as though she were merely continuing the thread of the conversation some hours ago, Lally told Eddie, "That was some honeymoon, wasn't it?"

"What?" Eddie Valdez said. He was trying on a pair of leather jeans and was struggling to zip the fly.

"Las Vegas," said Lally. "I still can't believe we won all that money."

"Sent by God," Eddie said.

"She's a nice girl, that Anna Marie," Lally said.

"Who?"

"The Barbra Streisand girl."

"Goddamn!" Eddie Valdez gave up pulling at the zipper.

"You've got two months to lose weight," Lally said. "You can do it."

"I wonder how Elvis did it," Eddie said, slipping the leather jacket on. He faced the mirror and looked at himself critically. "Do you think we should have gone to Graceland instead?"

"If we did, we would have ended up dirt poor," Lally said.

"We would have found a way to make ends meet," Eddie Valdez said. "We knew how to make money." But she was right. They used their winnings in Las Vegas to pay for two months' rent, because most of Lally's salary went to Eddie's immigration lawyers. How grateful he was to her back then, and—although he seldom acknowledged it—how disconcertingly dependent. But that didn't really matter. When they first arrived in America he not only stopped being a public figure. He became a shadow. He lived in the buffer zone of total anonymity, and could be anything he wanted to be.

That was long ago. *That was long ago* was something you said when things were beginning to change in your life, he thought. But he was in those moments before that, before things changed. He wanted change, and the thought filled him with trepidation, because he didn't know what he wanted to change into. "You know, I could really be Elvis all over again," he said to himself, and looked back to see if Lally had heard. But she was already in the bedroom, asleep before the TV, which had been left talking to itself.

On the night of the show he felt he was going to die. When was the last time he stood before a crowd? At Plaza Miranda, during one of the martial law anniversaries. No—at the Catholic Church in Encino, one Sunday, when the parish priest requested them to introduce themselves to the community of Filipino and Latino faithful. But that was different. He felt like he had walked into a party where he knew nobody, but the effusive camaraderie, superficial as a Sunday bazaar, soon engulfed him in the suffocating comfort of belonging. Tonight's performance, in comparison, was going to be hell. Why? Because Nostalgia Night was drawing bedroom communities from as far south as San Diego and as far north as Daly City. Because he had to show that once upon a time, in the Manila that everybody had forgotten, Elvis was alive and immortal as a pulsar. . . .

But by the time Simon and Garfunkel were strumming away onstage, his trepidation turned to panic. It didn't let up even as each number was boisterously applauded. People threw roses at Anna Marie Lepanto. Some sang along with Bob Dylan. And someone—a distant, disembodied voice from the balconies—shrieked shamelessly when John Travolta wiggled onstage.

"Good crowd, ha?" Carmen Miranda said to him as they stood by the wings. Even she seemed to be in high spirits, and conceding the finale to him— deftly negotiated by Sweetheart Pantig just a few days before the concert— seemed totally bygone. "People miss us, that's why," she said.

That was what he heard in his head the moment he went onstage. *People miss us.* But surely there was something else. When I swing my hips, he thought, the women in the orchestra seats scream and swoon, as though that gesture turned some automatic switch on. When I snarl, the faces in the front rows, all bathed in the garish stage lights, melt to sighs. Nobody can sing *Jailhouse Rock* like me. That's why I was Elvis of Manila. That's why everybody got lost in the bog of obscurity. That's why I'm here and they're some place I don't want to be: nowhere.

That feeling kept mounting to a crescendo even after the rousing curtain calls, even as they gathered backstage after the show and embraced one another with both elation and relief. He felt he was swirling in a daze, drunk and young and carefree. He looked around for Lally, but she was still in the orchestra rows, accepting kudos from friends. Anna Marie Lepanto, holding a bouquet of roses, walked to him and said, "You were the best." She planted a kiss, firm and confident, on his lips, her body pressed so close he could feel her warmth rising to him like a strong perfume. "I hope we see each other again," she said, as she placed a rose in his trembling hand. He stared at the rose and it seemed to enclose him in a cocoon of stillness while everything whirled around him: in that single flower was encapsulated the change that he knew was happening, now, in the eyes of the whole world, but only he could see it unfolding. He looked up and saw Anna Marie walking away, and wondered why he was filled with so much longing.

Then he saw Lally and started walking in her direction. But before he could reach her, a swarm of youngsters crowded around him, asking for his autograph. They were teenagers from one of the local high schools, and they were all dressed identically, with homeboy buzz cuts and oversized jeans.

"Man, that was *awesome*," one of the kids told him. "How long have you been doing that act?"

"A long time," he said. "Long before you were born."

"It's *great*, man," the boy continued. "Like, me and my friends, we were rolling down the aisles, you know? Like, it was *wild*."

"Glad you liked it," Eddie said.

"Hey," the boy continued, "I don't mean to put anybody down. I mean, I thought everyone was funny and shit, but you were the funniest of them all, man. Like, you were hysterical, man. You got real talent."

Later that evening, after all the wine, the food, and the interminable goodbyes, Eddie Valdez and his wife trudged up to their apartment in Encino. They walked straight to the bedroom, as was their habit. With their backs to each other, they changed into loose, frumpy, comfortable clothes—a cotton duster with lace hemming for her, boxer shorts and a loose undershirt for him. It was this transformation of apparel that delineated the borderzone between their life and the rest of the world, and it was a ritual that never failed to give them some sense of relief. Lally turned the coffeemaker on—only out of habit, because she wanted to slip right into bed but saw him sitting under the lamp in the living room.

"Best show you ever had," she said.

"Yes, it was," he said.

She turned the Panasonic player on and slipped in a tape of Elvis Presley standards. He smiled and tapped his feet to the music, but when she went into the kitchen to get the coffee, he pulled the tape out and was still looking for another when she came back.

"Didn't you like that one?" she asked him.

"I want to listen to something else," he said. But he didn't know what he wanted to listen to. Nothing. Silence. But it was never silent in Encino, at least not where they had lived since they first came here. There was always something that precluded even the idea of silence: the rumbling of traffic, the wailing of sirens, the chopping of helicopters beaming lights on runaway cars. When they first came here, he sat up all night listening to all the noises, still unable to believe that they had moved to another world.

From *Monkey King*

PATRICIA CHAO

Like most people I have many names. My father gave me "Delicate Virtue" in Chinese, but for the tough American world my parents decided that "Sarah Collisson Wang" had a ring to it. Herbert Collisson was the chairman of the Asian department at the Army Languages School in Monterey, where my parents were teaching then. But Sally is what I'm known as, Sally Wang-Acheson for the six years of my marriage, and since then I'm back to Sally Wang, those two flat *a*'s knocking against each other when Americans pronounce it, so graceless and so far off from what Daddy intended.

"What does it matter what Daddy intended?" I can hear my sister Marty saying. "He never gave a flying fuck about who we really were."

You should understand this: I am not the kind of person anyone ever expected to go crazy. That's more my sister's department. The only extreme thing I'd ever done in my life was to drop out of college to get married. I thought I'd never have to make a big decision again, except maybe whether or not to have children.

It's in my nature to hoard, and this turned out to be a godsend. My ex-husband, Carey, and I kept separate bank accounts, so when we got divorced the division of finances was simple. After I quit my job—telling my boss I wanted to freelance so I'd have more time to paint—I had enough savings to survive on for several months.

My new apartment in the East Village had a northeastern exposure and no coverings on the windows, so that I could sit in the baby rocking chair nights with the lights off and stare straight uptown to the silver spire of the Chrysler Building. Carey had kept most of the furniture, since it was originally from his family. My clothes were hung on exposed racks like a department store and I slept on a mattress on the floor. I had one mug, one glass, one plate, one set of cutlery, a single pair of chopsticks. Spare, the way I like things.

I actually did try working at home for a while, but it was just as excruciating as the office. Mornings I'd switch on the TV and just lie there, not getting to my drafting board until early afternoon, sometimes not at all. They fascinated me, those talk-show guests, bad skin slicked over with pancake makeup, as they related their dramas in quavering tones. I'd have to remind myself they were getting paid to do this.

I decided that what I needed to do was make my life extremely simple. Every Friday afternoon I went grocery shopping, always with the same list: a whole chicken, brown rice, and frozen vegetables. I'd stew up the chicken and live on it for a week. That was an old Wang tradition—even my sister, who can't boil an egg, has been known to call my mother long-distance for the recipe. One day at D'Agostino's a stock guy came up to me. "Hey, lady, are you all right?" I guess I'd been loitering in an aisle or something. Looking into his face, I realized he thought there was something wrong with me, maybe that I was mentally retarded.

I was cracking up and I knew it and I couldn't stop it.

It got worse. I couldn't tell anyone what I was seeing then. For one thing, my father was everywhere, a shock of white hair in the periphery of my vision, and then I'd turn and it would be a stranger, even a woman, or worse, nothing at all. Footsteps up the stairs at night, although I lived on the top floor and there shouldn't have been any.

I took the bus to Chinatown and wandered around scrutinizing every single little old man on the stoops, hoping this would break the spell. They mostly spoke Cantonese. Daddy's language had been a pure, educated Mandarin. Walking those teeming sidewalks, I felt totally alien although the tourists thought I was part of the scenery. When they stopped me to ask directions and I told them I didn't know, they were always amazed and put off by the fact that I spoke perfect English.

I found the old *bao zi* shop where my parents would take Marty and me. Chinese McDonald's Ma called it. I sat on a cracked green stool at the Formica counter and ordered a pork—*cha shao*—with an orange soda, like I used to. But when the steamed bun came I couldn't eat it. I drank my soda from the can through a bendable straw and watched old peasant women come in and order dozens of buns stacked in boxes tied with string. The women scolded the bakery man if he didn't have exactly what they wanted. He just smiled and was cheerfully rude back to them.

Chinese man the best to marry, Ma would tell Marty and me. Like American, basically tenderhearted.

Except Daddy. I had killed him in my head long ago, long before he actually died. What he had done to me was horrific. Still, I'd recovered. I'd even gotten married. So what was the problem? Why was he plaguing me now?

USELESS GIRL. WALKING PIECE OF MEAT.

I crossed Canal and went into Pearl Paint. It was mobbed, as usual, with serious and not-so-serious artists. On the second floor I meandered into the mezzanine, where the priciest oils were. Without thinking I picked up a couple of tubes of Old Holland cobalt violet light and slipped them into the pocket of my parka. My heart began to thud so hard I was sure it showed, but as far as I could see no one looked at me twice. I just clomped down those rickety loft stairs and strolled out of the store with eighty bucks worth of paint in my coat. No electronic beeper, no security guard grabbing my elbow.

In a store window I happened to catch a glance of myself and saw what a lowlife I looked, hair hanging down in a tangle. I hadn't even bothered to wash my face that morning. Amazing that I hadn't gotten stopped.

At a street vendor, I bought produce: pale chartreuse star fruit, persimmons, giant globes of winter melon. Then I went home and piled it all on a card table and tacked up a stretched canvas on my wall. Using a new palette, including the paint I'd stolen, I made several false starts. Nothing was happening—it was too static. I rearranged the fruit more gracefully, but this time it looked pockmarked and malevolent. I adjusted the light down and then the fruit looked dead again. *Nature morte.* Over the next couple of weeks I watched it all rot. It became a kind of pleasure to wake up and examine each new stage of decomposition. I almost couldn't bear to throw it out.

Fran suggested I try Chopin nocturnes. "Remember at school, when we'd get depressed? They always worked for you then." I dug out the tape and played it over and over, but the only thing it did was make me cry.

The bare night against the panes started to spook me. I unpacked one of my few boxes of marriage stuff, the steel blue Porthault sheets we'd never used, and stapled them up over the windows. The shroudlike heaviness of the drapery spilling down and pooling over the dusty floor was comforting. Now my apartment had two levels of brightness: dark or dim. I rarely turned on the lights.

I tried calling my sister. She was always out—at her job as a clown at the South Street Seaport, acting class, auditions, or the kinds of parties you read about in *New York* magazine. When I finally got hold of her she told me that her new boyfriend, a producer, had invited her to his villa in the south of France. The next thing I knew she was gone.

"Career connections," Ma explained to me from New Haven. By then I was hiding behind my machine, listening to the disembodied voices of the few friends who still called echoing in the empty apartment. My mother hates leaving messages and will just hang up and dial again, as if she could wear down the machine that way. She did this so many times in a row that one night I finally picked up, just so she would stop.

I told her I wasn't feeling well.

"New York City air," my mother diagnosed. "You come up to the country to rest. Stay as long as you want." Ma considers anything not Manhattan to be the country.

I decided it couldn't hurt. Although I had a set of perfectly good luggage Uncle Richard and Aunty Mabel had given me as a wedding present, I just threw some stuff into an old Macy's shopping bag. Maybe I wanted to make sure I wouldn't stay in New Haven long, which was a joke considering how soon after I arrived it became obvious that I would never leave.

Ma picked me up at the train station and then went back to Yale for a department meeting. We were in the middle of a January thaw, and I sat outside on the front steps and watched the snow melting off the eaves, plopping onto the gravel border. When you're clinically depressed something like drops falling can mesmerize you for hours. Then I wanted a cigarette and I'd forgotten to buy some before I left the city, so I went inside and up to my sister's room. Her desk was uncharacteristically bare, but in the top drawer I found used checkbooks, a letter from an old boyfriend ("My Winky" he called her), a ruffle-edged snapshot of the two of us on the swing set at our old house, and finally a pack of stale Larks.

The backyard was separated from the driveway by a concrete curb, beyond which the terrain sloped steeply into a flat meadow. I sat on the curb with my back to the house and lit up. Even in this season, through the acrid taste of old tobacco, I could smell the clean must of the evergreens. I felt a spark of hope. Perhaps after all it had been a good idea to come home. I could see myself leading a dull, comfortable life for a few weeks, doing errands for my mother until I got my brain back. I exhaled, watching the last of the smoke from my cigarette curl up in slow motion.

• • •

When I was still able to, I took the Honda over to our old house on Coram Drive. In physical distance, it was nothing, about five miles. When we lived there, the house, the last on a dead end, had been painted forest green with black shutters. It had changed hands a couple of times since my parents had sold it, and now it was buttercup yellow, with a neat white trim replacing the shutters. At some point the side porch had been insulated to serve as another room, because I saw white curtains at the windows. Thick ruffled curtains, not the delicate lace-trimmed ones my mother favors. The cozy effect was completed by a calico cat sitting on the sill, something that made me realize just how completely wiped out our presence there was. We never had any pets. Daddy said that animals belonged on farms, where they could pull their own weight and weren't just another mouth to feed.

The bedroom Marty and I had shared had a closet with a window. This had been my hiding place. From the window you could see past the grass island with its hawthorn bush and straight down the block to where the road made a sharp bend, by Witch Dugan's. You could check out who was out riding their bike, who was playing kickball, who was getting yelled at by their mother on their front steps. I peered up at the window but couldn't tell whether it was still being used as a closet or whether they had decided to make it into another tiny room.

It was too early in the season to tell if the daffodil bulbs my mother had planted along the front walk had survived. The hawthorn bush had been cut way back, almost to a stubble, and I couldn't see any berries. I looped the car slowly around the circle several times, wondering whether I should park in front and knock. Someone who'd paint their house yellow and owned a cat would certainly be friendly. Maybe they'd even give me a tour. I hoped my circling wasn't conspicuous. People were always getting lost on Coram Drive, it was such an odd little street, with its dramatic L-shaped bend and then suddenly the circle, which belonged to us, the neighborhood kids. We'd be out playing and have to scatter to the sidewalks or up onto the island when a stray car came by. "It's a dead end, stupid!" we'd hoot at the driver, who would either glare or look humiliated, depending on whether it was a man or a woman.

There were no kids out this time, not surprising on a bleak, tail-of-winter day. The Katzes' house next door had been knocked down a long time ago and someone had put up an ugly rawboned ranch that didn't go with the modest fake Colonials of the rest of the street. No doubt the goldfish pond out back had long since been filled in. I ended up not stopping at all but instead retraced my route out to Whitney Avenue, past St. Cecilia's and Lake Whitney and the wicked curve that was the last thing Darcy Katz saw in this life, and back home to the fancy house on the hill that contained only my mother, bent over the desk in Daddy's old study, paying bills. When she asked me where I'd been I told her out by the lake.

My lie gave me an idea. I needed to draw again. I couldn't read, and I couldn't paint, but there hadn't been a time in my life when I couldn't depend on that most elementary of connections between my eyes and the paper. I went up to the attic to look for the old box of drawing pencils and a half-filled sketch pad I knew were there from high school. The place was a mess: boxes brimming with schoolbooks, crates of Nai-nai's Limoges, which my mother thought was too good to use, packed in straw, ancient black fans with wicked-looking blades, bulging garment bags on hooks, moving cartons containing Daddy's old Chinese newspapers. Everything I touched brought up a puff of dust, making me sneeze.

And then I saw it, behind an old black trunk from China: the green plastic laundry basket filled with stuffed animals. They were battered almost beyond recognition, but I remembered them all: Buzzy the bear, Charlie the giraffe, Wilbur the donkey. I reached into the pile and pulled out the most raggedy one of all: Piggy. His fur, what was left of it, had been worn to a kind of sickly flesh color, the plastic snout with its two indentations still a garish orange. When his dark beady eyes caught the light from the overhead bulb, I felt a repulsion so great I almost dropped him.

In the next instant he looked benign, dirty and scarred, an old warrior.

I brushed him off and took him downstairs with me. For a while it would give me a jolt to see him sitting there on my pillow, plain and alone, but then I got used to it.

I had completely forgotten about my plan to go out by the reservoir and draw. By the time I remembered, it didn't seem worth it.

I began staying in bed all day. Every afternoon at one exactly Ma would come home from teaching, roaring up the driveway, clanging in the kitchen, and then rapping at my door. Without waiting for an answer, she'd push it open.

"You want cottage cheese? I make a nice salad, put fruit cocktail on it."

"No, Ma, I had something."

She knew I was lying and I knew she knew it, but we had to go through this ritual every day.

"Where all your grade school friends?" she asked me. "Maybe you call them, have party here."

"There's no one left," I said vaguely, and then I realized I had made it sound as if they were all dead.

I ventured out of my room only when I heard the door between the master bedroom and bathroom open as Ma went to bed and I could smell the soap from her bath in the hall.

Night was when I felt most comfortable. The house looked different then, the stark furnishings and Tudor arches friendlier in chiaroscuro. I wandered down to the kitchen and found food laid out on the counter: Chinese plum candies in blue and red wax papers, sesame crackers shaped like chickens, swollen-bellied pears in browns, greens, and yellows, tucked into the Rembrandt shadows of an earthenware bowl. Ma's own still life, to tempt me. The refrigerator was stocked with cottage cheese and plain yogurt, things that my mother herself never ate, but she must have remembered my vegetarian phase in boarding school. I sat down at the kitchen table and like an animal devoured what I had picked out, not knowing or remembering what I was cramming into my mouth, staring out at the black beyond the tiny window over the sink. Sometimes I'd take the food into the living room and consume it sitting on the floor with the TV on, sound off, even though I had no idea what was going on, watching simply in order to concentrate on something besides the static in my own head.

When even silent TV became unbearable, I went down into the basement and sat there in a dream until the sun came up.

My one-month visit had spilled into two. Ma made me an appointment with her doctor, who ordered a bunch of tests. The tests turned up nothing. I was underweight, but not seriously so. The doctor suggested that I see a psychotherapist.

My mother thought this was nonsense. "All you need is career. That takes your mind off personal problems. You seen my sewing scissors?"

"No," I said.

One afternoon Ma came to my room and announced that she had invited Lally Escobar to tea. "She especially wants to see you."

"I don't want to see her." I was lying in bed as usual, still in my pajamas.

"But she knows you're home. What am I suppose to say when she ask for you?"

"Tell her I'm asleep."

My mother said firmly, "You come down," and shut the door.

The only place I could think of to hide was the basement. I made it down to the first floor without Ma hearing. The teakettle began to whistle at the exact moment I opened the basement door and shut it behind me in a single motion. At the bottom of the stairs I held my breath. The kitchen floorboards creaked as my mother moved about above me. Then I heard the chimes of the doorbell and short quick creaks as she went to answer it.

I didn't dare turn on the light. When my eyes got used to the dark I edged my way deeper in through the maze of boxes and old furniture, the oil furnace growling in the middle, and finally reached the corner where I'd made a kind of nest for myself out of an old stadium blanket on top of several rolled-up rugs. I drew my bare feet up and tucked the bottom of the blanket around them.

Lally and my mother were talking. There was a package of Pepperidge Farm lemon nut cookies on the table between them. Because they were having Western tea, Ma was using her tulip tea set that had cups with handles. There was a bizarre rasping noise that I recognized as Lally's laugh. I pictured her in her gardening outfit—a pink-and-green-striped turtleneck and overalls—although she probably wouldn't be wearing that today.

I waited, growing colder. The dark pressed against my ears, so that I could hear my blood pounding. I covered the sides of my head and tried to slow down my breathing. The furnace rumbled. Lally wasn't laughing anymore. In fact, it was perfectly silent above. I imagined slowing down my breathing more, suppressing my heartbeat, like the yogis in India. Only I'd will it past suspended animation. I'd make myself die.

I reached down between the rolled-up rugs and felt for Ma's sewing shears. It wasn't the easiest thing to do in the dark, but I knew where there was virgin skin, up near the crook of my elbow. The feeling came, not as sharp as it would have been if it hadn't been so cold, and it didn't last nearly long enough.

There was one window high up in a corner that let in a bit of daylight, and I made myself concentrate on that. My cut began to throb. I pressed a corner of the blanket against it.

PIECE OF MEAT.

The window had gone completely dark by the time I finally decided it was safe. I unfolded myself from the rugs, stamped around a bit to get the circulation back in my legs, and then went up the basement stairs, slowly and deliberately this time. When I opened the door there was my mother sitting alone at the kitchen table, looking directly at me. The tea things had been cleared away, and the dishwasher was humming. I blinked hard, getting used to the light, and saw that my arm looked much worse than I'd imagined. I hadn't been so neat this time.

For a moment I thought she wasn't going to say anything at all. I turned to go on upstairs to my room.

"Lally gave me the name of someone. A woman doctor." I must have looked blank, for she added: "A doctor for your brain."

"A psychiatrist?"

"She has a medical degree from Yale. Good reputation."

So this was it. If my mother admitted it, I really was crazy.

I knew in my bones that no matter how brilliant this person was, she'd never be able to cure me.

From *A Cab Called Reliable*

PATTI KIM

My teacher usually loved anything I wrote that was about Korea. But my submission for the Young Writers Contest disappointed her. She told me that the writing in my story about aunt Han-il was technically just fine, nearly professional. However, the story itself was difficult to believe. "One is required to suspend an unreasonable amount of one's disbelief," she said with a friendly frown.

Within three pages, I had written my aunt's life story. She was abused and driven to insanity by her father, stepmother, and brothers. Her father sold her into a marriage in order to have his debts canceled. Her husband tormented her emotionally, physically, and mentally. My aunt then ran away from her home to live in a Buddhist temple, where she cooked meals for the monks. Haunted by past memories, she returned to the family with poisoned rice cakes. Her father, stepmother, and brothers gladly ate them and died instantly. Aunt Han-il burned down the house, emigrated to America, worked as a secretary in a doctor's office, married a Ph.D., had two daughters, and lived happily ever after.

My teacher said that I had enough material for an entire novel, and I could not possibly do justice to my aunt's life in three pages. The ending was artificial and contrived. Returning my story to me, she asked, "Ahn Joo, do you ever hear voices?" Without giving me a chance to respond, she told me to listen to them.

When I laid down in the center of my room with my palms pressed on the floor and my eyes closed, I heard the voice of my mother. She told me to do this and do that, don't do this and don't do that, you're good enough for this, but not good enough for that. I memorized the way she sounded, so that when I woke up, I could go to my notebook and record it.

Third place went to a Japanese girl, who wrote a diary comparing and contrasting her life in Kyoto with her life in Arlington; second place went to a boy, who wrote about his blind father reading him and his little brother bedtime stories in the dark; runner-up was awarded to an essay called "How to Save the World Through Arts and Crafts," written by my classmate, Jennifer Beechum, whose father was a well-known painter of some sort; and I was awarded first place for my piece, "The Voice of My Mother."

My teacher returned it to me with a gold star on the top right corner of the first page. She said that it was a mature, honest, powerful, poignant, and sophisticated piece of writing, and I should give serious thought to becoming a writer some day. Jennifer Beechum and I were to read our writings during our graduation ceremony.

My father could not attend my graduation ceremony, which was held on a Wednesday in the middle of the afternoon, because he was working in Washington, D.C. When I showed him my report card for the final marking period and told him I had won first place for a story I had written about Mother, he asked, "What did you say? What did you say about her?" To put him at ease, I lied and told him I had written about the time she made me mussel soup for my birthday.

"I'm reading it tomorrow for graduation," I said.

Glancing at my report card, he poured more milk into my glass and said that graduating from elementary school was only the first step. Graduating from college, now that would be a real accomplishment. He looked at my report card again, pointed at all my A's, and told me I was his only hope.

"I hate milk," I said.

"Drink it or you'll stop growing," he said and put a spoonful of rice into his mouth.

That night I went to bed early because I could not hold back my tears. In bed I told myself to stop or else my eyes would swell and reading with swollen eyes was impossible. Clearing my throat, I practiced saying aloud: "My name is Ahn Joo Cho, and my essay is called 'The Voice of My Mother.' I have written something called 'The Voice of My Mother,' which I will be reading to you today. 'The Voice of My Mother,' a prose poem by Ahn Joo Cho . . ." And I reminded myself never to say thank you. Why should I, like a leper, beggar, orphan, thank them for listening to me?

When the principal called my name, Ahn Joo Cho, as the recipient of this year's Young Writers Award, I stood up and walked with bowed head to the podium where the microphone was waiting for me. Jennifer Beechum had already read her essay and she had received great applause that I did not think my reading would match. She had family in the audience, who clapped and yelped and blew sharp whistles her way. The auditorium was full. At the foot of the stage the school band was getting ready to play the closing song. My teachers were scattered throughout the room. The clock on the opposite wall read 12:30. I pulled down the microphone, cleared my throat, and in my most confident voice said, "This is 'The Voice of My Mother.' She passed away a year ago.

"Chew on parsley if your mouth tastes old. Smear chicken grease on your lips so no one will think you go hungry. Boiled dandelion leaves with sesame oil and seeds make you go to the bathroom. Raisins soaked in *soju* relax your muscles. Chew gum, it'll help you digest. But don't chew gum like that with your teeth showing. Just like those country cows. No one wants to see your crooked teeth. When you smile, keep your lips together. Don't scrunch up your nose and eyes like that when you laugh—you'll get wrinkles. Why do you laugh so loudly? What do you have to laugh about? What do you have to cry about? Did your mother die? Is that why you cry? Or are you crying because your mother's still alive? Are you going to stop the tears or not? Stop biting your nails. They'll think you go so hungry, you have to eat yourself. Who taught you to eat your fish like that? You leave all the good parts. Suck out the fish eyes, they'll make you see better. Don't make me buy you eyeglasses.

Where do you go to buy eyeglasses here? Suck out the fish brain, it'll help you speak English. Then you can go buy your own eyeglasses. Chew on the bones, but don't swallow them. Chew and spit them out. America has no place to remove fish bones from a stupid girl's throat. Girls stupid enough to swallow fish bones deserve to choke. Don't hold your rice bowl in the palm of your hand. You want to make me a mother of a peasant? At home, eat slowly; outside, eat fast or everyone else will eat your seconds and thirds. But don't eat like you haven't been fed. Eat like a lady. Get your seconds and thirds, like a lady. But get your seconds and thirds. What do they feed you at school? Do you get enough? Crazy girl. Why aren't you eating? What are you going to live on? If you don't eat, you're going to be a midget. You'll never grow as tall as these American girls. Don't you want to look like them? Don't you want to be Miss America? Eat. Your hair won't grow. You won't ever need a bra. Your teeth will fall out. You'll stay ugly like that forever. Who's going to marry you? We'll have to send you back to the bridge where the lepers live. That's where we found you, underneath a bridge. You don't belong to me. No child of mine sucks on ice cubes used to freeze fish. Get away from me. You're so dirty. I can't believe you're sucking on those ice cubes. No one's going to marry you. Again? You're crying again? What do I have to do? You want butter and soy sauce in your rice? You want fried *kimchi*? You want fried anchovies, pork dumplings, kelp? Stop complaining. The cabbage here isn't the same. What do you want me to do, fly to Korea? How am I supposed to make you *shik keh* in this country? Even if I could, I wouldn't make it for a selfish, picky girl like you. You should know. You expect to find *jja jjang myun* here? *Been deh dduck, paht bing su, ho dduck*—in America? Eat what you have or starve. What do you want me to do? You want pink fish eggs, green fish cakes? You want rice cakes, don't you? You want dates and pine nuts? Where am I going to find rice cakes? Ahn Joo-yah, what are you crying for? Did your mother die? What are you crying for?"

There was an uncomfortable silence in the auditorium. When I looked up, I caught sight of my teacher, leaning against the kitchen door with her right hand over her heart. The two flute players below me yawned. There was a shuffling in the back where mothers began setting up trays of cookies, cakes, and donuts. When I said, "The end," the audience politely applauded. I reluctantly bowed, said thank you, and returned to my seat, where Jennifer Beechum, elbowing me, said, "Way too weird. Way too dark. Way too depressing."

That evening, my father brought home an electric typewriter that was missing its A and E keys and told me not to make any rice for tomorrow's dinner because he was going to take me to a Chinese restaurant. He asked how graduation ceremony went. Showing him my writing, proudly wearing its gold star, I told him I had read it aloud without making a single mistake, without stuttering once. He skimmed through the pages, palmed my head, tilted my neck back, and said that my writing was the prettiest he had ever seen.

The Goddess of Sleep

GINU KAMANI

Babies whose feet don't touch ground in their first seven months escape contamination by bad spirits. That's what they say. When Steven first heard of it he recognized immediately that this described the Goddess of Sleep. She had escaped the malevolence that plagued ordinary mortals, and did not even know it. She was a genius at sleep. In her own bed she excelled at slumber, but even in unfamiliar locations she rested peacefully, suffering marginally if it all. He marveled at this uncanny ability to surrender her body to the abyss.

Her talents as the Goddess of Sleep were masked at first by their shyness in bed. Though they embraced long and lovingly, skin touching skin, they separated before sleep settled in and spent the nights side-by-side. He awoke every night at two or three as was his habit, wishing he could fall back to sleep but too anxious to do so. He would watch her then for hours, watch her peaceful breathing, the stillness of her spread hair and gently curled fists. Sometimes she would open her eyes and catch him staring at her, his breath gentle on her cheek. She would smile and turn away, effortlessly reentering the wave of sleep without a ripple to mark her entrance. His panic would overwhelm him then, as if the bus for which he had been racing had abruptly left him sweating on a windy street.

A month or so into the relationship they found their timing, and the first time he unleashed the powerful ripples of her potent muscle, he counted more contractions than he had ever known in a woman. They prepared for sleep with some haste on his part that night because he sensed the possibility of a breakthrough.

Lying on his side he drew her body carefully around his so they formed twin curves extending from shoulder to heel. In minutes she was asleep, and her soft, unwavering breathing melted his body into a pliant liquid that entered into the vessel of her body and took on the shape of her restful peace. He awoke in confusion with the sun piercing his eyes, and cried with relief at having spent the night in dreams.

They discussed their night with great enthusiasm. She had never fallen asleep clasping a lover before. And he never being clasped. He worked steadily on closing the gap between his Goddess's crowning moment and the passage into sleep they took together now. He willed his fingers to grow, relax, twist with unimagined suppleness. He learned to drape himself around her so he could absorb the racking spasms, and while her body still pulsed from her release, their combined breathing slowed to a gentle roll that slid them effortlessly down the chute of sleep.

So many women had preceded his Goddess—his search for the Sleeping Beauty he could lie down with, break bed with, leach sleep from undisturbed.

Instead he had stumbled through years of mismatches—women who misunderstood his mission and faked orgasms for him; women who feared his clutching and had nightmares about him; chronic insomniacs who wanted nothing more than to keep company with him. But he definitely had the Goddess of Sleep this time. She smelled right, emitting pheromones of celebration, not fear. She felt right, her skin soft and smooth, covered with silky dark hair. She tasted like mother's milk. She had never rehearsed a climax. She never remembered her dreams.

Her parents came to visit. Unlike their daughter, they still carried the inflections of their native India in their accent, idioms, and pliant body language. They too slept the sleep of the blessed. Was this then a family trait? They laughed at Steven's question. Everyone in India sleeps, they insisted. No problem. In the heat, in the cold, in houses, out in the open, men, women, children. . . . The Goddess of Sleep assured him that this trait emanated from within the culture. He scoffed at her naiveté, mocking this explanation. The parents rose to the challenge and regaled him with stories of individuals sleeping through war, through marching bands, through doors being smashed in, violent storms at sea, on the median of the most congested urban streets. With every story, he felt his heart beating faster. Sweat poured down his back; he felt like a junkie in need of a fix. He turned to the Goddess with shaking limbs. "Why didn't you tell me?" he demanded, his tongue thick with desire. "Take me there now!"

The Air India flight proved the perfect introduction to his coveted kingdom of sleep. As he patrolled the aisles, he saw the Goddess's countrymen lost in snores in the most uncomfortable of positions. Crying babies did not awake them, nor did chattering stewardesses or announcements from the flight deck. They landed in Bombay in the darkness of predawn. The airport was brightly lit with fluorescent tubes, noisy and crowded with residents awaiting their loved ones. Impervious to the bustle, rows of plastic seats cradled human forms divinely suspended in slumber. On the pavements outside where taxi drivers pushed and shoved for access to passengers, prone bodies lay dissolved in rhythmic breathing, oblivious to those stepping over them. The uncomplicated abundance of sleep brought hot tears of envy to his eyes.

Don't you recall in childhood, mused the Goddess, falling asleep at parties, or at the cinema, or on the noisiest bus or train? We're trained in this kind of chaos. We have no choice but to make lullabies of this vitality.

The hotel was located in a crowded area. By day, hordes of office workers filtered through the streets. Book and magazine vendors spread their wares on the pavement, makeshift canvas stalls displayed imported goods, food stands fried up spicy snacks, all attracting commuters as they hurried between their trains and office buildings and back again. At night, families ventured out for a late stroll, wealthy patrons flocked to expensive restaurants, and pavement dwellers prepared their evening meals and settled down for the night.

But here sleep teased him too; rather than lying awake beside the Goddess, Steven found himself returning to the dark streets each night without her, reluctant to return to the hotel. Close to midnight, revellers still jostled by in groups, searching out a bite to eat. Kerosene lamps blazed brightly at each locus of activity, and within inches of the bustling commerce, humans spread themselves out in sleep.

Even later, Steven watched a solitary old man cook his late meal on a small stove, eat out of the pan, wash it out over the gutter with a cupful of water, then pack all his worldly belongings into a small bag. A body-length rectangle of plastic spread on the rough pavement was his bed, and in seconds he and his bag disappeared under a grimy sheet.

All night the inert, shrouded forms on the sidewalks beckoned him. Never had Steven experienced stepping over and around the various postures of sleep. Many times he paused amongst the cloaked forms, listening intently to their palpable exertions. Each body in trance concealed a body in healing.

The next night he was back to watch his solitary friend prepare for sleep. The old man recognized him and waved in greeting. Squatting on the pavement finishing his meal, he spoke to the nearby stall owner, who wryly translated in English. The foreigner was being invited to share a meal. Would he accept? No thanks, Steven replied, Already eaten. But he had a question for the kind street dweller: Where did he learn to sleep? The stall owner scratched his chin with amusement. He repeated the question once, twice to the old man. Back came the astonished reply: At his mother's breast, where else?

The dark man washed out his vessel with a great show of scrubbing and polishing, aware of being watched. Then he sat back and watched the foreigner watching him. They sat in silence for a while, and the man made no move toward rolling out his plastic sheet. Steven prodded the stall owner and pleaded: The man should sleep, he liked watching him sleep. Thoroughly entertained, surrounded by a gaping crowd, the translator conveyed Steven's request. Back came the irritated reply. In his country, did they not sleep?

The conversation transformed into a communal event, an impromptu convention on a busy street. A barrage of questions in broken English flowed unabated from the growing crowd. Dark eyes twinkled and flashed, hands touched him casually, ascertaining his corporeal nature. A feeling of deep benevolence descended on the American as he fielded inquiries on a vast array of topics. Even as he spoke, individuals thrust out their hands to be shaken, savoring the feel of having gone palm to palm with him. Others ran fingers down the crease of his pants and over the fine leather artistry of his Italian shoes. The crowd closed in on him with effortless coagulation. His skill tingled with waves of contact. His body filled with unfathomable well-being. Soon he had both arms over the shoulders of chatty young men who invited him for a cup tea. As they left the spot, he noticed that in the midst of his own adrenaline surging, the street dweller had veiled himself and fallen asleep.

Two nights stretched into five, and the Goddess seriously worried about her lover. He stayed out until dawn, then escorted her all day through family visits, shopping, sightseeing. He seemed to have given up sleeping, yet glowed with an unfamiliar light. Something had changed in their lovemaking, too. They made love as before and the Goddess relinquished herself to the depths but he held himself aloof, waiting for the tide of anxiety to wash over him, but it never came. Instead, each night he would feel a vague stirring within him and images of his street friends would dance again through his mind.

The groan of the ceiling fans, the horns of passing cars, the shouts of passersby swirled in a time-tested melody. He felt a yearning to lose himself in the dense crowds, to be ogled by the dark-eyed stares and the impulsive reachings for his skin. He liked the sensation of locking his gaze with every passing individual, of being endlessly consumed by the quizzical masses, of emotionally recharging through the powerful call and response expressed in a look, in a smile, in a posture that invited "Show Me."

Steven gazed a long last time at his sleeping Goddess and knew this was no longer where he belonged. He got up and slipped out the doors and into the beckoning human stream.

Ginu Kamani

From *The Necessary Hunger*

NINA REVOYR

In December of 1984, when Raina and I were sophomores, my high school held its first and last annual girls' winter basketball tournament, the Inglewood Christmas Classic. The next year, an hour before the first-round games were set to start, a light fixture fell from the ceiling and left a six-foot hole in the floor, and the indignity of having to cancel the tournament once convinced my coach we shouldn't host it anymore. This was a shame, because the first Classic was the only tournament we ever actually won. It was also the place I met Raina. I was running the clock on the first day when my coach came over and told me that Raina Webber had just walked in, and that I should pay attention to her. He didn't add—he couldn't have known—that a few months later, our parents would meet and fall in love, and that eventually the four of us would live together. All he knew then was that Raina and I were two of the top sophomores in Los Angeles County. That day, when her game began, I sat and watched her in awe, so dazzled by the way she slashed through the other team's defense that I kept forgetting to add points to the scoreboard. Midway through the second quarter, Raina dove for a loose ball and landed smack on the scorers' table. She'd knocked the scoreboard control box into my lap, and she lay facedown, her head between my hands where the box had just been and her legs trailing onto the floor. Dazed, she looked up into my face for a moment. Then her eyes began to focus.

"Hey," she said, smiling. "You're Nancy, right? I'm Raina. That was a hella sweet pass you threw against Crenshaw yesterday, and I know their coach called you a hot dog 'cos you passed behind your back, but shit, there *was* a defender kinda standin in your way, and besides, if you got it, you should use it, don't you think?"

She stood up, pulled the box off my lap and placed it on the table, and then ran back onto the court before I had time to answer. To me, that first encounter would repeat itself in various forms through all the years I knew her— Raina would land in front of me, and I would flounder.

Basketball, for Raina and me, was more a calling than a sport; it was our sustenance; it underpinned our lives. Every Sunday morning, as I drove the twenty-eight miles from our house in Inglewood to a gym in Cerritos, I saw well-dressed people on their way to the churches, mosques, and synagogues that were scattered throughout Southern California. I was en route to my Junior Olympic team's weekend practice, but my intention wasn't really so different. That drive to Cerritos was my weekend ritual, but it made up just a fraction of the time I gave to my sport. I was reverent and devout. The only differences between my faith and theirs were that I wore workout clothes instead of my Sunday best and that I worshipped every day.

Los Angeles was a great place to live if you were a basketball fanatic, because the sport was all around you. Besides being the only city that had two NBA teams—the Lakers and the Clippers—it was the home of half a dozen major colleges. Better yet, the players were part of the scenery. In the mid-eighties, when I was in high school there, it wasn't unusual to run into Magic Johnson at the mall; see Byron Scott drive through the neighborhood on his way to visit his mother; or spot Cheryl Miller, the great USC star, dancing up a storm at a local nightclub. Each August, Magic, Isiah Thomas, and other NBA stars would play pickup games at UCLA, and I'd go watch them as often as I could. The world was perfect on those summer afternoons. If Jesus himself had finally shown up, I wouldn't have noticed unless he'd worn sneakers and had a dangerous jump shot.

In our own small way, we high school players were celebrities, too. For one thing, we weren't subject to the same rules as other students. When my teammate Telisa got sent to the principal's office our junior year for calling her physics teacher an asshole (well, he *was* an asshole—he called Telisa a wench, because he referred to all women as wenches, and she finally got sick of it and told him off. All the girls in the class applauded when she did it, too), the principal just laughed and let her off without even listening to her side of the story. We were picked to win our league that year, and he refused to punish one of the people responsible for wresting glory away from the schools around us.

For another, we were always being recognized. This was especially true once our pictures started appearing regularly in the papers, and, in my case and in Raina's, after we'd been named third-team All-State our sophomore year and had begun to attract the attention of college scouts. I'd be shopping, or getting gas, or hanging out at the beach, and someone would come up and tell me that they'd seen me at such and such a place playing against this or that team, and that I'd scored however many points that day. Once, when I was with Raina at the movies our senior year, some little freshmen who'd seen her play in a tournament somewhere started screaming and asked for her autograph like she was a rock star.

The admiration was occasionally more ardent. I received a couple of suggestive fan letters, some players were given flowers or candy, and sometimes I even got phone calls from people who seemed impressed by things other than my skills on the court. After Raina moved in we got twice as many calls. She dealt with this better than I did. She talked to all her callers politely and said that she was sorry, but she already had someone and so it was impossible for her to meet them for a date. I, on the other hand, was not as composed—I always just got nervous and hung up.

If my teammates had ever heard me say I wasn't comfortable with being a big-time college recruit, they would have laughed long and hard, but it was true. As an only child, I lacked the social skills to shift easily into the role of semipublic figure, and I wasn't even gifted physically, except with height. Once, after a summer league game, I found a scouting report that a college coach had left in the bleachers, and so discovered that the official word on me was this:

Nancy Takahiro, Senior Forward—6´ 0˝, 155 lbs. Doesn't have the best athletic ability, but a great scorer and effective rebounder. Smart, consistent, tremendously hardworking, and can be counted on to get the little things done.

I always wondered what my father would have thought about the "getting little things done" part, since his refrain throughout those years was that I never cleaned my room. Still, it was the textbook portrait of a type-A only child. Takahiro means "tall and wide."

It wasn't easy being big. It seemed to me that the world had a grudge against big people, especially Asian ones, like me, who were supposed to be small. A few houses down from us there lived an old widow named Mrs. Cooper, a lady whose skin was both the color and the texture of a walnut shell, and every time I passed her on the street she clutched her purse a little tighter, although we'd lived on the same block together for the past eleven years. Short adults glanced up at my face suspiciously, even when I was being polite. Babies looked at me and burst out crying.

Maybe that's why I was drawn to Raina, because she was compact, her body well- proportioned and economical. At 5′ 7″ she wasn't tiny, but she was still five inches shorter than me. Tougher, too, or so I believed—and I felt qualified to say that because I watched her more closely than anyone else, with the possible exception of the scouts. The day she landed on the table and introduced herself, her team, which was seeded eighth, was going up against the number one seed. Raina was the shooting guard on that underdog team, and she was making all the other players look like they were standing still. She moved around the gym as if it had been built for her—not arrogantly, but with the casual assumption that everyone knew it was hers and wouldn't mind that she'd come there to claim it. She was always the first person up the court, always weaving through people like they were rooted to the floor, not because she was so much quicker than everyone else, but because it didn't seem to occur to her that she could fail. When she stood at the free throw line, she stared at the basket and held the ball at her waist as if she'd forgotten she had to shoot it, as if she could score the point just by concentrating hard enough. This attitude, I learned later, was typical Raina—she approached every aspect of the game as if it were a matter of will.

And who's to say it isn't? Over the years coaches and parents have encouraged kids to participate in sports on the grounds that sports build character. I've always thought it was more accurate to say that they *show* it. You live the way you play. A kid who blows an easy lay-up in the last few seconds of a close game is going to choke ten years later on the witness stand. A kid who can kick a field goal to win the state football championship could be trusted to land a plane in a tornado. If there is something to be known about a person, it will become evident on the court, or on the field. People with no experience in competitive sports don't understand how revealing they can be. Or how serious. Anyone who thinks traders on Wall Street are under pressure should try shooting a free throw in a packed gym with the game on the line.

When I saw Raina play that day, saw the way she stamped her foot against the floor in a stubborn refusal to give up, I knew my own devotion to basketball was just a shadow of what I was witnessing then. She played the game the way that it was meant to be played—as if her life depended on it. And she seemed driven by some need, or struggle, or fundamental resolve, that preceded the basketball and made it possible, and that I could never have accurately explained or described except to say that I myself didn't have it. The immediate effect of this resolve was that her team came back from ten points down that day to beat the top seed, which had finished second in the state the year before. Two days later, in the semifinals, her team would lose to the team *we* went on to beat for the championship, but that day, the day of the first-round games, was Raina's. As I sat at the scorers' table watching her team celebrate at midcourt, I wondered about the guts and will that had led to that improbable charge from behind. And later, when I noticed her strong, broad cheekbones, her suddenly hesitant step, the shy grin that flashed out of that smooth coffee-with-cream face, I wondered about the person who owned them.

Although Raina might have said I never made a fool of myself over her, I was a better judge, and I know that I did. I was fifteen when I met her, and at the beginning of an awkward phase that would last for roughly another decade, but I managed, somehow, to stumble my way into her life. We had some friends in common through summer league and the Amateur Athletic Union; through them I'd find out what game or party she planned to attend and then show up at it myself. My main source of information was Stacy Gatling—a high school teammate of Raina's who played on my spring league team that year. She was, like us, a lover of women, or as we put it, "in the family." Within a week of the beginning of spring league she informed me that Raina had a girlfriend, an older girl named Toni, and gave me her opinion of the calm, cool way I tried to deal with my attraction for her teammate.

"She knows you like her, Nance," Stacy told me in the middle of a game one day while we were both warming the bench. "It's fuckin obvious. You act like a fool around her."

"Shit," I answered. "Shit."

"Stop trippin, girl," she said. "It's all right. You know she don't want you, so just play it cool. She likes you, though, so don't mess the friendship up by actin all crazy and shit."

I hadn't known that Raina was spoken for, although I'd heard that she was gay. It was one of the great ironies of gossip that all the paranoid straight players who talked incessantly about who was gay actually did us the service of helping us find each other. That was how Stacy had heard about me, and I her. Anyway, Stacy went on to tell me that Raina's relationship with her girlfriend, Toni, was extremely rocky, or as she put it, "drop dead hella intense." This didn't surprise me, although I didn't say so. You live the way you play.

I would say that each love has a moment when it makes a mark on your poetic consciousness, when it rearranges the way you see both the love itself, and through it, your entire life. For me that mark was made the next July, when Raina and I, and a hundred other recruits, headed off to a nearby college to attend Blue Star. In theory Blue Star was a basketball camp, an instructional week, but in truth it was a glorified meat market—and it would become more so, in the next few years, as the popularity of women's basketball grew. That summer, two or three hundred vultures from colleges all over the country sat perched on one side of the stands and watched us, the main attraction, numbered and thrown onto the court like performing animals. Blue Star was big business, invitation only; we got free basketball shoes from Converse and a navy-and-red camp T-shirt that would unravel after the first time we washed it. Although we were all under great pressure to perform well and raise our stock with the scouts, the most important event of that week, for me, had nothing to do with basketball. On the second-to-last evening, after our afternoon games, Raina enlisted me to scoot back up to the dorms with her to beat the crowd for dinner. It was seven o'clock by then and still light outside, although the sun was low and muted. We took a shortcut and started through what looked like a little patch of woods, but after the initial clump of trees we stumbled into a clearing that wasn't visible from the road.

"Holy shit," said Raina softly, and I knew that all plans to be early for dinner were out the window. She walked off toward the little pond that was tucked into a corner of the clearing. Green and yellow stalks were shooting out of the water, and a few ducks sat communicating in the middle. All the greenery was darker than it might have been in broad daylight, as if the moisture from the insides of things had been pushed out to the surface, so that everything assumed a richer color. I followed Raina from maybe twenty feet behind, watching her steps get smaller as she got closer to the edge of the water. The grass extended halfway up her legs, and her thin shoulders rolled back as she turned her head to look at something.

"Nancy," she said without turning, "come here."

I worked my way towards her through the long yellow grass. A few feet in front of us were a bunch of ducklings, little brown balls of feather and fur. They were waddling around, bumping into each other, peeping, falling down. I turned to look at Raina and she was staring at them, eyes bright as if lit from within.

I felt, suddenly, that I was intruding on something, and backed away. She didn't seem to notice. She just kept standing in the grass, motionless, and as I stood there watching Raina watch the ducklings, it just hit me. Boom. I couldn't have explained what it was that moved me so much; all I knew was that the sight of Raina absorbed in something, oblivious to me and to everything else, touched off such a tangled surge of imagination, pain, and desire that I had to take a few steps away from her to keep from falling over. It was as if something had cracked in me, had opened up, suddenly, into some other place I knew nothing about.

So it was ironic, to say the least, when my father leaned forward at summer league the next week and asked about the gorgeous, straight-backed woman sitting in front of us in the bleachers. A few weeks later he asked Raina's mother out for dinner, and Claudia blinked a few times and said yes. I figured they'd go out once or twice maybe, and that would be it. It wasn't. Even after it became clear, though, that there was really something going on between them, it took a while to register with me. Part of it was that my dad had dated several women since my mother left when I was six, and I had learned not to have expectations. Also, I rarely saw them together—they tended not to spend much time at our place. And of course it was just too strange to consider the fact that my father was dating the mother of the girl I liked.

My father, Wendell, like me, was large. Twenty-three years before he'd been the only Asian named to the All-State high school football team, at linebacker. He got his optimism and sense of humor from *his* father, who was a shopkeeper before his internment during World War II, and a gardener after it. His size came from his unusually tall mother, and also from consuming—as he put it—"lotsa meat." Now he was a math teacher and assistant football coach at a high school a few miles from our house. My father was a popular teacher—kids came to talk to him about their problems, and he gave his players rough bear hugs when they did something good on the field. He was the kind of cheerfully macho big man who could get away with crying, which he did every year at his football banquet, and at home, during *Eight Is Enough.* He was thrilled to have an athlete for a daughter. The first time I beat him at one-on-one, the summer I turned twelve, he slapped me on the back and gave me a beer and moaned about getting old. Claudia said he was adorable. I didn't know about that. But when I looked at other people's fathers, or at least the few who were around, I knew that I was luckier than most.

I finally realized that his relationship with Claudia was serious when it occurred to me that he was almost never home. Normally, even when he was seeing someone, he wouldn't take her out very often. He blamed finances, claiming that it was too expensive to pay for a babysitter and then dinner for two; instead, he'd invite the woman over, cook dinner for her, and then all three of us would watch a rented movie. Occasionally, the woman would spend the night, and my father would look embarrassed in the morning. He'd never stay over at her place. The woman would eventually get tired of this arrangement, accusing my father of being cheap, antisocial, or completely unromantic. I didn't think that this was accurate or fair.

The truth was, he didn't want to leave me. I'd been his main companion since my parents got divorced, his sidekick, his second-in-command. When I was younger, we'd watch cartoons together—usually Bugs Bunny or the Road Runner—and if I left and went to a friend's house, he would watch them by himself. After I beat him at basketball, though, he started taking me to bars. We'd go to Gardena, a Japanese-American town, where it didn't matter that I was almost a decade from legal because the bartenders were all his friends. My father believed in the redemptive power of heartfelt talks with strangers. He taught me always to tip the bartender well, and never to drink cheap beer.

After he met Claudia, though, he started going out more, and leaving me at home by myself. From the way he'd behaved with past women, I'd expected him to make a big production out of presenting her to me, but he didn't; he was too far gone to care. He and Claudia went out to movies and dinner and basketball games, and he'd even spend the night at her apartment. I'd never been jealous of my father's girlfriends—his priorities had been so obvious— and I wasn't jealous of Claudia, either, but for an entirely different reason. I was sixteen by the time he met her, old enough to drive, and it was easier to have my own social life when my father wasn't around. With his attention taken up by Claudia, I could stay out later, have friends over, spend more time alone. Sometimes, though, he'd still go through the motions of asserting parental control. "You are *grounded*," he'd say after I'd broken some household rule. Then he would leave for the weekend.

Raina didn't seem too rattled by our parents' relationship, either. We ran into each other at college games and high school tournaments throughout the fall and winter of our junior year, but we didn't often refer to our parents' romance and only acknowledged that it existed when one of us asked the other to give the corresponding parent a message. "Ask my dad to pick up some cereal on the way home tomorrow," I'd say, or, "Tell him his friend Kenneth called." The novelty of it, the irony, soon wore off for both of us, and their relationship faded quickly into everyday life. There was something I noticed about the way children of divorce dealt with their parents' postmarital love lives—we never got our hopes up about anyone new, but on the other hand, we were never surprised.

They moved in on the third Sunday of August 1986. Although my father and Claudia had taken Raina and me out to dinner a month before to tell us this was happening, I didn't really believe it until they showed up that morning with a U-Haul full of their stuff. I was both annoyed and thrilled about the move—drunk with the idea of seeing Raina more often, but unhappy about sharing the house. I had no idea what Raina thought; she didn't talk much, to me or to anyone else. When I'd seen her at parties, there'd always been people around her, but they'd kept a respectful distance. I intended to do the same, as much as possible. Raina seemed poised, mature, in control of herself—completely out of my league.

The day they moved in, Raina and I helped bring boxes in from the truck, while our yellow Lab, Ann (after Ann Meyers, the first woman to try out for an NBA team), stood ears-up on the driveway, supervising. Occasionally a neighbor would stop by to help, and look at Claudia and Raina curiously, interested in the spectacle of two black women moving into a Japanese household. There were a couple of people, too—not people we were close with—who glared at my father disapprovingly, but they were the same ones who had always looked at us with vague suspicion and disapproval, so I tried not to pay them any mind. My more immediate concern, after I'd accepted that they were really staying, was what Claudia and Raina thought of the house. It had always looked, to me, like a huge cardboard box—it was exactly the right color, and the crumbling stucco gave it a rough, unfinished feel. The garage faced the front, but we didn't use it for the car, because the door was cracked so dramatically, the fissures running from ground to roof, that you couldn't lift it without it breaking into pieces. Our driveway was a network of small, interwoven cracks, like a flat expanse of bone-dry earth. The two shrubs by the front door reached up toward the sun halfheartedly, as if uncertain that they wanted to grow. Claudia watched all of the moving activity from the chair my father had set up for her on the scraggly front lawn. He'd told her to "take it easy," although she was muscular and fit and could probably have lifted as much as we jock types. "No problem at all," he gasped from under a large box. He was still trying hard to impress her.

Our place was big for that section of Inglewood—two stories and three bedrooms, one of which my father had used as a study. It had been cheap when he'd bought it in the mid-seventies, a time when—as its first owner, a white man, had put it—the neighborhood was starting to "turn." We'd moved there right after my parents' divorce because he'd wanted to escape the white suburb where my mother had insisted we live—a place that I, too, had hated, because the kids there hated me—and go back to a place more familiar to him, more like the racially mixed, working-class neighborhood in Watts where he'd grown up in the fifties and sixties. My mother had stayed behind in Redondo Beach, eventually marrying a white lawyer whose bully son had beaten me up on a regular basis. She was horrified by my father's choice of neighborhood. Inglewood, when we moved there, was already quite poor, but things had gotten worse in the next ten years, after the economic benefits that Reagan had promised, instead of trickling down, trickled out. At first, our neighborhood had also been more mixed, but gradually, the whites, Asians, and Latinos had moved on to other places, leaving a bunch of black families, and us.

I didn't sleep much the week that Claudia and Raina moved in. At night I lay rigid, eyes open, pondering the facts that there were two more people in the house, and that Raina was just on the other side of the wall. Daytime was awkward—we were all overly conscious of each other, and careful, especially my father, who ran around the house like a mad scientist tending to his wildest experiment. Raina, meanwhile, was friendly to my father and me, but distant, as if she were a temporary guest who had to be tolerant of us because we were putting her up for the night. My father didn't seem to notice because he had his hands full with Claudia. She often worked late at her job in the circulation department of the *Los Angeles Times,* but when she was home he floated around, grinning, as if he couldn't believe she was gracing our house with her royal presence. He'd bring her roses he'd bought from stoplight vendors, and serve her breakfast in bed in the morning. She indulged this behavior patiently, but she was obviously flattered. "I can't remember the last time a man spoiled me this way," she said. "I'm sure it won't last for long."

As for me, I moved around in a constant daze. I kept bumping into things, and was amazed to find that solid objects—tables, chairs, the dog—didn't dissolve right there in front of me. I tried to touch the image I saw in the mirror of a tall person with light brown skin and permed shoulder-length hair, and was surprised when my fingers encountered the cold, hard glass instead of that stranger's flesh. I sat down immediately upon entering the house and usually anchored myself in a chair for the rest of the night. That way, I knew, I couldn't hurt myself. People react to wonderful news and disastrous news in the same general manner—joy or sorrow does not immediately register on their faces; they are in such a state of shock that it takes them a while to absorb the information. Going through that first week with Raina in my house was like hearing a huge piece of dramatic news over and over again—the fact of it was constantly hitting me, but whether it was wonderful or disastrous I still didn't know.

Western Music

LINH DINH

Outside the glass door of Fish and Chick, the white noise of the motorcycle traffic sputtered: putt, putt, putt, putt. Inside, Skinny and Dercum sat at the bar, their sweat cooled by the air conditioning. Kurt Cobain was screaming on the stereo. It was the beginning of the summer, just before the monsoon season. Skinny was drunk on Jägermeister. He shouted: "I'm sick of this place!"

"So am I!" Dercum said.

"I've got to get out of here."

"We can go have a beer at M.I.G. or Bar Nixon if you like."

"No! No! No! No! What I mean is: I'm sick of Hanoi!"

"Do you want to go back to New York?"

"I don't want to go home. I just need to get away from Hanoi."

"We can go to Sapa."

"No, not Sapa." Skinny took a drag on his Perfume River cigarette. He jabbed his face over his shoulder towards the Israelis, Dutch, Germans, Aussies and Frenchmen sitting at tables behind them. "I'm tired of looking at these Eurotrash!"

"I'll talk to Mai tomorrow."

For $5 a day, Mr. Mai waited every day for Dercum outside the Victory Hotel to take him where he wanted to go. He was Dercum's personal cyclo driver. Wiry, with a bronze complexion, he was in his mid-fifties, a grandfather. He was too well-dressed for his profession. In public he wore a tailored shirt, tie, polyester slacks and imitation leather wing tips. Unlike most men his age, he was not a veteran. He was not allowed to serve because his parents were branded reactionaries by the Viet Minh, who executed his father in 1955 during the Land Reform Program. His mother committed suicide soon after.

Dercum walked out of the hotel lobby and found him, as usual, lounging in his cab beneath the flame tree: "Chao Ong!"

Mr. Mai roused himself from his seat: "How are you doing this morning, Dirt? Where we going?"

"I don't know yet. Maybe nowhere."

"Nowhere very good. I sit here and drink beer." Mr. Mai eased back down, lifted a plastic cup of beer to his lips. His eyes were bloodshot.

Dercum lit a Marlboro: "My friend is getting sick of Hanoi."

"Skin Knee sick of Hanoi?"

"Yes, Skinny is very sick of this place."

"Tell him to go home."

"But he does not want to go home yet."

"Tell him to go to Hanoi Hilton."

"Now, now, let's not get personal. Skinny is sick of looking at the Eu-ro-trash."

"Year-old trash?"

"Eu-ro-trash. Like White Trash," Dercum smiled good-naturedly, "like me, but Eu-ro-pean."

Mr. Mai finished his beer, burped, crossed his leg.

Dercum continued: "We want to go the countryside, somewhere where there's no Europeans or Americans."

Mr. Mai jiggled his empty cup: "For how long, Boss?"

"A week."

"To do what?"

"Do nothing. We just want to relax in the countryside."

Mr. Mai jiggled his cup, thought for a moment, then said: "We can go to my wife's home village."

"Where's that?"

"Three hundred kilometers from Hanoi."

"Nine hours by car?"

"Ten."

"Which direction?"

"West."

"In the mountain?"

"Yes."

"Near Son La?"

"Between Son La and Yen Chau."

"Is there a hotel there?"

"Hotel?!"

Dercum called Skinny at the Metropole: "It's all arranged. We're going to the sticks for a week."

"Sounds excellent."

"You should bring along cans of SPAM as a precaution."

"Don't worry. I've eaten ox penises and dogs."

"You have?"

"And sparrows."

"What else have you eaten?"

"Wouldn't you like to know."

"And we should bring along seven cases of beer. A case for each day."

"I'm really looking forward to this."

"I'll bring the toilet paper."

Dercum Sanders and Skinny, whose real name was Dave Levy, had met at Columbia. Dercum never finished college but dropped out after his sophomore year. First he worked as a bike messenger, then as a sous-chef at Coûte Que Coûte in midtown, then as a luggage handler for United Airlines, which allowed him to travel to Asia for free, and then his grandmother died . . . Before Dercum left New York, he said he was going to Vietnam to teach English, but after his first week in Hanoi, he thought, "Why should I feel apologetic about not working? Why shouldn't I just hang out?" After six months in Vietnam, he sent a fax to Skinny: "You must come over soon. This place is wild. COM-PLETE FREEDOM. One feels uninhibited here. I feel like a new man. I am a new man. I cannot wait to see your face again. I think about you day and night. I mean it. In New York nothing is possible. Now I see my past in a new light. You must come over."

It took Mr. Mai three days to make arrangements for the trip. Dercum and Skinny would split the cost of hiring a four wheel drive, at $600 a week, gas and driver included. The party would be comprised of Dercum, Skinny, the driver and Mr. Mai.

To avoid traffic, they decided to leave first thing in the morning. The car showed up promptly at 5 A.M. in front of the Victory Hotel. It was a Jeep Cherokee. They started loading. Dercum said to Mr. Mai: "All this beer is for you."

Mr. Mai stared at the cases of Heineken filling the luggage compartment and shook his head convulsively: "Not enough!"

"Not enough?!" Dercum shouted with feigned astonishment. Everyone laughed except the driver, a burly, bearded man in jeans and a pale blue T-shirt with "MOUNTAIN EVEREST IS THE HIGHEST MOUNTAIN IN THE WORLD" on the front and "SOLO FUCKER" on the back.

"You want a beer now?" Dercum asked Mr. Mai.

"Sure." Dercum handed him a beer. "And one for the driver."

Dercum handed a beer to the driver.

"Thank you, mate!" the driver said.

"Mr. Mai, please tell him that we're not Australians."

"They're not Australians."

"I'm Dercum." Dercum shook the driver's hand.

Mr. Mai interjected: "Dirt!"

"It's actually --Dirk'."

"Dirt," the driver said.

"And this is Skinny."

"Skin Knee."

"What is your name?"

"Long." On closer inspection, Long appeared to be only about 30, although his beard and scowl had made him seem much older.

"Long?"

"Long."

Skinny looked at Dercum with a twinkle in his eyes. "How long?" he blurted. Dercum burst out laughing. Long stared at Mr. Mai, his face blank.

"Never mind," Dercum said.

"I think I want a beer also," Skinny said.

"I didn't know you drink beer at five in the morning," Dercum said as he handed Skinny a Heineken.

"Skin Knee is becoming Vietnamese," Mr. Mai exclaimed.

Dercum and Skinny sat in the back. Mr. Mai sat up front. All except Long were elated as the car started moving. At that hour, the streets were filled with people of all ages: walking, jogging, doing tai chi, kicking a soccer ball or a shuttlecock, or playing badminton. They passed a squadron of legless men rolling briskly down Le Hong Phong Street on wheelchairs. "Old VC," Mr. Mai said. Long tapped a Morse-like staccato on his horn. On the tape deck was Louis Armstrong singing Fats Waller: "What did I do . . . to be so black and blue?"

"Do you like Louis Armstrong, Mr. Mai?" Dercum asked.

Mr. Mai didn't answer him. He was suddenly withdrawn, reflective, charmed by the sights of his home city. Each scene was made novel from the vantage point of a speeding car.

"I like jazz and blues," Long said.

Most of the motor traffic they encountered was going the other way: people coming into the city from outlying villages. Within twenty minutes, the houses thinned out on both sides. Long tapped on his horn constantly, passing motorcycles, bicycles, trucks, buses and cars while dodging chickens, pigs, cows, dogs, men and buffalo. After three hours, the road turned to gravel. Mr. Mai rolled the window down four times to throw up his three cans of beer.

Long said: "Easy, Grandfather."

Mr. Mai moaned: "I'm not used to sitting in a car."

Dercum said: "We should stop for lunch soon, Long."

Long turned his head around: "Good place to eat: twenty minutes." The car ran over a dog. Long could see a rapidly diminishing black shape twitching in the rear view mirror.

"Sounds good."

"Twenty minutes."

"Boys! I think we just ran over a dog!" Skinny yelped.

"Did we just run over a dog, Long?" Dercum asked.

"No."

"Can I have another beer?" Mr. Mai said.

Long drove the Cherokee onto the side of the road. The little eatery was fronted by a pool table beneath fiberglass awning propped up by bamboo poles. They walked past a glass cabinet displaying imported liquors and cigarettes, stepped over a dozing yellow dog and entered a bright, airy room. On its lime-colored walls were posters of busty white women hugging enormous beer bottles. Up high in one corner was a shelf-altar: In front of a framed, retouched black and white photograph of a handsome, smooth-faced, doe-eyed cadet was a sand-filled teacup holding joss sticks, a plate of mandarin oranges and a plate of boiled chicken. At the back of the room, a very old woman sat, all bunched up and immobile, on a bamboo settee in front of a very large, very loud TV, watching a soap opera. They sat down on little plastic stools at a low table. They were the only patrons. The waitress came out from the kitchen and said: "Today we have fried catfish and wild boar."

Mai ordered: "Bring those dishes, Sister. And fried tofu, boiled watercress, two bowls of soup."

"What nationality are these people, Uncle?"

"American."

"They look like Russians."

"They're gay."

"Gay!"

"Hurry up, Sister, we are all starving to death!"

The waitress went back to the kitchen.

"What did you tell her?" Skinny asked Mai.

"She said you look Russian. I said you are Americans."

Dercum asked: "Where are we?"

"Thao Nguyen."

Long said to Mai: "Are they really gay?"

"Of course!"

A gaggle of giggling children stood outside the restaurant to stare at Skinny and Dercum. Skinny smiled at them and said: "Boo!" The bravest of the children separated himself from the group and, with goading from the rest, shouted in English: "I love you!" before running away. The rest of them scattered, screaming: "I love you! I love you!"

Everyone but Skinny sat at the table picking their teeth with toothpicks after the meal. The waitress wiped the table cursorily with a rag, sweeping the little fish bones onto the tiled floor. She was wearing a lurid pink shirt with little black dots and red flowers. On her hair was a bright yellow bow. Long said to her: "Sister, do you want to go the mountain with us?"

"There is nothing but ghosts and savages in those mountains!" She smiled and walked back to the kitchen.

In college, Skinny and Dercum were not lovers. Each refused to acknowledge the unbearable fact of his attraction to the other by frantically trying to become a heterosexual. They dated many women, overlapping on occasions. But they remained emotional intimates, returning to each other for comfort after each failed relationship. When Dercum left for Vietnam, Skinny had just come out. Dercum was still undecided. Their love was consummated in Skinny's suite at the Metropole Hotel a day after his arrival.

The car climbed steadily. The road was mostly bad, alternating between asphalt, dirt and gravel. They passed tea plantations, a litchi forest, fields of maize and fields of tobacco. They drove through Viet towns of wooden and whitewashed brick houses; Black Thai *bản* of houses on stilts, with cows and buffalo beneath them; a Kha Mu village of thatch-roofed huts with walls of woven bark. In every Viet town there was at least one cafe with a sign outside advertising "karaoke." They saw a group of Flower Hmongs. One of the men carried a flintlock rifle. The women had woven horse hair into their own, creating enormous turbans. Neither Skinny nor Dercum said anything for a long time. Long glanced at the rear view mirror: the two men were asleep leaning against each other.

Mr. Mai said: "How long have you been a driver?"

"Just a year."

"It seems like a great job."

"You get to see places."

"And you get to meet foreigners."

Long chuckled: "There are classy foreigners, but there are some who are impossible to deal with."

"Like who?"

"Last week, I drove three Koreans. They were very unfriendly."

"How are the Americans?"

"They're actually not bad. Most of them tip."

"Any women?"

"Huh?"

"You know: you meet any women?"

Long chuckled: "A couple."

Mr. Mai waited for Long to continue. Long continued: "Most of them travel with a husband or a boyfriend. And then you have the old and Christian ones, who travel in pairs, but every now and then, you catch yourself an odd single."

Mr. Mai waited for Long to continue. Long continued: "For example, a couple months ago, I drove three people from New Zealand: a couple and a single girl, all college students. I drove them to Sapa, where we stayed in two rooms at The Auberge. The girl's name was Hillary. She was my girlfriend for a week."

Mr. Mai had a pained look on his face, made an unconscious sucking noise with his throat.

Long chuckled: "I evened the score a little, you know."

"Ah," Mr. Mai sighed, "but I'm an old man and a grandfather."

"And then there was this other one. American. Becky her name was. After I drove her to Halong Bay on a day trip, I would come to her hotel in Hanoi three or four times a week for a month. She was a sex maniac, this Becky was. I'm not your girlfriend, she said, I just want sex. Fine with me, I said. She was sleeping with at least two or three other guys, as far as I could tell. This girl couldn't get enough of it. She was delirious. She asked me, 'Am I pretty?' 'Sure you are,' I told her. And she was pretty. Maybe not that pretty, but pretty. She told me one night, 'I'm a very ugly girl, a very ugly girl.' She was actually crying over this, that's how crazy she was."

"Maybe in America they don't think she's so pretty."

Long furrowed his brows. He wasn't sure whether to become angry.

"You know, it's the same with some of the Vietnamese girls we see hanging on the arms of foreigners. We think these girls are ugly, but the foreigners think they're very pretty. They think some of these girls the most beautiful women on the face of this earth." Mr. Mai glanced at the back seat: "At least these two," he deepened his voice, "are not corrupting the chaste women of Vietnam with their decadent, imperialistic, materialistic pollution!"

"Ha! ha!"

"Actually, these two guys don't seem to like other white people. They requested that I take them somewhere where there's no Americans."

Long was glad the conversation had veered away from his sex life. What a dirty old man this Mai is, he thought. "But the whole country is crawling with Americans."

"That's true."

"If not live ones, then dead ones."

"That's true."

"How do you know there's no Americans in Muom Village?"

"I've been there three times. It's my wife's native village."

"How did she end up in Hanoi?"

"I kidnapped her!"

"Ha! Ha!"

"Actually, my wife served in the Army. That's how she made it to Hanoi."

"I figured."

"In my family, the decorated veteran is a woman!"

"Ha! Ha!"

"Hey, it worked out great for me: if she was near her family, there was no way they would have let her marry me."

"And how do they treat you now?"

"Like shit!"

"Ha! Ha!"

"Stop for a second."

Long stopped the car to let Mr. Mai out. Dercum opened his eyes, saw the back of Long's head, forgot where he was, panicked, recovered, closed his eyes again. Long thought: What a concept: gay Americans!!! But they all seem so . . . so . . . so . . . thick! So macho! All body hair and meat and sweat and swagger. Well, maybe not the Skin Knee guy . . . Were gays allowed in the US Army? Can there be such a thing as a gay imperialist? Mr. Mai climbed back in: "I feel much better."

After they started moving again, Mr. Mai said: "You know, Brother, there's an American ghost in Muom Village."

"Really?"

"My wife said that, in '69, a plane was shot down over Muom Village, and they found the pilot's leg in the forest."

"Just his leg?"

"Yes, but it was a very big leg. My wife told me it was as tall as a man's chest. This guy was a giant."

"They're all giants."

"But this guy was really a giant."

"People tend to be shorter in the mountains anyway."

"It's the lack of nutrients."

"No sodium."

"That's right. The villagers buried this leg where they found it, but his ghost began to show up at night, knocking on people's doors and asking for water."

Long took a sip from his Heineken: "Why do ghosts ask for water anyway?"

"Not all ghosts. Only the ones who have lost a lot of blood while dying."

"And did his entire body show up, or just his leg?"

"What do you mean?"

"When he knocked on people's doors at night, what did people see: a leg, or the entire body?"

"You really don't know?"

"No, I don't."

Mr. Mai raised his voice: "When you die, it doesn't matter if all that's left of you is your asshole, you come back as a whole person."

"I didn't know that."

"That's because you grew up in the city."

"You're right. There are no ghosts in the city."

"There are a few, but not many. There are not many ghosts in the city because of electricity."

"Tell me more about the American ghost."

"This guy kept bothering the villagers, always showing up at night and asking for water, so they went back to the burial site and erected a little shrine. After that, he stopped bothering them."

"He's getting more than he deserves for dropping bombs on them," Long chuckled.

"But you can't hold a grudge against a dead man. I've seen this shrine: There was a bottle of wine and a cassette player."

"A cassette player?"

"Yes, a cassette player playing Soviet music."

"Why Soviet music?"

"Because they didn't have tapes of American music. This was in 1989, in a place where 'monkeys cough, herons crow,' where 'dogs eat rocks, chickens eat pebbles!'"

"Whose idea was it to play him music?"

"I don't know. But it makes sense if you think about it. They probably thought that since he was so far away from home, he would appreciate hearing some Western music."

Dercum made a little noise. Without opening his eyes, he said: "Are we almost there, Mr. Mai?"

"We're almost there."

"The only Americans I want to see this week are these two guys back there," Long said. "I don't want to see any ghost."

"Don't worry."

But Mr. Mai did not explain to Long why the American ghost could not go home again. Maybe it was because he did not know the reason himself—he is, after all, also a city person.

When the American pilot was shot out of the sky, his body was scattered across several bodies of water. And a ghost, as any peasant will tell you, cannot cross a body of water, even a tiny brook, unless his own body is whole. So this American had nowhere to go but to stay where he was. From that point on, Muom Village would have to become his village. His asking for water from the villagers was only a ruse to be allowed inside someone's house. That is, until they decided to build him his own house: the shrine. What the peasants saw when they opened their door to the American was simply his wish to be whole again. They all noticed, for example, that his uniform was untorn, and unstained by blood.

They crossed a truss bridge spanning a deep, leafy ravine, then turned onto a twisting dirt road descending steeply into a narrow valley. Crowding the road on both sides were elephant grass, patches of daisies, mango trees, mangosteens, bamboo, creepers and a hundred different vines even the locals don't have names for. A copper-colored river appeared and disappeared through the foliage. Shafts of pale light pierced through the bluish gray clouds and in the sky, someone's kite was spiraling. Now they saw the first villager: a small girl walking towards them alongside an albino buffalo. As they passed, she stared at them blankly and did not wave. Now came the village: thirty houses clustered together, surrounded by rice paddies. The encircling mountains were covered by mist.

Chagrin

TAHIRA NAQVI

8:15 A.M.

It's a Sunday in March. Not of much account because Sunday is Sunday, the end of the weekend, the day before we all jump into work like clocked robots, rushing toward, well, the next weekend. And March is drab, a month when winter fights in insidious ways to show she's mistress. It's nothing like the March in Lahore I have almost forgotten. Spring, a slow season of abundance, flower shows in the Lawrence gardens, the cacti as large as trees on sidewalks, washed clean, small red roses leaping across any wall they can find.

Before going to bed last night we listened faithfully to the weather forecast so what I see from the bedroom window this morning doesn't surprise. The sky, the tall, bare-branched, stringy trees, and our winter-beaten front lawn, all seem to be wearing muted shades of the same color: a muddied, albescent lavender. We'll wait for the sun all day long.

"Damn!" Ali mutters, scratching the back of his head, as if he didn't know and has been caught off-guard. It's his turn at the window.

"I hope it doesn't snow," I mumble reflexively, although I know that it might, tomorrow if not today. We should have settled in Texas instead of Connecticut. Hot, predictable, flat, so much like the plains of Punjab. Perhaps we can retire there.

"Islamic class today," I remind Ali as he climbs back into bed.

"One-thirty?" he grunts.

"Yes," I say, wondering why he never remembers.

An empty plastic cover falls to the wooden floor with a sharp clang as I rummage through a scattered pile of tapes on our nightstand. Ignoring it, I select a tape and slip it into the stereo.

> *Zinda hun istarah ke gham-e-zindagi nahin*
> *Jalta hua diya hun magar roshni nahin*
> (I live with no thought to life's sorrows
> I am a candle that is lit but sheds no light)

Back in bed, I draw the covers over my shoulders as the mellow tones of Mukesh's voice dart from the stereo speakers, filling the bedroom, drowning out the noise of cartoons downstairs which had woven itself into the early morning silence of our house. The children are awake.

We can't see what's outside our windows anymore; gray, brown, lavender, it can be anything and we won't know. Together, our bodies close, we listen quietly, intently, to the song. I shut my eyes and the lyrics lilt in my head, moving faster than they do on the tape, the two sounds like voices in a fugue; my head nestled in the warmth between my husband's shoulder blades, I wait greedily for the next song, the next, and the next.

10:30 A.M.

"Islamic class today." The reminder is intended for the three boys who huddle together on the carpet in front of the television while Fred Flintstone and his prehistoric family with their anachronistic lifestyle *yabadabadoo* their way into their lethargic little heads. I hear a moan, a "*hmn*." Motionless, the children sit with their mouths half open, their eyes still glazed over from sleep, the lids heavy.

"Did you hear me?" I ask, loudly this time, forcing annoyance into my tone.

"Yes," Haider, the eldest, groans.

From the floor I retrieve a copy of *Time,* lying open, face down, embracing the carpet like a bat. On my way upstairs to the kitchen, I also pick up a stray cushion which, far from its destination on the sofa, betrays the energy generated in this room last night as the three boys wrestled, scuffled and threw things at each other.

Tea.

Ali is in the bathroom. I hear water swishing through the overhead pipes. He won't be down for another half-hour. Tea, I think, and *"O for a draught of vintage that hath been / Cool'd a long age in the deep-delved earth,"* ambles into my head. I try to dismiss Keats, but he follows me with *"My heart aches and a drowsy numbness pains my sense,"* and in the next moment, as if I had summoned her with those words, she's in my vision. Mrs. Kabir, the matronly Mrs. Kabir, incorrigible in her dedication, her mind racing along on a perpetual wave of English literature, Mrs. Kabir, who taught us English in high school and who goaded us into learning by heart poems of which we were sure we would have no need later in life.

The tea kettle screeches violently.

1:30 P.M.

The three cars in the parking lot at Brookfield Library stand apart from each other, like the estranged members of a warring family, turning the other way, sullen, reluctant parties at rapprochement.

"Well, looks like three families today," Haider mutters with a curl of the lips. *Why bother when no one else does,* he's telling himself. He had wanted to stay home and finish reading *The Once and Future King* for a test tomorrow. No excuses will do, I had said, bring the book along and read in the car.

"We're here, that makes four," I say firmly. But he's right. Four families for Islamic class is distressing. Sometimes we have seven or eight families which translate into ten or fifteen children. But that is rare. People have plans on weekends, no one can force anyone to come, and of course, the weather has been like a monster in a fairy story, standing in your way, demanding a heavy price for allowing you to pass.

The recreation room at Brookfield Library is large and bare of any furnishings that might lend it character. Two oversized prints, one with large-petaled yellowish flowers that could be chrysanthemums or blanched roses, another with a barn surrounded by a profusion of orange, red and brown tints and splashes meant to re-create a New England fall, hang on the walls forlornly. It is a room which can be made to wear any disguise; for us it is the Islamic Center, for the Girl Scouts who meet here weekly, it's a den, for another group it's something entirely theirs. It will be anything you want it to be.

In this room, which also has an adjoining kitchen, the Center has Eid prayers followed by socializing and food, *iftar* gatherings during Ramzan, even birthday parties. And, despite erratic attendance, the school continues, tenaciously, stubbornly, refusing to give up.

Today there are three children attending Mr. Ismail's Arabic language class. He has assigned them pages of writing, a task that seems to engross them. Slowly, laboriously, their small heads bent low over their notebooks, the children shape letters from the Arabic alphabet, struggling to maintain the right-to-left rhythm, their mouths open in tiny o's as they attend faithfully to the task at hand. The older children sit with the adults today since there aren't enough for a class. Mustafa, a Pakistani electric engineer turned handyman and builder, reads the Arabic text of sections 7 and 8 of *Sura Tauba* from the Koran. He is growing a beard, I notice. When he finishes, he asks Haider to read the English translation. For the first time I discover how much *zakat* we're supposed to give away. Two-and-a-half percent of our "merchandise," and 10 percent of the "fruits of the earth."

Mustafa begins to explain the point about the fruits of the earth, and Naheed, his wife, proposes that fruits don't necessarily imply agricultural goods.

"It's everything, all the things we have and all the money we make." She looks at me when she finishes. She wants me to agree.

Fruits of the earth, fruits of labor. We might be getting into metaphors here and one man's metaphor is another man's nightmare. "I don't know," I say, with forced emphasis, "it could mean just material possessions, like real estate, jewelry, you know, things like that."

"But money is material, and what about stocks and bonds? Or could all that be merchandise?" Ali rubs down the corners of his mustache thoughtfully.

We've probably been doing it all wrong all these years. Not giving enough, or giving too much of the wrong thing. For example, old, out-of-fashion clothes dumped at the door of the Salvation Army store constitute neither merchandise nor fruits.

Mustafa looks worried. "The question is, how do we determine 10 percent?" Because he was reading, he finds himself in a position to ask questions with a certain degree of authority.

Haider and Asghar, a year younger than his brother, are yawning.

"Let's read the notes," I say.

Continuing to frown, Mustafa turns to the notes at the end of the Arabic text. Silently we all wait for illumination. But none seems forthcoming. Soon it becomes clear that no one among us knows how alms are to be distributed.

"We'll have to consult the *hadith*," Naheed finally suggests, hitching her shoulders up and down. Her husband nods. With a sense of relief we all lean back in our seats.

"Let's go on. Asghar, will you please read the next section."

Asghar looks at me, I nod, he begins reading in a disinterested, droning voice, occasionally hindered by English transliterations of Arabic words. Suddenly he's stuck at a word. "Chagrin."

". . . the fathers whose spiritual chagrin was even worse than discomfiture in this world." Asghar pronounces the "ch" as "ch."

Haider snickers at his brother's mistake. Ali corrects the pronunciation, and I wonder idly if the boys know what chagrin means.

At Mr. Ismail's table across the room all is quiet. Kasim, who has just turned seven, is immersed in writing. Unlike his brothers, he takes some of his work here seriously. At the moment he's copying Arabic words from a xeroxed handout. He copies well and is conscientious about what has to be done, but he doesn't know what the words mean or why he must copy them. Mr. Ismail, who is Egyptian, continues, as others have done, to teach the children Arabic so they may be able to read and understand the Koran one day. He has little faith in translations because Arabic is his mother tongue. Once we tried telling him that for us a translation has done well all this time, but he was offended by our comments and implied a reluctance on our part to "understand the true meaning of the Koran."

Asghar has finished reading. That's all we will do today. I look at the pretty blue-eyed baby in Elizabeth Smith's lap and smile at her. A look of surprise spreads on her face and then she turns her head away. I lean over and tap her cheek.

"She's so cute," I tell Elizabeth, whose own eyes are darker than mine and whose hair, the little that has escaped from under her *hijab,* is so black I suspect she dyes it.

Elizabeth laughs. "She's a shrewd one," she says. Her voice is thick with a British accent because she and her husband have migrated from Britain recently. They are both displaced Palestinians. Her older daughter, Nadia, is at Kasim's table, writing the alphabet.

"Looks like snow." It's Naheed. Her eyes are directed to the window on the far side of the room, near the entrance.

"Oh, please!" Elizabeth and I turn to follow her gaze in alarm.

"Do you see flurries?" I ask apprehensively. I hate snow. It's so unpredictable, so hypocritical with its outward promise of beauty and its insidious power to hurt. So cold.

"No, no, it's just so dark out there." With a guilty smile Naheed pushes her glasses up on her nose and I notice she has strong hands, her nails clipped short, neat.

"Well, we've had snow in late March before," Ali offers wisely. I wait for "March comes in like a lamb, goes out like a lion," but today I think he feels he doesn't have the right audience for it.

"Let's not talk about snow. I couldn't take one more day of it." I start wrapping my copy of the Koran in a cotton cloth embroidered with tiny round mirrors.

Haider and Asghar get up and run toward the door. Ali shuffles to his feet. Mustafa and Naheed also rise from their chairs. Mr. Ismail's class is over. He walks in our direction and we all greet him with *"Salamalekum."* A chorus of "How are you?" follows with jumbled, mumbled, "Fine, fine," and *"Al-hamdo-lillah."*

The chairs and tables have to be put away. We must leave the room as we found it, with no traces of our anxious visitation, our quick, reluctant learning. Amidst the metallic *clitter clatter* of chairs being folded, the children, in a sudden burst of energy, begin bolting around the room, laughing, screaming. Within a few minutes, all of them, including Kasim, are embroiled in a game of tag.

4:30 P.M.

"Mom, what does chagrin mean?"

It's Asghar. We have been driving for nearly twenty minutes. "A feeling of disappointment, or sadness, like someone put you down or embarrassed you."

"Oh. I never thought I'd see a word like this in the Koran. It's weird." Asghar chuckles.

"But the Koran is full of words like this, ordinary, everyday words." We must teach, we must always teach. Especially when the children are listening.

"And ordinary everyday stories too," Ali volunteers sagely. "I know that," Asghar concedes hastily.

Ali slides a tape into the tape deck. It presses into place with a tiny click.

Mein ne samjha tha ke tu hai to darkhashaan hai hayat
Tera gham hai to gahm-e-dehr ka jhagra kiya hai
(I thought that if I were with you
Life would be glorious
That if I have your pain
The woes of the world will not torment me)
Yun na thaa mein ne faqat chaha tha ke ho jae
Mujh se pehli si muhabbat mere mehbub naa maang
(But that was not how it was, I had merely wished it to be thus.
Beloved, ask not for the love we once shared)

Humming along, Ali turns up the volume. It is Nur Jahan singing the verses of the poet Faiz. I hum too. "Beloved, ask not . . ." In the back, Asghar says something, Haider breaks into a laugh, and Kasim says, with a whine, "Tell me, tell me."

Outside our car, as we travel on Route 133 toward home, late afternoon slowly turns into dusk. The horizon is shot with crimson and the thready limbs of tall dark leafless trees seem to be lifted up toward a darkening sky in postures of supplication. There's to be snow, I tell myself. Slowly, the children's voices gain momentum.

From *The Foreign Student*

SUSAN CHOI

Katherine came to pick him up early in the morning, with the giddy whirr of the engine floating far ahead through the still air and her scarf and a ribbon of car exhaust streaming behind. It was unusually warm for November in the mountains, and she was driving with the top down and no hat. When she arrived at Strake House he was waiting for her on the front steps in a thin-looking suit. He was holding a cardboard box that had the slide projector in it, with a brown bag on top. Mrs. Wade had made him a lunch, which saved him some money. Added to what he had saved in not buying a bus ticket and in deciding to stick with old socks, he had the whole ten dollars left over, the bill still folded in half in the envelope that had come from Dean Bower. It was in his power to make some kind of gesture. He wasn't nervous anymore when she pulled up.

They slid down off the mountain and found the road that would carry them west to Jackson, which lay five hours away on the highway from Nashville to Memphis. Autumn had left the hills not so much bare as rubbed dull, like an old sofa's cushions. The road surged and stuttered, unrolling with growing momentum and then braking hard against towns where a post office and drugstore would spring up across from each other, with one traffic light strung between them. The wind roared too loudly to talk. At first they worried that perhaps they should shout to each other, but eventually this worry was gone, as if the wind peeled it away. One hour passed, and then another, until their wordless cocoon of loud wind in the midst of dull hills pouring past seemed ancient and permanent, and not requiring anything more. Around noon they had to change roads and he leaned toward her with a finger on the map. She hardly glanced at it, taking the sharp right without slowing down, and they slammed hard together against her door, and then slowly came upright again as the car headed north.

Jackson was a considerable small city of six churches, but they were all close together on the neat grid of main street and side streets that made up downtown. They wound through these, their eyes trained together on steeples and signs. Now, in the drowsy noontime hush that they moved through, the silence between them seemed huge. They found St. Paul's and pulled into the white gravel lot alongside it. They had arrived very early. Katherine turned off the engine and they sat listening to its reluctant rattles and clunks as it spun to a halt, and when these were finished, they listened to the birds.

"You must want lunch," she said at last. "You'd better have eaten before you give your talk."

He understood now that he had been expecting the drive to transport him to a place in which he would find himself very calmly buying Katherine lunch with his ten-dollar bill. The simple and absolute logic of such a plan almost guaranteed that it would take place. He fingered the envelope in his pocket.

"Maybe we go find something," he said, accidentally sounding reluctant.

"Mrs. Wade is too good a friend of mine for me to let you waste your lunch. It would break my heart. And I'm not hungry."

"But it must be."

"I'm not." She took her case from her pocketbook and lit herself a cigarette. "I'm going to stretch my legs and take a look around. That's what I need most." She got out of the car, lifted her arms above her head for a moment, and then strode away.

He watched her recede. She crossed the lawn to the front steps, craned her head to look up at the steeple, and then vanished around the side of the building. She had left a thin ghost of smoke near the car. He got the lunch bag from between his feet and unrolled it. The crackling of the paper seemed deafening. He glanced around, but there was no one outside on this street, which was lined with old spreading oaks, stripped bare, reaching sideways for each other. Then he peered into the bag and caught his breath. It held two sandwiches carefully folded in wax paper, two red pears, two slices of cake, and a thermos of water.

They ate sitting together in the small churchyard. "Mrs. Wade is an artist of sandwiches," Katherine said. The churchyard was only half full of grave markers, most of them of the sturdy, prosperous-looking kind, shaped like fat slices of bread, although some were badly leaning and no longer legible. "I never used to notice a church," she went on, balling up the wax paper that had contained her sandwich. She produced a pocket knife from her bag and cut up her pear; if there was a seed she nicked it out and sent it flying. "Churches used to seem like part of the landscape, like rocks or trees. It never occurred to me that there was any difference between them. Not just differences in appearance, but differences in faith. I never gave it any thought at all."

"You do now?"

"I guess I give it a little more thought. For example, this is a plain white shingled church and there's nothing very surprising about the proportions of the steeple. And it's Episcopal, but I don't know what that means from Methodist, or Baptist, or any of the others."

"My mother," he said, surprised to hear himself saying it, "becomes Episcopal some years ago."

"My father was a Catholic. That meant he didn't want any religion in the house at all. I think my mother might have been a Lutheran, but she had to please my father, which was wonderful for her because I'm sure she never wanted to bother with religion in the first place. When I was twelve years old I had a great longing for God. I prayed and mooned about the house and threatened to become a nun. I thought my situation was very tragic. But I outgrew that. You know, when you're a child you want so badly to set yourself apart, and you imagine you're something you're not. Other things came along that I was better at."

"What things?"

"It sounds like you don't think I'm good at anything."

"No!" He flushed. "No."

"I don't know. Other things. In any case, I was thinking that it's strange, because now I'm older and I seem to have come full circle, and started noticing churches. Why did your mother become an Episcopalian?"

"A missionary."

"Are there many Episcopal missionaries in Korea?"

"And Catholic."

"And she didn't want to be Catholic? Or did the Episcopals get to her first?"

"I don't know."

When he didn't elaborate she said, "And your father?"

"No."

"And you?"

"No." She had handed him part of the pear and its scent filled his nostrils. Flowers' perfume, he remembered, is their prayer to God. Where had he read that? He prayed sometimes, but mostly as a reflex. He might be struck, and then it would fly out of him: *please God.*

They saw the priest coming across the yard, frowning and nodding in welcome. "I'm Katherine Monroe," she announced when he'd drawn near, rising to offer her hand. He was looking at Chuck as he groped for it. "I didn't realize Mr. Ahn would be accompanied."

"I'm Sewanee's most famous idler, Father, so I'm always trying to be useful. I thought it would be nice if Mr. Ahn didn't have to take the bus. Shall we get your machine from the car?" she asked, turning back to him.

He followed them, half hearing Katherine's elaborate replies to the priest's inquiries about Sewanee. The hem of her skirt snapped around her knees as she walked. At the car she lifted his box to him and set about raising the top; the priest helped her. "Can you suggest any interesting places in town, Father? I thought I'd take a walk. I've never been in Jackson before."

"You're not going to listen to Mr. Ahn's talk?"

"I don't want to make him nervous. I think it's easier to speak in front of people you don't know. That's all right, isn't it, Chuck?"

He didn't know whether he was relieved or disappointed. He and the priest stood watching as she resecured her scarf around her neck and stowed her gloves in the glove box. Neither of them seemed able to proceed while she was still there. She popped open a compact and glanced at herself, and as quickly shut it again.

"I'm all set. Did you think of anything I should see, Father?"

"Our town hall is a pretty impressive building. If you follow this street to the corner and go left, you'll find some shopping."

"That would be lethal," she laughed.

"If you were a southerner I could think you'd take an interest in our monument square, but you might find it interesting anyway."

Katherine laughed again. "I am a southerner, Father."

"I'm sorry. I wouldn't have guessed it."

"What would you have guessed?"

"Oh, no. It was my mistake to assume in the first place."

"I lived up East awhile. I think I must have lost my accent there."

"My goodness," said the priest. She knew they were watching her all the way to the corner, where she turned left as he had suggested. Then she'd moved out of sight.

Inside the church the priest showed him a screen he had brought from the Sunday-school room, and together they dragged out a table to set the projector on. Chuck brought an extension cord out of the box and the priest complimented him on how prepared he was. Until now his compact self-sufficiency on these journeys was the one thing that he could rely on to steady his nerves. He liked to board the bus, in his thin suit, with his round-trip ticket, directions he'd made for himself from the library's atlas, a sum of money too small to seem unearned in his pocket, and the box in his arms that contained the projector and all of its needs: extension cord, slides, a spare bulb. All he required was electricity and a blank wall. He was an itinerant, as solitary as a country doctor, or the missionary who had converted his mother. He hadn't realized how much it gratified him to be independent this way until today.

He turned the projector on and a weak square of light swung around the room and fell short of the screen. He pushed a psalm book under the projector's front and glanced apologetically at the priest, but the priest was nodding and waving a hand. "That's just fine. I can tell that you've done this before."

"A few, two-three times." He put the slides in order and dropped them one by one into the carousel, checking that each had gone in right side up. Number one was the map: Korea After 1945. Number two was The U.S. Infantry Coming Out of the Seoul Railway Station. He put his thumb on the slide-changer button and fired the carousel through the full rotation. Then he fiddled for a while with the focus. His palms were sweating. He asked the priest to show him to the men's room and once alone rinsed his face and scrubbed it dry with a coarse paper towel. He bent over to touch his toes, and dragged his knuckles back and forth on the floor. Then the door swung open and he sprang upright in embarrassment.

"We're ready for you," the priest said.

The audience was mostly older, charity and book-circle women, and a few intent men. "Hi," he croaked, and they all smiled at once, in response. "I am Chang Ahn. I study at Sewanee, University of the South, but before this I live in Korea."

"How old are you?" a woman interrupted.

"Now I am twenty-five years old."

"You look so young," she said sadly.

He usually began his address by saying that his presence before them was the direct result of MacArthur's Inchon landing. "I'm not here, if this doesn't happen," he said, feeling melancholy suddenly. The faces in the audience blinked at him. He turned on the projector and Korea After 1945 appeared on the wall. He ducked through the beam apologetically. "Here it is," he said, letting the shadow from his forearm mar the picture. "I am sorry the map is not more big."

He explained the positions of Japan, China, and the Soviet Union, around the edges of the fuzzy square of light. "This is makes the fate of Korea. The Japanese colonize, at the beginning of this twentieth century, so when the Second World War is beginning, they are already there."

He paused and looked around. "Okay?" he asked anxiously. A few people nodded.

"You remember," he went on, "in the Second World War it is United States and Soviets together, Japanese with the Italians and Germans. The Japanese are in Korea, this is a terrible time," he sighed. "Okay. The Soviets, in the Second World War, fight against the Japanese, and they fight in Korea." He threw his arms wide.

When the Japanese surrendered at the end of the war, the Soviets and the Americans split the job of overseeing the Japanese withdrawal from the Korean peninsula. A line was drawn at the thirty-eighth parallel, which split the country roughly in half. The Soviet military would administer the northern half, the Americans the southern. This was, in theory, a temporary arrangement. Provisional governments were set up on each side for the duration of Korea's reconstruction. The Soviets, on their side, enabled the return from exile of a great people's hero, a revolutionary who had fought the Japanese throughout the thirties. Chuck cut himself short. "This man become the leader of Communist North Korea," he concluded. The Americans, for their part, imported a committed anti-Communist expatriate named Syngman Rhee, who had graduated Princeton and lived in the U.S. for the preceding forty years. Rhee was put in charge of South Korea. Over time the rival governments dug in, and in June of 1950, went to war.

He always felt hopeless, called upon to deliver a clear explanation of the war. It defied explanation. Sometimes he simply skipped over causes, and began, "Korea is a shape just like Florida. Yes? The top half is a Communist state, and the bottom half are fighting for democracy!" He would groundlessly compare the parallel to the Mason-Dixon line, and see every head nod excitedly. "In June 1950, the Communist army comes over the parallel and invades the South. They come by surprise, and get almost all to the sea." His hands swept: an amazing advance. The UN made a force to fight back, of the South's Republic of Korea army, ROKA, and the United States army, and some other armies, like Britain's.

The particularities of the UN force never interested anyone, and he quickly skipped ahead. "The Communists go fast, until the UN force is crowded into a very little space at the bottom of Korea, around the city Pusan." He pronounced it for them loudly: *Poos-ahn*. "This is like, if the war is all over Florida, and our side are trapped in Miami." Now MacArthur's genius showed itself: instead of trying to push back, over the land, he took his army to the sea, and sailed up the coast, to Inchon. He landed there and cut the Communists in half, off from themselves. Seoul was liberated, and the tide turned around.

He genuinely liked talking about the landing, and MacArthur. It all made for such an exciting, simple minded, morally unambiguous story. Each time he told it, the plot was reduced and the number of details increased, and the whole claimed more of his memory for itself and left less room for everything else. He punched the slide-changer now, and Korea After 1945 was replaced by The U.S. Infantry Coming Out of the Seoul Railway Station, a soap-scrubbed and smiling platoon marching into the clean, level street. This image made a much better illustration of the idea of MacArthur than any actual picture of the Korean war could have. People were often surprised by the vaulted dome of the train station, and the European-looking avenue of trees. "That's Seoul?" a woman asked, vaguely disappointed. The file of troops looked confident and happy, because the picture had not been taken during the Korean conflict at all, but in September 1945, after the Japanese defeat. The photo's original caption had read, "Liberation feels fine! U.S. and their Soviet allies arrive to clean house in Korea." No one was dreaming there would be a civil war.

He followed the U.S. Infantry slide with Water Buffalo in a Rice Paddy, and then Village Farmers Squatting Down to Smoke, which satisfied the skepticism of the woman who had asked about the Seoul railway station. Everyone murmured with pleasure at the image of the farmers, in their year-round pajamas and inscrutable Eskimos' faces, and then the double doors at the back of the sanctuary creaked loudly and Katherine was standing there, with her pocketbook held to her chin, looking lost.

Each of the twelve or so heads clustered in the front pews turned to look at her. She let the door fall shut and slipped into the rearmost pew. "I'm sorry," she said. A flush appeared on her cheeks to match his.

He couldn't remember where he'd left off. The awareness that he was blushing made him blush even more deeply. He wondered if anyone could see it. Often the darkness of his skin seemed to guard his emotions from notice, as if the fact of the color blotted out all that happened within it. He fingered the slide-changer nervously, and the carousel shot ahead, throwing a new picture onto the screen. For a terrifying eternity he stared at this without recognizing what it was. The rough grain of the image, fine rubble, a burial mound. . . . His gaze crisscrossed it wildly, searching for something that might help him locate himself.

When he remembered why the image was there, it was like remembering the plot of a childhood fable. Although the remembrance was deeply familiar, it wasn't convincing, because it didn't seem to make sense. The priest was in the front row, his eyebrows straining upward with encouragement. Chuck took a deep breath, and began again. "You maybe don't believe it, but Korea, the land, looks very much like Tennessee." He gestured at the picture of hills. So much, sometimes he woke in the morning and just for an instant was sure he was home. The mist coming out from the mountains. The soft shapes of hills. His hands formed them. At last he stopped seeing her.

Show and Tell

ANDREW LAM

Mr. K. brought in the new kid near the end of the semester during what he called oral presentations and everybody else called eighth grade Show and Tell. This is Cao Long Nguyen, he said, and he's from Vietnam and immediately mean old Billy said cool!

What's so cool about that? asked Kevin who sat behind him and Billy said, Idiot, don't you know anything, that's where my Daddy came back from with this big old scar on his chest and a bunch of grossed out stories. And that's where they have helicopters and guns and VCs and all this crazy shit. Billy would have gone on and on but Mr. K. said, Billy, be quiet.

Mr. K. stood behind the new kid and drummed his fingers on the kid's skinny shoulders like they were little wings flapping. He tried to be nice to the new kid, I could tell, but the kid looked nervous anyway. The new kid stood like he was waiting to be thrown into the ocean the way he was hugging his green backpack in front of him like a life saver.

Cao Long Nguyen is a Vietnamese refugee, Mr. K. said and he turned around and wrote "Cao Long Nguyen—Refugee" in blue on the blackboard. Cao doesn't speak any English yet but he'll learn soon enough so let's welcome him, shall we, and we did. We all applauded but mean old Billy decided to boo him just for the hell of it and Kevin and a few others started to laugh and the new kid blushed like a little girl. When we were done applauding and booing Mr. K. gave him a seat in front of me and he sat down without saying hello to anybody, not even to me, his neighbor, and I had gone out of my way to flash my cutest smile to no effect. But right away I started to smell this nice smell from him. It reminded me of eucalyptus or something. I was going to ask him what it was but the new kid took out his Hello Kitty notebook and began to draw in it like he'd been doing it forever, drawing and drawing even when Show and Tell already started and it was, I'm sorry to say, my turn.

Tell you the truth, I didn't want it to be my turn. I can be funny and all but I hated being in front of the class as much as I hated anything. But what can you do? You go up when it's your turn, that's what. So when Mr. K. called my name I brought my family-tree chart and taped it on the blackboard under where Mr. K. wrote "Cao Long Nguyen—Refugee" but before I even started Billy said Bobby's so poor he only got half a tree and everybody laughed.

I wanted to say something back real bad right then and there. But as usual I held my tongue on the account that I was a little afraid of Billy. OK, I lie, more than a little afraid. But if I weren't so fearful of that big dumb ox I could have said a bunch of things like Well at least I have half a tree. Some people they only have sorry ass war mongers with big old scars for a Daddy or I could have said what's wrong with half a tree. It's much better than having a quarter of a brain or something like that.

Anyway, not everybody laughed at Billy's butt swipe of a comment. Mr. K., for instance, he didn't laugh. He looked sad, in fact, shaking his head like he was giving up on Billy and saying, Shh Billy, how many times do I have to tell you to be quiet in my class? And the new kid he didn't laugh neither. He just stared at my tree like he knew what it was but I doubt it 'cause it didn't even look like a tree. Then when he saw me looking at him he blushed and pretended like he was busy drawing but I knew he wasn't. He was curious about my drawing, my half a tree.

If you want to know the awful truth it's only half a tree 'cause my Mama wouldn't tell me about the other half. Your Daddy was a jackass, she said, and so is his entire family and clan. That's all she said about him. But Mama, I said, it's for my Oral Presentation project and it's important but she said so what.

So nothing, that's what. So my Daddy hangs alone on this little branch on the left side. He left when I was four so I don't remember him very well. All I remember is him being real big and handsome. I remember him hugging and kissing and reading me a bedtime story once or twice and then he was gone. Only my sister Charlene remembers him well on account that she's three years older than me. Charlene remembers us having a nice house when my Daddy was still around and Mama didn't have to work. Then she remembers a lot of fighting and yelling and flying dishes and broken vases and stuff like that. One night when the battle between Mama and Daddy got so bad Charlene said she found me hiding in the closet under a bunch of Mama's clothes with my eyes closed and my hands over my ears saying Stop, please, Stop, please, Stop like I was singing or chanting or something. Charlene remembers us moving to California; not long after that Daddy left us. I don't remember any of that stuff. It just feels like my entire life is spent living in a crummy apartment at the edge of the city and that Mama had been working at Max's Diner forever, and that she smoked and drank and cussed too goddamn much and she was always saying we should move somewhere else soon, go back to the South maybe, to New Orleans where we came from, but then we never did.

So what did I do? I started out with a big lie. I had rehearsed the whole night for it. I said my Daddy's dead. Dead from a car accident a long long time ago. I said he was an orphan so that's why there's only half a tree—(so fuck you, Billy). Then I started on the other half. I know the other half real well 'cause all of Mama's relatives are crazy or suicidal and naturally I loved their stories. So I flew through them. There was my great-great-Granddaddy Charles Boyle the third who was this rich man in New Orleans and who had ten children and a big old plantation during the Civil War. Too bad he supported the losing side 'cause he lost everything and killed himself after the war ended. Then there was my Granddaddy Jonathan Quentin who became a millionaire from owning a gold mine in Mexico and then he lost it all on alcohol and gambling and then he killed himself. And there was my Grandma Mary who was a sweetheart and who had three children and who killed herself before the bone cancer got to her and there were a bunch of cousins who went north and east and west and became pilots and doctors and lawyers and maybe some of them killed themselves too and I wouldn't be a bit surprised 'cause my Mama said it's kinda like a family curse or something. I went on like that for some time, going through a dozen or so people before I got to the best part: See here, that's my great-aunt Jenny Ann Quentin, I said, all alone on this little branch 'cause she's an old maid. She's still alive too, I said, ninety-seven years old and with only half a mind and she lives in this broken-down mansion outside of New Orleans and she wears old tattered clothes and talks to ghosts and curses them Yankees for winning the war. I saw her once when I was young, I told my captive audience. Great-aunt Jenny scared the heck out of me 'cause she had an old shotgun and everything and she didn't pay her electric bills so her big old house was always dark and scary and haunted. You stay overnight and they'll pull your legs or rearrange your furniture. In summary, had we won the war a hundred years ago, we might have all stayed around in the South. But as it is, my family tree has its leaves fallen all over the States. So that's it, there, now I'm done, thank you.

Tommy went after me. He told about stamp collecting and he brought three albums full of pretty stamps, stamps a hundred years old and stamps as far as the Vatican and Sri Lanka. He told how hard it was for him to have a complete collection of Pope John Paul the Second. Then it was Cindy's turn. She talked about embroidery and she brought with her two favorite pillow-cases with pictures of playing pandas and dolphins that she embroidered herself. She even showed us how she stitches, what each stitch is called and how rewarding it was to get the whole thing together. And Kevin talked about building a tree house with his Daddy and how fun it was. He even showed us the blueprint which he and his Daddy designed together and photos of himself hanging out on the tree house, waving and swinging from a rope like a monkey with his friends and it looked like a great place to hide too if you're pissed off at your Mama or something and then the bell rang.

Robert, Mr. K. said, I wonder if you'd be so kind as to take care of our new student and show him the cafeteria. Why me, I said and made a face like when I had to take the garbage out at home when it wasn't even my turn but Mr. K. said why not you, Robert, you're a nice one.

Oh no I'm not, I said.

Oh yes you are, he said, and wiggled his bushy eye brows up and down like Groucho.

Oh no I'm not.

Oh yes you are.

OK, I said, but just today. OK, though I kinda wanted to talk to the new kid anyway, and Mr. K. said, thank you, Robert Quentin Mitchell. He called the new kid over and put one arm around his shoulders and another around mine. Then he said Robert, this is Cao, Cao, this is Robert. Robert will take care of you. You both can bring your lunch back here and eat if you want. We're having a speed tournament today and there's a new X-Men comic book for the winner.

All right! I said. You're privileged if you get to eat lunch in Mr. K.'s room. Mr. K. has all these games he keeps in the cabinet and at lunch-time it's sort of a club and everything. You can eat there if a) you're a straight-A student, b) if Mr. K. likes and invites you which is not often, or c) if you know for sure you're gonna get jumped that day if you play outside and you beg Mr. K. really really hard to let you stay. I'm somewhere in between the b) and c) category. If you're a bad egg like Billy, who is single-handedly responsible for my c) situation, you ain't never ever gonna get to eat there and play games, that's for sure.

So, Kal Nguyen—Refugee, I said, let's go grab lunch then we'll come back here for the speed tournament, what d' you say? But the new kid said nothing. He just stared at me and blinked like I'm some kinda strange animal that he ain't never seen before or something. Com'n, I said and waved him toward me, com'n, follow me, the line's getting longer by the sec', and so finally he did.

We stood in line with nothing to do so I asked him, hey, Kal, where'd you get them funny shoes?

No undostand, he said and smiled, *no sspeak engliss.*

Shoes, I said, Bata, Bata and I pointed and he looked down. *Oh, Ssues,* he said, his eyes shiny and black and wide opened like he just found out for the first time that he was wearing shoes. *Sssues . . . sssues . . . Saigon.* Yeah? I said, I guess I can't buy me some here in the good old U.S. of A then? Mine's Adidas. They're as old as Mrs. Hamilton, prehistoric if you ask me but they're still Adidas. A-di-das, go head, Kal, say it.

Adeedoos Sssues, Kal said, *Adeedoos.*

That's right, I said, very good, Kal. Adidas shoes. And yours, they're Bata shoes, and Kal said *theirs Bata sssues* and we both looked at each other and grinned like idiots and that's when Billy showed up. Why you want them gook shoes anyway, he said and cut in between us but nobody behind in line said nothing 'cause it's Billy. Why not, I said, trying to sound tough. Bata sounds kind of nice, Billy. They're from Saigon.

Bata sssues, the new kid said it again, trying to impress Billy.

But Billy wasn't impressed. My Daddy said them VCs don't wear shoes, he said. They wear sandals made from jeep tires and they live in fuck'n tunnels like moles and they eat bugs and snakes for lunch. Then afterwards they go up and take sniper shots at you with their AK-47s.

He don't look like he lived in no tunnel, I said.

Maybe not him, said Billy, but his Daddy I'm sure. Isn't that right, refugee boy? Your Daddy a VC? Your Daddy the one who gave my Daddy that goddamn scar?

The new kid didn't say nothing. You could tell he pretty much figured it out that Billy's an asshole 'cause you don't need no English for that. But all he could say was *no undohsten* and *sssues adeedoos* and those ain't no comeback lines and he knew it. So he just bit his lip and blushed and kept looking at me with them eyes.

So, I don't know why, maybe 'cause I didn't want him to know that I belonged to the c) category, or maybe 'cause he kept looking at me with those eyes, but I said leave him alone, Billy. I was kinda surprised that I said it. And Billy turned and looked at me like he was shocked too, like he just saw me for the first time or something. Then in this loud singsong voice, he said Bobby's protecting his new boyfriend. Everybody look, Bobby's got a boyfriend and he's gonna suck his VC's dick after lunch.

Everybody started to look.

The new kid kept looking at me like he was waiting to see what I was gonna do next. What I'd usually do next is shut my trap and pretend that I was invisible or try not to cry like last time when Billy got me in a headlock in the locker room and called me sissy over and over again 'cause I missed the softball in P.E. even when it was an easy catch. But not now. Now I couldn't pretend to be invisible 'cause too many people were looking. It was like I didn't have a choice. It was like now or never. So I said, you know what, Billy, don't mind if I do. I'm sure anything is bigger than yours and everybody in line said Ooohh.

Fuck you, you little faggot, Billy said.

No thanks, Billy, I said, I already got me a new boyfriend, remember?

Everybody said Ooohh again and Billy looked real mad. Then I got more scared than mad, my blood pumping. I thought oh my God, what have I done? I'm gonna get my lights punched out for sure. But then, God delivered stupid Becky. She suddenly stuck her beak in. And he's cute too she said, almost as cute as you, Bobby. A blond and a brunette. You two'll make a nice faggot couple, I'm sure. So like promise me you'll name your first born after me, OK?

So like I tore at her. That girl could never jump me, not in a zillion years. And I'm sure you're a slut, I said, I'm sure you'd couple with anything that moves. I'm sure there are litters of strayed mutts already named after you. You know, Bitch Becky One, Bitch Becky Two, and, let's not forget, Bow Wow Becky Junior and Becky called me asshole and looked away and everyone cracked up, even mean old Billy.

Man, he said, shaking his head, you got some mean mouth on you today. It was like suddenly I was too funny or famous for him to beat up. But after he bought his burger and chocolate milk, he said it real loud so everybody could hear, he said, I'll see you two bitches later. Outside.

Sure, Billy, I said and waved to him, see yah later, and then after we grabbed our lunch the new kid and me, we made a beeline for Mr. K.'s.

Boy, it was good to be in Mr. K.'s, I tell you. You don't have to watch over your shoulders every other second. You can play whatever game you want. Or you can read or just talk. So we ate and afterward I showed the new kid how to play speed. He was a quick learner too, if you asked me, but he lost pretty early on in the tournament. Then I lost too pretty damn quickly after him. So we sat around and I flipped through the X-Men comic book and tried to explain to the new kid why Wolverine is so cool 'cause he can heal himself with his mutant factor and he had claws that cut through metal, and Phoenix, she's my favorite, Phoenix's so very cool 'cause she can talk to you psychically and she knows how everybody feels without even having to ask them, and best of all, she can lift an eighteen-wheeler truck with her psycho-kinetic energy. That's way cool, don't you think, Kal. The new kid, he listened and nodded to everything I said like he understood. Anyway, after a while, there were more losers than winners and the losers surrounded us and interrogated the new kid like he was a POW or something.

You ever shoot anybody, Cao Long?

Did you see anybody get killed?

How *long* you been here Long? (Haha).

I hear they eat dogs over there, is that true? Have you ever eaten a dog?

Have you ever seen a helicopter blown up like in the movies?

No undohsten, the new kid answered to each question and smiled or shook his head or waved his hands like shooing flies but the loser flies wouldn't shoo. I mean where else could they go? Mr. K.'s was it. So the new kid looked at me again with them eyes and I said, OK, OK, Kal, I'll teach you something else. Why don't you say Hey, fuckheads, leave me alone! Go head, Kal, say it.

Hey-fuck-heads, I said, looking at him.

Hee, Foock headss, he said, looking at me.

Leave. Me. Alone! I said.

Leevenme olone! he said. *Hee, Foock headss. Leevenme olone!*

And everybody laughed. I guess that was the first time they got called fuckheads and actually felt good about it, but Mr. K. said Robert Quentin Mitchell, you watch your mouth or you'll never come in here again but you could tell he was trying not to laugh himself. So I said OK, Mr. K., but I leaned over and whispered *hey fuckheads, leave me alone* again in the new kid's ear so he'd remember and he looked at me like I'm the coolest guy in the world. Sthankew Rowbuurt, he said.

Then after school when I was waiting for my bus, the new kid found me. He gave me a folded piece of paper and before I could say anything he blushed and ran away. You'd never guess what it was. It was a drawing of me and it was really really good. I was smiling in it. I looked real happy and older, like a sophomore or something, not like in the 7th grade yearbook picture where I looked so goofy with my eyes closed and everything and I had to sign my name over it so people wouldn't look. When I got home I taped it on my family-tree chart and pinned the chart on my bedroom door and, I swear, the whole room had this vague eucalyptus smell.

Next day at Show and Tell Billy made the new kid cry. He went after Jimmy. Jimmy was this total nerd with thick glasses who told us how very challenging it was doing the New York Times crossword puzzles 'cause you got to know words like ubiquitous and undulate and capricious, totally lame and bogus stuff like that. When he took so long just to do five across and seven horizontal we shot spitballs at him and Mr. K. said stop that. But we got rid of that capricious undulating bozo ubiquitously fast and that was when Billy came up and made the new kid cry.

He brought in his Daddy's army uniform and a stack of old magazines. He unfolded the uniform with the name Baxter sewed under U.S. ARMY and put it on a chair. Then he opened one magazine and showed a picture of this naked and bleeding little girl running and crying on this road while these houses behind her were on fire. That's Napalm, he said, and it eats into your skin and burns for a long, long time. This girl, Billy said, she got burned real bad, see there, yeah. Then he showed another picture of this monk sitting cross-legged and he was on fire and everything and there were people standing behind him crying but nobody tried to put the poor man out. That's what you call self-immolation, Billy said. They do that all the time in 'Nam. This man, he poured gasoline on himself and lit a match 'cause he didn't like the government. Then Billy showed another picture of dead people in black pajamas along this road and he said these are VCs and my Daddy got at least a dozen of them before he was wounded himself. My Daddy told me if it weren't for them beatniks and hippies we could have won, Billy said, and that's when the new kid buried his face in his arms and cried and I could see his skinny shoulders go up and down like waves.

That's enough, Billy Baxter, Mr. K. said, you can sit down now, thank you.

Oh, man! Billy said, I didn't even get to the part about how my Daddy got his scar, that's the best part.

Never mind, Mr. K. said, sit down, please. I'm not sure whether you understood the assignment but you were supposed to do an oral presentation on what you've done or something that has to do with you, a hobby or a personal project, not the atrocities your father committed in Indochina. Save those stories for when you cruise the bars when you're old enough.

Then Mr. K. looked at the new kid like he didn't know what to do next. That war, he said, I swear. After that it got real quiet in the room and all you could hear was the new kid sobbing. Cao, Mr. K. said finally, real quiet like, like he didn't really want to bother him. Cao, are you all right? Cao Long Nguyen?

The new kid didn't answer Mr. K. so I put my hand on his shoulder and shook it a little. Hey, Kal, I said, you OK?

Then it was like I pressed an ON button or something, 'cause all of a sudden Kal raised his head and stood up. He looked at me and then he looked at the blackboard. He looked at me again, then the blackboard. Then he marched right up there even though it was Roger's turn next and Roger, he already brought his two pet snakes and everything. But Kal didn't care. Maybe he thought it was his turn 'cause Mr. K. called his name and so he just grabbed a bunch of colored chalk from Mr. K.'s desk and started to draw like a wild man and Mr. K. he let him.

We all stared.

He was really really good but I guess I already knew that.

First he drew a picture of a boy sitting on this water buffalo and then he drew this rice field in green. Then he drew another boy on another water buffalo and they seemed to be racing. He drew other kids running along the bank with their kites in the sky and you could tell they were laughing and yelling, having a good time. Then he started to draw little houses on both sides of this river and the river ran toward the ocean and the ocean had big old waves. Kal drew a couple standing outside this very nice house holding hands and underneath them Kal wrote *Ba* and *Ma*. Then he turned and looked straight at me, his eyes still wet with tears. *Rowbuurt,* he said, tapping the pictures with his chalk, his voice sad but expecting, *Rowbuurt.*

Me? I said. I felt kinda dizzy. Everybody was looking back and forth between him and me now like we were tossing a softball between us or something.

Rowbuurt. Kal said my name again and kept looking at me until I said what, what'd you want, Kal?

Kal tapped the blackboard with his chalk again and I saw in my head the picture of myself taped on my family-tree and then I don't know how but I just kinda knew. So I just took a deep breath and then I said, OK, OK, Kal, uhmm, said he used to live in this village with his Mama and Papa near where the river runs into the sea, and Kal nodded and smiled and waved his chalk in a circle like he was saying *Go on, Robert Quentin Mitchell, you're doing fine, go on.*

So I went on.

And he went on.

I talked. He drew.

We fell into a rhythm.

He had a good time racing them water buffaloes with his friends and flying kites, I said. His village is, hmm, very nice, and . . . and . . . and . . . at night he goes to sleep swinging on this hammock and hearing the sound of the ocean behind the dunes and everything.

Then one day, I said, the soldiers named VCs came with guns and they took his Daddy away. They put him behind barbed wire with other men, all very skinny, skinny and hungry and they got chains on their ankles and they looked really, really sad. Kal and his mother went to visit his Daddy and they stood on the other side of the fence and cried a lot. Yes, it was very, very sad. Then, hmm, one day his Daddy disappeared. No, he didn't disappear, he died, he died.

And Kal and his mother buried him in this cemetery with lots of graves and they lit candles and cried and cried. After that, there was this boat, this really crowded boat, I guess, and Kal and his Mama climbed on it and they went down the river out to sea. Then they got on this island and then they got on an airplane after that and they came here to live in America.

Kal was running out of space. He drew the map of America way too big but he didn't want to erase it. So he climbed on a chair and drew these high-rises right above the rice fields and I recognized the Trans-American building right away, a skinny pyramid underneath a rising moon. Then he drew a big old heart around it. Then he went back to the scene where the man named Ba stood in the doorway with his wife and he drew a heart around him. Then he went back to the first scene of the two boys racing on the water buffaloes in the rice field and paused a little before he drew tiny tennis shoes on the boys' feet and I heard Billy say that's Bobby and his refugee boyfriend but I ignored him.

Kal loves America very much, especially San Francisco, I said, he'd never seen so many tall buildings before in his whole life and they're so pretty. Maybe he'll live with his mother someday up in the penthouse when they have lots of money. But he misses home too and he misses his friends and he especially misses his Daddy who died. A lot. And that's all, I said. I think he's done, thank you.

And he was done. Kal turned around and climbed down from the chair. Then he looked at everybody and checked out their faces to see if they understood. Then in this real loud voice he said, *Hee, Foock headss, leevenme olone!* and bowed to them and everybody cracked up and applauded.

Kal started walking back. He was smiling and looking straight at me with his teary eyes like he was saying *Robert Quentin Mitchell, ain't we a team or what?* and I wanted to say yes, yes, Kal Long Nguyen—Refugee, yes we are but I just didn't say anything.

Mrs. Sen's

JHUMPA LAHIRI

Eliot had been going to Mrs. Sen's for nearly a month, ever since school started in September. The year before he was looked after by a university student named Abby, a slim, freckled girl who read books without pictures on their covers, and refused to prepare any food for Eliot containing meat. Before that an older woman, Mrs. Linden, greeted him when he came home each afternoon, sipping coffee from a thermos and working on crossword puzzles while Eliot played on his own. Abby received her degree and moved off to another university, while Mrs. Linden was, in the end, fired when Eliot's mother discovered that Mrs. Linden's thermos contained more whiskey than coffee. Mrs. Sen came to them in tidy ballpoint script, posted on an index card outside the supermarket: "Professor's wife, responsible and kind, I will care for your child in my home." On the telephone Eliot's mother told Mrs. Sen that the previous baby-sitters had come to their house. "Eliot is eleven. He can feed and entertain himself; I just want an adult in the house, in case of an emergency." But Mrs. Sen did not know how to drive.

• • •

"As you can see, our home is quite clean, quite safe for a child," Mrs. Sen had said at their first meeting. It was a university apartment located on the fringes of the campus. The lobby was tiled in unattractive squares of tan, with a row of mailboxes marked with masking tape or white labels. Inside, intersecting shadows left by a vacuum cleaner were frozen on the surface of a plush pear-colored carpet. Mismatched remnants of other carpets were positioned in front of the sofa and chairs, like individual welcome mats anticipating where a person's feet would contact the floor. White drum-shaped lampshades flanking the sofa were still wrapped in the manufacturer's plastic. The TV and the telephone were covered by pieces of yellow fabric with scalloped edges. There was tea in a tall gray pot, along with mugs, and butter biscuits on a tray. Mr. Sen, a short, stocky man with slightly protuberant eyes and glasses with black rectangular frames, had been there, too. He crossed his legs with some effort, and held his mug with both hands very close to his mouth, even when he wasn't drinking. Neither Mr. nor Mrs. Sen wore shoes; Eliot noticed several pairs lined on the shelves of a small bookcase by the front door. They wore flip-flops. "Mr. Sen teaches mathematics at the university," Mrs. Sen had said by way of introduction, as if they were only distantly acquainted.

She was about thirty. She had a small gap between her teeth and faded pockmarks on her chin, yet her eyes were beautiful, with thick, flaring brows and liquid flourishes that extended beyond the natural width of the lids. She wore a shimmering white sari patterned with orange paisleys, more suitable for an evening affair than for that quiet, faintly drizzling August afternoon. Her lips were coated in a complementary coral gloss, and a bit of the color had strayed beyond the borders.

Yet it was his mother, Eliot had thought, in her cuffed, beige shorts and her rope-soled shoes, who looked odd. Her cropped hair, a shade similar to her shorts, seemed too lank and sensible, and in that room where all things were so carefully covered, her shaved knees and thighs too exposed. She refused a biscuit each time Mrs. Sen extended the plate in her direction, and asked a long series of questions, the answers to which she recorded on a steno pad. Would there be other children in the apartment? Had Mrs. Sen cared for children before? How long had she lived in this country? Most of all she was concerned that Mrs. Sen did not know how to drive. Eliot's mother worked in an office fifty miles north, and his father, the last she had heard, lived two thousand miles west.

"I have been giving her lessons, actually," Mr. Sen said, setting his mug on the coffee table. It was the first time he had spoken. "By my estimate Mrs. Sen should have her driver's license by December."

"Is that so?" Eliot's mother noted the information on her pad.

"Yes, I am learning," Mrs. Sen said. "But I am a slow student. At home, you know, we have a driver."

"You mean a chauffeur?"

Mrs. Sen glanced at Mr. Sen, who nodded.

Eliot's mother nodded, too, looking around the room. "And that's all . . . in India?"

"Yes," Mrs. Sen replied. The mention of the word seemed to release something in her. She neatened the border of her sari where it rose diagonally across her chest. She, too, looked around the room, as if she noticed in the lampshades, in the teapot, in the shadows frozen on the carpet, something the rest of them could not. "Everything is there."

Eliot didn't mind going to Mrs. Sen's after school. By September the tiny beach house where he and his mother lived year-round was already cold; Eliot and his mother had to bring a portable heater along whenever they moved from one room to another, and to seal the windows with plastic sheets and a hair drier. The beach was barren and dull to play on alone; the only neighbors who stayed on past Labor Day, a young married couple, had no children, and Eliot no longer found it interesting to gather broken mussel shells in his bucket, or to stroke the seaweed, strewn like strips of emerald lasagna on the sand. Mrs. Sen's apartment was warm, sometimes too warm; the radiators continuously hissed like a pressure cooker. Eliot learned to remove his sneakers first thing in Mrs. Sen's doorway, and to place them on the bookcase next to a row of Mrs. Sen's slippers, each a different color, with soles as flat as cardboard and a ring of leather to hold her big toe.

He especially enjoyed watching Mrs. Sen as she chopped things, seated on newspapers on the living room floor. Instead of a knife she used a blade that curved like the prow of a Viking ship, sailing to battle in distant seas. The blade was hinged at one end to a narrow wooden base. The steel, more black than silver, lacked a uniform polish, and had a serrated crest, she told Eliot, for grating. Each afternoon Mrs. Sen lifted the blade and locked it into place, so that it met the base at an angle. Facing the sharp edge without ever touching it, she took whole vegetables between her hands and hacked them apart: cauliflower, cabbage, butternut squash. She split things in half, then quarters, speedily producing florets, cubes, slices, and shreds. She could peel a potato in seconds. At times she sat cross-legged, at times with legs splayed, surrounded by an array of colanders and shallow bowls of water in which she immersed her chopped ingredients.

While she worked she kept an eye on the television and an eye on Eliot, but she never seemed to keep an eye on the blade. Nevertheless she refused to let Eliot walk around when she was chopping. "Just sit, sit please, it will take just two more minutes," she said, pointing to the sofa, which was draped at all times with a green and black bedcover printed with rows of elephants bearing palanquins on their backs. The daily procedure took about an hour. In order to occupy Eliot she supplied him with the comics section of the newspaper, and crackers spread with peanut butter, and sometimes a Popsicle, or carrot sticks sculpted with her blade. She would have roped off the area if she could. Once, though, she broke her own rule; in need of additional supplies, and reluctant to rise from the catastrophic mess that barricaded her, she asked Eliot to fetch something from the kitchen. "If you don't mind, there is a plastic bowl, large enough to hold this spinach, in the cabinet next to the fridge. Careful, oh dear, be careful," she cautioned as he approached. "Just leave it, thank you, on the coffee table, I can reach."

She had brought the blade from India, where apparently there was at least one in every household. "Whenever there is a wedding in the family," she told Eliot one day, "or a large celebration of any kind, my mother sends out word in the evening for all the neighborhood women to bring blades just like this one, and then they sit in an enormous circle on the roof of our building, laughing and gossiping and slicing fifty kilos of vegetables through the night." Her profile hovered protectively over her work, a confetti of cucumber, eggplant, and onion skins heaped around her. "It is impossible to fall asleep those nights, listening to their chatter." She paused to look at a pine tree framed by the living room window. "Here, in this place where Mr. Sen has brought me, I cannot sometimes sleep in so much silence."

Another day she sat prying the pimpled yellow fat off chicken parts, then dividing them between thigh and leg. As the bones cracked apart over the blade her golden bangles jostled, her forearms glowed, and she exhaled audibly through her nose. At one point she paused, gripping the chicken with both hands, and stared out the window. Fat and sinew clung to her fingers.

"Eliot, if I began to scream right now at the top of my lungs, would someone come?"

"Mrs. Sen, what's wrong?"

"Nothing. I am only asking if someone would come."

Eliot shrugged. "Maybe."

"At home that is all you have to do. Not everybody has a telephone. But just raise your voice a bit, or express grief or joy of any kind, and one whole neighborhood and half of another has come to share the news, to help with arrangements."

By then Eliot understood that when Mrs. Sen said home, she meant India, not the apartment where she sat chopping vegetables. He thought of his own home, just five miles away, and the young married couple who waved from time to time as they jogged at sunset along the shore. On Labor Day they'd had a party. People were piled on the deck, eating, drinking, the sound of their laughter rising above the weary sigh of the waves. Eliot and his mother weren't invited. It was one of the rare days his mother had off, but they didn't go anywhere. She did the laundry, and balanced the checkbook, and, with Eliot's help, vacuumed the inside of the car. Eliot had suggested that they go through the car wash a few miles down the road as they did every now and then, so that they could sit inside, safe and dry, as soap and water and a circle of giant canvas ribbons slapped the windshield, but his mother said she was too tired, and sprayed the car with a hose. When, by evening, the crowd on the neighbors' deck began dancing, she looked up their number in the phone book and asked them to keep it down.

"They might call you," Eliot said eventually to Mrs. Sen. "But they might complain that you were making too much noise."

From where Eliot sat on the sofa he could detect her curious scent of mothballs and cumin, and he could see the perfectly centered part in her braided hair, which was shaded with crushed vermilion and therefore appeared to be blushing. At first Eliot had wondered if she had cut her scalp, or if something had bitten her there. But then one day he saw her standing before the bathroom mirror, solemnly applying, with the head of a thumbtack, a fresh stroke of scarlet powder, which she stored in a small jam jar. A few grains of the powder fell onto the bridge of her nose as she used the thumbtack to stamp a dot above her eyebrows. "I must wear the powder every day," she explained when Eliot asked her what it was for, "for the rest of the days that I am married."

"Like a wedding ring, you mean?"

"Exactly, Eliot, exactly like a wedding ring. Only with no fear of losing it in the dishwater."

By the time Eliot's mother arrived at twenty past six, Mrs. Sen always made sure all evidence of her chopping was disposed of. The blade was scrubbed, rinsed, dried, folded, and stowed away in a cupboard with the aid of a stepladder. With Eliot's help the newspapers were crushed with all the peels and seeds and skins inside them. Brimming bowls and colanders lined the countertop, spices and pastes were measured and blended, and eventually a collection of broths simmered over periwinkle flames on the stove. It was never a special occasion, nor was she ever expecting company. It was merely dinner for herself and Mr. Sen, as indicated by the two plates and two glasses she set, without napkins or silverware, on the square Formica table at one end of the living room.

As he pressed the newspapers deeper into the garbage pail, Eliot felt that he and Mrs. Sen were disobeying some unspoken rule. Perhaps it was because of the urgency with which Mrs. Sen accomplished everything, pinching salt and sugar between her fingernails, running water through lentils, sponging all imaginable surfaces, shutting cupboard doors with a series of successive clicks. It gave him a little shock to see his mother all of a sudden, in the transparent stockings and shoulder-padded suits she wore to her job, peering into the corners of Mrs. Sen's apartment. She tended to hover on the far side of the door frame, calling to Eliot to put on his sneakers and gather his things, but Mrs. Sen would not allow it. Each evening she insisted that his mother sit on the sofa, where she was served something to eat: a glass of bright pink yogurt with rose syrup, breaded mincemeat with raisins, a bowl of semolina halvah.

"Really, Mrs. Sen. I take a late lunch. You shouldn't go to so much trouble."

"It is no trouble. Just like Eliot. No trouble at all."

His mother nibbled Mrs. Sen's concoctions with eyes cast upward, in search of an opinion. She kept her knees pressed together, the high heels she never removed pressed into the pear-colored carpet. "It's delicious," she would conclude, setting down the plate after a bite or two. Eliot knew she didn't like the tastes; she'd told him so once in the car. He also knew she didn't eat lunch at work, because the first thing she did when they were back at the beach house was pour herself a glass of wine and eat bread and cheese, sometimes so much of it that she wasn't hungry for the pizza they normally ordered for dinner. She sat at the table as he ate, drinking more wine and asking how his day was, but eventually she went to the deck to smoke a cigarette, leaving Eliot to wrap up the leftovers.

· · ·

Each afternoon Mrs. Sen stood in a grove of pine trees by the main road where the school bus dropped off Eliot along with two or three other children who lived nearby. Eliot always sensed that Mrs. Sen had been waiting for some time, as if eager to greet a person she hadn't seen in years. The hair at her temples blew about in the breeze, the column of vermilion fresh in her part. She wore navy blue sunglasses a little too big for her face. Her sari, a different pattern each day, fluttered below the hem of a checkered all-weather coat. Acorns and caterpillars dotted the asphalt loop that framed the complex of about a dozen brick buildings, all identical, embedded in a communal expanse of log chips. As they walked back from the bus stop she produced a sandwich bag from her pocket, and offered Eliot the peeled wedges of an orange, or lightly salted peanuts, which she had already shelled.

They proceeded directly to the car, and for twenty minutes Mrs. Sen practiced driving. It was a toffee-colored sedan with vinyl seats. There was an AM radio with chrome buttons, and on the ledge over the back seat, a box of Kleenex and an ice scraper. Mrs. Sen told Eliot she didn't feel right leaving him alone in the apartment, but Eliot knew she wanted him sitting beside her because she was afraid. She dreaded the roar of the ignition, and placed her hands over her ears to block out the sound as she pressed her slippered feet to the gas, revving the engine.

"Mr. Sen says that once I receive my license, everything will improve. What do you think, Eliot? Will things improve?"

"You could go places," Eliot suggested. "You could go anywhere."

"Could I drive all the way to Calcutta? How long would that take, Eliot? Ten thousand miles, at fifty miles per hour?"

Eliot could not do the math in his head. He watched Mrs. Sen adjust the driver's seat, the rearview mirror, the sunglasses on top of her head. She tuned the radio to a station that played symphonies. "Is it Beethoven?" she asked once, pronouncing the first part of the composer's name not "bay," but "bee," like the insect. She rolled down the window on her side, and asked Eliot to do the same. Eventually she pressed her foot to the brake pedal, manipulated the automatic gear shift as if it were an enormous, leaky pen, and backed inch by inch out of the parking space. She circled the apartment complex once, then once again.

"How am I doing, Eliot? Am I going to pass?"

She was continuously distracted. She stopped the car without warning to listen to something on the radio, or to stare at something, anything, in the road. If she passed a person, she waved. If she saw a bird twenty feet in front of her, she beeped the horn with her index finger and waited for it to fly away. In India, she said, the driver sat on the right side, not the left. Slowly they crept past the swing set, the laundry building, the dark green trash bins, the rows of parked cars. Each time they approached the grove of pine trees where the asphalt loop met the main road, she leaned forward, pinning all her weight against the brake as cars hurtled past. It was a narrow road painted with a solid yellow stripe, with one lane of traffic in either direction.

"Impossible, Eliot. How can I go there?"

"You need to wait until no one's coming."

"Why will not anybody slow down?"

"No one's coming now."

"But what about the car from the right, do you see? And look, a truck is behind it. Anyway, I am not allowed on the main road without Mr. Sen."

"You have to turn and speed up fast," Eliot said. That was the way his mother did it, as if without thinking. It seemed so simple when he sat beside his mother, gliding in the evenings back to the beach house. Then the road was just a road, the other cars merely part of the scenery. But when he sat with Mrs. Sen, under an autumn sun that glowed without warmth through the trees, he saw how that same stream of cars made her knuckles pale, her wrists tremble, and her English falter.

"Everyone, this people, too much in their world."

Two things, Eliot learned, made Mrs. Sen happy. One was the arrival of a letter from her family. It was her custom to check the mailbox after driving practice. She would unlock the box, but she would ask Eliot to reach inside, telling him what to look for, and then she would shut her eyes and shield them with her hands while he shuffled through the bills and magazines that came in Mr. Sen's name. At first Eliot found Mrs. Sen's anxiety incomprehensible; his mother had a p.o. box in town, and she collected mail so infrequently that once their electricity was cut off for three days. Weeks passed at Mrs. Sen's before he found a blue aerogram, grainy to the touch, crammed with stamps showing a bald man at a spinning wheel, and blackened by postmarks.

"Is this it, Mrs. Sen?"

For the first time she embraced him, clasping his face to her sari, surrounding him with her odor of mothballs and cumin. She seized the letter from his hands.

As soon as they were inside the apartment she kicked off her slippers this way and that, drew a wire pin from her hair, and slit the top and sides of the aerogram in three strokes. Her eyes darted back and forth as she read. As soon as she was finished, she cast aside the embroidery that covered the telephone, dialed, and asked, "Yes, is Mr. Sen there, please? It is Mrs. Sen and it is very important."

Subsequently she spoke in her own language, rapid and riotous to Eliot's ears; it was clear that she was reading the contents of the letter, word by word. As she read her voice was louder and seemed to shift in key. Though she stood plainly before him, Eliot had the sensation that Mrs. Sen was no longer present in the room with the pear-colored carpet.

Afterward the apartment was suddenly too small to contain her. They crossed the main road and walked a short distance to the university quadrangle, where bells in a stone tower chimed on the hour. They wandered through the student union, and dragged a tray together along the cafeteria ledge, and ate french fries heaped in a cardboard boat among students chatting at circular tables. Eliot drank soda from a paper cup, Mrs. Sen steeped a tea bag with sugar and cream. After eating they explored the art building, looking at sculptures and silk screens in cool corridors thick with the fragrance of wet paint and clay. They walked past the mathematics building, where Mr. Sen taught his classes.

They ended up in the noisy, chlorine-scented wing of the athletic building where, through a wide window on the fourth floor, they watched swimmers crossing from end to end in glaring turquoise pools. Mrs. Sen took the aerogram from India out of her purse and studied the front and back. She unfolded it and reread to herself, sighing every now and then. When she had finished she gazed for some time at the swimmers.

"My sister has had a baby girl. By the time I see her, depending if Mr. Sen gets his tenure, she will be three years old. Her own aunt will be a stranger. If we sit side by side on a train she will not know my face." She put away the letter, then placed a hand on Eliot's head. "Do you miss your mother, Eliot, these afternoons with me?"

The thought had never occurred to him.

"You must miss her. When I think of you, only a boy, separated from your mother for so much of the day, I am ashamed."

"I see her at night."

"When I was your age I was without knowing that one day I would be so far. You are wiser than that, Eliot. You already taste the way things must be."

The other thing that made Mrs. Sen happy was fish from the seaside. It was always a whole fish she desired, not shellfish, or the fillets Eliot's mother had broiled one night a few months ago when she'd invited a man from her office to dinner—a man who'd spent the night in his mother's bedroom, but whom Eliot never saw again. One evening when Eliot's mother came to pick him up, Mrs. Sen served her a tuna croquette, explaining that it was really supposed to be made with a fish called bhetki. "It is very frustrating," Mrs. Sen apologized, with an emphasis on the second syllable of the word. "To live so close to the ocean and not to have so much fish." In the summer, she said, she liked to go to a market by the beach. She added that while the fish there tasted nothing like the fish in India, at least it was fresh. Now that it was getting colder, the boats were no longer going out regularly, and sometimes there was no whole fish available for weeks at a time.

"Try the supermarket," his mother suggested.

Mrs. Sen shook her head. "In the supermarket I can feed a cat thirty-two dinners from one of thirty-two tins, but I can never find a single fish I like, never a single." Mrs. Sen said she had grown up eating fish twice a day. She added that in Calcutta people ate fish first thing in the morning, last thing before bed, as a snack after school if they were lucky. They ate the tail, the eggs, even the head. It was available in any market, at any hour, from dawn until midnight. "All you have to do is leave the house and walk a bit, and there you are."

Every few days Mrs. Sen would open up the yellow pages, dial a number that she had ticked in the margin, and ask if there was any whole fish available. If so, she would ask the market to hold it. "Under Sen, yes, S as in Sam, N as in New York. Mr. Sen will be there to pick it up." Then she would call Mr. Sen at the university. A few minutes later Mr. Sen would arrive, patting Eliot on the head but not kissing Mrs. Sen. He read his mail at the Formica table and drank a cup of tea before heading out; half an hour later he would return, carrying a paper bag with a smiling lobster drawn on the front of it, and hand it to Mrs. Sen, and head back to the university to teach his evening class. One day, when he handed Mrs. Sen the paper bag, he said, "No more fish for a while. Cook the chicken in the freezer. I need to start holding office hours."

For the next few days, instead of calling the fish market, Mrs. Sen thawed chicken legs in the kitchen sink and chopped them with her blade. One day she made a stew with green beans and tinned sardines. But the following week the man who ran the fish market called Mrs. Sen; he assumed she wanted the fish, and said he would hold it until the end of the day under her name. She was flattered. "Isn't that nice of him, Eliot? The man said he looked up my name in the telephone book. He said there is only one Sen. Do you know how many Sens are in the Calcutta telephone book?"

She told Eliot to put on his shoes and his jacket, and then she called Mr. Sen at the university. Eliot tied his sneakers by the bookcase and waited for her to join him, to choose from her row of slippers. After a few minutes he called out her name. When Mrs. Sen did not reply, he untied his sneakers and returned to the living room, where he found her on the sofa, weeping. Her face was in her hands and tears dripped through her fingers. Through them she murmured something about a meeting Mr. Sen was required to attend. Slowly she stood up and rearranged the cloth over the telephone. Eliot followed her, walking for the first time in his sneakers across the pear-colored carpet. She stared at him. Her lower eyelids were swollen into thin pink crests. "Tell me, Eliot. Is it too much to ask?"

Before he could answer, she took him by the hand and led him to the bedroom, whose door was normally kept shut. Apart from the bed, which lacked a headboard, the only other things in the room were a side table with a telephone on it, an ironing board, and a bureau. She flung open the drawers of the bureau and the door of the closet, filled with saris of every imaginable texture and shade, brocaded with gold and silver threads. Some were transparent, tissue thin, others as thick as drapes, with tassels knotted along the edges. In the closet they were on hangers; in the drawers they were folded flat, or wound tightly like thick scrolls. She sifted through the drawers, letting saris spill over the edges. "When have I ever worn this one? And this? And this?" She tossed the saris one by one from the drawers, then pried several from their hangers. They landed like a pile of tangled sheets on the bed. The room was filled with an intense smell of mothballs.

"'Send pictures,' they write. 'Send pictures of your new life.' What picture can I send?" She sat, exhausted, on the edge of the bed, where there was now barely room for her. "They think I live the life of a queen, Eliot." She looked around the blank walls of the room. "They think I press buttons and the house is clean. They think I live in a palace."

The phone rang. Mrs. Sen let it ring several times before picking up the extension by the bed. During the conversation she seemed only to be replying to things, and wiping her face with the ends of one of the saris. When she got off the phone she stuffed the saris without folding them back into the drawers, and then she and Eliot put on their shoes and went to the car, where they waited for Mr. Sen to meet them.

"Why don't you drive today?" Mr. Sen asked when he appeared, rapping on the hood of the car with his knuckles. They always spoke to each other in English when Eliot was present.

"Not today. Another day."

"How do you expect to pass the test if you refuse to drive on a road with other cars?"

"Eliot is here today."

"He is here every day. It's for your own good. Eliot, tell Mrs. Sen it's for her own good."

She refused.

They drove in silence, along the same roads that Eliot and his mother took back to the beach house each evening. But in the back seat of Mr. and Mrs. Sen's car the ride seemed unfamiliar, and took longer than usual. The gulls whose tedious cries woke him each morning now thrilled him as they dipped and flapped across the sky. They passed one beach after another, and the shacks, now locked up, that sold frozen lemonade and quahogs in summer. Only one of the shacks was open. It was the fish market.

Mrs. Sen unlocked her door and turned toward Mr. Sen, who had not yet unfastened his seat belt. "Are you coming?"

Mr. Sen handed her some bills from his wallet. "I have a meeting in twenty minutes," he said, staring at the dashboard as he spoke. "Please don't waste time."

Eliot accompanied her into the dank little shop, whose walls were festooned with nets and starfish and buoys. A group of tourists with cameras around their necks huddled by the counter, some sampling stuffed clams, others pointing to a large chart illustrating fifty different varieties of North Atlantic fish. Mrs. Sen took a ticket from the machine at the counter and waited in line. Eliot stood by the lobsters, which stirred one on top of another in their murky tank, their claws bound by yellow rubber bands. He watched as Mrs. Sen laughed and chatted, when it was her turn in line, with a man with a bright red face and yellow teeth, dressed in a black rubber apron. In either hand he held a mackerel by the tail.

"You are sure what you sell me is very fresh?"

"Any fresher and they'd answer that question themselves."

The dial shivered toward its verdict on the scale.

"You want this cleaned, Mrs. Sen?"

She nodded. "Leave the heads on, please."

"You got cats at home?"

"No cats. Only a husband."

Later, in the apartment, she pulled the blade out of the cupboard, spread newspapers across the carpet, and inspected her treasures. One by one she drew them from the paper wrapping, wrinkled and tinged with blood. She stroked the tails, prodded the bellies, pried apart the gutted flesh. With a pair of scissors she clipped the fins. She tucked a finger under the gills, a red so bright they made her vermilion seem pale. She grasped the body, lined with inky streaks, at either end, and notched it at intervals against the blade.

"Why do you do that?" Eliot asked.

"To see how many pieces. If I cut properly, from this fish I will get three meals." She sawed off the head and set it on a pie plate.

In November came a series of days when Mrs. Sen refused to practice driving. The blade never emerged from the cupboard, newspapers were not spread on the floor. She did not call the fish store, nor did she thaw chicken. In silence she prepared crackers with peanut butter for Eliot, then sat reading old aerograms from a shoebox. When it was time for Eliot to leave she gathered together his things without inviting his mother to sit on the sofa and eat something first. When, eventually, his mother asked him in the car if he'd noticed a change in Mrs. Sen's behavior, he said he hadn't. He didn't tell her that Mrs. Sen paced the apartment, staring at the plastic-covered lampshades as if noticing them for the first time. He didn't tell her she switched on the television but never watched it, or that she made herself tea but let it grow cold on the coffee table. One day she played a tape of something she called a raga; it sounded a little bit like someone plucking very slowly and then very quickly on a violin, and Mrs. Sen said it was supposed to be heard only in the late afternoon, as the sun was setting. As the music played, for nearly an hour, she sat on the sofa with her eyes closed. Afterward she said, "It is more sad even than your Beethoven, isn't it?" Another day she played a cassette of people talking in her language—a farewell present, she told Eliot, that her family had made for her. As the succession of voices laughed and said their bit, Mrs. Sen identified each speaker. "My third uncle, my cousin, my father, my grandfather." One speaker sang a song. Another recited a poem. The final voice on the tape belonged to Mrs. Sen's mother. It was quieter and sounded more serious than the others. There was a pause between each sentence, and during this pause Mrs. Sen translated for Eliot: "The price of goat rose two rupees. The mangoes at the market are not very sweet. College Street is flooded." She turned off the tape. "These are things that happened the day I left India." The next day she played the same cassette all over again. This time, when her grandfather was speaking, she stopped the tape. She told Eliot she'd received a letter over the weekend. Her grandfather was dead.

A week later Mrs. Sen began cooking again. One day as she sat slicing cabbage on the living room floor, Mr. Sen called. He wanted to take Eliot and Mrs. Sen to the seaside. For the occasion Mrs. Sen put on a red sari and red lipstick; she freshened the vermilion in her part and rebraided her hair. She knotted a scarf under her chin, arranged her sunglasses on top of her head, and put a pocket camera in her purse. As Mr. Sen backed out of the parking lot, he put his arm across the top of the front seat, so that it looked as if he had his arm around Mrs. Sen. "It's getting too cold for that top coat," he said to her at one point. "We should get you something warmer." At the shop they bought mackerel, and butterfish, and sea bass. This time Mr. Sen came into the shop with them. It was Mr. Sen who asked whether the fish was fresh and to cut it this way or that way. They bought so much fish that Eliot had to hold one of the bags. After they put the bags in the trunk, Mr. Sen announced that he was hungry, and Mrs. Sen agreed, so they crossed the street to a restaurant where the take-out window was still open. They sat at a picnic table and ate two baskets of clam cakes. Mrs. Sen put a good deal of Tabasco sauce and black pepper on hers. "Like pakoras, no?" Her face was flushed, her lipstick faded, and she laughed at everything Mr. Sen said.

Behind the restaurant was a small beach, and when they were done eating they walked for a while along the shore, into a wind so strong that they had to walk backward. Mrs. Sen pointed to the water, and said that at a certain moment, each wave resembled a sari drying on a clothesline. "Impossible!" she shouted eventually, laughing as she turned back, her eyes teary. "I cannot move." Instead she took a picture of Eliot and Mr. Sen standing on the sand. "Now one of us," she said, pressing Eliot against her checkered coat and giving the camera to Mr. Sen. Finally the camera was given to Eliot. "Hold it steady," said Mr. Sen. Eliot looked through the tiny window in the camera and waited for Mr. and Mrs. Sen to move closer together, but they didn't. They didn't hold hands or put their arms around each other's waists. Both smiled with their mouths closed, squinting into the wind, Mrs. Sen's red sari leaping like flames under her coat.

In the car, warm at last and exhausted from the wind and the clam cakes, they admired the dunes, the ships they could see in the distance, the view of the lighthouse, the peach and purple sky. After a while Mr. Sen slowed down and stopped by the side of the road.

"What's wrong?" Mrs. Sen asked.

"You are going to drive home today."

"Not today."

"Yes, today." Mr. Sen stepped out of the car and opened the door on Mrs. Sen's side. A fierce wind blew into the car, accompanied by the sound of waves crashing on the shore. Finally she slid over to the driver's side, but spent a long time adjusting her sari and her sunglasses. Eliot turned and looked through the back window. The road was empty. Mrs. Sen turned on the radio, filling up the car with violin music.

"There's no need," Mr. Sen said, clicking it off.

"It helps me to concentrate," Mrs. Sen said, and turned the radio on again.

"Put on your signal," Mr. Sen directed.

"I know what to do."

For about a mile she was fine, though far slower than the other cars that passed her. But when the town approached, and traffic lights loomed on wires in the distance, she went even slower.

"Switch lanes," Mr. Sen said. "You will have to bear left at the rotary."

Mrs. Sen did not.

"Switch lanes, I tell you." He shut off the radio. "Are you listening to me?"

A car beeped its horn, then another. She beeped defiantly in response, stopped, then pulled without signaling to the side of the road. "No more," she said, her forehead resting against the top of the steering wheel. "I hate it. I hate driving. I won't go on."

She stopped driving after that. The next time the fish store called she did not call Mr. Sen at his office. She had decided to try something new. There was a town bus that ran on an hourly schedule between the university and the seaside. After the university it made two stops, first at a nursing home, then at a shopping plaza without a name, which consisted of a bookstore, a shoe store, a drugstore, a pet store, and a record store. On benches under the portico, elderly women from the nursing home sat in pairs, in knee-length overcoats with oversized buttons, eating lozenges.

"Eliot," Mrs. Sen asked him while they were sitting on the bus, "will you put your mother in a nursing home when she is old?"

"Maybe," he said. "But I would visit every day."

"You say that now, but you will see, when you are a man your life will be in places you cannot know now." She counted on her fingers: "You will have a wife, and children of your own, and they will want to be driven to different places at the same time. No matter how kind they are, one day they will complain about visiting your mother, and you will get tired of it too, Eliot. You will miss one day, and another, and then she will have to drag herself onto a bus just to get herself a bag of lozenges."

At the fish shop the ice beds were nearly empty, as were the lobster tanks, where rust-colored stains were visible through the water. A sign said the shop would be closing for winter at the end of the month. There was only one person working behind the counter, a young boy who did not recognize Mrs. Sen as he handed her a bag reserved under her name.

"Has it been cleaned and scaled?" Mrs. Sen asked.

The boy shrugged. "My boss left early. He just said to give you this bag."

In the parking lot Mrs. Sen consulted the bus schedule. They would have to wait forty-five minutes for the next one, and so they crossed the street and bought clam cakes at the take-out window they had been to before. There was no place to sit. The picnic tables were no longer in use, their benches chained upside down on top of them.

On the way home an old woman on the bus kept watching them, her eyes shifting from Mrs. Sen to Eliot to the blood-lined bag between their feet. She wore a black overcoat, and in her lap she held, with gnarled, colorless hands, a crisp white bag from the drugstore. The only other passengers were two college students, boyfriend and girlfriend, wearing matching sweatshirts, their fingers linked, slouched in the back seat. In silence Eliot and Mrs. Sen ate the last few clam cakes in the bag. Mrs. Sen had forgotten napkins, and traces of fried batter dotted the corners of her mouth. When they reached the nursing home the woman in the overcoat stood up, said something to the driver, then stepped off the bus. The driver turned his head and glanced back at Mrs. Sen. "What's in the bag?"

Mrs. Sen looked up, startled.

"Speak English?" The bus began to move again, causing the driver to look at Mrs. Sen and Eliot in his enormous rearview mirror.

"Yes, I can speak."

"Then what's in the bag?"

"A fish," Mrs. Sen replied.

"The smell seems to be bothering the other passengers. Kid, maybe you should open her window or something."

One afternoon a few days later the phone rang. Some very tasty halibut had arrived on the boats. Would Mrs. Sen like to pick one up? She called Mr. Sen, but he was not at his desk. A second time she tried calling, then a third. Eventually she went to the kitchen and returned to the living room with the blade, an eggplant, and some newspapers. Without having to be told Eliot took his place on the sofa and watched as she sliced the stems off the eggplant. She divided it into long, slender strips, then into small squares, smaller and smaller, as small as sugar cubes.

"I am going to put these in a very tasty stew with fish and green bananas," she announced. "Only I will have to do without the green bananas."

"Are we going to get the fish?"

"We are going to get the fish."

"Is Mr. Sen going to take us?"

"Put on your shoes."

They left the apartment without cleaning up. Outside it was so cold that Eliot could feel the chill on his teeth. They got in the car, and Mrs. Sen drove around the asphalt loop several times. Each time she paused by the grove of pine trees to observe the traffic on the main road. Eliot thought she was just practicing while they waited for Mr. Sen. But then she gave a signal and turned.

The accident occurred quickly. After about a mile Mrs. Sen took a left before she should have, and though the oncoming car managed to swerve out of her way, she was so startled by the horn that she lost control of the wheel and hit a telephone pole on the opposite corner. A policeman arrived and asked to see her license, but she did not have one to show him. "Mr. Sen teaches mathematics at the university" was all she said by way of explanation.

The damage was slight. Mrs. Sen cut her lip, Eliot complained briefly of a pain in his ribs, and the car's fender would have to be straightened. The policeman thought Mrs. Sen had also cut her scalp, but it was only the vermilion. When Mr. Sen arrived, driven by one of his colleagues, he spoke at length with the policeman as he filled out some forms, but he said nothing to Mrs. Sen as he drove them back to the apartment. When they got out of the car, Mr. Sen patted Eliot's head. "The policeman said you were lucky. Very lucky to come out without a scratch."

After taking off her slippers and putting them on the bookcase, Mrs. Sen put away the blade that was still on the living room floor and threw the eggplant pieces and the newspapers into the garbage pail. She prepared a plate of crackers with peanut butter, placed them on the coffee table, and turned on the television for Eliot's benefit. "If he is still hungry give him a Popsicle from the box in the freezer," she said to Mr. Sen, who sat at the Formica table sorting through the mail. Then she went into her bedroom and shut the door. When Eliot's mother arrived at quarter to six, Mr. Sen told her the details of the accident and offered a check reimbursing November's payment. As he wrote out the check he apologized on behalf of Mrs. Sen. He said she was resting, though when Eliot had gone to the bathroom he'd heard her crying. His mother was satisfied with the arrangement, and in a sense, she confessed to Eliot as they drove home, she was relieved. It was the last afternoon Eliot spent with Mrs. Sen, or with any baby-sitter. From then on his mother gave him a key, which he wore on a string around his neck. He was to call the neighbors in case of an emergency, and to let himself into the beach house after school. The first day, just as he was taking off his coat, the phone rang. It was his mother calling from her office. "You're a big boy now, Eliot," she told him. "You okay?" Eliot looked out the kitchen window, at gray waves receding from the shore, and said that he was fine.

The Shylocks

CYNTHIA IGNACIO

Forty-second Street is a diamond ring on the finger of a whore.

That's what I'm thinking when I arrive there by subway from Brooklyn. I pop a nosebleed. I'm tired because I pay ninety dollars a month to sleep on a couch in someone's living room, and all I eat is Ramen noodles and a little pseudo-orange juice. "Punch," they call it. Here I am, going to attend the graduation of an old buddy, an old buddy who has a car when I don't, but makes me take the goddamn bus all the way from Manhattan to Jersey to attend his stupid graduation.

I scavenge Port Authority for the ticket booth, and barely have time to catch the next bus that goes out of Manhattan to Rauchenburg University, N.J. I board the proper bus with minimal problems and major paranoia—I didn't want to take the wrong one and end up in fucking Nebraska. I get this terrible scratchy feeling in my throat and I suck on a couple of nasty-tasting Halls Mentho-lyptus during the trip out of Manhattan. I'm not sorry to see all the skyscrapers disappear behind me.

New Jersey's a different story. Once you get past the stinking factories on the fringe, with their space-age power plants and iron-wrought, gothic-looking stairwells, you get to a land that's green all over. In Jersey you could tell it was spring. You could tell a person was from Jersey when they complained about mowing a lawn like anyone could mow a goddamn lawn in Brooklyn.

I look out the oily bus window, watching the trees go by, looking at them with strange uncertainty, like a country bumpkin looking at the Empire State for the first time. I also notice that it's drizzling in a miserable half-assed way.

The weather was beautiful, fucking gorgeous just two days before, when I was filming at the studio, taking care of continuity and other assistant shit like that on a crappy Cracker Jack commercial. It was by accident that Gervasi saw me at the studio. Otherwise I wouldn't have attended this pomp and circumcision. Anyway, it's getting chilly, and clouds keep rolling in. I realize I don't know which stop is the right one, and I have a few anxiety attacks apiece during each bus stop, wondering, Is this one it? Or this one? I finally give up my New York pride, and walk haltingly to the front of the bus to ask the driver for the correct stop. He lets me off on the opposite side of the street. I manage to cross the road to the university in under an hour—the traffic is fast and deadly in these no-traffic-light 'burbs.

I trudge across campus, examining all buildings cautiously. I figure I would eventually run in to the graduation ceremony, which is arranged to occur outdoors. I finally locate the area via sound.

Evidently Rauchenburg University is full of a bunch of pretentious bastards who like playing garbled opera tapes they bought for a Nice Price at Waxie

Maxie's. After being treated to a tortuous twenty minutes of jangling banjo-like arias, some guy comes out to give the obligatory speech. The most embarrassing thing about the speaker is that he thinks he's at Cambridge. The old geezer keeps on saying Cambridge, Cambridge, Cambridge, Cambridge, here at Cambridge, there at Cambridge, everywhere at Cambridge. And it isn't that Old MacDonald here graduated at Cambridge. I checked the graduation booklet. He's an ancient alumnus of Harvard. The whole school is suffering from an identity crisis.

I'm so impressed by all this—especially by the mysterious garbage bags that are handed out with the graduation booklets. For all the shit that's being shoveled? Their high-class purpose reveals itself when the sky opens up with cold rain. I stand for a brief moment of token pride, miserable, sharp and sarcastic, biting back curses. Then I finally give in to idiocy and put the garbage bag over my head, a hole punched through so I can breathe. I while the time away by reading the program through the clear plastic bag, to see how many fuckers are left to graduate, and could they please hurry up, I'm freezing my ass off.

There's a refreshment "tent," as it were, off to the side. More like a circus tent, which would be appropriate, because this school is full of clowns. I have some coffee and cheap deli cookies. I refuse to get any Koolaid from the big plastic punch bowl, because it has some goddamn ice in it and I am cold enough, thank you. Then I see champagne, of all things, being handed out. This is happening behind one of the trees, guys yanking bottle after bottle out of a huge cardboard box. Probably compliments of some rich brat frat guy. The lawn is turning to mud underneath the feet of a thousand or more people. It looks like someone had dumped truckloads of writhing spaghetti on the mud—I look closely and see that there are hundreds of squirming earthworms everywhere.

At last, my prayers have been answered, and the ceremony ends. I hunt high and low for Gervasi, but the lawn is milling with so many people that it's impossible to find him. So I ask this usher for directions to the dormitory.

The ushers are girls from Staten Island, with black frumpy skirts that are too tight and too short, showing their ample stomach bulges of maybe being pregnant at too young an age. They all have wrinkled white blouses with dyed green carnations pinned to their pockets. Their dead-give-away "big hair" defies the elements with its cast-iron hair-spray coating. Their lips are fat, rounded, like their double chins and gold-filled heavy earrings that droop their earlobes down to a Buddhalike length. They look like hired help. The difference is obvious. On one side, the students are busy saying "Dahling" like fake Kennedys, showing off $500 gold brick tie tacks and parading around in Anne Klein heels that sink into the wet ground. On the other side, the ushers are scratching their asses and saying stuff like "dunno" and "ain't."

I get to the dorm and go up a flight. I walk down the hall of open doors, checking numbers for twenty-five, Gervasi's room. I'm almost at the end of the corridor before I realize that all the eyes that are looking at me are female.

"This is the girls' floor," an amber-eyed brunette calls out to me. "Guys are upstairs."

"Uh, yeah," I say, embarrassed. "Thanks." I quick-walk to the stairwell.

She scrutinizes me. "Are you Gervasi's brother? You look a lot like Gervasi."

I stop, surprised, open my mouth to say no, I'm not. But I'd turned to glance at her, standing in the doorway in a '50s-style black dress, with white polka dots. When I see her, I change my mind. "Yes, I'm his brother," I say, bowing grandiosely, backing off, then winking and heading up the stairs.

The floor above is noisy with blaring radios and deep laughter. Empty cases of beer are stacked up by piles of trash. I target number twenty-five right next door to a bathroom. In the hall, Gervasi's door is one of the few closed ones. I give the doorknob a perfunctory turn, but my guess is right—Gervasi isn't back yet. I steer myself into the bathroom.

The quaint bathroom stalls have window-style two-door Venetian wooden shutters. Kinda like in cowboy movies—those doors that were entrances to the saloons. There are no latches on the inside. The handles to the flusher are above, to a gravity-powered water supply. I look at myself in the mirror. I did look a little like Gervasi. Wasn't it always my dream to be Gervasi? Was that why, impulsively, I had done the little fancy bow downstairs, just like he would have in a similar situation? My head aches. I don't want to look at myself.

The gratings to the window are old decorative wrought iron. I look through one, thinking what a great shot it would make in a film. Down below, the new grads, with parents and assorted relatives, are milling about like ants. The speakers by the podium are blaring jazz now—is there no end to this university's retarded attempts at culture? Graduation, I would guess, is a happy occasion, not a funeral. Ironically, the jazz is of the blues kind, with the wailing, lowing tremor of prolonged sax and trumpet in B flat, a sad, moody New York sound. It reminded me of Gervasi. Two days ago.

Two days ago, I was in a film studio bathroom, sorting things out, calming myself down.

I recalled my old film teacher, Lorenzo—a loud-mouthed brilliant bastard of an Italian. We all figured he'd been in the military, or the police, or the Mafia, or the priesthood. He had that kind of Don't-Mess-With-Me attitude. He called bathrooms "baccasas." And a "baccasa" was the only way the studio bathroom could be described. The stall had a heavy solid wooden door (white paint peeling), and two locks on the inside. You knew this fucking baccasa was built by some trusting New Yorker—there was a deadbolt and there was a slide chain. There was even a peephole so you could check who was standing outside before you opened the door. Anyway, this particular baccasa also had a mirror hanging on the wall about seven feet up from the ground. I had to stand on the toilet seat and crouch down to see my face. Did I look calm? Not in the least.

After sufficiently locking myself inside the Lysol-scented haven, I had started making obscene gestures in Gervasi's general direction. What the hell is he doing here? I don't know. I took deep glaring breaths. I recapped to myself the events of the Day:

New York was a madhouse.

The air was perforated by angry shouting, bricks being thrown, scared cops running away. All this was going on outside our window. We were filming some godforsaken Cracker Jack commercial in a studio on Broadway.

There were riots in the city because of the ruling during the King trial, just yesterday in L.A. Even Wall Street shut down early. But not us. The director was screaming for us to get back to work—we were all crammed into the producer's office, so we could look out and wonder at the two o'clock traffic jam down below. One of the secretaries started handing out friggin' Häagen-Dazs ice cream bars to salve our worries. Mick, our sound man and resident comedian, sent a salvo of sarcasm at the cameraman sitting next to him—everyone was on the edge of their seat, no one was in the mood for the Fighting Irishman's shenanigans. No one wanted to risk their life for Mr. Cracker Jack. He could keep his crappy toy surprise in his little box.

The honking horns of the cars outside built up like a migraine. It was only two o'clock in the afternoon and already it was rush hour.

Someone switched the radio from Muzak to news. Demonstrations were happening everywhere. Someone in the studio started telling an old college joke about pulling over to the roadside to film a dead cow. At that moment, someone paged me over the intercom, whoop de doop and I'm pushing my way through sweating film crews, heading over to the editing room, telling myself that things couldn't get any worse than this. A voice says my name, and I look all around, and then I see who it is.

"Hey, how ya been?" A heavy hand descends on my shoulder—it's Gervasi. "This fucking graduation *gown*," he smirks at the word, "is soaking wet!" Already he's shucking it off. He wrings it with a broad grimace, a waterfall splashing noisily onto the white floor of the dormitory bathroom. "Can you fucking believe this weather? Jeezuschrist—can't the director of ceremonies do his job already? I got pneumonia is what I got, never mind the diploma—are they gonna pay for my hospital bills or what?" His Brooklyn voice rings in the tiled room, filling it with his presence. He notices this. "Here I come, to saaave the daaay," he sings loudly, slapping the wet gown against a sink, and "Mighty Mouse is on his waay!"

A faint voice penetrates the bathroom door. "What is that gross sound? That you, Gervasi?" The door bursts open, and this guy flies in, grinning widely. He has the word *Galileo* tattooed on his left arm. "Keep it down, ya faggot! How can I sleep when you're always making so much goddamn noise?"

"I didn't make any noise during the ceremony. You slept pretty well through *that*, shithead." He snaps the gown like a wet towel. The spraying drops of water send Galileo howling back into the main hallway. Gervasi grabs a handful of my sleeve and yanks me out of the bathroom. Outside, he tosses a key at me.

"Hurry up, and get in," he says out of the corner of his mouth. A bunch of grinning football goons starts towards him. I open the door of number twenty-five.

"You'll never take me alive, ya bastards! Take that! And that! Oh, woiseguy, eh?" he says, like one of the three stooges. "And how would you like some-a *dis*?" Gervasi cracks the gown like a whip, then shoves me through the door, slamming it shut behind him.

The window to his room has a semicircle archway. Above is a network of water sprinkler pipes. It's clean-cut, conservative. Most of his stuff is gone— today is his deadline to move out.

"Crazy bastards," Gervasi says with a smile. "Heard you told Lonette that you're my brother! Now every fucking Mary and Joe in this burg thinks I been holding out on them, that I have some secret twin in a box someplace."

I collapse onto his futon on the floor, nearly breaking my back in the process.

"No springs in that thing, bud, watch it," he says.

I always wonder about Markalan, Gervasi's dead brother. Am I supposed to be Markalan to Gervasi? My hand begins to itch for a cigarette.

Why do you smoke?

For the nostalgia.

The old automatic question-answer. It always recites itself in my head whenever I get that craving. Maybe I should call it the old automatic question-*excuse*.

I look at Gervasi, pulling on his mustard-colored Armani suit. Gervasi has blond hair that's thinning on top. It's cut short and moussed up spiky. His eyebrows are dark, his jaw cut square. Like a gangster-comedian from *Guys and Dolls,* he has a cigarette drooping off his bottom lip, and a dimpled smile.

Gervasi notices the silence, and starts telling me some boring nostalgic story about the Climbing Tree, we called it, out on my front lawn where my family lives in Long Island. Weren't those great times, he's saying as he admires himself in the mirror, and I tell him that the tree is gone, the government came by and chopped it down.

He swings around, a perfect look of surprise on his face. "Why the hell'd they do that?"

I shrug. "I don't know. Maybe it was like the Giving Tree. Maybe it didn't have anything left to give." I feel his stare and I shrug again. "I don't know. It was a long time ago. It happened while I was away."

Gervasi starts to say something, then changes his mind. He grabs his hair drier instead, and the Hoover-like sound of it fills the silence. On his dresser are a bunch of paperweights, athletic trophies, about twenty dollars of loose change, and a bottle of that French stuff, Egoiste. The cologne has a big red bow on it. Someone's idea of a joke graduation present. He also has one of those glass globes that has water and plastic snow inside. I notice that there's a space in the bottom of the globe for a battery, to light up the background. I turn it upside down, to check, and I see there's no battery inside.

"What made you go into film?" he says finally.

I shake the globe. "Hard to say. Why'd you go into business?"

"Money. Power. Girls." He laughs. "Did I mention money yet?"

I shake the globe again. "How old were you when you realized there's no Santa Claus?"

"When I was a bad boy, and I still got presents."

We step into the hall where some girls from his dorm are complaining about a roach crawling on the floor. He casually steps on it, and they all scream at him not to kill it, the poor thing. He does a little soft-shoe for the girls as he scrapes the cockroach off on the floor. It makes me want to puke as they squeal with delight.

We go out later with a bevy of girls, and a handful of guys—we eat Thai and Indian at a place off St. Mark's in the East Village. The guys are all grumpy in the shadow, while Gervasi's in the middle, smack-dab, the girls pointing at him, leaning right in, their faces like spotlights nailed to his figure, catching every nuance and gesture as he tells his latest story. I'm on the far side of a rickety table. A sympathetic, nervous, smiling waiter sticks a wad of paper towels underneath the table leg to give it balance. One of the guys talks to me about film. Another asshole tells me about the time Gervasi and he had gone skinny-dipping at a Jersey beach, and how the water was illuminated by some kind of luminescent seaweed and how the girls could see their erections in the water despite the fact that it was nighttime, etc. etc.

After we eat, we go to a dance club that's in an abandoned church. It costs an arm and a soul to get in. You have to pay to have your coat checked. We're not even talking tip here. And the coat check's in this dreary place in the basement that's like a goddamn dungeon, guarded by a punker with a mohawk and a Lee's Outdoors checkered cotton shirt, and combat boots that were made for walking all over you.

Upstairs is some kind of fashion show. The models keep bumping into each other on the runway. Some guys dismantle the stage after the show, so there's more dance floor space. There are girls dancing their little asses off inside suspended cages. Military men are all over the place like lice. I look again and see really they're choirboys in a whorehouse, Just Kids. Everyone dances like shit, even Gervasi. This is one of his weaknesses. The music is terrible. I feel like puking, a little. So I go to the men's room.

There are female skinheads in the john, and I feel a little intimidated while I'm pissing. Maybe they're men in dresses. The place is a shit hole. Paper towels in the trash can are overflowing, no toilet paper in the stalls. Graffiti and phone numbers are all over the plaster walls. I decide the best place to run is outside.

A few high school kids are lined up outside, with their crushed corsages and rented tuxes, and their battered bargain limos on the curb. I see Gervasi outside, rubbing his forehead like he's got a headache, and he looks tired and irritated. I remember him hiding in the goddamn attic, and the little boy that was Gervasi, pissed about always having to give himself—the great confident Gervasi. But I look at him, sitting on the planter, his one leg up and his elbow leaning on his knee like some sort of Bugle Boy model. Even his face has that kind of James Dean look, wrinkled forehead, frowning mouth. Even if the emotion is sincere, it's too self-conscious, too posed, and I don't talk to him. I don't talk to him at all. I want to leave, but I can't without him seeing me. I back into the lobby, with its leopard-skin-spotted carpet and cheesy plastic chandelier. There are all kinds of punkers and New York sleazes making out on the gothic pews lining the tomb corridor. I stand beneath a stained-glass window and think about the days when Gervasi and I used to think we were brothers. But that's not true after all, is it?

He once had this favorite hat. "If my brother wore a hat, he'd wear this." I had worn it for a little while, feeling honored. One day I eventually gave it back to him, and he threw it away.

There are mirrors all over the place in this church, for self-contemplation, self-worship. I'm wearing all black, because this is, after all, a funeral.

I walk over to a balcony overlooking the wooden-planked dance floor, and already Gervasi's back in action. I see him eyeing a blonde in a red dress—one of the sexpot models from the impromptu fashion show—he makes his move, edging his way over. He casually bumps into her, apologizes, and then starts dancing with her. After a few minutes he's already steering her towards the bar. The world is full of suckers. I could imagine the tales of conquest he would fill our ears with tomorrow morning—"If I was a girl," Gervasi always said, "I'd be a slut."

He told me how he'd bought a prostitute for one of his friends as a gift, along with a limo, and how he'd told the guy to hide his wallet cause she'd rip him off. "Yeah, well, he put it in the ice bucket, and a'course she found it so Chrissake I told him so—blah blah blah."

I do films. I go to NYU, and I work like a sonuvabitch to get where I'm going. One of the film students' shticks is to get their friends to do their acting, so they don't have to go out and get a real actor, har har. The camera loved Gervasi. When he was in front of the lens, he was electric. It was fucking amazing.

I remember I was doing some filming at Gervasi's house, this huge fucking mansion with el huge-o glass windows the size of two stories on the front of the house. I was filming some random action at the party and I get two of his cronies snorting, and Gervasi breaks my goddamn camera.

Why do you protect those bastards?

These are my friends—

What friends, you are dreaming, bastard, dreaming.

We are driving to Six Flags Great Adventure and he tries to wave a ten-dollar bill at a hooker who turns out to be a man in a dress.

He catches a venereal disease from an old high school classmate, Jane, who's abused by her boyfriend, Ted.

He has an illegitimate kid when he is sixteen.

We were playing hooky from high school—we stood under the trees. Gervasi had a BB rifle in his right hand. He was looking at me. "She's got nothing on me," Gervasi said casually, but I looked at his hand, the muscles showing white through the skin. We used to shoot people in the Jersey woods, taking pot shots at cars on Lovers' Lane, and smoking joints and going craw fishing. The woods were peaceful, far away from anything. For some reason, I broke into a sweat.

"You crazy fuck," I said. "You crazy fuck, what are you going to do?"

Gervasi came from a rich family, well off. They were harmless people, but he could be ruined if they found out about the girl.

"Shut up, you asshole," he muttered.

"Oh shit," I said, staring at him. "You—"

"You're not going to say anything," he said. Then he noticed my expression. "You're the only one I can trust. Why do you think I told you this? You gotta help me on this." A worried look passed over his face. "You're my best friend."

I wanted to hear that all my life. He trusted me. I could prove my loyalty to him by doing this. So—I backed him up.

I was eight years old, he was seven. We'd just got back from going rock hunting in a ditch near the neighborhood baseball field. We were cracking open these rocks that were as big as our fists. He'd found one that had beautiful rose crystals inside. I broke several more open, hoping to find more of the same. The rest were just plain, brown rocks inside, nothing worthwhile. And he was at another school at that point, and he was talking about a new friend he'd met at school, Terry. His best friend. And he asks me, "Who's your best friend?" And I say, "You are," and he doesn't say a thing.

Gervasi bought these two pit bulls. "Look how strong these bastards are," and there was a rope in his hand that was as thick as my wrist, and they clung to the damn thing like Cerebus on the neck of some pathetic sinner, yeah. They were like muscles, a huge fist. One of them jumped up to lick me in the face, and its jaw slammed into mine, practically knocking me out. This was about the time when the things were getting a rep for eating babies and all kinds of crazy shit.

Gervasi was built like a brick shit house. He was pissed off and passed out. The summer before going away to college, he was a wreck. We went to bars all the time, unshaven, smoking, drinking.

There were times when I doubted him. He sensed those moments, like a lie detector, the telltale line scrawling the rapid beating of my heart, and he would lose that cold mask and let a little humanity seep through. We would go into bars together and talk long hours into the night, he would cry automatic actor's tears into his beers, and like the sucker of an audience I was, I reacted as expected, laughed at all the boners, cried at all the heart-tugging setups. The only genuine moments were when he didn't speak at all, because whenever he spoke he lied, he lied about his anger and his grief. In those silent moments he inhabited that place all idols inhabit—and in that place, the more people they are surrounded by, the more lonely they become.

There was a gorgeousness about him at the bars, they were his pièce de résistance, his brutality and fire; beautiful brooding acting that he refined on me for the sake of saving his reputation. He wasted his finest moments of acting on me, in those bars, the summer before I went to college. He's a player, all the time. I realize nothing much matters to him now—if you can escape the worst kind of claptrap, what couldn't a person do?

The music's loud inside, an incessant tempo, matching the heat of the mating season inside. I see him at the bar with his hand on the girl. I have this sudden fantasy of ripping his arms out of his sockets, and blood dripping in gratuitous excess. When he sweet-talks a girl it's like having the president of the United States fart in my ear.

He's startled to see me. I make a few short, inaudible excuses and say goodbye, knowing that he won't leave the bimbo and follow me out, try to convince me to stay longer. And I'm right.

In my nightmares, when we meet, we never speak.

PART 4

DRAMA

Introduction
Asian American Theater Awake at the Millennium

ROBERTA UNO

On a desolate street, in a tiny hole-in-the-wall theater in San Francisco's blighted South of Market district, a full house is about to witness a performance by the ensemble Teatro ng Tanan (Tagalog for Theater for the People) or TnT.[1] Observing the audience of mostly young Fil Ams, Filipino Americans, I realize I have no preconceived notion of what to expect. The negative possibilities abound—will it be a plodding immigrant drama? An enhanced college skit? Self-righteous agitprop? Impenetrable performance art? It's obvious that, like other performance junkies, I have done time; I have spent that interminable sentence in the dark, fueled by the hope and possibility of a hit of magic.

As the house darkens and strange prehuman sounds become audible, I am startled by the fleeting warmth of breath in my ear, as a reptilian body slithers past my shoulder. Even as I catch my breath, my mind races toward recognition. I think, "Aha—this is going to be a retro-homage to the Living Theater," one of those earnest college-ensemble productions that treads well-traveled ground with the naiveté of generational discovery.

But as the lights dawn, it is an astonishing new world that appears before me, unpredictable, fresh, and completely engrossing. With minimal lighting, props, or scenic support, the ensemble innovatively creates a universe, a story, an experience that surprises, delights, and moves its audience. Here is Jojo (short for Joseph), a quirky, comical, fearful little boy, whose quintessentially hardworking, two-income, immigrant parents desperately need day care. With trepidation, they leave him in the hands of his grandmother, Lola Celia, an old woman who may need care herself as she teeters between lucidity and incoherence. The Collective Memories, seen only by the boy and his grandmother, and expertly enacted by the ensemble, lurk at the fringes of their world. They reveal themselves as both angelic and demonic. They become fanciful playmates; they interrupt, insist, and inject themselves where they aren't wanted, they evoke fantastic story-telling worlds. And as their presence becomes increasingly vivid, they become a harrowing, violent force that threatens to carry Jojo and Lola Celia away into the grandmother's unspeakable past and the dark realm of madness.

The production is *Awake,* the result of a laboratory exploration, in which the TnT ensemble trained for six months in physical theater, including stilt walking, mask and character work, and gymnastics. They developed the script and brought it to production, under the skillful and inventive direction of Chrystene R. Ells, the lab leader and TnT's artistic director, and Michelle Arellano, the stage director. I have just seen the last performance of this extraordinary play and am dismayed to learn from its director, who is also running lights this particular evening, that the cohesive ensemble work I saw is so much so that there is no existing script. Nor, in the stress of production, has this small company had time to videotape the piece. And after a three-week run, in a city where Asian Americans comprise 24.5 percent of the population, this remarkable production has also remained beyond the narrow scope of the press and has gone unreviewed and undocumented.

This is the exhilarating and precarious state of Asian American theater in the new millennium. It is a time when artistic production is being fueled by the vitality of burgeoning communities, particularly Korean and South and Southeast Asian, which are pushing the boundaries previously defined by an historical Chinese and Japanese immigrant presence. It is a time of artistic risk taking when interdisciplinary work, physical theater, solo performance, community-engaged theater, intercultural collaboration, and popular culture genres of comedy, spoken word, performance poetry, hip hop, and contemporary music are redefining theater performance beyond the revered well-made play. It is a time of geographical expansion, where Asian American theater, historically confined to the two coasts, is present in the heartland, in the Southwest, and in New England.

But it is also a time when the established Asian American theaters, entering their midlife decades, must struggle between the rising costs of balancing the bottom line and the marketplace risk of innovative theater work. It is also a time when only a handful of Asian American playwrights have broken the color line of production in mainstream venues, even in cities with an overwhelming percentage of Asian American residents. It is also a time when a considerable distance persists between funding and policy making for the arts, and Asian American theater artists. It is also a time when some of the most extraordinary theater evaporates with its final performance, a time when what is documented and commented upon is narrowly representative of a much wider movement.

Undocumented Aliens

As the artistic director of New WORLD Theater, a first-voice theater of artists of color founded in 1979 in Amherst, Massachusetts, I feel it is this issue of documentation, as well as the issues of new aesthetics, expanded identity, and enlarged geographies, which are resonating points of intersection with the work I do within the Asian American theater.[2] I am a third generation Japanese American woman, born in Hawai'i and raised in Los Angeles, who has chosen to locate my artistic work within a multiracial context. When I arrived in New England in the 1970s, a California transplant, I experienced a culture shock familiar to many. I was confronted with a homogenous environment that did not reflect me—from the food in the grocery stores to the theater on stage. I was clearly an alien, searching for cultural reflection, and finding invisibility, also undocumented.

This experience spurred me not only to make theater, but to actively document it, through publishing and archival projects. These have been efforts to make a presence known, from a primary perspective, precisely because what is omitted from the official record is often more noteworthy than what is included.

For example, Nobuko Miyamoto, a pioneering Asian American artist and social activist, whose career spans five decades from the Broadway stage, to Hollywood, to countless performance spaces and college campuses in between, has notably been absent from the official record of Asian American theater scholarship and mainstream theater criticism. Her theater work consists of multi-character and solo theater performances in the musical theater genre,[3] and for this reason it has not been included in Asian American theater anthologies. She is also a self-identified community-based artist, making theater for and in Asian American communities and other communities of color. For this reason, her work has existed outside the very limited radar of mainstream reviewers, despite the fact that she is based in Los Angeles, a city with several weekly publications and a major daily newspaper. This neglect, by both theater academics and the press, challenges how artistic work is documented and what work enters the official record and the canon.

Her musical *Chop Suey* (1980–1981) was performed at Los Angeles area colleges and eight Los Angeles county parks,[4] and toured the Pacific Northwest. It arguably had one of the largest Asian American audiences of any work of theater written by an Asian American, yet it (and by extension Miyamoto) has been omitted from Asian American theater histories because it was not produced in either an Asian American or mainstream theater and consequently was not reviewed. Finally, Miyamoto has chosen to align herself with other artists of color and this may have also caused her work to be placed outside of more narrowly defined Asian American ethnic theater projects.

Clearly this example of Miyamoto is intended to be historically restorative. But it also speaks to the widest arenas in which Asian American theater has been and is being made. The need to restore a major theater artist to the record underscores the situation faced by other Asian American artists who either work outside of ethnically specific or mainstream theaters, work in community-based settings, work in interdisciplinary genres, work within an alternative social or political context (feminist, multiracial, and/or queer, for example), or work beyond the confines of a bicoastal geography. These are the areas in which I see the most challenging Asian American theater work being made and which I feel will make the greatest impact in the coming decades.

Multiracialism and the Browning of Asian America

It is projected that, by the year 2050, Caucasians will become a minority in the United States, outnumbered by people of color, a monolithic category, which, while affirming unity, obscures the complexity of difference. In this prediction, demographers also question the diminishing relevance or new meanings of traditional assignations of race, as categories will increasingly blur due to racial, cultural, and ethnic hybridization. In Asian American studies, the accelerated rate of out-marriage for Asian Americans has been well documented. In the theater arena, this changing demographic has raised extremely challenging questions. Playwright Velina Hasu Houston, a hapa of Japanese, African American and Blackfoot Indian heritage, describes the difficulties she encounters working in both Asian American and African American theaters where her work is scrutinized for authenticity: "Odd comments or questions arise such as: Are these characters black enough? Are these characters Japanese enough? This black man's language isn't jive enough. Japanese people would never do these things. . . . Sometimes these self-appointed regulators have no authentic or direct understanding of the very cultures they criticize or attempt to represent, but still they feel compelled to present themselves as authorities despite my intimate connection to the cultures explored in my stories."[5] Her comments prompt the questions: Where will the work of multiracial Asian Americans be sited? And, how archaic/relevant/oppressive is "realistic" casting in an increasingly multiracial and multiethnic society?

The questions of multiethnicity and interculturalism have also been provoked from a generational perspective, particularly from Asian American youth in urban centers, where youth culture has created a blending and borrowing of cultures, pressed by both fashion and economic survival. Brenda Wong Aoki, an Asian American of Chinese, Japanese, Spanish, and Scots heritage, poignantly describes the impetus to write her solo work *The Queen's Garden*. Aoki creates a multiethnic world of Samoans, Hawaiians, Chicanos, Guamanians, Caucasians and Blacks, telling a love story that disintegrates as a neighborhood dies in gun violence and drug wars. Prior to writing the piece, she had been touring another solo work, *Obake*, based on traditional Japanese ghost stories. In the early 1990s, she was invited to perform the piece at a predominantly African American public high school in New Orleans, where there had been conflicts between Blacks and Vietnamese immigrant youth. She doubted the white administrator's logic in thinking that a Japanese play would ameliorate the situation; the silence and prompt departure of the Vietnamese youth in the audience confirmed her apprehension. Afterward, she recollects, "One Vietnamese girl approached me and said, 'Miss Aoki, we don't mean to be dissin' you, but this is N'ahlins (New Orleans). Here we don't got to be Vietnamese. We got to be Black.' It was like a Zen slap. My real life—my own teen years growing up in Long Beach, my work with street gangs, and as a community organizer—my real life was what they needed to know about."[6]

In the case of my own theater, I have tried to create a space for artists of color in the theater which would not reduce us to representatives of categories, but would create, through an expanded dramaturgy and deep relationships with communities, a new site of production. The artistic and political decision to align with Black, Latino, Native American, and allied white theater artists came not only from the palpable void I observed in New England, but emerged from the environment of my upbringing in Los Angeles. At the time I founded my theater, in 1979, I had never heard of the word *multiculturalism*, a term I became uneasily familiar with in the 1980s, as it ascribed meaning to my work which was neither present nor intended (multicultural = representative, celebratory, and essentialized theater). But this alliance and our geographical location appeared to place the work of my theater outside certain discussions of Asian American theater which centered on the ethnically specific. Somehow, the association with other artists of color diminished my theater's relevance to the Asian American theater, in a way that didn't happen with ethnically specific Asian American theaters whose artistic programs include Asian plays by

European American playwrights' work. I even have had other Asian Americans ask me if I'm "mixed"; they assume I must have biracial heritage because I work with Blacks and Latinos. As our theater enters its third decade, some Asian American scholars have graciously apologized for their late arrival in bringing our work into their purview. These experiences have not only provoked questions of Asian American ethnocentricity, but have compelled a further questioning of the validating eye and cultural authority. And ultimately, whether the work is documented or not, validated or not, understood or not, the movement toward 2050 has already begun, even if all of us have yet to "get on the bus."

Roberta Uno

Outside the Box

In his introduction to *Asian American Drama: 9 Plays from the Multiethnic Landscape,* playwright David Henry Hwang describes a younger "Third Wave" of Asian/Pacific playwrights who "explode the myth of an immutable cultural identity" through the themes and narratives of their work.[7] As the millennium dawns, we are seeing the swell of the next wave of theater artists who challenge immutability not only through thematic content, but also through the forms, modes, and structures of theater making as interdisciplinary and solo theater artists. Solo performance, the theatrical cottage industry of the 1980s, has become a means to redress stereotyping and misrepresentation and to assert ownership of theatrical production. For instance, solo artists Lane Nishikawa, Jude Narita, Amy Hill, Nobuko Miyamoto, and Brenda Wong Aoki have made Asian American theater known throughout the country with works of insight, wit, and originality. Adding to the evolution of this increasingly complex and sophisticated art form are artists like Denise Uyehara,[8] Dawn Akemi Saito, Alison de la Cruz, Alex Luu, Kip Fulbeck, Shishir Kurup, lê thi diem thúy or thúy lê, Dan Kwong, Sandra Tsing Loh, Alec Mapa, Leilani Chan, and Marcus Quiñones.

In this volume two such works are presented in excerpt, Shishir Kurup's *Assimilation* and thúy lê's *Mua He Do Lua/Red Fiery Summer.* In *Assimilation,* Kurup complicates conventional immigrant narratives of a one-way journey with the United States as ultimate destination. His is a transnational narrative which speaks to issues of Asian diaspora and postcoloniality. Its opening, underscored by a tri-continental soundscape of Malayalam, Hindi, Swahili, Gujarati, and American English, is the sonic metaphor for his personal epic of transmigration and layered identity.

thúy lê's *Red Fiery Summer* is constructed in two contrasting halves, the first in Viet Nam and the second in the United States (included in this volume). As unconventional an immigrant narrative as Kurup's, hers is not the expected refugee story of triumph over adversity, where resolution is equated with becoming American. Rather, she probes an unresolved memory space between violently fractured geographies. Using slides of French colonial postcards and photographs of her parents as the backdrop, lê contrasts her family's life in Viet Nam during the war with their life in southern California after the war. The decision to use French colonial postcards places the Viet Nam War within a larger frame of colonialism and a longer history of political conflict; it also raises, from an unexpected angle, the contemporary media issue of how images of Vietnamese bodies have been represented, commodified, and transmitted.

Like lê, other Asian Pacific theater artists employ multiple texts (literary, visual, auditory, movement) in innovative ways to convey their artistic statements. While several anthology projects have done an admirable job of representing the work of pioneering interdisciplinary artists such as Jessica Hagedorn and Ping Chong,[9] the performance texts for these works can only partially convey their full intent and effect. For example, while Dawn Akemi Saito's *HA!* is a powerful written text, it is hard to imagine it without her exquisite, disturbing post-Butoh movement twisted around each word. She is among a handful of actor/writer/dancer/movement artists, including Julie Tolentino Wood, Ananya Chatterjea, Muna Tseng, Pearl Ubungen, and Maura Nguyen Donohue, who meld physical rigor and spoken text on a canvas of solo and ensemble performance.[10]

Another force in this artistic wave is works which have resulted from intercultural and transnational collaboration. A far cry from gratuitous attempts to theatricalize a production through the performative exotic, these are works which draw from a deep cultural well to convey their meaning. In this collection, Rick Shiomi's *Mask Dance* is a poignant, visually arresting work which was the result of a collaboration between Shiomi and two Korean artists, theater director Dong-Il Lee and drummer JooYeo No, who helped Shiomi to explore the theme of Korean adoption in the United States and express its profound cultural and spiritual ramifications. The use of Korean mask dance from Pongsan and shamanistic ritual eloquently expresses the unseen, but felt; the unknown, but sensed. These connecting pieces about adoptees locate a place of origin. *Mask Dance* is an excellent example of the use of traditional performative elements that are not merely illustrative, but are essential to creating a transformative experience. The work is one of several noteworthy collaborative productions that have been created at Theater Mu in Minneapolis under the artistic direction of Shiomi, a Japanese Canadian playwright and taiko drum player. Another Minneapolis-based theater which has forged new directions for the Asian American theater drawing from world repertory, traditional performance, and political theater is the multiracial Pangea World theater led by Artistic Director Dipankar Mukherjee. Ma-Yi Theatre Company of New York City, headed by Artistic Director Ralph Peña, has fostered a rich, ongoing artistic dialogue between Filipino and Filipino American artists resulting in works like Peña's *Flipzoids* and Chris Millado's *Little Brown Brothers*. Ma-Yi is a fascinating artistic example of the connections between cultural and political geographies. Unlike many Japanese and Chinese American theater artists who have had to reestablish a cultural tie to a homeland, the work of Ma-Yi is strengthened by the continuous interaction of artists whose creative arenas are in the Philippines, the United States, and Hawai'i.[11] It has brought Filipino artists whose origins were in anti-Marcos activism together with Filipino American artists whose focus was Filipino American community activism, and Filipino American artists whose domain is the professional theater. Together they create theater works of rich artistic vision and high professional standards that make incisive social commentary.

Are We Finished Yet? Is the Work Done?

In May 1999, the Northwest Asian American Theatre (NWAAT) in Seattle held an historic event. The first national Asian American Theater Convening brought together ten theater groups from across the country and various individual theater artists. In attendance were representatives from the East West Players of Los Angeles (founded in 1965), the Asian American Theater Company of San Francisco (founded in 1973), Ma-Yi Theatre Company of New York City (founded in 1989), Theater Mu of Minneapolis (founded in 1992), QBD Ink of Arlington, Virginia (founded in 1996), Pan Asian Repertory of New York City (founded in 1977), the National Asian American Theater Company of New York City (founded in 1989), New WORLD Theater of Amherst, Massachusetts (founded in 1979), and the Asian American Theater Lab of the Mark Taper Forum (founded in 1967).

Over the course of two days, these artistic leaders grappled with the state and future of Asian American theater, closely examining shared themes and unique differences. The galvanizing moment of the conference occurred when Pamela Wu, producing director of the Asian American Theatre Company (AATC) of San Francisco, asked her peers, "Are we finished yet? Is the work done?" This poignant question emerged from AATC's beleaguered recent history. As one of the first Asian American theater companies in the nation, it purchased its own building in San Francisco in the late 1980s, only to see major funding for Asian American theater programming go to the neighboring American Conservatory Theater. While the funding opened the doors for individual Asian American artists to enter the mainstream, AATC found itself reduced to a casting agency and training ground; this underfunding was compounded by the devastating 1989 San Francisco earthquake which forced the theater to close its doors. Wu's painfully honest question pointed to the reality of a glass ceiling for established Asian American theater companies and demanded a redefinition of philosophy and mission, catalyzing further questions. Do these companies exist to prepare Asian American actors and playwrights for the mainstream? Is this a location where they can hone their skills until they "make it"? Is the reality that the theaters are a dramaturgical laboratory, where plays can be workshopped and exposed to audience response because mainstream theaters will not commit to their development?

Playwright Chay Yew provided an astute response from the inside, as head of the Mark Taper Forum's Asian American Theater Lab. He leapfrogged the Taper's troubled history with the majority "minority" population of Los Angeles and suggested creative, entrepreneurial strategies for working with the given circumstances.[12] His answer shifted the focus from an expectation that Asian American work should be appearing on the Taper main stage. Instead, he focused on how his laboratory resources could be most effectively used to create programs and partnerships that would ensure that the work of Asian American artists is done. He gave as examples coproductions with the East West Players, Highways, and the Actors' Gang, where his laboratory supplemented the development process, resulting in a stronger production. He also spoke of his own curatorial strategies for stimulating and supporting new work. He cautioned younger artists not to place their only hope in a mainstream response, but to self-produce, collaborate, find ways to get the work made, "Don't be the barbarian at the gate."[13]

Janet Tu reported in *American Theatre* magazine on the conclusions reached at the historic event:

> That Asian American theatres, which have until now focused on the histories of people who came to his country at the turn of the century, will increasingly find vitality in the influx of newer Asian immigrants; that many Asian American theatres feel disenfranchised when it comes to mainstream arts policy making and funding; that future works will likely include more collaborations between groups and with artists around the world; and that the theatres have done an admirable job of presenting Asian American plays to a broader audience, while training emerging Asian American artists.[14]

The concluding panel further emphasized the need to work more deeply with communities, especially with youth and newer immigrants, to creatively engage the issue of multiracialism, and to continue to take artistic risks.

And ultimately, the strength of the gathering was not only in the magnificent job NWAAT's interim artistic director, Rosa Joshi, had done in bringing together the sixty-plus participants, but also in the fact that there were many, many more Asian American theater practitioners who were not in the room. Whereas a decade earlier the meeting might have been a small conversation between fewer than a half dozen artistic leaders, this convening served to identify artistic leadership across a wide geography, across generations, and across genres.

Looking to the Margin: A Wake-Up Call

It is the nature of art that the margin is often the point of origin, the place where discovery, vitality, and new direction are found. Clearly the Asian American theater has come of age—some of its artists can be found in the mainstream. Its oldest theater companies—East West Players, Pan Asian Repertory, Northwest Asian American Theatre Company, and Asian American Theatre Company—are doing an admirable job maintaining high professional standards, while striving to become part of the institutional fabric of this nation through the owning and operation of permanent autonomous spaces. Across the country Asian American artists are finding new forums for expression and visibility. Writers like Naomi Iizuka, Diana Son, and Han Ong are taking flight from the well-traveled ground of identity to explore new universes. Some are solo performers who have redefined the territory of and access to performance, crossing and recrossing the country in a circuit of colleges, conferences, and communities. Other significant theaters which have expanded the reach and breadth of Asian American theater include Kumu Kahua in Honolulu; Teatro ng Tanan and Theater of Yugen in San Francisco; the San Diego Asian American Repertory Theatre; Great Leap, Te-A-Da Productions, and Club O'Noodles in Los Angeles; Theater Ma-Yi and the National Asian American Theater Company; New WORLD Theater; Theater Mu; Pangea World Theatre; and QBD Ink. Independent performance ensembles like SLANT, In Mixed Company, 18 Mighty Warriors, Tongue in a Mood, I Speak in Two Tongues, Here and Now, Cold Tofu, Peeling the Banana, and Isang Mahal are honing unique artistic visions as groups of mutually committed artists. Still other Asian American artists are shaping and redefining projects which are not identified as Asian American, like Sean San Jose at Campo Santo in San Francisco, Page Leong and Shishir Kurup at Cornerstone Theatre in Los Angeles, Stacey Makishi with Split Britches, Sokeo Ros with Everett Dance Theatre in Providence, Rhode Island, Jono Eiland with Sojourn Theatre, Alleluiah Panis at Brava! for Women in the Arts in San Francisco, Dan Kwong at Highways in Santa Monica, and Sixto Wagan at DiverseWorks in Houston. Together, these artists have given a wake-up call to the American theater—one that startles, stuns, jumpstarts, hijacks, invigorates and inspires. The collective creative body is awake at the millennium, vibrant and visible, in motion.

Notes

1. The theater, Bindlestiff Studios, is located in the SOMA district, the oldest Filipino neighborhood in San Francisco and a primary target for urban development. Currently, there is a petition being circulated stating the community's recognition of Bindlestiff as a cultural center fulfilling an irreplaceable social function. Developers are bidding on the building and whether or not Bindlestiff will survive through this current negotiation is unknown. Bindlestiff Studio's mission, as a consortium of Filipino American artists, is to provide an affordable, professional small theater venue where new and veteran artists can take risks. It is the home of Teatro ng Tanan, Tongue in A Mood, and PiNoisePop Music Festival.

2. Special thanks to *Bold Words* coeditor Rajini Srikanth, who directed me to write this introduction within the framework of my work with New WORLD Theater and my background on the West Coast. Thanks also to Golda Sargento and Cathy Schlund for research assistance.

3. Miyamoto began her performance career as a dancer with her film debut in *The King and I* starring Yul Brynner. She was a principal dancer in other Broadway and film classics including *Flower Drum Song* and *Kismet*. A dancer, choreographer, singer, playwright, actor, and movement activist, she began creating work for the Asian American theater in the early 1980s. She has developed a unique methodology for working with communities to create theater with her "To All Relations" project. A fuller biography is available in Miles X. Liu, ed. *Asian American Playwrights: A Bio- Bibliographical-Critical Sourcebook* (Westport, Conn.: Greenwood Press, 2001).

4. I saw *Chop Suey* performed at Griffith Park with a predominantly Asian Pacific crowd of five to six hundred in Los Angeles. Had I not seen it, I wouldn't know about this notable production, the music of which, composed by Benny Yee, stays with me until this day. It was co-produced by the East West Players, but did not run at their theater.

5. Velina Hasu Houston, "Notes from a Cosmopolite," in *The Color of Theater: A Critical Sourcebook on Race and Performance*, Roberta Uno, ed. (London: Continuum Press, 2001).

6. Author's interview with Brenda Wong Aoki, June 26, 2000. See also Brenda Wong Aoki interview and materials in the *Uno Asian American Women Playwrights'*

Script Collection 1924–Present, W.E.B. Du Bois Library, University of Massachusetts at Amherst.

7. Brian Nelson, ed., *Asian American Drama: 9 Plays from the Multiethnic Landscape* (New York: Applause Theatre Books, 1997), viii.

8. Denise Uyehara, *Maps of City and Body* (New York: Kaya Production, 2001).

9. Alvin Eng, ed., *Tokens?: The New York Asian American Experience on Stage* (New York: Asian American Writers' Workshop, 2000). Eng's groundbreaking construction of this collection uses play texts, interviews intercut as a verbal mural, and photographs, giving us a new model of artist-driven scholarship.

10. Dawn Akemi Saito is a Butoh practitioner, writer, and actor who works in solo performance, as well as in scripted work. A former member of African American choreographer David Rousseve's company, Julie Tolentino Wood is a Filipina/El Salvadorian choreographer and performer who created the dance theater piece *Mestiza* in 1998. Ananya Chatterjea works with Women in Motion in Minneapolis and is the creator of the dance theater piece *Unable to Remember Roop Kanwar.* Muna Tseng is Artistic Director of Muna Tseng Dance Projects (founded in 1986), located in New York City. *Slut for Art* is a tribute to the brother she lost to AIDS and a chronicle of East Village life in the 1980s. Pearl Ubungen is Artistic Director of Pearl Ubungen and Dancers in San Francisco. Her dance/theater piece, *I-Hotel*, is a site-specific work. Maura Nguyen Donohue is a Vietnamese Irish American choreographer and performer whose work with her dance theater ensemble, In Mixed Company, includes her piece *SKINning the surFACE* which examines the legacy of Amerasian Vietnamese.

11. Ralph Peña and Chris Millado, along with director Cecile Guidote, were all anti-Marcos cultural activists in the Philippines working with Philippine Educational Theatre Association. See Eugene Van Erven, *The Playful Revolution* (Bloomington, Ind.: Indiana University Press, 1992). In the United States, anti-Marcos activists formed Sining Bayan, the cultural arm of the KDP (Katipunan mg nga Demokratikong Pilipino: Union of Democratic Filipinos), which produced and toured four plays developed with Ermena Marlene Vinluan in the United States and in Hawai'i. Sining Bayan's activities are documented in *Ang Katipunan* and *Ang Kalayaan,* the newspapers of the KDP.

12. A June 7, 2000, article in the *Los Angeles Times* named Yew as one of the Taper's corps of play developers "who work on projects that usually are not ready or aesthetically appropriate for the Taper main stage." It announced "a modest festival of fully staged productions . . . at the 99–seat Actors' Gang in Hollywood." The article asserted that "the developmental troops were growing restless" waiting for the Taper to develop its own alternative space. Fellow play developer, writer Luis Alfaro, said, "Not being produced gets more and more frustrating. If we had not produced this season, it would have been time to go."

13. David Roman, "Interview of Chay Yew" in *The Color of Theater: A Critical Sourcebook on Race and Performance,* Roberta Uno, ed. (London: Continuum Press, 2001).

14. Janet Tu, "The Mainstream and Beyond," *American Theatre* (October 1999), 108.

From *Eye of the Coconut*

JEANNIE BARROGA

Dad plays Hawaiian music in a Midwestern town. His daughters are attracted to the white boys available. As this family is neither Hawaiian nor white, comedic drama ensues when relocated parents and Americanized daughters clash over intercultural relationships and assimilated identities.

TIME: Late 1960s

PLACE: The Midwest: family kitchen; Hawaiianized Polish bar; various street scenes, Owen's YMCA room, bus station

CHARACTERS: 5 females (Asian American, Filipino preferred); 3 males (2 Filipinos preferred; 1 Caucasian)

DAD: narrator, father of 3 daughters, leads Hawaiian band, lenient, accommodating (noticeable Ilocano dialect preferred)

MOM: his wife, reactionary, efficient housewife with a business sense, envies Teora (Visayan accent requires translation)

SUZIE: oldest (19), intellectual, loves Owen, somewhat naive about intermarriage

PAMMIE: youngest (16), church going, has crush on priest, a knack for wheedling money from people

EDIE: 18, tries to be bohemian, mouthy, considered the black sheep, banters with Petey

TEORA: 30s, Hawaiian dancer, streetwise, witty, Edie's mentor

Editors' note: The following characters appear in later sections of the play:

PETEY: mid-20s, slick, witty, sharp dresser, prefers Edie though chosen by Dad to be Suzie's suitor

OWEN: Caucasian, Suzie's boyfriend, rather proper
(preferred if he also doubles as:)

GROMSKI: Polish bar owner, Midwest dialect, loud, corny

Act One

TABLEAUX: MOM, SUZIE AND PAMMIE AT HOME. "MOONLIGHT SERENADE" IS HEARD, DAD SEEN STRUMMING UKELELE. SONG SEGUES INTO "BEER BARREL POLKA," THEN INTO "SWEET LEILANI." BY THEN DAD HAS MOVED DOWNSTAGE CENTER, AMIABLE:

DAD: I play the Club tomorrow in Polishtown. Where's that? ANYTOWN, U.S.A., east of the Mississippi. Yep, I play music for five hours, two breaks, free drinks, and bar pretzels. A fair trade for art, don't you think? Especially when you only play weekends.

(*indicates shirt*) See? Hawaiian. I play Hawaiian music in a Hawaiian shirt with a Hawaiian dancer. The native drums, the ocean waves, the call of the conch shell—*authentic,* all of it! (relents) Okay, they're taped, but it's authentic taping!

See, I came here to the States with an older brother and an itinerant father. They picked fruits and vegetables in the fields two thousand miles away from here. My brother, he stayed with the fields. Me, I moved with my music to this Midwestern town. You could say, to be an American, I adapted here, took a few chances, relinquished a few holds—because of music. I haven't complained, no need to complain, not yet. I can say I've done okay with, God willing, only a few regrets. *I make do,* you see. Like ocean waves and conch shells, taping will do.

Now from this, you might think that I myself am Hawaiian, so I should make a point . . . to be fair . . . uh, forthright . . . *honest.*

Okay, I want to get this out in the open: all of us in the band? *We're Filipinos!* Well, all except the dancer. She's from Tahiti. Yes, I know that's not Hawaiian, either . . . and it's really her mother who's from Tahiti . . . Teora's from New Jersey.

Aah, Americans don't know the difference.

DAD MOVES TOWARD FAMILY, INTRODUCING EACH AS THEY ACTIVATE (SUZIE SEALING HER LETTER, PAMMIE READING *THORN BIRDS,* MOM HANDSEWING HAWAIIAN SHIRT).

(*continues*) My family treats me like a celebrity!

THE ACTIVITY NOTICEABLY PUSHES DAD AROUND:

DAD: My wife of twenty years . . .

MOM: Ano, your shirt, it's been in the closet so long it smells like mothballs! Sewing, sewing, all day now, diba . . .

DAD: My oldest, Suzie . . .

SUZIE: All these letters! My hand's cramped. Daddy, when will I get my own phone? A girl's gotta have privacy at my age! Can we talk later? (*exits*)

DAD: My youngest, a beauty . . .

PAMMIE: Daddy, fork over a dollar, okay? Please? How about ten??

DAD: And my middle one . . . (looks around) My middle one . . . ?

EDIE BREEZES THROUGH.

EDIE: (*totes camera*) Got a gig, gang! Diane Arbus, look out! Ciao!

EXITS. A TEMPORARY CALM.

MOM: Oy, are you listening??

PAMMIE: (*holds out coin purse*) Other parents let *their* kids eat burgers after a movie!

DAD: There's food here! You come home if you're hungry!

MOM: Play here, play there! You should have MORE jobs by now, you play music so much! Now it's Polish bars, ay, naku . . .

DAD: Better than backyard bar mitzvahs!

PAMMIE: *Hawaiian* music in a *Polish* bar??

DAD: (*explains*) See, if the owner likes it, we'll play for his luau in April.

PAMMIE: Ooh, can we go?

DAD: We'll see.

PAMMIE: With a real pig and everything?

MOM: Oy, I get the pig's head, eh?

PAMMIE: (*grimaces*) Mom! I'd *die* of embarrassment! This isn't the Islands!

DAD: They might just throw that away . . .

MOM: Talaga! Waste of food! In the Islands . . .

PAMMIE: Oh, please!

MOM: (*Visayan*) Listen to her! (*English*) We saved everything, feet, tail, ears!

PAMMIE: You save everything here, too, even things that aren't food! Foil, tin, plastic, Saran Wrap . . .

MOM: You'll never know when you may need it. (*to* DAD) Tell her.

DAD: (*echoes*) You never know when you may need . . .

MOM: 'Susmarjosep, you all just mock me!

PAMMIE: Mom, we don't *need* everything! This is America! Families can have anything they want! *I* would . . . if I were married.

MOM: Ay, there she goes again . . .

PAMMIE: But I'm into being a *nun*.

DAD: No, you'll have the handsomest man in town. Maybe San Felipe's boy, Mark.

PAMMIE: Oh, he's so stuck up! He says his family's from the Ilocano part of the Islands, and we're only Visayan!

MOM: Oh, he did, did he?? Well, forget him then!

PAMMIE: We're all the same, aren't we?

MOM: No stuck-up San Felipe for MY daughter! Who does he think he is??

DAD: You're starting up again . . .

MOM: (*doesn't quit*) The Visayan in you comes from ME! He doesn't like me, well, I don't like HIM!

DAD: (*Ilocano*) Don't get upset . . .

MOM: And you can tell him he was left on a doorstep in an ILOCANO basket!

DAD: (*Ilocano*) Hush now, settle down . . . !

MOM: Tell him the Visayan neighborhood wouldn't take him!

DAD: I said, stop now!

MOM: Well, say something! The San Felipes are no better than us! We're just as good! We're BETTER!

DAD: I said, quiet now! We're all together here, the San Felipes, the Duhays, Estralitas, Aguasitos, all of us. We didn't come here to be little groups like we were in the Islands. We can't; there's not enough of us! San Felipe's boy said something stupid, that's all. I *know* his father, and he wouldn't say that. He'd say, as I do, that we're all American-Filipinos now.

PAMMIE: I don't know what all the fuss is about. I told you I'm going to be a nun, right here at Eternal Agony Parish. I'm celibous.

MOM: Ano? Celibous?

DAD: A pretty girl like you a nun? You'd be thrown out of the convent for distracting the priests! Now go on, here's five dollars . . . (*reconsiders*) Ten dollars.

MOM: (*shakes head*) Oy, you spoil her.

DAD: I spoil *all* of you. You walk all over me.

GLEEFULLY, PAMMIE STUFFS MONEY INTO COIN PURSE.

PAMMIE: (*checks watch*) Eleven o'clock. Matinee in an hour.

DAD: (*reminded*) I have rehearsal!

PAMMIE: Oh, Teora called. She said she might be late.

DAD: WHAT?? Why?

MOM: Always late, always busy . . .

PAMMIE: (*shrugs*) I don't know. Just late, she said.

MOM: Hungover . . . recovering . . .

DAD: That's not fair.

MOM: (*Visayan*) You know what kind of life she leads . . .

PAMMIE: (*sighs*) Mom, I *know* you're talking about her.

MOM: She drinks, she smokes, God knows what else . . .

DAD: Enough.

TEMPORARY TRUCE.

PAMMIE: Daddy, why do you play Hawaiian music?

DAD: 'Cause it's popular. Look at, at . . . ELVIS!

PAMMIE: Well, for him. But you??

DAD: (*explains*) Here, it's popular with Polish and Germans and Czechs and Slovaks who usually never see Filipinos much less hear Hawaiian music. It's a *treat*! It brings in a crowd, a curious crowd.

PAMMIE: But why Hawaiian? We're FILIPINO!

DAD: Who wants to hear Filipino music??

PAMMIE: Why isn't *our* music popular?

TINKLING MUSIC HEARD, FADES INTO HAWAIIAN MUSIC.

DAD: Well, I guess because of the war when the Japanese bombed Pearl Harbor. American soldiers stationed there brought back mementos of Hawai'i and leis and blue water. They took in the steel guitars and drums and dancing. War does that. In times like that, you want to remember paradise among the confusion. Cultures trade off parts of each other.

PAMMIE: Guess we lost out, huh? I mean, if the Japanese bombed the Philippines and if Americans were stationed there, maybe you'd be playing *our* music in a Polish bar instead.

DAD: The Japanese *did* bomb the Philippines, and Americans *were* stationed in the Islands!

PAMMIE: Wow, no popularity, no music. We got a pretty raw deal all the way around, didn't we?

MOM: No raw deal! The war made your father American! It brought him to my hometown! Then we came here and raised you kids.

PAMMIE: Thank God *one* thing's right.

MOM AND DAD EXCHANGE LOOKS.

MOM: If we had raised you in the Islands, you wouldn't be so sassy now! Now don't be late, and don't do anything *bad*. . . !

MOM AND PAMMIE EXIT. DAD ADDRESSES AUDIENCE ON APPROACH TO TEORA:

DAD: I had to think about that one, all the way to rehearsal at Joey Duhay's house. I had traveled the music circuit throughout this country and learned that music is an international language, one everyone can understand. If I thought jazz was more popular, I'd play jazz. Or if blues were, I'd play blues. Or swing, yes, I'd even play swing. But colored play better blues, and whites play better swing, and only Hawaiians play better Hawaiian. This is what I was told when I tried to get jobs playing music. So I took up the ukulele and now this Pinoy passes for Hawaiian. You see, it's more important to play *any* music than not to play at all . . .

(*impatiently waits for* TEORA) The band tries to rehearse once a week . . .

that is, the ones that make it. The dancer? From "New Jersey"? (*shakes his head*, to TEORA) Two hours, Teora.

LIKE EDIE LATER, TEORA CHARMS:

TEORA: (*bumps*) What do you think? Rehearsed it myself! (*grinds*)

DAD: The band's got a gig tomorrow and I want to know who'll BE there!

TEORA: (*fingers his neck*) Aw, you know I'm good!

DAD: Even good ones rehearse *with the band*! (*brushes her off*) Stop now! (*sighs*) Teora, I treat you like a daughter, don't I?

TEORA: (*not serious*) Yes, sweetkins, you do.

DAD: You've been to my home . . .

TEORA: *Lovely* home!

DAD: I've played for your wedding . . .

TEORA: Like an angel!

DAD: (*meaningfully*) *Both* of them! And this is how you pay me back! My own daughter, Edie, looks up to you, follows every move you make! She sees your marriages, your breakups . . .

TEORA: (*drops "act"*) I just missed one rehearsal! Do I deserve a lecture on childrearing?? I'm just not the kind to be married!

DAD: (*trump card*) To WHITE men, no.

TEORA: (*contained*) My two EX-husbands were JERKS who wanted the Orient, and they got it! And when someone more exotic came along, they disappeared.

DAD: Like I said, white.

TEORA: I don't want to talk about this . . .

DAD: Teora, you saw two ways of life, two kinds of cultures, and you picked the one that wasn't yours. What happened to you shouldn't happen to anyone's daughter or someone I consider my daughter. I can't have anyone I care for go through what you're going through!

TEORA: Daughters do what they do for love . . .

DAD: But . . .

TEORA: *Not* for blood.

DAD: I'm a father! I "know what's best"!

TEORA: And I'm just a woman who's had bad luck with men any color. And any man *any* color is NOT my favorite subject right now.

SILENCE.

DAD: (*breaking tension*) We heard the new Don Ho album.

TEORA: (*laughs in spite*) Oh, please! Again??

DAD: You know, if *we* use a little more pidgin . . .

TEORA: You're joking.

DAD: Just a little! Just to be more authentic!

TEORA: We're selling music, not dialects!

DAD: But he sounds Island . . .

TEORA: He *is* Island!

DAD: So am I!

TEORA: You're *another* one! They're not all alike!

DAD: (*pause*) He's made it, Teora.

TEORA: By making music, not kissing ASS!

SILENCE.

DAD: I dream we're going to be there, too . . . someday.

TEORA SIGHS, SMILES, THEN EXITS.

PRODUCTION HISTORY:

April 1987	Asian American Theatre, San Francisco (showcase)
October 1987	Northwest Asian American Theatre, Seattle (mainstage), Bea Kiyohara, Director
February 1991	Asian American Theatre, San Francisco (mainstage), Ann Fajilan, Director
January 1992	East West Players, Los Angeles (reading)
February 1993	East West Stage, Berkeley (production), Cary Hamaguchi, Director
June 1995	Asian American Repertory Theatre, Stockton (production), Maria Zaragoza, Director

From *Assimilation*
(*a monologue about immigration*)

SHISHIR KURUP

(*Out of the dark we hear a sweet Malayalam song*)

PAMBEGAL KU MALAM INDUH
PARAVUHGUL KAGASHUM INDUH
MANUSHA PUTHREN UM TALAH CHAIKAN
MANIL IDUM ILLA, MANIL IDUM ILLA (*Repeat*)

Mame, I'm going out to play
"Put some powder on, mone"
But I'm just going out to play
"Be a good boy now and put on some powder"
But I hate powder
"Be my golden son now"

(*Lights up in a center pool on man standing with a container of Cuticura tal-cum powder in his hand. Odd, dreamy theme music plays underneath as he pours an inordinate amount of powder into his hand, slaps it to his face and smears it on, giving him a ghastly, clown-like look. The Clown moves slowly in pool of light as we hear on tape . . .*)

Voiceover: Warm Bombay nights. We sleep on terraces. Rooftops! Because it's too damn hot to sleep indoors and the moon is huge and full and close enough to reach out and touch as I lay under the twinkle, twinkle little stars, how I wonder . . . flanked by my mother on one side and my father on the other with just a few grass mats below us and a thin bed sheet for cover. In my memory words and tastes, Jaggivanram Hospital. . .where I was born, Marine Drive and Choupati . . . where we went for seaside walks, roasted corn and bhel puri . . . what we ate on the seaside walks. They swirl in my mind like thinly veiled flashes of a past life, phantom experiences I sometimes doubt ever happened.

(*Another voice comes on with the previous audio in other languages: Malay-alam, English, Hindi, Swahili, Gujarati*)

Other voices: Ende ponnumon ah alle. Kainse ho behte? Tera bab! I can't, I can't, I can't, I can't, I can't, I can't, I can't, I can't!

Voiceover: Along with tastes and words, I to this day remember dreams I had as a child of hanging off the ledge of our fifth-floor balcony at the railway quarters in Bombay Central. Hanging on for dear life. These were vivid, panic-inducing dreams that had a startling clarity, the surroundings accurate in everyday detail, hanging on with three-year-old fingers unable to quite pull myself onto the ledge or to let go. Unable to do anything but hang there hoping for the kindness of strangers to haul me up onto a two-foot ledge of safety.

Other voices: This is not your home, you're only renting. Go back to where you came from. Go back Go back Go back Go back Go back . . . Jambo, Habari, Muzuri. Shiro puri, jalebi, tala dood pak. Huyu iko watu wa America. Me shire toh nehi.

(*The language phrases running concurrently become a cacophony. Music builds to a climax. The Clown appears to be hanging on a ledge. Music ends. Lights cross-fade to . . .*)

Mythic Fears

Mythic fears of coming to America. The United States, Los Estados Unidos, land of the free, home of the brave. Home of Clint Eastwood, Steve Mc-Queen, Charles Bronson, Bruce Lee, Elvis . . . and my main man, Carlos Santana.

Mythic fear number one: Americans loved to go streaking.

Mythic fear number two: Americans spoke in an English so slanged, we would have a very difficult time understanding them. They loved double negatives: "I didn't do nothin'."

Mythic fear number three: Like the British they didn't wash their ass, just wiped it with toilet paper. This frightened us. This frightened my mother, this frightened my father and this terrified me.

Mythic fear number four: Every single American had smoked marijuana by the age of twelve.

Mythic fear number five: Every single American girl had had sex by the age of twelve. I was twelve. I was in America. (*Blackout*)

Fat Family

(*A short burst from Jimi Hendrix's "Star-Spangled Banner" and lights go to a general wash. Clown wipes powder off face*)

I never saw the Statue of Liberty from the bow of a hulking steamship bound for freedom. The first symbol of America for me was that festive Arby's sign. You know, the giant cowboy hat with the flickering, colored lights around it. Kinda like the one Hoss wore on *Bonanza,* which I heard was a television show here, not just the comic books I'd read, and that there really was a Hoss and an Adam and a Little Joe and a Hop Sing.

Across the street from the Arby's was a Hardee's, which boasted charbroiled hamburgers! I had only recently discovered hamburgers before I came to the United States. Wimpy's had invaded Africa and the British were threatening to colonize once again. So I already understood the concept of convenient or fast food, and it appealed to me. Indian food is neither convenient nor fast. First you have to go to the big open bazaars where the Arabs display their wares; you go get your vegetables fresh, you go get your cheese fresh, you go get your chicken fresh . . . which the guy pulls out of this huge basket filled with twenty or thirty strangely silent chickens. Then he grabs its head and cuts its throat. Using his foot to pin it down, he drains the blood as the chicken shudders. Then he cuts the head off, throws it one way, takes the body, throws it another way—into a pot of boiling water, leaves it there for about thirty seconds, takes it out, pulls all the feathers off, skins it, cuts it, guts it, asks if we want the giblets, of course my mom says yes, innards is her thing, wraps it up in some newspaper, hands it to us and we head home. Meanwhile I'm thinking, I don't wanna eat this. All I keep seeing is that poor chicken flopping around. How'm I supposed to eat after that, hah? Give me a hamburger neatly wrapped in a piece of wax paper, with some kind of emblem on it, and all the condiments and an innocuous piece of charred meat, something I haven't had a history with and I'm happy. That's why the Hardee's across from the Arby's was so appealing. I could have a history-less hamburger, charbroiled, I think that means it's better, a large order of "French" fries and a thick, frosty strawberry milkshake, every day. It was so easy. For less than three dollars I could eat like a king! A Burger King. McDonalds. White Castle, the tiny little baby hamburgers, Kentucky Fried Chicken, the aforementioned Arby's and Hardee's, and, of course . . . Tastee Freeze! A veritable cornucopia of fast food joints. One for every day of the week. This was great. I was happy. I was eating fun food. And I was eating and eating and eating. And my mom . . . was eating and eating and eating. And my dad . . . was eating and eating and eating. Because we were happy! And soon we became (*pulls a photo out of his pocket and shows it to audience*) the fat family. We had a combined weight equal to that of the Bulgarian Olympic weight-lifting team. We were in our new home and we were happy.

(*Blackout. In the darkness we hear "Ballroom Blitz" by Sweet.*)

Tom

(*Lights up on . . .*)

Hey man, ya'll live in huts where you come from? Nah?

You ever swing from a vine, though, like Tarzan? Nah?
We got a swing line off a tree over a crik, you know the kind with a tire, swing out over the crik. What's a crik? I don't know. Don't ya'll have criks where you come from? I don't know. It's like a stream or something. Like a river, only smaller. A creek? It ain't no rusty hinge man, it's a crik. You talk funny. Kinda like that guy on *Man from U.N.C.L.E.* You know the blonde-haired guy. I mean how come you don't say can't. Say it. I can't. Not can! Can't!! See, see. You say . . . cunt or something like 'at. That's a bad word round here, man. I mean it's simple. You can, you can't! You can, you can't!! You can, you can't!!! The way you do it, one minute you're sayin' you can and the next you're cussin'. No, not cousin. Cussin'. I don't know. It's like swearin'. You know, like sayin', "You cocksucker!" Cocksucker? I don't know. Your cock! It's . . .

your dick! Your thing, man. So, COCK—SUCKER! Get it? Yeah! Hey, you know what pussy is. No, it's not a cat. (*beat*) It's a cock . . . only it's a girl's. You got a cock on a guy and a pussy on a girl. Beaver too. Pussy and beaver, same thing. Cock on one side, pussy and beaver on the other. (*beat*) Yeah, they're both named after animals, isn't that funny! I don't know why. (*beat*) Hey, how do you say cocksucker where you come from? We could say cocksucker all day long and nobody'd know what we were saying. You don't got a word for it? What, ya'll don't cuss? You do? Well, how do you do it? Cuss me out! Good one. (*beat*) What language? What do you mean? How many languages you speak? Get out. Really? Wow. I just speak American. (*beat*) So, go on man, cuss me out. I don't care, pick a language. (*beat*) Say it again! Kuma . . . ma . . . maa . . . ko. Kumamamako. Kumamamako. Kumamamako. I got it. What's it mean? Fuck . . . your . . . mother. MOTHERFUCKER! Ya'll say motherfucker. That's all right. What language was that? Swahili? That's African? Why don't they just call it African? That's confusing. Another one? All right, hit me. (*beat*) Mahder . . . chode. Mah . . . der . . . chode. Mahderchode. I got it. What's 'at mean? Wait a second. Is that motherfucker again? I'm catching on, ain't I? What language was that? Kut . . . chee? Kutchee. Gesundheit! (*beat*) That's a joke, man. Don't worry about it. It's an American thing. (*beat*) So, let's see now. We got Kuma . . . ma . . . mako, mahder . . . chode, motherfucker! Hey! I can say motherfucker in three languages! That's all right! (*Blackout*)

Tina's Food Mart

(*Lights up. Everything in this piece is spoken, including the words in parentheses*)

In Milwaukee,
living on Warren Avenue across from Tina's Food Mart
typical neighborhood store, a Paki shop in London
never seen Tina, just a coupla Middle Eastern guys
been checking me out every time I'm in there

And always the foreign chatter, which I recognize
as foreign chatter because I'm foreign
and I can tell the difference between
foreign chatter and . . . uh, American chatter
Never said nothin' to me, though
in fact the chatter stops whenever I come in
paranoia? perhaps

This day I enter Tina's
again the chatter stops
walk down the cramped miniaturized
replication of the Great American Supermarket aisle
picking out my bread or milk or whatever
checking them checking me out
the cornera their eyes

the cornera my eyes
Self-concious amble down the aisle
to the counter
to pay for my bread or milk or whatever
reach for some money
catch the older, heavier-set balding moustachioed fellow
stare me in the face eyes beg a question
"You are from where?" (Heavy accent)
Momentary pause as I reel from the contact.
"I'm from India originally." (All but faded accent)
"Oh." (Pause) "We like very much the Indian movie." (Heavy accent)
"Oh. Where have you seen Indian movies?" (All but faded accent)
(Pause). "In Jerusalem." (Heavy accent)
"Oh, so you're from Jerusalem." (All but faded accent)
(Awkward pause) "We're . . . uh . . . "
"We're Palestinian" chimes in the younger, curly-headed fellow
silent till now.
"Oh."
The air heavy checkin' out my reaction
no visible reaction not a flinch
"What's your name?" (Curlyhead)
more personal contact I guess I passed.
"Shishir"
"Shishir?" (Curlyhead)
"Yeah. What's your name?"
(Pause) "Art."
Bald-headed laugh
"His name not Art. His name Arteef." (Baldhead)
"Ohhh, Arteef!"
bigger bald-headed laugh
"Yes!!!"
"So, what's your name?"
"My name?" (Baldhead)
"Yeah."
"BILL."
(*Blackout*)

My Father's Name Is . . .

(*Out of the dark . . .*)

Could I have some house lights please? (*Lights up*) Thank you! My father's name is Karipott Thaivalipill Ravindran Kurup. Fine Irish name don't you think? Say it with me. Karipott Thaivalipill Ravindran Kurup. (*Repeats it several times with the audience*) Now let's do it in a round. We'll start with this section then this section then this section. Ready? (*Jumps off the stage and starts round with the three sections of the audience*) Keep it going, keep it going, it's a round! All right, all right. Valiant effort. Thank you. (*Returning to the stage*) Okay. So let me break this name down for you. Karipott Thaivalipill! That's my father's house name. Shared by all the siblings. Karipott Thaivalipill. House name. Ravindran! My father's first name. So, Karipott Thaivalipill Ravindran . . . Kurup, the family name. So, Karipott Thaivalipill Ravindran Kurup.

My mother's name. Leela Bhavani Nair. Married Karipott Thaivalipill Ravindran Kurup and became Leela Bhavani Ravindran. Common practice of taking your husband's first name as your last name.

My name. Shishir Ravindran Kurup. My father's first name, my mother's last name, my middle name.

All well and good until you move to another country. (*Pointing to the ground as if to indicate this land*) Then it's damn confusing.

Karipott Thaivalipill Ravindran Kurup became Ravindran Karipott or Ray Karapot.

Leela Bhavani Ravindran became Bhavani Ravindran or Bonnie Ravendran.

Shishir Ravindran Kurup became Shishir Kurup or (*pulling out yearbook and reading from it*) Shish, C.C., SeSe, Shishi, Shishink, Shirsha, Hosh Hosh, Sheer Energy, Shiser Krup, C.C. Corruption, Little Richard, Tutti Frutti, My Favorite Little Nigger, and last but not least . . . Shitsmear Karap. (*Blackout*)

An Actor Prepares

(*Spotlight up on Actor/Clown with script in hand. Throughout the scene he'll interact with the unseen casting director on audio*)

A: Hello. Is anybody there? Hello. (*Finding himself alone, he does a warm-up*) A big, black, bug, bit, a big, black, bear and the big, black, bear, bled, blood. A tutor who tooted the flute tried to tutor two tooters to toot. Said the two to the tutor is it harder to toot or to tutor two tooters to toot? (*Looks at his script sides and reads from it*) Mrs. Lieberman . . . I'm Dr. Habib. Your son has been diagnosed with chronic depression, which we feel more than likely contributed to his opening fire on those sixty-five innocent Armenians clearly enjoying their McDonalds Happy Meals at the Glendale Galleria. (*beat*) Who writes this stuff?
(*Bored with waiting, Clown starts to recite . . .*)
   Mislike me not for my complexion,
   The shadow'd livery of the burnish'd sun,
   To whom I am a neighbor, and near bred.
   Bring me the fairest creature northward born,
   Where Phoebus' fire scarce thaws the icicles,
   And let us make incision for your love,
   To prove whose blood is reddest—

B: Excuse me! Mr. Kapoor?

A: Kurup!

B: Right! Sorry . . . We're ready!

A: Oh, good.

B: What was that you were doing? Was that our script?

A: Ah, no . . . that was a little something from *Merchant of Venice*.

B: Bertolucci, right?

A: No . . . Shakespeare.

B: Oh right, right! Great stuff! . . . Okay, you ready?

A: Yeah . . . I think so.

B: All right, let's do it. L.A. Hospital, audition slate, Shishir Kapoor.

A: Kurup!

B: Right. Sorry. (*A looks to "camera" then to "voice," perplexed*)

A: Should I be looking at you or at the camera? I mean . . . is it better to . . . you know . . . look at the camera 'cause I could look at . . . but maybe it would be better if—

B: Whatever feels good.

A: Okay. (*Mouths to the casting director, "I'll look at the camera"*) Mrs. Lieberman . . . I'm Dr. Habib. Your son has been diagnosed with chronic depression—

B: Excuse me, Mr. Kapoor.

A: Kurup!

B: Right. Sorry. I think . . . I think we're missing an element of . . . how should I say this . . . of ethniticity.

A: Ethni-ti-city?

B: The . . . uh . . . producers feel that they need the Peter Sellers kind of . . . you know . . . the Gandhi thing.

A: The Gandhi thing?

B: Mmm hmm.

A: But . . . the guy's a doctor.

B: Mmm hmm.

A: (*beat*) So . . . Gandhi as doctor?

B: Exactly!

A: I see!

B: Look, I'm sorry about this . . . It's what the producers want. (*beat*) If you need more time?

A: No, no. I think I know exactly what you're looking for.

B: Great! Great! Let's do it. L.A. Hospital, take two . . . Shishir Kapurnik. (*Clown gives the casting director the evil eye*)

A: (*With heavy accent and head waggle*) Dr. Habib. Your son has been diagnosed with chronic depression which we feel more than likely contributed to his opening fire on those sixty-five innocent Armenians clearly enjoying their McDonalds Happy Meals at the Glendale Galleria. (*Clown is now over the top and as his emotions start to boil over, he appears to be blowing a gasket. He's manic*)

B: Perfect, perfect. That's it—

A: That's what you wanted—

B: We got it—

A: Gandhi as doctor—

B: Exactly!

A: Right, right. I wish you'd said that to begin with. Of course, the guy wouldn't be Jewish would he . . . of course he wouldn't be Jewish . . . you wouldn't have called me in for that.

(*Heavy stereotypical Jewish accent*) Mrs. Lieberman, your son's been diagnosed with chronic guilt, the meshuggener is a crazy bubeleh . . .

Could he possibly be English, I mean would you have called me in for that? (*His mania building, he does a priggish British accent*) Mrs. Lieberman, I believe your son's been diagnosed with a nasty case of hemorrhoids, they're as big as my head and I need to cut them out . . . cut them right out . . .

Or maybe he's Scottish. (*Over-the-top Scottish accent*) Mrs. Lieberman, your son's suffering from a chronic case of diarrhea . . . he's lettin' it go . . . he's lettin' it flow . . . it's comin' out like a river—

B: MR. KURUP!!! (*beat*) Thank you!

A: No! Thank you.

(*The lights, toward the end of the tirade, have been getting darker till they have backlit Clown as we transition into . . .*)

Africa

(*Lights cross-fade to a red background. Clown holds chalk in hand*)

Africa! Mother of us all. Black. White. Yellow. Brown
East Africa! Olduvai Gorge. Possible womb of the mother
Kenya! Land of Masai, Samburu and Kikuyu. Land of red elephants.

(*A voice on tape speaks. As the words and their definitions are spoken, the Clown repeats each African term and writes it on the floor of the stage*)

Swahili: An African, Arab, Indian hybrid language.

Banyani: Brown-skinned Indian shopkeepers who wore banyans, Italian undershirts. Not loved by the Africans.

Muarabu: Light-skinned offspring of the intermarriage of Arabs and Africans. Not loved by the Indians.

Muzungu: The European or white skinned. Envied but not loved by either Indians or Africans.

Mafrique: The African or black skinned. Feared and exploited by both Banyanis and Muzungus.

Makai: Corn or maize.

Mogo: The cassava root.

Mzee: Old man.

Toto: Child.

Jambo: Hello.

Muzuri: Good.

Kwa heri: Good-bye.

Rafiki: Friend.

(*The strains of a guitar playing a familiar African pop song, "Malaika," begin. Clown puts on the costume of Mzee*)

Mombasa

I am called Mzee. Mzee means "old man" in Swahili. A term of respect. But, anyone who is over thirty-five is called Mzee so . . . (*Laughs*) I was born right here in Mombasa and I've lived here all my life. Mombasa is a very old city. Over two thousand years old. I bet you didn't know that, did you? I didn't know it either until I read it in the *National Geographics*. Sailors have been coming here since before Christ was a twinkle in God's eye and they still come and get drunk and fight and vomit in the street. In fact somebody vomited over there last night. I don't like that. It's not good for business. I sell makai on the street (*shows it*) and mogo, which is cut and roasted, then sprinkled with salt and chili powder and a squeeze of lime. It's very good. And very cheap. Only ten cents. By the end of the day I can make about fifteen or twenty shillings, which is not much, but it's better than begging, don't you think? I was in the Mau-Mau and I fought for independence . . . against the Muzungu . . . and beat them . . . and sent them back to Britain and got our independence . . . and now . . . I'm selling makai on the street.(*Pause. To customer*) Ten cents, memsaab. (*Hands her a piece of corn*) Be careful, it's hot! (*Taking money*) Thank you, memsaab. (*She leaves*) She's an Indian woman. Very beautiful. But she puts a lot of powder on her face because she doesn't want to look like an African. She wants to be fair like the Muzungus. But she's dark like we are.

We've got a lot of Indians here. We call them Banyanis. It's not a good word. They don't like it. But, they call us names too. So, there you have it (*beat*). I have a little friend, a Banyani boy. I have taught him Swahili. He calls me Mzee. I call him Toto. We are rafikis. Good friends.

Eh, Toto. Toto. Kuja hapa. Kuja hapa, Toto. Jambo . . . muzuri. Why you don't come visit Mzee anymore? Doesn't Mzee give you free makai and mogo? I have seen you going to the Arabs to get your mogo because they have the oil to fry it in, eh? I don't blame you, Toto. Mzee's fire is no match for the Arab's oil. Let me ask you something. What are they charging now? Twenty cents?!! Those Arabs, I tell you. They're just like the Banyanis. Your people. They know how to make the money. They are too rich, like the Muzungu. The Muzungu, the Muarabu, the Banyani, they all know how to make money. Only the African doesn't know how to make money. Why is that, Toto? (*beat*) No matter. (*beat*) Toto, you know who is coming to visit Mombasa? Emperor Haile Selassie. You don't know who he is? He's the great man from Ethiopia. Many people say that he is the Christ come back to free the black man. Who is the Christ? My god, Toto, Jesus Christ! A very famous African who lived in Israel. No, not as famous as Pelé, but . . . very famous indeed! He said many good words, like "The meek shall inherit the earth" and "All we are saying is give peace a chance" and "You've got to change your evil ways, bay-beh." (*beat*) Anyhow, the emperor will be traveling right down Kilindini Road and there will be a lot of people lined up to see him and I will sell all my makai and mogo, so, I don't need your money, Toto, you can keep it. Put it away! Put it away! (*Hands Toto a piece of corn*) Be careful, it's hot. (*beat*) So where have you been? I've not seen you all week. Nairobi? What you're doing in Nairobi, Toto? Passport? Where are you going, Toto, back to India? (*beat*) No lie . . . Toto . . . you're going to America? That's good. That's very good. The United States of America is a good place. Because there the black man is free . . . and respected. Not like here. There a black man can be a film star like Mr. Jim Brown and Mr. Richard Roundtree "talking 'bout Shaft, John Shaft, he's a bad mother—shut your mouth" . . . and Mr. Sidney Poitier, a great actor. And the women here love their American accent. They think it's great. Not like our African accent. It's bad. (*beat*) I think you are going to like it there, Toto . . . but . . . you must promise me one thing, Toto. You must promise to write to me. I must get a card or some sort of correspondence from you so I can show people my rafiki from America. (*beat*) Toto, I don't have a P.O. box . . . I don't have an address. You can't write to me. I'm sorry, Toto . . . .I'm sorry. (*beat*) No matter. Just . . . think of Mzee once in a while. That will be enough. And say "Jambo" to Mr. Sidney Poitier. From Mzee. Kwaheri, Toto. And don't forget your Swahili. Kwaheri, rafiki. Kwaheri.

(*Lights cross-fade as Mzee strips off costume to become Clown again and . . .*)

April 1st, 1994. April Fools' Day. After twenty years of ambivalence I became an American! (*Clown puts on a tux, tails, and an Uncle Sam striped top hat and rolls video monitor slowly forward as it plays. The footage is his natural-ization ceremony, where over 3,500 people are being naturalized. In concert with the video he does a patriotic small flag dance. During the "Star-Spangled Banner" section he drops flags and moves the monitor ever so slowly stage left and eventually offstage. He comes back into the spotlight still in tux and top hat, picks up a flag and puts it in his pocket and . . .)*

Siam

In Milwaukee
Hole-in-the-wall Thai place. Siam.
Great food. Motherly waitress. Dahng.
Married to German-American Kluss. So, Dahng Kluss.
Spicy food. Warm human being. Comfort to my frozen tropical ass
Out of place in that Lake Michigan bone-cutting chill.
Reminiscent of my mother's South Indian chow.
Reminiscent of my mother.
Dahng's eight-year-old, Susie. Beautiful child. Loveofherlife.
Really her niece but adopted and brought here to have a better life as American.
This day I enter Siam
leaving the howling windy street to the warmth of Dahng's
"Come in, come in. Sit down, sit down. It cold outside, huh?
You cold, huh? Want some spicy shrimp? Spicy shrimp and rice?
It hot! Good for you! Warm you up. I know, I know. No M.S.G."
Our usual introductory ritual.
Today, however, her warmth was tempered by a sadness in her eyes.
"What's the matter Dahng?"
"Oh . . . you know my Susie?"
"Yeah."
"She come home today. She crying. She say her friends call her a chink. I say,
    you not a chink, you not a chink."
Then she told me a story of when Susie was five.
Time for her to become a citizen.
The child is taken to the naturalization office to be sworn in.
When the ceremony is complete and the oath of allegiance taken
The judge leans over and says to the five-year-old
"Susie you're now an American."
The child looks back and says, "When I get my blue eyes?"
Dahng said, "You know, when I hear that, my tear wanna fall down."

(Lights slowly fade to black as Assimilation *theme starts up and rises to cacophonous climax.)*

Note: Shishir Kurup wrote *Assimilation* and first performed it at The Institute of Contemporary Arts in London in 1994. He has since extensively toured the university and theater circuit in the United States.

Mask Dance

RICK SHIOMI

[This play is based upon interviews with a number of Korean adoptees who were participants in Theater Mu, Minneapolis, in the early years.]

Mask Dance Drama in Folk Korea

In Korea, masks were first used to communicate with the spirit world. Shamans used masks as mediums to communicate with the world of spirits and ancestors. Over time, mask dances became secular folk plays put on by rural villages at planting and harvest festivals, each village having a different style of masks and dances, but similar themes and stock characters. These masked plays were often comic and bawdy in nature, populated by the wily servant, the lecherous monk, and the crone, lampooning the aristocracy, Buddhist monks, errant husbands, and other institutions of power.

The mask dance in this play is based on the Eight Monk Dance and the Shaman Dance from the Pongsan T'alch'um style. The Pongsan style is fast, bold, and free in spirit, emphasizing expression and energy over tight choreography. The earthy, rooted movements, set against the free flow of the hansam (fabric sleeves worn over the hands), the masks, and the heartbeat rhythms of the drum speak of a sublime and familiar spirit which is Korea.

—Andrew Kim

CAST:
    KAREN: 18–year-old Korean adoptee
    CARL: 17–year-old Korean adoptee
    LISA: 15–year-old Korean adoptee
    MOTHER: Caucasian female in late 50s
    FATHER (JIM): Caucasian male in late 50s
    P.K.: Female Korean adoptee in early 20s
    SPIRIT: Asian Spiritual character with half-white face
    MASK DANCER: Asian Movement Character wearing Chwibari mask

The Setting is a middle-class home in a small town in Minnesota.

The Time is the 1990s.

Act One

SCENE ONE

(*There is a window hanging downstage right. Upstage right is a dresser with the frame of a mirror hung above it. Upcenter is a low riser with steps at the* front and sides. Up center of the riser is a flat with white and black cloths attached to it and angled to the ceiling. Upstage left a long white cloth [about forty-eight inches wide] is hung from the ceiling. Midstage right is a bedroom, down center is the living room, and down left is the garage. The low riser is used for the performance stage and an apartment. There are black boxes used as furniture for the various locations.)

MASK DANCE #1: *Lights go to black and the changgo drummer plays a slow basic introduction to the mask dance rhythm. Lights come up slowly as several dancers with traditional Korean mask dance masks and hansam enter, led by the MASK DANCER. They circle around the stage and then in two lines kneel to the floor. The drummer pauses, then begins the main dance rhythm, and the dancers begin to move as if being born again. They rise and begin the ritual Pongsan mask dance. At the end of the dance they end up kneeling with their faces to the ground again. Then with a slow rhythm, they sit up to face the audience and lights fade to black.*

MASK DANCE #2: *Lights come up downstage left and the MASK DANCER and the SPIRIT dance a short duet that is playful yet reflects the darker emotional tones of the next scene. Lights cross-fade to the bedroom on stage right.*

The MASK DANCER exits but the SPIRIT remains behind the white cloth. Lights cross-fade to Karen in her bedroom packing her clothes into a suitcase. She finds a Korean doll in her dresser drawer and stops to stare at it.

LISA (*Offstage*): Karen? . . . Karen? . . . Mom bought some rice cakes . . .

(*Lisa appears in the doorway to the bedroom*)

LISA: You want some?

(*Karen simply shakes her head and puts the doll down*)

LISA: What's wrong?

KAREN: Nothing . . .

LISA: You sad about leaving?

(*Karen crosses to the suitcase to continue packing*)

KAREN: I was just thinking . . .

LISA: You don't have to . . .

KAREN: What, think?

LISA: No . . . go to college this year . . . Why not wait a year and we can go together . . .

KAREN: That's not how it works . . .

(*Karen crosses back to the dresser. Lisa picks up a sweater from the suitcase*)

LISA: You taking this too?

KAREN: You want it?

LISA: I'd think of you when I wear it . . .

KAREN: Sure . . .

(*Karen crosses back to the suitcase with more clothes as Lisa notices the doll in the suitcase*)

LISA (*picks it up gingerly*): Where'd you dig this up?

KAREN: In the dresser . . .

LISA: God, it's so old . . .

KAREN (*she stops packing*): It's only faded . . .

(*The SPIRIT uncovers itself from the white cloth*)

SPIRIT: Like the color of our pain.

KAREN: And the gold trim's nice . . .

SPIRIT: It can't hide the yellowed skin . . .

LISA: I'd dump it . . .

(*Lisa crosses away to the window downstage*)

SPIRIT: It's like our time of despair . . .

KAREN: It seems so far away now . . . when we first came here . . . You, me and Carl . . .

(*Karen finishes up her packing*)

LISA: Why'd you have to talk like that?

KAREN: Sorry . . .

LISA (*pause*): It'll feel kind of empty in the house . . .

KAREN: Mom and Dad'll be here . . .

LISA: You and Carl won't . . .

KAREN: Maybe we can talk Carl into moving back home. . . .

LISA: No way . . .

KAREN: Come on, he's broke half the time . . .

LISA: He'd rather live on the streets . . . than with Dad here . . .

KAREN (*crosses back to suitcase*): Well, I'll be home for Thanksgiving and Christmas . . .

LISA: I know . . . but still . . .

KAREN: I know . . .

(*Karen embraces Lisa as the SPIRIT dances center stage*)

SPIRIT: From our unknown home . . .
To the orphanage . . .
(*pause*)
From Korea . . .
To the United States . . .
To this small town . . .
(*pause*)
From our birth mothers . . .
To our parents here . . .
To Carl leaving . . .
(*pause*)
It's different for us . . .
(*pause*)
Going away for a few months . . .
For a few days . . .
A few moments . . .
(*pause*)
Could be . . . forever . . .

(*The SPIRIT returns to the cloth and the two girls let go, almost embarrassed at their mutual show of emotion. Karen closes up her suitcase as Lisa looks out a window*)

LISA: Is Carl really coming today?

KAREN: He promised me he would . . .

LISA: I wish Dad would take a fishing trip . . . then Carl might stay over . . .

KAREN: Maybe he will anyway . . .

(*Karen pauses and holds up the doll to Lisa*)

KAREN: Would you keep this for me?

LISA: Me?

KAREN: Mom bought it for us, our first Christmas here, remember? Don't you think it's special?

LISA: It's so . . . Koreanish . . .

(*Lights fade to transition blue*)

MOTHER (*offstage*): Karen! . . . Lisa! . . . Come down here!

Carl's here! Carl's come home!

SCENE TWO

(*The bed is now the living-room couch and a single seat is stage left of it. Lights come up on the living room. Carl stands in front of the couch while the Father sits in the seat and the Mother enters stage right. The SPIRIT stands up center*)

FATHER: Welcome home, Carl . . .

MOTHER: It's wonderful to see you . . .

CARL: Yeah . . .

(*Lisa and Karen come in first from stage right. Lisa and Carl embrace while Karen watches smiling*)

LISA: Carl!

CARL: Hi, kiddo . . .

KAREN: Thanks for coming . . .

CARL: Didn't want to miss the party . . .

LISA: I miss you . . .

CARL: Yeah . . . sure . . .

KAREN: We all do . . .

FATHER: Let's have something to drink, Mom.

(*Lisa and Carl sit down with Karen standing behind them*)

MOTHER: It's been such a long time, since we've all been together like this . . .

SPIRIT: Don't start that now, Mom . . .

FATHER: Can you get the drinks?

MOTHER: Okay . . . okay . . . I just wanted to make Carl feel at home again . . .

SPIRIT: It's all right, Mom . . . we can work this out ourselves . . .

MOTHER: What would you like to drink, Carl?

CARL: Got any beer?

MOTHER: How about a coke?

CARL: Whatever . . .

(*The Mother exits right*)

FATHER: You look tired, Carl . . .

SPIRIT: Not you too, Dad . . .

FATHER: Is everything all right?

CARL: It's cool . . .

FATHER: Still got that job, at the Burger King?

CARL: Naw, gave it up . . . no future in it, right?

FATHER: How're you paying the bills?

CARL: I don't . . . I got my friends to kick in on the apartment and stuff . . .

FATHER: Why not give up this hand-to-mouth stuff . . . and go to college?

SPIRIT: Hoof-in-mouth disease!

CARL: I don't need this . . .

KAREN: Come on, Carl . . . relax . . .

CARL: Then tell him to stop buggin' me . . .

SPIRIT: That's why he ran away . . .

CARL: I'm a free agent, get it?

SPIRIT: Like the last rays of the sun . . .

FATHER: Are they offering you millions to play a bum of the street?

CARL: Naw, just the chance to breathe . . .

(*The Mother enters with a Coke can*)

LISA: Let's talk about something else . . .

MOTHER: Yes . . . this is a farewell party for Karen . . . Let's not forget that . . .

SPIRIT: We can't ever forget that . . .

MOTHER: Does anyone want to help me set the table?

LISA: I will . . .

FATHER: I'll check the barbecue . . .

(*Lisa and the Mother exit right. The Father exits up left. Karen crosses down to Carl. The SPIRIT comes off her riser*)

KAREN: Carl . . . could you try not to talk like that in front of Mom and Dad?

CARL: You ever wonder who our birth parents were?

KAREN: Where did that come from?

CARL: I was thinking . . . there a law against that?

KAREN: Just don't bring it up in front of Mom and Dad, okay?

CARL: Mom and Dad? . . . What planet are they from?

KAREN: It's not that bad . . .

CARL: Getting dumped here wasn't my choice.

KAREN: This is better than any orphanage.

CARL: Is that what's important to you? All this fake happiness . . . You wanna be a Barbie doll? Go ahead . . . but don't suck me into that game, okay?

KAREN: Maybe we're the lucky ones . . . You know what it'd be like for us, back in Korea?

CARL: No. Do you?

MOTHER (*Offstage*): Dinner's ready!

(*Lights go to transition blue*)

SCENE THREE

(*Lights come up in a line upstage where the family members Carl, Karen, Lisa, Mother and Father walk into the light*)

LISA: Where'd you get this kim chee, Mom?

MOTHER: At United Noodle, in the city . . .

FATHER: I like Lee's grocery . . . where we went the day you kids arrived . . .

KAREN: Dad, please . . .

FATHER: What'd I say now?

KAREN: Nothing . . . forget it, all right?

FATHER: I just remember it was a great day . . . and we wanted to get you something special.

KAREN: We know that, Dad . . .

(*As the drum begins beating quietly, the SPIRIT enters stage left, dragging in the steamer trunk. The trunk is placed downstage left in the garage area*)

MOTHER: Carl, you haven't eaten a thing.

CARL: I'm not hungry . . .

FATHER: This stuff's still too hot for me . . .

MOTHER: You don't have to touch it, Jim . . .

LISA: What'll we do after dinner?

CARL: Anything on MTV?

MOTHER: Why don't we all do something together?

LISA: You don't like MTV, Mom . . .

KAREN: What about the trunk out in the garage?

LISA: The one with all our old stuff in it?

KAREN: Yeah, let's take a look at it . . .

MOTHER: Why don't you do that . . .

LISA: I'd rather watch MTV . . .

KAREN: We can do that later . . .

(*MASK DANCE #3: The drum plays louder and the MASK DANCER enters. He joins the SPIRIT in the dance and they move offstage left. Lights fade to transition blue. Sound of applause*)

SCENE FOUR

(The set is up as a café during the announcer's speech. There is one table with two chairs downstage right and the single box stage left. Lights come up on Carl sitting at the table and waiting for somebody)

CLUB ANNOUNCER (*Voiceover*): Thank you, that was Gilbert Davidson doing "Parrot Impersonations and other Reverse Paradigms."

(pause)

And now, let's welcome the final performer of our Performance Slam at Club Indigo!

(Sound of polite applause. MASK DANCE #4: A spotlight comes up on the riser where P.K. enters wearing a Pongsan mask and hansam. She makes a few dance moves and stops, taking off her mask and hansam. She turns to the audience, still holding the mask. She plays with the mask during the first part of the monologue)

P.K.: Hi, my name's Annie Oakley . . .

(pause)

You don't believe me? You think because I know how to dance with this mask on that I'm Oriental? Ann Hyundai . . . or Annie B. Toyota? . . . How about Anna Luisa Pilipino? You want to see my birth certificate? My Minneapolis library card? . . . Hey, how about this, my driver's license?

(She pauses to look at her picture on card)

Well . . . actually I am Korean . . . at least I was . . . way back . . . before I was, you know . . . "adopted" . . . Yeah . . . there's ten thousand of us Korean adoptees out there in the backwoods of Minnesota . . . about one for every lake . . .

(pause)

I came over when I was five . . . got picked up at the airport gate . . . Most people have birthday parties . . . I get a gate day party . . . 'cause they don't really know when I was born . . . but that's getting a little grim, right? And I'm here to entertain you people . . .

(puts down mask)

So . . . you ever shoot anybody? I know most of you have wanted to shoot plenty of people . . . your boss, your wife, your husband, your in-laws . . . yahoo! . . . Hell . . . what's America without a decent shootout? And you know . . . I once did it . . . Yeah . . . that's how I got my nickname, "Annie Oakley" . . .

(pause)

Anyway, my folks, they were pretty well off, and they had these parties. They'd invite over all their friends and relatives . . . I never really liked those parties so I used to hide out, in the closet . . . with my pair of six-guns . . .

(*pause*)

I never liked them . . . 'cause my Mom would take me out and show me off, you know? Like it was kind of . . . show and tell . . . and I was the show . . . And all these strange smelling people would smile and stare down at me . . . like I was some kind of freak . . .

(*pause*)

There was this one big fat guy . . . breathing down on me . . . and he asked my Mom if I had had my shots . . . like I was some kind of little animal . . .

(*pause*)

I pulled out my six gun, real slow . . . raised it up . . . and took aim at that sucker, right between the eyes . . . He laughed and thought it was cute . . . me playing Annie Oakley . . . Then I pulled the trigger and bang . . . He was dead . . .

(*pause*)

Everybody thought it was funny . . .

(*pause*)

But for me, it was real . . .

(*P.K. picks up the mask again, does a quick 360–degree turn and stamps her foot, holding the mask in front of her face. Lights cross-fade back to the club as sound of applause is heard*)

CLUB ANNOUNCER (*Voiceover*): That was P.K. Lee performing "Life Behind the Mask" . . . and thank you for being such a great audience for our Club Indigo Performance Slam!

(*P.K. crosses down to the box and sits, noticing Carl as she does so. She smiles and talks to several offstage people. Carl stares at her*)

P.K.: Hey, Ruby . . . thanks for coming . . . no sex intended!

(*pause*)

Tammy . . . good to see you . . . thanks . . .

(*pause*)

Danielle! Good luck with your show . . . I'll try to make it!

(*P.K. turns to see Carl staring at her*)

P.K.: You staring at me?

CARL: What?

P.K.: I said, are you staring at me . . .

CARL: No . . .

P.K.: I just happen to be in the way, huh?

CARL: No . . .

P.K.: Don't be afraid. I don't bite . . . unless I'm really mad . . .

CARL: You're pretty funny . . .

P.K.: That a delayed reaction, or what?

CARL: No . . .

P.K.: You know, you should enter one of those twenty-five-words-or-less contests . . .

CARL: I'm not much good with words . . .

P.K.: You wouldn't have to do much editing . . .

CARL: Am I bothering you?

P.K.: Me? . . . Not at all . . . I was looking for some avid conversation tonight . . .

CARL: I'm not much at talking . . .

P.K.: No problem, I can do it for both of us . . .

CARL: You always like this?

P.K.: Like what?

CARL: Jokin' around . . .

P.K.: It eases the burden, you know?

CARL (*pause*): That true?

P.K.: What?

(*pause*)

Now you got me talkin' like you . . .

CARL: About bein' . . . you know . . .

P.K.: What? . . . Adopted?

CARL: Yeah . . .

P.K.: In twenty-five words or less?

CARL: Doesn't it bother you?

P.K.: No . . . it's kind of like . . . riding a razor on pain killers . . . you bleed but you don't feel a thing . . .

(*pause*)

That less than twenty-five words?

CARL: Depends . . .

P.K.: On what?

CARL: How you count the contractions . . .

P.K.: Very funny . . .

(*Carl looks across the stage*)

CARL: You better get back . . . Your friends are callin' . . .

P.K. (*turning*): Hey, Julie! Thanks . . .

(*pause*)

That's just Julie . . . old buddy . . .

CARL: You lesbian or somethin'?

P.K.: Where did that come from?

CARL: All your friends . . .

P.K.: Does it bother you?

CARL: I got nothing against gays . . .

P.K.: What about lesbians and bisexuals?

CARL: I don't care much one way or the other.

P.K.: You know, that's almost funny . . .

CARL: Yeah?

P.K.: No . . . Yes . . . and so what . . .

CARL: What?

P.K.: I'm not lesbian . . . I am bisexual . . . and so what?

CARL: I don't know . . .

P.K.: You Asian guys all talk the same . . .

CARL: Me?

P.K.: Has somebody else joined us, or are you a multiple personality?

CARL: I'm just me . . .

P.K.: You are Asian . . .

CARL: I guess so . . .

P.K.: You don't know if you're Asian or not?

CARL: I'm probably part . . . Korean . . . the rest . . . I don't know . . .

P.K. (*pause*): Are you like me?

CARL: Yeah . . . in a way I guess . . .

P.K.: You mind if I join you?

CARL: What for?

P.K.: Well . . . I don't know . . . maybe we could strike up a conversation . . . Seein' as we have something . . . in common . . .

CARL: Okay . . . if you like . . .

(*P.K. gets up and crosses to table to join Carl*)

P.K.: Hey, an open-minded Asian guy . . . You're a rare bird, you know?

CARL: I'm not a bird . . .

P.K.: Sorry if you were offended . . .

CARL: You don't like me bein' Asian?

P.K.: Can you be something else?

CARL: I'm not really Korean . . .

P.K.: You're not a banana, are you?

CARL: I don't like them either . . .

P.K.: Are you pullin' my leg?

CARL: I'm not the comedian . . .

P.K.: I wouldn't be so sure about that . . .

CARL: So . . . what you wanna talk about?

P.K.: I don't know . . . how about you fill me in on your story . . . then maybe I'll tell you mine . . . and then who knows . . . we might both get crazy and keep talkin' till the cows come home . . .

CARL: Cool . . .

P.K.: Look . . . before we get into anything here . . . you've got to give up this monosyllabic male thing, okay?

CARL (*pause*): Okay . . . I'll do that . . .

P.K. (*looks up*): Max . . . another round, please!

CARL: Uh . . . can we go somewhere else, to talk?

P.K.: You don't like it here?

CARL: I feel like walkin' . . .

P.K.: Sure . . . I can walk and talk at the same time . . .

CARL: You don't mind?

P.K.: Let's take it one step at a time, okay?

CARL: Sure . . .

P.K. (*as they leave*): Forget the round, Max . . .

(*They both get up and exit as lights fade to black. End of Scene Four*)

SCENE FIVE

(*The garage has simply the steamer trunk in the middle of it with a lamp hanging above downstage left. Lights come up on Carl, Karen and Lisa seated around the steamer trunk. The SPIRIT stands on the up left riser*)

KAREN: So that's why I missed you at the café. . .

CARL: It's what you get for being late.

KAREN: You could've waited a few more minutes . . .

LISA: So what was she like?

CARL: Crazy . . . like us . . . only she can talk about it . . .

KAREN: You spent the night with her?

CARL: I was curious . . .

LISA: You mean . . . you're seeing a Korean girl?

CARL: This ain't *Married with Children* . . .

KAREN: No, that would take some thought . . .

CARL: You think I always mess up, right?

KAREN: Come on . . . it's not like that . . . You always make things so extreme . . . You make going to the store a life and death decision.

CARL: I don't need this . . .

(*Carl gets up*)

LISA: Don't go!

(*The SPIRIT stretches out her hand and Carl stops as if held by some invisible thread*)

SPIRIT: You can't go yet . . . We have plans for you . . .

LISA: We're sorry . . .

KAREN: Yeah . . . let's have some fun . . . This could be the last time we're together for a while . . .

CARL: Now who's getting dramatic?

(*The SPIRIT lowers her hand and Carl returns to his seat*)

KAREN: Let's see what's inside this old trunk . . .

(*Karen opens the trunk and pulls out a traditional Korean gown*)

KAREN: Wow . . . I didn't know this was in here!

CARL: Mom probably stashed it in there . . . I hate all that Korean stuff she tries to shove down our throats . . .

KAREN: She's never done that . . .

CARL: Didn't she start up that dumb Kamp Bulgogi, just so we'd meet other Korean kids?

LISA: I didn't mind it . . .

CARL: That place had more losers than mosquitoes!

KAREN: We should know more about Korean things.

CARL: Go ahead . . . just don't start pushing that junk on me . . .

KAREN (to Lisa): Why don't you try this on?

LISA: Me?

CARL: Watch out, Lisa . . . you could turn Korean.

LISA: You put it on first . . .

KAREN (pause): Okay . . .

(Karen turns and faces upstage as she puts on the gown and the drum beat begins. The SPIRIT mimics Karen from the riser. Lights change to more surreal tone. Then Karen turns and picks out two fans from the trunk and begins to do moves from the traditional fan dance. The SPIRIT comes off her riser and touches Karen's elbows and Karen drops the fans. Lights fade to a blue spot on Karen and the SPIRIT as the SPIRIT moves Karen like a puppet)

KAREN: Don't you think I'm pretty? Don't you think I'm lovely? Look at my wonderful gown . . . and my smooth skin . . . my rich black hair . . . Don't you wish you could be like me? . . . Don't you wish you had all these wonderful things? . . .

(pause)

I could be a princess . . . and if you were like me . . . You could be too . . .

(The SPIRIT stops moving Karen and steps back onto the riser. Karen comes out of her trance. The lights return to normal)

CARL: Hey, Karen . . . you can come out of it . . .

KAREN: What?

CARL: Cut the games, okay?

KAREN: What games?

CARL: That mystic dance shit . . . How long you been practicing that, huh?

KAREN: I wasn't dancing . . .

LISA: Yes you were . . .

CARL: I got a witness . . .

LISA: But it was beautiful . . .

KAREN: I don't remember anything.

CARL: Convenient . . .

LISA: You better take that off . . .

KAREN: You want to try it on?

LISA: No thanks . . .

KAREN: What are you afraid of?

CARL: Losing her marbles . . .

KAREN: You think I'm crazy?

LISA: No.

KAREN: I wasn't dancing . . .

(*Karen takes off the gown and puts it back into the trunk*)

CARL: Come on, Lisa . . . let's go upstairs . . .

LISA: Yeah . . .

(*As they get up to leave, Karen pulls out a small locket*)

KAREN: Do you remember this?

LISA: That's mine . . . Mom gave it to me . . .

CARL: What's inside?

LISA (*taking locket from Karen*): A lock of my hair . . .

(*Lisa walks downstage and lights change to surreal lighting*)

LISA: I remember sitting in the sandbox . . . with all the other girls walking around me . . . they were calling me things . . . I didn't know what they were saying . . . but it didn't feel good . . . and then they'd laugh . . . and throw sand at me . . . I remember the sand flying all over my head . . . covering me . . . getting caught in my hair . . . till my head felt matted down with it . . . the sand was everywhere . . . like the girls . . . and I didn't know why . . .

(*pause*)

I got up and ran home . . . crying for my mother . . . she came out and I could see she was angry . . . She shouted at the girls . . . and I felt funny . . . kind of embarrassed . . . then the tears began to roll down my cheeks . . . I looked down at the wooden floor of the porch . . . that was covered with sand . . . and my tears bubbled up with the sand . . .

(*pause*)

I cut my hair after that . . . I always cut my hair . . . short . . .

(*MASK DANCE #5: The MASK DANCER returns, this time dancing around Lisa along with the SPIRIT. Lisa swings out at them but misses each time*)

LISA: No . . . get . . . away from me . . . I don't need you . . . so leave me alone . . . No . . . No! . . . I don't want that crap! NO! . . . NOOO!!!

(*Lights change back to the garage, as Carl grabs Lisa and holds her close*)

CARL: It's all right, Lisa . . . it's all right . . . we're here with you . . .

(*Lisa puts her head on Carl's shoulder. Lights fade to black. End of Scene Five*)

SCENE SIX

(*The bedroom is set up as in Scene One. Lights come up in the bedroom, where Karen is lying on her bed, reading a book. The Mother enters*)

MOTHER: Can't get any sleep?

KAREN: I just felt like reading . . .

MOTHER: What's the book?

KAREN: *Dr. Zhivago* . . .

MOTHER: I loved that story . . . It's so romantic, isn't it?

KAREN: It's kind of sad to me . . . Them being separated like that.

MOTHER: But they had that time together . . . That's rare, you know?

KAREN: Yeah, I guess . . .

MOTHER (*pause*): So . . . how was Carl? He still seemed so upset when he left.

KAREN: He didn't really enjoy looking through the stuff in the trunk . . .

(*pause*)

You know how it is when he sees Korean things . . .

MOTHER: Why does Carl feel like that? You and Lisa don't . . .

KAREN: Well, actually I think it upsets Lisa too . . .

MOTHER: I just wanted you to know about your own . . . heritage . . .

KAREN: I know . . . and that's been great . . .

(*pause*)

It's just that Carl and Lisa feel different about it . . .

(*pause*)

It's not you, Mom . . .

MOTHER: Then what is it?

KAREN: I don't know . . .

MOTHER (*pause*): What about you . . . are you all right?

KAREN: I think so . . .

MOTHER: You know, I'm so proud of you, going off to college . . .

KAREN (*pause*): Why did you do it?

MOTHER: What?

KAREN: Adopt us?

MOTHER: Because we loved you . . .

KAREN: I mean, why us? Why not some other kids?

MOTHER: Well, I guess because fate was kind enough to bring you to us . . .

KAREN: But we're Korean . . . didn't you want some American kids?

MOTHER: That didn't happen, and I haven't regretted it . . .

(*pause*)

It's a blessing that you're Korean . . . That we have three beautiful children.

KAREN (*pause*): Some people say it's because Koreans were the easiest to adopt . . . that's all . . .

MOTHER: Adoption isn't easy . . .

(*pause*)

Becoming your parents was not something we decided lightly.

(*pause*)

It was like a two-year pregnancy . . . Holding onto your pictures . . . going to classes to help us understand Korean culture . . . and waiting . . . always waiting . . .

KAREN: Could you feel us, in those pictures? Feel who we were?

MOTHER: I thought so . . .

KAREN: You must have wanted us badly . . .

MOTHER: I needed you . . .

KAREN (*pause*): Because you couldn't have your own children?

MOTHER (*stands*): It was more than that . . .

KAREN: What do you mean?

MOTHER (*pause*): For a long time . . . it was like a curse, not having my own babies.

(*pause*)

I had to stop feeling guilty for something . . . unknowable . . . and listen to the voices inside me . . .

(*walks away*)

I must sound crazy to you . . .

KAREN: No . . . what did the voices say?

MOTHER: Nothing . . . it was nothing, really . . . Now you better go to sleep . . .

KAREN: Why won't you tell me?

MOTHER: It's something personal . . . I mean . . . maybe one day . . .

KAREN: If that day never comes . . . And you never tell us . . . What then?

MOTHER: I've never told anyone . . . not even your father . . .

KAREN: Then when will we ever understand?

MOTHER (*pause*): Okay . . . but it was . . . one of those strange experiences . . .

(*pause*)

I was on an airline flight . . . visiting my mother . . . And . . . I began to hear these voices . . . of all the unborn babies inside me, singing out to me . . . All of my babies . . . singing sweet songs of sorrow . . . And crying out to me . . . Mommy I need you . . . Hold me . . . rock me . . .

(*pause*)

They had died a strange death . . . My babies . . . They died before they were born . . . Before they were conceived . . .

(*pause*)

Most people ask, Does life begin at conception? No one asks when death begins . . . But death can begin before conception. My babies died with no one to mourn them. No one except me . . . But they'll always live within me . . . They'll always sing to me . . .

(*pause*)

Then I looked at the child in the seat next to mine . . . She was traveling alone . . . And when she looked up at me . . . I thought she looked just like me . . . when I was her age . . . And in my rage . . . I thought . . . this child could be mine . . . This child could be mine . . .

(*pause*)

Then the voices of my babies . . . cried out to me, Mommy give us peace . . . Please . . . leave your grief . . . We are happy where we are . . . deep and unborn . . . within your soul . . .

(*pause*)

I guess that's when I knew . . . that I needed to find you.

(*Karen walks over to her mother and they embrace. Lights go to transition blue*)

SCENE SEVEN

(*The center stage becomes a street at night with the boxes now becoming a park bench. P.K. and Carl enter from downstage left. They are laughing and enjoying each other's company*)

CARL: You know, you're all right . . . for someone who does weird things on stage . . .

(*P.K. jumps up on bench*)

P.K.: How many people get to play out their personal lives in front of a crowd?

CARL: Who'd want to?

P.K.: It's like getting paid for going to therapy . . .

CARL: Right . . .

P.K.: You're regressing . . .

CARL: So where is this apartment of yours?

P.K.: Not far . . . just a few more blocks . . .

CARL: You got anything to drink?

P.K.: Like what?

CARL: Beer . . . hard stuff . . .

P.K.: No . . . you got any money?

CARL: Don't you?

P.K.: I'm broke, till next week . . . I got one more check coming from my show . . .

(*Cross-fade to spot in bedroom in front of mirror where Lisa enters and picks up a telephone*)

LISA: Hello, Carl?

(*blues rock music plays in background*)

CARL'S VOICE: Hi, this is Carl, Jonas, George, Jake and friends . . . can't talk so leave a message . . . and we'll get back to you . . . some day . . .

(*sound of beep*)

LISA: Carl? . . . Carl? . . . I have to talk to you, okay? . . . I called Karen, but she wasn't home either . . . call me as soon as you can . . . okay? . . . Please?

(*Lisa hangs up the phone*)

MOTHER'S VOICE: Lisa? . . . Lisa? . . . It's time for school . . .

(pause)

Are you all right?

LISA: I'm feeling kind of sick . . .

MOTHER'S VOICE: Shall I call the doctor?

LISA: No . . . it's not that bad, Mom . . .

(Lisa stares into the mirror and then exits. Cross-fade to center)

CARL: Don't you feel bad . . . going through that stuff about being adopted, again and again?

P.K.: Nope . . . I kind of enjoy it now . . . I push this button . . . and wham . . . I'm back there . . . living it all over again . . . ready to squeeze that trigger . . .

(pause and smile)

You know that story I tell about shooting the fat man? The funny thing is . . . what I remember most is being in the living room . . . feeling like this spotlight has me trapped on stage, I want to hide . . . but I can't get out of the light . . .

(pause)

Now I love it . . . the spotlight . . . It's almost like I need it . . . You hear those people clapping . . . and it feels good . . . 'cause you just opened your veins, and showed them your blood . . . and they love you . . .

CARL: I still couldn't do it . . .

P.K.: Can you tell me?

CARL: What?

P.K.: What's buggin' you . . . inside . . .

CARL: It's nothin' you don't know . . .

P.K.: Come on . . . I've been spilling my guts out for you . . . and you've hardly told me a thing . . .

CARL *(pause)*: Okay . . . but it's not much . . .

P.K.: I'm listening . . .

(Lights cross-fade to center stage where Carl sits on the bench. P.K. sits on the ground downstage. There is the sound of a train starting up and rolling away)

CARL: When did I know? . . . I saw it in her eyes . . . Where were we? . . . On a bench . . . it was in a park . . . no . . . across the street from the park . . . at a train station . . . we were . . . waiting there . . . for the train . . . I was sitting on the bench, swinging my legs . . . and she was there beside me . . . watching me . . . I thought of running off into the park, and disappearing.

But I couldn't leave her, she was my friend . . . she was nice to us . . . she was the only one at the orphanage who cared

(*pause*)

That's how I could see it . . . in her eyes . . . I was four years old . . . and I knew she was saying good-bye . . . before she even said a word . . . How did I know?

(*pause*)

I saw the tears in her eyes . . . before they even came out . . .

(*Lights cross-fade back to street. P.K. gets up and crosses to Carl. She wants to embrace him, but then just sits down beside him and holds his hand. He slowly looks over at her. MASK DANCE #6: The drum begins to play and the MASK DANCER leads the cast with masks in a series of movements around the frozen Carl and P.K. The dance ends with the dancers in a semicircle facing Carl and P.K. Lights go to black. End of Act One*)

Act Two

SCENE ONE

(*Upstage on the riser is a low sofa in P.K.'s apartment. It is several weeks later. MASK DANCE #7: The MASK DANCER comes out with the SPIRIT and P.K. They dance around center stage in a ritual dance. Carl watches from the sofa. At the end of the dance, P.K. takes off her mask and walks over to Carl. The MASK DANCER takes his place left of the riser. The SPIRIT walks up on the riser and stands behind Carl. The stagehands stand by the riser wearing masks, one of which is the concubine mask*)

P.K.: What do you think?

CARL: There's a family resemblance . . .

P.K.: What?

CARL: Between you and the mask . . .

P.K.: I was asking about the dance . . .

CARL: Why're you stuck on that stuff?

P.K.: You have to take a journey . . .

CARL: Where're we going?

SPIRIT: Bungee jumping . . .

P.K.: We're on an archeological dig of the subterranean caves in your head . . .

CARL: Sorry, I'm not donating my brain to science . . .

P.K.: Look at these masks . . . they have power.

SPIRIT: A woman with a little knowledge . . .

CARL: Is this the twilight zone?

SPIRIT: Could brighten up your day . . .

P.K.: Why don't you try one on?

(*pause*)

      It's up to you . . . Can you handle that?

CARL (*pause*): What's that one supposed to be . . .

P.K.: The pregnant concubine . . .

CARL: Not my type, thanks . . .

SPIRIT: What about your fate?

CARL (*pointing to the Mask Dancer*): How about that one . . .

P.K.: Chwibari? That's the playboy . . . the prodigal son . . . sometimes the monk gone bad . . . He's a real prankster . . .

(*pause*)

      Put it on . . . let's see what happens . . .

CARL: I don't think so . . .

P.K.: Okay . . . try it without the mask first. Put on these hansam . . .

CARL: What're they for?

P.K.: They're extensions of our bodies . . . that connect us to nature . . . That's what gives us the power . . .

(*Lights on Carl and P.K. fade to low. Two spots downstage left and right come up on Karen and the Mother as they talk on the phone*)

KAREN: Mom . . . Lisa's lonely out there . . .

MOTHER: Lisa will be all right . . . she's just getting used to being without you and Carl . . . that's all . . . it's good for her.

KAREN: That's not what she told me.

(*Spot comes up on Lisa upstage. The SPIRIT puts on a white mask and comes down to Lisa. The two stagehands, wearing white masks too, join the SPIRIT in walking around Lisa, staring at her like she's some kind of alien. Lisa watches them with growing anxiety*)

MOTHER: What did she say?

KAREN: It's not easy, being the only Korean in that town . . .

MOTHER: All of you grew up here . . .

KAREN: But we had each other . . .

MOTHER: Why don't you and Carl come visit more often?

KAREN: That's not the answer . . .

MOTHER: But I don't think it's right for Lisa to live with you in the city . . .

KAREN: Mom, I thought it wouldn't be a big deal . . . leaving her there . . . and I know it doesn't seem fair . . . but . . . Lisa . . . needs Carl and me . . . We need to be together . . .

MOTHER: I won't let Lisa go off with you, she's only sixteen.

(*The Mother exits. Cross-fade from spotlights to riser where P.K. resumes regular speed in her movements. She stops*)

P.K.: You ready to try it?

CARL: Why do I have to be into it? Why can't we just be together? Isn't that more fun?

P.K.: You think I do this for kicks? Some kind of small-town sport, like ice fishing? Or duck hunting?

(*pause*)

My whole life is somewhere out there, in here . . . and you know what . . . It's important to me . . .

CARL (*pause*): Okay . . . I'll try it, when I'm ready . . .

P.K.: Sure . . . whenever, huh?

(*pause*)

I got to clean up for my show . . .

(*P.K. exits and Carl sits on the steps, staring at the masks. The light on him fades to low as spotlight on Karen comes up. She's still holding the phone. The SPIRIT stands behind Karen*)

KAREN: Mom . . . Mom . . . you don't understand . . . this thing with Carl and Lisa and me . . . It's special . . . It's what gave us hope . . . more than anything else . . .

(*pause*)

I know you love us . . . and we love you too . . . but this is different . . .

(*General lights come up center stage. The SPIRIT speaks Karen's lines as Karen, Carl and Lisa walk around center stage as if young children exploring the space*)

SPIRIT: You see . . . when I got to the orphanage, there were all these kids . . . coming and going . . . you couldn't get close to anyone . . . But with Lisa and Carl . . . we just connected.

(*Karen, Carl and Lisa make eye contact*)

They were only two and four . . . I was only five myself . . . but we got so close . . .

(They hold hands and circle center stage)

    I don't know how it happened . . . Maybe God reached down and touched us . . .

(They kneel and huddle center stage)

    We were just three more kids in that place . . . we weren't even related by blood . . . but we became a family . . . and it was more than blood . . . more than love . . .

(Karen, Carl and Lisa look out at the audience. MASK DANCE #8: The stagehands enter as orphanage officials. They point at Lisa and circle her. They try to take Lisa away but Karen and Carl grab her other arm. The MASK DANCER enters and jumps between the stagehands and the kids. A battle ensues with the stagehands finally pulling the MASK DANCER away. The stagehands return to grab Lisa, but the other two hold her again. This time the stagehands take all three kids. Lights fade to transition blue.

MASK DANCE #9: Lights cross-fade upstage to the riser, where Carl picks up the Chwibari mask. Suddenly the MASK DANCER and SPIRIT enter from both sides. The SPIRIT leads Carl around the stage as the drumming builds. The SPIRIT stops Carl in front of the MASK DANCER. SPIRIT takes the mask and puts it on Carl while the MASK DANCER dances in front of Carl, who is facing upstage. The MASK DANCER and SPIRIT lead Carl through a series of dance moves. Carl goes from being hesitant to being confident but in the end he falters and falls to his knees. The MASK DANCER and SPIRIT exit. Carl takes off the mask and looks dazed and yet exhilarated.

Lisa enters from upstage right and crosses downstage right with her hands over her face. The stagehands, wearing white masks, follow her)

CARL: Lisa? . . . Lisa!

(Carl stands and waves at the stagehands, who step into Lisa's path. In slow motion Carl tries to push them out of the way)

CARL: Get out of my way! Get out of . . . my way!

(MASK DANCE #10: The MASK DANCER dances toward the stagehands, who back away. Carl crosses to embrace Lisa. Lights cross-fade to the riser, where P.K. enters, having cleaned up)

P.K.: Carl? . . . Carl?

(Carl breaks away from Lisa, who kneels in low light. Carl crosses to get the mask and take it back up to the riser)

CARL: I'm out here . . .

P.K.: You ready to go?

CARL: Yeah . . .

P.K.: What're you doing with that mask?

CARL: Just looking at it . . .

P.K.: Did it bite?

CARL: No . . .

P.K.: That was a joke . . .

(*The phone rings. P.K. goes upstage to pick up the receiver*)

P.K.: Yeah? . . . Yeah . . . Who? . . .

(*to Carl*)

It's for you . . .

(*Carl looks across to where Lisa is still kneeling in low light. Lights fade to transition blue*)

SCENE TWO

(*Lights come up on the living room of the family home. Karen sits on the single seat. The Father and Mother sit together on the sofa. SPIRIT sits where Lisa was kneeling*)

MOTHER: We should have gotten some counseling . . .

FATHER: But Lisa seemed fine . . . She never said a word about anything like this . . .

MOTHER: A therapist could help us . . . I know a woman who specializes in children like Lisa . . .

KAREN: She needs more than therapy, Mom . . .

FATHER: And I suppose you have all the answers.

MOTHER: Please, let's not argue now.

SPIRIT: Yes . . . time to put our heads together . . .

(*Carl enters from left*)

CARL: Sorry I'm late . . . How is Lisa?

FATHER: She'll be all right . . . for now . . . The doctor said if she'd been in the car much longer . . . she would have slipped into a coma . . .

MOTHER: It's lucky we came back early from next door . . . Dad heard the car engine running in the garage . . .

CARL: Can I see her?

MOTHER: Let's wait a bit . . . She's still asleep . . .

CARL: I won't wake her up . . .

FATHER: The doctor said—

MOTHER: Maybe it'll be okay . . . but promise me you won't get her up . . .

KAREN: We won't . . .

(*The SPIRIT leads Karen and Carl downstage right and then upstage right to stand in front of the dresser. At the same time Lisa enters from up right and lies on the bed as the Mother and Father exit left. Lights cross-fade to the bedroom*)

KAREN: Did Lisa talk to you?

CARL: No . . . she just left some messages for me to call . . .

KAREN: I should've known this would happen . . .

CARL: It's not your fault . . .

KAREN: We have to do something for Lisa . . .

CARL: What?

KAREN: I don't know . . .

SPIRIT: The answer's right here in this room . . . (*SPIRIT exits*)

CARL: She looks beautiful . . . doesn't she?

KAREN: Yeah . . . like when she was a baby . . .

CARL: You know . . . it's weird . . . but I had this dream . . . about Lisa . . . like she was saying good-bye to me . . . And this Masked Dancer . . . helped me save her . . .

KAREN: Mask Dancer?

CARL: I can't explain it.

KAREN: When did this happened?

CARL: Yesterday . . . Just before you called me about Lisa.

(*Lisa wakes up*)

LISA: Karen? . . . Carl? . . . What're you two doing here?

KAREN: We came to see you.

CARL: How're you doing, kiddo?

LISA (*pause*): All right, I guess . . . I'm sorry . . .

KAREN: Why'd you do it?

LISA: I don't know . . .

(*pause*)

Living here now . . . it's like a nightmare . . . it's like nobody understands . . .

CARL: You don't have to be alone . . . we were thinking of a plan so you could live with Karen, in the city . . .

LISA: You were?

KAREN: Well, we haven't worked it out yet . . .

CARL: I might even move in with you . . . so we could all be together again . . .

KAREN: You what?

LISA: That's great!

KAREN: What's going on, Carl?

CARL: Nothing . . . I Just thought . . . it 'd be better . . . if we were all together again . . .

(*Lights fade to transition blue*)

SCENE THREE

(*Karen, Carl and the Mother and Father are back standing in a line upstage center. The SPIRIT and the MASK DANCER enter and watch them from upstage. When the family begins to speak they walk around the center stage area*)

FATHER: That was a good dinner, Mom . . .

MOTHER: Thanks. Could you pick up a few things at the grocery store?

FATHER: Okay . . .

MOTHER: Here's the list . . . and don't forget the tofu . . .

FATHER: I won't . . .

KAREN: Mom, could we talk?

FATHER: Is it important?

KAREN: No . . .

FATHER: Why don't you and Carl come along with me . . . make sure I buy the right stuff . . .

KAREN: It's all right . . . Dad . . . we just want to talk with Mom . . .

FATHER: I see . . . okay . . . don't let me get in the way . . .

KAREN: We'll let you know what happened . . .

FATHER: Yeah . . . sure . . .

(*The MASK DANCER and the SPIRIT lead the Father away while lights cross-fade to the living room where the Mother sits on the single seat, Karen sits on the sofa and Carl stands right of the sofa*)

KAREN: Mom . . . remember that talk we had on the phone a while back?

MOTHER: I won't ever forget it . . .

(*pause*)

And I've decided we should move into the city . . . so Lisa isn't alone out here.

KAREN: Really?

MOTHER: You and Carl could move in with us, if you like . . . that way we'd all be together again . . .

CARL: What about Dad?

MOTHER: I'll talk to him . . . I think he'll understand . . .

KAREN: What do you think, Carl?

CARL: That could help you and Lisa . . .

MOTHER: You're not thrilled by it . . .

CARL: We had our own plan . . .

MOTHER: What was that?

KAREN: Well . . . it was just an idea

CARL: We want to live together . . . Karen, Lisa and me . . . in the city . . .

MOTHER: And what about your father and me?

KAREN: It wouldn't work . . .

CARL: You didn't say that before . . .

KAREN: Well I am now . . .

MOTHER: Carl . . . I know you've had your problems with Dad . . . and me . . . but can't we get beyond them?

CARL: I'm trying to . . .

MOTHER: We're a family, Carl . . . I know you haven't thought about us like that . . . for a long time . . . but we are a family . . . and I will do whatever it takes to keep us together . . .

(*pause and to Karen*)

You know how much I love you . . .

(*The Mother sits down and Karen crosses to her*)

KAREN (*pause*): Mom, we're sorry . . . we didn't mean to exclude you . . . we were only thinking about how maybe . . . Lisa needed to be with Carl and me . . . that's all . . .

MOTHER: You are my children . . . I am your mother . . .

CARL: We're not walking out on you . . .

MOTHER: It feels like it . . .

KAREN: We can work on this together . . . okay?

(*Carl walks over and touches the Mother on the shoulder. Lights go to transition blue*)

SCENE FOUR

(*The living room. The Father is alone in his chair reading the newspaper. He puts down the newspaper and paces for a moment then sits down again. The Mother enters and the Father looks up*)

FATHER: So what crazy idea did the kids come up with?

MOTHER: They wanted to take Lisa into the city to live with them . . .

FATHER: I knew it . . .

MOTHER: But I had a better idea . . .

FATHER: What?

MOTHER: I think we should move into the city ourselves . . .

FATHER: You do?

MOTHER: Yes . . . what do you think of that?

FATHER: Are you asking me? Or telling me?

MOTHER: I'm asking you.

FATHER: Well I think it's a damned stupid idea . . .

MOTHER: Come on, Jim . . . We can work this out as a family . . .

FATHER: Hogwash! . . . This is our home . . . we've been here over twenty-five years and overnight you're going to pack it all in?! What am I supposed to do, give up my job and just go looking for another one in the city?

(*pause*)

I'm not a young guy anymore . . . I've set down some roots here in this house . . .

(*pause*)

I know we got a problem here with poor Lisa . . . but moving into the city isn't the solution . . . it's not just a matter of where we live . . . for Christ's sake, why don't we move back to Korea?!

(*pause*)

I don't know . . . I just work and bring home the bread, right? I'm the donkey that pulls the cart and to hell with what I think, right?!

(*pause*)

Sure, you got to talk things over? Send me down to the store . . . Yeah, get me outa the way . . . because I'm not sensitive enough to deal with these things . . . I'm just a big dumb donkey you can whip when you're frustrated . . . Whoa, donkey . . . Giddyup . . . turn left . . . turn right.

(*pause*)

I don't know all about this Korean stuff . . . and what's good for them . . . I just tried to give them a roof over their heads and somebody to love them . . . and maybe I didn't even do a decent job of that . . .

(*pause*)

But let me tell you . . . when they told us Lisa had a brother and sister who had to come along with her . . . I could've caused a fuss and said, "You can't pull that trick on me" . . . but I didn't . . . and when I saw those three little kids at the airport gate . . . three of them instead of one . . . I thanked God he blessed us with more than we expected . . . only what do I get for all that? My kids and wife can't get out of here fast enough . . .

MOTHER (*pause*): Then you know how important this is to all of us . . .

FATHER (*pause*): Yeah . . . sure . . . I'll do whatever it takes to work this thing out . . .

(*The Mother and Father embrace. Lights go to transition blue with a spotlight stage left, where Karen and the SPIRIT pick up the trunk and bring it center stage. They do a dance around the trunk, with Karen mimicking the fans with her hands and the SPIRIT mimicking the puppet moves. The spot fades as Karen sits on the trunk with her back to the audience*)

SCENE FIVE

(*A few months later. P.K. and Carl are in her apartment. He's sitting on the floor, she's behind him on the sofa*)

P.K.: So . . . your folks are going to move into the city . . .

CARL: Yeah . . . I never thought they'd do that.

P.K.: Are you moving back in with them?

CARL: Back in with my parents? . . . No way . . .

P.K.: You said you never talked about them as your parents . . .

CARL: Things have changed . . . Dad's not so bad now . . . like something happened to him . . . something broke inside . . . and it made him better . . . funny, huh?

P.K.: Yeah . . .

CARL: You want to move in together?

P.K.: Me and you?

CARL: Anybody else here?

P.K.: I would . . . except . . . well . . . I'm thinking of moving . . .

CARL: Where?

P.K.: San Francisco . . . . or maybe New York . . .

CARL: When you planning to go?

P.K.: Next year sometime . . .

(*pause*)

You want to come with me?

CARL: Maybe I'll take a trip out to see you . . . once you get settled and everything . . .

P.K.: Sure . . .

(*pause*)

I ran into Lisa downtown . . . she said the three of you are taking a trip
back to Korea . . .

CARL: Yeah . . . next summer . . .

(*pause*)

Our folks are paying for it . . .

P.K.: I remember when you hated everything about Korea . . . you wouldn't
even try on my masks . . .

CARL: I said I'd try it when I was ready . . .

(*Lights come up on Karen opening up the trunk and pulling out the Korean
dress*)

KAREN: I'm beautiful . . . can't you tell?

P.K.: Karen must be looking forward to the trip . . .

CARL: I'm not sure she is . . .

P.K.: Why not?

CARL: I don't know . . .

KAREN: I'm really a princess . . .

(*The SPIRIT crosses as Karen begins to put it on again, but this time the
SPIRIT grabs the dress and pulls at it, making it more difficult for Karen to
put it on*)

CARL: I never told you . . . but it kind of helped me . . . you talking about all
that mask dance stuff . . .

P.K.: It's nice to know some things get through . . .

KAREN: Let go of it . . . this is my dress!

CARL: We're going next summer, so I'm taking a Korean language class.

KAREN: I'm not an orphan . . .

CARL: My folks have a contact with the orphanage . . . you know . . . they still remember us . . .

P.K.: Don't get your hopes up too high . . .

KAREN: I'm not like the others . . . I'm only lost . . .

CARL: Why not?

KAREN: I'm a lost princess! That's who I am! So don't ever ask me again . . . Is that clear?!

(*Lights go to black on Karen*)

P.K.: When I went back . . . I had my real name and birth date . . . on the papers my folks had . . . so I figured, I could find my birth parents . . . I went all the way back to the orphanage . . . got them to open up their record books . . . and the woman showed me this sheet of names . . . of all the babies registered that week . . . there were a dozen of us . . . and so they gave us all the same birth dates . . . and the same last name . . .

SPIRIT: Lee . . . It's kind of like Smith . . .

P.K.: I remember sitting in the hotel room . . . on the bed . . . holding the piece of paper with my name and birth date on it . . . looking out the window . . . realizing it was just made up . . . like everything else. And I'd never know the answer . . .

CARL: I'm sorry . . .

P.K.: Just don't get your hopes up too high, okay?

(*Lights fade to transition blue with a spot coming up on the trunk, which the SPIRIT drags back to the garage*)

SCENE SIX

(*Lights come up on the SPIRIT downstage left*)

SPIRIT: Whatever it takes . . . A journey of a thousand miles . . . begins with one airline ticket . . . one passport . . . one will to face the past . . .

(*The fan of the MASK DANCER appears in the spotlight. The MASK DANCER enters, followed by Carl and Lisa. MASK DANCE #11: The SPIRIT joins them. They perform a journey dance together and then kneel upstage. Carl stands and walks down left to speak*)

CARL: We took that trip back to Korea . . . and went to the orphanage . . .

(*pause*)

    Their records showed they'd found me one morning . . . in the alley, behind the building . . . in a plain brown basket . . .

(*Lisa stands and walks center stage to speak to the audience*)

LISA: I was luckier . . . I found out that my mother had left her true name, when she turned me over to the orphanage . . .

(*Karen enters from upstage right and walks downstage right*)

KAREN: I decided not to go on that trip . . . I thought it was a waste of time . . .

CARL: I asked for the nurse . . . the one who'd taken me to the train station . . . but she'd died . . .

LISA: When I finally tracked her down . . . my mother begged me to forgive her . . . that she was so young . . . and my father had passed away . . . she had to marry again . . . and it wouldn't have been possible to keep me . . .

(*Karen faces Carl*)

KAREN: I'm Korean American . . . and I'm proud of that . . . so I don't need to know who my birth parents are . . .

CARL: I went back to that train station . . . and stood there . . . waiting for the train . . . just so I could see it again . . .

(*Lisa turns to Karen*)

LISA: I tried to understand her . . . it's the old-fashioned Korean way . . . somebody else's daughter wouldn't fit . . .

KAREN: I have one set of parents already . . . and that's enough for me . . . They love me . . . what more can I want?

CARL: And this old man came up to me . . . In broken Korean, I asked about the train . . . In bits and pieces of English . . . he said the station was closed . . . They were going to tear it down . . . and put up a new one . . .

(*Karen turns her back to the others, who speak to audience*)

LISA: I stayed with my mother and her husband, and all their kids . . . in one small apartment . . . it wasn't easy . . .

CARL: I was sitting on the bench, swinging my legs . . . And she was there, beside me . . .

LISA: I realized how American I was . . . and I didn't want to change that . . . But I didn't want them to change to suit me . . .

CARL: I thought of running off into the park, and disappearing. But I couldn't leave her, she was my friend . . . she was nice to us . . .

LISA: My birth mom wanted me to be like them . . . and stay . . .

(*pause*)

I couldn't . . . and then we cried again . . .

CARL: I was four years old . . . and I knew she was saying good-bye . . . before she even said a word . . . How did I know?

(pause)

    I saw the tears in her eyes . . . before they even came out . . .

(Lisa and Carl exit left together. During the next section the MASK DANCER, SPIRIT and other dancers take positions up left)

KAREN: Look at Lisa . . . she came back thankful she lived here . . . and Carl? Why travel thousands of miles to find out you'll never know anyway? Sometimes it's better not to know . . .

(MASK DANCE #12: The MASK DANCER enters with Carl, Lisa, the SPIRIT, the Mother, Father and P.K. The MASK DANCER begins to lead the other dancers in an exorcism dance to drive the troubled spirit out of Karen. Karen curls up on the floor while the others dance around her. The others exit as the MASK DANCER remains and waves his hansam over Karen, who looks up at him. The MASK DANCER dances around her and then exits. Karen turns downstage, deep in thought. Fade to transition blue)

SCENE SEVEN

(It's the fall of the next year. Karen, Lisa and Carl are sitting in Carl's apartment. The Spirit watches from the side)

KAREN: This is a great apartment . . .

LISA: How can you afford all this space?

CARL: I'm the new janitor for the house, P.K. recommended me . . .

KAREN: Have you heard from her lately?

CARL: Not for a week . . . She seems to like living in San Francisco . . .

LISA: You miss her?

CARL: Yeah . . . I do . . . but she's the independent kind . . .

KAREN: Like you . . .

CARL: Lisa says you're studying Korean . . .

KAREN: I hope it'll help me . . .

(pause)

    I'm taking a trip to Korea . . .

LISA: You never told me.

KAREN: I didn't want everyone to know . . . before I was sure of going . . .

CARL: You going alone?

KAREN: No . . . It's a college tour group . . . I'll only be there for two weeks . . .

CARL: You going to visit the orphanage?

KAREN: I don't know . . .

LISA: You could visit my birth mom . . .

KAREN: Maybe I could . . .

(*to Carl*)

You know, Mom and Dad would like to see more of you . . .

CARL: I'm still sorting a lot of things out, okay?

KAREN: I guess we all are . . .

SPIRIT: Time to open up the presents . . .

(*Lisa and Karen pick up presents from behind the sofa*)

LISA: We brought these for you . . .

CARL: What for?

KAREN: Your new apartment . . .

(*Carl opens one and pulls out the Korean doll*)

CARL: I remember this . . .

LISA: Karen gave it to me . . . but I thought you should have it . . .

CARL: Thanks . . .

(*Carl opens the second present and pulls out a Chwibari mask*)

CARL: Where did you get this?

KAREN: We ordered it . . . from Korea . . .

CARL (*pause*): It's kind of amazing, isn't it?

LISA: What?

CARL: The three of us . . . sitting here . . .

(*They all hold hands*)

SPIRIT:
How we found each other in that orphanage . . .
So many years ago . . .
and flew like seeds in the wind . . .
across oceans and mountains . . .
from breaking hearts to hopeful hands . . .
from east to west and back again . . .
It's kind of amazing, isn't it?

(*They sit together on the riser, a mirror image of their being together at the orphanage. Lights cross-fade downstage to the Mask Dancer, who does a solo dance— MASK DANCE #13—downstage left in a spotlight. At the end of his solo, the MASK DANCER leads the line of all the dancers until they form two lines facing the audience. MASK DANCE #14: The dancers do several crossing moves and come to a halt facing each other closely in two lines. They make*) *several more moves and then step away into another long line that forms a tight circle center stage. They all hold their hansam in the middle and slowly, to the beat of the drum, pull up and finally out to face the audience in a pose. Lights go to black)*

END OF PLAY

Note: *Mask Dance* was performed at the Theater Mu in Minneapolis in 1995.

From *Mua He Do Lua/Red Fiery Summer*

lê thi diem thúy

SET AND COSTUMES:

The set consists of two rusted metal pipes positioned fifteen feet from each other. The stage right pipe should be a foot shorter than the stage left pipe. Both pipes are topped with conical straw hats. Cinder blocks surround the base of each pipe. The stage right pipe is surrounded by broken blocks while the stage left pipe is surrounded by whole blocks. A rubber band jump rope is tied to the stage right pipe, hidden in the cinder blocks. The jump rope will later be used as a clothesline.

Upstage left, in front of the stage left pipe, sit two low bamboo stools. A San Diego Padres baseball cap sits atop one stool, with the insignia visible to the audience.

Upstage right, beside the stage right pipe, are two bamboo baskets, large enough to sit in. One basket contains: a large off-white bed sheet, suit pants, a dress shirt and wooden clothespins. The other basket contains: a matching suit jacket, a tattered turquoise-colored silk shirt, a fedora, a string of fake poinsettias, a red ribbon and wooden clothespins. The costumes should be treated as other personas sharing the stage. When they are hung on the clothesline in the first half of the show, they are right side up, their fronts to the audience. In the second half of the show, they are hung upside down, a literal rendering of the world turned upside down. At various points in the narrative, each costume becomes emblematic of a character, a voice, a mood or a persona. Costumes, set pieces and props also double, becoming other than whatever they were initially introduced as. As with all aspects of this piece, the emphasis is on the fluidity of elements, whether they be text, gesture, set, costume or prop.

Red Fiery Summer

Light Cue #14: Cross-fade General with Silhouette Special.

(*T puts on black pajama pants behind curtain. Comes out while putting on blue shirt.*) People often ask me, Do you have memories of Vietnam? You must not remember much about the war because wasn't it over by the time you were born? I grew up asking my mother,

When was I born?
You were born in Red Fiery Summer.
But I was born in January.
You were still born in Red Fiery Summer.

Red Fiery Summer. I used to think this was my mother, being poetic and contrary, painting a winter month in words which hold the heat of summer. But recently I found out that to many South Vietnamese, Mua He Do Lua describes a particular season of warfare.

In April of 1972, the Communists launched a series of strategic attacks all across Vietnam in response to U.S. bombings of the North. Officially, these attacks are referred to as the Easter Offensive of 1972 but Mother, and many Vietnamese like her, who remember the fires which scorched the countryside that summer, invoke the entire year of 1972 in this one phrase.

So when my mother said to me, You were born in Red Fiery Summer, she was saying, as far as I'm concerned, You were born in the burning heart of war.

Red Fiery Summer. The history of this phrase in my life is off center, askew. Explosive and poetic, it gives a collage perspective. I've used it to lure you here tonight, a vision of summer at the beginning of winter. A promise of heat before the first snowfall.

This is how I know war, in its seductive contrasts. People say the U.S. lost its innocence in Vietnam. But how can we speak of innocence and genocide in one breath?

There is an unofficial prayer which Marines recited during the Vietnam War. It goes something like this:

(*T takes center stage, crosses arms.*)

Though I walk through the valley
in the shadow of death
I fear no evil
for I am the biggest
baddest motherfucker
in the valley

Now I lay me down to sleep
I pray the lord the WAR to keep
so MARINES can come and save the day
and I can earn my goddamn pay

God bless the United States
God bless the drill instructors
God bless the Marine Corps.

THIS PRAYER WILL BE MEMORIZED.

(*Long beat.*)

Fuck you . . . I know barbed wire. I know bombing. I know blown-off hands, heads, legs, missing bodies, twisted into improbable formations, mutations, fishes floating with their bellies up. Breathing becomes poison.

I know gutting, leveling, locating, targeting, searching, destroying, sweeping in, and blasting to high water.

I know fucking in, fucking with, getting fucked, fucked over, fucked again, fucked from all sides, fuck till you bleed, fuck till you scream, a relentless fucking!

But no. No. I don't want to fuck you here tonight. I just want to seduce you. With a story.

FOB

(*T walks to stage right stool.*) **Light Cue #15**: Dim General, bring up Slide Special.

(*T sits down.*) **Slide Cue #9**: FOB: family photo of T as a child.

it begins with a dream i had
about a shoddy boat moving through water
heavy
fragile
something about the sun
it gets so hot
so warm so
longing for your touch
water is to drown in
i cried all my tears away
it's all a true story
it's a lie
it's a dream

(*T stands.*) I remember a young Vietnamese girl being carried out of the officers' quarters on the big, grey naval ship. She was carried high on the shoulder of one officer while another officer followed close behind, beaming a proud smile. She was expressionless like a statue and they carried her like a trophy. They brought her onto the deck of the ship where a large group of Vietnamese refugees stood huddled, close together.

I felt sorry for this girl. They picked her out of the crowd of people and took her away. She disappeared into the grey hold of the ship and emerged scrubbed clean, dressed in new clothes, her hair washed and combed and parted.

I asked my father, What happened to that girl?

I remember she didn't say anything. Even when the villagers turned away from her. Ashamed at the sight of her so changed from them. Even her father, who took one step forward to receive her, stopped suddenly. Unable to bring himself to touch her. I thought, How terrible. They took her away and changed her so that even her father, the only member of her family on the ship with her, couldn't look at her without seeing their mark on her.

I asked my father, What happened to that girl?

He said, Ah, Thúy . . . I'm sorry.

(*T snaps fingers, assumes wrestling stance.*) Me and my father wrestling because when I was fifteen I was lying in bed, trying to fall asleep, when I heard my father's voice say, I hate her! Every time I look at her, I just hate her. I don't understand why, but I can't stand the sight of her. I hate her!

I asked my mother why my father had said this about me. At first she said, He didn't mean it. But then she said, Are you sure you didn't dream it? Didn't you say you were half asleep already?

(*T snaps fingers, assumes wrestling stance.*) Me and my father wrestling because I can speak better English than him. I'm his translator. I'm filling out school applications and work applications for both of us while he's walking around the house, muttering the spelling of his name in English. (*T slowly walks in a circle, pointing out each letter in the air, as it is uttered, as though writing the name in the air.*) M-I-N-H. M-I-N-H. M-I-N-H.

I am wanting to beat him up because I miss his bad-ass swagger. I am wanting to beat the sadness out of him before he turns it on me, breaking it across my body until I am down on my knees in front of him screaming, Ba, Ba! It's me! It's me!

Ah, Thúy . . . I'm sorry.

Slide Cue #10: FOB out.

Our Time in Linda Vista

Light Cue #16: General up, Slide Special out as T carries the suit jacket, which has been on the floor beside the stage right stool, to the clothesline and hangs the jacket upside down. T begins speaking after the suit pants are hung upside down. T continues speaking as she hangs the remainder of the costumes upside down. The clothesline from stage right to stage left consists of: suit jacket, suit pants, sheet, fedora, baseball cap, pj top, dress shirt.

We live in the country of California, the province of San Diego, the village of Linda Vista. We live in old Navy Housing bungalows which were built in the '40s and '50s. Since the '80s these bungalows house Vietnamese, Cambodian, and Laotian refugees from the Vietnam War.

When we moved in, we had to sign a form promising not to put fish bones down the garbage disposal.

We are happy in Linda Vista. As happy as we could ever be outside of Vietnam. So many of us here in Linda Vista, it's as good as Vietnam. For now. My family goes crazy in Linda Vista. This is where my father begins dancing in the alley at night. Where my mother shaves her hair off in a fit of rage. Where my grandparents arrive suddenly one day and then just as suddenly are taken from us.

In Linda Vista, we grow a garden full of lemongrass, mint, cilantro and basil. The family next door raises chickens for eggs. In the morning, their rooster sits on the fence and crows off and on, all day long, until dark comes. We throw day-old rice into a shallow pit in the middle of a dirt field which separates our row of yellow houses from an identical row of yellow houses which sits across from ours and faces us like a sad twin. Pigeons flock to this rice, cooing.

Linda Vista makes us hungry for Vietnam but it is not Vietnam. To compensate, Ba begins to drink more. Ma begins to gamble. I begin listening to Vietnamese New Wave music. (*T sings "get in my car, boy / you know I'll drive you far / you know I've got a car . . ." which is interrupted by T shouting in Ba's voice. T boxes during the following lines.*) At night, I hear my father boxing shadows outside my bedroom window. Every time Ba gets drunk, he wants to debate the story about the water buffalo crossing the bridge.

(*T stumbles drunkenly, assumes Ba's voice.*)

I don't think it went over the bridge. No. It went under the bridge. Yeah, that's right. The water went up to its neck and almost into its ears but it still went under the bridge. What do you mean it couldn't have happened that way? What do you mean it doesn't matter whether the water buffalo went under the bridge or over the bridge? It matters! It's what I remember. What I remember matters!

Then my mother shaved her hair off and that's when people in Linda Vista began to say that my parents, especially my mother, were crazy.

(*T puts hand on hip, assumes posture of gossiping women.*)

She's got poison in her, that girl. So spiteful . . .
And she was so pretty too!
What a poisonous temper she's got.
He must be so mad at her, huh?
Mad? Because she looks so stupid?
You think she looks stupid? She looks scary to me.
She looks like a man.
Yes, the way she sets her jaw when she walks down the street.
She looks meaner than a man.
Meaner than a man?
She looks meaner than my man.
And your man is pretty mean!

(*T leans against "door" with one hand up.*) My mother has locked herself in the bathroom while my father is passed out drunk on the bed. I am leaning against the bathroom door, listening for her movements:

Ma, you can come out now. Everything's quiet. Ma, everything is quiet now. Ma, oi . . .

(*T stands up straight, extends hand toward audience. Assumes Ma's voice.*) Thúy, don't be afraid. It's me. It's still me. Don't you recognize me? These are my hands. I told you you would always know me by my hands. Do you remember when you were a little girl, I showed you how to wash the rice with your hands? (*T begins washing rice motion.*) Your two big eyes focused on my hands going round and round. I said just follow the motion of my hands and you began to sway back and forth, back and forth, moving your body in the rhythm of my hands.

(*T runs hands through hair then "cuts" hair with fingers.*) Thúy, it gets so hot in my head, all my thoughts racing in a fever. This hair gets too heavy. Weighs me down. Makes it hard for me to stand up straight so . . . I am just going to cut some of this off, move things around and make more room for. Me. To. Breathe. (*T rests head in the palm of the left hand while stroking hair and face with the right hand.*)

(*T pulls poinsettias from basket and strings them along the clothesline.*) At Christmas, my father decorates a plastic tree with fake snow and shiny red and gold bulbs. I am sent to the store to collect empty boxes. When I bring them home, my mother pulls out rolls of generic "Season's Greetings" wrapping paper and reams of red ribbon. My parents sit down in the living room and wrap the empty boxes. Now, these boxes should be the model for every professional gift wrapper. The presentation is impeccable. Our Christmas tree, with its base surrounded by beautifully wrapped gift boxes, is the perfect picture of Christmas. (*T makes a "gift box" by tying a bow around one of the stools.*) But my parents said to me, We are not concerned with the perfect picture of Christmas. (*T holds "gift box" up.*) It is often hollow inside. (*T turns "gift box" on its side and pushes it against base of stage right pipe with bow visible to the audience.*)

(*T walks to stage left stool and sits down.*) In Linda Vista, my mother received the black-and-white photograph of her parents sitting in bamboo chairs in their front courtyard. Her sister Nga sent it to her from Vietnam. When my mother opened the envelope and held the photograph in her hand, she began to cry. She had not lingered over her parents' features since the day she left home to be with my father. So to my mother, this photograph was more than the image of her parents. It was her parents.

She enlisted me to help her move them in. (*T stands on stool.*) She lifted me high up in her arms and I slipped the stiff envelope into the open spaces of the attic. I pushed the envelope the length of my arms and down to my fingertips. I pushed it so far it was beyond reach but Ma said it was enough, they had come to live with us and sometimes you don't need to see or touch people to know that they're there. I was so happy my grandparents had come to help ease the fire in my mother's head.

(*T steps off stool.*) A month after my mother and I moved my grandparents into the attic, everyone on our square block of Navy Housing received an eviction notice. It said we had a month to get out. We had a new owner who wanted to tear everything down and build again. We were priority tenants for the new complex but we couldn't afford the new rent so it didn't matter. If we didn't get out in time, all our possessions would be confiscated in accordance with some section of a law book we were supposed to have known about but had never seen. We couldn't believe this notice so we threw it away. But one day, we came home to find a fence surrounding our entire block.

The fence is tall, silver and see-through. Chain-link, it rattles when you shake it and wobbles when you lean against it. It circles the block like a bad dream. It is not funny like a line of laundry whose flying shirts and empty pants suggest human birds and vanishing acts. This fence presses sharply against my brain. We three stand still as posts looking at it, then at each other, in disbelief.

At night, we come back. (*T draws a circle in the air and steps through.*) Ba cuts a hole in the fence and we step through. Quiet, we break into our own house through the back window. Quiet (*T picks up stool, using it as trash bag while running in a circle*), we steal back everything that is ours. We fill ten-gallon garbage bags with pots and pans, flip-flops, the porcelain figure of Mary and our wooden Buddha. When we are done, we are clambering and breathless. We can hear police cars coming to get us, though it's quiet! (*T stops running, continues holding stool.*)

We tumble out the window like people tumbling across continents. We are time traveling, weighed down by heavy furniture and bags of precious junk. We find ourselves leaning against Ba's yellow truck. Ma calls his name, her voice reaching like a hand feeling for a tree trunk in the darkness:

   Minh, anh Minh, oi. Minh, anh Minh . . .

(*T sits down on stool. Every time T assumes Ma's voice, she is crying.*) In the car, Ma starts to cry and then she screams,

   Take me back. Oh my god, take me back. I can't believe . . . I've left them there to die. I can't go with you. Take me back!

Ma wants Ba to stop the car but Ba doesn't know why. He thinks it's just that her head is in a fever. He says, My, we'll come back tomorrow. It's too late now. Ba puts his foot on the gas pedal. Our car races through the empty streets. We drive for hours, going nowhere and Ma keeps crying,

   I need air, water. Thúy, roll the window down. I can't breathe. I can't breathe.

(*T stands and walks to center stage.*) In the morning, we come back and the world is flat. Linda Vista is laying down like a jagged brush stroke of sunburnt yellow. There is a big sign inside the fence which reads, Coming Soon: Townhouses; Condominiums; Family Homes.

Beside these words is a water-color drawing of a large, pink complex.

We stand on the edge of the chain-link fence, sniffing the air for the scent of lemongrass, scanning this flat world for a sign of our blue sea. A wrecking ball dances madly through our house. Everything has burst wide open and sunk down low. Then I hear her calling them. She is whispering, Ma/Ba, Ma/Ba, Ma/Ba. The whole world becomes two butterfly wings rubbing against my ears.

Listen, they are sitting in the attic, sitting like royalty. Shining in the dark, buried by a wrecking ball. Paper fragments floating across the surface of the sea and there's not a trace of blood anywhere except here, in my throat, where I am telling you all this.

Song: a mosh pit of blues in no particular language
The performance opens and ends with a song. In the begining of the perform-ance, it is sung with the performer's back to the audience. At the end, it is sung with the performer facing the audience. This song is sung to a melody which sounds like a traditional Vietnamese lullaby. The lyrics consist of Vietnamese and Vietnamese-sounding words, arranged in an order which, in fact, makes no "sense." Translated, the song is gibberish, though its mood —one of long-ing and sorrow—is genuine. The song must convey this mood.

Light Cue #17: Cross-fade Center Special with General as T begins singing, this time facing the audience.

Light Cue #18: Fade to black as T spreads arms while singing.

END

Note: *Mua He Do Lua/Red Fiery Summer* was first performed on December 2, 1994 at the Northampton Center for the Arts.
Writer/performer—lê thi diem thúy
Set and costume design—Emily Park
Lighting design—Aimee Schneider

From *Three Lives*

ALEX LUU

House goes to black.

BEGIN SOUND CUE 1. (War Sound FX) PROJECT SLIDES.

Slide 1: Sepia-toned photograph of an Asian woman in her 20s. She is holding a parasol and smiling; she is natural, effervescent, and radiant. An Asian Ingrid Bergman in her prime.

Slide 2: Sepia-toned photograph of same Asian woman. A close-up that is even more striking than the parasol picture.

Slide 3: Sepia-toned photograph of Asian woman and handsome Asian man in his early 20s; they are standing side by side, smiling and full of hope.

Slide 4: Sepia-toned photograph of baby Alex and sister Irene standing in front of a classic '60s-model motorcycle with shiny rims and stainless steel handlebars.

Slide 5: Sepia-toned photograph of family portrait: Asian woman (mother), Asian man (father), baby Alex and sister Irene.

Slide 6: Close-up of baby Alex.

Narration on SOUND CUE 1:

Saigon. 1975. The Viet Congs are coming. When you're nine years old, it didn't matter who was wrong or who was right. Faceless Communist soldiers with enough firepower to wipe out a village, even a city. Thousands and thousands of families are leaving their homeland.

On last slide, END SOUND CUE 1.

Alex enters stage in darkness.

Lights up.

I wake up to faces and voices. Some I recognize some I do not.
(in Chinese) *"Wake up! Wake up! Hurry up and eat! We can't be late. Eat your rice and put your clothes on! Hurry up. We can't be late."*
Mom hands me a bowl of barbecue pork fried rice. Aaaahhhh . . . barbecue pork fried rice. My favorite. Grandpa's favorite. Soft shiny white rice mixed perfectly with little pieces of succulent barbecue pork, finely diced green onions and thin layers of egg yolk with a dash of black pepper and mild soy sauce. Through sleepy, watery eyes, it is like a surreal dream—a great, big party at my house. Look, there's fourth uncle, chomping on a *cha su bao*. There's first uncle, sipping hot tea. All my loved ones are here. The men are

with the men, whispering in hushed voices, as if plotting some secret operation. The women are with the women, crying and hugging each other. Why are
they crying? I thought this was a party . . .

Did somebody die . . . ?

*Alex sits down and begins to eat his bowl of fried rice. After a few mouthfuls,
Alex gets up.*

Grandpa, what are you doing? Why . . . why are you tearing up the family pictures? Why are you throwing them into the fire? What are you doing? Ah-ma,
why is Grandpa tearing the family pictures? My baby pictures . . . Ah-ma, Ah-ba,
sis and me at the American embassy . . . our trip to Cho Lon with a few of Ah-
ma's ITT friends . . . Tet celebration with Ah-ma's American and French work
mates . . . look . . . my favorite picture . . . me sitting on your lap at your birthday
party . . . but why are you tearing them up? Ah-ma, why is Grandpa doing that?

*"Because if the Viet Congs know we have any ties to the Americans they
will kill everyone who's left behind after we leave."*

My baby pictures, my pictures . . . burning . . . burning. My childhood . . .
just ashes fluttering in the wind . . . fluttering in the wind.

Alex runs in place.

The wind. The wind hot and dry, whipping up sand and dirt. Can barely
see. Have to get there on time. Get to the American embassy. Get there on
time. Can't be late. Just another day in Saigon, just another day to be shot and
killed if we don't make it on time. Run faster. Get there on time. Mom and
Dad have been planning for this too long for it to fail. In the distance, a swarm
of black hornets swoop over the mountainside, heading straight towards us.
They increase speed and momentum, yet appearing immobile to the naked eye.
They fly in perfect formation. In a matter of seconds, the hornets become
larger and larger.

"Cover your face! Cover your face!"
"We're all going to die! This is the end! We're going to die!"
"I'm scared! Ah-ba, I'm scared!"
"Be strong! We'll be all right, son!"
"Ah-ba, I'm so scared! I think I'm peeing in my pants!"
"Be strong! Don't pee! Be strong! Hold it in!"
"Ah-ba, I think I'm going to pee . . . !"
"Be strong! No pee!"

"Ah-ba, I peed! I peed in my pants! I'm scared! I'm so scared! I'm . . . I'm
. . . I'm hungry! I'm so hungry! I should have eaten last night!"

Lights change (FLASHBACK).

BEGIN SOUND CUE 2. (Crickets Sound FX)

The night before, we are evacuated out of the hangar and ordered to jump
into ditches dug by MP soldiers. Dusty, rock-filled ditches no higher than four-
and-a-half feet by three feet wide. Jump in and shut up and pray. Pray you
don't get hit by shrapnel or grenades. Could blind you or worse, slice your
head clean off at the neck. The VCs are inching their way near the airfield . . .

I can't breathe . . . choking on grimy dust and body odor . . . It's so cramped in here. I'm starving. . . . The night drags on . . .

MANUAL FADE SOUND CUE 2.

Finally . . . the MP soldiers pass out small Styrofoam bowls of rice. Rice! Yes! Finally, RICE!!

Alex wolfs down rice like there's no tomorrow, cheeks ballooning with each massive scoop from bowl to mouth.

Mmmm . . . AAAAARRRRGGGHHHHH!!! (*spits out rice*) This isn't rice! It looks like rice, but it is not rice! It has no taste!

"Ah-ma, are you sure this is rice?"

"*Shhhh!! Just eat it.* "

"Ah-ma, do the *gwailo* think this is rice? The *gwailo* use this to make fried rice?"

"*Be quiet. Just eat it.*"

"But Ah-ma . . . this is not rice! Did the *gwailo* cook it in a rice cooker? Did the *gwailo* use the 'finger method'?"

"*Shhh!! Just eat it! Be quiet and just eat it.*"

(pause) "Mom . . . who's Uncle Ben?"

Blackout.

My first taste of America. Rice that doesn't taste like rice.

I'm hungry . . . I'm hungry . . .

Lights up.

BEGIN SOUND CUE 3. (Helicopters Sound FX)

"Ah-ba . . . I'm hungry . . . "

"*Be strong. Hold on, be strong!*'

About fifty yards away, the black hornets descend, transforming into squadrons of gigantic military helicopters.

"*Run for your lives!*'

"*Run for the helicopters!*"

We scramble in, bodies slamming against bodies, bones knocking against bones. Ten, twenty, thirty, pile in, there's more room, forty, fifty, sixty, we can all fit in, squeeze, squeeze! Seventy, eighty . . . ninety . . . come on, come on, get in! There's more room, we can all fit in! Come on, more room, we can fit in! Hurry! Wait . . . .wait! we're shaking, rumbling. No! We're taking off, we're taking off! No, not yet! There's more people, there's more people! Don't close the door yet! Women and children are hanging on, let them in! American soldiers pry their fingers loose! No! Bodies falling! Ah-ma, tell the American soldiers to let them in! There's more room! Ah-ma, they're falling, they're falling! NOOOO!!!

END SOUND CUE 3.

Blackout.

My second taste of America. Every man for himself. No one there to lift you up. You're on your own now.

From *Texas*

JUDY SOO HOO

Act One

SCENE ONE: GO WEST, COLLEGE BOY

SETTING: A small, cramped trailer. Dirty dishes stack up on the counter. Machine parts litter the tables and chairs. Hubcaps and car parts scatter. License plates from places like Missouri or Mississippi are tacked to the wall.

(DANNY, *nervous in tank top and jeans, enters carrying a suitcase, followed by* STEVEN, *a young college student dressed in a button-down and trousers.*)

DANNY: I'm glad I found you at the airport, when I did. I've never been at the airport. Never had a reason to go anywhere. All the planes flying in the air makes me a little high strung. Whoosh! I don't like to be wired and jammed up. My brother is high strung.

STEVEN: I was waiting for a while.

DANNY: You weren't waiting long.

STEVEN: Two hours.

DANNY: Hey, I found you with my sign. I made that sign myself with magic markers.

(DANNY *holds up a crudely drawn sign that reads,* "College Boy Wanted.")

DANNY: You're a College Boy. Yes, you are. Yes, I did find you. Magic markers. I don't know what magic is in markers, maybe it would make me go fly.

STEVEN: Is this the place?

DANNY: You like it, huh? I can tell.

(DANNY *sweeps several machine parts into a bucket.*)

STEVEN: It's rather small.

DANNY: No, it's not. No. No.

STEVEN: Yes, it rather is.

DANNY: Nah, me and my brother think of it as large. Roomy.

(STEVEN *sits on the lone recliner with duct tape strapped around it to keep the filling from spilling out.*)

DANNY: You can't sit there. Not there. That's my brother's chair. Get off. Get off it before he comes home.

STEVEN: Wait a minute. You mean . . .

DANNY: I'm not mean. My brother is mean.

STEVEN: No, no. You mean that I'm sharing this space with you and your brother?

DANNY: Yeah.

STEVEN: No, no. The college arranged this housing and they said that I would have a guest room. In a lovely house.

DANNY: We had a house. A big house with see-through windows and a bathroom and running water. We had a house since last week. But because of the fire, not his fault, not his fault, we have to live here.

STEVEN: I don't have a room?

DANNY: We have plenty of room. Look around. Look around. We can share.

STEVEN: I'm going to see the college housing board.

DANNY: No, you can't do that. No can do. No, my brother won't like it.

STEVEN: What's your name again? Who's your brother?

DANNY: I'm not Duke. He's Duke, named after the Hawaiian surfer. But he's a crazy motherfucker. He bites women on the back. Men too. Cuts men up. Cuts up cars. Cuts cars to ship over there. Chops up the engine two by two. Rolls out the tires so the car's just a stump. He's been in the can for cutting up cars. Locked up in a cell, four by four, for months, years. He bites bullets. Shoots guns, two in hands, two by two. He's a wild boy. He's a crazy motherfucker. He's Duke. I'm not.

STEVEN: Who are you?

DANNY: I'm Danny. I'm not a crazy motherfucker.

STEVEN: And I'm not stupid. I'm going to the housing board.

DANNY: Oh, that's not good. Not good.

STEVEN: I've been traveling for miles on miles on an airplane. When the plane dipped and buckled, my stomach turned and landed in my throat. Now, I've landed on firm ground and I'm going to school on a scholarship and I just can't stay in a rinny, tin tin trailer.

DANNY: It's a Winnebago.

STEVEN: Fine, Winnebago. I would appreciate it if you would drive me to the housing board.

DANNY: I can't.

STEVEN: We just came from your delightfully rusty truck.

DANNY: The housing board can't help you. Not today. No way.

STEVEN: I'll be the judge of that.

DANNY: They're closed. It's Sunday. Everything is closed today, except for the drinking bars. We can go for dollar beer with the little foam heads.

STEVEN: I've landed in an ungodly hell.

DANNY: Not Hell. Not Hell. You landed in Texas.

STEVEN: Tomorrow you're taking me to the housing office.

DANNY: I see. I see. I've got to talk to Duke.

STEVEN: No talking. Just drive me there.

DANNY: I'll ask Duke.

STEVEN: Don't ask Duke. He's a crazy motherfucker.

DANNY: I'm not Duke.

STEVEN: No, you're not.

(DUKE, *wearing a tank top and jeans identical to those of his brother,* DANNY, *enters, slamming doors.*)

DANNY: This is the College Boy, Duke.

DUKE: College Boy, what's your name?

STEVEN: Steven.

DUKE: Steven. That's an awful name. Cheap and tawdry.

DANNY: Duke, Steven wants to go away.

DUKE: Go away? You just came? Are we bad company?

STEVEN: You're great company. Real cheerful. But I wanted my own room.

DUKE: You have it. This is your own room. It's also my brother's and mine.

STEVEN: I don't want to share. I'm funny like that.

DANNY: We like to share. We're funny like that.

DUKE: Shut up! We like to share. We're funny like that. Look, sit down.

(DUKE *points to the recliner covered in duct tape.*)

STEVEN: Is that your chair?

DUKE: I like to share. Sit.

(STEVEN *sits.* DUKE *sits next to him, the two of them in the lone recliner chair.*)

DUKE: A man gots to sit when he gets home from work. He has to find a place to land or he'll just float away.

STEVEN: What do you do?

DUKE: I chop things up.

STEVEN: Cars?

DUKE: Have you been talking to my brother?

DANNY: I just told him the truth.

DUKE: The truth is I haven't chopped up a car in months. Three months. I work in the meat packing industry.

DANNY: Duke's a meat chopper.

DUKE: I'm a butcher.

STEVEN: I've never met a butcher.

DUKE: We butchers work in a meat-packing plant, that's what they call it. To me, it's just the slaughterhouse. I work with a bunch of Mexicans, a couple of Armenians, ex-rice farmers from Cambodia, runaways from Laos and a sprinkling of Chinese from Vietnam. We work in the cutting room, the chopping yard, splitting open an Angus or a porter or a Hereford with our swirling saws, carving up the carcass, scooping out the cow guts, vacuuming out the insides. Then we hack, chop through the thick white creamy layer of fat, down to the marbled meat, down further to the bone and way down to the spongy marrow. Texas is a cow. We ship beef to forty-nine states and beyond, hanging on a freezer hook or shrink-wrapped in plastic.

DANNY: Duke's good at chopping.

DUKE: I'm good at chopping.

STEVEN: It's good that you're good at chopping.

DUKE: Yeah, a man has to be good at something. What are you good at?

STEVEN: I'm studying architecture.

DANNY: What's architecture?

STEVEN: I study buildings.

DUKE: That won't do you any good.

STEVEN: I study how to build buildings.

DANNY: Duke, he can build our house up again. The one that got burnt.

DUKE: He can't build up what was burnt.

STEVEN: I just started studying. I'm not very good.

DANNY: You'll build it, won't you? Yes, you'll build it.

DUKE: Stop that wheezing! Or I'll put you back in the bughouse.

DANNY: Not the bugs. Not the bughouse. Don't take me back to the bug-house!

DUKE: I know you don't want to go back to the bughouse.

DANNY: I just want my house back. My room.

DUKE: Stop it! Time to go to bed. Aren't you tired, College Boy?

STEVEN: I'm very tired. Maybe I should stay at a motel.

DUKE: Nonsense, College Boy, you're staying with us, the college housing board said so. Me and Danny signed a contract saying that we'll take Prime A Select care of you. Now, we'll help you get ready for bed.

DANNY: Yep, yep, we'll take Prime A Select care of you. What made you come to Texas, College Boy?

STEVEN: Well, I needed to get out.

DUKE: Yeah, so you wanted to get out?

STEVEN: I just wanted to get out, get out over there, get out in the middle of out there. I never been out in the middle of Texas, never been out in the middle of out there. I got a flying ticket, an interest-free scholarship from a college in Texas who was recruiting minority students to fluff up their demographics. And college housing board said I would be staying with a nice Asiatic family in a house. When I landed at the airport, the twinkling neon sign said, "Welcome to Eden. Welcome to Eden, Texas."

DUKE: Yep, we're a nice Asiatic family.

DANNY: Duke, what's Asiatic?

DUKE: Shut up! College Boy, you're stuck with us for a while. Let's go to sleep.

(DANNY *and* DUKE *climb into the single bed on stage.* DANNY *and* DUKE *sandwich* STEVEN *in the middle as they clamber into bed, looking like three little boy babies in a too narrow bed.*)

STEVEN: Is this the only bed?

DANNY: Yeah. We broke the rest.

STEVEN: I could sleep on that recliner.

DUKE: Nobody sleeps in that recliner. You can sit but you can't sleep.

STEVEN: I could sleep on the floor.

DANNY: You don't want to do that. Rats.

STEVEN: I could sleep outside. Outside there are no rats.

DUKE: Nope. Wild, feral dogs run unchained. College Boy, you're green and tender like a newly sprung alfalfa sprout. Out there is a wild untamed unbroken country that could break you, snap you, snip you in two. You're safer in here with us. Between us.

DANNY: Tell us a story, Duke. Tell us a scary story.

DUKE: You want to hear it? You want to hear it?

STEVEN: I'll hear it.

DUKE: He lives in the basement. Under the baseboards. Under the house we live on top of. On top we scream because bombs are falling on Cambodia. On top we are crazy-stupid. He's on the bottom, crazy-fucked up. He's old we are told. Older than Cambodia, older than the basement he lives up in. Down we go if we scream for ice cream. Bottom up we tumble when we scream for ice cream. He will grab our ankles by the baseboard as we go down on the wood boards. With our feet, we will tumble. Upstairs, bombs are falling. London Bridge is falling. The sky is falling. Bombs are dropping. We scream for ice cream. The walls are falling. The door is closing. Locking us up with the man, who is old. Older than we are told.

DANNY: We scream for ice cream!

STEVEN: That was strangely moving.

DUKE: Yeah. Time to go to sleep. Lights out.

(*The stage is pitch black. The sound of crickets punctuates the air with a steady, melodic pitch. A soft whimper breaks through the song of the crickets, followed by a louder whimper and louder until it is a beating drum.*)

DUKE: What's that wheezing? Who's doing all that sneezing? Is that you, Danny Boy?

DANNY: Not me. Not me. Okay me. Okay, it's me. I'm scared.

DUKE: Lights up! What is it?

(*Lights up in the trailer.*)

DANNY: You told a scary story.

DUKE: College Boy, was that a scary story?

STEVEN: It was the most unusual scary story.

DUKE: But you told me to tell.

DANNY: I can't sleep. Can't sleep. You know what happens when I can't sleep.

STEVEN: What happens when he can't sleep?

DUKE: He gets bugged. He gets bugged out.

DANNY: I don't want to get bugged out. I can't get bugged out. Do you know what happens when I get bugged out?

STEVEN: Don't let him get bugged out. I don't want to know what happens when he gets bugged out.

DANNY: In the bughouse, bugs crawl on your skin. They creep up on your face, go up your nose, down your mouth, in your eyehole, out your butthole. They burrow in deep, make nests in the folds of your skin, lick your fat, eat your dick. Bugs devour you, man, spit you out, turn you around, make you go down on your knees. Make you plead, beg on your little knees. So you're a little man begging, pleading, begging and pleading,

"Don't make me go back to the bughouse! Don't make me go back to the bughouse! Don't make me go back!"

DUKE: Nobody's going back, Danny Boy.

STEVEN: What's the bughouse?

DUKE: The bughouse is where they keep the bugs.

DANNY: I'm scared. I'm silly scared.

DUKE: Let's play a game. Do you like games? (*To* STEVEN) What's your name?

STEVEN: I told you. My name is Steven. I like games. But I thought we were going to sleep.

DUKE: Can't go to sleep yet. Danny's scared of the bugs.

DANNY: Big bugs. Little bugs. Crawling. Creeping. Burrowing. Digging.

DUKE: We have to ride him out of his scared spell.

STEVEN: Now? We ride now?

DUKE: Do you have something to do? What do you have happening on? He needs to get ridden out of his scared spell.

DANNY: College Boy, play with us. We are good players.

STEVEN: I'm not good at playing.

DANNY: We'll teach you how to play good.

DUKE: Danny needs you to play.

DANNY: I want you to play. Play fun. Play good.

STEVEN: I don't want to play. We can watch TV.

DUKE: We don't have TV. TV makes you docile, dead. We need to be alert, expecting, playing.

DANNY: Just one game, College Boy, and then we can sleep the rest of the night.

STEVEN: Just one game? One game?

DUKE: Just one.

STEVEN: Well, what are we playing?

DUKE: Let me think and see.

STEVEN: What do you know? What did your Daddy teach you how to play?

DANNY: Pa taught us how to play Mahjongg Poker.

DUKE: Don't talk about Pa.

DANNY: Ma and Pa owned a poker and pool house. But it got blown away.

DUKE: I told you not to talk about Pa. Quit your wheezing.

DANNY: I was just being friendly.

DUKE: I am friendly. Aren't I? So what games do you know, Steven?

STEVEN: We could play Scrabble. We could spell out words.

DANNY: Duke's not good at spelling. I can spell though. I spell good.

DUKE: I can too spell. I can spell *police*.

STEVEN: No, that's not a good idea. I'll play your game. What do you want to play?

DUKE: Hold on to your hats, boys. Let's play piggy.

DANNY: Oh, good. Oh, good. I like piggy. Piggy. Piggy.

STEVEN: What's piggy?

DUKE: Hurry up. You two play piggy.

STEVEN: What are you playing?

DUKE: I'm playing the wolf.

DANNY: Good. Good. I don't like being the wolf.

STEVEN: Do I have to play piggy?

DANNY: Be quiet. We have to hide now.

(DANNY *and* STEVEN *hide behind the lone recliner chair.* DUKE *crouches and then stands.*)

DUKE: Come out, come out wherever you are. I'll huff and puff and I'll blow your house down.

DANNY: You're not getting in this house. You're not breaking down our house.

STEVEN: Let him have the house.

DUKE: I'm coming in.

DANNY: Don't let him in.

(DANNY *shoves* STEVEN *into the path of* DUKE.)

STEVEN: Get out, wolf!

DUKE: I'm the wolfman. I don't get out. I get it on!

(DUKE *climbs on* STEVEN's *back.*)

DUKE: Ride it, cowboy. Give me your best piggyback ride.

DANNY: Ride him, College Boy. Ride him. Give him a piggyback ride like he's never been ridden before.

STEVEN: You huffed and you puffed and you blew the house down. By the hair of my chinny, chin, chin you blew the house down. Big bad wolf.

DUKE: I'm the wolfman.

DANNY: He's the wolfman.

STEVEN: Shut up! He's not the wolfman.

(DUKE *rides* STEVEN *around the trailer.*)

DUKE: I'll huff and puff and blow the house down.

STEVEN: You huffed and puffed and blew the house down. What happened to the big house? The housing board told me I would be living in a big house. Did you blow your house down? Did you huff, big bad wolfman? Did you blow it down? Blow the house down with your big bad breath? Blow. Blow. Blow.

(DUKE *bites* STEVEN *on the back.* STEVEN *yells a big throaty cry of a wounded pig.*)

STEVEN: He bit me on the back.

DANNY: I told you he bites people on the back. He's a crazy motherfucker.

STEVEN: You didn't have to bite me on the back.

DUKE: I bit you on the back because you weren't playing fair.

STEVEN: I was playing. I was playing fair.

DUKE: You didn't. You didn't play fair. Nobody talks. Nobody talks about the big house.

DANNY: Not his fault. Not his fault.

STEVEN: Nobody talks about the big house. What's in the big house?

DANNY: Ma and Pa lived in the big house. Danny and Duke, too.

DUKE: We used to live in the big house. One big happy family in the big house. Quit it. Quit it. We can't go back. We can't go back to the big house. We live in the driveway, now. We live in the underbushes. We live in a trailer now.

DANNY: Winnebago, Duke. We live in a Winnebago.

DUKE: We're just trash. We're cast-off people. We're left-behind riffraff. We're throwaways. We're the bottom feeders of the weed-eaters.

DANNY: I'm Danny. I'm not Duke. He's Duke.

STEVEN: I'm the College Boy. Steven.

DANNY: Duke went to college. City college in the city. Went for half a year.

STEVEN: What did you study?

DUKE: It's better to ask, what didn't I study.

DANNY: Duke didn't study.

DUKE: I threw down the studying and stayed blue collar.

DANNY: Duke studied truck driving after that.

DUKE: Eighteen wheeler. I drove an eighteen wheeler. Passed the driving test. Passed on the first try. But I threw away my trucking papers, turned down the poetics of the highway, and learned how to chop up cars.

DANNY: Duke didn't like driving.

DUKE: Didn't like the moving. Losing yourself on the highways. I cut up cars. Cut them up so that they'll stay put. Stay still.

STEVEN: I should get moving. I appreciate your hospitality. Your grace.

DANNY: We like being friendly.

DUKE: Believe it or not, we don't have many friends over.

STEVEN: I believe it.

DANNY: We haven't had company over in four, five, six . . .

DUKE: Seven years. Not since the accident.

DANNY: That's right, Duke. Not since the accident.

STEVEN: I best be going. I'll call a cab.

DUKE: We don't have a phone. I threw it against the wall.

STEVEN: I'll walk to town.

DUKE: This flat plain is pockmarked with gopher holes and scorpion nests. There's no counting what you could fall into without a good looking out for.

STEVEN: I'll borrow a flashlight. I have matches. Night is a good time for a long walk.

DUKE: Not this time of night. Danny Boy, what time is it?

DANNY: Nearly midnight, Duke.

DUKE: It's a bad time.

STEVEN: Why is it a bad time?

DANNY: It's the hour of the dogs.

DUKE: In this hour, in the hour of the dogs, wild unchained dogs run free. Our neighbor, Mr. Tom, has a pack of dogs, a pack of pit bulls, with collapsed-in faces and smashed-up noses. Every night about so, about now, about midnight, he lets them out, lets them run. Mr. Tom has funny ideas. This ex-colonel in the Taiwanese army thinks funny things. He thinks that insurance and banks are part of big government. He thinks in his funny mind that these dogs keep gangs of robbers away from his funny collection of jade monkeys. He calls the hours, about now, about midnight, when he lets his pack of dogs out, "the running of the pit bulls." The pit bulls will run after you, run you down, bite you in the heel, bite it off so it's just a bony stub. This hour, this time of night, is the time we stay in, stay put. Stay away.

DANNY: From the running of the pit bulls!

(DUKE *slides open a small window. Sound of pit bulls barking, snarling thunders through the room.*)

STEVEN: I'm stuck tonight with a nice Asiatic family.

DUKE: Yep, you're stuck with a nice Asiatic family.

DANNY: I'm hungry now, Duke. Are you hungry?

STEVEN: I'm not. I'm not hungry.

DUKE: Okay, we're hungry. Let's eat.

DANNY: Duke, chop us up some vegetables, cut up a side of beef, a slab of cow, a rump roast, a T- bone, a Kansas City cut. I like meat.

DUKE: We like meat. We like beef. We like cow.

STEVEN: I don't like meat. I don't like beef. I don't like cow.

DUKE: I'll chop and then cook. I'll let the pot simmer, let all the spices mingle, let all the juices mix, let the mixture stir and boil and then we'll eat. And you'll stay with us for a while. Stay with us.

(DUKE *goes into the cramped kitchen, opens the refrigerator. He takes out a head of lettuce and whacks it in two with a sharp swing of a knife. Lights out.*)

End of Scene.

SCENE TWO: YES, I'LL BUILD A BIG HOUSE

(DUKE *and* DANNY *are in the cramped kitchen.* DUKE *is cooking and* DANNY *is setting the table.*)

DUKE: Where's College Boy?

DANNY: He's washing up, washing up his bite mark.

DUKE: He's a marked man. He's been Duke marked.

DANNY: He's been marked up. Yep, I marked him on my calendar, too. I marked the day that he would come. Yep, yep, I circled it in red, circled the date, the 27th, and wrote "College Boy Comes To Stay." See.

(DANNY *shows* DUKE *a calendar with the 27th marked in red ink and an arrow pointing to the words* "College Boy Stays with Duke and Danny.")

DUKE: He better stay or we don't get our stipend from the housing board.

DANNY: Duke, what's a stipend?

DUKE: A stipend is like an allowance.

DANNY: We need an allowance.

DUKE: This allowance is gonna change our luck around, spin it, twist it, turn it around into something good. For seven years, for seven long years, ever since Ma and Pa . . .

DANNY: Kaboom. Kaboom.

DUKE: Our luck has been knotted and kinked, gnarled and hunched, full of misery and despair.

DANNY: Our luck has been prickly as a cactus tree.

DUKE: Smelly and rotten like day-old water.

(STEVEN *enters from the bathroom door.*)

STEVEN: I checked my bite and it didn't break any skin.

DUKE: It's a love bite.

STEVEN: Listen, I don't love you. I hate you. You're a biter. I hate biters. I'm going to the housing board and tell them that you bit me. You're a crazy motherfucker.

DANNY: I told you so.

DUKE: Listen, I'm sorry I bit you, but I bite people on the back. It's part of my nature. So sit and we'll have something to eat. Well, where are you going this time of night? Outside the pit bulls are running. The only motel around here smells of urine and day-old sex and the owner is an one-eyed weasel. Come sit and have something to eat.

(STEVEN *sits at the small table.* DANNY *and* DUKE *sit next to him.* DUKE *heaps food on the plates.*)

DANNY: Say grace, College Boy.

STEVEN: Grace.

DANNY: That's not good. Not good. That's horrible. Horrible. You're supposed to thank everyone that you know. Everyone.

DUKE: Danny, show him.

DANNY: Thank you Ma and Pa, all blown up in bits and pieces, now in heaven. Thank you Grandpa, now in heaven, died with an apple stick sword plunged into your pear heart. Thank you Auntie Bess and Uncle Clyde, drowned three summers ago in a freak flood, now in heaven. Thank you Doggie Patches, my collie terrier that was pulled apart, haunch by haunch, by coyotes, now in heaven. Thank you all. Grace.

DUKE: Everyone eat.

(DUKE *and* DANNY *eat.*)

STEVEN: That was the most unusual grace.

DUKE: We were paying respect to our folks.

DANNY: Duke, pass the meat platter.

DUKE: Have a porterhouse, still hot and black on the outside.

(DUKE *spears a slab of meat and drops it on* STEVEN*'s plate*)

DANNY: Duke, mash up my food.

(DUKE *takes a bite from* DANNY*'s plate, chews it up hard like a mother bird and spits it out on* DANNY*'s plate for Danny bird to eat.*)

DUKE: Do you want your food mashed up, College Boy?

DANNY: Duke's a masher. He can mash it up good like Ma used to do.

STEVEN: No, no. I can mash my own food.

DUKE: Why can't I mash up your food? I mash up Danny's food.

DANNY: Show him your molars, Duke. Take a look at his bicuspids.

STEVEN: I don't want to look at his bicuspids.

DUKE: What? You don't like my bicuspids?

STEVEN: No, no. They're lovely bicuspids. I just want . . .

DUKE: What? What do you want?

STEVEN: I want you to mash up my food for me with your bicuspids.

(DUKE *mashes a slab of beef and spits it out in a little ball on* STEVEN *plate.*)

DUKE: I love meat. I love the taste of it, all gritty and raw, blood oozing with
each bite.

DANNY: I love Pooh Bear.

DUKE: Danny's in his girly phase.

STEVEN: He's in love with Pooh Bear?

DANNY: Hiep Li Anh Tran, a.k.a. Pooh Bear. She's my Pooh Bear. She has
hair as black as hell and a smile as kinked as the fiercest bombing run in
Saigon. She wakes up scared as a fox in a foxhole with a pack of hounds
chasing her. She wakes up with firebombs holed up in her head. She wakes
up with the rattle-tat-tat of machine guns, of missiles bursting in midair,
of raining shrapnel. She wakes up with shots shooting past her ear, blowing it off in little itty-bitty shreds. She wakes up war-spooked. But she's
my Pooh Bear, my honey, my baby, a little spawn born in a hell called
Vietnam.

DUKE: She's spooky looking too.

DANNY: All right. All right. She's a little spooky looking. It's on account of
her face. Her left side of her face is fissured, cracked, creviced with burn
scars from a nappy explosion of Napalm. But her right side of her face is
lovely, creamy and smooth. Her left, burnt. Her right, beautiful. Burnt.
Beautiful. Burnt. Beautiful.

(DANNY *illustrates by covering alternate sides of his face with the palms of his hands.*)

DANNY: The left side of her face will make your stomach turn over, turn black, turn away. But on the right side of her face, she's an angel, a honey, a sweet nectar of a peach.

DUKE: They fooled around.

DANNY: We fooled around. My Pooh Bear's stomach poofed up and poofed out.

DUKE: Pooh Bear is going to have a bear cub.

DANNY: When Pooh Bear's stomach poofed out, something snapped and broke, something fractured and fizzled, something happened to Pooh Bear.

STEVEN: What? What?

DANNY: Pooh Bear has scary dreams. She dreams scary dreams even when her eyes are open wide. In her waking dreams, things burn up, fire rolls on the ground, falls into cracks. She's running away from Communists shooting at her back, from the killer firecracker weapons falling from the American planes high bombing. She sidesteps a minefield, swims across the South China Sea, survives a pirate attack. With the help of missionary men, she runs straight into the arms of Texas. She asks me, "What the hell am I doing in Texas?" (*Pause.*) We had such a short time together, then she snapped and then she's gone.

STEVEN: What do you mean gone?

DANNY: She's gone over. She's gone over the deep walls, the electric fence and the metal gate. She's gone in the dark cave, the marked corners, the belly of the beast. She's gone into the bughouse. My bear cub is in there, too, trapped. She's gone in and I have to get her out. I have to get her out and our bear cub too! But I don't want to go back. I don't want to go in.

STEVEN: I don't want you to go in.

DANNY: You'll stay with me for a while?

STEVEN: I have to go to college.

DANNY: You have to learn and study. Learn how to build houses. College Boy, you have to build our big house up again.

DUKE: Danny, he's just a College Boy. What does he know?

DANNY: He'll learn. He'll learn how to build a big house.

STEVEN: I can learn. I'm a College Boy.

DUKE: Aren't you going to learn anything? It ain't coming back. And if it rose from the charred ashes, like a miracle from the ground, it wouldn't be the same. It wouldn't be our big house. (*Pause.*) College Boy, why aren't you eating my mashed-up meat? I thought you liked it.

STEVEN: Well I didn't want to say.

DANNY: Do you want Duke to spoon-feed you, College Boy?

DUKE: I can spoon-feed you, College Boy. Open up.

STEVEN: No, no.

DANNY: Duke spoon-feeds me. He can do you.

STEVEN: He can't do me.

DUKE: Open wide. I got a heaping spoonful.

STEVEN: I don't want to eat it.

DUKE: You don't like my cooking. I'm a bad cook?

STEVEN: It smells tasty, but I . . .

DUKE: It is tasty, but what? But what, spit it out, College Boy!

STEVEN: I . . . I'm a vegan.

DUKE: So College Boy is a vegan.

DANNY: Duke, what's a vegan?

DUKE: A celery eater. A lettuce chomper. A carrot lover.

DANNY: College Boy's a carrot lover? What does this mean, Duke?

DUKE: He don't like meat. He don't like cow. He don't like a good Kansas City cut.

DANNY: Oh no. Oh no. Look what you did, College Boy.

STEVEN: What did I do?

DUKE: Nobody gets between me and my cooking.

DANNY: Duke's a crazy motherfucker. And you, College Boy, you did bewitched his cookery.

DUKE: College Boy, you cursed my sautéing, my broiling, my barbecuing.

STEVEN: I didn't mean it.

DUKE: You sullied all my culinary skills that I learned from Ma. You disgraced the ways of my family.

DANNY: Oh, it's not good, College Boy. Duke, you have to do what you have to do.

STEVEN: Maybe, it's not a good idea to have Duke do what he has to do.

DUKE: I got to do what I gotta do.

DANNY: Go ahead. I sharpened your axe, Duke.

DUKE: I got to do some cutting. I gotta go chopping.

STEVEN: I don't think he should be chopping.

DANNY: Stick three fingers out, College Boy.

STEVEN: Why do you need me to stick out three fingers?

DANNY: Just stick out your fingers.

STEVEN: No, no.

DUKE: I like my chopping.

DANNY: Then I'll stick three fingers out.

(DANNY *holds three fingers up.*)

STEVEN: No. No. Don't stick your three fingers out.

DANNY: Duke's gotta do his chopping.

DUKE: I gotta go chopping.

DANNY: One, two, three. (DANNY *counts down with his fingers.*) Go, Duke. Go.

(DUKE *slams the end of the axe handle against the table and exits out the door, slamming it.*)

STEVEN: Where did he go?

DANNY: He went to chop wood.

STEVEN: But wild unchained pit bulls run free outside.

DANNY: He's got an axe.

STEVEN: Listen, tomorrow, when the sun comes up—

DANNY: The rooster crows.

STEVEN: What?

DANNY: The rooster crows every day when the sun comes up unless it's been run over by a

roving truck.

STEVEN: Tomorrow after the rooster crows unless it's been run over by a roving truck, can you drive? Can you drive me in your truck? Drive me to college?

DANNY: Why do you need to be driven to college? Don't you like your situation?

STEVEN: I love my situation. I just need to iron out my classes.

DANNY: I don't know. I don't know. I have to ask Duke.

STEVEN: Don't ask Duke. Don't ask Duke. Ask me. (*Beat.*) I'll help you iron things out. I'll help you with your situation.

DANNY: How are you going to help?

STEVEN: I'll help by drawing up plans for your burnt-down big house.

DANNY: Plans for my big house?

STEVEN: I had two years of drafting. I'm good at right angles and straight lines. I'll draw your big house with right angles and straight lines. I'll draw your big house, if you take me to town, after the rooster crows unless it's been run over by a roving truck.

DANNY: You'll draw me a room for me and Pooh and baby, too? Draw a bathroom so we can take baths? Draw a kitchen so I can cook? Draw a TV room so we can watch TV with our feet up? Draw a front porch with a swinging chair so we can swing with our toes touching the ground? You have to draw a room for Duke, too. And draw a garage for Duke's cars, the ones he cuts up, chops in twos and fours.

STEVEN: I'll do it. I'll draw it all. Give me some paper and a ruler to draw right angles and straight lines. Give me a pencil with an eraser. I'm apt to make mistakes.

(DANNY *gives* STEVEN *all his supplies and* STEVEN *starts to draw on a piece of butcher paper.*)

DANNY: Oh, no. Oh, no. Duke won't like that! No, he won't. Not at all.

STEVEN: What will he won't like?

DANNY: You're building a house. He ain't going to like that. He wants to let sleeping dogs lie.

STEVEN: We won't tell.

DANNY: I have to tell. I have to tell Duke everything. He told me to.

STEVEN: I'm telling you not to tell.

DANNY: But he's going to run after us.

STEVEN: We have to make sure he doesn't run after us.

DANNY: Well, he has a bad foot.

STEVEN: How bad is his foot?

DANNY: During the running of the pit bulls one dark night under an unlit moon, the pit bulls ran flat-footed through rot weed and tall trees to where Duke was and with their teeth, long and sharp, they chewed his left foot down to the bone, chomped it in two, bit it clean off. All that was left was a little stub.

STEVEN: The pit bulls did that to him?

DANNY: The pit bulls tore it right off.

STEVEN: Tore it off?

DANNY: It was a clean tear.

STEVEN: I'm scared of dogs.

DANNY: They're mean dogs.

STEVEN: Duke . . . Duke. What about Duke's leg?

DANNY: He's got a peg leg.

STEVEN: I see. I see that . . . We have to steal it. We have to steal his peg leg.

DANNY: Duke's not going to like that we are stealing his peg leg.

STEVEN: Like it or not, we have to steal his leg to keep him from running after us. Is it the twist-off kind or the pull-off kind?

DANNY: It's the snap-off kind. But what are we going to do with his leg once we steal it?

STEVEN: We'll just have to bury it in the backyard.

DANNY: Don't hurt his leg. Not his leg. I won't like it if you hurt his leg.

STEVEN: I won't hurt his leg. It's the snap-off kind.

DANNY: I don't know. I don't know. Duke's a crazy motherfucker.

STEVEN: That's right. That's right. You're not Duke. You're not a crazy motherfucker.

DANNY: I'm Danny.

STEVEN: I'm Steven, the College Boy. I'm going to draw you and Pooh Bear a house, and you are going to take me to town to the housing board. We are going to leave this trailer, we are going to walk out that door.

DANNY: I'm scared of walking out the door.

STEVEN: Think of it as choosing a door. You got two doors in front of you. One door opens and it's Pooh Bear and her bear cub. Open another door and it's a tiger ready to eat you up, it's Duke, it's the crazy motherfucker.

DANNY: I got to choose two doors?

STEVEN: You got to choose one door. The lady Pooh Bear and her cub or the tiger, Duke. Pooh Bear or Duke?

DANNY: I can't choose one door.

STEVEN: There's only one door. There is only one way out.

DANNY: What if I choose the wrong door?

STEVEN: You won't. You got me, Danny Boy, and I'll stay with you.

DANNY: I know you will. I wrote it down on my calendar. College Boy comes to stay. But I don't know. I don't.

STEVEN: You do know.

DANNY: I have to take a pill now.

STEVEN: What pill?

DANNY: The pill.

STEVEN: What does that pill do? It's not going to make you nervous, is it?

DANNY: It keeps me from getting nervous. You don't want me to be nervous, do you?

STEVEN: No, I don't want you nervous.

DANNY: If I'm nervous, there's no counting what I'll do.

(DANNY *takes a pill.*)

STEVEN: Danny feel better?

DANNY: Whoa! Whee! I feel like a new dollar bill. I just have to take my pills. Big balls of pills. Round ones, square ones, skinny ones, fat ones, purple, green and orange. I have to take twelve every day or else.

STEVEN: I'm glad you took your pill and swallowed it quick. Now, we have to think of a way to steal Duke's peg leg. Got a twisted idea?

DANNY: We can't twist it off. We got to snap it off.

STEVEN: When we snap it off, it's going to hurt bad.

DANNY: I don't want it to hurt bad. I want it to be sweet.

STEVEN: We gonna have to do it when Duke's sleeping then.

DANNY: He's not the sleeping kind. He sleeps with one eye open.

STEVEN: In your pill bottle, do you have a sleeping pill, a knockout pill?

DANNY: I got a pill that makes me see dots.

STEVEN: What kind of dots?

DANNY: Big polka dots.

STEVEN: Then, the big polka dot pill is the pill we give Duke.

DANNY: But there's a problem.

STEVEN: What's the problem?

DANNY: The pill is sour.

STEVEN: Then we got to find a way to make it sweet. We'll just take that pill and slip it in a glass of lemonade to make the sourness go away.

DANNY: I don't know. I don't know how to slip a pill in a glass of lemonade.

STEVEN: Listen, you don't know it and I may not look like it. But I'm a wild boy. I push old women and old men too, down on the ground. I roll drunks, roll them over and pick their pockets, take the cash and scoot. I burrow in men's pockets and women's pocketbooks and take what's there without them knowing. So I can slip a pill, slide it in, stir it in Duke's lemonade. I may look like a College Boy, but I'm not just a College Boy. I'm . . . I'm . . . I'm . . . a mean College Boy.

DANNY: You are not.

STEVEN: I am too.

DANNY: You're a College Boy. A smart one.

STEVEN: I've been in the cathouse.

DANNY: I've been there too.

STEVEN: Well, I've been in the tiger's cave.

DANNY: I like tigers. They're greeaat.

STEVEN: I've been . . .

DANNY: You've been where?

STEVEN: I've been . . . I've been in the snakepit.

DANNY: No, no, no. Not the snakepit.

STEVEN: Yes, yes, yes, the snakepit.

DANNY: I don't like the snakepit.

STEVEN: In the snakepit, I've been slithered on.

(STEVEN *lightly runs his fingers along* DANNY's *arm*.)

DANNY: You've been snake walked on?

STEVEN: I've been hissed on.

(STEVEN *hisses in* DANNY's *ear*.)

DANNY: You've been snake talked to?

STEVEN: I've been slimed on.

(STEVEN *licks* DANNY's *arm*.)

DANNY: No, no . . . You've been snake licked.

STEVEN: Yes, I've been snake licked.

DANNY: I've never been slimed.

STEVEN: You don't want to be slimed.

DANNY: I don't like snakes. They're worse than bugs.

STEVEN: No, no, the worst thing is when they squeeze you like a desperate, lonely girlfriend. With their snake bodies, those long cylinder bodies that go on for miles and miles, they can wrap their bodies around your chest two, three dozen times, and then squeeze you, so you can't breathe, can't exhale, can't inhale. And then, they crack the rib bones, and then break the rib bones, and then break them again until you're lying on the floor, ready to ring death's door, ready to say, "Let me in, Death. Let me in."

DANNY: I hate snakes.

STEVEN: That's right. That's right. I've been in the snakepit and I'll take you there.

DANNY: No, No. I can't be snaked out. Don't let me get slimed.

(STEVEN *licks* DANNY's *arm.*)

STEVEN: I won't let you get slimed.

DANNY: You're a good College Boy.

STEVEN: Give me a pill. You don't want to get slimed. Get hissed at. Get squeezed.

DANNY: Not that. Not that. No, not that. I'll give you a pill that'll make Duke see polka dots.

(DANNY *gives* STEVEN *a pill.* STEVEN *places it in his pocket.*)

STEVEN: That's a good Danny Boy. When Duke walks through that door, we'll spike his lemonade. He'll see big polka dots and then he'll lie down, he'll go down sweet, he'll go down soft. In the meantime, I'll finish drawing your house.

(STEVEN *continues to draw on a piece of paper.*)

(*End of Scene*)

Appendix 1: Themes and Topics

We offer this categorization with some reluctance, recognizing that most texts provoke multiple interpretations. Please note that many of the selections appear in more than one category. At best, these are only suggestions for how to approach the material; readers will undoubtedly discover their own ways in.

Acculturation/Assimilation

Chin, F., "Railroad Standard Time"
Dinh, "The Dead"
Kurup, from *Assimilation*
Lim, from *Among the White Moon Faces*
Mirikitani, "Recipe"
Hagedorn, "Smokey's Getting Old"

Childhood

Duong, "Sister Play"
Gotera, "Beetle on a String"
Kim, P., from *A Cab Called Reliable*
Kim R., from *Clay Walls*
Lam, "Show and Tell"
Yamamoto, "Seventeen Syllables"
Yamanaka, "Kala Gave Me Anykine Advice Especially about Filipinos When I Moved to Pahala"

Community

Lei-lanilau, from *Ono Ono Girl's Hula*
Mori, "He Who Has the Laughing Face"
Pak, "The Valley of the Dead Air"
Yamashita, from *Through the Arc of the Rain Forest*

Communities in Conflict

Kim R., from *Clay Walls*
Yamanaka, "Kala Gave Me Anykine Advice Especially about Filipinos When I Moved to Pahala"

The Creative Act

Alexander, "News of the World," "The Voice That Passes Through Me"

Bulosan, "How My Stories Were Written"
Kim, P., from *A Cab Called Reliable*
Langworthy, "Projections"
Lew, "Ch'onmun Hak"
Lim, from *Among the White Moon Faces*
Pak, "In That Valley Beautiful Beyond"
Sze, from "The Redshifting Web"
Tabios, "Absorbing and Being Absorbed by Poetry"
Yamamoto, "Seventeen Syllables"

Critiquing the American Dream

Apostol, "Fredo Avila"
Bulosan, "The Story of a Letter"
Gamalinda, "Elvis of Manila"

Family/Intergenerational Conflicts

Barroga, from *Eye of the Coconut*
Bulosan, "The Story of a Letter"
Chin, F., "Railroad Standard Time"
Duong, "Sister Play"
Kim, P., from *A Cab Called Reliable*
Lee, C., "The Faintest Echo of Our Language"
Lee, L., "The Gift"
Lim, from *Among the White Moon Faces*
Shiomi, *Mask Dance*
Song, "A Conservative View"
Soo Hoo, excerpt from *Texas*
Tran, "Zenith"
Yamamoto, "Seventeen Syllables"

Health

Chao, from *Monkey King*
Verghese, from *My Own Country*

Heritage/Identity

Chin, F., "Railroad Standard Time"
Chin, M., "The Floral Apron"
Hagedorn, "Smokey's Getting Old"
Kurup, from *Assimilation*
Lei-lanilau, from *Ono Ono Girl's Hula*
Naqvi, "Chagrin"
Shiomi, *Mask Dance*
Vazirani, "Reading the Poem about the Yew Tree"

Homeland/Nostalgia

Ali, from "In Search of Evanescence"
Amirthanayagam, "Not Much Art," "Ceylon"
Bulosan, "The Story of a Letter"
Choi, from *The Foreign Student*
Hongo, "Yellow Light"
Kamani, "The Goddess of Sleep"
Lahiri, "Mrs. Sen's"
Okada, from *No-No Boy*
Ung, from *First They Killed My Father*
Vazirani, "Reading the Poem about the Yew Tree"

Internment of Japanese Americans

Okada, from *No-No Boy*

Immigrant/Diasporic Experiences

Ali, excerpt from "In Search of Evanescence"
Bulosan, "The Story of a Letter"
Chung, untitled poem
Divakaruni, "The Founding of Yuba City"
Hagedorn, "Smokey's Getting Old"
Hongo, "Yellow Light"
Kabir, "A Difference of Background"
Kim, P., from *A Cab Called Reliable*
Kim R., from *Clay Walls*
Kingston, from *China Men*
Lahiri, "Mrs. Sen's"
Lim, from *Among the White Moon Faces*
Sui Sin Far, "In the Land of the Free"

Truong, "Seeds"
Vazirani, "Reading the Poem about the Yew Tree"
Yamamoto, "Seventeen Syllables"
Yamashita, from *Through the Arc of the Rain Forest*

Love/Relationships

Choi, from *The Foreign Student*
Chu, "The Bitterness of Bodies We Bear"
Dinh, "The Dead"
Ignacio, "The Shylocks"
Inada, "Filling the Gap"
Kabir, "A Difference of Background"
Lahiri, "Mrs. Sen's"
Lam, "Show and Tell"
Langworthy, "Prints"
Lee, L., "The Gift," "This Room and Everything in It"
Lum, "Urban Love Songs"
Monji, "Kim"
Mori, "He Who Has the Laughing Face"
Revoyr, from *The Necessary Hunger*
Soo Hoo, from *Texas*
Yamamoto, "Seventeen Syllables"
Yau, "A New Beginning"

Racism/Stereotypes

Francia, "Walls"
Mirikitani, "Recipe"
Salanga, "They Don't Think Much about Us in America"
Yamada, "Thirty Years Under," "Cincinnati"
Yuson, "Andy Warhol Speaks to His Two Filipino Maids"

Refugee Experiences

Lam, "Show and Tell"
lê, from *Red Fiery Summer*
Luu, from *Three Lives*
Ung, from *First They Killed My Father*

Resistance

Chock, "Strawberries"
Mirikitani, "Why Is Preparing Fish a Political Act?"
Yamada, "Thirty Years Under"

Sensuality/Sexuality/Gender

Chock, "Strawberries"
Kamani, "The Goddess of Sleep"
Koyama, "The Chocolatier"
Lei-lanilau, from *Ono Ono Girl's Hula*
Linmark, from *Rolling the R's*
Monji, "Kim"
Mura, from *Where the Body Meets Memory*
Revoyr, from *The Necessary Hunger*

War/Violence

Alexander, "The Young of Tienanmen"
Amirthanayagam, "Ceylon," "Not Much Art"
Cha, from *DICTEE*
Chu, "The Bitterness of Bodies We Bear"
Dinh, "Western Music," "The Dead"
Lam, "Show and Tell"
lê, from *Red Fiery Summer*
Luu, from *Three Lives*
Ung, from *First They Killed My Father*

Appendix 2: Ethnicity of Authors

D = Drama, E = Essay, F = Fiction, M = Memoir, P = Poetry

Bi/Multiracial

Langworthy, Christian (P)
Lei-lanilau, Carolyn (M)
Revoyr, Nina (F)
Song, Cathy (P)
Sui Sin Far (F)

Chinese

Chao, Patricia (F)
Chin, Frank (F)
Chin, Marilyn (P)
Chock, Eric (P)
Kingston, Maxine Hong (M)
Lee, Li-Young (P)
Lim, Shirley Geok-Lin (M)
Lum, Wing Tek (P)
Soo Hoo, Judy (D)
Sze, Arthur (P)
Yau, John (F)

Filipina/Filipino

Apostol, Gina (F)
Barroga, Jeannie (D)
Bulosan, Carlos (M, F)
Francia, Luis H. (P)
Gamalinda, Eric (F)
Gotera, Vince (P)
Hagedorn, Jessica (P)
Ignacio, Cynthia (F)
Linmark, R. Zamora (F)
Salanga, Alfrredo Navarro (P)
Tabios, Eileen (E)
Yuson, Alfred (P)

Japanese

Hongo, Garrett (P)
Inada, Lawson Fusao (P)
Koyama, Tina (P)
Mirikitani, Janice (P)
Monji, Jana (F)
Mori, Toshio (F)
Mura, David (M)

Okada, John (F)
Shiomi, Rick S. (D)
Uno, Roberta (E)
Yamada, Mitsuye (P)
Yamamoto, Hisaye (F)
Yamanaka, Lois-Ann (P)
Yamashita, Karen Tei (F)

Korean

Cha, Theresa Hak Kyung (F)
Choi, Susan (F)
Chung, Frances (P)
Kim, Patti (F)
Kim Ronyoung (F)
Lee, Chang-rae (M)
Lew, Walter K. (P)
Pak, Gary (E, F)

South Asian

Alexander, Meena (E, P)
Ali, Agha Shahid (P)
Amirthanayagam, Indran (P)
Divakaruni, Chitra (P)
Kabir, Nurul (F)
Kamani, Ginu (F)
Kurup, Shishir (D)
Lahiri, Jhumpa (F)
Naqvi, Tahira (F)
Vazirani, Reetika (P)
Verghese, Abraham (M)

Southeast Asian

Chu, Bao-Long (P)
Dinh, Linh (F, P)
Duong, Lan (P)
Lam, Andrew (F)
lê thi diem thúy (D)
Luu, Alex (D)
Tran, Barbara (P)
Truong, Monique T. D. (F)
Ung, Loung (M)

Glossary

We have glossed only terms whose meanings cannot be guessed at from context. Words are Hawaiian unless otherwise indicated. Some definitions are based on entries in the *New Pocket Hawaiian Dictionary* by Mary Kawena Pukui and Samuel H. Elbert (University of Hawai'i Press 1992).

An den conversational move asking for information or signaling that information will follow (Hawaiian Creole, variant pronunciation of "and then")

auē exclamation of despair, wonder, fear, pity

'aumākua family or personal gods. Lei-lanilau's 'aumākua are the shark and owls.

ayecudiyou sound/word made up by Lei-lanilau's father

bonzai (variant pronunciation of Japanese *banzai*) a cheer or toast

boo look (Chinese) kind of citrus fruit

deshi/desi (Hindi) fellow countryman

hadith (Urdu) the traditions of the Prophet Muhammad which form an integral part of Islamic beliefs

hana work, job, activity of any kind

hansam (Korean) white fabric extensions on sleeves of the costumes of mask dancers, believed to connect the earth with the heavens

haole Anglo, a white person

hauna unpleasant odor

hele to go, come, move

iftar (Urdu) the ritual of breaking the fast during the month of Ramadan, the time being soon after sunset

I mua Forward!

kāhili ginger variety of ginger whose blossoms grow in cylindrical clusters reminiscent of *kāhili*, a feather standard that symbolizes royalty.

kahuna priest, minister, sorcerer, expert in any profession

Kamapua'a a pig demigod famous in legend

kaona pulse or impulse

kāne man, male, husband

keiki child

kī a plant in the lily family. also referred to as a ti plant kino body, self

lau lau a traditional Hawaiian dish

lele to jump, leap, burst forth

liao (Hakka) to pause and visit a while

li hing mui (Chinese) dried salty seed eaten as a snack

mā hū homosexual

ma'i genitals

maka'āinana people in general

mane'o impulse from the groin

mone (Malayalam) son

'ohana family

'ōkole buttocks

'ono delicious

pakalana Chinese violet

pākē Chinese

pau finished, completed, final

pī kai to sprinkle with rain or salt water in order to bless or to remove a taboo

pī kake jasmine

pua flower

puta (Spanish) prostitute

sake (Japanese) rice wine

skoosh a little (from Japanese *sukōshi*, a little bit)

ti see kī

tūtū grandmother

wahine woman, female, wife

zakat (Urdu) the portion of one's income that one is required to give away in charity

About the Contributors

Meena Alexander is an internationally renowned poet and writer whose work has been widely published, anthologized, and translated. She is Distinguished Professor of English at the Graduate Center and Hunter College, The City University of New York. Alexander has written novels, critical essays, the memoir *Fault Lines* (selected as one of the best books of 1993 by *Publishers Weekly*), and several volumes of poems.

Agha Shahid Ali teaches at the University of Utah. Among his recent collections of poetry are *The Country without a Post Office* and *Rooms Are Never Finished*.

Indran Amirthanayagam was born in Sri Lanka in 1960 and educated in the United States. His poems have appeared in *The Open Boat: Poems from Asian America, Grand Street, The Kenyon Review,* and *The Massachusetts Review.* A collection of his poems, *The Elephants of Reckoning,* was published in 1992.

Gina Apostol's novel *Bibliolepsy* won the 1997 Philippine National Book Award. Her stories have appeared in the anthologies *Babaylan: Filipina and Filipina-American Writers, Balikbayan: Filipino Stories Translated into the Italian, Flippin': Filipinos on America,* and *Catfish Arriving in Little Schools.* Apostol lives in New York.

Jeannie Barroga is an active member of the Dramatists Guild, and has been writing plays since 1981. Her plays *Walls, Talk-Story, Rita's Resources, The Revered Miss Newton,* and *Kenny Was a Shortstop* have been produced nationwide and published. Barroga received the Maverick award from the Los Angeles Women's Festival in 1996 and has been Literary Manager at Theatreworks, Menlo Park, since 1985.

Carlos Bulosan (1911–1956) was born in the Philippines and immigrated to the United States in 1931, where he worked as a seasonal laborer and union activist. He began writing while hospitalized with tuberculosis in Los Angeles. Best known for his autobiographical novel *America Is in the Heart* (1946), Bulosan also wrote poems, short stories, and magazine articles.

Theresa Hak Kyung Cha (1952–1982) was born in Pusan, Korea, and immigrated to the United States with her family in 1962. In addition to writing, she produced, directed and performed in numerous video and film projects. Her published works include DICTEE (1982) and *Pravda/Istina.*

Patricia Chao lives in New York City. *Monkey King* is her first novel.

Frank Chin is the author of numerous novels, short stories, plays, and essays. With Shawn Wong, Jeffrey Chan, and Lawson Fusao Inada, he co-edited *Aiiieeeee! An Anthology of Asian American Writers* (1974) and *The Big Aiiieeeee!*

An *Anthology of Chinese-American and Japanese-American Literature* (1991). Chin's most recent collection of writing is *Bulletproof Buddhists and Other Essays* (1998).

Marilyn Chin was born in Hong Kong and raised in Portland, Oregon. Her poems have appeared in *The Iowa Review, Ploughshares, The Kenyon Review,* and *Parnassus,* as well as in her collections *Dwarf Bamboo* (1987) and *The Phoenix Gone, The Terrace Empty* (1994). She is the recipient of a National Endowment for the Arts writing fellowship and the Stegner Fellowship.

Eric Chock was born in Honolulu, Hawai'i, in 1950. He is program coordinator for the Hawai'i Poets in the Schools Program and, with Darrell Lum, a founding coeditor of Bamboo Ridge Press. A collection of his poems, *Last Days Here,* was published in 1990.

Susan Choi was born in Indiana, grew up in Texas, and lives in New York City. Her short fiction has appeared in *Iowa Review* and *Epoch Magazine. The Foreign Student* is her first novel.

Bao-Long Chu is currently program director for Writers in the Schools, a nonprofit organization that places poets and writers in schools and community settings in and around Houston. His poems have appeared in *The Asian Pacific American Journal, The Viet Nam Forum,* and *Watermark: Vietnamese American Poetry and Prose.*

Frances Chung (1950–1990) was a bilingual (English and Spanish) mathematics teacher in New York City public schools. Two posthumously discovered book manuscripts of her writings are collected in *Crazy Melon and Chinese Apple: The Poems of Frances Chung* (2000). Chung was awarded poetry fellowships by the New York Times Company Foundation and New York State Council on the Arts.

Linh Dinh, born in Saigon in 1963, is the author of a chapbook of poems, *Drunkard Boxing* (1998), and a collection of short stories, *Fake House* (2000). His work has appeared in many journals, including *Sulfur, New American Writing, Chicago Review, Skanky Possum, Threepenny Review,* and *Mānoa.* Dinh also edited *'Night, Again: Contemporary Fiction from Vietnam* (1996).

Chitra Divakaruni, a widely published fiction writer and poet, is a founding member of Maitri, a South Asian women's helpline. Her collections of poetry include *Black Candle* and *Leaving Yuba City.* Divakaruni received an American Book Award and the Oakland PEN Josephine Miles Award for her short story collection *Arranged Marriage.* Her novel *Mistress of Spices* is being made into a film. Her most recent collection of fiction is *The Unknown Errors of Our Lives* (2001).

Lan Duong immigrated to the United States at the age of two. She studied comparative literature at the University of California at Irvine, focusing on Vietnamese and French film and literature. Her work has appeared in *Watermark: Vietnamese American Poetry and Prose* (1998).

Luis H. Francia, a resident of New York City, has published two collections of poetry: *Her Beauty Likes Me Well* (with David Friedman), and *The Arctic Archipel-*

ago and Other Poems. He edited *Brown River, White Ocean: An Anthology of Twentieth-Century Philippine Literature,* and co-edited *Flippin': Filipinos on America.* Francia is co-editing *Vestiges of War,* an anthology about the aftermath of the 1899 Philippine-American War.

Eric Gamalinda was born in Manila, where he worked as an editor and journalist, and where he published four novels—the latest of which, *My Sad Republic,* won the Philippine Centennial Award in 1998—as well as a collection of stories and poetry. He is a recipient of a fellowship from the New York Foundation for the Arts. His latest work, *Zero Gravity,* a collection of poems, won the 2000 Asian American Literary Award.

Vince Gotera is the editor of the *North American Review* (established 1815). He has published a book of poems, *Dragonfly,* and a work of literary criticism, *Radical Visions: Poetry by Vietnam Veterans.* Gotera teaches creative writing and literature at the University of Northern Iowa.

Jessica Hagedorn was born in the Philippines in 1949. In 1983 she received an American Book Award for her collection *Food and Tropical Apparitions.* Her novels include *Dogeaters,* which was nominated for a National Book Award in 1990, and *The Gangster of Love* (1996). Hagedorn is the editor of *Charlie Chan Is Dead: An Anthology of Contemporary Asian American Fiction* (1993).

Garrett Hongo was born in 1951 in Volcano, Hawai'i. His collection of poems *The River of Heaven* was a finalist for the 1989 Pulitzer Prize in Poetry and the Lamont poetry selection of the Academy of American Poets. Hongo edited *The Open Boat: Poems from Asian America* (1993).

Cynthia Ignacio has participated in the David Henry Hwang Writers Institute, and had her work published in *Disorient* and *YOLK Magazine.* An animation artist, Ignacio worked on *The Lion King, Pocahontas,* and *The Hunchback of Notre Dame.* Currently she is the lead stylist for the *Jackie Chan Adventures* animated series.

Lawson Fusao Inada was born in 1940. He coedited *Aiiieeeee! An Anthology of Asian American Writers* (1974) and *The Big Aiiieeeee!* Inada teaches multicultural literature and creative writing at Southern Oregon State College. His most recent collection of poetry is *Drawing the Line: Poems* (1997).

Nurul Kabir was born in Bangladesh in 1959 and came to the United States as a teenager. His writing has appeared in the anthologies *Living in America* (1995) and *Contours of the Heart: South Asians Map North America* (1996). A software engineer by profession, he divides his time between Cambridge, Massachusetts, and Dakha, Bangladesh.

Ginu Kamani, author of the short story collection *Junglee Girl,* was born in Bombay, India, in 1962. Her short fiction and essays appear in collections of erotica, most recently *Best American Erotica 2000.* Kamani has taught creative writing and lives in Northern California.

Patti Kim was born in Pusan, Korea, in 1970. She came to the United States in 1974 and graduated from the University of Maryland in 1994. *A Cab Called Reliable* is her first novel.

Kim Ronyoung (1926–1987), also known as Gloria Hahn, was born in Los Angeles to immigrant parents from North Korea. She began writing *Clay Walls* when she was diagnosed with cancer in 1976. The semi-autobiographical novel was published just before her death.

Maxine Hong Kingston was born in 1940 in Stockton, California. Her book *The Woman Warrior: Memoir of a Girlhood among Ghosts* (1976) was the first work by an Asian American to win national acclaim and a broad popular readership. Kingston's other works include *China Men*, the novel *Tripmaster Monkey*, poetry, and a collection of essays, *Hawai'i One Summer.*

Tina Koyama studied at the University of Washington. Her work has appeared in *The Seattle Review*, *Breaking Silence: An Anthology of Contemporary Asian American Poets,* and *Willow Springs.* Koyama received the Oberg Award for poetry in 1983.

Shishir Kurup is an actor/playwright/composer/director. A perpetual hyphenate, he was born in Bombay, India, raised in Mombasa, Kenya, resides in Los Angeles, California, and calls himself an Indo/African/American. He is a member of the ensemble of the Cornerstone Theater Company where he is currently in the throes of birthing his latest work, *An Antigone Story.*

Jhumpa Lahiri was born in London in 1967 and grew up in Rhode Island. Her short fiction has appeared in *The New Yorker.* Lahiri's first collection, *Interpreter of Maladies,* was awarded the Pulitzer Prize for fiction in 2000.

Andrew Lam is an associate editor with the Pacific News Service in San Francisco, a short story writer, and a regular commentator on NPR's *All Things Considered.* He was born in Saigon, Vietnam, and came to the United States at the end of the Vietnam war in 1975 when he was eleven years old. Lam has an M.A. in creative writing from San Francisco State University. He is working on his first short story collection.

Christian Langworthy's poetry appears or will appear in these anthologies and journals: *Premonitions, Watermark, From Both Sides Now, Poetry Nation, Asian American Poetry, In the Mix, Tongue's Afire, PBS Experience, Fence, Mudfish,* and *The Asian Pacific American Journal.* His novel *War Child* is forthcoming.

lê thi diem thúy, a writer and solo performance artist, was born in Phan Thiet, South Vietnam, in 1972 and came to the United States in 1978. She has presented her work at the International Women Playwrights Festival in Galway, Ireland, and the Third New Immigrants' Play Festival in New York City. Her essay "The Gangster We All Are Looking For" appears in *Best American Essays 1997.*

Chang-rae Lee is the author of the novels *Native Speaker* and *A Gesture Life.*

Li-Young Lee was born in Jakarta, Indonesia, in 1957 to parents who had fled from Communist China in 1951. He and his family immigrated to the United States in 1964. His published works include the collections of poetry *Rose* (1986) and *The City in Which I Love You* (1990), and a memoir, *Winged Seed* (1994).

Carolyn Lei-lanilau's art and writing reflect her Hawaiian/Hakka/Chinese background as well as her interests in linguistics, gender/ethnic identity, and sexuality. Her award-winning work has been widely published and includes *Wode Shuofa (My Way of Speaking)* (1988), *Ono Ono Girl's Hula* (1997), and her research on the secret language of the women of Hunan Province.

Walter K. Lew is the author of a forthcoming volume of poems and intermedia pieces and editor of *Crazy Melon and Chinese Apple: The Poems of Frances Chung, Muae 1,* and a historical anthology of Korean American fiction, co-edited with Heinz Insu Fenkl. He is preparing a translation of works by the Korean author Yi Sang (1910–1937) with commentary.

Shirley Geok-lin Lim was born in Malacca, Malaysia, in 1944. She earned her Ph.D. in English and American Literature at Brandeis University. Lim has written poetry, short stories, essays, and a memoir, *Among the White Moon Faces,* which received the National Book Award in 1997. She teaches English and women's studies at the University of California, Santa Barbara.

R. Zamora Linmark was born in 1970 in Manila and studied at the University of Hawai'i. His work has appeared in numerous anthologies, including *Charlie Chan Is Dead* (1993), *Premonitions: The Kaya Anthology of New Asian North American Poetry* (1995), and *The Best Gay American Fiction of 1997.*

Wing Tek Lum lives in Honolulu, Hawai'i. A collection of his poetry, *Expanding the Doubtful Points,* was published in 1987.

Alex Luu is a teacher, performance artist and independent filmmaker based in Los Angeles. His plays have been performed at numerous venues including San Francisco's Asian American Theater Center, New York's National Asian American Theatre Company, Boston's Tremont Theater, and the Japanese American National Museum. Luu has been the editor-in-chief of *YOLK Magazine* since 1999.

Janice Mirikitani was born in Stockton, California, in 1942. A poet, activist, teacher, dancer, and editor, she has worked with the Glide Church/Urban Center and Glide Theater Group and edits several publications, including *Third World Women* and *AYUMI.* Mirikitani's writing has appeared in *Awake in the River* (1978) and *Shedding Silence* (1987).

Jana Monji, a third-generation Japanese American, was born in San Diego, California. She received a B.A. in both Studio Arts and Asian Studies from the University of California at Santa Barbara. She earned an M.A. in East Asian Languages and Cultures from the University of California at Los Angeles and later an M.A. in print journalism from the University of California at Santa Cruz. She wrote theater reviews for the *L.A. Weekly* before moving to her current freelance position as a theater critic for the *Los Angeles Times.* When she's not at the theater, she's either working as a photographer or learning about the mysteries of the universe from her three dogs.

Toshio Mori (1910–1980) was born in Oakland, California. His short stories describe life in pre–World War II Japanese American communities, but publication of his collection *Yokohama, California* was delayed until after the war. Mori was interned at Topaz Relocation Center, where he served as camp historian.

David Mura, born in Illinois in 1952, has received numerous awards and fellowships. His poetry collections include *After We Lost Our Way* (1989) and *The Colors of Desire* (1995). Mura is also the author of *Where the Body Meets Memory: An Odyssey of Race, Sexuality, and Identity* (1996), *Turning Japanese: Memoirs of a Sansei* (1991), and *A Male Grief: Notes on Pornography and Addiction* (1987).

Tahira Naqvi grew up in Lahore, Pakistan. Her first collection of stories, *Attar of Roses and Other Stories of Pakistan,* was published in 1998. She has translated the works of Sa'adat Hasan Manto, Ismat Chughtai, and most recently Khadija Mastur, a well-known Pakistani writer of Urdu fiction. Naqvi is currently completing her first novel.

John Okada (1923–1971) was born in Seattle, Washington. His novel *No-No Boy* (1957) focuses on the Japanese American community in the period immediately following World War II. Initially met with a poor reception, *No-No Boy* was rediscovered in the 1970s and has since become critically acclaimed and widely studied.

Gary Pak lives in Kane'ohe, Hawai'i. He is the author of the novel *A Ricepaper Airplane* (1998) and the collection *The Watcher of Waipuna and Other Stories* (1992), which won the Association for Asian American Studies 1993 National Book Award for Literature. Pak teaches writing at Kapi'olani Community College in Honolulu. His play for children, *Beyond the Falls,* was produced in spring 2001.

Nina Revoyr was born in Japan and raised in Tokyo and Los Angeles. She is of Japanese and Polish American descent. Revoyr earned her M.F.A. at Cornell University, where she is currently a lecturer. *The Necessary Hunger* is her first novel.

Alfrredo Navarro Salanga (1948–1988) worked as a journalist and editor, and was a founding member of the Philippine Literary Arts Council. A collection of his poems, *Turtle Voices in Uncertain Weather,* was published the year after his death.

Rick Shiomi has been involved in the Asian American theater movement since 1980. His play *Yellow Fever* was produced Off Broadway in New York, around North America, and in Tokyo, Japan. Relocating to Minnesota, he was one of the founders of Theater Mu and is presently its Artistic Director. He has written *Mask Dance, Tale of the Dancing Crane,* and *Song of the Pipa* for the company.

Cathy Song was born in 1955 in Honolulu, Hawai'i. Her first collection of poetry, *Picture Bride,* won the Yale Series of Younger Poets competition and was nominated for the National Book Critics Circle Award. Song's other collections include *Frameless Windows, Squares of Light* (1988), and *School Figures* (1994).

Judy Soo Hoo's play *Texas* won the 1999 Yukon Pacific New Play Award at the Edward Albee Theatre Conference and had its world premiere at Lodestone Theatre Ensemble in Los Angeles. She is a PEN/West Emerging Voices Fellow and one of the winners of the 1997 East/West Players/AT&T New Voices Playwriting Competition.

Sui Sin Far (1865–1914) was born Edith Maud Eaton, the daughter of a Chinese mother and English father. Eaton chose her Chinese pen name when she began her writing career in the 1880s. Her writings are collected in *Mrs. Spring Fragrance* and *Leaves from the Mental Portfolio of a Eurasian*.

Arthur Sze lives in Pojoaque, New Mexico, and teaches at the Institute of American Indian Arts. He has published six books of poetry, including *The Redshifting Web* (1998). *The Silk Dragon: Translations of Chinese Poetry* is forthcoming.

Eileen Tabios, a poet and wine taster, is the editor of *Black Lightning: Poetry-in-Progress* (1998) and *The Anchored Angel: Selected Writings by José Villa Garcia* (1999). Her poetry has been widely anthologized and is collected in *Beyond Life Sentences* (1998). Tabios recently stepped down as editor of the *Asian Pacific American Journal*.

Barbara Tran is a recipient of the MacDowell Colony's Gerald Freund Fellowship and a Pushcart Prize. She is coeditor of *Watermark: Vietnamese American Poetry Prose* published by the Asian American Writers' Workshop (1998).

Monique T. D. Truong received her B.A. in literature from Yale University and her J.D. from Columbia University School of Law. She is the coeditor of the anthology *Watermark: Vietnamese American Poetry Prose* by Asian American Writers' Workshop (1998). Truong is currently at work on her first novel.

Loung Ung was eight years old when she lost her parents and two siblings to the violence of Pol Pot's regime in Cambodia, and ten when she and her brother came to the United States, sponsored by a church in Vermont. Ung now serves as a national spokesperson for the Campaign for a Landmine-Free World, a program of the Vietnam Veterans of America Foundation (VVAF). She lectures extensively throughout the United States.

Roberta Uno is the artistic director of the New WORLD Theatre and professor of theater at the University of Massachusetts at Amherst. She is the editor of *Unbroken Thread: An Anthology of Plays by Asian American Women*, coeditor of *Contemporary Plays by Women of Color*, and editor of the forthcoming *The Color of Theater: A Critical Sourcebook on Race and Performance*.

Reetika Vazirani was born in India and grew up in Maryland. Her poems have been published in *Callaloo, The Kenyon Review, The International Quarterly,* and elsewhere. In 1994, Vazirani received the Discovery Award from *The Nation*.

Abraham Verghese was born in Ethiopia to parents from Kerala, India. He is professor of medicine and chief of infectious diseases at the Texas Tech Health Sciences Center in El Paso and a frequent contributor to *The New Yorker*. Verghese is the author of two memoirs, *My Own Country* (1994) and *The Tennis Partner* (1998).

Mitsuye Yamada was born in Kyushu, Japan, in 1923 and grew up in Seattle. She founded Multi-Cultural Women Writers of Orange County and was a board member of Amnesty International. Her work is collected in *Camp Notes and Other Poems* (1976) and *Desert Run: Poems and Stories* (1988).

Hisaye Yamamoto was born in California in 1923 and began writing as a teenager. She was interned in Poston, Arizona, during World War II and continued to work as a reporter and columnist. Her stories have been published in anthologies and her own collection, *Seventeen Syllables and Other Stories* (Rutgers University Press, 1998).

Lois-Ann Yamanaka was born in 1961 on the Hawaiian island of Moloka'i. Her collection of poetry, *Saturday Night at the Pahala Theatre,* received the Pushcart Prize XVIII, 1993. Yamanaka's novels include *Wild Meat and the Bully Burgers* (1996), *Blu's Hanging* (1997), and *Heads by Harry* (1999).

Karen Tei Yamashita lived for nine years in Brazil, the setting of her first two novels, *Through the Arc of the Rain Forest* (1990) and *Brazil-Maru* (1992). Her third novel, *Tropic of Orange* (1997), is set in Los Angeles.

John Yau was born in Lynn, Massachusetts, in 1950. An art critic, poet, teacher, and curator, he has received many fellowships and awards and published numerous collections including *Radiant Silhouette: New and Selected Work 1974–1988, Edificio Sayonara* (1992), *Hawaiian Cowboys* (1995), and *My Symptoms* (1998).

Alfred A. Yuson has authored two novels, three poetry collections, two essay compilations, a short fiction collection, and two children's stories. Among numerous distinctions, he has received the SEA Write (South East Asian Writers) Award for lifetime achievement. Yuson currently writes literary reviews for a Manila broadsheet.

About the Editors

Esther Yae Iwanaga was born and grew up in Honolulu, Hawai'i. She is a lecturer in Asian American literature, Vietnam war literature, and writing at the University of Massachusetts, Boston and Wellesley College.

Rajini Srikanth teaches in the English department and Asian American Studies program at the University of Massachusetts, Boston. She coedited the award-winning anthology *Contours of the Heart: South Asians Map North America* (1996) and *A Part Yet Apart: South Asians in Asian America* (1998).

Copyrights and Permissions

Lew, Walter K. "Ch'onmun Hak" reprinted by permission of the author.

Lim, Shirley Geok-lin. Reprinted by permission of the author and The Feminist Press at The City University of New York, from Shirley Geok-lin Lim, *Among the White Moon Faces: An Asian-American Memoir of Homelands* (New York: The Feminist Press at The City University of New York, 1996). Copyright © 1996 by Shirley Geok-lin Lim.

Linmark, R. Zamora. "Rated-L" and "Our Lady of Kalihi" from *Rolling the R's*. Copyright © 1995 by R. Zamora Linmark. Reprinted by permission of Kaya Production.

Lum, Wing Tek. "Urban Love Songs" reprinted by permission of the author.

Luu, Alex. Excerpt from *Three Lives* reprinted by permission of the author.

Mirikitani, Janice. "Recipe" and "Why Is Preparing Fish a Political Act?" excerpted from *Shedding Silence*, copyright © 1987 by Janice Mirikitani. Reprinted by permission of Celestial Arts, P. O. Box 7123, Berkeley, CA 94707.

Monji, Jana. "Kim" reprinted by permission of the author. Copyright © 1995 by Jana J. Monji.

Mori, Toshio. "He Who Has the Laughing Face" from *Yokohama, California*. Reprinted by permission of Caxton Press, Caldwell, Idaho.

Mura, David. Excerpt from *Where the Body Meets Memory* by David Mura, copyright © 1996 by David Mura. Used with permission of Doubleday, a division of Random House, Inc.

Naqvi, Tahira. "Chagrin" reprinted by permission of the author.

Okada, John. Excerpt from *No-No Boy*. Copyright © 1976 by Dorothy Okada. Reprinted by permission of the University of Washington Press.

Pak, Gary. "The Valley of the Dead Air" from *The Watcher of Waipuna and Other Stories* by Gary Pak (Bamboo Ridge Press 1992). Reprinted by permission of the author.

Revoyr, Nina. Excerpt from *The Necessary Hunger* by Nina Revoyr reprinted by permission of Simon & Schuster. Copyright © 1997 by Nina Revoyr.

Salanga, Alfrredo Navarro. "They Don't Think Much about Us in America" reprinted by permission of Alicia Loyola Salanga.

Shiomi, Rick. *Mask Dance* is reprinted with permission from R. A. Shiomi.

Song, Cathy. "A Conservative View" from *School Figures* by Cathy Song, © 1994. Reprinted by permission of University of Pittsburgh Press.

Soo Hoo, Judy. Excerpt from *Texas* used by permission of the author.

Sze, Arthur. "The Redshifting Web," section one from *The Redshifting Web* © 1998 by Arthur Sze. Reprinted by permission of Copper Canyon Press, P. O. Box 271, Port Townsend, WA 98369.

Tran, Barbara. "Zenith" published by permission of the Yale University Council on Southeast Asia Studies.

Truong, Monique T. D. "Seeds" reprinted by permission of the author.

Ung, Loung. Pages 101–112 from *First They Killed My Father: A Daughter of Cambodia Remembers* by Loung Ung. Copyright © 2000 by Loung Ung. Reprinted by permission of HarperCollins Publishers, Inc.

Vazirani, Reetika. "Reading the Poem about the Yew Tree" reprinted by permission of the author.

Verghese, Abraham. Excerpt reprinted with the permission of Simon & Schuster, from *My Own Country: A Doctor's Story of a Town and Its People in the Age of AIDS* by Abraham Verghese. Copyright © 1994 by Abraham Verghese.

Yamada, Mitsuye. "Thirty Years Under" and "Cincinnati" from *Camp Notes and Other Poems*, copyright © 1992 by Mitsuye Yamada. Reprinted by permission of Rutgers University Press.

Yamamoto, Hisaye. "Seventeen Syllables" from *Seventeen Syllables and Other Stories,* copyright © 1988 by Hisaye Yamamoto DeSoto. Reprinted by permission of Rutgers University Press.

Yamanaka, Lois-Ann. "Kala Gave Me Anykine Advice Especially about Filipinos When I Moved to Pahala" from *Saturday Night at the Pahala Theatre.* Copyright © 1993 by Lois-Ann Yamanaka. Published by Bamboo Ridge Press. First published in *Bamboo Ridge: The Hawai'i Writer's Quarterly.* Reprinted by permission of Susan Bergholz Literary Services, New York. All rights reserved.

Yamashita, Karen Tei. Excerpt from *Through the Arc of the Rain Forest* (Coffee House Press 1990). Copyright © 1990 by Karen Tei Yamashita. Reprinted by permission of Coffee House Press.

Yau, John. "A New Beginning" copyright © 1995 by John Yau. Reprinted from *Hawaiian Cowboys* with the permission of Black Sparrow Press.

Yuson, Alfred. "Andy Warhol Speaks to His Two Filipino Maids" first appeared in *Caracoa XX,* the quarterly literary journal of the Philippine Literary Arts Council, published in Manila, Philippines in November 1998. Reprinted by permission of author.

Index of Authors and Titles